Lindsay Ames

LATIN EROTIC ELEGY

The first comprehensive elegiac anthology for several decades, this volume is an invaluable resource for all those studying elegiac poetry, and will also be important for courses on Augustan culture and gender in the ancient world.

The detailed introduction looks at major figures, the evolution of the form, and the Roman context, with a particular focus on the changing relations between the sexes. The texts that follow range from the earliest manifestations of erotic elegy in Catullus, through Tibullus, Sulpicia (Rome's only female elegist), Propertius and Ovid.

The accessible commentary explores the historical background, issues of language and style, and the relation of each piece to its author's larger body of work. The volume closes with an anthology of critical essays representing the main trends in scholarship; these illuminate the genre's most salient features and help the student understand its modern reception.

Paul Allen Miller is Director of Comparative Literature and Associate Professor of Classics at the University of South Carolina. He is the author of *Lyric Texts and Lyric Consciousness* (Routledge 1994) and numerous articles on Latin, Greek, English and French poetry. He has also edited several volumes of essays including *Rethinking Sexuality* (1998), and the journal *Intertexts*.

D1484755

LATIN EROTIC ELEGY

An anthology and reader

Edited with an introduction and
commentary by Paul Allen Miller

London and New York

TO SAM, WITH ALL MY LOVE

First published 2002
by Routledge
11 New Fetter Lane, London EC4P 4EE

Simultaneously published in the USA and Canada
by Routledge
29 West 35th Street, New York, NY 10001

Routledge is an imprint of the Taylor & Francis Group

© 2002 Selection and editorial matter, Paul Allen Miller; individual
extracts, the contributors

Typeset in Garamond by RefineCatch Limited, Bungay, Suffolk
Printed and bound in Great Britain by
Biddles Ltd, King s Lynn, Norfolk

All rights reserved. No part of this book may be reprinted or
reproduced or utilised in any form or by any electronic,
mechanical, or other means, now known or hereafter
invented, including photocopying and recording, or in any
information storage or retrieval system, without permission in
writing from the publishers.

British Library Cataloguing in Publication Data
A catalogue record for this book is available from the British Library

Library of Congress Cataloging in Publication Data
Latin erotic elegy: an anthology and reader / Paul Allen Miller.
p. cm.
Includes bibliographical references and index
1. Elegiac poetry, Latin.   2. Elegiac poetry, Latin – History and
criticism.   3. Erotic poetry, Latin – History and criticism.   4. Love
poetry, Latin – History and criticism.   5. Erotic poetry, Latin.   6.
Love poetry, Latin.   I. Miller, Paul Allen, 1959–   , II. Title.
PA6127.L38   2002
871′.01083543—dc21   2001048560

ISBN 978-0-415-24371-1 (hbk)
ISBN 978-0-415-24372-8 (pbk)

CONTENTS

CONTENTS

PREFACE

This text is designed primarily for students and teachers of advanced undergraduate and MA level classes, although scholars may find it useful as well. The Introduction provides a general overview of the genre of Latin erotic elegy in its historical and literary context. The commentary is designed to aid students in understanding both the language and the poetry. Discussion of textual matters and of sources has been limited to those cases where it is necessary for linguistic or artistic intelligibility. The critical anthology at the conclusion of the volume is designed to allow the student both a greater comprehension of the poems themselves and of the history of the debates surrounding them. The essays chosen, while they are all important, have been selected on the basis of their representing certain trends in scholarship on elegy rather than on any claim that they are intrinsically better than others that might have been chosen. Only essays that deal with the genre as a whole rather than single authors or poems have been used. Unfortunately, this means that many fine pieces of scholarship have been left out.

Citations have been kept to the bare minimum to aid in accessibility. Those wishing to do further reading should refer to the select bibliography at the end of the Introduction, which does not begin to reflect my debt to the previous scholarship in the field. The texts for the poems are all taken from the OCT editions, with the exception of Catullus where I have relied on Quinn and of the *Heroides* where I have used the Budé.

ACKNOWLEDGEMENTS

I owe debts of gratitude to many people and institutions. My thanks go first
to my colleague Ward Briggs who suggested this project to me and then to
Barbara K. Gold who introduced me to the elegists so many years ago. I
should also thank Kevin Herbert whose love for Catullus first sparked my
own. The manuscript could not have been prepared without the aid of my
research assistant and student, Christel Brown, and of the secretary of the
Comparative Literature Program at the University of South Carolina, Noreen
Doughty. I owe a debt of gratitude to Micaela Janan of Duke University and
Deborah Lyons of Johns Hopkins as well as to their students who used a draft
of this text in their classes and provided invaluable feedback. Micaela, you
were, as always, a helpful and supportive friend. I can't thank you enough for
countless favors large and small. Ellen Greene read over the final versions of
the manuscript, provided insightful criticism and invaluable moral support.
All remaining faults are my own. Of course, I would be and do nothing were
it not for the love and support of my wife, Ann Poling, and of Sam, the only
person who still asks me to play tag.

Two University of South Carolina College of Liberal Arts Scholarship
Support awards provided the time and funds necessary to travel to the
Classics Library at the University of Texas at Austin to complete my research
and to finish the manuscript.

George Luck, "Introduction" to *Latin Love Elegy*, copyright © 1968; repro-
duced by permission of Routledge, Inc, part of the Taylor and Francis group.
J. P. Sullivan, "The Politics of Elegy," *Arethusa* 5:1 (1972), 17–34, copyright
© Johns Hopkins University Press; reprinted with permission of the Johns
Hopkins University Press. Judith P. Hallett, "The Role of Women in Roman
Elegy: Counter-Cultural Feminism." *Arethusa* 6:1 (1973), 103–24, copyright
© Johns Hopkins University Press; reprinted with permission of the Johns
Hopkins University Press. R. O. A. M. Lyne, "The Life of Love" from *The
Latin Love Poets from Catullus to Horace*, copyright © 1980 by Oxford Uni-
versity Press; reprinted by permission of Oxford University Press. Paul
Veyne, *Roman Erotic Elegy: Love, Poetry, and the West*, translated by Davis

Pellauer, copyright © 1988 by University of Chicago Press; originally published in French as *Elégie érotique romaine*, copyright © 1983 by Edition du Seuil; reprinted by permission of Georges Borchardt Inc. and the University of Chicago Press. Maria Wyke, "Mistress and Metaphor in Augustan Elegy," *Helios* 16:1 © 1989; reprinted by permission of Texas Tech University Press. Duncan Kennedy, "Representation and the Rhetoric of Reality" from *The Arts of Love: Five Studies in the Discourse of Roman Love Elegy*, copyright © 1993; reprinted with the permission of Cambridge University Press. Barbara K. Gold, "'But Ariadne Was Never There in the First Place': Finding the Female in Roman Poetry," from *Feminist Theory and the Classics*, copyright © 1993; reproduced by permission of Routledge, Inc, part of the Taylor and Francis group. David Fredrick, "Reading Broken Skin: Violence in Roman Elegy" from J. Hallett and M. Skinner, *Roman Sexualities*, copyright ©1997 by Princeton University Press; reprinted by permission of Princeton University Press.

Every effort has been made to trace copyright holders of printed material. If a copyright holder has not been acknowledged, please contact the publisher.

INTRODUCTION

General

1. Roman erotic elegy is one of the most influential genres in the history of western poetry. It is not too much to say that our conception of romantic love as the passionate attachment of one person to another, to the exclusion of all other concerns – money, fame, social propriety – was first codified by the Roman elegists. It was from the elegists, and Ovid in particular, that the medieval poets of courtly love derived their most famous and influential conceits. Likewise, the love sonnets of the Renaissance poets from Petrarch to Shakespeare would be unimaginable without the elegiac predecessors from which they self-consciously drew. The sonnet tradition, in turn, established the conventions for romantic devotion and the life of love that have dominated western culture until at least the beginning of the twentieth century. In short, to study the elegiac poets is not just to study a genre of poetry practiced by a people long dead, in a tongue no longer spoken, and in a far away place. To study Latin elegy is to uncover the storehouse of themes and images from which our modern notions of love and commitment have been constructed.

2. The familiarity of this poetry's themes and images, however, can be deceptive. We must be wary of assuming that the same gesture or image in one time and place has the same meaning when used again in another. The metaphor of love's slavery, for example, is a much more abstract affair in a society such as ours, in which slavery is not a fact of everyday life, than it was for the ancient Romans. Elegy, then, is not only the common property of all the cultures that trace their origins to the ancient Mediterranean; it is also a discrete, time-bound phenomenon. Indeed, one of its great paradoxes is that, despite its extraordinary influence on literature for more than two thousand years after its birth, the genre lasted barely fifty years. Thus, Latin elegy not only continues to have a modern appeal, it is also inextricably bound to a particular context. Therefore, if we want to understand what erotic elegy meant to the Romans, we have to examine both the history of its development and of the social and political conditions that made it possible. In the

1

process, we shall discover not only how our present has grown from the past, but also how the past was radically different from the present.

3. The surviving erotic elegists are Catullus, Tibullus, Sulpicia, Propertius, and Ovid, all of whom were active in the last two-thirds of the first century BCE. The defining features of their poetry are relatively few in number. First, all elegies are written in elegiac couplets. The couplet consists of two different lines. The first is a dactylic hexameter, the meter used for epic verse. The second line is a pentameter that is largely dactylic in rhythm. We shall talk more about meter later in this introduction. For the present, it is sufficient to note that this was a common meter in ancient poetry, used by archaic Greek poets for everything from political advice to marching songs. In Rome, before Catullus, the elegiac couplet was used for epitaphs and short witty epigrams. Both forms were based on Greek practice, and the epigrams were either translations or close imitations of works by Alexandrian poets such as Callimachus.

4. One of the ways elegy differs from epigram is length. An epigram is a short poem of roughly two to ten lines. Its brevity demands rigorous concision on the part of the poet and allows little scope for narrative development. Roman erotic elegies vary in size, but are usually substantially larger than epigrams written in the same meter. The average poem of Tibullus runs about 75 lines. The typical elegy of Propertius in the first three books is around 35 lines, though that number grows to 86 in Book 4, while the poems in Ovid's *Amores* average about 50 lines. Elegy's greater length offers more opportunity for rhetorical and narrative elaboration, as well as for the creation of structural complexities, impossible to achieve in the more restrictive format of epigram. Likewise, whereas epigrams are, with certain exceptions, occasional compositions in which one poem's relation to the next is *ad hoc*, the elegists write books in which the reader can follow the course of a love affair from beginning to end. These stories are not as linear as was once believed, when critics strove to reconstruct the poets' biographies from their poetry. Nonetheless, to cite only one example, Ovid's *Amores* takes us from the moment the poet first falls in love to the end of the affair in three books that are arranged in roughly chronological order. Sulpicia's poetry, as we shall see, while closer to epigram than elegy in terms of length, shares this focus on narrative complexity that is one of erotic elegy's most distinguishing characteristics. Thus, one thing that all the elegists share is the way in which each poem in a book relates to another, creating a whole that is greater than the sum of its parts. The nature of an anthology such as this will limit the degree to which this aspect of elegiac style can be fully appreciated, but we shall bring out the connections between texts in the notes.

5. The thematic principle around which all the elegiac collections are organized was the love affair. Each book of the canonical elegists was primarily devoted to a single beloved of the opposite sex. Like all generic laws, this is more a rule of thumb than an unalterable law of nature. Catullus's mistress, Lesbia, is the central focus of his most famous poetry, but much of that poetry is not written in elegiac couplets and much of what is written in the meter is on topics other than the poet's affair. For this reason, Catullus is best considered not an elegist proper, but a precursor. Cornelius Gallus is the first true elegist, and all four of his books were devoted to his beloved, Lycoris. Unfortunately, while the figure of Gallus looms large in the poetry of Vergil, Propertius, and Ovid, his own poetry has all but disappeared. He rose to be the prefect of Egypt under Augustus, and when he became too bold in proclaiming his own accomplishments, he was forced to commit suicide. Hence, while there was no systematic effort on the part of the imperial regime to destroy his poetry, its preservation and dissemination were not encouraged. Little can be said of his depiction of Lycoris with any real assurance. Tibullus wrote two books of poetry. The first is devoted to Delia, but also features three pederastic poems (1.4, 1.8, and 1.9) dedicated to a certain Marathus. Tibullus here is following Hellenistic precedent in which erotic poetry written in elegiac meters was generally homoerotic in nature. Catullus did the same, writing erotic epigrams about his love for Juventius. Tibullus dedicates his second book exclusively to his travails with the ominously named Nemesis. Sulpicia's slight *œuvre* recounts her love affair with Cerinthus. The first three books of Propertius are devoted to his love for Cynthia. In his fourth book, however, the historical limitations of the elegiac genre are becoming manifest. While love and Cynthia are not wholly absent, Propertius here embarks on a program of historical and political elegies in the Alexandrian mode. Ovid's case is the most complex. The three books of the *Amores* recount the course of his affair with Corinna. However, Ovid's engagement with erotic elegy does not end here. He also produces both the *Heroides*, a series of letters from amorous heroines recounting their misadventures in flawless elegiac verse, and the *Ars Amatoria*, a manual of seduction based on the conventions of erotic elegy. Augustus deemed the latter work sufficiently subversive that he cited it as one of the reasons for the poet's exile to the Black Sea town of Tomis.

6. Ovid's exile, however, points to a problem. How could love poetry be subversive? How could it be cited as a reason, even if as only a pretext, for exile? This is hard for us to understand in a society that takes the expression of individual emotion for granted and in which romantic love is seen as the foundation of the nuclear family. Such, however, was not the case in Rome or throughout the ancient Mediterranean. Indeed, the attempt to make heterosexual, romantic love the foundation of the family has been a uniquely modern and western experiment. Not only do elegiac love affairs focus on love outside of marriage; they call into question the basic power relations that lay at the heart of traditional Roman life. The defining characteristic of the focus on an exclusive or dominant love affair as the genre's thematic center of gravity already casts it outside the mainstream of Roman cultural life. Love, in genres such as comedy and satire, was a regrettable extravagance to be

tolerated in young men. They could have their flings with a courtesan or *meretrix*, provided they did not despoil the family fortune, but were then expected to settle down in a traditional arranged marriage and pursue a career in law, the military, or politics. Love was tolerated so long as it was temporary and did not endanger another man's fortune or legitimate sexual prerogatives. In Horace's lyric poetry, which was written during the twenties BCE, the heyday of the elegiac genre, love is a pleasant diversion to be indulged in with a variety of Greek flute girls and *meretrices*. In epic, which elegy always defines as its generic opposite, amorous intrigues such as Aeneas's with Dido are portrayed as endangering the very foundations of the state by distracting the hero from his divine mission.

7. In elegy, however, the beloved is always portrayed as the *domina* or *era* of the poet. Whereas Catullus uses both terms, the former would become canonical in the later tradition. Both, however, refer to the woman of the house or *domus*, the *matrona* who ruled its domestic slaves. She was their literal "mistress," and it is from this metaphor that our own use of the term derives. The lovers, in turn, adopt the pose of the slave of love, *seruus amoris*, in which they pretend to subject themselves completely to the will of their beloveds. This subjection is an abdication of the normal rights of masculine domination that went without question in Roman society. For a man to submit to the will of a woman was to accept the label of effeminate softness or *mollitia*. Moreover, the elegists go further still and cast themselves in the role of *praeceptores amoris*, teachers of love. They present themselves not only as sexual nonconformists but also as the advocates of a lifestyle that, if taken literally, threatens the very bases of traditional power relations between the genders.

8. Too much can be made of these declarations of masculine subjection. It is not always clear who had the upper hand in these relationships. Ovid and Tibullus, for example, write poems that show the lover using violence toward the beloved. Likewise, Ovid's poems on Corinna's abortion reveal that certain imbalances of power remained inherent in the sexual situation of most women in the ancient world regardless of the metaphors employed. Moreover, the male lovers in an elegiac relationship always retain the option of pursuing a conventional career in law, politics, the military, agriculture, or large-scale commerce. These were not options for their mistresses. The question, then, of who was free and who was a slave in these relationships is more complicated than the theme of *seruitium amoris* might make it appear. Casting yourself as the slave of someone who has very little real social power is a pretty risk-free proposition. Nonetheless, the elegists by questioning the nature of relations between the sexes and by envisioning their own subjugation to women – even if in an often ironic and humorous manner – present an interrogation of sexual norms unparalleled in Roman poetry.

9. Elegy not only defines itself as *mollis*, or soft, it does so in direct opposition to epic, which it terms *durus*, or hard. The sexual connotations of

such terms do not need to be belabored, but there is an elaborate pun here that is foundational to the genre: for *mollis* is a stylistic term as well as a sexual one. *Mollitia* represents the soft style of composition advocated by the Alexandrian poet Callimachus, as opposed to the harsh style of epic associated with Homer. The soft style eschews lengthy continuous narrative in favor of indirect forms of exposition. It avoids the harsh alliterations and enjambments characteristic of the Roman epic style represented by Ennius, in favor of smooth and flowing verse. It focuses on delicate psychological portraiture rather than broad description. Elegy is thus *mollis* because it portrays men subjected to women, because it defines itself thematically as the opposite of epic, and because it is composed in the soft style of Callimachus. This kind of elaborate word play, moreover, in which sexual and literary registers of language become conflated, is typical of the genre. When Ovid or Propertius speak of their *amores*, it is impossible to tell if they mean their loves, their love poetry, or both.

10. Elegy's potential to unsettle traditional mores, the *mos maiorum*, the return to which was a major part of the political program of the emperor Augustus, was not limited to its depiction of men subjected to women. The situations depicted by the genre also threatened what were considered the legitimate relations of power and property that governed the commerce between men and women. Elegiac romance, like that of the medieval courtly lovers who would follow in its wake, is always by definition extramarital. Catullus describes his relationship with Lesbia as adulterous in poem 68. Ovid uses the term *uir* to refer to Corinna's man. It is ambiguous and may mean her husband or her established lover. In either case, Ovid is stepping on what is acknowledged to be another man's sexual territory and upsetting the balance of power. The relationship is *de facto*, if not *de iure*, adulterous. Likewise, in *Amores* 2.19 and 3.4 when Ovid is having a fling with a woman other than Corinna, he refers to her as an *uxor*, or wife, and to her *uir* as a *maritus*, or spouse. The cases of Cynthia, Delia, and Nemesis are less clear, but, as Copley pointed out half a century ago, one of the set pieces of the elegiac genre is the *paraclausithyron*, the song of the 'locked out lover' or *exclusus amator*. In these poems, the door is barred to the lover for one of three reasons: the *uir* has posted a *ianitor*, or door slave; the *domina* is with another lover; or, a *lena*, or madam, has locked the lover out for lack of funds. In all three instances, the relationship between poet and mistress is an irregular one that violates either the marital or proprietary rights of another.

11. This conflation of marital and property rights may seem strange to us, but it was not in Roman life. As Catullus tells the bride in his second marriage hymn, her maidenhood is only one-third hers, the other two-thirds belong to her parents. Marriage, while nominally consensual between the two parties, was in fact a political and economic transaction between families in which emotional ties played little if any role. This is not to say that spouses did not sometimes grow to have a real affection for one another, but

emotional satisfaction was not the primary concern in contracting a marriage. This can be clearly demonstrated by the high rate of divorce and remarriage among the upper classes in the last century of the republic, the same period that saw the rise of elegy. At this time, marriage was a tool of *amicitia*, a relationship of mutual obligation that might entail personal friendship or merely political alliance, between powerful aristocrats. The chief role of marriage was the production of legitimate heirs and the consequent cementing of economic and political relations between extended families or *gentes*. The nature of this peculiar institution is perhaps nowhere better illustrated than by the story of that paragon of Stoic virtue, Cato the younger, who, when his friend Hortensius was childless, divorced his wife Marcia so that she could marry Hortensius and produce legitimate heirs. He promptly remarried her upon Hortensius's death.

12. Under such a system of interfamilial alliance, the property and the power relations marriage entailed could only be preserved if the women in question remained faithful to the men into whose control they were remanded. Only then could the legitimacy of heirs be insured. Thus, *marita fides*, or "marital fidelity," was an expectation of women but not of men. The essential ethical obligation for men was not faithfulness but the respect of other men's property, which included their wives and long-term sexual partners. Hence, Horace in *Satire* 1.2, "Against Adultery," urges young men to release their pent up sexual energies on whatever slave boy or girl is handy, but not to grind another man's grain. The elegists, however, claim it is they, not their *dominae*, who are faithful, thereby deliberately reversing normal sexual roles even as they undermine the very virtue in the name of which they assert their amorous servitude. The elegists, therefore, are doubly subversive. Not only do they invert the power relations between men and women by adopting the position of the *seruus amoris* they also trouble the power relations between men by threatening the property rights of other men over their women.

13. The deliberate ambiguity of the last statement reflects our ignorance of the identity and social status represented by the elegiac *dominae*. This issue has been at the center of many debates in recent years. It seems clear that Lesbia is meant to be a *matrona*, or aristocratic wife, and, on the basis of internal evidence and a statement by Apuleius, she has been identified as Clodia Metelli, the wife of the consul Metellus Celer and sister of Cicero's arch-enemy Clodius Pulcher. Gallus's Lycoris is universally conceded to be the actress Cytheris, who scandalized and titillated the provincial Cicero and who was also the mistress of Marc Antony before becoming Gallus's paramour. Delia, Nemesis, Cynthia, and Corinna are, however, impossible to identify with any conviction. Different scholars have seen them as other men's wives, other men's concubines, and as courtesans on the make. The poetry gives indications of all these different statuses and makes a clear identification of who they were supposed to represent, let alone who they "really

6

were," impossible to determine. In a period that witnessed an increasing anxiety about sexual mores, declining birth rates among the upper classes, and the first legislation criminalizing adultery in the history of the Roman state, such vagueness was perhaps desirable. Nonetheless, in all cases these relationships are portrayed as illegitimate and, if not directly adulterous, then involved in poaching on what could legitimately be seen as another man's territory.

14. Sulpicia, the sole female elegist to survive, represents the exception. She neither submits to the rule of a *domina* nor threatens the property rights of others. Yet, if we grant the generally accepted identification of her as the niece and ward of Messalla Corvinus, then her poetry too becomes transgressive. As the daughter of one of Rome's most honored aristocratic houses, her declaration of open love for a man not identified as her husband marks a clear departure from the expected rules of feminine conduct. As she herself writes, "pecasse iuvat" ["it is a pleasure to have done wrong"] (3.13.9). She does not portray herself as the traditional *matrona*-to-be whose chief concerns would be faithfulness to her husband's household and the raising of his children, but as a lover. At the same time, she deliberately undermines the traditional power relations that defined love and marriage in male-dominated Rome, not by merely inverting those relations, as her male counterparts did, but by reconceiving love as a relation between equals: "cum digno digna fuisse ferar" ["Let me be said to have been a worthy woman with a worthy man"] (3.13.10).

Historical background

15. Sulpicia and the *dominae* portrayed in elegy are symptomatic of larger trends in Roman society. The literature of the period is full of anxious statements about the decline in the sexual morality of the upper classes, their increasing effeminacy, and the emancipation of their women. In the middle of the second century BCE, when republican Rome was at the height of its power with the end of the Third Punic War and as foreign treasure filled the coffers of the aristocracy creating greater social inequality and political disruption (Sallust, *Bellum Catalinae* 9–11), a series of female scare-figures begin to appear. These are powerful and sexually liberated women epitomized by Sallust's portrait of Sempronia (*Bellum Catalinae* 25) and Cicero's of Clodia Metelli in the *Pro Caelio*. In all cases, the portraits of these women are embedded in larger narratives of social decay and corruption. As such, they are best seen not as providing independent evidence regarding the lives of real Roman women, but rather as symptoms of a crisis in the way sexuality was conceived in relation to traditional republican norms. Such women represent less a new "reality" than traditional Roman thought's inability to conceptualize such women as anything other than impossible monsters. These new figures of feminine power and masculine subjection, like the

dominae and *serui amoris* of elegy, point to a crisis in Roman society that produced a disruption in sexual and social norms and made the position of the elegist possible.

16. Any attempt to date such turning points in history is necessarily arbitrary. Every beginning always has its origin in some prior state of affairs. Still, one could do worse than to date the crisis in Roman life and culture that eventually made elegy possible to the land and grain reforms proposed by the Gracchi. In 133 BCE, Tiberius Gracchus, a landed aristocrat descended from Scipio Africanus, was elected tribune of the people. His most important act was the passing of a sweeping land reform that provided small allotments to Rome's landless peasants and urban poor. In the wake of Rome's wars of conquest and the successful conclusion of the Punic Wars, vast amounts of wealth and slaves had flooded into the capital. Much of that wealth took the form of land owned by the state, or public land. This public land was leased to private landowners who were supposed to pay a percentage of their harvest to the state in return for its use. Over time, however, the rich magnates who acquired this land and worked it with slaves came to regard it as theirs by right and ceased paying the fee. During this same period, many small farmers lost their livelihoods. They had been called up for military service and their families were unable to maintain their farms in their absence and so went into debt to the wealthy landowners living in the area. The result was that many of these small freeholders lost their land and were forced to move into Rome, creating a growing urban proletariat that was underemployed and a source of political instability. Moreover, the Roman army was not a professional fighting force but a citizen's militia. To serve in it one had to be a property owner. The traditional image was that of the farmer-soldier who, like Cincinnatus, was called from his plough to defend the fatherland. The decline in the number of landowners thus represented a crisis. Rome, through its military success, was eroding the traditional base of its army at the same time as it was dispossessing the very class of small freeholders upon whose back its new wealth was built.

17. Tiberius Gracchus, whether for patriotic motives or through political opportunism, saw the redistribution of public land as a method to address this problem. His proposal would have allowed the aristocratic families who were squatting on this land to retain up to a thousand acres. Nonetheless, much of the senatorial class found the proposition an unbearable infringement on their traditional prerogatives and refused to consider the legislation. When Gracchus took the controversial step of presenting his proposal directly to the people, where it passed easily, his outraged opponents viewed this as an attempt to overthrow the state. After a series of complex and constitutionally questionable maneuvers on both sides, a gang of senators caught, cornered, and beat to death the tribune and more than one hundred of his followers. In 123 and 122 BCE, Tiberius's brother Gaius was elected to the tribunate with the avowed purpose of carrying forward the program of reforms cut short by his brother's murder. One of his most important and controversial measures was the passing of a bill requiring subsidized grain sales to the urban poor. This would become the norm by the middle of the next century, but at the time it was viewed as an infringement upon the economic rights of the well-to-do. Another Gracchan reform was the proposal to extend full citizenship rights to Rome's Latin allies. The conflicts between the senate and Gaius like those between it and Tiberius grew increasingly intense. Eventually, Gaius resorted to armed insurrection in the attempt to keep his opponents from overturning his reform program after he left office in 121. He and many of his supporters were killed in the attempt, and the senate promptly annulled his reforms. His brother's land reform remained official policy until 91 BCE, although the commission executing it was disbanded in 129.

18. The story of the Gracchi is important for the subsequent cultural, political, and sexual history of Rome on several counts. First, it marks the beginning of a century of civil strife that would eventually lead to Julius Caesar's dictatorship (48 BCE), assassination (44 BCE), and to the emergence of his heir and nephew, Octavian, as the sole ruler of Rome (31 BCE). The latter, as the *princeps* or first citizen, would be styled Augustus by the senate in 27 BCE. Second, the story of the Gracchi reveals how a number of issues, which might seem unrelated to us, were deeply intertwined in the Roman imagination, for the questions both brothers addressed went to the heart of what it meant to be a Roman. How is the citizen body, and hence its army, able to reproduce itself in a situation in which its traditional bases of self-definition no longer obtain? How can the senatorial oligarchy respond to these changing conditions without undermining the very conditions that maintained its rule? How do we determine who is a legitimate Roman citizen and who is not? What the story of the Gracchi makes apparent is the ways in which issues of sexuality and population (the production of legitimate citizen soldiers), political power, and class conflict were interrelated throughout this period. What starts in 133 BCE reaches its fullest fruition a hundred years later with the emergence of the principate and Augustus's moral reform legislation, which was designed to promote legitimate childbirth and prohibit adultery among the upper classes. The latter, rather than being something radically new, was part of an ongoing political process designed to produce a stable citizen population that could maintain the state and the position of those who controlled it. Elegy was a product and symptom of this social, political, and cultural revolution. Propertius's declaration in 2.7 that he would not marry and that no son of his would serve in Rome's armies acquires its full meaning only when this context is understood. From this perspective, elegy and the conflicts of power, sexuality, and legitimacy it dramatized did not just happen to arise in the last half of the first century BCE. Indeed, if elegy had not existed, someone would have had to invent it.

19. Finally, the story of the Gracchi is exemplary because of the role of their mother Cornelia. The daughter of Scipio Africanus, she was a well-educated and strong-willed woman who, due to the early death of her husband, was in charge of the upbringing of her two sons. Cornelia was not only an extraordinary mother but also an accomplished woman of letters whose published correspondence survived for more than two centuries after her death. She represents the rise of a new, powerful, and independent female figure who, while admired, nonetheless represented a challenge to the traditional hierarchies of gendered power in Rome. She was the positive image of a new Roman woman, of which Sempronia and Clodia represent the negative caricature. The existence of powerful, independent, and cultured women made the character of the *domina* believable as a literary construct and threatening as an object of desire.

20. The problems that the Gracchi had tried to address did not disappear with their deaths. The brothers were more symptoms of structural problems in Roman culture and politics than causes *per se*. Thus in 107 BCE, Marius was elected consul for the first of an eventual seven times. One of his first acts was to remove the property qualification for serving in the army. In effect, he was merely regularizing a situation that had increasingly become the case over the years, but by doing so and establishing a specified term of service he turned the army into a professional fighting force. The professionalization of the army eroded the traditional ideology that bound the soldiery to a republic in which they as landholders had a definite stake. Instead, they professed loyalty to their individual commanders, the sole authorities who had an interest in insuring that they received their just rewards, generally an allotment of land supplied by despoiling either foreign or domestic enemies.

21. In light of this changing military and political situation, the leadership of the senatorial oligarchy became beholden to the generals – Marius, Sulla, Pompey, Caesar, and eventually Octavian and Antony – to crush both their rivals and, if need be, popular resistance. The soldiers' alienation from the traditional instances of state power was augmented by the practice of some of this senatorial elite of driving the families of these soldiers off their lands while they were away on campaign. The ruling class became increasingly fragmented as they were forced to line up behind various warlords, like Caesar and Pompey, and the factions they represented. At the same time, certain members of the elite, such as Clodius Pulcher, who claimed to represent the interests of the *plebs urbana* were engaging in new forms of political organizing. They sought to create alternative organs of power through the mobilization of *collegia*, or guilds of tradesmen, *uici*, or neighborhood councils, and the worshippers of nontraditional cults such as those of Isis and Bacchus. Thus, at this period in Roman history, power became more diffuse as it broke away from its traditional institutional basis even as it became more concentrated in the hands of the generals whose troops were the final arbiters of political conflict.

22. In this context, by the time of the assassination of Julius Caesar the republican constitution no longer existed. The return to it was impossible. The Augustan settlement would step into this breach. The Augustan program of moral revival and religious reconstruction was consistently presented in terms of a return to the virtues of the past, the *mos maiorum*, and the restoration of the republic (Augustus, *Res Gestae* 8, 19–21, 34). At the same time, it was laying the ideological groundwork for consolidating what was to be the most sweeping transformation of the Roman state since the expulsion of the Etruscan kings. Moreover, in spite of its self-proclaimed conservative nature, the regime did not scruple to appropriate concepts of sacred kingship and other ideas foreign to traditional republican political thought where it deemed them useful. Augustan imperial ideology was less a coherent, theoretical edifice than an *ad hoc* construction designed to meet specific needs. It was more concerned with power and stability than ideological purity.

23. To that end, the Augustan regime consistently presented the final round of the civil wars between Antony and Octavian, the two claimants to Julius Caesar's legacy, as a battle to preserve Rome's masculine integrity or *uirtus* (derived from the word *uir*) against an onslaught from the effeminized East. Thus in Horace *Odes* 1.37, the chief opponent of Augustus at the battle of Actium (31 BCE) is not Antony, a Roman general, but his consort Cleopatra, an eastern queen surrounded by eunuchs. And while Horace's portrait of Cleopatra is ultimately a good deal more nuanced than this thumbnail sketch might lead one to believe, nonetheless its echoes of official Augustan propaganda are unmistakable. This propaganda aimed to produce a revisionist history. Octavian was not to be presented as the bloody victor of a protracted civil conflict. He was not to be portrayed as the one-time ally of Mark Antony, who had willingly joined in the proscriptions that killed or despoiled thousands of their political opponents. He was to be the *pater patriae*, the establisher of peace, restorer of the republic, and defender of Roman *uirtus*. In short, Augustus sought to portray himself as a bulwark against the very kind of irrationality, or *furor*, and effeminacy, or *mollitia*, that were the essence of elegy's self-representation. Cleopatra too was an avatar of the *domina*.

The elegiac tradition

24. The roots of elegy, however, like those of virtually all the poetic genres, were not to be found in Rome alone, but also in Greece. Greek poetry set the standard for cultural achievement. This is not to deny the strong influence of domestic poetic forms on elegy's unique evolution. Greek new comedy, as adapted by Plautus and Terrence, with its tales of young love run riot, expensive courtesans, and outraged parents, had a major influence on the themes and dramatic situations of elegy. Likewise, the uniquely Roman tradition of satire, starting with Lucilius (second century BCE), had established a poetic

precedent for the pose of frank personal revelation and autobiographical intent. Nonetheless, in Book 10 of the *Institutio*, when Quintilian says, "in elegy too we challenge the Greeks," he is clearly setting Latin love elegy against the background of its Greek antecedents. In addition, when Catullus, Propertius, and Ovid speak of their literary predecessors Mimnermus, Antimachus, and above all Callimachus loom large.

25. The elegiac meter is as old as Greek poetry itself. The first recorded practitioner is Archilochus (seventh century BCE), but cognate meters in other Indo-European languages show it more ancient still. It was often etymologized to mean *e e legein*, "to say woe, woe," and from the beginning it appeared on funeral steles, but its use was much wider by the archaic Greek period. Until the fifth century, it is a frequent medium of political and military exhortation. The poet Theognis combines political commentary with poems of a frankly pederastic intent (although since the institution of pederasty was as much educational as sexual in archaic Greece one should refrain from making too sharp a distinction). By the end of the seventh century, Mimnermus had composed poems that were at some point collected in an edition termed the *Nanno*, possibly named for a courtesan. As best as can be judged from the five remaining fragments, while their style was elegant, their subject matter was largely concerned with history, mythology, and popular wisdom. The first elegiac poet clearly to devote a collection of poetry to his beloved was Antimachus of Colophon (*c.*400 BCE). His work, *Lyde*, named after his deceased mistress was nonetheless a compilation of mythological narratives, which, while serving as a memorial to his lost love, very little resembled the first-person narratives that were central to Latin erotic elegy. Antimachus's collection of long narrative elegies on mythological themes does seem to have served as a precedent for the later Alexandrian poets, although Callimachus criticized it as fat and inelegant.

26. By far the most important influence on Latin elegy, however, was Callimachus (third century BCE). Catullus, Propertius, and Ovid list him as among their chief influences, and Tibullus, who refrains from making overt theoretical statements, alludes to him on several occasions. A brief introduction cannot do justice to his importance. The best that can be hoped for is to give a general idea of this complex and elusive poet, who was a scholar and librarian at the Museum in Alexandria. His poetry is characterized by learning, wit, and studied indirection. Unfortunately, most of his work survives only in fragments.

27. One of the longest extant examples of his verse is a translation by Catullus of a poem called the "Lock of Berenice." A short excerpt gives a sense of its flavor. It tells how a tress cut from the hair of Queen Berenice of Egypt was miraculously transformed into a new constellation discovered by the royal astronomer to the court at Alexandria, Conon. Berenice sheared the lock as an offering for the safe return of her husband and brother, Ptolemy

III, from a campaign in Syria on which he had left immediately after their marriage.

> Idem me ille Conon caelesti in limine uidit
>   e Bereniceo uertice caesariem,
> fulgentem clare, quam multis illa dearum
>   leuia protendens bracchia pollicita est,
> qua rex tempestate nouo auctus hymenaeo
>   uastatum finis iuerat Assyrios,
> dulcia nocturnae portans uestigia rixae,
>   quam de uirgineis gesserat exuuiis.

That same Conon saw me shining clearly on the threshold of the sky, a flowing lock from the top of Berenice's head, which she stretching forth her slight arms had promised to many of the goddesses, in that season when it had pleased the king, blessed with a new marriage, carrying with him the sweet traces of their nocturnal struggle, when he had borne off the young girl's spoils, to lay waste to the Assyrians. (66.7–14)

The precious imagery, the coy psychology of the pampered tress, the witty compliments to the royal couple, and the complex sentence structure are typically Callimachean. We are a long way from Homer, archaic Greek elegy, or a typical Roman panegyric of a triumphant general. In this passage, we see the thematic and stylistic *mollitia* that the Latin elegists so admired in the Alexandrian poet. At the same time, the conflation of the amorous with the soldierly in the evocation of the king and queen's nocturnal struggle would become one of the signature motifs of Roman erotic elegy, the *militia amoris* or "soldiering of love."

28. For all the convergences between the styles of Callimachus and those of his later elegiac followers, there are certain clear differences as well. Callimachus's poem does not adopt the autobiographical pose that distinguishes the Latin elegists nor, despite its clear interest in the erotic, does it form part of a larger narrative of an amorous affair. The "Lock of Berenice" is from Callimachus's most famous collection of poems, the *Aitia* or *Causes*. This four-volume anthology of learned elegies recounts stories that purport to give the origins or causes of a variety of cultural, religious, and natural phenomena. "The Lock of Berenice," therefore, offers an explanation, however facetious it may be, of the origin of the new constellation discovered by Conon.

29. These poems are anything but dry and scholarly, however recondite their subject matter or abstruse their approach. They are the clever constructions of a court poet who appears in his poems as an opinionated narrator and polemical poetic theorist. Thus, the *Aitia* opens with a prologue in which the

poet defends himself against the charge that he is incapable of producing a single continuous narrative of epic proportions. His witty response is that Apollo had told him to make his sacrifices fat, but to keep his muse slender. This notion of the slender style, as opposed to the fat bombast of epic, became one of the most important ways Roman elegy defined itself in contrast to epic. Thus in 2.1, for example, Propertius speaks of his inability to write heroic verse in his narrow bed, a metaphor that cleverly identifies love-making with the production of verse in the Callimachean style. Likewise, at the end of Callimachus's "Hymn to Apollo," the poet concludes not with the god's praises but with a swipe at his critics:

> And Envy whispered in Apollo's ear:
> "I am charmed by the poet who swells like the sea."
> But Apollo put foot to Envy and said:
> "The River Euphrates has a powerful current
> but the water is muddy and filled with refuse.
> The cult of Bees brings water to Deo
> but their slender libations are unsullied and pure,
> the trickling dew from a holy spring's height."
> (Lombardo and Rayor 1988:10)

The contrast between the slender purity of the Callimachean style and the swollen flotsam of epic bombast could not be better expressed. More importantly, however, what is clear from both this passage and the prologue to the *Aitia* is that we have in Callimachus not an unobtrusive or self-effacing narrative voice, but the very clear assertion of a singular point of view. Hence, simplistic distinctions between subjective and objective elegy, which were once common in discussions of the ways in which the Latin poets differed from their Greek predecessors, have to be abandoned. This does not however mean that anyone would confuse the stance of the Callimachean narrator with the Latin poet's pretense to writing confessional verse.

30. In the end, Hellenistic models for elegy, while important, are all partial at best. Where Antimachus's *Lyde* possessed an erotic subjective frame for a series of narrative elegies, and Callimachus had presented an interventionist and opinionated narrator for the mythological tales told in the *Aitia*, no precedent for Catullus 68's combination of "autobiographical" narrative and mythological exempla, nor for Catullus 76's agonized internal dialogue, can be found in Hellenistic poetry. Likewise, the Latin elegiac poet's complete subjection (*seruitium amoris*) to a single mistress (*domina, era*) is unprecedented in ancient Greek poetry of any era. Indeed, as I have argued before, Catullus represents the beginning of that uniquely interiorized voice that is commonly termed lyric poetry in the modern sense of the term and of which Latin erotic elegy is a subgenre. What Hellenistic literature offered at the end of the first century BCE was not a model to be slavishly copied by the erotic elegists, but an alternative value system to the Roman republic's traditional emphasis on *domus, dignitas,* and *gloria,* the *mos maiorum.* The Callimachean dedication to poetic excellence and the rejection of the common path were rhetorical tools the elegists deployed in their rejection of the traditional life of duty. Catullus and the elegists would exploit this resource, but from the unique perspective offered by a Roman cultural and political system that was at this time in the process of restructuring. Indeed, one of the great ironies of the relationship between Hellenistic poetics and the development of Roman erotic elegy is that the rhetoric of Alexandrian absolutism, which aided the elegists in their resistance to traditional republican ideology, may also have unwittingly prepared them for the emergence of Rome's own monarchy, the Augustan principate.

Meter

31. The elegiac couplet in the hands of the Roman elegists is as much a stylistic as a metrical unit. The first line of each distich is a dactylic hexameter.* The second line has two parts, consisting of two and a half dactyls apiece:

In Catullan practice, the resolution of the dactyl ($-\smile\smile$) into a spondee ($--$) is occasionally found in the fifth foot, but becomes very rare thereafter. In general, Catullus's elegiacs tend toward a heavily spondaic rhythm. The later poets have more dactyls per line, rendering their verse lighter and more fluent. Ovid in particular is fond of dactylic rhythms. His verse represents the culmination of a long line of stylistic development.

32. Catullus also has a high proportion of elision, giving a sense of emotional urgency to his verse but at times rendering the diction harsh. A couplet such as the following from Catullus would be unthinkable in Ovid, Tibullus, or Propertius:

Nam quaecumque_homines bene cuiquam_aut dicere possunt

aut facere,_haec a te dictaque factaque sunt.

For whatever good things men are able to say or do for anyone, these things have been said and done by you. (76.7–8)

---

* The rules for scansion can be found in any reference grammar.

The three elisions and predominantly guttural diction distinguish this couplet from the smoother composition found in the later elegists. In addition, while this passage may not be typical of Catullus's versification, it is hardly the most extreme example in his corpus (compare 73.5–6, 75.3–4, 76.13–14, 87.3–4, or 116.7–8). Tibullus's poetry, in contrast, features not only smoothly flowing diction but also the frequent use of devices such as internal rhyme (indicated by italics), to give the couplet a greater aural coherence:

$$- \; \smile \; \smile | - \smile \smile | - \; \neg | - \quad - | - \; \smile \; \neg | - -$$

Non ego divitias patrum fructusque requir*o*

$$- \quad \smile \smile | - \; \neg \; \neg | | - \quad \smile \smile | - \smile \smile | -$$

quos tulit antiqu*o* condita messis au*o*.

I do not seek the riches and crops of my ancestors, what the stored up harvest brought my ancient grandfather. (1.1.41–42)

Likewise, a Propertian distich, though less musical than its Tibullan counterpart, is noticeably more refined than its Catullan relative.

$$- \; \smile \; \neg | - \smile \; \neg | - \quad \smile \neg \quad \smile \neg | - \; \sim | - -$$

Tu mihi sola places: placeam tibi, Cynthia, solus.

$$- \; \smile \smile | - \; \smile \; \neg | | - \quad \smile \neg \quad - \smile \neg | -$$

hic erit et patrio sanguine pluris amor.

You alone are pleasing to me: may I alone be pleasing to you, Cynthia. This love will be worth more than even a father's blood. (2.7.19–20)

In all three cases, however, the resources of the line are exploited for maximum, if differing, poetic effects, and the impossibility of spondaic resolution after the pentameter's caesura, or break, marks the end of the couplet, sealing it as a complete metrical unit.

33. This recurring metrical refrain at once makes the elegiac couplet less fluid than its cousin, the dactylic hexameter, and allows even greater opportunities for rhetorical elaboration. There is a stanzaic quality to the couplet that becomes increasingly marked in later elegiac practice. Thus, while Catullus follows the Greek precedent and allows enjambment from one couplet to the next, his successors treat each couplet as a complete unit of sense, if not always of syntax. The emphasis on end-stopped couplets increases over the course of the genre's development so that by the time of Ovid the pentameter invariably finishes with a disyllabic word, doubly marking the closure of the line. As the couplet develops, the hexameter becomes the line of assertion or declaration, while the pentameter becomes the line of

expansion, qualification, or continuation. Ovid embodies these tendencies in metrical and stylistic practice and marks their contrast with the epic hexameter's gradually unfolding grandeur in the following couplet:

$$- \ \smile\smile \ | - \ \smile \ \smile | - \ \smile \ \gamma - \ - \ | \ - \ \ \smile \ \smile \gamma \ -$$

sex mihi surgat opus numeris, in quinque residat;

$$- \ \smile | \ - \ \ \ \gamma \ - \| - \ \smile \ \smile \ | - \ \smile \ \ \gamma \ -$$

ferrea cum uestris bella ualete modis.

My work rises in six numbers, it falls back in five; farewell to you, iron wars, and to your meters (1.1.27–28)

This distich provides a brief conspectus of the poetics of the elegiac couplet in their fullest flower and is remarkable on several counts. The opening line describes an antithesis between the hexameter and the pentameter, even as it enacts the elegiac couplet's rising and falling rhythm. That antithesis is then resolved in the pentameter where the poet bids farewell to epic and hence to the conflict between elegiac distichs and dactylic hexameters. At the same time, the nature of the elegiac couplet as a synthesis of epic meter and the pentameter is enacted by the word order's interweaving of *ferrea . . . bella* with *uestris . . . modis* around *ualete*, in effect healing the breech marked by the caesura. The meters of "iron war" are bid farewell in the very moment that they reassert their coherence across the pentameter's break. The disyllabic ending of the couplet marks its finality, while the use of the word *modis* or 'meters' reinforces semantically the metrical lesson the couplet has taught. Ovid's verse represents the pinnacle of this stylistic achievement.

Catullus

34. As Catullus's metrical practice was the least regular, his work is also the most diverse. Little is known about the poet's background. Born in Verona in the late eighties, he is generally thought to have died around the age of 30, *c.*50 BCE. He was from a wealthy provincial family that was sufficiently prominent to host Julius Caesar while wintering during the campaign in Gaul. Catullus shares two qualities with all the later elegists except Sulpicia: he is an equestrian and of provincial origins. The equestrian order was just below the senatorial. Its members had to possess a net worth of at least 400,000 sesterces, sufficient to live off their income and rents without other employment. This economic fact is of no little literary importance. These were men with the means and the leisure to pursue poetry and learning as a full-time occupation, with no need for external remuneration. Before Catullus, professional poets had been drawn from the lower classes and were often of Greek or servile origins. To make a living, they had to produce the kind of poetry for which Roman aristocrats were willing to pay. In practice,

this meant made-to-order panegyrics of military and political triumphs or historical epics recounting the deeds of famous ancestors. The equestrian status of Catullus and his successors freed them from this necessity, at the same time as their provincial status made their entry into Roman politics unlikely. They were *noui homines*, men without consular ancestors. While it was possible for a talented *nouus homo*, such as Cicero or Marius, to claw his way to the top of the political heap and to achieve not only senatorial but consular status, it was rare. Thus all the elegists, like Catullus, were men of wealth, leisure, and learning, who were disengaged from the all-consuming political obsessions of the scions of the great aristocratic families. They were members of the first generation for which the duties of being a poet were compatible with those of being a free man.

35. Catullus traveled to Rome in his late teens or early twenties where he made the acquaintance of many of the most accomplished literary men of his age, people such as Licinius Calvus, Gaius Helvius Cinna, and Cornelius Nepos. Together they formed a loosely affiliated group referred to in modern scholarship as the neoterics. Although bound by no formal doctrine, they were all committed to the Alexandrian concepts of brevity, wit, polish, and learning in poetry, qualities summed up in two of Catullus's favorite words, *urbanitas* and *uenustas*. *Urbanitas* was a quality of charm and sophistication that implied both learning and a refusal of pedantry. Its opposite was *rusticitas*, the quality of being a country bumpkin. *Uenustas* was seductive elegance. It refers to being under the sign of Venus. It thus has an erotic charge, but can refer to any behavior that has the capacity to enchant the beholder.

36. Catullus's corpus comes down to us in three distinct sections. The polymetrics (poems 1–60) are short pieces written in iambic and lyric meters. They vary in subject matter from tender love poems to harsh invective. In one poem, Catullus will rejoice in the homecoming of his friend Veranius from Spain (c. 9), and in another threaten Furius and Aurelius with oral and anal rape (c. 16). This same section includes both a moving translation of Sappho 31 (c. 51) and a poem in which Julius Caesar's henchman, Mamurra, is referred to as a gigantic, all-consuming prick, *mentula* (c. 29).

37. The *carmina maiora* or "longer poems" (61–68) occupy the central section of the corpus. The shortest (65) is 24 lines and the longest (64) is 408. The *carmina maiora* are written in a variety of meters, but 65–68 are in elegiac couplets. The *carmina maiora* contain Catullus's only poems in dactylic hexameters, the miniature epic on the marriage of Peleus and Thetis (64) and a choral marriage hymn (62). Like the polymetrics, these poems vary in subject matter, but the overarching theme of marriage is a constant throughout. Poems 61 and 62 are thus marriage hymns or epithalamia. Poem 63 tells the tale of Attis's ecstatic commitment to the great mother goddess, Cybele, in which he castrates himself in a mystical marriage that insures the returning fertility of the soil. The poem focuses on the morning after the ritual frenzy when Attis wakes to regret what he has done. Poem 64,

on the marriage of Peleus and Thetis, closes with an ironic epithalamium sung by the Fates. Poem 65 is an introductory missive accompanying poem 66, which as we saw earlier celebrates Queen Berenice of Egypt's devotion to her brother and new husband, Ptolemy III. Poem 67 is a version of the paraclausithyron, but, rather than the song of the lover at the door, this is the song of the door itself recounting its mistress's infidelity and the impotence of her husband. Poem 68 is by most accounts the first full-fledged love elegy in Latin literature. It continues the marriage theme by both portraying Lesbia's adulterous liaison with Catullus as a marriage and by emphasizing that she was in fact married to somebody else. The *carmina maiora* thus begin with ideal marriage and progress through ironic and perverse unions to adulterous ones.

38. The last section of the Catullan corpus is the epigrams (69–116). These are short poems written in elegiac meter. They range from two (85, 93, 94, 95b) to twenty-six lines (76), the last representing Catullus's other main claimant for the title of a fully-fledged love elegy. The epigrams, like the polymetrics, vary widely in subject matter. Unlike the latter, they are less concerned with *uenustas* and *urbanitas* than with traditional Roman concepts such as *amicitia* (friendship, but also political alliance), *fides* (good faith), *foedus* (a formal agreement based on *fides*), *officium* (duty), and *pietas* (formal obligations to the family, the state, and the gods). All of these terms refer to the system of mutual obligations that bound Roman aristocratic males in complex webs of friendship, political alliance, and clientage. One of Catullus's most revolutionary innovations was the systematic use of this vocabulary to describe his relationship with Lesbia. He uses this vocabulary to describe a relation of mutual respect and affection between a man and a woman that to this point had only been conceived as existing between men. Thus in one poem (72), Catullus famously compares his love for Lesbia to that of a father for his sons and sons-in-law. The epigrams are also distinguished by their analytical mode of presentation. In them, the poet often states an initial problem or premise and then draws what seem, to him at least, to be the necessary consequences. A good example is poem 92:

> Lesbia mi dicit semper male nec tacet umquam
> de me: Lesbia me dispeream nisi amat.
> quo signo? quia sunt totidem mea: deprecor illam
> assidue, uerum dispeream nisi amo.

> Lesbia always speaks ill of me and is never silent about me: I'll be damned if Lesbia doesn't love me. Why do I say this? Because it's the same with me: I run her down constantly, but I'll be damned if I don't love her.

In using this rhetoric, Catullus wittily combines a Roman bent toward the reduction of problems to their bare essentials with a gesture inherited from Alexandrian epigram, the twist in the final line. While all the elegists are clearly familiar with the subject matter of the epigrams, Ovid is their clearest inheritor. Not only does he share a fondness for the final coda, he also loves to take an initial premise and work out all its logical permutations, expanding what in Catullus would be an epigram to the length of an entire elegy.

39. Whether this tripartite arrangement of the Catullan corpus is the product of the author's own hand or the work of a posthumous editor has been the subject of much long and bitter debate. The majority opinion, at present, leans toward the view that the poet himself is responsible for the arrangement, but many scholars refuse to pronounce one way or the other. What does not seem in doubt is that Catullus expected his audience to read his poems in terms of one another, whether they were presented in the order we now have them or not. Thus, in the opening sequence of the polymetrics (2, 3, 5, 7, 8, 11), we find a brief conspectus of the entire affair, from the poet's early love through his dawning awareness of Lesbia's infidelity to his final bitter dismissal:

> cum suis uiuat ualeatque moechis,
> quos simul complexa tenet trecentos,
> nullum amans uere, sed identidem omnium
>   ilia rumpens;
>
> nec meum respectet, ut ante, amorem,
> qui illius culpa cecidit uelut prati
> ultimi flos, praetereunte postquam
>   tactus aratro est. (11.17–24)

> Let her live and prosper with her adulterers, whom she holds three hundred at a time in her embrace, loving none truly, but time and again breaking their loins; nor should she look for my love as before, which has fallen by her fault, just like a flower in the farthest meadow when touched by the passing plough.

The final image of the flower and the plough is one of the most striking in the Catullan corpus and features an inversion of traditional gender stereotypes that is common both in Catullus and the later elegists. The epigrams included in this anthology produce another similar narrative of the affair, moving from mistrust (70, 72) through despair (75, 76) to resignation (85).

Tibullus

40. Information on Tibullus's life is not much more plentiful than that on Catullus's. He was born between 60 and 55 BCE and died in 19. Ancient testimony links him to the area near the village of Pedum in the Alban hills east of Rome. He was closely associated with the orator and general, M. Valerius Messalla Corvinus (64 BCE to 8 CE), whom he appears to have accompanied on his Acquitanian campaign and perhaps on others. Messalla was a Roman aristocrat and politician who cultivated the arts and would have been a natural patron for Tibullus, as he was later for the young Ovid. After some hesitation, Messalla supported Augustus in his conflict with Antony, but shortly after celebrating his Acquitanian triumph in 27 BCE, he retired from active participation in politics. Tibullus's poetry, unlike Propertius's or Ovid's, is all but free of references to Augustus and the nascent imperial regime. From a statement in poem 1.1, we can reasonably deduce that Tibullus's family, like many others, suffered a reduction of fortune during the proscriptions carried out by the members of the second triumvirate (Antony, Octavian, and Lepidus) after the defeat of the republican assassins of Caesar.

41. Quintilian's famous statement, "mihi tersus atque elegans maxime uidetur auctor Tibullus. Sunt qui Propertium malint" ["In my opinion Tibullus is a very elegant and concise author. There are those who prefer Propertius"] (*Inst.* 10.1.93), nicely sums up ancient opinion. Ovid terms Tibullus *cultus* or "polished" (*Amores* 3.9.66). The ancients held Tibullus in high regard and valued him above all for his style and cultivation. He has fared less well among the moderns, particularly during the twentieth century. One of the commonplaces of Tibullan criticism is a focus on the dreamlike quality of his text, a view that normally goes hand in hand with the devaluation of his poetry as smooth or soft, and lacking the formal integrity, imaginative leaps, and sharp juxtapositions that characterize Propertius. One commentator went so far as to attribute Tibullus's style to a brain abnormality. Even his supporters often damn him with faint praise. Thus, Smith, in the first modern English commentary on the poet, writes, "He is not a man of brilliant passages" (68). Others characterize his poetry as "smooth" and "drifting." The fact is that all agree, whether friend or foe, that Tibullus's poetry is nonlinear, and often seems to move from one topic to the next "through the mere associations of ideas and words" (Veyne 1988: 36). These texts are less a series of coherent rhetorical arguments in the manner of Ovid than complex tissues of related, interwoven, and sometimes contradictory themes.

42. In poem 1.1, the poet starts with the contrast between the life of the farmer and the soldier, modulates into praise of Messalla, and finishes with an evocation of his life as Delia's *seruus amoris*. Yet, the entire poem, although the setting and characters change, proceeds effortlessly and returns to certain key oppositions such as *labor* ("struggle") versus *inertia* ("inactivity"), and *diuitiae* ("riches") versus *paupertas* ("poverty") throughout. His poems are more like symphonies composed of a series of recurring and contrasted themes than linear expositions or dramatic narratives. Contemporary readers familiar with the experimental narrative techniques used in recent film, fiction, and music videos, may be better able to appreciate these poems than were scholars raised on romantic poetry and realist fiction at the beginning of the last century.

43. One of the ways Tibullus achieves unity of composition in the presence of such thematic diversity is with anaphora, the systematic repetition of the same word at the beginning of successive lines or couplets. The following passage gives a good example of this very sophisticated technique. I have used italics to draw attention to words that are repeated in the passage, related to repeated words, or similar in sound and shape to repeated words:

> *nam neque* tunc plumae *nec* stragula picta soporem
> *nec* sonitus placidae ducere possit aquae.
> *num* Veneris magnae uiolaui *num*ina uerbo,
> et mea *nunc* poenas impia lingua luit?
> *num* feror incestus sedes adiisse deorum
> sertaque de sanctis deripuisse focis?
> *non ego*, si merui, dubitem procumbere templis
> et dare sacratis oscula liminibus,
> *non ego* tellurem genibus perrepere supplex
> et miserum sancto tundere poste caput.

For then neither feather pillows nor painted spreads nor the pleasing sounds of water would be able to bring sleep. Have I violated the godhead of great Venus by my speech and does my impious tongue now pay the penalty? Am I now said to have approached the temples of the gods in a state of pollution and to have stolen garlands from the holy altars? I would not hesitate, if I deserved it, to prostrate myself before temples and give kisses to their sanctified thresholds. I would not hesitate to crawl upon the earth on my knees as a suppliant and beat my wretched head against the holy doorpost. (1.2.77–86)

The poet effortlessly carries us from his sleepless bed, adorned with rich coverlets, to the threshold of the temple of Venus, where he pounds his head, by subtly intertwining negations (*neque*, *nec*, *non*), interrogatives (*num*), and their near homophones (*nam*, *numina*, *nunc*). The door of Venus, of course, doubles for the house of his beloved before which he sings his fruitless paraclausithyron.

44. Tibullus published his work in two books. The first, *c.*26 BCE, is largely concerned with his love for Delia (1.1, 1.2, 1.3, 1.5, 1.6), a woman of

indeterminate origins and status. It includes pederastic poems written for a certain Marathus (1.4, 1.8, 1.9), a poem celebrating Messalla's birthday (1.7), and a closing poem on Tibullus's pet themes of love and the virtues of rural simplicity (1.10). Delia is generally thought to be a *meretrix*, because of the emphasis the poet places on the rich rivals who compete for her favors. The opposition of the *diues amator* ("rich lover") to the poor poet is part of the book's general emphasis on the preference of genteel poverty to the exertion and dangers associated with acquiring riches through warfare or mercantile adventures. Given Tibullus's equestrian status, this latter theme must be regarded as a pose. The celebration of the virtues of poverty is, in fact, part of the pastoral genre's praise of country life. Tibullus alone among the extant elegists casts the rural ideal as the background to his poetry. Thus, the theme of the *diues amator*, from which the social identity of Delia is deduced, is as much a part of this poetry's generic as its social context. By the same token, the preference for amorous *otium* ("leisure") to a more socially and fiscally remunerative *negotium* ("business") is typical of erotic elegy from it inception. It is part of what makes it suspect from a traditional Roman perspective.

45. Tibullus's second book is devoted to his affair with Nemesis or 'Revenge' (2.3, 2.4, 2.6). While he portrays his love for Delia as anything but ideal, things deteriorate in Book 2. Nemesis is depicted as a cold and calculating mistress whose one interest is money. The poet's self-abasement before his beloved becomes complete in Book 2 when he proposes to become a field slave so that he can be close to his mistress when she goes to the country estate of his rich rival. There is a strong element of comedy as well as pathos in this literalization of the metaphor of *seruitium amoris*. Gone in Book 2 is the idealized country life portrayed in 1.1. This field hand gets blisters and a sunburn, where the farmer in Book 1 planted fruit trees with an "easy hand" (*facilis manus*). The rest of Book 2 is devoted to Tibullus's friends and patrons. Poem 2.1, dedicated to Messalla, recounts the celebration of the Ambarvalia, the ceremonial purification of crops, animals, and farmers. Poem 2.2 is a short piece celebrating the birthday of Tibullus's friend Cornutus. Poem 2.5 is long narrative elegy celebrating the election of Messalla's son, Messalinus, to the priestly college of the *quindecemuiri sacris faciundis*, the keepers of the Sibylline oracles. The second book is substantially shorter than the first and is thought by some to be a posthumous collection.

Sulpicia

46. The poems of Sulpicia come down to us in what is known as the *corpus Tibullianum*, the collection in which Tibullus's poetry was transmitted to us from antiquity. The first two books of the corpus are his. The last is a miscellany of poems by poets in the circle gathered around Messalla. This

third book was divided in two by the Renaissance humanists, but the present custom is to follow the ancient precedent. Poems 3.1 through 3.6 are elegies by an otherwise unknown poet named Lygdamus on his separation from a woman named Neaera. Poem 3.7 is an anonymous *Panegyric of Messalla* written in hexameters. Poems 3.8 to 3.12 are a series of anonymous elegies about Sulpicia's love for Cerinthus. They are designed to serve as an introduction to Sulpicia's own poems and are sometimes thought to have been written by Tibullus himself. Poems 3.13 through 3.18 are Sulpicia's own poems, while the last two poems are epigrams by Tibullus.

47. Sulpicia's poetry is important on several counts. First, she is the only woman writer of classical Latin poetry whose work has survived. Second, her obvious sophistication and independent spirit gives us insight into the character of the young women who frequented the circles in which elegiac poetry was read and composed. As the daughter of the jurist Servius Sulpicius and the niece of Messalla, she hailed from the most respectable of backgrounds but does not scruple to speak publicly of her affair. One cannot help but feel she could have held her own easily with the likes of Lesbia, Cynthia, or Delia, although her self-characterization is very different. Where the *dominae* are portrayed by their male poets as fickle and interested only in gifts, Sulpicia presents herself as the articulate daughter of a noble house who does not scruple to tread on convention and who expects fidelity and respect from her lover, Cerinthus. Third, her poetry represents an interesting fusion of the Catullan epigrammatic tradition and later elegiac practice. In general, her couplets are end-stopped. Her pentameters terminate in disyllabic words in every case but one. No poem is over ten lines long, and her prosody is heavily spondaic, although she scrupulously avoids resolution in the fifth foot. Her syntax is at times convoluted and difficult, but the narrative line of her brief collection is clear. Poem 3.13 is a programmatic poem that announces the impossibility of her remaining silent about her love. 3.14 and 3.15 are on the possibility of her being led out of town by her uncle on her birthday. 3.16 and 3.17 are poems of jealousy on Cerinthus's affair with a low-class *scortum* ("hussy") and his seeming indifference to Sulpicia's having taken ill. The final poem looks to reconciliation with Cerinthus after Sulpicia had stormed out of a tryst in an ill-conceived attempt to hide the intensity of her passion. The link between elegy and epigram is nowhere clearer than in Sulpicia where Catullan precedent is married with a strong narrative line and stylistic refinements characteristic of later elegy. The critical tradition that once saw these poems as the spontaneous effusions of an artless young girl has recently been shown to be more the product of romanticism and condescension than a careful reading of the poems.

Propertius

48. Sextus Propertius, born 49–47 BCE, was an equestrian from the city of Asissi. In the last poem of his first book, the *Monobiblos*, he tells us that he lost a kinsman in the siege of Perusia. This epigram serves as a *sphragis* or 'signature' to the first book. It deserves to be quoted in full:

> Qualis et unde genus, qui sint mihi, Tulle, Penates,
>   quaeris pro nostra semper amicitia.
> si Perusina tibi patriae sunt nota sepulcra,
>   Italiae duris funera temporibus,
> cum Romana suos egit discordia ciuis,
>   (sic mihi praecipue, puluis Etrusca, dolor,
> tu projecta mei perpessa es membra propinqui,
>   tu nullo miseri contegis ossa solo),
> proxima supposito contingens Umbria campo
>   me genuit terris fertilis uberibus.

On account of our friendship, Tullus, you are always asking of what sort and from where is my family, and who are my household gods. If the Perusine graves of the Italian fatherland are known to you, as well as the deaths from that hard time when discord drove Rome's citizens (for this reason, you are especially painful to me, Etruscan dust that allowed the bones of my kinsman to be scattered, that covered them with no soil), fertile Umbria, right next door, touching the field below, gave birth to me in her rich land. (1.22)

The Perusine war, referred to in this poem, was among the most savage of those fought during the period of civil turmoil that marked the early life of Propertius.

49. Ostensibly a conflict over where to settle the veterans of Octavian and Mark Antony's victory over Caesar's assassins, the Perusine war represents an early round in the political maneuvering that would culminate in the battle of Actium. While Marc Antony regulated affairs in the east after the battle of Philippi (42 BCE), his brother, Lucius, served as Octavian's colleague in the consulship for 41 BCE. When the Northern Italian landowners protested against Octavian's plan to seize land for the veterans, Lucius took the opportunity to portray his brother as the landowners' champion. Riots broke out in Rome, and both sides assembled their troops. After some initial victories, Octavian cornered Lucius in the town of Perusia, where a siege was laid. Relief from other legions loyal to the Antonian cause never materialized due to factional infighting and an unwillingness on the part of the soldiers to fight against a plan whose purpose was to insure their own rewards. In the end, Octavian, although allowing Lucius to surrender and return to Rome, put to death the entire town council of Perusia as well as three hundred senators and equestrians who had accompanied Lucius's army. It was a massacre that sent a chilling message, but one that Octavian, once he became Augustus, preferred to forget.

50. Propertius's choice to end his first collection of poetry with a poem that links his identity to those dying at Perusia marks a definitive distance from the Augustan regime, which retrospectively colors the whole book. Published in 28 BCE, the *Monobiblos* is not at first glance a book of political poetry. It is a collection of love poetry by a clever young poet. Yet, the refusal of politics is itself a political gesture and the significance of that gesture is woven into the order of the poems. Thus, poem 1.4, addressed to the iambic poet Bassus, proclaims Propertius's exclusive devotion to Cynthia despite the temptations Bassus dangles before him. Poem 1.5 warns Gallus – generally believed to be Cornelius Gallus, Propertius's predecessor in the genre – to keep away from Cynthia. Poem 1.6, like 1.22, is addressed to Tullus, the poet's patron. He is a rich young aristocrat about to embark on a tour of government service and invites Propertius to accompany him. Such a voyage would normally represent a highly valued entrée into the world of public affairs that a young man was expected to make his own. Propertius, however, refuses to leave Cynthia and rejects the invitation. The next poem, 1.7, purports to teach Ponticus the superiority of elegy over epic, while 1.8a and 1.8b demonstrate the efficacy of elegy in persuading Cynthia not to leave on a journey. Thus, the poet begins the sequence by proclaiming the superiority of his elegiac devotion to a single beloved over the traditional light-hearted promiscuity of iambic poetry. He then argues for the superiority of his love poetry over that of his predecessor, Gallus. In 1.6, this same poetry, in the person of its dedicatee, Cynthia, prohibits the poet from following a normal career path, which would involve direct participation in the political structures sponsored by the Augustan regime. In 1.7, he argues for elegy's superiority over the genre that celebrates the virtues of the career path he has just rejected, epic. Lastly, 1.8 is an object lesson in the power of elegy itself. In sum, the heart of the *Monobiblos* weaves together the life of love, the superiority of the elegiac genre to its competitors, and the refusal of traditional Roman values into a single indissoluble whole. Read in light of 1.22's evocation of the slaughter at Perusia, it is hard not to see the poet's choice of genre as necessarily, though not exclusively, politically motivated. *Seruitium amoris* is portrayed as an antidote to the *seruitium* inherent in normal life.

51. Yet, such a picture of Propertius as an anti-Augustan aesthete, while in one sense accurate, is too black and white. His second book, published in 25 or 26, complicates this two-dimensional picture. In the first poem, we discover that our poet has now moved into the circle of Maecenas, a close advisor and political ally of Augustus. Maecenas has been styled Augustus's minister of culture. This is an oversimplification. He was a man of letters and a patron of the arts with a keen eye for talent. Among the writers in his circle

when Propertius joined it were Horace and Vergil. These poets were clearly in sympathy with the Augustan program, although they were not uncritical of it. Thus, while parts of the *Aeneid* have been read as veiled warnings to Augustus on the dangers of *furor* ("rage") and revenge, the poem nonetheless celebrates the Augustan peace and Rome's *imperium sine fine* ("rule without end"). Likewise, though Horace counsels moderation and gently warns of the dangers of tyranny, he also pictures Augustus as the earthly representative of Jupiter himself. Neither poet produced anything like Propertius 1.22's harsh reminder of the slaughter at Perusia.

52. Still, there is little evidence that Maecenas demanded made-to-order verse from his poets and there was good reason for many to be optimistic about the reign of Augustus. The victor at Actium in 31 BCE proved clement in a way that the young *triumvir* of 41 had not. By 29 BCE, the era of the civil wars was at an end and Augustus, while retaining *de facto* power (*auctoritas*), chose to respect traditional republican forms of government. In addition, he launched an ambitious building program for the city that included the refurbishing of many temples and the revival of the ancient rites celebrated in their precincts. Lastly, under the slogan of a return to the *mos maiorum*, Augustus passed a series of laws promoting marriage and childbirth among the upper classes while penalizing adultery. These latter measures were controversial, and they had to be amended and revised on several occasions due to popular outcry. Nonetheless, to many, the *auctoritas* (as opposed to *imperium*, "formal legal power") of the victor of Actium meant a return to stability and normalcy after a hundred years of unrest and civil slaughter. Maecenas, therefore, did not have to dictate patriotic topics to his poets, and their occasional straying from the strict party line merely showed his and Augustus's respect for the traditional republican virtue of *libertas*, "freedom of speech."

53. Propertius, however, strayed more than most in Maecenas's circle. Poem 2.1 is a *recusatio*, a common type of poem in the period, in which a poet alleges his inability to write one kind of verse, normally epic, and indicates his preference for staying with a less strenuous form such as lyric or elegy. In itself, the *recusatio* is not necessarily a subversive gesture. Horace writes them as well as Propertius, and they are an expected part of the Callimachean poet's arsenal of weapons for fending off the threat of epic composition. Nonetheless, when Propertius tells Maecenas that if he were able to write epic he would compose a poem on Augustus's feats during the civil wars, including the battle of Perusia, one can only imagine that both the *princeps* and the patron were relieved by Propertius's refusal. The massacre of Roman senators and equestrians was hardly in keeping with the image Augustus wished to project as the guarantor of peace and the restorer of traditional morality. In poem 2.7, the interdependence of the poetic, the political, and the sexual in elegy is demonstrated when Propertius and Cynthia celebrate the repeal of a law that would have forced the poet to marry and break off

27

their irregular relationship. There has been considerable debate over whether the law in question is one of Augustus's moral reform laws or a piece of earlier triumviral legislation taxing unmarried men. In either case, poem 2.7 shows Propertius in particular, and elegy in general, as out of keeping with the spirit of the Augustan reforms. By the same token, poems 2.15 and 2.16, both of which deal with the battle of Actium, show the poet identifying with the cause of Antony as much as with that of Augustus.

54. It would be a mistake, then, to see Propertius's move into the circle of Maecenas as a recantation of the position he adopts at the end of the *Monobiblos*. Moreover, the politics of this are very complex. On the one hand, the poet shows his acceptance of the new regime by becoming the close associate of one the *princeps*'s most trusted advisors. On the other, the *princeps* is able to demonstrate his liberality by, in effect, sponsoring his own critic. Thus, the poet, by becoming the client of Maecenas, is able, at least temporarily, to be both pro- and anti-Augustan at the same time. The nature of this carefully balanced position is perhaps best illustrated by the opening couplets of two poems from Book 3, published *c*.23 BCE:

Arma deus Caesar dites meditatur ad Indos,
  et freta gemmiferi findere classe maris.

Caesar, the god, is planning arms against rich India and to split the straits of the gem-bearing sea with his fleet. (3.4.1–2)

Pacis Amor deus est, pacem ueneramur amantes:
  Stant mihi cum domina proelia dura mea.

Love is the god of peace, we lovers worship peace, and hard are my battles with my mistress. (3.5.1–2)

The couplet from the first poem appears to be a piece of typical Roman panegyric celebrating the plans of a fearless leader to conquer a foreign enemy and come home covered in glory and booty. The next poem, however, parodies the first and counterposes Love and peace to Caesar and arms. Poem 3.5, then, proceeds to evoke the standard elegiac conceit of *militia amoris*, while the fact that the lover's battles with his girl are termed "hard" is a clear sexual *double entendre*.

55. Book 4 of Propertius, published *c*.16 BCE, represents a fundamental change in the way the poet thinks of the elegiac genre. In part, this book represents a return to the genre's Callimachean roots. As the poet writes in 4.1, he shall become the Roman Callimachus, offering us a new *Aitia* dedicated to the *urbs aeterna* itself: "sacra diesque canam et cognomina prisca locorum" ["I shall sing rites and days and the ancient names of places"] (4.1.69). Two lines later a second speaker, the Babylonian astrologer Horos,

interrupts the poet with a warning that Apollo opposes the poet's new direction. Propertius's task is to serve in the legions of Venus: "militiam Veneris blandis patiere sub armis" ["you will suffer the soldiery of Venus, wielding pleasing arms"] (4.1.137). This alternation of the aitiological with the amatory in large part characterizes Book 4 as a whole. Thus in 4.4, the poet tells the tale of how the Tarpeian rock, off which murderers and traitors were thrown, received its name from the treachery of Tarpeia, a Vestal virgin. In the traditional story, Tarpeia betrays the Roman citadel to Tatius, the Sabine commander, after being bribed. She is then executed on the spot by the Sabines themselves. In Propertius's version of the myth, however, Tarpeia betrays Rome for love not money. She is smitten with Tatius's beauty. In this fashion, the poet manages to combine the erotic with the aitiological to create a recognizably hybrid form. Poem 4.6 is, on the surface at least, a purely patriotic poem celebrating Augustus's victory at Actium. This poem is read by some as evidence of the poet's reconciliation with Augustus and by others as an exercise in satire. Poems 4.7 and 4.8 are the only poems on Cynthia in the last book. In 4.7, Cynthia returns from the dead to accuse Propertius of giving her a cheap funeral, abusing her slaves, and being unfaithful to her memory. It is a poem commemorating the death of elegy, as we have known it. Poem 4.8 takes us back to an earlier time, before Cynthia's death. It includes an aitiological element, when it recounts the story of an obscure snake cult in Lanuvium. At the same time, it vividly tells the tale of Cynthia surprising Propertius with two girls.

56. Overall, Book 4 shows Propertius searching for a new direction. There is a clear gesture in several poems toward embracing the national and patriotic through the aitiological. The Augustan regime is now firmly established and it has become obvious that there neither are, nor will be, any alternatives to it in the foreseeable future. The poet had best make his peace. Yet, every time the gesture of reconciliation is made it is accompanied by one of distancing. The story of Tarpeia's criminal love is told, but it is a story of love not very different from the elegist's own. The victor of Actium is celebrated, but in such an over-the-top fashion that it is impossible to tell the difference between panegyric and parody. Cynthia is dead, but in the next poem comes back to life. Perhaps the most significant factor in the whole of Book 4, however, is the increasing prominence of third person narrative. It is as if the very space that made the voice of the elegist possible was vanishing as the Augustan regime hardened into an established fact.

Ovid

57. Of course, on one level, we know that this was not true. In the very period when Propertius is writing Book 4, Ovid is beginning to publish the first edition of the Amores (c.19 BCE). Born in Sulmo in 43 BCE, Ovid was only 12 at the time of the battle of Actium. By the time he had reached his late

teens, when young people begin to develop a political consciousness, the Augustan regime was not only well entrenched; it was all he had ever known. Thus while many have tried to read Ovid's ironic stance in relation to the Augustan program of moral and religious restoration as political opposition, this seems to be based more on wishful thinking than hard-nosed analysis. Ovid is certainly irreverent, even flippant, but we find none of the bitterness expressed by Propertius in poems such as 1.22. Augustus is for Ovid a fact of life, and as such a potential target for Ovid's wit. Since Augustus is a very a big fact in Rome, he is naturally a very big target. Yet, Ovid is a creature of Augustan Rome and can imagine living nowhere else. He has no illusions about the desirability of returning to a simpler world of republican virtue. For him, this is the golden age.

58. The textual history of the *Amores* is complex, as is the dating of all of Ovid's work. A brief overview of his career will help situate our discussion. In a prefatory epigram to the present edition of the *Amores* Ovid tells us that this is a revised second edition. The first edition, which contained five books instead of the present three, is generally thought to have been published in installments over the course of the teens. The second edition is dated variously by scholars to any time between 9 BCE and 1 CE, with most people placing it within a few years of the turn of the millennium. After Ovid finished the first edition, he is generally believed to have produced the first volume of the *Heroides*, which contained poems 1–15. Where the *Amores* were love elegies in the same sense as those found in Catullus, Tibullus, and the first three books of Propertius, the *Heroides* are a series of love letters from mythological heroines to their lovers who have under one pretext or another left them. Propertius established the precedent for this variation on the elegiac genre in 4.3, the letter of Arethusa to Lycotas. The second volume of the *Heroides*, poems 16–21, which consists of pairs of letters between heroines and their absent lovers, is a later addition, from the period shortly before the poet's exile to Tomis (4–8 CE). The clearest successor to the *Amores* in both spirit and form, however, is the *Ars Amatoria* and its companion piece, the *Remedia Amoris*. The *Ars* takes the pose of the *praeceptor amoris*, which already figured prominently in love elegy, and uses it to create a how-to book on the art of seduction. It was published between 1 BCE and 1 CE.

59. Ovid published two other main bodies of work in the elegiac meter, the *Fasti* and the exilic poetry. The *Fasti*, a versified calendar of Roman religious observances, was half finished at the time of Ovid's exile in 8 CE. Although there is evidence he did some more revision on it, the poem was never completed. The *Fasti* owes very little to the Roman erotic elegiac tradition and will not be treated any further in the present collection. The exilic poetry, on the other hand, comes down to us in two primary collections, the *Tristia* and the *Epistulae ex Ponto*. The *Tristia* presents a speaker who is at times very reminiscent of the persona presented in *Amores* and the *Ars Amatoria*. In the early poems, in particular, he is witty and unbowed. He recognizes

Augustus's authority but is not above deflating it with a rude *double entendre*. In Book 2 (9 CE), the poet offers a defense of his career as an erotic elegist. The last three books of the *Tristia* and the four books of the *Epistulae ex Ponto* are progressively more somber, and in them one can see the progressive extinction of the elegiac genre. In the world of Augustan absolutism and under the Julio-Claudian monarchy that succeeded it, there was no longer any place for elegiac subversion.

60. Ovid is the most wide-ranging of the elegists. Not only does he take erotic elegy into uncharted territory in works such as the *Heroides*, the *Ars*, and to a lesser extent the *Tristia*; he is also the only one after Catullus to have produced a substantial body of work outside the elegiac meter. Ovid wrote a tragedy, the *Medea* (*c*.10 BCE), which Quintilian praises but is lost to us. His most famous work, however, is the *Metamorphoses*. A narrative poem written in hexameters, it recounts a series of tales of miraculous transformation from the beginning of the world to the present. Ovid tells us that exile prevented him from giving it a final revision. Nonetheless, we have a highly polished narrative poem in fifteen books. It is an epic to rival the *Aeneid*, but its tone is very different from Vergil's poem of melancholy grandeur. The poem ends with a panegyric of Augustus in which he is equated with Jupiter's earthly representative, a gesture familiar from Horace, *Odes* 3.1, "Iuppiter arces | temperat aetherias et mundi regna triformis, | terra sub Augusto est" ["Jupiter controls the heavenly citadels and the kingdoms of the tri-formed world, the earth is under Augustus"] (15.858–60). There then follows a coda, which again is an imitation of Horace, but this time of *Odes* 3.30, "Iamque opus exegi, quod nec Iouis ira nec ignis | nec poterit ferrum nec edax abolere uetustas" ["Now I have completed a work that neither the anger of Jupiter nor fire nor the sword nor gnawing age will be able to destroy"] (15.871–72). Such vaunts are traditional, and the anger of Jupiter is a standard metaphor for lightning. Yet, coming immediately after the equation of Jupiter and Augustus in their respective realms, this coda seems to retract the earlier praise of the *princeps*'s absolute power over things on earth. The immediate juxtaposition of the two passages cannot help but issue an invitation to read them ironically. This is the kind of epic only an elegist could write. Its ironic defiance of the power of Jupiter and Augustus, however, was shortly answered by the poet's exile to Tomis. Still, Ovid had the last laugh. His poetry did survive. Not even the anger of Jupiter was able to destroy it.

61. The causes of Ovid's exile are shrouded in mystery. He lists two, "carmen et error" ["poetry and a mistake"] (2.207). He was not permitted to discuss the error. He tells us he saw something that he should have reported but did not. What he saw is a matter of speculation. It is generally believed that he was privy either to one of the sexual indiscretions for which Augustus's granddaughter, Julia, was exiled or to the intrigues surrounding the imperial succession late in Augustus's reign – although it is by no means clear that the one was not linked to the other. Beyond that nothing can be

said. The *carmen* in question, however, is clear. Ovid sets out to defend the *Ars Amatoria* in *Tristia* 2. Yet, whatever would have given offense in the *Ars* was already present in the *Amores*.

62. The opening sequence of the *Amores* is particularly revealing. Poem 1.1 presents the poet in the midst of trying to write epic, when Cupid appears and steals a foot from every other line, producing elegiac couplets rather than dactylic hexameter. The first line of the poem is a clear parody of the *Aeneid*'s "arma uirumque cano" ["arms and the man I sing"] (1.1). Poem 1.2 presents Cupid's triumph over the poet. The triumph represented the pinnacle of success for a Roman commander in the republican period. By this point in the principate, it had been restricted to members of the imperial family. Ovid's parody of it in an amorous context represents a form of near sacrilege. In 1.3, the poet's beloved finally receives a name. Up to this point, love had been an abstract concept. Ovid, here, is clearly revealing the artificial nature of the elegiac genre as a whole. In 1.4, the poet gives instructions on how Corinna can deceive her *uir* when they attend a dinner party, and in 1.5, we see their adulterous affair consummated. In sum, Ovid presents his enterprise as an artificial game that positions itself as the opposite of epic and the traditional values it represents. The artificiality of the genre, while on the one hand defusing any real political bite, on the other hand is calculated to offend by its very flippancy. Likewise, the fact that the affair itself is essentially adulterous is sure to give offense to an emperor who prided himself on the re-establishment of antique virtue and passed the first recorded legislation against adultery in the history of the Roman state. The fictional nature of the situation and the ambiguous status of Corinna may have been designed to give the poet cover, but the sequence can in no way be seen as an endorsement of the *princeps*'s stated program.

63. Nonetheless, this is a collection of poems that could only have been written in the Augustan age. It assumes the *pax Augusta* and civil peace as givens. Ovid does not reject the possibility of a real triumph because that possibility does not exist for him or anyone else outside the imperial family. The rococo life of sophisticated distraction he imagines in the *Amores* is the life left a Roman aristocrat once the political arena has been reduced to an ornament of an unchanging regime. Augustus's maintenance of republican forms of government was a fig leaf that would be dropped by his successors. In such a world, the revival of the *mos maiorum* is an impossible fiction, since the conditions that made those values meaningful no longer obtained. The artificiality of the world of Ovidian elegy is a faithful reflection of the artificiality of the Augustan enterprise as whole. Ovid represents not so much the opposite of Augustan culture as its fullest flowering.

64. The *Ars*, however, must have been particularly galling to Augustus since it adopted the pose of didactic poetry. Certainly, the position of *praeceptor amoris* was a common trope in elegy, but it had never been developed in this kind of systematic fashion. The poet's warning that he did not intend his

manual of seduction to be used against lawfully protected *matronae* does nothing to guarantee that such a book would not "fall into the wrong hands." Indeed, this sort of caveat positively plants the suggestion of adultery at the very moment that it proclaims its acceptance of traditional morality. Like Augustus's claim to have restored the republic, Ovid's warning is most meaningfully read as signifying the opposite of what it says. This game of reflection is extended even further in the *Ars* when Ovid, in the passage we have chosen for the present anthology, names the very monuments that Augustus had restored or built as prime hunting grounds for young Don Juans.

65. The *Heroides* is unique in ancient literature in its systematic attempt to present the other side of the great love affairs mythology had preserved for Ovid. Here we see Penelope's complaint to Ulysses, Briseis's love letter to Achilles, and Phaedra's self-justification to Hippolytus. Such a perspective is consonant with the elegiac practice of inverting traditional gender roles discussed above. At the same time, mythological exempla and learning had always played an important role in love elegy, beginning with Catullus 68's evocation of the Laudamia and Protesilaus myth. *Heroides* 7, the poem chosen for this volume, is particularly important. As the letter of Dido to Aeneas, it allows Ovid to invert the perspective of the great love story of the *Aeneid*. Here, Aeneas is not the self-sacrificing hero who gives up personal happiness to insure the foundation of Rome. He is depicted as a callous and deceptive lover who abandons his possibly pregnant beloved. What was tragic in Vergil becomes pathetic in Ovid.

66. The *Tristia* and *Epistulae ex Ponto* were not widely read in the twentieth century. The complaints of exile, however moving, become tedious after a time. Ovid's wheedling before Augustus and later Tiberius can be unseemly. Recently, however, a number of scholars have shown that there is more to these poems than meet the eye. The poet's compliments to Augustus can be read as thinly disguised barbs, his apologies as indictments. These are not the monotonous texts they sometimes seem. They require careful reading, however, for the full scope of their range and subtlety to become apparent. Thus in *Tristia* 2 we find the poet defending the *Ars Amatoria* by arguing that the literary and artistic tradition is full of stories of rape and seduction. The very gods who occupy the temples Augustus restored were participants in those stories, the same gods whose temples are recommended as good places to pick up girls in the *Ars Amatoria*. The poet thus defends the *Ars* by invoking the very passage that would have most given offense. It is a stroke of rhetorical brilliance, because if Augustus is to make the argument that Ovid's art encourages immorality, then Ovid's invocation of the numerous myths of rape and seduction associated with these sites would make Augustus as guilty as Ovid. The *princeps* is left with the choice of either refusing to recognize his own reflection in Ovid's verse, in which case there is no longer a justification for his anger at the poet, or to see himself

and thereby admit that Ovid is no more guilty than he is in the corruption of morals.

67. Augustus, of course, had one more option that Ovid's strategy cannot take into account. That is the possibility of not reading. Augustus can refuse to play Ovid's rhetorical game and simply leave him in Tomis until his death in 17 CE. The years go by and every year Ovid writes another volume of verse. Each is met with stony silence on the part of both the *princeps* and his successor. Yet, not one of those volumes is suppressed. Ovid is allowed to write and publish. In fact, he was exiled to Tomis under the terms of what was called a *relegatio* rather than *exilium*, which meant that he kept his citizen's rights and property. He simply was not allowed to leave Tomis. As such, he was able to serve simultaneously as an example of the *princeps*'s clemency toward his enemies and his implacable anger. In such a world, where everything already means the opposite of what it says, there is no longer a place for elegiac subversion. The values on which it depended no longer exist. The genre had reached its end and would have to await the courtly poets of the high Middle Ages before it would experience a revival.

Select bibliography

Albrecht, M. von. (1997) *A History of Roman Literature from Livius Andronicus to Boethius with Special Regard to its Influence on World Literature*, vol. 1, rev. G. Schmeling and M. von Albrecht, trans. M. von Albrecht and G. Schmeling with the assistance of F. and K. Newman, Leiden: Brill.

Badian, E. (1985) "A Phantom Marriage Law," *Philologus* 129: 82–98.

Barsby, J. (ed. and trans.) (1979) *Ovid: Amores I*, Bristol: Bristol Classical Press.

Beard, M. (1980) "The Sexual Status of Vestal virgins," *Journal of Roman Studies* 70: 12–27.

Booth, J. (1991) *Ovid: The Second Book of the* Amores, Warminster, UK: Aris and Phillips.

Boyd, B. W. (1984) "*Parva seges satis est*: The Landscape of Tibullan Elegy in 1.1 and 1.10," *Transactions of the American Philological Association* 114: 273–80.

Bradley, J. R. (1995) "The Elegies of Sulpicia: An Introduction and Commentary," *New England Classical Newsletter and Journal* 22: 159–64.

Bright, D. F. (1978) *Haec mihi Fingebam: Tibullus and His World*, Leiden: Brill.

Butler, H. E. and Barber, E. A. (1969) *The Elegies of Propertius*, Hildesheim: Olms. Original 1933.

Cairns, F. (1979) *Tibullus: A Hellenistic at Rome*, Cambridge: Cambridge University Press.

Camps, W. A. (1961) *Propertius: Elegies Book I*, Cambridge: Cambridge University Press.

—— (1965) *Propertius: Elegies Book IV*, Cambridge: Cambridge University Press.

—— (1966) *Propertius: Elegies Book III*, Cambridge: Cambridge University Press.

—— (1967) *Propertius: Elegies Book II*, Cambridge: Cambridge University Press.

Conte, G. B. (1994) *Latin Literature: A History*, trans. J. B. Solodow, rev. D. Fowler and G. W. Most, Baltimore: Johns Hopkins University Press.

Copley, F. O. (1956) *"Exclusus Amator": A Study in Latin Love Poetry*, Madison, WI: American Philological Association.

Fedeli, P. (1985) *Il libro terzo delle elegie: Properzio*, Bari: Adriatica.

Fitzgerald, W. (1995) *Catullan Provocations: Lyric Poetry and the Drama of Position*, Berkeley: University of California Press.

Gold, B. K. (1993) " 'But Ariadne Was Never There in the First Place': Finding the Female in Roman Poetry," in N. S. Rabinowitz and A. Richlin (eds), *Feminist Theory and the Classics*, New York: Routledge, 75–101.

Goold, G. P. (1990) *Propertius: Elegies*, Cambridge, MA: Harvard University Press.

Green, P. (ed. and trans.) (1982) *Ovid: The Erotic Poems*, London: Penguin.

—— (1994) *Ovid: The Poems of Exile*, London: Penguin.

Greene, E. (1998) *The Erotics of Domination: Male Desire and the Mistress in Latin Love Poetry*, Baltimore: Johns Hopkins University Press.

Gruen, E. S. (1995) *The Last Generation of the Roman Republic*, Berkeley: University of California Press. Original 1974.

Gurval, R. A. (1995) *Actium and Augustus: The Politics and Emotions of Civil War*, Ann Arbor: University of Michigan Press.

Hallett, J. P. (1973) "The Role of Women in Roman Elegy: Counter-Cultural Feminism," *Arethusa* 6: 103–23.

—— and M. B. Skinner (eds) (1997) *Roman Sexualities*, Princeton: Princeton University Press.

Hubbard, T. K. (1984) "Catullus 68: The Text as Self-Demystification," *Arethusa* 17: 29–49.

Jacobson, H. (1974). *Ovid's Heroides*, Princeton: Princeton University Press.

Janan, M. (1994) *"When the Lamp is Shattered": Desire and Narrative in Catullus*, Carbondale: Southern Illinois University Press.

—— (2000) *The Politics of Desire: Propertius IV*, Berkeley: University of California Press.

Kennedy, D. (1993) *The Arts of Love: Five Essays in the Discourse of Roman Love Elegy*, Cambridge: Cambridge University Press.

Knox, P. E. (1995) *Ovid:* Heroides: *Selected Epistles*, Cambridge: Cambridge University Press.

Lachmann, K. (1973) *Sextus Propertius: Carmina*, Olms: Hildesheim. Original 1816.

Lilja, S. (1965) *The Roman Elegists' Attitude to Women*, Helsinki: Academia Scientiarum Fennicae.

Lombardo, S. and D. Rayor (trans.) (1988) *Callimachus: Hymns, Epigrams, Select Fragments*, Baltimore: Johns Hopkins University Press.

Lowe, N. J. (1988) "Sulpicia's Syntax," *Classical Quarterly* 38: 193–205.

Luck, G. (1968) *The Latin Love Elegy*, 2nd edn, London: Methuen.

Lyne, R. O. A. M. (1980) *The Latin Love Poets: From Catullus to Ovid*, Oxford: Oxford University Press.

Mack, S. (1988) *Ovid*, New Haven: Yale University Press.

McKeown, J. C. (1987) *Ovid:* Amores, Text, Prolegomena and Commentary in Four Volumes, vol. 1, Leeds: Francis Cairns.

—— (1989) *Ovid:* Amores, Text, Prolegomena and Commentary in Four Volumes, vol. 2, Leeds: Francis Cairns.

—— (1998) *Ovid:* Amores, Text, Prolegomena and Commentary in Four Volumes, vol. 3, Leeds: Francis Cairns.

Melville, A. D. (trans.) (1990) *Ovid: The Love Poems*, Oxford: Oxford University Press.

Merriam, C. U. (1990) "Some Notes on the Sulpicia Elegies," *Latomus* 35: 95–98.

Miller, P. A. (1994) *Lyric Texts and Lyric Consciousness: The Birth of a Genre from Archaic Greece to Augustan Rome*, London: Routledge.

—— (1999) "The Tibullan Dream Text," *Transactions of the American Philological Association* 129: 181–224.

—— and C. Platter, (1999) "Crux as Symptom: Augustan Elegy and Beyond," *Classical World* 92: 445–54.

Murgatroyd, P. (1991) *Tibullus 1*, Bristol: Bristol Classical Press.

—— (1994) *Tibullus: Elegies II*. Oxford: Oxford University Press.

Owen, S. G. (1924) *P. Ovidi Nasonis: Tristium Liber Secundus*, Oxford: Oxford University Press.

Putnam, M. C. J. (1973) *Tibullus: A Commentary*, Norman: University of Oklahoma Press.

Quinn, K. (1973) *Catullus: The Poems*, New York: St. Martin's.

Richardson, L., Jr. (1977) *Propertius: Elegies I–IV*, Norman: University of Oklahoma Press.

Roessel, D. (1990) "The Significance of the Name *Cerinthus* in the poems of Sulpicia," *Transactions of the American Philological Association* 120: 243–50.

Santirocco, M. S. (1979) "Sulpicia Reconsidered," *Classical Journal* 74: 229–39.

Ste. Croix, G. E. M. de (1981) *The Class Struggle in the Ancient Greek World: From the Archaic Age to the Arab Conquests*, Ithaca: Cornell University Press.

Smith, K. F. (1964) *The Elegies of Albius Tibullus*, Darmstadt: Wissenschaftliche Buchgesellschaft. Original 1913.

Stahl, H. P. (1985) *Propertius: "Love" and "War": Individual and State Under Augustus*, Berkeley: University of California Press.

Stapleton, M. L. (1996) *Harmful Eloquence: Ovid's Amores from Antiquity to Shakespeare*, Ann Arbor: University of Michigan Press.

Sullivan, J. P. (1976) *Propertius: A Critical Introduction*, Cambridge: Cambridge University Press.

Syme, R. (1960) *The Roman Revolution*, Oxford: Oxford University Press.

Tränkle, H. (1990) *Appendix Tibulliana*, Berlin: de Gruyter.

Tschiedel, H. J. (1992) "Die Gedichte der Sulpicia (Tib. 3, 13–18): Frauenlyrik?" *Grazer Beiträge* 18, 87–102.

Veyne, P. (1988) *Roman Erotic Elegy: Love Poetry and the West*, trans. D. Pellauer, Chicago: University of Chicago Press.

Walter, H. (1999) "Zum Gedichtschluss von Ovid Am. 1,2," in W. Schubert (ed.) *Ovid Werk und Wirkung: Festgabe für Michael von Albrecht zum 65 Geburtstag*, vol. 1, Frankfurt am Main: Lang, 87–98.

Williams, G. (1968) *Tradition and Originality in Roman Poetry*, Oxford: Clarendon Press.

—— (1980) *Figures of Thought in Roman Poetry*, New Haven: Yale University Press.

Wiseman, T. P. (1985) *Catullus and His World: A Reappraisal*, Cambridge: Cambridge University Press.

Wyke, M. (1989) "Mistress and Metaphor in Augustan Elegy," *Helios* 16: 25–47.

—— (1995) "Taking the Woman's Part: Engendering Roman Love Elegy," in A. J. Boyle (ed.), *Roman Literature and Ideology: Ramus Essays for J. P. Sullivan*, Bendigo, Australia: Aureal, 110–28.

TEXTS

CATULLUS

68B

Non possum reticere, deae, qua me Allius in re
    iuuerit aut quantis iuuerit officiis,
ne fugiens saeclis obliuiscentibus aetas
    illius hoc caeca nocte tegat studium:
sed dicam uobis, uos porro dicite multis   45
    milibus et facite haec carta loquatur anus.

  .   .   .   .

    notescatque magis mortuus atque magis,
nec tenuem texens sublimis aranea telam
    in deserto Alli nomine opus faciat.   50
nam, mihi quam dederit duplex Amathusia curam,
    scitis, et in quo me torruerit genere,
cum tantum arderem quantum Trinacria rupes
    lymphaque in Oetaeis Malia Thermopylis,
maesta neque assiduo tabescere lumina fletu   55
    cessarent tristique imbre madere genae,
qualis in aerii perlucens uertice montis
    riuus muscoso prosilit e lapide
(qui cum de prona praeceps est ualle uolutus,
    per medium densi transit iter populi,   60
dulce uiatori lasso in sudore leuamen,
    cum grauis exustos aestus hiulcat agros).
hic uelut in nigro iactatis turbine nautis
    lenius aspirans aura secunda uenit
iam prece Pollucis, iam Castoris implorata,   65
    tale fuit nobis Allius auxilium.
is clausum lato patefecit limite campum,
    isque domum nobis isque dedit dominae,
ad quam communes exerceremus amores.
    quo mea se molli candida diua pede   70

intulit et trito fulgentem in limine plantam
    innixa arguta constituit solea,
coniugis ut quondam flagrans aduenit amore
    Protesilaeam Laudamia domum

75   inceptam frustra, nondum cum sanguine sacro
    hostia caelestis pacificasset eros.
nil mihi tam ualde placeat, Ramnusia uirgo,
    quod temere inuitis suscipiatur eris.
quam ieiuna pium desideret ara cruorem,

80   docta est amisso Laudamia uiro,
coniugis ante coacta noui dimittere collum,
    quam ueniens una atque altera rursus hiems
noctibus in longis auidum saturasset amorem,
    posset ut abrupto uiuere coniugio,

85   quod scibant Parcae non longo tempore abesse,
    si miles muros isset ad Iliacos.
nam tum Helenae raptu primores Argiuorum
    coeperat ad sese Troia ciere uiros,
Troia (nefas!) commune sepulcrum Asiae Europaeque,

90   Troia uirum et uirtutum omnium acerba cinis,
quaene etiam nostro letum miserabile fratri
    attulit. ei misero frater adempte mihi,
ei misero fratri iucundum lumen ademptum,
    tecum una tota est nostra sepulta domus,

95   omnia tecum una perierunt gaudia nostra,
    quae tuus in uita dulcis alebat amor.
quem nunc tam longe non inter nota sepulcra
    nec prope cognatos compositum cineres,
sed Troia obscena, Troia infelice sepultum

100   detinet extremo terra aliena solo.
ad quam tum properans fertur <lecta> undique pubes
    Graeca penetralis deseruisse focos,
ne Paris abducta gauisus libera moecha
    otia pacato degeret in thalamo.

105   quo tibi tum casu, pulcerrima Laudamia,
    ereptum est uita dulcius atque anima
coniugium: tanto te absorbens uertice amoris
    aestus in abruptum detulerat barathrum,
quale ferunt Grai Pheneum prope Cyllenaeum

110   siccare emulsa pingue palude solum,
quod quondam caesis montis fodisse medullis
    audit falsiparens Amphitryoniades,
tempore quo certa Stymphalia monstra sagitta
    perculit imperio deterioris eri,

pluribus ut caeli tereretur ianua diuis,   115
   Hebe nec longa uirginitate foret.
sed tuus altus amor barathro fuit altior illo,
   qui tamen indomitam ferre iugum docuit.
nam nec tam carum confecto aetate parenti
   una caput seri nata nepotis alit,   120
qui, cum diuitiis uix tandem inuentus auitis
   nomen testatas intulit in tabulas,
impia derisi gentilis gaudia tollens,
   suscitat a cano uolturium capiti;
nec tantum niueo gauisa est ulla columbo   125
   compar (quae multo dicitur improbius
oscula mordenti semper decerpere rostro,
   quam quae praecipue multiuola est mulier).
sed tu horum magnos uicisti sola furores,
   ut semel es flauo conciliata uiro.   130
aut nihil aut paulo cui tum concedere digna
   lux mea se nostrum contulit in gremium,
quam circumcursans hinc illinc saepe Cupido
   fulgebat crocina candidus in tunica.
quae tamen etsi uno non est contenta Catullo,   135
   rara uerecundae furta feremus erae,
ne nimium simus stultorum more molesti.
   saepe etiam Iuno, maxima caelicolum,
coniugis in culpa flagrantem concoquit iram,
   noscens omniuoli plurima furta Iouis.   140
atqui nec diuis homines componier aequum est –
   ingratum tremuli tolle parentis onus;
nec tamen illa mihi dextra deducta paterna
   fragrantem Assyrio uenit odore domum,
sed furtiua dedit mira munuscula nocte,   145
   ipsius ex ipso dempta uiri gremio.
quare illud satis est, si nobis is datur unis
   quem lapide illa dies candidiore notat.
hoc tibi, quod potui, confectum carmine munus
   pro multis, Alii, redditur officiis,   150
ne uestrum scabra tangat rubigine nomen
   haec atque illa dies atque alia atque alia.
huc addent diui quam plurima, quae Themis olim
   antiquis solita est munera ferre piis.
sitis felices et tu simul et tua uita,   155
   et domus in qua <nos> lusimus et domina,
et qui principio nobis †terram dedit aufert†,
   a quo sunt primo omnia nata bono,

160 et longe ante omnes mihi quae me carior ipso est,
lux mea, qua uiua uiuere dulce mihi est.

70

Nulli se dicit mulier mea nubere malle
quam mihi, non si se Iuppiter ipse petat.
dicit: sed mulier cupido quod dicit amanti,
in uento et rapida scribere oportet aqua.

72

Dicebas quondam solum te nosse Catullum,
Lesbia, nec prae me uelle tenere Iouem.
dilexi tum te non tantum ut uulgus amicam,
sed pater ut gnatos diligit et generos.
5 nunc te cognoui: quare etsi impensius uror,
multo mi tamen es uilior et leuior.
qui potis est, inquis? quod amantem iniuria talis
cogit amare magis, sed bene uelle minus.

75

Huc est mens deducta tua mea, Lesbia, culpa
atque ita se officio perdidit ipsa suo,
ut iam nec bene uelle queat tibi, si optima fias,
nec desistere amare, omnia si facias.

76

Siqua recordanti benefacta priora uoluptas
est homini, cum se cogitat esse pium,
nec sanctam uiolasse fidem, nec foedere nullo
diuum ad fallendos numine abusum homines,
5 multa parata manent in longa aetate, Catulle,
ex hoc ingrato gaudia amore tibi.
nam quaecumque homines bene cuiquam aut dicere possunt
aut facere, haec a te dictaque factaque sunt.
omnia quae ingratae perierunt credita menti.
10 quare cur te iam amplius excrucies?
quin tu animo offirmas atque istinc teque reducis,
et dis inuitis desinis esse miser?
difficile est longum subito deponere amorem?
difficile est, uerum hoc qualubet efficias:

una salus haec est, hoc est tibi peruincendum,   15
    hoc facias, siue id non pote siue pote.
o di, si uestrum est misereri, aut si quibus umquam
    extremam iam ipsa in morte tulistis opem,
me miserum aspicite et, si uitam puriter egi,
    eripite hanc pestem perniciemque mihi,   20
quae mihi subrepens imos ut torpor in artus
    expulit ex omni pectore laetitias.
non iam illud quaero, contra me ut diligat illa,
    aut, quod non potis est, esse pudica uelit:
ipse ualere opto et taetrum hunc deponere morbum.   25
    o di, reddite mi hoc pro pietate mea.

85

    Odi et amo. quare id faciam, fortasse requiris?
    nescio, sed fieri sentio et excrucior.

87

    Nulla potest mulier tantum se dicere amatam
    uere, quantum a me Lesbia amata mea est.
    nulla fides ullo fuit umquam foedere tanta,
    quanta in amore tuo ex parte reperta mea est.

101

Multas per gentes et multa per aequora uectus
    aduenio has miseras, frater, ad inferias,
ut te postremo donarem munere mortis
    et mutam nequiquam alloquerer cinerem.
quandoquidem fortuna mihi tete abstulit ipsum,   5
    heu miser indigne frater adempte mihi,
nunc tamen interea haec, prisco quae more parentum
    tradita sunt tristi munere ad inferias,
accipe fraterno multum manantia fletu,
    atque in perpetuum, frater, aue atque uale.   10

TIBULLUS

1.1

Diuitias alius fuluo sibi congerat auro
　　et teneat culti iugera multa soli,
quem labor adsiduus uicino terreat hoste,
　　Martia cui somnos classica pulsa fugent:
5　me mea paupertas uita traducat inerti,
　　dum meus adsiduo luceat igne focus.
ipse seram teneras maturo tempore uites
　　rusticus et facili grandia poma manu:
nec Spes destituat sed frugum semper aceruos
10　　praebeat et pleno pinguia musta lacu.
nam ueneror, seu stipes habet desertus in agris
　　seu uetus in triuio florida serta lapis:
et quodcumque mihi pomum nouus educat annus,
　　libatum agricolae ponitur ante deo.
15　flaua Ceres, tibi sit nostro de rure corona
　　spicea, quae templi pendeat ante fores;
pomosisque ruber custos ponatur in hortis
　　terreat ut saeua falce Priapus aues.
uos quoque, felicis quondam, nunc pauperis agri
20　　custodes, fertis munera uestra, Lares.
tunc uitula innumeros lustrabat caesa iuuencos:
　　nunc agna exigui est hostia parua soli.
agna cadet uobis, quam circum rustica pubes
　　clamet 'io messes et bona uina date.'
25　iam mihi, iam possim contentus uiuere paruo
　　nec semper longae deditus esse uiae,
sed Canis aestiuos ortus uitare sub umbra
　　arboris ad riuos praetereuntis aquae.
nec tamen interdum pudeat tenuisse bidentem
30　　aut stimulo tardos increpuisse boues;

non agnamue sinu pigeat fetumue capellae
    desertum oblita matre referre domum.
at uos exiguo pecori, furesque lupique,
    parcite: de magno praeda petenda grege.
hinc ego pastoremque meum lustrare quot annis   35
    et placidam soleo spargere lacte Palem.
adsitis, diui, neu uos e paupere mensa
    dona nec e puris spernite fictilibus. –
fictilia antiquus primum sibi fecit agrestis
    pocula, de facili composuitque luto. –   40
non ego diuitias patrum fructusque requiro,
    quos tulit antiquo condita messis auo:
parua seges satis est; satis est, requiescere lecto
    si licet et solito membra leuare toro.
quam iuuat immites uentos audire cubantem   45
    et dominam tenero continuisse sinu
aut, gelidas hibernus aquas cum fuderit Auster,
    securum somnos imbre iuuante sequi!
hoc mihi contingat. sit diues iure, furorem
    qui maris et tristes ferre potest pluuias.   50
o quantum est auri pereat potiusque smaragdi,
    quam fleat ob nostras ulla puella uias.
te bellare decet terra, Messalla, marique,
    ut domus hostiles praeferat exuuias:
me retinent uinctum formosae uincla puellae,   55
    et sedeo duras ianitor ante fores.
non ego laudari curo, mea Delia: tecum
    dum modo sim, quaeso segnis inersque uocer.
te spectem, suprema mihi cum uenerit hora,
    et teneam moriens deficiente manu.   60
flebis et arsuro positum me, Delia, lecto,
    tristibus et lacrimis oscula mixta dabis
flebis: non tua sunt duro praecordia ferro
    uincta, nec in tenero stat tibi corde silex.
illo non iuuenis poterit de funere quisquam   65
    lumina, non uirgo sicca referre domum
tu manes ne laede meos, sed parce solutis
    crinibus et teneris, Delia, parce genis.
interea, dum fata sinunt, iungamus amores:
    iam ueniet tenebris Mors adoperta caput;   70
iam subrepet iners aetas, nec amare decebit,
    dicere nec cano blanditias capite.
nunc leuis est tractanda uenus, dum frangere postes
    non pudet et rixas inseruisse iuuat.

75   hic ego dux milesque bonus: uos, signa tubaeque,
            ite procul, cupidis uulnera ferte uiris,
        ferte et opes: ego composito securus aceruo
            dites despiciam despiciamque famem.

1.2

        Adde merum uinoque nouos compesce dolores,
            occupet ut fessi lumina uicta sopor:
        neu quisquam multo percussum tempora baccho
            excitet, infelix dum requiescit amor.
5   nam posita est nostrae custodia saeua puellae,
            clauditur et dura ianua firma sera.
        ianua difficilis domini, te uerberet imber,
            te Iouis imperio fulmina missa petant.
        ianua, iam pateas uni mihi uicta querellis,
10   neu furtim uerso cardine aperta sones.
        et mala si qua tibi dixit dementia nostra,
            ignoscas: capiti sint precor illa meo.
        te meminisse decet quae plurima uoce peregi
            supplice cum posti florida serta darem.
15   tu quoque ne timide custodes, Delia, falle.
            audendum est: fortes adiuuat ipsa Venus.
        illa fauet seu quis iuuenis noua limina temptat
            seu reserat fixo dente puella fores:
        illa docet molli furtim derepere lecto,
20   illa pedem nullo ponere posse sono,
        illa uiro coram nutus conferre loquaces
            blandaque compositis abdere uerba notis.
        nec docet hoc omnes, sed quos nec inertia tardat
            nec uetat obscura surgere nocte timor.
25   en ego cum tenebris tota uagor anxius urbe,

        . · . · . · . · . · . · . · . · . ·

25a   nec sinit occurrat quisquam qui corpora ferro
            uulneret aut rapta praemia ueste petat.
        quisquis amore tenetur, eat tutusque sacerque
            qualibet; insidias non timuisse decet.
        non mihi pigra nocent hibernae frigora noctis,
30   non mihi cum multa decidit imber aqua.
        non labor hic laedit, reseret modo Delia postes
            et uocet ad digiti me taciturna sonum.
        parcite luminibus, seu uir seu femina fiat
            obuia: celari uult sua furta Venus.
35   neu strepitu terrete pedum neu quaerite nomen

neu prope fulgenti lumina ferte face.
si quis et imprudens aspexerit, occulat ille
  perque deos omnes se meminisse neget:
nam fuerit quicumque loquax, is sanguine natam,
  is Venerem e rapido sentiet esse mari. 40
nec tamen huic credet coniunx tuus, ut mihi uerax
  pollicita est magico saga ministerio.
hanc ego de caelo ducentem sidera uidi,
  fluminis haec rapidi carmine uertit iter,
haec cantu finditque solum manesque sepulcris 45
  elicit et tepido deuocat ossa rogo:
iam tenet infernas magico stridore cateruas,
  iam iubet aspersas lacte referre pedem.
cum libet, haec tristi depellit nubila caelo:
  cum libet, aestiuo conuocat orbe niues. 50
sola tenere malas Medeae dicitur herbas,
  sola feros Hecatae perdomuisse canes.
haec mihi composuit cantus, quis fallere posses:
  ter cane, ter dictis despue carminibus.
ille nihil poterit de nobis credere cuiquam, 55
  non sibi, si in molli uiderit ipse toro.
tu tamen abstineas aliis: nam cetera cernet
  omnia: de me uno sentiet ille nihil.
quid credam? nempe haec eadem se dixit amores
  cantibus aut herbis soluere posse meos, 60
et me lustrauit taedis, et nocte serena
  concidit ad magicos hostia pulla deos.
non ego totus abesset amor, sed mutuus esset,
  orabam, nec te posse carere uelim.
ferreus ille fuit qui, te cum posset habere, 65
  maluerit praedas stultus et arma sequi.
ille licet Cilicum uictas agat ante cateruas,
  ponat et in capto Martia castra solo,
totus et argento contextus, totus et auro,
  insideat celeri conspiciendus equo; 70
ipse boues mea si tecum modo Delia possim
  iungere et in solito pascere monte pecus,
et te dum liceat teneris retinere lacertis,
  mollis et inculta sit mihi somnus humo.
quid Tyrio recubare toro sine amore secundo 75
  prodest cum fletu nox uigilanda uenit?
nam neque tunc plumae nec stragula picta soporem
  nec sonitus placidae ducere posset aquae.
num Veneris magnae uiolaui numina uerbo,

80 et mea nunc poenas impia lingua luit?
 num feror incestus sedes adiisse deorum
  sertaque de sanctis deripuisse focis?
 non ego, si merui, dubitem procumbere templis
  et dare sacratis oscula liminibus,
85 non ego tellurem genibus perrepere supplex
  et miserum sancto tundere poste caput.
 at tu, qui laetus rides mala nostra, caueto
  mox tibi: non uni saeuiet usque deus.
 uidi ego qui iuuenum miseros lusisset amores
90 post Veneris uinclis subdere colla senem
 et sibi blanditias tremula componere uoce
  et manibus canas fingere uelle comas:
 stare nec ante fores puduit caraeue puellae
  ancillam medio detinuisse foro.
95 hunc puer, hunc iuuenis turba circumterit arta,
  despuit in molles et sibi quisque sinus.
 at mihi parce, Venus: semper tibi dedita seruit
  mens mea: quid messes uris acerba tuas?

1.4

 'Sic umbrosa tibi contingant tecta, Priape,
  ne capiti soles, ne noceantque niues:
 quae tua formosos cepit sollertia? certe
  non tibi barba nitet, non tibi culta coma est;
5 nudus et hibernae producis frigora brumae,
  nudus et aestiui tempora sicca Canis.'
 sic ego: tum Bacchi respondit rustica proles
  armatus curua sic mihi falce deus.
 'o fuge te tenerae puerorum credere turbae:
10 nam causam iusti semper amoris habent.
 hic placet, angustis quod equum compescit habenis
  hic placidam niueo pectore pellit aquam;
 hic, quia fortis adest audacia, cepit: at illi
  uirgineus teneras stat pudor ante genas.
15 sed ne te capiant, primo si forte negabit,
  taedia; paulatim sub iuga colla dabit.
 longa dies homini docuit parere leones,
  longa dies molli saxa peredit aqua;
 annus in apricis maturat collibus uuas,
20 annus agit certa lucida signa uice.
 nec iurare time: ueneris periuria uenti
  inrita per terras et freta summa ferunt.

gratia magna Ioui: uetuit Pater ipse ualere,
  iurasset cupide quidquid ineptus amor:
perque suas impune sinit Dictynna sagittas   25
  adfirmes, crines perque Minerua suos.
at si tardus eris errabis. transiet aetas
  quam cito! non segnis stat remeatque dies.
quam cito purpureos deperdit terra colores,
  quam cito formosas populus alta comas.   30
quam iacet, infirmae uenere ubi fata senectae,
  qui prior Eleo est carcere missus equus.
uidi iam iuuenem, premeret cum serior aetas,
  maerentem stultos praeteriisse dies.
crudeles diui! serpens nouus exuit annos: 35
  formae non ullam fata dedere moram.
solis aeterna est Baccho Phoeboque iuuentas:
  nam decet intonsus crinis utrumque deum.
tu, puero quodcumque tuo temptare libebit,
  cedas: obsequio plurima uincet amor.   40
neu comes ire neges, quamuis uia longa paretur
  et Canis arenti torreat arua siti,
quamuis praetexens picta ferrugine caelum
  uenturam admittat imbrifer arcus aquam.
uel si caeruleas puppi uolet ire per undas,   45
  ipse leuem remo per freta pelle ratem.
nec te paeniteat duros subiisse labores
  aut opera insuetas atteruisse manus;
nec, uelit insidiis altas si claudere ualles,
  dum placeas, umeri retia ferre negent.   50
si uolet arma, leui temptabis ludere dextra;
  saepe dabis nudum, uincat ut ille, latus.
tunc tibi mitis erit, rapias tum cara licebit
  oscula: pugnabit, sed tibi rapta dabit.
rapta dabit primo, post adferet ipse roganti,   55
  post etiam collo se implicuisse uelit.
heu male nunc artes miseras haec saecula tractant:
  iam tener adsueuit munera uelle puer.
at tua, qui uenerem docuisti uendere primus,
  quisquis es, infelix urgeat ossa lapis.   60
Pieridas, pueri, doctos et amate poetas,
  aurea nec superent munera Pieridas.
carmine purpurea est Nisi coma: carmina ni sint,
  ex umero Pelopis non nituisset ebur.
quem referent Musae, uiuet, dum robora tellus,   65
  dum caelum stellas, dum uehet amnis aquas.

at qui non audit Musas, qui uendit amorem,
    Idaeae currus ille sequatur Opis,
et tercentenas erroribus expleat urbes
70   et secet ad Phrygios uilia membra modos.
blanditiis uult esse locum Venus ipsa: querellis
    supplicibus, miseris fletibus illa fauet.'
haec mihi, quae canerem Titio, deus edidit ore:
    sed Titium coniunx haec meminisse uetat.
75 pareat ille suae: uos me celebrate magistrum,
    quos male habet multa callidus arte puer.
gloria cuique sua est: me, qui spernentur, amantes
    consultent: cunctis ianua nostra patet.
tempus erit, cum me Veneris praecepta ferentem
80   deducat iuuenum sedula turba senem.
eheu quam Marathus lento me torquet amore!
    deficiunt artes, deficiuntque doli.
parce, puer, quaeso, ne turpis fabula fiam,
    cum mea ridebunt uana magisteria.

1.5

Asper eram et bene discidium me ferre loquebar:
    at mihi nunc longe gloria fortis abest.
namque agor ut per plana citus sola uerbere turben
    quem celer adsueta uersat ab arte puer.
5 ure ferum et torque, libeat ne dicere quicquam
    magnificum post haec: horrida uerba doma.
parce tamen, per te furtiui foedera lecti,
    per uenerem quaeso compositumque caput.
ille ego cum tristi morbo defessa iaceres
10   te dicor uotis eripuisse meis:
ipseque te circum lustraui sulpure puro,
    carmine cum magico praecinuisset anus;
ipse procuraui ne possent saeua nocere
    somnia, ter sancta deueneranda mola;
15 ipse ego uelatus filo tunicisque solutis
    uota nouem Triuiae nocte silente dedi.
omnia persolui: fruitur nunc alter amore,
    et precibus felix utitur ille meis.
at mihi felicem uitam, si salua fuisses,
20   fingebam demens sed renuente deo.
rura colam, frugumque aderit mea Delia custos,
    area dum messes sole calente teret,
aut mihi seruabit plenis in lintribus uuas

pressaque ueloci candida musta pede.
consuescet numerare pecus; consuescet amantis 25
    garrulus in dominae ludere uerna sinu.
illa deo sciet agricolae pro uitibus uuam,
    pro segete spicas, pro grege ferre dapem.
illa regat cunctos, illi sint omnia curae:
    at iuuet in tota me nihil esse domo. 30
huc ueniet Messalla meus, cui dulcia poma
    Delia selectis detrahat arboribus:
et, tantum uenerata uirum, hunc sedula curet,
    huic paret atque epulas ipsa ministra gerat.
haec mihi fingebam, quae nunc Eurusque Notusque 35
    iactat odoratos uota per Armenios.
saepe ego temptaui curas depellere uino:
    at dolor in lacrimas uerterat omne merum.
saepe aliam tenui: sed iam cum gaudia adirem,
    admonuit dominae deseruitque Venus. 40
tunc me discedens deuotum femina dixit,
    a pudet, et narrat scire nefanda meam.
non facit hoc uerbis, facie tenerisque lacertis
    deuouet et flauis nostra puella comis.
talis ad Haemonium Nereis Pelea quondam 45
    uecta est frenato caerula pisce Thetis.
haec nocuere mihi. quod adest huic diues amator,
    uenit in exitium callida lena meum.
sanguineas edat illa dapes atque ore cruento
    tristia cum multo pocula felle bibat: 50
hanc uolitent animae circum sua fata querentes
    semper, et e tectis strix uiolenta canat:
ipsa fame stimulante furens herbasque sepulcris
    quaerat et a saeuis ossa relicta lupis;
currat et inguinibus nudis ululetque per urbes, 55
    post agat e triuiis aspera turba canum.
eueniet; dat signa deus: sunt numina amanti,
    saeuit et iniusta lege relicta Venus.
at tu quam primum sagae praecepta rapacis
    desere: nam donis uincitur omnis amor. 60
pauper erit praesto tibi semper: pauper adibit
    primus et in tenero fixus erit latere:
pauper in angusto fidus comes agmine turbae
    subicietque manus efficietque uiam:
pauper ad occultos furtim deducet amicos 65
    uinclaque de niueo detrahet ipse pede.
heu canimus frustra nec uerbis uicta patescit

ianua sed plena est percutienda manu.
    at tu, qui potior nunc es, mea furta timeto:
70   uersatur celeri Fors leuis orbe rotae.
non frustra quidam iam nunc in limine perstat
    sedulus ac crebro prospicit ac refugit
et simulat transire domum, mox deinde recurrit
    solus et ante ipsas exscreat usque fores.
75   nescio quid furtiuus amor parat. utere quaeso,
    dum licet: in liquida nam tibi linter aqua.

2.3

Rura meam, Cornute, tenent uillaeque puellam:
    ferreus est, heu heu, quisquis in urbe manet.
ipsa Venus latos iam nunc migrauit in agros,
    uerbaque aratoris rustica discit Amor.
5   o ego, cum aspicerem dominam, quam fortiter illic
    uersarem ualido pingue bidente solum
agricolaeque modo curuum sectarer aratrum,
    dum subigunt steriles arua serenda boues!
nec quererer quod sol graciles exureret artus,
10   laederet et teneras pussula rupta manus.
pauit et Admeti tauros formosus Apollo,
    nec cithara intonsae profueruntue comae,
nec potuit curas sanare salubribus herbis:
14   quidquid erat medicae uicerat artis amor.
14a ipse deus solitus stabulis expellere uaccas

   . . . .

14b et miscere nouo docuisse coagula lacte,
14c   lacteus et mixtis obriguisse liquor.
15   tunc fiscella leui detexta est uimine iunci,
    raraque per nexus est uia facta sero.
o quotiens illo uitulum gestante per agros
    dicitur occurrens erubuisse soror!
o quotiens ausae, caneret dum ualle sub alta,
20   rumpere mugitu carmina docta boues!
saepe duces trepidis petiere oracula rebus,
    uenit et a templis inrita turba domum:
saepe horrere sacros doluit Latona capillos,
    quos admirata est ipsa nouerca prius.
25   quisquis inornatumque caput crinesque solutos
    aspiceret, Phoebi quaereret ille comam.
Delos ubi nunc, Phoebe, tua est, ubi Delphica Pytho?
    nempe Amor in parua te iubet esse casa.

felices olim, Veneri cum fertur aperte
   seruire aeternos non puduisse deos. 30
fabula nunc ille est: sed cui sua cura puella est,
   fabula sit mauult quam sine amore deus.
at tu, quisquis is es, cui tristi fronte Cupido
   imperat ut nostra sint tua castra domo

. . . .

ferrea non uenerem sed praedam saecula laudant: 35
   praeda tamen multis est operata malis.
praeda feras acies cinxit discordibus armis:
   hinc cruor, hinc caedes mors propiorque uenit.
praeda uago iussit geminare pericula ponto,
   bellica cum dubiis rostra dedit ratibus. 40
praedator cupit immensos obsidere campos,
   ut multa innumera iugera pascat oue:
cui lapis externus curae est, urbisque tumultu
   portatur ualidis mille columna iugis,
claudit et indomitum moles mare, lentus ut intra 45
   neglegat hibernas piscis adesse minas.
at mihi laeta trahant Samiae conuiuia testae
   fictaque Cumana lubrica terra rota.
heu heu diuitibus uideo gaudere puellas:
   iam ueniant praedae, si Venus optat opes 50
ut mea luxuria Nemesis fluat utque per urbem
   incedat donis conspicienda meis.
illa gerat uestes tenues, quas femina Coa
   texuit, auratas disposuitque uias:
illi sint comites fusci, quos India torret 55
   Solis et admotis inficit ignis equis:
illi selectos certent praebere colores
   Africa puniceum purpureumque Tyros.
nota loquor: regnum ipse tenet, quem saepe coegit
   barbara gypsatos ferre catasta pedes. 60
at tibi, dura seges, Nemesim quae abducis ab urbe,
   persoluat nulla semina Terra fide.
et tu, Bacche tener, iucundae consitor uuae,
   tu quoque deuotos, Bacche, relinque lacus.
haud impune licet formosas tristibus agris 65
   abdere: non tanti sunt tua musta, pater.
o ualeant fruges, ne sint modo rure puellae:
   glans alat et prisco more bibantur aquae.
glans aluit ueteres, et passim semper amarunt:
   quid nocuit sulcos non habuisse satos? 70
tunc, quibus aspirabat Amor, praebebat aperte

mitis in umbrosa gaudia ualle Venus.
nullus erat custos, nulla exclusura dolentes
   ianua: si fas est, mos precor ille redi.

75   . . . .

horrida uillosa corpora ueste tegant.
nunc si clausa mea est, si copia rara uidendi,
   heu miserum, laxam quid iuuat esse togam?
ducite: ad imperium dominae sulcabimus agros:

80   non ego me uinclis uerberibusque nego.

SULPICIA

3.13

Tandem uenit amor, qualem texisse pudori
  quam nudasse alicui sit mihi fama magis.
exorata meis illum Cytherea Camenis
  attulit in nostrum deposuitque sinum.
exoluit promissa Venus: mea gaudia narret,   5
  dicetur si quis non habuisse sua.
non ego signatis quicquam mandare tabellis,
  me legat ut nemo quam meus ante, uelim,
sed peccasse iuuat, uultus componere famae
  taedet: cum digno digna fuisse ferar.   10

3.14

Inuisus natalis adest, qui rure molesto
  et sine Cerintho tristis agendus erit.
dulcius urbe quid est? an uilla sit apta puellae
  atque Arretino frigidus amnis agro?
iam, nimium Messalla mei studiose, quiescas;   5
  non tempestiuae saepe, propinque, uiae.
hic animum sensusque meos abducta relinquo,
  arbitrio quamuis non sinis esse meo.

3.15

Scis iter ex animo sublatum triste puellae?
  natali Romae iam licet esse suo.
omnibus ille dies nobis natalis agatur,
  qui nec opinanti nunc tibi forte uenit.

3.16

Gratum est, securus multum quod iam tibi de me
  permittis, subito ne male inepta cadam.
sit tibi cura togae potior pressumque quasillo
  scortum quam Serui filia Sulpicia:
5 solliciti sunt pro nobis, quibus illa dolori est
  ne cedam ignoto maxima causa toro.

3.17

Estne tibi, Cerinthe, tuae pia cura puellae,
  quod mea nunc uexat corpora fessa calor?
ego non aliter tristes euincere morbos
  optarim, quam te si quoque velle putem.
5 at mihi quid prosit morbos euincere, si tu
  nostra potes lento pectore ferre mala?

3.18

Ne tibi sim, mea lux, aeque iam feruida cura
  ac uideor paucos ante fuisse dies,
si quicquam tota commisi stulta iuuenta
  cuius me fatear paenituisse magis,
5 hesterna quam te solum quod nocte reliqui,
  ardorem cupiens dissimulare meum.

PROPERTIUS

1.1

Cynthia prima suis miserum me cepit ocellis,
  contactum nullis ante cupidinibus.
tum mihi constantis deiecit lumina fastus
  et caput impositis pressit Amor pedibus,
donec me docuit castas odisse puellas   5
  improbus, et nullo uiuere consilio.
et mihi iam toto furor hic non deficit anno,
  cum tamen aduersos cogor habere deos.
Milanion nullos fugiendo,Tulle, labores
  saeuitiam durae contudit Iasidos.   10
nam modo Partheniis amens errabat in antris,
  ibat et hirsutas ille uidere feras;
ille etiam Hylaei percussus uulnere rami
  saucius Arcadiis rupibus ingemuit.
ergo uelocem potuit domuisse puellam: 15
  tantum in amore preces et bene facta ualent.
in me tardus Amor non illas cogitat artis,
  nec meminit notas, ut prius, ire uias.
at uos, deductae quibus est fallacia lunae
  et labor in magicis sacra piare focis,   20
en agedum dominae mentem conuertite nostrae,
  et facite illa meo palleat ore magis!
tunc ego crediderim uobis et sidera et amnis
  posse Cytaeines ducere carminibus.
et uos, qui sero lapsum reuocatis, amici,   25
  quaerite non sani pectoris auxilia.
fortiter et ferrum saeuos patiemur et ignis,
  sit modo libertas quae uelit ira loqui.
ferte per extremas gentis et ferte per undas,
  qua non ulla meum femina norit iter: 30

57

uos remanete, quibus facili deus annuit aure,
    sitis et in tuto semper amore pares.
in me nostra Venus noctes exercet amaras,
    et nullo uacuus tempore defit Amor.
35   hoc, moneo, uitate malum: sua quemque moretur
    cura, neque assueto mutet amore locum.
quod si quis monitis tardas aduerterit auris,
    heu referet quanto uerba dolore mea!

1.3

Qualis Thesea iacuit cedente carina
    languida desertis Cnosia litoribus;
qualis et accubuit primo Cepheia somno
    libera iam duris cotibus Andromede;
5   nec minus assiduis Edonis fessa choreis
    qualis in herboso concidit Apidano:
talis uisa mihi mollem spirare quietem
    Cynthia non certis nixa caput manibus,
ebria cum multo traherem uestigia Baccho,
10   et quaterent sera nocte facem pueri.
hanc ego, nondum etiam sensus deperditus omnis,
    molliter impresso conor adire toro;
et quamuis duplici correptum ardore iuberent
    hac Amor hac Liber, durus uterque deus,
15   subiecto leuiter positam temptare lacerto
    osculaque admota sumere et arma manu,
non tamen ausus eram dominae turbare quietem,
    expertae metuens iurgia saeuitiae;
sed sic intentis haerebam fixus ocellis,
20   Argus ut ignotis cornibus Inachidos.
et modo soluebam nostra de fronte corollas
    ponebamque tuis, Cynthia, temporibus;
et modo gaudebam lapsos formare capillos;
    nunc furtiua cauis poma dabam manibus;
25   omniaque ingrato largibar munera somno,
    munera de prono saepe uoluta sinu;
et quotiens raro duxti suspiria motu,
    obstupui uano credulus auspicio,
ne qua tibi insolitos portarent uisa timores,
30   neue quis inuitam cogeret esse suam:
donec diuersas praecurrens luna fenestras,
    luna moraturis sedula luminibus,
compositos leuibus radiis patefecit ocellos.

sic ait in molli fixa toro cubitum:
'tandem te nostro referens iniuria lecto   35
  alterius clausis expulit e foribus?
namque ubi longa meae consumpsti tempora noctis,
  languidus exactis, ei mihi, sideribus?
o utinam talis perducas, improbe, noctes,
  me miseram qualis semper habere iubes!   40
nam modo purpureo fallebam stamine somnum,
  rursus et Orpheae carmine, fessa, lyrae;
interdum leuiter mecum deserta querebar
  externo longas saepe in amore moras:
dum me iucundis lapsam sopor impulit alis.   45
  illa fuit lacrimis ultima cura meis.'

1.6

Non ego nunc Hadriae uereor mare noscere tecum,
  Tulle, neque Aegaeo ducere uela salo,
cum quo Rhipaeos possim conscendere montis
  ulteriusque domos uadere Memnonias;
sed me complexae remorantur uerba puellae,   5
  mutatoque graues saepe colore preces.
illa mihi totis argutat noctibus ignis,
  et queritur nullos esse relicta deos;
illa meam mihi iam se denegat, illa minatur,
  quae solet ingrato tristis amica uiro.   10
his ego non horam possum durare querelis:
  a pereat, si quis lentus amare potest!
an mihi sit tanti doctas cognoscere Athenas
  atque Asiae ueteres cernere diuitias,
ut mihi deducta faciat conuicia puppi   15
  Cynthia et insanis ora notet manibus,
osculaque opposito dicat sibi debita uento,
  et nihil infido durius esse uiro?
tu patrui meritas conare anteire securis,
  et uetera oblitis iura refer sociis.   20
nam tua non aetas umquam cessauit amori,
  semper at armatae cura fuit patriae;
et tibi non umquam nostros puer iste labores
  afferat et lacrimis omnia nota meis!
me sine, quem semper uoluit fortuna iacere,   25
  hanc animam extremae reddere nequitiae.
multi longinquo periere in amore libenter,
  in quorum numero me quoque terra tegat.

non ego sum laudi, non natus idoneus armis:
30   hanc me militiam fata subire uolunt.
at tu seu mollis qua tendit Ionia, seu qua
       Lydia Pactoli tingit arata liquor;
seu pedibus terras seu pontum carpere remis
       ibis, et accepti pars eris imperii:
35   tum tibi si qua mei ueniet non immemor hora,
       uiuere me duro sidere certus eris.

2.1

Quaeritis, unde mihi totiens scribantur amores,
       unde meus ueniat mollis in ora liber.
non haec Calliope, non haec mihi cantat Apollo.
       ingenium nobis ipsa puella facit.
5   siue illam Cois fulgentem incedere †cogis†,
       hac totum e Coa ueste uolumen erit;
seu uidi ad frontem sparsos errare capillos,
       gaudet laudatis ire superba comis;
siue lyrae carmen digitis percussit eburnis,
10   miramur facilis ut premat arte manus;
seu cum poscentis somnum declinat ocellos,
       inuenio causas mille poeta nouas;
seu nuda erepto mecum luctatur amictu,
       tum uero longas condimus Iliadas;
15   seu quidquid fecit siue est quodcumque locuta,
       maxima de nihilo nascitur historia.
quod mihi si tantum, Maecenas, fata dedissent,
       ut possem heroas ducere in arma manus,
non ego Titanas canerem, non Ossan Olympo
20   impositam, ut caeli Pelion esset iter,
nec ueteres Thebas, nec Pergama nomen Homeri,
       Xerxis et imperio bina coisse uada,
regnaue prima Remi aut animos Carthaginis altae,
       Cimbrorumque minas et bene facta Mari:
25   bellaque resque tui memorarem Caesaris, et tu
       Caesare sub magno cura secunda fores.
nam quotiens Mutinam aut ciuilia busta Philippos
       aut canerem Siculae classica bella fugae,
euersosque focos antiquae gentis Etruscae,
30   et Ptolemaeei litora capta Phari,
aut canerem Aegyptum et Nilum, cum attractus in urbem
       septem captiuis debilis ibat aquis,

aut regum auratis circumdata colla catenis,
    Actiaque in Sacra currere rostra Via;
te mea Musa illis semper contexeret armis,   35
    et sumpta et posita pace fidele caput:
Theseus infernis, superis testatur Achilles,
    hic Ixioniden, ille Menoetiaden.
sed neque Phlegraeos Iouis Enceladique tumultus
    intonet angusto pectore Callimachus,   40
nec mea conueniunt duro praecordia uersu
    Caesaris in Phrygios condere nomen auos.
nauita de uentis, de tauris narrat arator,
    enumerat miles uulnera, pastor ouis;
nos contra angusto uersantes proelia lecto: 45
    qua pote quisque, in ea conterat arte diem.
laus in amore mori: laus altera, si datur uno
    posse frui: fruar o solus amore meo!
si memini, solet illa leuis culpare puellas,
    et totam ex Helena non probat Iliada.   50
seu mihi sunt tangenda nouercae pocula Phaedrae,
    pocula priuigno non nocitura suo,
seu mihi Circaeo pereundum est gramine, siue
    Colchis Iolciacis urat aena focis,
una meos quoniam praedata est femina sensus,   55
    ex hac ducentur funera nostra domo.
omnis humanos sanat medicina dolores:
    solus amor morbi non amat artificem.
tarda Philoctetae sanauit crura Machaon,
    Phoenicis Chiron lumina Phillyrides,   60
et deus exstinctum Cressis Epidaurius herbis
    restituit patriis Androgeona focis,
Mysus et Haemonia iuuenis qua cuspide uulnus
    senserat, hac ipsa cuspide sensit opem.
hoc si quis uitium poterit mihi demere, solus   65
    Tantaleae poterit tradere poma manu;
dolia uirgineis idem ille repleuerit urnis,
    ne tenera assidua colla grauentur aqua;
idem Caucasia soluet de rupe Promethei
    bracchia et a medio pectore pellet auem.   70
quandocumque igitur uitam mea fata reposcent,
    et breue in exiguo marmore nomen ero,
Maecenas, nostrae spes inuidiosa iuuentae,
    et uitae et morti gloria iusta meae,
si te forte meo ducet uia proxima busto,   75
    esseda caelatis siste Britanna iugis,

taliaque illacrimans mutae iace uerba fauillae:
  'Huic misero fatum dura puella fuit.'

2.7

Gauisa est certe sublatam Cynthia legem,
  qua quondam edicta flemus uterque diu,
ni nos diuideret: quamuis diducere amantis
  non queat inuitos Iuppiter ipse duos.
5 'at magnus Caesar.' sed magnus Caesar in armis:
  deuictae gentes nil in amore ualent.
nam citius paterer caput hoc discedere collo
  quam possem nuptae perdere more faces,
aut ego transirem tua limina clausa maritus,
10 respiciens udis prodita luminibus.
a mea tum qualis caneret tibi tibia somnos,
  tibia, funesta tristior illa tuba!
unde mihi patriis natos praebere triumphis?
  nullus de nostro sanguine miles erit.
15 quod si uera meae comitarem castra puellae,
  non mihi sat magnus Castoris iret equus.
hinc etenim tantum meruit mea gloria nomen,
  gloria ad hibernos lata Borysthenidas.
tu mihi sola places: placeam tibi, Cynthia, solus:
20 hic erit et patrio sanguine pluris amor.

2.15

O me felicem! o nox mihi candida! et o tu
  lectule deliciis facte beate meis!
quam multa apposita narramus uerba lucerna,
  quantaque sublato lumine rixa fuit!
5 nam modo nudatis mecum est luctata papillis,
  interdum tunica duxit operta moram.
illa meos somno lapsos patefecit ocellos
  ore suo et dixit 'sicine, lente, iaces?'
quam uario amplexu mutamus bracchia! quantum
10 oscula sunt labris nostra morata tuis!
non iuuat in caeco Venerem corrumpere motu:
  si nescis, oculi sunt in amore duces.
ipse Paris nuda fertur periisse Lacaena,
  cum Menelaeo surgeret e thalamo:
15 nudus et Endymion Phoebi cepisse sororem
  dicitur et nudae concubuisse deae.

quod si pertendens animo uestita cubaris,
　scissa ueste meas experiere manus:
quin etiam, si me ulterius prouexerit ira,　　　　　　　　20
　ostendes matri bracchia laesa tuae.
necdum inclinatae prohibent te ludere mammae:
　uiderit haec, si quam iam peperisse pudet.
dum nos fata sinunt, oculos satiemus amore:
　nox tibi longa uenit, nec reditura dies.
atque utinam haerentis sic nos uincire catena　　　　25
　uelles, ut numquam solueret ulla die!
exemplo iunctae tibi sint in amore columbae,
　masculus et totum femina coniugium.
errat, qui finem uesani quaerit amoris:
　uerus amor nullum nouit habere modum.　　　　　　30
terra prius falso partu deludet arantis,
　et citius nigros Sol agitabit equos,
fluminaque ad caput incipient reuocare liquores,
　aridus et sicco gurgite piscis erit,
quam possim nostros alio transferre dolores:　　　　35
　huius ero uiuus, mortuus huius ero.
quod mihi si secum talis concedere noctes
　illa uelit, uitae longus et annus erit.
si dabit haec multas, fiam immortalis in illis:
　nocte una quiuis uel deus esse potest.　　　　　　　40
qualem si cuncti cuperent decurrere uitam:
　et pressi multo membra iacere mero,
non ferrum crudele neque esset bellica nauis,
　nec nostra Actiacum uerteret ossa mare,
nec totiens propriis circum oppugnata triumphis　　45
　lassa foret crinis soluere Roma suos.
haec certe merito poterunt laudare minores:
　laeserunt nullos pocula nostra deos.
tu modo, dum lucet, fructum ne desere uitae!
　omnia si dederis oscula, pauca dabis.　　　　　　　50
ac ueluti folia arentis liquere corollas,
　quae passim calathis strata natare uides,
sic nobis, qui nunc magnum spiramus amantes,
　forsitan includet crastina fata dies.

2.16

Praetor ab Illyricis uenit modo, Cynthia, terris,
　maxima praeda tibi, maxima cura mihi.
non potuit saxo uitam posuisse Cerauno?

a, Neptune, tibi qualia dona darem!
5   nunc sine me plena fiunt conuiuia mensa,
      nunc sine me tota ianua nocte patet.
    quare, si sapis, oblatas ne desere messis
      et stolidum pleno uellere carpe pecus;
    deinde, ubi consumpto restabit munere pauper,
10   dic alias iterum nauiget Illyrias!
    Cynthia non sequitur fascis nec curat honores,
      semper amatorum ponderat una sinus.
    at tu nunc nostro, Venus, o succurre dolori,
      rumpat ut assiduis membra libidinibus!
15   ergo muneribus quiuis mercatur amorem?
      Iuppiter, indigna merce puella perit.
    semper in Oceanum mittit me quaerere gemmas,
      et iubet ex ipsa tollere dona Tyro.
    atque utinam Romae nemo esset diues, et ipse
20   straminea posset dux habitare casa!
    numquam uenales essent ad munus amicae,
      atque una fieret cana puella domo;
    numquam septenas noctes seiuncta cubares,
      candida tam foedo bracchia fusa uiro;
25   non quia peccarim (testor te), sed quia uulgo
      formosis leuitas semper amica fuit.
    barbarus exclusis agitat uestigia lumbis –
      et subito felix nunc mea regna tenet!
    aspice quid donis Eriphyla inuenit amaris,
30   arserit et quantis nupta Creusa malis.
    nullane sedabit nostros iniuria fletus?
      an dolor hic uitiis nescit abesse tuis?
    tot iam abiere dies, cum me nec cura theatri
      nec tetigit Campi, nec mea mensa iuuat.
35   at pudeat certe, pudeat – nisi forte, quod aiunt,
      turpis amor surdis auribus esse solet.
    cerne ducem, modo qui fremitu compleuit inani
      Actia damnatis aequora militibus:
    hunc infamis amor uersis dare terga carinis
40   iussit et extremo quaerere in orbe fugam.
    Caesaris haec uirtus et gloria Caesaris haec est:
      illa, qua uicit, condidit arma manu.
    sed quascumque tibi uestis, quoscumque smaragdos,
      quosque dedit flauo lumine chrysolithos,
45   haec uideam rapidas in uanum ferre procellas:
      quae tibi terra, uelim, quae tibi fiat aqua.
    non semper placidus periuros ridet amantis

Iuppiter et surda neglegit aure preces.
uidistis toto sonitus percurrere caelo,
    fulminaque aetheria desiluisse domo: 50
non haec Pleiades faciunt neque aquosus Orion,
    nec sic de nihilo fulminis ira cadit;
periuras tunc ille solet punire puellas,
    deceptus quoniam fleuit et ipse deus.
quare ne tibi sit tanti Sidonia uestis, 55
    ut timeas quotiens nubilus Auster erit.

2.34

Cur quisquam faciem dominae credat Amori?
    sic erepta mihi paene puella mea est.
expertus dico, nemo est in amore fidelis:
    formosam raro non sibi quisque petit.
polluit ille deus cognatos, soluit amicos, 5
    et bene concordis tristia ad arma uocat.
hospes in hospitium Menelao uenit adulter:
    Colchis et ignotum nonne secuta uirum est?
Lynceu, tune meam potuisti, perfide, curam
    tangere? nonne tuae tum cecidere manus? 10
quid si non constans illa et tam certa fuisset?
    posses in tanto uiuere flagitio?
tu mihi uel ferro pectus uel perde ueneno:
    a domina tantum te modo tolle mea.
te socium uitae, te corporis esse licebit, 15
    te dominum admitto rebus, amice, meis:
lecto te solum, lecto te deprecor uno:
    riualem possum non ego ferre Iouem.
ipse meas solus, quod nil est, aemulor umbras,
    stultus, quod stulto saepe timore tremo. 20
una tamen causa est, qua crimina tanta remitto,
    errabant multo quod tua uerba mero.
sed numquam uitae fallet me ruga seuerae:
    omnes iam norunt quam sit amare bonum.
Lynceus ipse meus seros insanit amores! 25
    solum te nostros laetor adire deos.
quid tua Socraticis tibi nunc sapientia libris
    proderit aut rerum dicere posse uias?
aut quid Erecthei tibi prosunt carmina lecta?
    nil iuuat in magno uester amore senex. 30
tu satius memorem Musis imitere Philitan
    et non inflati somnia Callimachi.

nam rursus licet Actoli referas Acheloi,
 fluxerit ut magno fractus amore liquor,
35 atque etiam ut Phrygio fallax Maeandria campo
 errat et ipsa suas decipit unda uias,
qualis et Adrasti fuerit uocalis Arion,
 tristis ad Archemori funera uictor equus:
 †non Amphiareae prosint tibi fata quadrigae†
40 aut Capanei magno grata ruina Ioui.
desine et Aeschyleo componere uerba coturno,
 desine, et ad mollis membra resolue choros.
incipe iam angusto uersus includere torno,
 inque tuos ignis, dure poeta, ueni.
45 tu non Antimacho, non tutior ibis Homero:
 despicit et magnos recta puella deos.
sed non ante graui taurus succumbit aratro,
 cornua quam ualidis haeserit in laqueis,
nec tu tam duros per te patieris amores:
50 trux tamen a nobis ante domandus eris.
harum nulla solet rationem quaerere mundi,
 nec cur fraternis Luna laboret equis,
nec si post Stygias aliquid restabimus undas,
 nec si consulto fulmina missa tonent.
55 aspice me, cui parua domi fortuna relicta est
 nullus et antiquo Marte triumphus aui,
ut regnem mixtas inter conuiua puellas
 hoc ego, quo tibi nunc eleuor, ingenio!
me iuuet hesternis positum languere corollis,
60 quem tetigit iactu certus ad ossa deus;
Actia Vergilium custodis litora Phoebi,
 Caesaris et fortis dicere posse ratis,
qui nunc Aeneae Troiani suscitat arma
 iactaque Lauinis moenia litoribus.
65 cedite Romani scriptores, cedite Grai!
 nescio quid maius nascitur Iliade.
tu canis umbrosi subter pineta Galaesi
 Thyrsin et attritis Daphnin harundinibus,
utque decem possint corrumpere mala puellas
70 missus et impressis haedus ab uberibus.
felix, qui uilis pomis mercaris amores!
 huic licet ingratae Tityrus ipse canat.
felix intactum Corydon qui temptat Alexin
 agricolae domini carpere delicias!
75 quamuis ille sua lassus requiescat auena,
 laudatur facilis inter Hamadryadas.

tu canis Ascraei ueteris praecepta poetae,
    quo seges in campo, quo uiret uua iugo.
tale facis carmen docta testudine quale
    Cynthius impositis temperat articulis.   80
non tamen haec ulli uenient ingrata legenti,
    siue in amore rudis siue peritus erit.
nec minor hic animis, ut sit minor ore, canorus
    anseris indocto carmine cessit olor.
haec quoque perfecto ludebat Iasone Varro,   85
    Varro Leucadiae maxima flamma suae;
haec quoque lasciui cantarunt scripta Catulli,
    Lesbia quis ipsa notior est Helena;
haec etiam docti confessa est pagina Calui,
    cum caneret miserae funera Quintiliae.   90
et modo formosa quam multa Lycoride Gallus
    mortuus inferna uulnera lauit aqua!
Cynthia quin uiuet uersu laudata Properti –
    hos inter si me ponere Fama uolet.

3.4

Arma deus Caesar dites meditatur ad Indos,
    et freta gemmiferi findere classe maris.
magna, uiri, merces: parat ultima terra triumphos;
    Tigris et Euphrates sub tua iura fluent;
sera, sed Ausoniis ueniet prouincia uirgis;   5
    assuescent Latio Partha tropaea Ioui.
ite agite, expertae bello date lintea prorae
    et solitum armigeri ducite munus equi!
omina fausta cano. Crassos clademque piate!
    ite et Romanae consulite historiae!   10
Mars pater, et sacrae fatalia lumina Vestae,
    ante meos obitus sit precor illa dies,
qua uideam spoliis oneratos Caesaris axis,
    ad uulgi plausus saepe resistere equos,
inque sinu carae nixus spectare puellae   15
    incipiam et titulis oppida capta legam,
tela fugacis equi et bracati militis arcus,
    et subter captos arma sedere duces!
ipsa tuam serua prolem, Venus: hoc sit in aeuum,
    cernis ab Aenea quod superesse caput.   20
praeda sit haec illis, quorum meruere labores:
    me sat erit Sacra plaudere posse Via.

3.5

Pacis Amor deus est, pacem ueneramur amantes:
　　stant mihi cum domina proelia dura mea.
nec tamen inuiso pectus mihi carpitur auro,
　　nec bibit e gemma diuite nostra sitis,
5　nec mihi mille iugis Campania pinguis aratur,
　　nec miser aera paro clade, Corinthe, tua.
o prima infelix fingenti terra Prometheo!
　　ille parum caute pectoris egit opus.
corpora disponens mentem non uidit in arte:
10　　recta animi primum debuit esse uia.
nunc maris in tantum uento iactamur, et hostem
　　quaerimus, atque armis nectimus arma noua.
haud ullas portabis opes Acherontis ad undas:
　　nudus in inferna, stulte, uehere rate.
15　uictor cum uictis pariter miscebitur umbris:
　　consule cum Mario, capte Iugurtha, sedes.
Lydus Dulichio non distat Croesus ab Iro:
　　optima mors Parcae quae uenit acta die.
me iuuat in prima coluisse Helicona iuuenta
20　　Musarumque choris implicuisse manus:
me iuuat et multo mentem uincire Lyaeo,
　　et caput in uerna semper habere rosa.
atque ubi iam Venerem grauis interceperit aetas,
　　sparserit et nigras alba senecta comas,
25　tum mihi naturae libeat perdiscere mores,
　　quis deus hanc mundi temperet arte domum,
qua uenit exoriens, qua deficit, unde coactis
　　cornibus in plenum menstrua luna redit,
unde salo superant uenti, quid flamine captet
30　　Eurus, et in nubes unde perennis aqua;
sit uentura dies mundi quae subruat arces,
　　purpureus pluuias cur bibit arcus aquas,
aut cur Perrhaebi tremuere cacumina Pindi,
　　solis et atratis luxerit orbis equis,
35　cur serus uersare boues et plaustra Bootes,
　　Pleiadum spisso cur coit igne chorus,
curue suos finis altum non exeat aequor,
　　plenus et in partis quattuor annus eat;
sub terris sint iura deum et tormenta gigantum,
40　　Tisiphones atro si furit angue caput,
aut Alcmaeoniae furiae aut ieiunia Phinei,
　　num rota, num scopuli, num sitis inter aquas,

num tribus infernum custodit faucibus antrum
    Cerberus, et Tityo iugera pauca nouem,
an ficta in miseras descendit fabula gentis,   45
    et timor haud ultra quam rogus esse potest.
exitus hic uitae superest mihi: uos, quibus arma
    grata magis, Crassi signa referte domum.

3.11

Quid mirare, meam si uersat femina uitam
    et trahit addictum sub sua iura uirum,
criminaque ignaui capitis mihi turpia fingis,
    quod nequeam fracto rumpere uincla iugo?
uenturam melius praesagit nauita mortem,   5
    uulneribus didicit miles habere metum.
ista ego praeterita iactaui uerba iuuenta:
    tu nunc exemplo disce timere meo.
Colchis flagrantis adamantina sub iuga tauros
    egit et armigera proelia seuit humo,   10
custodisque feros clausit serpentis hiatus,
    iret ut Aesonias aurea lana domos.
ausa ferox ab equo quondam oppugnare sagittis
    Maeotis Danaum Penthesilea ratis;
aurea cui postquam nudauit cassida frontem,   15
    uicit uictorem candida forma uirum.
Omphale in tantum formae processit honorem,
    Lydia Gygaeo tincta puella lacu,
ut, qui pacato statuisset in orbe columnas,
    tam dura traheret mollia pensa manu.   20
Persarum statuit Babylona Semiramis urbem,
    ut solidum cocto tolleret aggere opus,
et duo in aduersum mitti per moenia currus
    nec possent tacto stringere ab axe latus;
duxit et Euphraten medium, quam condidit, arcis,   25
    iussit et imperio subdere Bactra caput.
nam quid ego heroas, quid raptem in crimina diuos?
    Iuppiter infamat seque suamque domum.
quid, modo quae nostris opprobria uexerit armis,
    et famulos inter femina trita suos?   30
coniugii obsceni pretium Romana poposcit
    moenia et addictos in sua regna Patres.
noxia Alexandria, dolis aptissima tellus,
    et totiens nostro Memphi cruenta malo,
tris ubi Pompeio detraxit harena triumphos!   35

tollet nulla dies hanc tibi, Roma, notam.
issent Phlegraeo melius tibi funera campo,
   uel tua si socero colla daturus eras.
scilicet incesti meretrix regina Canopi,
40   una Philippeo sanguine adusta nota,
ausa Ioui nostro latrantem opponere Anubim,
   et Tiberim Nili cogere ferre minas,
Romanamque tubam crepitanti pellere sistro,
   baridos et contis rostra Liburna sequi,
45 foedaque Tarpeio conopia tendere saxo,
   iura dare et statuas inter et arma Mari!
quid nunc Tarquinii fractas iuuat esse securis,
   nomine quem simili uita superba notat,
si mulier patienda fuit? cape, Roma, triumphum
50   et longum Augusto salua precare diem!
fugisti tamen in timidi uaga flumina Nili:
   accepere tuae Romula uincla manus.
bracchia spectaui sacris admorsa colubris,
   et trahere occultum membra soporis iter.
55 'Non hoc, Roma, fui tanto tibi ciue uerenda!'
   dixit et assiduo lingua sepulta mero.
septem urbs alta iugis, toto quae praesidet orbi,
58   femineo timuit territa Marte minas.
67 nunc ubi Scipiadae classes, ubi signa Camilli,
68   aut modo Pompeia, Bospore, capta manu?
59 Hannibalis spolia et uicti monumenta Syphacis,
60   et Pyrrhi ad nostros gloria fracta pedes?
Curtius expletis statuit monumenta lacunis,
   at Decius misso proelia rupit equo,
Coclitis abscissos testatur semita pontis,
   est cui cognomen coruus habere dedit:
65 haec di condiderant, haec di quoque moenia seruant:
66   uix timeat saluo Caesare Roma Iouem.
69 Leucadius uersas acies memorabit Apollo:
70   tantum operis belli sustulit una dies.
at tu, siue petes portus seu, nauita, linques,
   Caesaris in toto sis memor Ionio.

4.4

Tarpeium nemus et Tarpeiae turpe sepulcrum
   fabor et antiqui limina capta Iouis.
lucus erat felix hederoso conditus antro,
   multaque natiuis obstrepit arbor aquis,

Siluani ramosa domus, quo dulcis ab aestu 5
    fistula poturas ire iubebat ouis.
hunc Tatius fontem uallo praecingit acerno,
    fidaque suggesta castra coronat humo.
quid tum Roma fuit, tubicen uicina Curetis
    cum quateret lento murmure saxa Iouis? 10
atque ubi nunc terris dicuntur iura subactis,
    stabant Romano pila Sabina Foro.
murus erant montes: ubi nunc est Curia saepta,
    bellicus ex illo fonte bibebat equus.
hinc Tarpeia deae fontem libauit: at illi 15
    urgebat medium fictilis urna caput.
et satis una malae potuit mors esse puellae,
    quae uoluit flammas fallere, Vesta, tuas?
uidit harenosis Tatium proludere campis
    pictaque per flauas arma leuare iubas: 20
obstipuit regis facie et regalibus armis,
    interque oblitas excidit urna manus.
saepe illa immeritae causata est omina lunae,
    et sibi tingendas dixit in amne comas:
saepe tulit blandis argentea lilia Nymphis, 25
    Romula ne faciem laederet hasta Tati:
dumque subit primo Capitolia nubila fumo,
    rettulit hirsutis bracchia secta rubis,
et sua Tarpeia residens ita fleuit ab arce
    uulnera, uicino non patienda Ioui: 30
'Ignes castrorum et Tatiae praetoria turmae
    et formosa oculis arma Sabina meis,
o utinam ad uestros sedeam captiua Penatis,
    dum captiua mei conspicer ora Tati!
Romani montes, et montibus addita Roma, 35
    et ualeat probro Vesta pudenda meo:
ille equus, ille meos in castra reponet amores,
    cui Tatius dextras collocat ipse iubas!
quid mirum in patrios Scyllam saeuisse capillos,
    candidaque in saeuos inguina uersa canis? 40
prodita quid mirum fraterni cornua monstri,
    cum patuit lecto stamine torta uia?
quantum ego sum Ausoniis crimen factura puellis,
    improba uirgineo lecta ministra foco!
Pallados exstinctos si quis mirabitur ignis, 45
    ignoscat: lacrimis spargitur ara meis.
cras, ut rumor ait, tota potabitur urbe:
    tu cape spinosi rorida terga iugi.

lubrica tota uia est et perfida: quippe tacentis
50   fallaci celat limite semper aquas.
o utinam magicae nossem cantamina Musae!
      haec quoque formoso lingua tulisset opem.
te toga picta decet, non quem sine matris honore
      nutrit inhumanae dura papilla lupae.
55 Sic, hospes, pariamne tua regina sub aula?
      dos tibi non humilis prodita Roma uenit.
si minus, at raptae ne sint impune Sabinae,
      me rape et alterna lege repende uices!
commissas acies ego possum soluere: nuptae
60   uos medium palla foedus inite mea.
adde Hymenaee modos, tubicen fera murmura conde:
      credite, uestra meus molliet arma torus.
et iam quarta canit uenturam bucina lucem,
      ipsaque in Oceanum sidera lapsa cadunt.
65 experiar somnum, de te mihi somnia quaeram:
      fac uenias oculis umbra benigna meis.'
dixit, et incerto permisit bracchia somno,
      nescia se furiis accubuisse nouis.
nam Vesta, Iliacae felix tutela fauillae,
70   culpam alit et plures condit in ossa faces.
illa ruit, qualis celerem prope Thermodonta
      Strymonis abscisso pectus aperta sinu.
urbi festus erat (dixere Parilia patres),
      hic primus coepit moenibus esse dies,
75 annua pastorum conuiuia, lusus in urbe,
      cum pagana madent fercula diuitiis,
cumque super raros faeni flammantis aceruos
      traicit immundos ebria turba pedes.
Romulus excubias decreuit in otia solui
80   atque intermissa castra silere tuba.
hoc Tarpeia suum tempus rata conuenit hostem:
      pacta ligat, pactis ipsa futura comes.
mons erat ascensu dubius festoque remissus
      nec mora, uocalis occupat ense canis.
85 omnia praebebant somnos: sed Iuppiter unus
      decreuit poenis inuigilare suis.
prodiderat portaeque fidem patriamque iacentem,
      nubendique petit, quem uelit, ipsa diem.
at Tatius (neque enim sceleri dedit hostis honorem)
90   'Nube' ait 'et regni scande cubile mei!'
dixit, et ingestis comitum super obruit armis.
      haec, uirgo, officiis dos erat apta tuis.

A duce Tarpeia mons est cognomen adeptus:
O uigil, iniustae praemia sortis habes.

4.6

Sacra facit uates: sint ora fauentia sacris,
 et cadat ante meos icta iuuenca focos.
serta Philiteis certet Romana corymbis,
 et Cyrenaeas urna ministret aquas.
costum molle date et blandi mihi turis honores,   5
 terque focum circa laneus orbis eat.
spargite me lymphis, carmenque recentibus aris
 tibia Mygdoniis libet eburna cadis.
ite procul fraudes, alio sint aere noxae:
 pura nouum uati laurea mollit iter.   10
Musa, Palatini referemus Apollinis aedem:
 res est, Calliope, digna fauore tuo.
Caesaris in nomen ducuntur carmina: Caesar
 dum canitur, quaeso, Iuppiter ipse uaces.
est Phoebi fugiens Athamana ad litora portus,   15
 qua sinus Ioniae murmura condit aquae,
Actia Iuleae pelagus monumenta carinae,
 nautarum uotis non operosa uia.
huc mundi coiere manus: stetit aequore moles
 pinea, nec remis aequa fauebat auis.   20
altera classis erat Teucro damnata Quirino,
 pilaque feminea turpiter acta manu:
hinc Augusta ratis plenis Iouis omine uelis,
 signaque iam patriae uincere docta suae.
tandem aciem geminos Nereus lunarat in arcus,   25
 armorum et radiis picta tremebat aqua,
cum Phoebus linquens stantem se uindice Delon
 (nam tulit iratos mobilis una Notos)
astitit Augusti puppim super, et noua flamma
 luxit in obliquam ter sinuata facem.   30
non ille attulerat crinis in colla solutos
 aut testudineae carmen inerme lyrae,
sed quali aspexit Pelopeum Agamemnona uultu,
 egessitque auidis Dorica castra rogis,
aut qualis flexos soluit Pythona per orbis   35
 serpentem, imbelles quem timuere lyrae.
mox ait 'O Longa mundi seruator ab Alba,
 Auguste, Hectoreis cognite maior auis,
uince mari: iam terra tua est: tibi militat arcus

40   et fauet ex umeris hoc onus omne meis.
            solue metu patriam, quae nunc te uindice freta
                imposuit prorae publica uota tuae.
            quam nisi defendes, murorum Romulus augur
                ire Palatinas non bene uidit auis.
45   et nimium remis audent prope: turpe Latinis
                principe te fluctus regia uela pati.
            nec te, quod classis centenis remigat alis,
                terreat: inuito labitur illa mari:
            quodque uehunt prorae Centaurica saxa minantis,
50   tigna caua et pictos experiere metus.
            frangit et attollit uires in milite causa;
                quae nisi iusta subest, excutit arma pudor.
            tempus adest, committe ratis: ego temporis auctor
                ducam laurigera Iulia rostra manu.'
55   dixerat, et pharetrae pondus consumit in arcus:
                proxima post arcus Caesaris hasta fuit.
            uincit Roma fide Phoebi: dat femina poenas:
                sceptra per Ionias fracta uehuntur aquas.
            at pater Idalio miratur Caesar ab astro:
60   'Sum deus; est nostri sanguinis ista fides.'
            prosequitur cantu Triton, omnesque marinae
                plauserunt circa libera signa deae.
            illa petit Nilum cumba male nixa fugaci,
                hoc unum, iusso non moritura die.
65   di melius! quantus mulier foret una triumphus,
                ductus erat per quas ante Iugurtha uias!
            Actius hinc traxit Phoebus monumenta, quod eius
                una decem uicit missa sagitta ratis.
            bella satis cecini: citharam iam poscit Apollo
70   uictor et ad placidos exuit arma choros.
            candida nunc molli subeant conuiuia luco;
                blanditiaeque fluant per mea colla rosae,
            uinaque fundantur prelis elisa Falernis,
                terque lauet nostras spica Cilissa comas.
75   ingenium positis irritet Musa poetis:
                Bacche, soles Phoebo fertilis esse tuo.
            ille paludosos memoret seruire Sycambros,
                Cepheam hic Meroen fuscaque regna canat,
            hic referat sero confessum foedere Parthum:
80   'Reddat signa Remi, mox dabit ipse sua:
            siue aliquid pharetris Augustus parcet Eois,
                differat in pueros ista tropaea suos.
            gaude, Crasse, nigras si quid sapis inter harenas:

ire per Euphraten ad tua busta licet.'
sic noctem patera, sic ducam carmine, donec   85
    iniciat radios in mea uina dies.

4.7

Sunt aliquid Manes: letum non omnia finit,
    luridaque euictos effugit umbra rogos.
Cynthia namque meo uisa est incumbere fulcro,
    murmur ad extremae nuper humata uiae,
cum mihi somnus ab exsequiis penderet amoris,   5
    et quererer lecti frigida regna mei.
eosdem habuit secum quibus est elata capillos,
    eosdem oculos: lateri uestis adusta fuit,
et solitum digito beryllon adederat ignis,
    summaque Lethaeus triuerat ora liquor.   10
spirantisque animos et uocem misit: at illi
    pollicibus fragiles increpuere manus:
'Perfide nec cuiquam melior sperande puellae,
    in te iam uires somnus habere potest?
iamne tibi exciderant uigilacis furta Suburae   15
    et mea nocturnis trita fenestra dolis?
per quam demisso quotiens tibi fune pependi,
    alterna ueniens in tua colla manu!
saepe Venus triuio commissa est, pectore mixto
    fecerunt tepidas pallia nostra uias.   20
foederis heu taciti, cuius fallacia uerba
    non audituri diripuere Noti.
at mihi non oculos quisquam inclamauit euntis:
    unum impetrassem te reuocante diem:
nec crepuit fissa me propter harundine custos,   25
    laesit et obiectum tegula curta caput.
denique quis nostro curuum te funere uidit,
    atram quis lacrimis incaluisse togam?
si piguit portas ultra procedere, at illuc
    iussisses lectum lentius ire meum.   30
cur uentos non ipse rogis, ingrate, petisti?
    cur nardo flammae non oluere meae?
hoc etiam graue erat, nulla mercede hyacinthos
    inicere et fracto busta piare cado.
Lygdamus uratur – candescat lamina uernae –   35
    sensi ego, cum insidiis pallida uina bibi –
aut Nomas – arcanas tollat uersuta saliuas;
    dicet damnatas ignea testa manus.

quae modo per uilis inspecta est publica noctes,
40   haec nunc aurata cyclade signat humum;
at grauiora rependit iniquis pensa quasillis,
    garrula de facie si qua locuta mea est;
nostraque quod Petale tulit ad monumenta coronas,
    codicis immundi uincula sentit anus;
45 caeditur et Lalage tortis suspensa capillis,
    per nomen quoniam est ausa rogare meum.
te patiente meae conflauit imaginis aurum,
    ardente e nostro dotem habitura rogo.
non tamen insector, quamuis mereare, Properti:
50   longa mea in libris regna fuere tuis.
iuro ego Fatorum nulli reuolubile carmen,
    tergeminusque canis sic mihi molle sonet,
me seruasse fidem. si fallo, uipera nostris
    sibilet in tumulis et super ossa cubet.
55 nam gemina est sedes turpem sortita per amnem,
    turbaque diuersa remigat omnis aqua.
una Clytaemestrae stuprum uehit, altera Cressae
    portat mentitae lignea monstra bouis.
ecce coronato pars altera rapta phaselo,
60   mulcet ubi Elysias aura beata rosas,
qua numerosa fides, quaque aera rotunda Cybebes
    mitratisque sonant Lydia plectra choris.
Andromedeque et Hypermestre sine fraude maritae
    narrant historiae tempora nota suae:
65 haec sua maternis queritur liuere catenis
    bracchia nec meritas frigida saxa manus;
narrat Hypermestre magnum ausas esse sorores,
    in scelus hoc animum non ualuisse suum.
sic mortis lacrimis uitae sanamus amores:
70   celo ego perfidiae crimina multa tuae.
sed tibi nunc mandata damus, si forte moueris,
    si te non totum Chloridos herba tenet:
nutrix in tremulis ne quid desideret annis
    Parthenie: potuit, nec tibi auara fuit.
75 deliciaeque meae Latris, cui nomen ab usu est,
    ne speculum dominae porrigat illa nouae.
et quoscumque meo fecisti nomine uersus,
    ure mihi: laudes desine habere meas.
pelle hederam tumulo, mihi quae pugnante corymbo
80   mollia contortis alligat ossa comis.
ramosis Anio qua pomifer incubat aruis,
    et numquam Herculeo numine pallet ebur,

hic carmen media dignum me scribe columna,
    sed breue, quod currens uector ab urbe legat:
HIC TIBVRTINA IACET AVREA CYNTHIA TERRA: 85
    ACCESSIT RIPAE LAVS, ANIENE, TVAE.
nec tu sperne piis uenientia somnia portis:
    cum pia uenerunt somnia, pondus habent.
nocte uagae ferimur, nox clausas liberat umbras,
    errat et abiecta Cerberus ipse sera.   90
luce iubent leges Lethaea ad stagna reuerti:
    nos uehimur, uectum nauta recenset onus.
nunc te possideant aliae: mox sola tenebo:
    mecum eris, et mixtis ossibus ossa teram.'
haec postquam querula mecum sub lite peregit,   95
    inter complexus excidit umbra meos.

4.8

Disce, quid Esquilias hac nocte fugarit aquosas,
    cum uicina nouis turba cucurrit agris.
turpis in arcana sonuit cum rixa taberna;   19
    si sine me, famae non sine labe meae.   20
Lanuuium annosi uetus est tutela draconis,
    hic ubi tam rarae non perit hora morae;
qua sacer abripitur caeco descensus hiatu,   5
    qua penetrat (uirgo, tale iter omne caue!)
ieiuni serpentis honos, cum pabula poscit
    annua et ex ima sibila torquet humo.
talia demissae pallent ad sacra puellae,
    cum temere anguino creditur ore manus;   10
ille sibi admotas a uirgine corripit escas:
    uirginis in palmis ipsa canistra tremunt.
si fuerint castae, redeunt in colla parentum,
    clamantque agricolae 'Fertilis annus erit.'
huc mea detonsis auecta est Cynthia mannis: 15
    causa fuit Iuno, sed mage causa Venus.
Appia, dic quaeso, quantum te teste triumphum
    egerit effusis per tua saxa rotis!   18
spectaclum ipsa sedens primo temone pependit,   21
    ausa per impuros frena mouere locos.
serica nam taceo uulsi carpenta nepotis
    atque armillatos colla Molossa canis,
qui dabit immundae uenalia fata saginae,   25
    uincet ubi erasas barba pudenda genas.
cum fieret nostro totiens iniuria lecto,

mutato uolui castra mouere toro.
Phyllis Auentinae quaedam est uicina Dianae,
30   sobria grata parum: cum bibit, omne decet.
altera Tarpeios est inter Teia lucos,
      candida, sed potae non sat is unus erit.
his ego constitui noctem lenire uocatis,
      et Venere ignota furta nouare mea.
35   unus erat tribus in secreta lectulus herba.
      quaeris concubitus? inter utramque fui.
Lygdamus ad cyathos, uitrique aestiua supellex
      et Methymnaei Graeca saliua meri.
Nile, tuus tibicen erat, crotalistria †phillis†,
40   haec facilis spargi munda sine arte rosa,
Magnus et ipse suos breuiter concretus in artus
      iactabat truncas ad caua buxa manus.
sed neque suppletis constabat flamma lucernis,
      reccidit inque suos mensa supina pedes.
45   me quoque per talos Venerem quaerente secundos
      semper damnosi subsiluere canes.
cantabant surdo, nudabant pectora caeco:
      Lanuuii ad portas, ei mihi, solus eram;
cum subito rauci sonuerunt cardine postes,
50   et leuia ad primos murmura facta Laris.
nec mora, cum totas resupinat Cynthia ualuas,
      non operosa comis, sed furibunda decens.
pocula mi digitos inter cecidere remissos,
      palluerantque ipso labra soluta mero.
55   fulminat illa oculis et quantum femina saeuit,
      spectaclum capta nec minus urbe fuit.
Phyllidos iratos in uultum conicit unguis:
      territa uicinas Teia clamat aquas.
lumina sopitos turbant elata Quiritis,
60   omnis et insana semita nocte sonat.
illas direptisque comis tunicisque solutis
      excipit obscurae prima taberna uiae.
Cynthia gaudet in exuuiis uictrixque recurrit
      et mea peruersa sauciat ora manu,
65   imponitque notam collo morsuque cruentat,
      praecipueque oculos, qui meruere, ferit.
atque ubi iam nostris lassauit bracchia plagis,
      Lygdamus ad plutei fulcra sinistra latens
eruitur, geniumque meum protractus adorat.
70   Lygdame, nil potui: tecum ego captus eram.
supplicibus palmis tum demum ad foedera ueni,

cum uix tangendos praebuit illa pedes,
    atque ait 'Admissae si uis me ignoscere culpae,
      accipe, quae nostrae formula legis erit.
tu neque Pompeia spatiabere cultus in umbra,   75
    nec cum lasciuum sternet harena Forum.
colla caue inflectas ad summum obliqua theatrum,
    aut lectica tuae se det aperta morae.
Lygdamus in primis, omnis mihi causa querelae,
    ueneat et pedibus uincula bina trahat.'   80
indixit leges: respondi ego 'Legibus utar.'
    riserat imperio facta superba dato.
dein quemcumque locum externae tetigere puellae,
    suffiit, at pura limina tergit aqua,
imperat et totas iterum mutare lucernas,   85
    terque meum tetigit sulpuris igne caput.
atque ita mutato per singula pallia lecto
    respondi, et toto soluimus arma toro.

OVID

Amores 1.1

Arma graui numero uiolentaque bella parabam
    edere, materia conueniente modis.
par erat inferior uersus; risisse Cupido
    dicitur atque unum surripuisse pedem.
5   'quis tibi, saeue puer, dedit hoc in carmina iuris?
    Pieridum uates, non tua, turba sumus.
quid si praeripiat flauae Venus arma Mineruae,
    uentilet accensas flaua Minerua faces?
quis probet in siluis Cererem regnare iugosis,
10   lege pharetratae uirginis arua coli?
crinibus insignem quis acuta cuspide Phoebum
    instruat, Aoniam Marte mouente lyram?
sunt tibi magna, puer, nimiumque potentia regna:
    cur opus affectas ambitiose nouum?
15   an, quod ubique, tuum est? tua sunt Heliconia tempe?
    uix etiam Phoebo iam lyra tuta sua est?
cum bene surrexit uersu noua pagina primo,
    attenuat neruos proximus ille meos.
nec mihi materia est numeris leuioribus apta,
20   aut puer aut longas compta puella comas.'
questus eram, pharetra cum protinus ille soluta
    legit in exitium spicula facta meum
lunauitque genu sinuosum fortiter arcum
    'quod' que 'canas, uates, accipe' dixit 'opus.'
25   me miserum! certas habuit puer ille sagittas:
    uror, et in uacuo pectore regnat Amor.
sex mihi surgat opus numeris, in quinque residat;
    ferrea cum uestris bella ualete modis.
cingere litorea flauentia tempora myrto,
30   Musa per undenos emodulanda pedes.

Amores 1.2

Esse quid hoc dicam, quod tam mihi dura uidentur
    strata, neque in lecto pallia nostra sedent,
et uacuus somno noctem, quam longa, peregi,
    lassaque uersati corporis ossa dolent?
nam, puto, sentirem, si quo temptarer amore –   5
    an subit et tecta callidus arte nocet?
sic erit: haeserunt tenues in corde sagittae,
    et possessa ferus pectora uersat Amor.
cedimus, an subitum luctando accendimus ignem?
    cedamus: leue fit, quod bene fertur, onus.   10
uidi ego iactatas mota face crescere flammas
    et uidi nullo concutiente mori;
uerbera plura ferunt quam quos iuuat usus aratri,
    detractant prensi dum iuga prima, boues;
asper equus duris contunditur ora lupatis: 15
    frena minus sentit, quisquis ad arma facit.
acrius inuitos multo que ferocius urget,
    quam qui seruitium ferre fatentur, Amor.
en ego, confiteor, tua sum noua praeda, Cupido;
    porrigimus uictas ad tua iura manus.   20
nil opus est bello: pacem ueniamque rogamus;
    nec tibi laus armis uictus inermis ero.
necte comam myrto, maternas iunge columbas;
    qui deceat, currum uitricus ipse dabit;
inque dato curru, populo clamante triumphum,   25
    stabis et adiunctas arte mouebis aues.
ducentur capti iuuenes captaeque puellae:
    haec tibi magnificus pompa triumphus erit.
ipse ego, praeda recens, factum modo uulnus habebo
    et noua captiua uincula mente feram.   30
Mens Bona ducetur manibus post terga retortis
    et Pudor et castris quidquid Amoris obest.
omnia te metuent, ad te sua bracchia tendens
    uolgus 'io' magna uoce 'triumphe' canet.
Blanditiae comites tibi erunt Errorque Furorque,   35
    adsidue partes turba secuta tuas.
his tu militibus superas hominesque deosque;
    haec tibi si demas commoda, nudus eris.
laeta triumphanti de summo mater Olympo
    plaudet et adpositas sparget in ora rosas.   40
tu pinnas gemma, gemma uariante capillos,
    ibis in auratis aureus ipse rotis.

tunc quoque non paucos, si te bene nouimus, ures;
    tunc quoque praeteriens uulnera multa dabis.
45   non possunt, licet ipse uelis, cessare sagittae;
    feruida uicino flamma uapore nocet.
talis erat domita Bacchus Gangetide terra:
    tu grauis alitibus, tigribus ille fuit.
ergo cum possim sacri pars esse triumphi,
50   parce tuas in me perdere uictor opes.
aspice cognati felicia Caesaris arma:
    qua uicit, uictos protegit ille manu.

Amores 1.3

Iusta precor: quae me nuper praedata puella est,
    aut amet aut faciat cur ego semper amem.
a, nimium uolui: tantum patiatur amari;
    audierit nostras tot Cytherea preces.
5   accipe, per longos tibi qui deseruiat annos;
    accipe, qui pura norit amare fide.
si me non ueterum commendant magna parentum
    nomina, si nostri sanguinis auctor eques,
nec meus innumeris renouatur campus aratris,
10   temperat et sumptus parcus uterque parens:
at Phoebus comitesque nouem uitisque repertor
    hac faciunt et me qui tibi donat Amor
et nulli cessura fides, sine crimine mores,
    nudaque simplicitas purpureusque pudor.
15   non mihi mille placent, non sum desultor amoris:
    tu mihi, si qua fides, cura perennis eris;
tecum, quos dederint annos mihi fila sororum,
    uiuere contingat teque dolente mori;
te mihi materiem felicem in carmina praebe:
20   prouenient causa carmina digna sua.
carmine nomen habent exterrita cornibus Io
    et quam fluminea lusit adulter aue
quaeque super pontum simulato uecta iuuenco
    uirginea tenuit cornua uara manu.
25   nos quoque per totum pariter cantabimur orbem
    iunctaque semper erunt nomina nostra tuis.

Amores 1.4

Vir tuus est epulas nobis aditurus easdem:
    ultima cena tuo sit precor illa uiro.

ergo ego dilectam tantum conuiua puellam
    aspiciam? tangi quem iuuet, alter erit,
alteriusque sinus apte subiecta fouebis?   5
    iniciet collo, cum uolet, ille manum?
desine mirari, posito quod candida uino
    Atracis ambiguos traxit in arma uiros;
nec mihi silua domus, nec equo mea membra cohaerent:
    uix a te uideor posse tenere manus.   10
quae tibi sint facienda tamen cognosce, nec Euris
    da mea nec tepidis uerba ferenda Notis.
ante ueni quam uir; nec quid, si ueneris ante,
    possit agi uideo, sed tamen ante ueni.
cum premet ille torum, uultu comes ipsa modesto   15
    ibis ut accumbas, clam mihi tange pedem;
me specta nutusque meos uultumque loquacem:
    excipe furtiuas et refer ipsa notas.
uerba superciliis sine uoce loquentia dicam;
    uerba leges digitis, uerba notata mero.   20
cum tibi succurret Veneris lasciuia nostrae,
    purpureas tenero pollice tange genas;
si quid erit, de me tacita quod mente queraris,
    pendeat extrema mollis ab aure manus;
cum tibi, quae faciam, mea lux, dicamue, placebunt,   25
    uersetur digitis anulus usque tuis;
tange manu mensam, tangunt quo more precantes,
    optabis merito cum mala multa uiro.
quod tibi miscuerit, sapias, bibat ipse iubeto;
    tu puerum leuiter posce quod ipsa uoles: 30
quae tu reddideris, ego primus pocula sumam,
    et, qua tu biberis, hac ego parte bibam.
si tibi forte dabit quod praegustauerit ipse,
    reice libatos illius ore cibos;
nec premat impositis sinito tua colla lacertis,   35
    mite nec in rigido pectore pone caput,
nec sinus admittat digitos habilesue papillae;
    oscula praecipue nulla dedisse uelis.
oscula si dederis, fiam manifestus amator
    et dicam 'mea sunt' iniciamque manum.   40
haec tamen aspiciam, sed quae bene pallia celant,
    illa mihi caeci causa timoris erunt.
nec femori committe femur nec crure cohaere
    nec tenerum duro cum pede iunge pedem.
multa miser timeo, quia feci multa proterue,   45
    exemplique metu torqueor ipse mei:

saepe mihi dominaeque meae properata uoluptas
    ueste sub iniecta dulce peregit opus.
hoc tu non facies; sed ne fecisse puteris,
50   conscia de tergo pallia deme tuo.
uir bibat usque roga (precibus tamen oscula desint),
    dumque bibit, furtim, si potes, adde merum.
si bene conpositus somno uinoque iacebit,
    consilium nobis resque locusque dabunt.
55   cum surges abitura domum, surgemus et omnes,
    in medium turbae fac memor agmen eas:
agmine me inuenies aut inuenieris in illo;
    quidquid ibi poteris tangere, tange, mei.
me miserum! monui, paucas quod prosit in horas;
60   separor a domina nocte iubente mea.
nocte uir includet; lacrimis ego maestus obortis,
    qua licet, ad saeuas prosequar usque fores.
oscula iam sumet, iam non tantum oscula sumet:
    quod mihi das furtim, iure coacta dabis.
65   uerum inuita dato (potes hoc) similisque coactae:
    blanditiae taceant sitque maligna Venus.
si mea uota ualent, illum quoque ne iuuet opto;
    si minus, at certe te iuuet inde nihil.
sed quaecumque tamen noctem fortuna sequetur,
70   cras mihi constanti uoce dedisse nega.

Amores 1.5

Aestus erat, mediamque dies exegerat horam;
    apposui medio membra leuanda toro.
pars adaperta fuit, pars altera clausa fenestrae,
    quale fere siluae lumen habere solent,
5   qualia sub lucent fugiente crepuscula Phoebo
    aut ubi nox abiit nec tamen orta dies.
illa uerecundis lux est praebenda puellis,
    qua timidus latebras speret habere pudor.
ecce, Corinna uenit tunica uelata recincta,
10   candida diuidua colla tegente coma,
qualiter in thalamos formosa Sameramis isse
    dicitur et multis Lais amata uiris.
deripui tunicam; nec multum rara nocebat,
    pugnabat tunica sed tamen illa tegi;
15   quae cum ita pugnaret tamquam quae uincere nollet,
    uicta est non aegre proditione sua.
ut stetit ante oculos posito uelamine nostros,

in toto nusquam corpore menda fuit:
quos umeros, quales uidi tetigique lacertos!
    forma papillarum quam fuit apta premi!   20
quam castigato planus sub pectore uenter!
    quantum et quale latus! quam iuuenale femur!
singula quid referam? nil non laudabile uidi,
    et nudam pressi corpus ad usque meum.
cetera quis nescit? lassi requieuimus ambo.   25
    proueniant medii sic mihi saepe dies.

Amores 2.5

Nullus amor tanti est (abeas, pharetrate Cupido),
    ut mihi sint totiens maxima uota mori.
uota mori mea sunt, cum te peccasse recordor,
    ei mihi, perpetuum nata puella malum.
non mihi deceptae nudant tua facta tabellae   5
    nec data furtiue munera crimen habent.
o utinam arguerem sic, ut non uincere possem!
    me miserum, quare tam bona causa mea est?
felix, qui quod amat defendere fortiter audet,
    cui sua 'non feci' dicere amica potest.   10
ferreus est nimiumque suo fauet ille dolori,
    cui petitur uicta palma cruenta rea.
ipse miser uidi, cum me dormire putares,
    sobrius apposito crimina uestra mero:
multa supercilio uidi uibrante loquentes;   15
    nutibus in uestris pars bona uocis erat.
non oculi tacuere tui conscriptaque uino
    mensa, nec in digitis littera nulla fuit.
sermonem agnoui, quod non uideatur, agentem
    uerbaque pro certis iussa ualere notis.   20
iamque frequens ierat mensa conuiua relicta;
    compositi iuuenes unus et alter erant:
improba tum uero iungentes oscula uidi
    (illa mihi lingua nexa fuisse liquet),
qualia non fratri tulerit germana seuero,   25
    sed tulerit cupido mollis amica uiro;
qualia credibile est non Phoebo ferre Dianam,
    sed Venerem Marti saepe tulisse suo.
'quid facis?' exclamo 'quo nunc mea gaudia defers?
    iniciam dominas in mea iura manus.   30
haec tibi sunt mecum, mihi sunt communia tecum:
    in bona cur quisquam tertius ista uenit?'

haec ego, quaeque dolor linguae dictauit; at illi
   conscia purpureus uenit in ora pudor.
35   quale coloratum Tithoni coniuge caelum
   subrubet, aut sponso uisa puella nouo;
quale rosae fulgent inter sua lilia mixtae
   aut ubi cantatis Luna laborat equis;
aut quod, ne longis flauescere possit ab annis,
40   Maeonis Assyrium femina tinxit ebur:
his erat aut alicui color ille simillimus horum,
   et numquam casu pulchrior illa fuit.
spectabat terram: terram spectare decebat;
   maesta erat in uultu: maesta decenter erat.
45   sicut erant, et erant culti, laniare capillos
   et fuit in teneras impetus ire genas;
ut faciem uidi, fortes cecidere lacerti:
   defensa est armis nostra puella suis.
qui modo saeuus eram, supplex ultroque rogaui
50   oscula ne nobis deteriora daret.
risit et ex animo dedit optima, qualia possent
   excutere irato tela trisulca Ioui:
torqueor infelix, ne tam bona senserit alter,
   et uolo non ex hac illa fuisse nota.
55   haec quoque, quam docui, multo meliora fuerunt,
   et quiddam uisa est addidicisse noui.
quod nimium placuere, malum est, quod tota labellis
   lingua tua est nostris, nostra recepta tuis.
nec tamen hoc unum doleo, non oscula tantum
60   iuncta queror, quamuis haec quoque iuncta queror:
illa nisi in lecto nusquam potuere doceri;
   nescioquis pretium grande magister habet.

Amores 2.7

Ergo sufficiam reus in noua crimina semper?
   ut uincam, totiens dimicuisse piget.
siue ego marmorei respexi summa theatri,
   elegis e multis unde dolere uelis;
5   candida seu tacito uidit me femina uultu,
   in uultu tacitas arguis esse notas;
si quam laudaui, miseros petis ungue capillos,
   si culpo, crimen dissimulare putas;
siue bonus color est, in te quoque frigidus esse,
10   seu malus, alterius dicor amore mori.
atque ego peccati uellem mihi conscius essem:

aequo animo poenam, qui meruere, ferunt.
nunc temere insimulas credendoque omnia frustra
    ipsa uetas iram pondus habere tuam:
aspice, ut auritus miserandae sortis asellus   15
    adsiduo domitus uerbere lentus eat.
ecce, nouum crimen: sollers ornare Cypassis
    obicitur dominae contemerasse torum.
di melius, quam me, si sit peccasse libido,
    sordida contemptae sortis amica iuuet!   20
quis Veneris famulae conubia liber inire
    tergaque complecti uerbere secta uelit?
adde quod ornandis illa est operosa capillis
    et tibi per doctas grata ministra manus:
scilicet ancillam, quae tam tibi fida, rogarem?   25
    quid, nisi ut indicio iuncta repulsa foret?
per Venerem iuro puerique uolatilis arcus
    me non admissi criminis esse reum.

Amores 2.8

Ponendis in mille modos perfecta capillis,
    comere sed solas digna Cypassi deas,
et mihi iucundo non rustica cognita furto,
    apta quidem dominae sed magis apta mihi,
quis fuit inter nos sociati corporis index?   5
    sensit concubitus unde Corinna tuos?
num tamen erubui? num uerbo lapsus in ullo
    furtiuae Veneris conscia signa dedi?
quid quod, in ancilla si quis delinquere possit,
    illum ego contendi mente carere bona?   10
(Thessalus ancillae facie Briseidos arsit,
    serua Mycenaeo Phoebas amata duci:
nec sum ego Tantalide maior nec maior Achille;
    quod decuit reges, cur mihi turpe putem?)
ut tamen iratos in te defixit ocellos,   15
    uidi te totis erubuisse genis.
at quanto, si forte refers, praesentior ipse
    per Veneris feci numina magna fidem!
(tu, dea, tu iubeas animi periuria puri
    Carpathium tepidos per mare ferre Notos.)   20
pro quibus officiis pretium mihi dulce repende
    concubitus hodie, fusca Cypassi, tuos.
quid renuis fingisque nouos, ingrata, timores?
    unum est e dominis emeruisse satis.

25 quod si stulta negas, index ante acta fatebor
   et ueniam culpae proditor ipse meae,
   quoque loco tecum fuerim quotiensque, Cypassi,
   narrabo dominae quotque quibusque modis.

Amores 2.19

Si tibi non opus est seruata, stulte, puella,
   at mihi fac serues, quo magis ipse uelim.
quod licet, ingratum est; quod non licet, acrius urit:
   ferreus est, si quis, quod sinit alter, amat.
5 speremus pariter, pariter metuamus amantes,
   et faciat uoto rara repulsa locum.
quo mihi fortunam, quae numquam fallere curet?
   nil ego, quod nullo tempore laedat, amo.
uiderat hoc in me uitium uersuta Corinna,
10 quaque capi possem callida norat opem.
a, quotiens sani capitis mentita dolores
   cunctantem tardo iussit abire pede!
a, quotiens finxit culpam, quantumque licebat
   insonti, speciem praebuit esse nocens!
15 sic ubi uexarat tepidosque refouerat ignis,
   rursus erat uotis comis et apta meis.
quas mihi blanditias, quam dulcia uerba parabat!
   oscula, di magni, qualia quotque dabat!
tu quoque, quae nostros rapuisti nuper ocellos,
20 saepe time insidias, saepe rogata nega,
et sine me ante tuos proiectum in limine postis
   longa pruinosa frigora nocte pati.
sic mihi durat amor longosque adolescit in annos:
   hoc iuuat, haec animi sunt alimenta mei;
25 pinguis amor nimiumque patens in taedia nobis
   uertitur et, stomacho dulcis ut esca, nocet.
si numquam Danaen habuisset aenea turris,
   non esset Danae de Ioue facta parens;
dum seruat Iuno mutatam cornibus Io,
30 facta est quam fuerat gratior illa Ioui.
quod licet et facile est quisquis cupit, arbore frondes
   carpat et e magno flumine potet aquam;
si qua uolet regnare diu, deludat amantem.
   (ei mihi, ne monitis torquear ipse meis!)
35 quidlibet eueniat, nocet indulgentia nobis:
   quod sequitur, fugio; quod fugit, ipse sequor.
at tu, formosae nimium secure puellae,

88

incipe iam prima claudere nocte forem;
  incipe, quis totiens furtim tua limina pulset,
    quaerere, quid latrent nocte silente canes,   40
quas ferat et referat sollers ancilla tabellas,
    cur totiens uacuo secubet ipsa toro:
mordeat ista tuas aliquando cura medullas,
    daque locum nostris materiamque dolis.
ille potest uacuo furari litore harenas,   45
    uxorem stulti si quis amare potest.
iamque ego praemoneo: nisi tu seruare puellam
    incipis, incipiet desinere esse mea.
multa diuque tuli; speraui saepe futurum,
    cum bene seruasses, ut bene uerba darem.   50
lentus es et pateris nulli patienda marito;
    at mihi concessi finis amoris erit.
scilicet infelix numquam prohibebor adire?
    nox mihi sub nullo uindice semper erit?
nil metuam? per nulla traham suspiria somnos?   55
    nil facies, cur te iure perisse uelim?
quid mihi cum facili, quid cum lenone marito?
    corrumpit uitio gaudia nostra suo.
quin alium, quem tanta iuuet patientia, quaeris?
    me tibi riualem si iuuat esse, ueta.   60

Amores 3.4

Dure uir, inposito tenerae custode puellae
    nil agis: ingenio est quaeque tuenda suo.
si qua metu dempto casta est, ea denique casta est;
    quae, quia non liceat, non facit, illa facit.
ut iam seruaris bene corpus, adultera mens est   5
    nec custodiri, ne uelit, ulla potest;
nec corpus seruare potes, licet omnia claudas:
    omnibus occlusis intus adulter erit.
cui peccare licet, peccat minus: ipsa potestas
    semina nequitiae languidiora facit.   10
desine, crede mihi, uitia irritare uetando;
    obsequio uinces aptius illa tuo.
uidi ego nuper equum contra sua uincla tenacem
    ore reluctanti fulminis ire modo;
constitit, ut primum concessas sensit habenas   15
    frenaque in effusa laxa iacere iuba.
nitimur in uetitum semper cupimusque negata:
    sic interdictis imminet aeger aquis.

centum fronte oculos, centum ceruice gerebat
20   Argus, et hos unus saepe fefellit Amor;
in thalamum Danae ferro saxoque perennem
       quae fuerat uirgo tradita, mater erat:
Penelope mansit, quamuis custode carebat,
       inter tot iuuenes intemerata procos.
25   quidquid seruatur, cupimus magis, ipsaque furem
       cura uocat; pauci, quod sinit alter, amant.
nec facie placet illa sua, sed amore mariti:
       nescioquid, quod te ceperit, esse putant.
non proba fit, quam uir seruat, sed adultera cara:
30   ipse timor pretium corpore maius habet.
indignere licet, iuuat inconcessa uoluptas:
       sola placet, 'timeo' dicere si qua potest.
nec tamen ingenuam ius est seruare puellam;
       hic metus externae corpora gentis agat.
35   scilicet ut possit custos 'ego' dicere 'feci',
       in laudem serui casta sit illa tui?
rusticus est nimium, quem laedit adultera coniunx,
       et notos mores non satis Vrbis habet,
in qua Martigenae non sunt sine crimine nati
40   Romulus Iliades Iliadesque Remus.
quo tibi formosam, si non nisi casta placebat?
       non possunt ullis ista coire modis.
si sapis, indulge dominae uultusque seueros
       exue nec rigidi iura tuere uiri
45   et cole quos dederit (multos dabit) uxor amicos:
       gratia sic minimo magna labore uenit;
sic poteris iuuenum conuiuia semper inire
       et, quae non dederis, multa uidere domi.

Ars Amatoria 1.61–228

Seu caperis primis et adhuc crescentibus annis,
       ante oculos ueniet uera puella tuos;
siue cupis iuuenem, iuuenes tibi mille placebunt:
       cogeris uoti nescius esse tui.
65   seu te forte iuuat sera et sapientior aetas,
       hoc quoque, crede mihi, plenius agmen erit.
tu modo Pompeia lentus spatiare sub umbra,
       cum sol Herculei terga leonis adit,
aut ubi muneribus nati sua munera mater
70   addidit, externo marmore diues opus;
nec tibi uitetur quae priscis sparsa tabellis

porticus auctoris Liuia nomen habet,
quaque parare necem miseris patruelibus ausae
    Belides et stricto stat ferus ense pater;
nec te praetereat Veneri ploratus Adonis   75
    cultaque Iudaeo septima sacra Syro,
nec fuge linigerae Memphitica templa iuuencae
    (multas illa facit, quod fuit ipsa Ioui);
et fora conueniunt (quis credere possit?) amori,
    flammaque in arguto saepe reperta foro.   80
subdita qua Veneris facto de marmore templo
    Appias expressis aera pulsat aquis,
illo saepe loco capitur consultus Amori,
    quique aliis cauit, non cauet ipse sibi;
illo saepe loco desunt sua uerba diserto,   85
    resque nouae ueniunt, causaque agenda sua est.
hunc Venus e templis, quae sunt confinia, ridet;
    qui modo patronus, nunc cupit esse cliens.
sed tu praecipue curuis uenare theatris;
    haec loca sunt uoto fertiliora tuo.   90
illic inuenies quod ames, quod ludere possis,
    quodque semel tangas, quodque tenere uelis.
ut redit itque frequens longum formica per agmen,
    granifero solitum cum uehit ore cibum,
aut ut apes saltusque suos et olentia nactae   95
    pascua per flores et thyma summa uolant,
sic ruit ad celebres cultissima femina ludos;
    copia iudicium saepe morata meum est.
spectatum ueniunt, ueniunt spectentur ut ipsae;
    ille locus casti damna pudoris habet.   100
primus sollicitos fecisti, Romule, ludos,
    cum iuuit uiduos rapta Sabina uiros.
tunc neque marmoreo pendebant uela theatro,
    nec fuerant liquido pulpita rubra croco;
illic, quas tulerant nemorosa Palatia, frondes   105
    simpliciter positae, scena sine arte fuit;
in gradibus sedit populus de caespite factis,
    qualibet hirsutas fronde tegente comas.
respiciunt oculisque notant sibi quisque puellam
    quam uelit, et tacito pectore multa mouent;   110
dumque rudem praebente modum tibicine Tusco
    ludius aequatam ter pede pulsat humum,
in medio plausu (plausus tunc arte carebant)
    rex populo praedae signa petita dedit.
protinus exiliunt animum clamore fatentes   115

uirginibus cupidas iniciuntque manus;
ut fugiunt aquilas, timidissima turba, columbae
utque fugit uisos agna nouella lupos,
sic illae timuere uiros sine lege ruentes;
120   constitit in nulla qui fuit ante color.
nam timor unus erat, facies non una timoris:
pars laniat crines, pars sine mente sedet;
altera maesta silet, frustra uocat altera matrem;
haec queritur, stupet haec; haec manet, illa fugit.
125   ducuntur raptae, genialis praeda, puellae,
et potuit multas ipse decere timor.
si qua repugnarat nimium comitemque negarat,
sublatam cupido uir tulit ipse sinu
atque ita 'quid teneros lacrimis corrumpis ocellos?
130   quod matri pater est, hoc tibi' dixit 'ero.'
Romule, militibus scisti dare commoda solus:
haec mihi si dederis commoda, miles ero.
scilicet ex illo sollemni more theatra
nunc quoque formosis insidiosa manent.
135   nec te nobilium fugiat certamen equorum:
multa capax populi commoda Circus habet.
nil opus est digitis per quos arcana loquaris,
nec tibi per nutus accipienda nota est;
proximus a domina nullo prohibente sedeto,
140   iunge tuum lateri qua potes usque latus.
et bene, quod cogit, si nolis, linea iungi,
quod tibi tangenda est lege puella loci.
hic tibi quaeratur socii sermonis origo,
et moueant primos publica uerba sonos:
145   cuius equi ueniant facito studiose requiras,
nec mora, quisquis erit cui fauet illa, faue.
at cum pompa frequens caelestibus ibit eburnis,
tu Veneri dominae plaude fauente manu;
utque fit, in gremium puluis si forte puellae
150   deciderit, digitis excutiendus erit;
etsi nullus erit puluis, tamen excute nullum:
quaelibet officio causa sit apta tuo;
pallia si terra nimium demissa iacebunt,
collige et immunda sedulus effer humo:
155   protinus, officii pretium, patiente puella
contingent oculis crura uidenda tuis.
respice praeterea, post uos quicumque sedebit,
ne premat opposito mollia terga genu.
parua leuis capiunt animos: fuit utile multis

puluinum facili composuisse manu;   160
profuit et tenui uentos mouisse tabella
   et caua sub tenerum scamna dedisse pedem.
hos aditus Circusque nouo praebebit amori
   sparsaque sollicito tristis harena foro.
illa saepe puer Veneris pugnauit harena   165
   et, qui spectauit uulnera, uulnus habet:
dum loquitur tangitque manum poscitque libellum
   et quaerit posito pignore uincat uter,
saucius ingemuit telumque uolatile sensit
   et pars spectati muneris ipse fuit.   170
quid, modo cum belli naualis imagine Caesar
   Persidas induxit Cecropiasque rates?
nempe ab utroque mari iuuenes, ab utroque puellae
   uenere, atque ingens orbis in Vrbe fuit.
quis non inuenit turba, quod amaret, in illa?   175
   eheu, quam multos aduena torsit amor!
ecce, parat Caesar, domito quod defuit orbi
   addere: nunc, Oriens ultime, noster eris.
Parthe, dabis poenas; Crassi gaudete sepulti
   signaque barbaricas non bene passa manus.   180
ultor adest primisque ducem profitetur in annis
   bellaque non puero tractat agenda puer.
parcite natales timidi numerare deorum:
   Caesaribus uirtus contigit ante diem.
ingenium caeleste suis uelocius annis   185
   surgit et ignauae fert male damna morae:
paruus erat manibusque duos Tirynthius angues
   pressit et in cunis iam Ioue dignus erat;
nunc quoque qui puer es, quantus tum, Bacche, fuisti,
   cum timuit thyrsos India uicta tuos?   190
auspiciis annisque patris, puer, arma mouebis
   et uinces annis auspiciisque patris.
tale rudimentum tanto sub nomine debes,
   nunc iuuenum princeps, deinde future senum;
cum tibi sint fratres, fratres ulciscere laesos,   195
   cumque pater tibi sit, iura tuere patris.
induit arma tibi genitor patriaeque tuusque;
   hostis ab inuito regna parente rapit.
tu pia tela feres, sceleratas ille sagittas;
   stabit pro signis iusque piumque tuis.   200
uincuntur causa Parthi, uincantur et armis:
   Eoas Latio dux meus addat opes.
Marsque pater Caesarque pater, date numen eunti:

205

nam deus e uobis alter es, alter eris.

auguror en, uinces, uotiuaque carmina reddam

et magno nobis ore sonandus eris:

consistes aciemque meis hortabere uerbis

(o desint animis ne mea uerba tuis!);

tergaque Parthorum Romanaque pectora dicam

210

telaque, ab auerso quae iacit hostis equo.

qui fugis ut uincas, quid uicto, Parthe, relinques?

Parthe, malum iam nunc Mars tuus omen habet.

ergo erit illa dies, qua tu, pulcherrime rerum,

quattuor in niueis aureus ibis equis;

215

ibunt ante duces onerati colla catenis,

ne possint tuti, qua prius, esse fuga.

spectabunt laeti iuuenes mixtaeque puellae,

diffundetque animos omnibus ista dies;

atque aliqua ex illis cum regum nomina quaeret,

220

quae loca, qui montes quaeue ferantur aquae,

omnia responde, nec tantum si qua rogabit;

et quae nescieris, ut bene nota refer:

hic est Euphrates, praecinctus harundine frontem;

cui coma dependet caerula, Tigris erit;

225

hos facito Armenios, haec est Danaeia Persis;

urbs in Achaemeniis uallibus ista fuit;

ille uel ille duces, et erunt quae nomina dicas,

si poteris, uere, si minus, apta tamen.

Heroides 7

[Accipe, Dardanide, moriturae carmen Elissae;

quae legis, a nobis ultima uerba legis.]

sic ubi fata uocant, udis abiectus in herbis

ad uada Meandri concinit albus olor.

5

nec quia te nostra sperem prece posse moueri,

adloquor (aduerso mouimus ista deo),

sed merita et famam corpusque animumque pudicum

cum male perdiderim, perdere uerba leue est.

certus es ire tamen miseramque relinquere Didon,

10

atque idem uenti uela fidemque ferent?

certus es, Aenea, cum foedere soluere naues

quaeque ubi sint nescis, Italia regna sequi?

nec noua Carthago, nec te crescentia tangunt

moenia nec sceptro tradita summa tuo?

15

facta fugis, facienda petis; quaerenda per orbem

altera, quaesita est altera terra tibi.

ut terram inuenias, quis eam tibi tradet habendam?
  quis sua non notis arua tenenda dabit?
†alter amor tibi restat? habenda est altera Dido?†
  quamque iterum fallas, altera danda fides?   20
quando erit ut condas instar Carthaginis urbem
  et uideas populos altus ab arce tuos?
omnia si ueniant nec di tua uota morentur,
  unde tibi, quae te sic amet, uxor erit?
uror, ut inducto ceratae sulpure taedae;   25
  Aenean animo noxque diesque refert.
ille quidem male gratus et ad mea munera surdus
  et quo, si non sim stulta, carere uelim.
non tamen Aenean, quamuis male cogitat, odi,
  sed queror infidum questaque peius amo.   30
parce, Venus, nurui, durumque amplectere fratrem,
  frater Amor! castris militet ille tuis
atque ego quem coepi (neque enim dedignor) amare,
  materiam curae praebeat ille meae.
fallor et ista mihi falso iactatur imago;   35
  matris ab ingenio dissidet ille suae.
te lapis et montes innataque rupibus altis
  robora, te saeuae progenuere ferae,
aut mare, quale uides agitari nunc quoque uentis,
  quo tamen aduersis fluctibus ire paras.   40
quo fugis? obstat hiemps. hiemis mihi gratia prosit.
  adspice ut euersas concitet Eurus aquas.
quod tibi malueram, sine me debere procellis;
  iustior est animo uentus et unda tuo.
non ego sum tanti (quamuis merearis, inique)   45
  ut pereas, dum me per freta longa fugis.
exerces pretiosa odia et constantia magno,
  si, dum me careas, est tibi uile mori.
iam uenti ponent strataque aequaliter unda
  caeruleis Triton per mare curret equis.   50
tu quoque cum uentis utinam mutabilis esses!
  et, nisi duritia robora uincis, eris.
quid, si nescires insana quid aequora possunt,
  expertae totiens tam male credis aquae?
ut pelago suadente etiam retinacula soluas,   55
  multa tamen latus tristia pontus habet.
nec uiolasse fidem temptantibus aequora prodest;
  perfidiae poenas exigit ille locus,
praecipue cum laesus amor, quia mater Amorum
  nuda Cytheriacis edita fertur aquis.   60

perdita ne perdam, timeo, noceamue nocenti,
  neu bibat aequoreas naufragus hostis aquas.
uiue, precor; sic te melius quam funere perdam;
  tu potius leti causa ferere mei.
65 finge, age, te rapido (nullum sit in omine pondus)
  turbine deprendi; quid tibi mentis erit?
protinus occurrent falsae periuria linguae
  et Phrygia Dido fraude coacta mori;
coniugis ante oculos deceptae stabit imago
70   tristis et effusis sanguinulenta comis.
"Quicquid id est, totum merui; concedite," dicas,
  quaeque cadent, in te fulmina missa putes.
da breue saeuitiae spatium pelagique tuaeque;
  grande morae pretium tuta futura uia est.
75 nec mihi tu curae; puero parcatur Iulo.
  te satis est titulum mortis habere meae.
quid puer Ascanius, quid commeruere Penates?
  ignibus ereptos obruet unda deos?
sed neque fers tecum, nec quae mihi perfide, iactas,
80   presserunt umeros sacra paterque tuos.
omnia mentiris, neque enim tua fallere lingua
  incipit a nobis primaque plector ego.
si quaeras ubi sit formosi mater Iuli,
  occidit a duro sola relicta uiro.
85 haec mihi narraras et me mouere. merentem
  ure: minor culpa poena futura mea est.
nec mihi mens dubia est quin te tua numina damnent;
  per mare, per terras septima iactat hiemps.
fluctibus eiectum tuta statione recepi
90   uixque bene audito nomine regna dedi.
his tamen officiis utinam contenta fuissem,
  et mihi concubitus fama sepulta foret!
illa dies nocuit, qua nos decliue sub antrum
  caeruleus subitis compulit imber aquis.
95 audieram uocem; nymphas ululasse putaui;
  Eumenides fatis signa dedere meis.
exige, laese pudor, poenas, uiolate Sychaeeu,
  ad quem, me miseram, plena pudoris eo.
est mihi marmorea sacratus in aede Sychaeus
100   (oppositae frondes uelleraque alba tegunt);
hinc ego me sensi noto quater ore citari;
  ipse sono tenui dixit: "Elissa, ueni."
nulla mora est, uenio, uenio tibi dedita coniunx;
  sum tamen admissi tarda pudore mei.

da ueniam culpae; decepit idoneus auctor; 105
  inuidiam noxae detrahit ille meae.
diua parens seniorque pater, pia sarcina nati,
  spem mihi mansuri rite dedere uiri;
si fuit errandum, causas habet error honestas;
  adde fidem, nulla parte pigendus erit. 110
durat in extremum uitaeque nouissima nostrae
  prosequitur fati, qui fuit ante, tenor.
occidit Herceas coniunx mactatus ad aras,
  et sceleris tanti praemia frater habet.
exul agor cineresque uiri patriamque relinquo 115
  et feror in duras hoste sequente uias.
adplicor ignotis fratrique elapsa fretoque
  quod tibi donaui, perfide, litus emo;
urbem constitui lateque patentia fixi
  moenia finitimis inuidiosa locis. 120
bella tument; bellis peregrina et femina temptor,
  uixque rudis portas urbis et arma paro;
mille procis placui, qui me coiere querentes
  nescio quem thalamis praeposuisse suis.
quid dubitas uinctam Gaetulo tradere Iarbae? 125
  praebuerim sceleri bracchia nostra tuo.
est etiam frater, cuius manus impia poscit
  respergi nostro, sparsa cruore uiri.
pone deos et quae tangendo sacra profanas.
  non bene caelestis impia dextra colit; 130
si tu cultor eras elapsis igne futurus,
  paenitet elapsos ignibus esse deos.
forsitan et grauidam Didon, scelerate, relinquas,
  parsque tui lateat corpore clausa meo.
accedet fatis matris miserabilis infans 135
  et nondum nati funeris auctor eris,
cumque parente sua frater morietur Iuli,
  poenaque conexos auferet una duos.
sed iubet ire deus. uellem uetuisset adire
  Punica nec Teucris pressa fuisset humus. 140
hoc duce nempe deo uentis agitaris iniquis
  et teris in rabido tempora longa freto.
Pergama uix tanto tibi erant repetenda labore,
  Hectore si uiuo quanta fuere forent.
non patrium Simoenta petis, sed Thybridas undas; 145
  nempe ut peruenias quo cupis, hospes eris,
utque latet uitatque tuas abstrusa carinas,
  uix tibi continget terra petita seni.

hos potius populos in dotem, ambage remissa,
150   accipe et aduectas Pygmalionis opes;
       Ilion in Tyriam transfer felicius urbem
          resque loco regis sceptraque sacra tene.
       si tibi mens auida est belli, si quaerit Iulus
          unde suo partus Marte triumphus eat,
155   quem superet, ne quid desit, preabebimus hostem;
          hic pacis leges, hic locus arma capit.
       tu modo, per matrem fraternaque tela, sagittas,
          perque fugae comites, Dardana sacra, deos,
       (sic superent quoscumque tua de gente reportas,
160   Mars ferus et damni sit modus ille tui,
       Ascaniusque suos feliciter impleat annos,
          et senis Anchisae molliter ossa cubent!)
       parce, precor, domui, quae se tibi tradit habendam.
          quod crimen dicis praeter amasse meum?
165   non ego sum Phthia magnisque oriunda Mycenis
          nec steterunt in te uirque paterque meus.
       si pudet uxoris, non nupta, sed hospita dicar;
          dum tua sit, Dido quodlibet esse feret.
       nota mihi freta sunt Afrum plangentia litus;
170   temporibus certis dantque negantque uiam;
       cum dabit aura uiam, praebebis carbasa uentis;
          nunc leuis eiectam continet alga ratem.
       tempus ut obseruem, manda mihi; serius ibis,
          nec te, si cupies, ipsa manere sinam.
175   et socii requiem poscunt, laniataque classis
          postulat exiguas semirefacta moras.
       pro meritis et siqua tibi debebimus ultra,
          pro spe coniugii tempora parua peto;
       dum freta mitescant et amorem temperet usus
180   fortiter ediscam tristia posse pati.
       si minus, est animus nobis effundere uitam;
          in me crudelis non potes esse diu.
       adspicias utinam quae sit scribentis imago;
          scribimus, et gremio Troicus ensis adest,
185   perque genas lacrimae strictum labuntur in ensem,
          qui iam pro lacrimis sanguine tinctus erit.
       quam bene conueniunt fato tua munera nostro!
          instruis impensa nostra sepulcra breui.
       nec mea nunc primum feriuntur pectora telo;
190   ille locus saeui uulnus amoris habet,
       Anna soror, soror Anna, meae male conscia culpae,
          iam dabis in cineres ultima dona meos.

nec consumpta rogis inscribar Elissa Sychaei;
   hoc tamen in tumuli marmore carmen erit:
'Praebuit Aeneas et causam mortis et ensem;   195
   ipsa sua Dido concidit usa manu.'

Tristia 2.207–468

perdiderint cum me duo crimina, carmen et error,
   alterius facti culpa silenda mihi:
nam non sum tanti, renouem ut tua uulnera, Caesar,
   quem nimio plus est indoluisse semel.   210
altera pars superest, qua turpi carmine factus
   arguor obsceni doctor adulterii.
fas ergo est aliqua caelestia pectora falli,
   et sunt notitia multa minora tua;
utque deos caelumque simul sublime tuenti   215
   non uacat exiguis rebus adesse Ioui,
de te pendentem sic dum circumspicis orbem,
   effugiunt curas inferiora tuas.
scilicet inperii princeps statione relicta
   inparibus legeres carmina facta modis?   220
non ea te moles Romani nominis urget,
   inque tuis umeris tam leue fertur onus,
lusibus ut possis aduertere numen ineptis,
   excutiasque oculis otia nostra tuis.
nunc tibi Pannonia est, nunc Illyris ora domanda,   225
   Raetica nunc praebent Thraciaque arma metum,
nunc petit Armenius pacem, nunc porrigit arcus
   Parthus eques timida captaque signa manu,
nunc te prole tua iuuenem Germania sentit,
   bellaque pro magno Caesare Caesar obit.   230
denique, ut in tanto, quantum non extitit umquam,
   corpore pars nulla est, quae labet, inperii,
urbs quoque te et legum lassat tutela tuarum
   et morum, similes quos cupis esse tuis.
non tibi contingunt, quae gentibus otia praestas,   235
   bellaque cum multis inrequieta geris.
mirer in hoc igitur tantarum pondere rerum
   te numquam nostros euoluisse iocos?
at si, quod mallem, uacuum tibi forte fuisset,
   nullum legisses crimen in Arte mea.   240
illa quidem fateor frontis non esse seuerae
   scripta, nec a tanto principe digna legi:
non tamen idcirco legum contraria iussis

sunt ea Romanas erudiuntque nurus.
245   neue, quibus scribam, possis dubitare, libellos,
      quattuor hos uersus e tribus unus habet:
'este procul, uittae tenues, insigne pudoris,
      quaeque tegis medios instita longa pedes!
nil nisi legitimum concessaque furta canemus,
250   inque meo nullum carmine crimen erit.'
ecquid ab hac omnes rigide summouimus Arte,
      quas stola contingi uittaque sumpta uetat?
'at matrona potest alienis artibus uti,
      quoque trahat, quamuis non doceatur, habet.'
255 nil igitur matrona legat, quia carmine ab omni
      ad delinquendum doctior esse potest.
quodcumque attigerit siqua est studiosa sinistri,
      ad uitium mores instruet inde suos.
sumpserit Annales (nihil est hirsutius illis)
260   facta sit unde parens Ilia, nempe leget.
sumpserit 'Aeneadum genetrix' ubi prima, requiret,
      Aeneadum genetrix unde sit alma Venus.
persequar inferius, modo si licet ordine ferri,
      posse nocere animis carminis omne genus.
265 non tamen idcirco crimen liber omnis habebit:
      nil prodest, quod non laedere possit idem.
igne quid utilius? siquis tamen urere tecta
      comparat, audaces instruit igne manus.
eripit interdum, modo dat medicina salutem,
270   quaeque iuuet, monstrat, quaeque sit herba nocens
et latro et cautus praecingitur ense uiator
      ille sed insidias, hic sibi portat opem.
discitur innocuas ut agat facundia causas:
      protegit haec sontes, inmeritosque premit.
275 sic igitur carmen, recta si mente legatur,
      constabit nulli posse nocere meum.
'at quasdam uitiat.' quicumque hoc concipit, errat,
      et nimium scriptis arrogat ille meis.
ut tamen hoc fatear, ludi quoque semina praebent
280   nequitiae: tolli tota theatra iube:
peccandi causam multi quam saepe dederunt,
      Martia cum durum sternit harena solum.
tollatur Circus; non tuta licentia Circi est:
      hic sedet ignoto iuncta puella uiro.
285 cum quaedam spatientur in hoc, ut amator eodem
      conueniat, quare porticus ulla patet?
quis locus est templis augustior? haec quoque uitet,

in culpam siqua est ingeniosa suam.
cum steterit Iouis aede, Iouis succurret in aede
   quam multas matres fecerit ille deus.   290
proxima adoranti Iunonis templa subibit,
   paelicibus multis hanc doluisse deam.
Pallade conspecta, natum de crimine uirgo
   sustulerit quare, quaeret, Erichthonium.
uenerit in magni templum, tua munera, Martis,   295
   stat Venus Vltori iuncta, uir ante fores.
Isidis aede sedens, cur hanc Saturnia, quaeret,
   egerit Ionio Bosporioque mari?
in Venerem Anchises, in Lunam Latmius heros,
   in Cererem Iasion, qui referatur, erit.   300
omnia peruersas possunt corrumpere mentes:
   stant tamen illa suis omnia tuta locis.
et procul a scripta solis meretricibus Arte
   summouet ingenuas pagina prima manus.
quaecumque erupit, qua non sinit ire sacerdos,   305
   protinus huic dempti criminis ipsa rea est.
nec tamen est facinus uersus euoluere mollis,
   multa licet castae non facienda legant.
saepe supercilii nudas matrona seueri
   et Veneris stantis ad genus omne uidet.   310
corpora Vestales oculi meretricia cernunt,
   nec domino poenae res ea causa fuit.
at cur in nostra nimia est lasciuia Musa,
   curue meus cuiquam suadet amare liber?
nil nisi peccatum manifestaque culpa fatenda est: 315
   paenitet ingenii iudiciique mei.
cur non Argolicis potius quae concidit armis
   uexata est iterum carmine Troia meo?
cur tacui Thebas et uulnera mutua fratrum,
   et septem portas, sub duce quamque suo?   320
nec mihi materiam bellatrix Roma negabat,
   et pius est patriae facta referre labor.
denique cum meritis inpleueris omnia, Caesar,
   pars mihi de multis una canenda fuit,
utque trahunt oculos radiantia lumina solis,   325
   traxissent animum sic tua facta meum.
arguor inmerito. tenuis mihi campus aratur:
   illud erat magnae fertilitatis opus.
non ideo debet pelago se credere, siqua
   audet in exiguo ludere cumba lacu.   330
forsan (et hoc dubitem) numeris leuioribus aptus

sim satis, in paruos sufficiamque modos:
　　at si me iubeas domitos Iouis igne Gigantas
　　　dicere, conantem debilitabit onus.
335　diuitis ingenii est inmania Caesaris acta
　　　condere, materia ne superetur opus.
　　et tamen ausus eram. sed detractare uidebar,
　　　quodque nefas, damno uiribus esse tuis.
　　ad leue rursus opus, iuuenalia carmina, ueni,
340　　et falso moui pectus amore meum.
　　non equidem uellem: sed me mea fata trahebant,
　　　inque meas poenas ingeniosus eram.
　　ei mihi, quod didici! cur me docuere parentes,
　　　litteraque est oculos ulla morata meos?
345　haec tibi me inuisum lasciuia fecit, ob Artes,
　　　quis ratus es uetitos sollicitare toros.
　　sed neque me nuptae didicerunt furta magistro,
　　　quodque parum nouit, nemo docere potest.
　　sic ego delicias et mollia carmina feci,
350　　strinxerit ut nomen fabula nulla meum.
　　nec quisquam est adeo media de plebe maritus,
　　　ut dubius uitio sit pater ille meo.
　　crede mihi, distant mores a carmine nostro
　　　(uita uerecunda est, Musa iocosa mea)
355　magnaque pars mendax operum est et ficta meorum:
　　　plus sibi permisit compositore suo.
　　nec liber indicium est animi, sed honesta uoluptas:
　　　plurima mulcendis auribus apta feres.
　　Accius esset atrox, conuiua Terentius esset,
360　　essent pugnaces qui fera bella canunt.
　　denique composui teneros non solus amores:
　　　composito poenas solus amore dedi.
　　quid, nisi cum multo Venerem confundere uino,
　　　praecepit lyrici Teia Musa senis?
365　Lesbia quid docuit Sappho, nisi amare, puellas?
　　　tuta tamen Sappho, tutus et ille fuit.
　　nec tibi, Battiade nocuit, quod saepe legenti
　　　delicias uersu fassus es ipse tuas.
　　fabula iucundi nulla est sine amore Menandri,
370　　et solet hic pueris uirginibusque legi.
　　Ilias ipsa quid est aliud, nisi adultera, de qua
　　　inter amatorem pugna uirumque fuit?
　　quid prius est illi flamma Briseidos, utque
　　　fecerit iratos rapta puella duces?
375　aut quid Odyssea est, nisi femina propter amorem,

dum uir abest, multis una petita procis?
quis, nisi Maeonides, Venerem Martemque ligatos
    narrat in obsceno corpora prensa toro?
unde nisi indicio magni sciremus Homeri
    hospitis igne duas incaluisse deas?   380
omne genus scripti grauitate tragoedia uincit:
    haec quoque materiam semper amoris habet.
numquid in Hippolyto, nisi caecae flamma nouercae?
    nobilis est Canace fratris amore sui.
quid? non Tantalides agitante Cupidine currus   385
    Pisaeam Phrygiis uexit eburnus equis?
tingeret ut ferrum natorum sanguine mater,
    concitus a laeso fecit amore dolor.
fecit amor subitas uolucres cum paelice regem,
    quaeque suum luget nunc quoque mater Ityn.   390
si non Aeropen frater sceleratus amasset,
    auersos Solis non legeremus equos.
inpia nec tragicos tetigisset Scylla coturnos,
    ni patrium crinem desecuisset amor.
qui legis Electran et egentem mentis Oresten,   395
    Aegisthi crimen Tyndaridosque legis.
nam quid de tetrico referam domitore Chimaerae,
    quem leto fallax hospita paene dedit?
quid loquar Hermionen, quid te, Schoeneia uirgo,
    teque, Mycenaeo Phoebas amata duci?   400
quid Danaen Danaesque nurum matremque Lyaei
    Haemonaque et noctes cui coiere duae?
quid Peliae generum, quid Thesea, quiue Pelasgum
    Iliacam tetigit de rate primus humum?
huc Iole Pyrrhique parens, huc Herculis uxor,   405
    huc accedat Hylas Iliacusque puer.
tempore deficiar, tragicos si persequar ignes,
    uixque meus capiet nomina nuda liber.
est et in obscenos commixta tragoedia risus,
    multaque praeteriti uerba pudoris habet.   410
nec nocet auctori, mollem qui fecit Achillem,
    infregisse suis fortia facta modis.
iunxit Aristides Milesia crimina secum,
    pulsus Aristides nec tamen urbe sua est.
nec qui descripsit corrumpi semina matrum,   415
    Eubius, inpurae conditor historiae,
nec qui composuit nuper Sybaritica, fugit,
    nec qui concubitus non tacuere suos.
suntque ea doctorum monumentis mixta uirorum,

420	muneribusque ducum publica facta patent.
	neue peregrinis tantum defendar ab armis,
	et Romanus habet multa iocosa liber.
	utque suo Martem cecinit grauis Ennius ore,
	Ennius ingenio maximus, arte rudis:
425	explicat ut causas rapidi Lucretius ignis,
	casurumque triplex uaticinatur opus:
	sic sua lasciuo cantata est saepe Catullo
	femina, cui falsum Lesbia nomen erat;
	nec contentus ea, multos uulgauit amores,
430	in quibus ipse suum fassus adulterium est.
	par fuit exigui similisque licentia Calui,
	detexit uariis qui sua furta modis.
	quid referam Ticidae, quid Memmi carmen, apud quos
	rebus adest nomen nominibusque pudor,
435	Cinna quoque his comes est, Cinnaque procacior Anser,
	et leue Cornufici parque Catonis opus.
	et quorum libris modo dissimulata Perillae est
	nomine, nunc legitur dicta, Metelle, tuo?
	is quoque, Phasiacas Argon qui duxit in undas,
440	non potuit Veneris furta tacere suae.
	nec minus Hortensi, nec sunt minus improba Serui
	carmina. quis dubitet nomina tanta sequi?
	uertit Aristiden Sisenna, nec offuit illi,
	historiae turpis inseruisse iocos.
445	non fuit opprobrio celebrasse Lycorida Gallo,
	sed linguam nimio non tenuisse mero.
	credere iuranti durum putat esse Tibullus,
	sic etiam de se quod neget illa uiro:
	fallere custodes idem docuisse fatetur,
450	seque sua miserum nunc ait arte premi.
	saepe, uelut gemmam dominae signumue probaret,
	per causam meminit se tetigisse manum,
	utque refert, digitis saepe est nutuque locutus,
	et tacitam mensae duxit in orbe notam;
455	et quibus e sucis abeat de corpore liuor,
	inpresso fieri qui solet ore, docet:
	denique ab incauto nimium petit ille marito,
	se quoque uti seruet, peccet ut illa minus.
	scit, cui latretur, cum solus obambulet, ipsas
460	cui totiens clausas excreet ante fores,
	multaque dat furti talis praecepta docetque
	qua nuptae possint fallere ab arte uiros.
	non fuit hoc illi fraudi, legiturque Tibullus

et placet, et iam te principe notus erat.
inuenies eadem blandi praecepta Properti: 465
    destrictus minima nec tamen ille nota est.
his ego successi, quoniam praestantia candor
    nomina uiuorum dissimulare iubet.

COMMENTARY

CATULLUS

68B

This poem is generally considered the first example of the elegiac genre. It offers the length and complexity typical of the form and anticipates later uses of mythological exempla. The poem is also important because it gives us a rare glimpse into the overall narrative of the Lesbia affair. Here Catullus clearly states that it is an adulterous affair, but that he nonetheless conceives of his relationship to Lesbia as a kind of marriage [10, 13, 37].* Such a demand for fidelity in an adulterous liaison would have been highly unusual in the Roman world and highlights the eccentric nature of the affair portrayed by Catullus [12]. It is this commitment to a woman to whom one would normally owe no such thing that signals the unique status of the elegiac romance in Roman life. This poem also foreshadows later developments in the genre by showing that Catullus's sense of commitment was not shared by his beloved. It is this presumed inequality of feeling that lies behind the common elegiac theme of *servitium amoris* or "the slavery of love" [8]. One feature of this theme is the casting of the beloved in the figure of the *domina* [7], the poet's literal mistress, an inversion of the normal Roman hierarchy of gender relations. This poem features the first use of the word *domina* in an erotic context.

   While 68B does much to clarify the narrative of the Lesbia affair and its status as model for the later elegists, from a formal point of view the poem is fraught with difficulties. In all the surviving manuscripts, it is printed with a 40-line preface addressed to a certain Mallius or Manius. This preface takes the form of a letter in which Catullus explains that he is unable to provide a poem as Mallius requests because he is wracked with grief on his brother's death, and in any case he is away from his library in Rome. What follows is

---

* Bold numbers in brackets (e.g. [1]) refer to paragraphs in the Introduction where a more expanded discussion of the topic can be found.

either a substitute poem addressed to an Allius or a belated answer to the original request (in which case Allius is the addressee's *nomen* and Mallius his *praenomen*). The problem has vexed scholars for the last two centuries.

Nonetheless, 68B reads as a complete poem. It exhibits a clear ring composition in which recurring motifs are paired around the central panel on the death of the poet's brother. It alone concerns the poet's own love affair and so 68A can be left aside for our purposes.

41–46. The poet offers a poem of praise to his friend Allius, promising him poetic immortality in return for the latter's good offices in the early stages of the Lesbia affair. The Muses will spread his name through centuries to come. **Deae** is vocative plural.

47. The hexameter from this couplet has dropped out. It presumably referred to the renown Allius would receive while still living, as opposed to the posthumous fame addressed in the pentameter.

49–50. The spider web is a good example of the imagistic style Catullus uses in this poem.

51–66. Here begins the first of several complex similes found throughout the poem. Each is a miniature masterpiece of the Alexandrian art of allusion and aesthetic symmetry and each turns out to illustrate a point far different from what it initially claims. Thus this simile ostensibly illustrates how great Allius's aid was in Catullus's time of distress, and hence how deserving it is to be memorialized in poetry. However, if the reader pays careful attention, the tears that Catullus sheds become the stream that comforts the weary traveler. The welcomeness of this cool water is in turn compared to the aid brought by the gods Castor and Pollux to sailors in a storm at sea, who are the very image of Allius in his good offices to Catullus. The poet's tears and sorrow are thus compared to the aid that Allius gave to relieve them! Could this ambiguity be traced to the fact that, by facilitating the affair with Lesbia, Allius has caused more pain than if he had never done the poet any such favor?

The reader should note the extraordinary symmetry of the description as the poet moves from the dry heat of **torruerit**, to the volcanic lava of Etna and the hot springs of Thermopylae. These hot springs become the poet's eyes, which melt (**tabescere**) and are transformed into the rain that moistens his cheeks. This shower is, in turn, compared to a mountain spring that flows through a valley providing relief to the sweat-covered (**sudore**) traveler, when the dry summer heat splits open the parched earth. The progression thus is from dry heat to hot liquid, then to cool liquid, and finally back to warm liquid and dry baking heat. The traveler's salty sweat recalls the poet's tears while anticipating the storm at sea still to come.

51. Amathusia = Venus. She is **duplex** as the bringer of pleasure and pain.

53. Trinacria rupes = Mt. Etna.

54. Oetaeis Malia Thermopylis = the warm springs at the base of Mt. Oeta in Thessaly near the pass of Thermopylae, hence the latter's name: "hot gates."

65. Castor and Pollux, the divine brothers of Helen and Clytemnestra, are the traditional gods of sailors.

67–69. Allius's service was to provide his country home as a secluded spot where Catullus and Lesbia could have their first adulterous rendezvous. Some argue that *domina* could not refer to Lesbia since Allius did not provide her, and therefore it must mean that he provided a mistress of the house to give them proper cover for their dangerous liaison. Nonetheless, by providing his *domus*, Allius in effect created the conditions under which Lesbia became Catullus's *domina*. Compare **erae** (135); **domina** (156).

Note the way the sentence spills over the bounds of the couplet. Later elegiac practice would tend to make each couplet a self-contained syntactical unit. Catullus's metrical practice in this poem is closer to that of his Hellenistic sources than his Latin successors {33}.

70–76. This sentence is extraordinary on several levels. 1. Its depiction of Lesbia as a shining goddess is striking and underlines the inversion of normal power relations between the genders. 2. The image is clearly that of a bride crossing the threshold. Catullus is the awestruck groom waiting inside the house to receive his divine bride. 3. But this is an ill-omened marriage because Lesbia's sandal squeaks (**arguta . . . solea**) as it crosses the threshold (**limine**). How could things be otherwise since this is in fact not a marriage but adultery? 4. This sentence introduces the longest simile of poem (73–130) in which Lesbia is compared to Laudamia approaching Protesilaus on the day of their ill-fated wedding.

Like the previous similes, this one too is not what it seems. As more than one commentator has noted, while Catullus says he is comparing Lesbia to Laudamia, the situation described in the simile as a whole applies far better to him than to her. This takes the inversion of gender roles to another level, as the poet figuratively becomes the bride rather than the groom.

74. Protesilaus was the first soldier killed in the Trojan War. He departed the morning after his wedding night. The theme was popular in ancient literature, with some versions featuring a return from the realm of the dead for one night and others Laudamia's fashioning a likeness of him that she takes to her bed. In all versions, the pathetic futility of their love is central.

77–78. Ramnusia virgo = Nemesis, goddess of divine retribution. This aside is ironic since Catullus's relation with Lesbia had not been sanctified by sacrifice, and hence his *domus* too (household, but also the physical building) had been begun in vein (**frustra**).

79. The hungry altars (**ieiuna . . . ara**), desiring blood (**cruorem**), are a powerful image of the doomed nature of Laudamia and Protesilaus's marriage, and a foreshadowing of the description of the Trojan war as well as of the tomb of Catullus's brother, which immediately follows. **Pium** refers both to the blood sacrifice duty (*pietas*) owed the altars and to the blood of the dutiful or innocent who will pay the ritual debt.

81–84. The syntax here is difficult. Laudamia is forced (**coacta**) to give up the embrace of her husband before (**ante . . . quam**) the coming of a second winter would have filled (**saturasset**, syncopated pluperfect subjunctive) her love's hunger during its long nights. As we find out later in the poem, it is Catullus who must live with his desire for Lesbia unfulfilled.

85–86. Quod refers back to the entire idea expressed in line 84. **Isset** is a syncopated form.

87–100. The set of associations woven into this passage is extremely complex. In outline, the mention of the Trojan War that occasioned Laudamia's loss of Protesilaus recalls to Catullus the loss of his brother whose tomb was to be found near the site of Troy. The Trojan War was the cause of the death of countless young men who, like Catullus's brother, were struck down in their prime. Thus, Catullus's sense of loss for his brother is implicitly compared to Laudamia's for Protesilaus. At the same time, the cause of the Trojan War, Helen's infidelity, recalls that of Lesbia to whom Laudamia is explicitly compared. The conflation of the poet's grief for his brother with his sorrow over a love affair gone wrong, in the context of a simile comparing the first night of that affair to Laudamia's wedding night, makes this one of the most difficult and powerful passages in all of Latin poetry.

91. Quaene: the interrogative *-ne* is equivalent to the colloquial English, "isn't it?" or the French "n'est-ce pas?".

92–96. This passage echoes 68A.20–24. **Adempte** is vocative. The **domus sepulta** recalls both Laudamia and Protesilaus's **domus incepta frustra** (74–75) as well as the **domus** loaned to Catullus and Lesbia by Allius (68).

101–04. The syntax again is difficult. **Pubes**, the subject of **fertur**, is modified by **properans, lecta**, and **Graeca**. In the second clause, the hyperbaton, or disruption of normal prose word order, is again difficult. **Gauisus** modifies

Paris and takes its complement in the ablative (**abducta** . . . **moecha**), making **libera** . . . **otia** the object of **degeret**.

105. Quo . . . casu: the main narrative of the Laudamia simile is resumed after the digression on the death of Catullus's brother.

107–28. Here the reader finds a series of three similes that rival in complexity those in lines 51–66, with the added twist that this second series occurs within the larger framework of the Laudamia simile that dominates the central portion of the poem. The complexities of these similes and the difficulty of determining that to which they ultimately refer must surely be deliberate. It is an artful confusion that mirrors the confusion of gender roles in Catullus's relation with Lesbia, the undermining of accepted standards of social conduct in his carrying on an adulterous affair, and the conflation of his loss of Lesbia through infidelity with the loss of his brother seen here and elsewhere in the corpus.

107–18. The violence of Laudamia's passion is compared to a whirlpool in a chasm (**barathrum**) such as that dug by Hercules when he drained the swamp at Pheneus while killing the man-eating birds of Stymphalus during his fifth labor.

109. Cyllenaeum = pertaining to Cyllene, a mountain in Northwest Arcadia.

111–22. audit = *dicitur*, a Greek idiom. Hence **fodisse** = perfect infinitive in indirect discourse. The polysyllabic **falsiparens Amphitryoniades** for Hercules is a wonderful example of Catullus's Hellenistic *doctrina*. It demonstrates his knowledge of the myth – Amphitryon was only nominally Hercules's father – while serving as an example of metrical pyrotechnics and a reminder of the themes of adultery and infidelity. It looks forward to the **plurima furta Iovis** (140), inasmuch as Jupiter's deceptive seduction of Alcmene is the true cause of Hercules's birth.

114. Deterioris eri = Eurystheus, who ordered the twelve labors. The fact that he was actually Hercules's inferior serves as another example of the inversion of normal power relations.

115–16. As a reward for his labors, Hercules upon his death becomes a god and marries **Hebe**, the goddess of youth.

118. The paradox of the still untamed (**indomitam**) Laudamia being taught by the depth of her love to bear the yoke (of sadness? of continuing fidelity to an absent spouse?) rests on a metaphor common in ancient poetry, comparing the marriage of a young girl to the taming of a colt, best captured in the Greek verb *damazō*, "to break a horse, to marry."

119–24. This second simile within a simile is based on a passage in Pindar's *Olympian* 10, whose complex embedded style this poem resembles. The syntax here is difficult owing to the rhetorical foregrounding of **carum . . . caput.** Only with **nata** does the reader realize that **caput** is the object and not the subject of the verb. **Qui,** referring back to **nepos,** is modified by **inventus** and **tollens,** and is the subject of **suscitat. Testatas . . . tabulas** refer to the grandfather's will.

125–28. The third simile embedded within the larger Laudamia simile directly interlocks with the second and the pair recall in their structure the double simile at 51–66.

Doves were proverbial for their passion and fidelity. The **multiuola . . . mulier,** while an analogue to the dove in the intensity of her desire, also suggests a woman who wants more than one man (compare **omniuoli . . . Iouis** at 140). This hint of infidelity applies better to Lesbia than Laudamia, and it signals that we are coming to the end of the central portion of the poem and returning to the outer frame.

129–30. Laudamia's passion in the one night of love she had with her blond hero was greater than even that of the doves over the course of a lifetime.

131. Aut paulo = a telling concession.

132–33. Cupido in his saffron robe recalls Hymen as portrayed in Catullus's marriage hymn, 61.8. The substitution of Desire for Marriage reveals the unfortunate reality of his relation with Lesbia.

136. Era = *domina*, an invocation of *servitium amoris* in the context of Catullus's recognition of the need to accept Lesbia's *furta*.

138–40. Juno must overlook Jupiter's infidelities, as any Roman wife was expected to do of her husband. The existence of this sexual double standard makes Catullus's self-comparison with Juno striking.

142. Catullus adopts the stance of urbane acceptance of infidelity, a pose of enlightened cynicism that Ovid will make his own.

143–46. Catullus here explicitly acknowledges that he has no legitimate claims on Lesbia's fidelity. Indeed, he is the beneficiary of her infidelity to her husband. **Furtiua** recalls **furta** (136, 140) and makes a sharp juxtaposition with the luminous **mira . . . munuscula** of the same line. **Dempta** recalls

adempte (92) and **ademptum** (93) used of Catullus's brother. All such losses are irrecoverable.

147–48. Is looks forward to **dies. Lapide . . . candidiore** refers to the Roman practice of marking holidays on calendars with brightly colored stones, our red-letter days.

149–50. In light of the foregoing, it hard not to read this couplet as at least in part ironic.

151. Themis = the goddess of justice.

156. A deliberate echo of line 68.

157. This line is normally considered hopelessly corrupt. If correct as printed, **qui** must refer to Allius, and the asyndeton **dedit aufert** is extraordinarily harsh. The gist seems clear. Allius in providing his **domus** supplied the occasion from which **sunt . . . omnia nata** (158). If **aufert** is correct, it may well be a reference to the double-edged nature of this gift.

70

This poem is the first of a series of epigrams that outlines a narrative progression from mistrust to disillusion to resignation in the Lesbia affair [39]. It is also the first of a pair on the same topic. This is a common procedure in Catullus, who frequently writes pairs of poems that examine the same situation from different perspectives (see poems 2 and 3, 5 and 7, 69 and 71, 107 and 109). Thus, poem 70 sets the stage for 72's greater disillusion. The basic theme of the poem, that lovers' oaths are not to be trusted, is found in Callimachus's twenty-fifth epigram.

1–2. This couplet is artfully ambiguous. Would Lesbia rather marry Catullus than anyone, or rather marry no one than Catullus? The marriage theme carries over from poem 68. Elsewhere Catullus refers to Lesbia as *mea puella*, the choice of **mulier** here indicating both increased gravity and the possibility of marriage. **Petat** = potential subjunctive.

3–4. The poem's triple repetition of **dicit** sets up an opposition between speaking and writing (**scribere**). But the contrast between the permanence of writing and the impermanence of speech is undermined by the media in which Catullus says Lesbia's promise should be written – wind and water. Writing on wind and water is proverbial of impermanence.

72

This poem takes up where 70 left off. It is remarkable on several counts. The contrast between the love the common man has for his *amica* and Catullus's feeling of respect and affection for Lesbia is made all the more striking by the poet's resort to comparing his feelings to those of a father for his sons [38]. Traditional Latin vocabulary had no way of expressing affection between a man and a woman that was not fundamentally sexual in nature. Catullus is making an analytical distinction that is unprecedented, and he has no way to do so other than to express his feelings in terms used to describe relations between men or homosociality.

The contrast between Catullus and the common man is balanced by one between present and past. Catullus now is disillusioned, but his passion burns the more, even as Lesbia has fallen in his esteem. The opposition between present and past, in turn, refers us back to poem 70.

1–2. The couplet restates the basic thesis of poem 70. **Dicebas** recalls the triple repetition of *dicit*. The substitution of **nosse** and **tenere** for 70's *nubere* gives the poem a frankly more sensual tone. **Nosse** = a syncopated form of *novisse*, the perfect infinitive. It can refer to either mental or carnal knowledge.

3–4. The perfect **dilexi** contrasts present disillusion with the continuing integrity of relations between a father and his sons, **gnatos**, and sons-in-law, **generos**, signified by the present **diligit**. Note the sharp repeated ts in line 3 as well as the elision between **tantum** and **ut**, giving **tant'ut** [32]. The choice of the archaic **gnatos** in place of the more usual **natos** creates an alliteration that underlines the parallelism between **gnatos** and **generos**.

5–6. **Cognoui** recalls **nosse** from line one. The primary sense is "now I have gotten to know you," but a sexual meaning is also present. Note the harsh elision of **quare etsi impensius**, giving **quar'ets'impensius**. The rhyming of **uror** with **uilior** and **leuior** underlines the correlation between an increase in the poet's sexual desire for Lesbia and a decrease in his respect. As other poems make clear, this is a function of Lesbia's infidelities, which both fire the poet's erotic imagination and cause him disgust.

7–8. **Qui** = the adverb, "how". The rhetorical question is a common device in the epigrams. **Iniuria** is an offense against *amicitia*, a formal relation of friendship between men, that would normally constitute grounds for its dissolution [38]. *Amor* and *amicitia* are here seen as opposed terms. The paradox of **amare magis** and **bene uelle minus**, articulated around the caesura, is the focus of poems 75 and 85.

75

This epigram draws the psychological consequences of the conflicting emotions expressed in the concluding couplet of 72.

1–2. The interlocking word order of nominative **mens deducta . . . mea** and ablative **tua . . . culpa** effectively embodies Catullus's dilemma. **Ipsa** refers back to **mens**. Catullus's mind is destroying itself by doing its duty, **officium**, toward Lesbia [38]. This is a perverse relationship since the performance of one's **officium** would normally be conceived as the guarantor of emotional health. Catullus harms himself by doing what he should, i.e., by being loyal to Lesbia. Yet, there is an ambiguity in Catullus's formulation. Does his mind destroy itself, **se . . . perdidit ipsa**, or is it led astray by Lesbia's fault, **mens deducta tua . . . culpa**? Is the perversity Catullus's, Lesbia's, or both?

3–4. Bene uelle recalls 72.8. The situation is beyond hope; should Lesbia become the best of women, **optima**, he could not respect her, nor could he cease to desire her no matter what she did, **omnia**. The elision of **amare** with **omnia** destroys the effect of the caesura. This was generally avoided by the later elegists.

76

This is the sole poem by Catullus, other than 68, to have the length and range of emotional development to be able to lay claim to being a true elegy rather than an epigram. In many ways, it is a summary of the affair. Catullus claims that he has been *pius* (respectful of his obligations) and shown *fides* in his affair with Lesbia, but these good works have gone unrewarded. He therefore prays to the gods for justice. He does not seek to make Lesbia love him, but asks merely to be freed from the bonds of this affair, which is pictured as a disease that gnaws at the poet's entrails. This is a powerful poem and a fitting summary of the affair as portrayed in 70, 72, and 75.

More than one commentator, however, has pointed out that there is no small irony in Catullus's calling upon the gods to recognize his *fides* in the *foedus* between him and Lesbia. These are the terms used for formal agreements between aristocratic men [38], whose end-result would be the formal declaration of *amicitia*. Yet, Catullus's affair, inasmuch as it was adulterous, had little claim to the rewards normally associated with these virtues [12]. Rather, from a traditional point of view he had been *impius* toward Metellus, Lesbia's husband, although the latter died in 59 BCE, after the likely dramatic date of this poem. As Catullus tells us in 68.143–46, however, Lesbia was still married when the affair began.

1–2. The postponement of **homini** to the second line makes the first line difficult.

3–4. **Violasse** = *uiolauisse*. It is an infinitive in indirect discourse dependent on **cogitat** in the previous line. The last clause in normal word order would read *nec abusum foedere nullo diuum numine ad fallendos homines*. *Esse* has to be assumed. *Abutor* takes the ablative. A *foedus* is a formal pact sealed by religious ceremony, hence it necessarily invokes the *diuum numen*. **Nec . . . nullo** is emphatic rather than a double negative. This is normal in Greek.

5–6. The long-awaited apodosis of the initial conditional statement. The postponement of **gaudia** makes the syntax more difficult but allows for its rhetorically effective framing by **ingrato . . . amore**.

7–8. This couplet sums up the first section of the poem. The poet has done and said what he should [32].

9–10. This couplet begins the second section of the poem. If I have been *pius* – *pietas* brings its own ultimate reward – why do I continue to torture myself? The mode of address changes from that of making generic moral statements to direct self-interrogation. **Te** = Catullus. **Ingratae . . . menti** responds to 76.6's **ingrato . . . amore**. **Excrucies** is a common metaphor, but Catullus here recalls the literal meaning. Crucifixion killed through a combination of exposure and the slow tearing apart of the joints by the pull of gravity leading to suffocation. Catullus is emotionally tearing himself apart.

11–12. Why don't you shape up? The pentameter is very condensed. Owing to the ambiguity of the ablative absolute, **dis inuitis**, it could mean either, "why do you not cease to be miserable if the gods do not approve of this behavior (i.e., that made you miserable)"; or, "why do you not cease to be miserable, since the gods are unwilling for you to be happy if you continue doing this." The question is: are the gods unwilling for him to be happy, are they unwilling for him to be unhappy (and so he should change his behavior), or both? The questions are not mutually exclusive, but they are not identical. The implication of the rest of the poem is that Catullus cannot be happy if he ceases to love Lesbia nor if he continues.

13–14. Note the anaphoric repetition [43] of **difficile est**. The elision is emotionally effective. **Efficias** is hortatory subjunctive. **Qualubet** indicates desperation.

15–16. The metaphor of disease that will dominate the last third of the poem begins here with **salus**. The passive periphrastic, **est . . . peruincendum**, continues the effort at self-persuasion begun with line 14's use of the subjunctive and continued in line 16's **facias**. The syntax of the final line effectively obliterates the caesura while making a statement on the impossibility but necessity of making a break.

17–18. This couplet begins the final section of the poem, a ten-line prayer in which love is pictured as a form of disease. **Vestrum** = your affair. **Extremam . . . ipsa in morte . . . opem** = final aid to those on the verge of death, as in extreme unction.

19–20. The violence of **eripite** indicates a kind of radical surgery. This disease must be ripped from the poet's entrails.

21–22. Subrepens . . . ut torpor = "creeping like a paralysis."

23–24. Contra = adverb, "in return."

25–26. Note the large number of elisions. **Valere opto et taetrum hunc** gives **ualer'opt'et taetr'unc**, and **mi hoc** gives **m'oc**.

85

The greatest two-line poem ever written, 85 sums up the whole dilemma of the Lesbia affair as outlined in 70, 72, 75, and 76, while its language enacts the wrenching conflict it describes.

1–2. The problem is stated immediately in two strong active verbs **odi** and **amo**. The questions that follow move the speaker into a more passive, receptive position. **Nescio** is a verb that negates action, while **fieri sentio**, although still grammatically active in the main verb, describes a passive perception. **Excrucior** presents the subject as hapless victim of his own emotional torture, torn apart by the conflicting emotions of **od'et amo**. Note also the opposition between knowing and feeling in the pairing of **nescio** and **sentio**.

87

This poem looks back to an earlier, more hopeful stage of the affair. It is a declaration of the unique nature of Catullus's affair. It is important for its use of the homosocial language of aristocratic mutual obligation to describe the affair [38].

1–2. A direct statement of Catullus's unique love for Lesbia. The large number of elisions heightens the impression of immediacy. *Esse* must be understood with **amatam**.

3. **Foedere**: a *foedus* is normally a contractual relationship between two aristocratic men guaranteed by **fides**. Catullus says not only was his love for Lesbia unique in the history of relations between men and women, but even between men themselves. Note that the Romans conceived of true mutual respect as only existing between men.

4. The implication is that the **fides ex parte mea** was not reciprocated in **amore tuo**.

101

One of the most moving poems in the Latin language, this epigram on the death of Catullus's brother is important for two reasons. First, it shows the use of the elegiac meter in what may have been its originary function, as a song of lamentation. Second, it continues the story of the death of Catullus's brother from poem 68.

1–2. We know from poem 68 that Catullus's brother died somewhere near Troy. Catullus has come to visit the grave. **Aduenio** should be translated as a present perfect, "I have come." **Inferias** are offerings to the *manes*, spirits of the dead, at the tomb. They consisted of gifts of honey, milk, and flowers and were a ritual obligation of the family.

3–4. **Donarem** takes the accusative of the recipient and ablative of thing given. **Mortis** = genitive of definition. **Nequiquam** nicely underlines the pathos of the attempt to address the dead.

5. **Tete** = emphatic *te*. **Mihi**, the person from whom something is taken, is always in the dative. **Abstulit** = perfect of **aufero**.

6. The entire line is a vocative addressed to the brother. Note that **indigne** is an adverb. This line directly recalls 68.92.

7. **Interea** strengthens the adversative force of **tamen**, "but even so."

7–9. An example of Catullus's use of enjambment [33]. **Haec** is the direct object of **accipe** in line 9 and the antecedent of **quae**. It is modified by **manantia**.

8. **Tristi munere** = a modal ablative, "as a sad gift."

9. **Multum** = adverb.

10. **Aue atque uale**: the formula is common on gravestones.

TIBULLUS

1.1

This poem begins as the statement of a contrast between the life of the contented farmer and the hectic existence of the soldier, but rapidly becomes more complex [40–42]. What poses as artless nonchalance is in fact a carefully crafted interweaving of ideas and poetic language. The initial basis of the contrast is *labor*. But the idea that the farmer does less labor than the soldier rapidly appears absurd as the poet enumerates the various tasks it would not shame him to do (**nec . . . pudeat**, line 29). Manual labor was not something a member of the equestrian order would normally undertake. The frequent use of the optative subjunctive emphasizes the dreamlike quality of the fantasy of rural contentment. The emphasis on the simplicity of rural religious piety is typically Tibullan.

We slowly modulate from the poet contentedly working on the farm to the picture of him holding his *domina* [7, 13, 15] to his breast in his modest hut as the winds howl outside. This mention of love, however, signals the end of the georgic portion of the poem (lines 1–48). There follows a brief transitional section in which the poet refuses the life of an ocean-going merchant on the grounds that such a journey might cause his beloved grief (lines 49–52). Adventures of this kind are not his province but those of his mighty patron Messalla [40] whose lot in life is glory (lines 53–54), while that of Tibullus is the shame and humiliation of being Delia's *seruus amoris* (lines 55–76). The rural context of the poem disappears completely and is only alluded to again in the final couplet that serves as the poem's coda (lines 77–78).

The parallel between the *seruitium* of real, manual labor and the *seruitium* of subjection to a woman is implicitly drawn in the poem. In either case, a man is not free in the Roman sense of the term. Only Messalla is free in those terms, but the opening of the poem makes clear that the soldier too is subject to the cruel exactions of *labor*. The poem establishes three different positions, the farmer, the soldier, and the lover, and then proceeds to muddy the distinctions between them. In the final analysis, this poem is a profound meditation on the power of fantasy and desire to create an ideal world, and

121

on the ways in which that ideal world is constantly brought up short before
the demands of the real. It is programmatic for the first book, introducing
themes that will be dealt with more fully in later poems.

1–4. It is not until the second couplet that we realize that we are dealing
with a soldier and not a well-to-do equestrian farmer. The average soldier did
not possess vast acreages. The confusion between farmer and soldier and the
clear fantasy component is present from the first couplet. Note that all the
main verbs in the opening sequence are in the optative subjunctive, "let this
be the case."

3–4. Labor = both labor and conflict, it is the opposite of the *uita iners* the
poet describes in line 5. The vivid image of the martial trumpet blast driving
away sleep sets up the later contrast with the poet holding his love next to
his breast while the storm rages outside (see lines 45–46).

5–6. The wish for poverty can only be considered perverse in Roman
ideology. It should be recalled that the both the senate and the equestrian
order had very strict limits on who could join their ranks based on net worth
and according to Cicero these men alone constituted the *boni*. Rome was
essentially a plutocracy. The small farmer, nonetheless, was traditionally
considered the backbone of Rome [16]. He was revered for his hard work
and selfless dedication to the state. **Traducat** in this context becomes very
difficult to translate. It should mean something like "hand over" or
"entrust," but it can also mean "betray" or "traduce."

Tibullus through his fantasy of rural ease has put his finger on a contradiction at the very heart of traditional Roman ideology. The farmer-soldier of
Roman tradition is split into two antithetical images whose common ground
is alluded to in the repetition of the adjective **adsiduus**. In line 3 it modified **labor**; here it modifies the farmer's hearth (**focus**). Yet, labor is the
condition of the farmer as much as it is of the soldier.

7–8. The figure of the **rusticus** is an odd pose for a poet who in neoteric
terms should be the image of *urbanitas* [35].

Ipse emphasizes the strangeness of an equestrian planting and sewing
with his own hand. Of course, manual labor as the object of fantasy represents the height of sophistication. It can be a dream only to those for whom
it is not a fact of daily life.

The juxtaposition of **teneras** with **maturo** captures the entire cycle from
planting seedlings to the harvest of ripe fruit, although **maturo tempore**
can mean simply "the right time." **Grandia poma** emphasizes the fruits
of the harvest rather than seedlings, and so picks up on the other meaning of
maturus, "ripe." **Poma** is synecdoche for *pomus*, the tree itself. The entire
couplet is very condensed.

Facili manu is difficult. *Facilis* normally means "easy, without effort." However, the planting of vines and fruit trees is hardly effortless. Many commentators argue for a less common, active meaning, "ready, skillful." But, of course, if the farmer's life is to be contrasted with the soldier's on the basis of who endures *adsiduus labor*, then the first meaning becomes necessary. In the end, the question is undecidable and we should assume that the ambiguity is deliberate.

9–10. The images of abundance in this couplet contrast with the modesty of means implied by **paupertas** in line 5. **Lacus** = "vat." **Pinguia musta** = "rich new-pressed wine."

11–12. Note **ueneror** is the first indicative in the poem. The shift in mood makes the image of rural piety vivid, although it does not necessarily connote any greater reality as evidenced by the return to the subjunctive in line 15.

The worshipping of boundary markers (**stipes**) and crossroads (**uetus in triuio . . . lapis**) was part of early Roman religion, which was an animistic cult of small farmers. The anthropomorphic mythological veneer we are familiar with from poetry is a later Greek overlay. Tibullus's fantasy of a Golden Age of ideal agriculture ease and genteel poverty is set in the world of this simple rural piety.

13–14. The offering of first fruits was traditional. **Educat** = brings to maturity. **Agricolae . . . deo** is deliberately vague, "the god of the farmer." **Ante** = in front of the shrine or statue.

15–16. We return to the optative subjunctive with the invocation of **flaua Ceres** in the vocative. **Ceres** = goddess of the grain harvest. **Corona spicea** = garlands of grain spikes, a primitive offering from early Roman religion.

17–18. Statues of the phallic god, **Priapus**, were often painted red (**ruber**) and placed in the fields as scarecrows (**custos**). He is portrayed wielding a pruning hook (**falx**). Priapus will be the main speaker of poem 1.4.

19–22. The reason for the farmer's **paupertas** now becomes clearer. He is the heir to a reduced estate. No explanation for this reduction is offered, but from the echo of Vergil's first *Eclogue* it can be assumed that Tibullus is referring to the proscriptions undertaken by the second triumvirate, in which many lost land, wealth, and sometimes their lives [23, 40, 48–49]. It is notable that Tibullus alone of the poets of this period is silent on the topic of Augustus.

19–20. The opposition of **felicis** with **pauperis** is telling of the way Roman ideology identifies wealth with good fortune, even in a poem that ostensibly celebrates the virtues of poverty.

The **Lares** are primitive gods whose origins are shrouded in mystery. The *Lar familiaris* was a household guard of the hearth. The *Lares compitales* were gods of the crossroads where the paths between four farms met. They were thus boundary gods. Most commentators have assumed that the reference here is to the *Lares compitales*. But since a reference to offerings made at crossroads occurred in line 12, it is best to assume that the poet left the designation deliberately vague. The ambiguity allows him to round off the sequence of rural gods begun in lines 11–12. We have moved from the rocks and posts of early animistic faith, to the more fully anthropomorphic Ceres and Priapus, and finally to the *Lares*, who both stand for the household whose fortune has been reduced and represent a personified spirit of the crossroads invoked at the beginning of the passage.

The switch to the indicative **fertis** has almost an imperative force. The *Lares do* bring their accustomed gifts. It is not just a wish.

21–22. The image of the small sacrifice may be a reference to Callimachus's preference for the slender style [29].

The switch to the imperfect indicative, **lustrabat**, contrasts a past, actual state of affairs with the ideal outlined at the poem's opening.

23–24. The shift to the future indicative, **cadet**, prepares for the return to the subjunctive in the following couplet. **Circum** = postposition.

25–26. The repetition of **iam** effectively emphasizes the contrast between past abundance, present constraint, and longed-for future ease. The use of the subjunctive, **possim**, seems odd at first, given that the previous couplets indicated that the speaker already lives in straitened circumstances. The essential term is **contentus**; the speaker wishes to be able to be happy in this condition. This implies that he is tempted by the life of restless acquisition represented by the soldier in the poem's opening couplets. It is the soldier and the traveling merchant, two images of discontented acquisitiveness often associated with one another in Roman culture, who are normally **semper longae deditus uiae. Deditus**, "surrendered," is military terminology chosen to recall the poem's beginning.

The image of the *uia* is common in Tibullus (see 1.3.36 and 1.4.41). It is a sign of the fallen state of the present age as compared to the Golden Age. Travel implies a lack of contentment. Roads are built by soldiers and used by merchants. In 1.7, Messalla is praised as the builder of a road that allows farmers to bring their products to market. In the present poem, he represents the opposite of the Tibullan ideal of rural ease. Messalla and the roads he builds stand for what is approved (see 1.1.57) by conventional Roman ideology.

27–28. The rising of the Dog Star, **Canis**, signals the beginning of the oppressive heat of the Italian summer. The notion that the farmer can avoid it by taking a siesta in the shade next to a babbling brook is a clear indication that we are in the realm of pastoral fantasy and not real agricultural labor.

29–30. On **nec . . . pudeat**, see the introductory note to this poem. **Tenuisse** and **increpuisse**: the use of the perfect for the present infinitive is a common stylistic trait of erotic elegy.

31–32. Non . . . pigeat is parallel to **nec . . . pudeat** in both meaning and metrical position. Together they represent a comical class anxiety. **Oblita matre** = ablative absolute. **Domum** = locative.

33–34. Exiguo . . . magno: the opposition recalls that between the farmer and the soldier in the opening lines. It is also a truism of Callimachean poetics [29]. Tibullus's fantasy of rural poverty is thus a subtle statement of poetic principle.

Petenda assumes *est*.

35–36. We return to the image of rural piety. **Quot annis** = year after year. **Pales** is a primitive pastoral divinity. Her festival, the *Parilia*, was celebrated on 21 April, the foundation day of Rome. **Placidam** = predicative, the goddess is rendered "calm" through offerings of milk (**lacte**) and oil.

37–38. Adisitis, divi is a regular ritual invitation. **Fictilibus** = earthenware vessels symbolic of the humble table; gold and silver would be common in the sacrifices of the wealthy. This is one of the rare examples of a pentameter not ending with a disyllabic word in Tibullus [33]. As Murgatroyd (1991) has calculated, Tibullus adheres to the rule 92 per cent of the time.

39–40. Note the repetition of **fictilia** from the previous line [43].

41–44. These two couplets end the opening section of the poem. **Diuitias** recalls line 1, while **patrum** recalls 19–22. The **parua seges** looks to 22's **exigui . . . soli**, to 25's **uiuere paruo**, and to 33's **exiguo pecori** [42]. As noted above, all these can be read as allusions to Callimachus. The images of the bed (**lecto**) and couch (**toro**) subtly prepare for the introduction of the **domina** in the following couplet, so that images of slenderness and erotic themes are subtly juxtaposed. Tibullus here signals that he is a Callimachean erotic elegist. Compare the **angusto . . . lecto**, "narrow bed," in Propertius 2.1.45.

41–42. The personified **messis**, once it had been stored away (**condita**), brought **diuitias** and **fructus** to Tibullus's aged grandfather (**auo**).

43–44. Note the artful construction of the couplet, with the repetition of **satis est** around the first caesura as well as the internal rhyme of **lecto**, **solito**, and **toro** to mark the line ends and the second caesura. All three words either modify one another or are semantically related [32, 43].

45–48. These two couplets mark the shift to the erotic portion of the elegy, although their setting remains rural.

45–46. Note the opposition between the pitiless outside and the closed world of elegiac love.

47–48. Note the repetition of **iuuat** from the preceding couplet, now in the participial form, **iuuante**. The freezing rain (**imbre**) becomes a source of positive joy when the poet holds his *domina* to his breast.

49–54. Observe the highly unusual sequence of three rhyming couplets, as the rain (**pluuias**) endured by the **diues**, "rich man," becomes the **uias** he must travel to gain his wealth, only to be transformed into the spoils of war (**exuuias**) Messalla displays in his home. The fact that two out of the three pentameter endings violate the disyllabic ending rule draws closer attention to the relations between these words [33]. The **pluuias** refer back to the previous line's **imbre iuuante**. The **diues** endures the elements from which the elegiac lover is sheltered in his rural erotic idyll.

49–50. Hoc mihi contingat: the situation described in 45–48 is the Tibullan ideal, not love's reality.

 Iure: the wealthy man deserves the riches he braves the elements to acquire.

51–52. Better that all the gold and emeralds in the world should perish (**pereat**) than any girl cry (**fleat**) on account of my voyages (**uias**)! The real reason for the poet's faintheartedness becomes clear: he does not wish to make his girl weep. This is an unRoman sentiment; compare Aeneas and Dido.

53–54. It is appropriate that **Messalla** [40] makes his entrance immediately following **uias. Terra . . . marique** expands on the notion of travel, at the same time as Messalla is presented as the traditional Roman aristocrat for whom warfare is a fitting occupation (**te bellare decet**), the result of which is increased glory for his household (**domus**).

 Hostiles . . . exuuias: enemy spoils were often displayed in the *uestibulum* of a Roman household. This same space featured the death masks of the owner's consular ancestors. Every morning at dawn the great man's clients would gather here for the formal *salutatio* before accompanying him to the forum for the morning's business in the senate or the courts. The entrance to the *domus* thus is the space of a spectacle of traditional republican *uirtus* that brings glory on the household and serves as a tangible symbol of its power. This is Messalla's world, the opposite of Tibullus's ideal elegiac *otium* [44].

Praeferat = displays.

55–56. Where Messalla has the spoils of war displayed before his house, Delia's trophy is Tibullus. He adopts the position of a slave. The **ianitor** was among the lowest ranking of the slaves in household and was chained to the door. The poet thus pictures himself at the opposite end of the social hierarchy from Messalla. He is the *seruus amoris* [8, 12, 15, 42]. The lover is chained to his beloved's door because this is where the *exclusus amator* sings his paraclausithyron [10].

Note that we have definitively left the world of rural life. It will not be mentioned again in this poem.

57–58. Tibullus rejects the traditional pursuit of *laus*, "military and political glory," and actively seeks terms of opprobrium in the name of subjection to his beloved. **Segnis** = sluggish, inactive. **Iners** = idle, but also impotent. The lover thus loses his manhood, *uirtus*, through the *mollitia* of refusing **laudari** [7–9, 23, 27].

59–62. The graveside fantasy is a recurring motif in elegy, see Propertius 2.1.47–48 and 77–78. The association of love and death is one of the constants in the western imagination of the erotic, from Platonic visions of immortality to nineteenth-century opera's duets between dying lovers.

61–62. Note the images of flame, associated with passion, combined with their opposite, the water of Delia's tears of grief. **Arsuro** = future participle of *ardeo*.

63–64. The anaphoric repetition of **flebis** moves us from the subjunctive wish of lines 59–60, to the confident expectation of the future indicative in 61–62, to the melancholy hope expressed in this couplet. The use of the present indicative with the negation leads the reader to believe that Delia, in fact, has given every indication that her *praecordia sunt uincta duro ferro* and that *silex stat* in her *tenero corde*. Tibullus, however, imagines that with death Delia's "true feelings" will be expressed. This is a portrait of comical and pathetic self-delusion.

65–66. Tibullus's death will be the cause of universal grief among the young because, as an elegist, he is the *praeceptor amoris* [7]. **Domum** = locative.

67–68. Delia is begged not to torment Tibullus's ghost (**manes**) by marring her beauty with traditional acts of mourning. Note the artful construction of the couplet with the parallel endings, **parce solutis** and **parce genis**.

69–70. The whole elaborate death fantasy is now revealed as a ploy introducing the traditional **carpe diem** motif. **Caput** = a Greek accusative of respect. The image of Death's head veiled in shadows is striking.

71–72. This is the third appearance of **iners**. In line 3 it contrasts the peaceful and contented life of the poor farmer with the labor of the wealthy soldier. In line 58 it contrasts the life of the powerless lover with the glorious Messalla, and here it contrasts present vigor with the creeping impotence of old age. Tibullus uses this repetition of key terms to achieve compositional unity in a text that weaves together a variety of different themes. **Decebit** looks back to **decet** in line 53 and points to the contrast between the unconventional elegiac lover and the respectable Messalla.

Note how the previous couplet's head of death, shrouded in darkness, here becomes the white head of old age.

73–78. The major themes of the poem are recalled in these last three couplets as the poem is brought to a close.

73–74. Nunc leuis est tractanda uenus: this not only states that love is appropriate to youth, but also announces Book 1's poetic program. **Leuis** is the opposite of the traditional Roman virtue of *grauitas*, "seriousness;" see Catullus 72.6.

Frangere postes: the violent image prepares for the next couplet's explicit invocation of the *militia amoris* motif [27, 54–55].

Non pudet: the use of the indicative contrasts with line 29's **nec ... pudeat**. There the potential subjunctive speaks of how it *would* not shame the equestrian to Tibullus to pick up the hoe in his own hands. Here the indicative states that it *does* not shame him to break down the door of his beloved. The pastoral dream is revealed as the cover for an altogether more sordid, and more comical, urban reality.

75–76. Like Messalla, Tibullus too is a **dux** and a **miles**, but of a very different sort. He is a soldier of love. **Signa tubaeque** recalls line 4's **classica pulsa**.

77–78. Despite his earlier protestations of poverty, Tibullus already has his own "pile" (**aceruo composito**, compare line 10). **Dites** recalls line 1's **diuitias**.

The poem ends with a perfectly balanced pentameter that calls for a mean between poverty and wealth. Its note of resolution is deceptive, however. Can the conflicting positions of the lover and the soldier, the farmer and the merchant, the poet and Messalla, Tibullus and Delia really be so easily resolved? The constantly shifting setting of this poem would suggest not.

1.2

Poem 1.2's urban setting picks up where 1.1 left off. The image of the poet breaking down his beloved's door in the previous poem's antepenultimate couplet directly prepares us for the present elegy's use of the paraclausithyron. The poet has not simply written poems that express the feelings of the moment, but he has carefully constructed a book.

Tibullus's poetry nowhere earns its reputation of being dreamlike so much as in 1.2 [41]. Even the setting is contradictory. When the poem opens, the poet is calling for more wine to induce sleep and seems to be in a private or sympotic setting. Later in the same poem, he is portrayed as the *exclusus amator* standing before his beloved's door where she is kept under strict guard [10]. From a logical point of view, both cannot be true. He must be either in the bar or at the door. This confusion has given rise to much debate. The partisans of each view line up the reasons why their opponents' reading could not be true and why the imagery either of the symposium or the paraclausithyron must be an illusion. Yet, the question is not which context is correct, but what does it mean to create poetry capable of being read in such contradictory ways? Why does Tibullus go to such lengths to subvert his own dreams?

This is not the sole example of such self-subverting contradictions within the poem. In lines 41–64, the poet urges Delia to let him in because he has obtained magical powers from a witch that will make him invisible to her *coniunx* ("husband" or "regular lover"). The bathos of the ploy is clear on its own terms, but the poet then proceeds to tell how the same witch's spell had failed to free him from the love of Delia – ostensibly because he secretly wished not for separation but for their love to be mutual. The spell, however, as the poem makes clear, was a failure on both counts. The absurdity of pretending that this kind of argument will persuade Delia only undercuts the speaker's credibility. In cases such as this, to insist on univocal meaning is to apply a standard alien to Tibullus's text and its time. The contradictions are not flaws in the poem's structure, but its subject matter in the deepest sense.

1–2. The poet calls for unmixed wine (**merum**) so that he might fall into a drunken stupor and escape his pain. The Romans normally drank their wine mixed with water.

Fessi is ambiguous. Does he seek the sleep of the exhausted man through strong drink (**fessi sopor**), or does that drink provide sleep to one who is exhausted but sleepless from love (**fessi lumina**)? Both readings are possible.

3–4. Percussum ... baccho is a memorable metaphor for the effects of wine. Its violence contrasts with the peacefulness of the slumber that results from it. **Tempora** = Greek accusative of respect.

The delayed appearance of **amor** is effective. Only now are we sure this is a poem about love.

5–6. The cause of the poet's **dolor** is made clear. Delia is under guard and held behind a locked door. **Sera** = the bar with which the door is shut. The **dura ... sera** contrasts with the implied *mollitia* of the poet [7, 9]. Note the couplet's repeated **as** and **ae** diphthongs.

7–8. Let the door be exposed to the elements and the anger of Jupiter! **Ianua** is vocative. I have changed the punctuation of the OCT by adding a comma after **domini** at the caesura.

The placement of **difficilis** is happy. Morphologically it can be either vocative or genitive. We thus naturally take it with **ianua** before realizing it goes with **domini**. Effectively it modifies both.

Domini is the first indication we have that Delia may already have a lover. He is the master of the *domus*. The parallel with **domina** points up the disparity between the real power of the man to control the house and its slaves and the imagined power of the mistress over her *seruus amoris* [7, 8].

9–10. Note the anaphoric repetition of **ianua** linking this with the previous couplet, and ultimately looking back to line 6 [43].

Uni mihi: the poet fears he has other rivals as well.

Victa recalls **uicta lumina** in line 2. Note the subtle use of military metaphors throughout.

Furtim implies stealth, but also the poet's status as a thief. He would steal the love of *dominus* [10–12]. Therefore, the door must be bid to open without a sound.

11–12. If in my madness I have cursed you, may those curses fall upon my head! The poet's tone has changed from threats (lines 7–8), to hopeful prayer (lines 9–10), to abject wheedling.

Dicere mala = both to speak ill of and to curse.

Dementia is the madness of both love and drink. Its personification distances the poet, thereby diminishing his responsibility.

13–14. The poet prays to the door as one would to a deity. The basic prayer formula of Roman religion was *do ut des*. The relation to the gods was conceived in terms of contractual exchange relations. I give you x so that you may give me y. The poet here beseeches the door not to think of his recent impiety but to recall (**te meminisse decet**) the garlands (**florida serta**) he has left on it as a suppliant. Leaving garlands on the door of the beloved is a commonplace in Alexandrian and Latin erotic poetry. This closes the address to the door.

15–16. Venus helps those who help themselves! The poet addresses Delia directly. The anaphora of **te** and **tu** eases the transition and creates the appearance of unity. This next section, lines 15–40, focuses on Venus's aid to Tibullus and Delia in their efforts to deceive her **coniunx** (41).

17–22. Note the anaphoric repetition of **illa** as the poet presents his catechism of Venus. Venus is the patron saint of illegitimate love. She teaches how to open closed doors and how to creep from bed on silent feet.

21–22. **Docet** governs **conferre** and **abdere**. The husband or *dominus* (**uiro**) is not only to be fooled, but right before his very eyes (**coram**). **Nutus . . . loquaces** = "nods that speak what mouths cannot" (Putnam 1973: 64).

Compositis . . . notis = an agreed-upon code. Ovid will take this conceit of the lover's secret signs and turn it into an entire poem in *Amores* 1.4.

23–24. **Inertia** here becomes the enemy of Venus, where in 1.1.5 and 1.1.58 it was her ally. It should be remembered, however, that one possible meaning of *iners* is "impotent." Love is by nature *mollis*, but only to a certain point. Judging where that point was part of what made Roman masculinity a perilous venture. The heterosexual Don Juan could be considered *mollis* in Roman terms as well as the passive homosexual (*cinaedus*). Neither exemplified the *grauitas* and self-control expected of the aristocratic male. At the same time, terms like *mollis* and *durus* take their meaning from a context that privileges masculine potency. The dangers of *mollitia*, then, loom on all sides. In elegy, Roman masculinity is in a perpetual state of crisis.

The repetition of **docet** from line 19 continues the anaphoric pattern.

Timor is banished. The lover like the soldier must lead the *uita actiua*.

25. Behold, I am one of Venus's protected few! The missing pentameter says words to the effect that, though the poet wanders (**uagor**) throughout the city (**tota urbe**) at night (**cum tenebris**), "he nonetheless remains safe."

25a–26. After dark, brigands roamed freely in Rome where there was no official police force.

Occurrat = final subjunctive without **ut**, a poetic construction.

27–28. The lover enjoys divine protection. Horace treats the same commonplace with equal humor in *Odes* 1.22, "*Integer uitae . . . .*"

29–30. This divine protection extends even to the very elements (**imber**) whose punishing blows he earlier wished upon the recalcitrant door and would normally affect the *exclusus amator* who stands outside it. See line 7. **Pigra** = "numbing."

Note the anaphoric repetition of **non**.

31–32. The lover suffers the hardships of **labor** just like the soldier in 1.1.3. Note the shift from the confident indicative of **non laedit** to the optative subjunctive of **reseret** and **uocet**.

The object of the preposition **ad** is the delayed **sonum**. The emphasis therefore falls on **digiti**: "at the sound of her finger." The hyperbaton, or disruption of normal word order, allows for the juxtaposition of **taciturna** with **sonum**. On the lovers' agreed-upon signs, see lines 21–22.

33–36. Parcite luminibus could be addressed to the slaves who are carrying torches and accompanying the lover on his late-night rendezvous. "Whether a man or a woman should be met on the road, spare the lights." The gnomic quality of the statement could also make it a general statement of amorous wisdom addressed by the *praeceptor amoris* to his pupils. As noted above, this poem has no one setting nor a single addressee. The more common reading translates **parcite luminibus** as "avert your eyes," citing *parce oculis* in Propertius 4.9.53. The addressee then becomes a generic "you." *Lumina*, while it refers to "eyes" in line 2, clearly means "torches" in 36, just two lines later. A shift in meanings from one couplet to the next would be harsh, but the repetition of the same meaning without alteration would be otiose. Either alternative is problematic. The ambiguity, however, is purposeful. Love's thievery prospers in the dark, and we should avert our eyes since lovers are protected by Venus.

Furta picks up on **furtim** in lines 10 and 19.

37–38. Occulat: optative subjunctive, with *id* understood.

39–40. The threat here is castration. Venus traditionally arose from the foam and blood of Uranus's testicles when they were cut off and tossed into the sea by Saturn. Love was born from an act of unmanning and whoever gossips about the poet and his trysts will discover this truth. The paradox of love as both *durus* and *mollis*, masculine and effeminizing, continues.

Rapido . . . mari recalls Catullus 70.4's *rapida . . . aqua*.

41–42. This couplet opens the third section of the poem on the **saga** or "witch," which stretches to line 64. The witch is a stock figure in elegy; see 1.5.59 and Propertius 1.1.19–24. See also the introduction to the notes on this poem.

Huic refers back to **quicumque loquax** in line 39 and eases the transition from one section to the next.

Coniunx most often means spouse but can refer to anyone with whom a woman has a long term and exclusive relationship.

Verax suggests that such promises would not normally be trusted.

43–44. In light of the poet's later equivocation as to the witch's power, his claims to having been an eyewitness to her powers lose credibility. Leading the stars from the sky and making rivers reverse course are standard wonders attributed to witches in poetry. See Propertius 1.1.23–24.

Carmen originally referred to ritual chanting and hence spells. It later became a generic word for song. Tibullus and other Augustan poets play on both meanings. Note the use of anaphora in lines 43–56 to give the sense of a heightened ritual language.

45–46. The list of wonders continues. **Finditque solum manesque sepulcris | elicit** = "both cleaves the soil and conjures the spirits of the dead from their graves." **Manes** can mean either ghosts or corpses, though the former is more common.

47–48. The witch is comically pictured as commanding an army of zombies with her shrill magic cry (**stridore**). Milk is a frequent part of rituals involving the dead; see the note on Catullus 101.1–2.

49–50. Even the natural world is at her disposal. **Aestiuo . . . orbe** = summer sky.

51–52. Dicitur: we have now left the realm of "eyewitness" reporting and are dealing with hearsay. The poet's claims to credibility are progressively weakened.

Malas Medeae . . . herbas: these are not good omens given the results of Jason's love for Medea: the murder of her father, brother, and of her and Jason's children.

Hecate: a goddess of the underworld. She is an aspect of Diana in Roman religion. Her cult featured dog sacrifice and her apparitions were often accompanied by packs of dogs.

53–54. The number three is common in magic. Hecate was also known as the triform goddess. **Quis** = archaic *quibus*.

55–56. Seeing is not believing for the *coniunx*! **Sibi** is pleonastic, and **uiderit** assumes *nos*. The ironic contrast with Tibullus's claim to authenticate the witch's miraculous powers through eyewitness testimony in line 43 is to be savored.

57–58. The poet catches himself up short. If Delia's *coniunx* cannot see Tibullus when he lies in the former's bed with his beloved, then presumably he cannot see Delia with others as well. He issues a rapid correction that undercuts his already thin credibility.

The enjambment of **omnia** and the splitting of the last clause by the caesura in the pentameter gives the couplet a jerky rhythm reminiscent of hasty improvisation.

59–60. The poet anticipates Delia and the reader's obvious question: **quid credam?** The response is comically ridiculous: because the witch said she could make Tibullus fall out of love. Yet, he is still in love. The poet, however, has laid his rhetorical trap with all due skill. Readers are lulled into a false sense of security through the postponement of **soluere** until after the caesura in the pentameter. We are led to believe that this will be another tale of the power of the witch to produce *amor*, not destroy it.

61–62. The poet without skipping a beat describes the ceremony. First he is purified with the sulfur from torches, and then a dark victim (**hostia pulla**) is offered to the gods of the underworld who were appealed to in magic (**magicos . . . deos**).

63–64. Now comes the poet's explanation for why the spell did not work: it was his fault not the witch's. He prayed for mutual love not separation. But this is rhetorical sleight-of-hand. What the poet offers as proof of the witch's power already presumes that Delia has consented to join in the effort to deceive the *coniunx*, which would mean that she had been persuaded by his argument. If not, their love is not mutual and the spell failed.

65–74. The theme of separation alluded to in the previous couplet (**abesset**) prepares for the next section of the poem, which inveighs against military adventurism in favor of a life of agrarian simplicity like that envisioned in 1.1.

65–66. Ille is generally assumed to be the *coniunx* but could well be Tibullus himself. Poem 1.3 shows him after he has fallen ill on the island of Corcyra while accompanying Messalla on just the kind of expedition he here condemns.

Ferreus is a pun. War is characteristic of the Iron Age whereas agrarian repose is a traditional mark of the Golden Age. See 2.3.35. Thus, the soldier is not only hard-hearted he is also symptomatic of the fallen age in which the poet lived. Note that **praedas** are the natural corollary of **arma**. The soldier and the merchant are both men of the Iron Age who travel in search of wealth on the *uiae* Messalla builds. These are the "iron" or *durus* men of traditional *uirtus*.

67–68. Cilicum = genitive plural. The Cilicians were noted pirates whom

Pompey had defeated in 66 BCE. They also figured in Messalla's eastern campaign. **Ante** = adverb.

69–70. The **ferreus** hero, now woven out of silver and gold, sits upon his horse.

71–72. The idyll of rural poverty makes its return, but the poet says he *would* be able (**possim**) to adopt this lifestyle, not that he actively seeks it. His real interest, as before, is Delia, and there is no sign that she shares his pastoral reveries.

Boues . . . iungere = to hitch oxen to the plough.

73–74. The tentative **liceat** is to be contrasted with the soldier's more assured **licet** in line 67.

The interweaving of **mollis . . . somnus** and **inculta . . . humo** (uncultivated and hence hard earth) nicely captures the pastoral paradox. It is only those who are *culti* (cultivated in the sense of cultured) who imagine the shepherd's sleep to be soft. *Cultus* and *mollis* are practically synonymous for cultural refinement.

75–86. This section continues the theme of sleep but now focuses on the sleepless nights the poet spends because of the tortures of Venus. It is one of the most artfully constructed passages in Tibullus [43].

75–76. Tyrian purple was an expensive dye, synonymous with luxury.

77–78. **Plumae** = feather pillows. **Stragula** = coverlets. **Sonitus placidae . . . aquae** = a fountain in a wealthy house.

79–80. Are my sleepless nights the result of a rash or slanderous word against Venus? **Numina** = poetic plural.

81–82. Or perhaps I am said (**feror**) to have committed sacrilege? **Incestus** = the negative of *castus*. **Serta**: see line 14. Are these the same garlands the poet has left on Delia's door?

83–84. The poet's self-flagellation reaches a fevered pitch. The combination of self-abasement with eroticism implicit in the pose of the *seruus amoris* here becomes explicit in the image of the poet on his hands and knees kissing the threshold to the temple of Venus. This of course is exactly the position of the *exclusus amator*. The poet returns to the themes that opened the poem.

85–86. The image is one of comic masochism even as it recalls 1.1.73–74's **frangere postes | non pudet**.

87–98. The final section returns to the poem's second theme, the powers of Venus.

87–88. Caueto = future imperative, "beware!" **Tu** is either one of the poet's drinking companions or the reader. **Usque** = "forever."

89–90. The aging lover is a standard figure of ridicule. See 1.1.72.

91–92. The pathos of **tremula . . . uoce** adds to the comic effect. We should probably assume *tremulis* with **manibus** as well.

93–94. The figure of the *exclusus amator* returns. **Nec . . . puduit** recalls 1.1.29 and 1.1.74. The **ancilla** is detained while doing errands in the forum (**medio . . . foro**) in order to carry a message from the aged lover to his *domina*.

95–96. Circumtero = a Tibullan coinage, to rub around. The crowd of boys and youths jostles around the old man as they mock him and spit. **Despuit** = apotropaic magic to ward off such a fate. See lines 53–54.

 Molles: primarily because of their youth, but also because they are the right age for elegy, the *mollis* genre. See 1.1.71–74.

97–98. The prayer that Venus spare him is too late. He is her slave (**seruit**), and she should not burn her own harvest. The shift to the agricultural metaphor recalls 1.1.

1.4

Priapus introduces the figure of the *praeceptor amoris* in a poem that looks back to the pederastic content of Hellenistic elegy. This poem has been neglected in previous textbooks. It is not hard to understand why. It features a speaker who is iconographically represented as either having or being a giant penis giving advice on how to pick up young boys. Yet, to ignore this poem is to ignore much of the fundamental background that separates the world of the elegists from our own.

 Roman society, while possessed of a strict sexual code in terms of what acts were allowed and with whom, was also frankly erotic. Roman sexuality was understood almost exclusively in phallic terms, that is to say in terms of the symbolic representation of the male genitals. Phalloi hung from small children's necks as amulets to guard them from harm. Winged phalloi decorated oil lamps that hung over dining tables and sexual scenes not infrequently decorated the walls of the homes of the wealthy. The moral code that regulated this culture of sexual display was one that privileged masculine penetration and that stigmatized as *mollis* [9], and hence effeminate, whoever was penetrated. Penetration equaled power and dominance.

Homosexuality *per se*, then, was not stigmatized nor considered mutually exclusive from heterosexuality, as demonstrated by Catullus's Lesbia and Juventius poems. Indeed, these terms are themselves misleading since they imply a stable sexual identity based on the gender of one's beloved. This was not the case in the Greco-Roman world. What was stigmatized, however, was a man allowing himself to be penetrated by another man. Pederasty was not effeminate since the older male partner was always imagined as the active penetrating party. In this light, the truly subversive nature of the elegists' self-depiction as *mollis* becomes clear. Although on one level they remain active penetrating males, their submission to their mistresses (*dominae*) casts them in the role of the passive. In this context, Priapus's role as *praeceptor amoris* [7] seems obvious.

Poem 1.4 is important for two other reasons. First, it demonstrates Roman erotic elegy's roots in Alexandrian poetry, which was predominantly pederastic [5, 25, 44]. Indeed, almost every theme in this poem can be directly paralleled somewhere in the corpus of Hellenistic poetry. Second, it introduces the theme of *munera*, gifts. Boys only yield to the *dives amator*. The same thing is true of Delia and Nemesis, confirming the analogy between the feminine and the effeminate positions in Roman thought.

Indeed, the interesting question is not "why is there pederastic poetry in elegy?" but, given its ideological and Hellenistic background, "why is heterosexual love so dominant?" The answer may well have to do with the unstable power relations that characterized Rome during this time of civil upheaval at the beginning of principate. The *servus amoris/domina* relationship represented an inversion of normal relations that were deeply embedded in Roman society. Marriage, family, and the inheritances dependent on them were all parts of the ideological matrix from which elegy's peculiar understanding of love sprang. Elegiac love embodied a felt instability in power relations that could at any moment be reversed, an instability that Augustus attempted to address through his moral reform program [22–23]. The pederastic relationship was more rule-bound and by definition more temporary. The elder lover might claim to be the young boy's slave, but he could never slip into the passive role. The much-maligned figure of the adult passive, the *cinaedus*, was always pictured as an adult man who was penetrated by other adult men. Within the sexual terminology of the day, a man who liked to be penetrated by boys simply did not exist. In the ancient world, the pederast was less subversive than the elegist.

1–6. The poet prays to Priapus to teach him how to attract boys.

1–2. The poet following the standard formula of Roman prayer, *do ut des*, prays that the statue of Priapus be protected from the elements so that it might teach him the precepts of love. As noted, in 1.1.17–18, statues of Priapus were featured in fields and gardens as scarecrows where they would be exposed to sun and snow. As a phallic god, Priapus was naturally associated with fertility.

3–4. Priapus is a rustic deity who is not particularly handsome. It thus cannot be the neatness of his beard (**barba**) or the sophistication of his coiffure (**culta coma**) that accounts for his success. There must be some trick (**sollertia**).

5–6. **Nudus**: Priapus's nudity is symbolic of his raw sexuality, but also of his being *incultus*, and hence his exposure to the elements. **Producis** = intransitive, "you endure."

7–14. Priapus responds initially with a warning about the dangers posed by boys.

7–8. **Sic ego** = "I said." **Bacchi . . . proles**: Priapus was the son of Bacchus, himself a god of fertility and, in his guise as god of wine, the frequent father of desire. On **falce**, see 1.1.17–18.

9–10. Boys cannot be trusted in love! The majestic tone of the *praeceptor amoris* is in comic contrast to his actual status as a crude garden statue.
  Te . . . credere = "to entrust yourself."
  Causam . . . habent = an idiom meaning "have as a pretext." Boys always allege true love (**iusti . . . amoris**) as a pretext.

11–14. Every type of boy elicits desire. Ovid will later expand these four lines into an entire poem. See *Amores* 2.4.
  Niueus is normally a feminine attribute. Men were supposed to be sunburnt from outdoor exercise and activity. Note the sensuous quality of the description.

13–14. Where the first two types differed only in accidentals, horse riding versus swimming, the second pair are more fundamentally opposed as indicated by the use of **hic** and **ille**. If both the bold and the shy are equally attractive, what kind is not?
  Virgineus and **teneras** are effeminizing epithets. See **tenerae . . . turbae** in line 9.

15–20. Knowing that his warnings will be ignored, Priapus launches into the main body of his lesson. The lover must be willing to endure anything. The central portion of the poem is written in paragraphs of three couplets apiece. Lines 21–26 advise the poet to promise freely, lines 27–32 remark on the swift passage of time, and lines 33–38 note that only the gods have eternal youth.

15–16. Perseverance wins the day. **Taedia** = subject of **capiant**. The *puer* is the assumed subject of **negabit** and **dabit**. Note how the rhyming couplet sets off the opposition between initial refusal and eventual yielding.

17–18. Note the characteristic use of anaphora (**longa dies**), and the rhetorical contrast between the hard stone (**saxa**) and the soft water (**molli aqua**).

19–20. The days turn into years as love ripens. **Apricis . . . collibus** = open and hence sunny hills.

21–22. This and the next couplet clearly recall Catullus 70. **Freta** = a common synecdoche (part for the whole) for seas.

23–24. Amor is **ineptus** both in itself and in the effect it has on the lover.

25–26. Dictynna = a cult name for Diana. As goddess of the hunt, her arrows were one of her most prominent attributes. **Minerua** was especially proud of her hair. Both goddesses were perpetual virgins and odd choices in an erotic context. Even odder is Priapus's claim that they would aid and abet perjury in the service of desire.

27–38. Priapus's credibility, like that of all Tibullan speakers, soon starts to wear thin. Where before he counsels patience, here he advises haste. Note the anaphoric repetition of **quam cito**.

27–28. Aetas: the window during which pederastic activity was acceptable was very narrow, from the age of about 13 or 14 to the appearance of a beard and prominent body hair. Pederasty with the sons of freeborn men was illegal in Rome, but the *lex Scantinia* appears to have been sporadically and inconsistently enforced. Such encounters were discouraged as interfering with a boy's later ability to become an active male citizen.
Segnis: compare 1.1.58 where this is the mark of the lover as opposed to the soldier.

29–30. Purpureos . . . colores = the bright colors of spring.
The fall of the leaves in autumn is proverbial of the passage of time.

31–32. Quam provides an elegant variation on the anaphoric repetition of **quam cito**.
Iacet = "lies prostrate, dejected, lifeless."
Eleo . . . carcere: the starting gate at Olympia, site of the games.

33–38. Only the gods have the eternal beauty of youth.

33–34. Iuuenem ... maerentem stultos praeterisse dies: the maturing youth regrets that he has not spent more days on love and hence he was foolish, but days spent on love would be considered foolish from a traditional Roman perspective. Tibullus nicely captures the ambiguity.

35–36. Crudeles diui: the irony is that Priapus himself is a god, if a relatively minor one. The image of the **serpens** shedding the years with his skin was proverbial.

37–38. Intonsus crinis: uncut hair was a symbol of youth and hence of avail-ability as the object of pederastic desire. There is humorous sacrilege in impli-citly casting Bacchus and Apollo in the roles of pederastic beloveds. Roman youths normally cut their hair at age 16 when they received the *toga virilis*.

39–56. The successful lover will yield to the boy's every wish. The illustra-tions are all commonplaces of Hellenistic and Roman erotic poetry.

39–40. Obsequio plurima uincet amor: a recollection of Vergil's famous *omnia uincit amor* (*Eclogues* 10.69), it foregrounds the paradox of conquest through submission that lies at the heart of *seruitium amoris*.

41–42. Where he leads you will follow. Such journeys (*uiae*) represent the opposite of the ideal of rural and amorous ease put forward in 1.1. On **Canis**, the Dog Star, see 1.1.27.

43–44. The image of the deep purple of the rainbow against the clouds sets up a nice rhetorical contrast with the baking heat of the Dog Star in the previous couplet.

Praetexens picta ferrugine caelum = "bordering the sky painted with deep purple." *Ferrugo* = a deep rust color, ranging from greenish-blue to dark red and purple.

Imbrifer arcus: a vivid metaphor for the vault of the sky covered with storm clouds and the presence of rainbow. The rainbow in the Greco-Roman world was considered a harbinger of rain rather than a sign of the storm's end.

I have accepted **admittat** for the metrically impossible **amiciat**. This yields a less vivid image, but it makes for good Latin, and it is easy to see how the corruption could have occurred. The OCT prints the line with daggers indicating an insoluble crux.

45–46. The willingness of the lover to undertake manual labor well below his social station recalls the opening of 1.1.

Puppi: commonly synecdoche for the ship as a whole.

47–48. Nec . . . paeniteat: compare **nec . . . pudeat** (1.1.29) and **nec . . . pigeat** (1.1.31).

Opera = ablative of means.

49–50. If he wishes to go hunting, you will carry his gear. Again, a servile occupation.

Insidiis altas . . . claudere ualles: Roman hunters would close off both ends of a valley to trap the animals within.

51–52. If he wants to fence, let him win. **Leui . . . dextra** = a right hand that does not make full use of its strength.

Nudum = "unprotected." The erotic pun is obvious.

53–54. Mitis: a double meaning, (1) ripe, the lover's labors have reached fruition, (2) mellow, the boy no longer harshly rejects the lover.

The interplay of resistance and yielding is perfectly captured by the three rhyming words placed at the main metrical pauses in the couplet: **licebit, pugnabit,** and **dabit.** Their sequence tells the whole story.

55–56. At first he will yield what you take, soon he will not be able to get enough. The narrative ends with normative power relations restored as the ideal pederastic lover finds himself restored to his "natural" position of dominance. The disruption in power relations occasioned by pederastic *seruitium amoris* is only temporary.

Se implicuisse: the elision of the caesura is purposeful. The prosody enacts the inseparability of the beloved from the lover.

57–72. Money, however, has the capacity to corrupt the ideal pederastic pattern. In a moment where the poet's self-interest is humorously revealed, he has Priapus argue that boys should yield to the poet rather than the *diues amator* [44].

57–58. Haec saecula: the fallen age of the present is consistently contrasted with the Golden Age of the past in Tibullus. On the theme of *munera*, see the introductory note on this poem.

59–60. The celebration of the *heuretes* or "founder" of a certain practice is a topos in Hellenistic poetry. Tibullus here works an elegant variation on this motif by turning it into a malediction. The curse of a heavy tombstone is also a reversal of the common sepulchral dedication, *sit terra tibi leuis.*

61–62. The mask falls away and the poet's face is visible. His self-interest in making these statements is clear.

Pieridas = the Muses, the daughters of Pierus. Note the elegance of beginning and ending the couplet with them.

63–68. A traditional celebration of the Muses' power to confer immortality.

63–64. The use of mythological exempla is an integral part of elegiac style (see the Laodamia and Protesilaus simile in Catullus 68). They are less common in Tibullus than Propertius and Ovid, but this passage is a notable example in his corpus.

Purpurea . . . Nisi coma: Nisus was a king of Megara. His kingdom's safety depended on the existence of a single purple hair. His daughter, Scylla, sometimes confused with the mythological beast in the *Odyssey*, cut it off to gain the love of Minos, king of Crete. Tibullus's point in this and the other exemplum is that these stories would not be known were it not for their immortalization by poetic song.

Ex umero Pelopis . . . ebur: Pelops was served by his father, Tantalus king of Phrygia, as an offering to the gods. When they realized what they were to eat, they refused it in horror. It was too late, however. Demeter had already swallowed his shoulder. Jupiter replaced it with one of ivory. Tantalus was condemned to eternal hunger and thirst in Hades. See Propertius 2.1.65.

65–66. Referent = "tell of." **Vehet** = "bears" and is the verb for all three **dum** clauses.

67–68. Audit = "hear," as in who is sensitive to poetry, but also "heed."

Idaeae currus ille sequatur Opis: Idan Ops is a reference to the Great Mother goddess Cybele who lived on Mount Ida [37]. She was often equated with the Roman goddess of plenty, Ops. Her processions were famous. The chariot carrying the cult statue was followed by her priests, the Galli, who were ritually castrated. Tibullus wishes this fate on those who would sell their love. The source for this curse is Callimachus's third *Iambus*, in which the poet declares that he might as well be a eunuch priest of Cybele, since a poor poet cannot compete with rich rivals for the love of boys.

69–70. Phrygios . . . modos refers to the exotic music that accompanied Cybele's rites.

Vilia membra = a generic reference to the sacrificed genitalia. There is also a joke. Those *membra* that were once so expensive shall become quite cheap.

71–72. Blanditiis . . . querellis supplicibus, miseris fletibus: these are the themes of elegy, and Venus is claimed as their sponsor.

73–84. Priapus's speech is at an end. The poet now makes three succeeding claims, each of which contradicts the one before it. (1) This speech was not given for my benefit. The god gave me this information for Titius whose wife will not let him pay attention to these sorts of things. (2) With this information, I will become a powerful *praeceptor amoris* respected by all. (3) All my skills fail me in my love for Marathus. In fact, the final section allows the whole poem to be read as a failed effort to persuade Tibullus's beloved to yield to him. This in turn explains those passages where Priapus sounds more like a self-interested poet than a rustic garden god.

73–74. Titius is other wise unknown. **Meminisse** is striking. Titius's wife not only forbids him to act on this knowledge but even to remember it! Titius is either extraordinarily compliant or Tibullus is searching for a pretext to explain his inaction.

75–76. Pareat ille suae = "let him obey his wife," hardly an orthodox sentiment in Roman sexual ideology. **Male habet** is unparalleled in elegy, but the sense is clear, "to have in a bad way."

77–78. Gloria cuique sua est = "to every man his own glory." Mine shall be as a consultant to the lovelorn!

79–80. The gradual shift to the future in this final section reveals the unreality of the poet's dream. He pictures himself as an honored elder being led to the forum (**deducat**) by a crowd of adoring youths, much as a Roman aristocrat with his *clientes* after the morning *salutatio*. See the note on 1.1.53–54.

81–82. The abrupt switch from future success to present failure is marked by the cry **eheu**. The introduction of **Marathus** forces the reader to reread the whole poem from a more interested and ironic point of view. Tibullus is not the objective seeker of knowledge he posed as, and Priapus's principles are ineffective.

83–84. The poet is reduced to powerlessness and can only beg for mercy. The humor is that it is this very poetry, with its power to immortalize, that has made him a **turpis fabula**. The poem, thus, ends with an ironic smile.

1.5

Tibullus envisions his pastoral ideal of Delia as mistress of his farm serving the first fruits to Messalla, while acknowledging the impossibility of his dream in the famous phrase *haec mihi fingebam*. The poem begins with Tibullus standing firm and ready to call an end to the affair but his resolution melts away before the first couplet is through. The poet compares himself to a top spun now here, now there by a group of young boys. He reminds Delia of how he cared for her in a recent illness before proceeding to envision his ideal rural life, with her playing the mistress of his domain and hostess to Messalla. That ideal, however, represents a dream now passed. Delia is in the possession of the *diues amator* [44] and the poet offers to serve as her *seruus amoris*, even facilitating her liaisons with other men. In the meantime, as the *exclusus amator*, he will wait outside her door for the wheel of fortune to turn once more.

In truth, of course, Delia was never a creature of the country and the dream was always just that. She lives in the city, an urban sophisticate whose life represents the opposite of Tibullus's pastoral imaginings, and whose existence is only joined to the country by the roads that Messalla builds, the very presence of which marks the limits of the Tibullan agrarian utopia. Messalla, the city, and Delia, then, all stand in the same essential relation to the Tibullan dream. They supply the necessary conditions for the dream's poetic content and forms, as well as the leisure and sophistication necessary to create it – yet they ultimately prevent its actualization in real life. They are, then, profoundly related figures. Love and desire depend on this structure of fantasy and lack of satisfaction. It is in the tension between these two poles that elegy finds itself at home.

1–2. The contrast between present and past that is fundamental to this poem is immediately introduced with the imperfect tenses (**eram, loquebar**) in line 1, followed by the present (**abest**) and **nunc** in line 2.

Asper = "harsh," a term more at home in a military than amatory context.

Gloria = a term used for fame acquired through military prowess. See Propertius 2.1.74, 2.7.17–18, and 3.11.60. Tibullus's victory is short-lived.

3–4. Tibullus is the plaything of conflicting emotions turning now this way, now that. Compare the ironic tone of this image to Catullus's anguished *odi et amo* (85.1). **Turben** = top. **Uerbere** = the "blow" of the string used to make the top spin.

5–6. **Vre ferum et torque**: slaves were sometimes branded on their faces to prevent them from running away. Tibullus, as the run-away *seruus amoris*, demands the appropriate punishment from his *domina* [7, 8, 12–13]. Such an exchange of roles not only inverts normative gender roles, but also normative social roles since Delia as a *meretrix* would most likely be a freed woman and hence from a lower social class than the equestrian Tibullus [6, 44].

Doma: the wild slave is to be tamed, his behavior to brought under the control of his *domina*. On the erotic overtones of the verb, see Propertius 1.1.15–16.

7–8. Te = direct object of **quaeso**.

Per . . . furtiui foedera lecti: this phrase is a wonderful oxymoron. A *foedus* is normally a pact reached between two aristocratic males (see Catullus 76.3, 87.3). "The pacts of a stolen bed" would represent agreements whose substance was the undermining of the culture of homosocial obligation. *Furta* would normally constitute an *iniuria* that would be the grounds for dissolving a *foedus* (see Catullus 72.7). Tibullus, however, not only cites such a *foedus*, but also invokes it as the power in whose name he begs mercy!

Venerem could be either the act of love or the goddess herself.

Compositumque caput refers to the arrangement of her hair, but *componere* is also a technical term for laying out a corpse. It thus prepares the way for the next five couplets on Delia's illness.

9–10. We move from the bed of love to the bed of sickness. **Ille ego . . . dicor**: Tibullus's devotion has become the talk of the town.

Votis = both the prayer and the thing pledged if the prayer is granted.

11–12. The poet himself (**ipse**) performed the act of ritual purification by walking around (**circum**) Delia with purifying (**puro**) sulfur, when the wise woman had chanted for Delia's recovery. Is the **anus** the *uerax saga* from 1.2.41? On **carmen**, see 1.2.54. Note the anaphoric repetition of **ipse** in this and the next two couplets.

13–14. The poet not only assisted the wise woman but himself made sure that Delia was not harmed by bad dreams. **Procuraui** = obtained by means of sacrifice. On **ter** as a magic number, see 1.2.54. **Mola** = salted meal regularly strewn at sacrifices.

Deueneranda: appears only here in extant Latin. From context, it would appear to mean "ward off by rites or ritual." The **saeua somnia** of fever are offered sacrifice in return for their agreement not to torment Delia. Hence, they are done reverence, *uenerata*.

15–16. Velatus: Romans covered their heads when praying. **Filo** = a fillet, a thin ribbon of wool worn round the head by priests.

Tunicisque solutis: in many ancient cultures magic powers were attributed to knots. To insure that nothing interfered with the proper performance of the rites, they were always to be performed in clothing without knots.

Triuiae = Diana of the crossroads, an aspect of Hecate, see 1.2.53–54.

17–18. A great comic anticlimax. Another reaps (**fruitur**) what Tibullus has sown. **Persolui omnia** = I rendered all the gods were due. This concludes the section on Delia's illness and prepares us for the next section on Tibullus's dream of rural happiness (19–36).

19–20. Felicem uitam: the happy life his rival now enjoys, Tibullus once envisioned (**fingebam**) for himself.

Fingebam is from the same root that gives us *fiction*. It means to make or fashion something, like the Greek verb *poiein* from which we get *poet*.

Renuente deo = "with the god nodding up," which is the ancient equivalent to shaking the head in disapproval. I have followed the oldest manuscript readings and left **sed** rather than accept the OCT reading **et**. The OCT's comma then becomes superfluous.

21–22. The switch from the imperfect indicative to the potential subjunctive shows that we have now entered the poet's dream world. That dream is the unity of the two halves of poem 1.1. In 1.1, we begin with Tibullus's ideal of rural simplicity and then move to Delia in the city. In this dream, we have Delia in the country playing the perfect farmer's wife.

Colam = "inhabit, cultivate, care for."

Custos: where in 1.2 Delia has a **custos** who keeps her under lock and key in the city, in Tibullus's dream she will become the guardian of his farm.

Area = subject of **teret**. Neither Tibullus nor Delia has to do any real manual labor on this farm, thus underlining its unreality.

23–24. Lintribus = vats where the grapes were held before pressing. On **musta**, see 1.1.10.

25–26. Consuescet: note the artful repetition. It is given variety by making **uerna** the subject of the second.

Amantis ... dominae: Tibullus returns the term *domina* to its literal meaning. What he has wanted from the beginning is to be the *seruus* of an *amantis dominae*, but here it is the *garrulus uerna*, the literal, house-born slave, who enjoys the affections of the mistress. This ironic return to the literal meaning of *domina* also signals Tibullus's progressive effacement from his dream. After **rura colam** (line 21), he is merely a passive spectator. This is a subtle acknowledgement of the dream's impossibility. Only in a world in which Tibullus does not exist could the contrary realms of the urban Delia and the rural paradise, of elegiac love and the aristocratic Messalla become one.

27–28. Deo ... agricolae: see 1.1.14. **Spicas**: see 1.1.16. Delia here takes over Tibullus's imagined role in poem 1.1.

Dapem = a sacrificial meal.

29–30. Delia as *domina* will be in charge of all. Tibullus will rejoice in doing nothing, but **esse nihil** literally means "to be nothing." It is as if he does not exist.

31–32. In 1.1.53–56, Messalla's *uestibulum* displaying the spoils of the conquered and Delia's *fores* are fundamentally opposed. In the dream, these two contradictory forces are reconciled as Delia plays the ideal hostess.

33–34. Delia treats Messalla as if he were a god and she the slave (**ministra**). It is fitting that this role reversal for the *domina* represents the climax of the dream, which is then deflated in the next couplet. Note the shift back to the subjunctive.

There is no elision (hiatus) between **uirum** and **hunc** because of the word division falling on the caesura of the line and due to the strong exclamatory tone of **tantum uenerata uirum.**

35–36. The repetition of **fingebam** rounds off this section of the poem and reminds us that the dream was a fiction that Tibullus created in the past. It was a delusion and he recognizes it as such.

Eurus = the southeast wind. **Notus** = the south wind. The perfumed Armenians are a suitably eastern and effeminate image to represent the fate of the dream of elegiac decadence.

37–42. Since my disillusionment I have sought comfort in wine and the arms of another, but to no avail.

37–38. Merum: see 1.2.1. The image of turning unmixed wine into water reverses the normal order.

39–40. Gaudia = a euphemism for orgasm. **Admonuit dominae deseruitque Venus:** the recollection of Delia makes the poet impotent, i.e., *mollis*.

41–42. The poem's earlier images of the powers of witchcraft to cure Delia are here inverted (see lines 9–16) as the new girl accuses the incapacitated poet of having been bewitched (**deuotum**) by Delia.

A pudet: compare 1.1.29 and 1.1.74. In both cases, the topic of *inertia*, which can be translated "impotence," forms the subtext.

Meam = the subject of **scire** in indirect discourse. Understand *dominam*.

43–44. Delia bewitches me not with spells, but with her beauty.

45–46. "So once was the sea-blue Nereid, Thetis, carried to Thessalian Peleus on a bridled fish." Another use of the mythological exemplum. See 1.4.63–65. The complexity of the word order mirrors the learned quality of the simile and contrasts with the previous couplet's relative simplicity.

47–60. The benevolent *anus* (line 12) of the beginning of the poem, whose magical powers identified her with the *saga* in 1.2.41–64, is here transformed into Delia's **lena** or madam [10]. The identification of these two figures was common in Roman poetry. Both were older women who had the potential to wield power over men through magic or control of their mistress.

47–48. The *diues amator* [44] here makes his formal entrance into the poem. See 1.4.57–72.

49–50. The poet prays for the *lena* to feast upon the causes of madness, blood and gall.

51–52. The **animae** are deliberately vague. Are they the evil spirits she calls upon, or as Putnam (1973) suggests, the spirits "of lovers she has ruined"? Through metonymy – the rhetorical figure of contiguity – the *lena* and her *animae* are then metamorphosed into a screech owl that stands as a portent of violence to come.

53–54. Where the *uerax saga* of 1.2.51 knew how to control the *malas Medeae ... herbas*, the mad *lena* is to be driven by hunger to consume the cursed grass of tombs. There is a pun in **lupis**. *Lupa* was slang for prostitute, and hence appropriate for a *lena*.

55–56. The recollection of 1.2 continues. In 1.2.52, the *saga* is said to have tamed the wild dogs of Hecate, who is often identified with *Diana triuia*, the goddess of the crossroads. Here the *lena* is to be chased by dogs from the crossroads (**e triuiis**). In this poem, all the power relations from 1.2 are inverted. The powers that the *saga* was said to possess are pictured as those that control the *lena*. Yet, as in the earlier picture of Delia as the mistress of Tibullus's country estate, the repeated use of the optative subjunctive indicates that this too is a mere fantasy. Tibullus will not dominate the old woman who limits his access to Delia's sexuality, but, as the next section makes clear, he will be subjected to that sexuality, even serving as the go-between for Delia and her lovers. Tibullus will be unmanned, hence the repeated images of impotence throughout the poem.

    Inguinibus nudis: the sexuality of older women is considered grotesque by Roman poets, inciting both ridicule and fear. See Horace's poems on Canidia.

57–58. The confident tone of this couplet's opening future indicative is belied by the next couplet's affirmation that **donis uincitur omnis amor**.

59–60. The identification of the *lena* with *saga* here becomes explicit, but she is no longer *uerax* but *rapax* (**rapacis**). On **donis uincitur omnis amor**, see 1.4.40.

61–66. The poor poet is to be preferred to the *diues amator* because only he will be his mistress's faithful slave. Note the anaphora of **pauper**.

61–62. The image of the poet cleaving to his mistress's tender flank is not only one of faithful devotion but also of frank sexuality.

63–64. It would normally be the job of a slave to clear the way for his mistress. The irony of Tibullus making a *uia*, normally associated with Messalla, should not be missed. See 1.1.25–26, 49–54 and 1.4.40–41.

65–66. The poet in his ultimate debasement will lead Delia to meet her secret lovers. The *deductio* was part of the wedding ceremony where the bride was led to the house of her husband. This is a perverse parody of that procession. See the marriage theme in Catullus 68.
   Vincla = sandals.

67–68. Even the fantasy of servile debasement is revealed as a hollow. Delia's door is only to be struck by a hand full of money (**plena . . . manu**). The image of the closed door brings us back to the world of the paraclausithyron [10, 43].

69–70. The wheel of fortune was a common image in the Hellenistic world. Delia's current lover should remember that his **furta** from Tibullus could be balanced by Tibullus's **furta** from him or by those of a third party. The condensation of **mea furta timeto** allows for both possibilities. **Timeto** = future imperative.

71–74. The low realism of the description of the would-be lover lurking outside the beloved's door recalls the world of Roman comedy [24]. The poet's affirmation that the lover waits not in vain (**non frustra**) is contradicted by his previous experience with Delia as the affair is portrayed in the poetry (see 1.2). Is the figure described Tibullus or a third lover?

75–76. Enjoy love while you can. The standard idiom, **nescio quid** ["something"], is nicely literalized in this passage. Tibullus does not know what love prepares.
   The image of the lover's skiff (**linter**) captures the instability of the situation, recalling Catullus 70.3–4.

2.3

This poem captures the harsher tone of Book 2's Nemesis cycle [5, 13, 45]. It both reveals the artificiality of Tibullus's earlier rural ideal by focusing on the brutalizing manual labor performed on an ancient estate and literalizes the metaphor of *seruitium amoris* [7–8] by picturing Tibullus as a common field slave. It also contains the single longest mythological exemplum in the Tibullan corpus, the story of Apollo's love for Admetus (lines 11–32). The basic scenario is calculated to reinforce the poet's sense of comic self-abasement. Nemesis has gone to the country with her new paramour, a wealthy freed-slave who gained vast estates through his career as a soldier. This new lover represents the opposite of everything Tibullus idealizes in Book 1. The poet concludes that if he cannot beat his rival he will join him and, if necessary, rob temples to provide Nemesis with the expensive gifts she desires (lines 49–60). The poem ends with one of the longest and most detailed evocations of the Golden Age in the Tibullan corpus. One of this poem's greatest artistic achievements is the subtle way it weaves together the serious and ironic, the humorous and the pathetic.

1–2. The opening of this poem is deceptive on several levels. First, **rura** is normally a positive term. We assume the same is true here until lines 9–10. Second, the dedication to Cornutus, the addressee of 2.2, a short poem expressing Tibullus's good wishes on the occasion of his birthday, leads the reader to believe there will be some sort of thematic continuity between the poems, though there is none. Third, the vague **puellam** naturally brings to mind Delia, since neither 2.1 nor 2.2 has been an erotic poem. It is not until line 51 that we discover the poet has a new love named Nemesis. The poet, then, establishes a number of expectations in the mind of the reader and undermines them in a systematic fashion.

Ferreus = "hard, unyielding." See 1.2.65. In the context of the whole poem, such a person must be imagined as a representative of the fallen Iron Age as opposed to the ideal world of the Golden Age imagined at the poem's end.

3–4. At first this seems to be a summation of Tibullus's rural ideal as expressed in poems such as 1.5. It is only with further reading that we understand the ironic nature of this "migration."

5–8. These couplets echo 1.1.29–30. But here Tibullus is a common slave and not an idealized farmer. The image of the equestrian Tibullus assuming such a position would have been humorous to his sophisticated audience.

5–6. Hiatus after o is a common mark of exclamation.

7–8. **Subigunt** = "turn up." **Steriles . . . boves** = steers as opposed to bulls. Oxen were normally castrated. The word choice reflects the futility of Tibullus's labors, both amatory and agricultural.

9–10. In this couplet, the blisters and sunburn the poet receives indicate that we have left behind the effortless agricultural ideal of 1.1.8's *facilis manus*. Rather, the poet's **teneras . . . manus** bear the marks of a harsh labor for which the *mollis* elegist is by nature unfit. The diminutive **graciles** is indicative of the slenderness and preciosity of the Callimachean style that elegy claimed as its own {9, 26–29}.

Pussula = an uncommon word in poetry, designed to give the illusion of realism.

11–32. The next section is given over to the exemplum of Apollo's tending of the herds of Admetus, king of Pherae in Thessaly. In Hesiod's version of the myth, this humiliation was a punishment meted out by Zeus for killing the Cyclopes. But in Callimachus's *Hymn to Apollo* (lines 47–54) it is a form of *seruitium amoris*. Apollo as god of poetry is an obvious choice as a parallel for Tibullus. Admetus was unmoved by Apollo's gesture just as Nemesis is unmoved by Tibullus's.

11–12. By dwelling on Apollo's good looks, the poet implicitly compliments himself.

Pauit = perfect of *pasco*.

Cithara: Apollo, as god of the lyre, is also god of poetry.

Intonsae comae: the god's uncut hair was a sign of his eternal youthfulness; see 1.4.37–38.

13–14. The god, as patron deity of medicine, is nonetheless unable to cure himself of the sickness of love. On the power of **herbae** in this context, see 1.2.59–60.

14a–14c. The text here is corrupt. In the best manuscript, 14a and 14b are joined together without any space between them. At minimum, one pentameter is missing. The sense nonetheless is clear. We have an enumeration of the tasks Apollo undertook for Admetus, including turning the cows out from their pens and the making of cheese. As Murgatroyd points out, *dicitur*, or something like it, must be assumed in the lacuna, with Apollo as its subject in 14b and **lacteus . . . liquor** in 14c.

Ipse, as in 1.1.7, brings out the impropriety of one of high social station undertaking such menial tasks.

Docuisse implies that Apollo both invented and taught the art of making cheese by adding rennet (**coagula**) to fresh milk.

15–16. The homely touch of describing the how the cheese-straining basket is made is typically Callimachean. It adds an incongruous realism to a humorous tale. **Vimine** = "a switch." **Iunci** = "a reed."

The **rara uia** is an allusion to Apollo's admonition to Callimachus in the preface to the *Aitia* to follow only *keleuthous atriptous* (1.27–28), "unworn paths." The allusion to the words of Apollo in one work by Callimachus while retelling a version of a myth about the same god from another is an excellent example of the subtlety of Tibullus's Alexandrian art. In addition, the use of such elaborate artistic and rhetorical effects in such a humble context is the essence of the Tibullan aesthetic. The simplicity of the Tibullan ideal and the naive quality of his art is constantly belied by the sophistication of the means used to produce it.

17–18. On the carrying of stray livestock back to their mothers as the work of those of low social station, and hence the cause of Diana's blush, see 1.1.31–32.

The incongruity implicit in this image and others is one of the organizing principles of Tibullan elegy. It presents a world out of joint and is symptomatic of the contradictory nature of Augustan Rome.

19–20. The bathos of using anaphora (**o quotiens**) to juxtapose Diana's blush with the cows, whose lowing dared to interrupt the learned (**docta**, i.e., Callimachean) song of the god, is to be savored. The displacement of **boues** to the end of the couplet leaves the reader waiting until at least **mugitu** to find out the identity of the women who are the subject of **ausae** and who, given the anaphora, should be parallel figures to Diana. The logical assumption, given the context of song, is that these would be the Muses. The revelation that they are cows is another moment of deliberate incongruity.

Sunt must be assumed with **ausae**.

Sub = "down in."

Note the juxtaposition of the onomatopoetic **mugitu** with **carmina docta**.

21–22. Like the typical elegiac lover, Apollo neglects his duties in favor of love. As the god of prophecy, Apollo's oracles at Delphi and elsewhere were commonly consulted by leaders preparing to undertake risky ventures.

Inrita = without a response.

23–24. Apollo was famed for the beauty of his hair. See 1.4.37–38. **Horrere** = "to bristle." **Latona** = Apollo's mother. His stepmother (**nouerca**) is Juno, since Jupiter was his father. The **nouerca** is proverbially a hostile figure, yet even she admired the beauty of his tresses before they became unkempt through the performance of menial labor.

25–26. Note the artistic pattern. After two couplets beginning **o quotiens** come two beginning **saepe**, a virtual synonym. Thus we have both anaphora, properly speaking, and anaphoric repetition on the semantic level as well. This fifth couplet continues the pattern by extending the discussion of

Apollo's hair from 23–24, thus extending the repetitions on the level of meaning [43].

Quaereret = "would seek in vain."

27–28. Even Apollo is a slave of love, abandoning his magnificent temples on Delos and Delphi for a rustic shack. **Pytho** = the original name of Delphi.

29–32. In the past, men were happy when it shamed not even the god to serve love, but now Apollo's behavior is a source of scandal. This passage both provides a bridge from the exemplum to Tibullus's own situation and prepares for the contrast between the Golden Age of the past and the fallen present age introduced later in the poem.

29–30. Felices: understand *erant*.

31–32. Fabula = a scandal, a tale told by many. **Sit** = optative subjunctive. The elegist prefers scandal to celibate gods.

33–34. This couplet is difficult and its thought is obviously incomplete, resulting in the lacuna posited by most editors between it and the next distich. It is most reasonably addressed to Tibullus's rival, who by capturing Nemesis has set up camp (**castra**) in the poet's own house (**nostra ... domo**).

Quisquis is es is contemptuous.

Tristi fronte may be deliberately vague. Whether the god of love's disapproval is directed primarily at Tibullus or his rival is an open question.

35–36. The theory of the four ages, gold, silver, bronze, and iron, is first found in Hesiod and becomes a favorite topos for Roman poets in the Augustan age. In Vergil and Horace, the implication is that the *pax Augusta* represented the return to the Golden Age [23, 51–53, 63]. In Tibullus, the present age is fallen and this may be seen to represent an ideological distance between the poet and the emerging regime, consistent with his choice of Messalla [40, 42] as his patron rather than Maecenas [51–54]. Ovid would later invert the whole topos by claiming that the present age was golden [57], because anything could be bought with gold (*Ars Amatoria* 2.277–78).

This couplet begins a long anaphoric series (lines 35–42) centered on **praeda** and its cognates. The Iron Age (**ferrea ... saecula**) was associated with the acquisition of wealth through violence and rapine, whereas the Golden Age represented a period before money and private property when the earth spontaneously provided for all of one's needs. Tibullus's rival is *ferreus* (see 1.2.65–70 and 2.3.2).

Est operata = "is concerned with."

37–38. Greed is the source of violence. Given the recent civil wars, this characterization of the origins of civil strife would hardly have been flattering.

Feras = uncivilized and echoes **ferrea**.

Proprior modifies **mors**. War makes men die before their time.

39–40. The beginning of sea travel is proverbial of the fall from the Golden Age and associated with greed throughout ancient literature. The pentameter considers naval warfare as the natural consequence of seafaring in search of **praeda**. Note how, as in 1.1, warfare and trade are practically indistinguishable. **Dubiis** = "unstable, unreliable."

41–42. The **praedator** desires to possess vast *latifundia* worked by gangs of slaves [16–17]. See 1.1.1–2. Note the elision between **multa** and **innumera** thus drawing attention to the **praedator**'s insatiable greed.

Obsidere = "to occupy."

Pasco = "to use as pasture."

43–44. Lapis externus is a phrase rich in significance. First, it means "stone that would go on the outside of the building" and hence would not be functional but ostentatious. Second, it would therefore also mean "extrinsic or superficial decoration" and serve as a reflection of the moral character of its owner. Finally, it means "foreign stone." Such decorative and exotic marbles generally had to be imported.

Tumultu = ablative of attendant circumstances. **Vrbis** = both objective genitive, the disruption caused by transporting massive blocks of stone through the city, and subjective genitive, the stones are transported through the hustle and bustle of the vast metropolis. The disruption caused by heavy wagons transporting building materials was so great that by 45 BCE it was illegal for them to enter the city until two hours before sundown.

Columna = an unusually effective use of the poetic singular, allowing it to stand both for a single column so grotesquely large it could only be transported by a thousand strong teams of oxen (**ualidis mille . . . iugis**) and for a thousand individual columns pulled by strong teams of oxen. In either case, the hyperbole indicates the kind of luxury and excess that came in for frequent criticism.

45–46. Fishponds were a common luxury of the period often pointed to as a sign of excess. One purpose of such ponds was to provide fresh fish for the increasingly demanding palates of the wealthy.

Lentus . . . piscis: the fish themselves, like their owner, have become decadent and lazy in their new environment, no longer needing to concern themselves when the threats of winter weather (**hibernas . . . minas**) arrive (**adesse**).

47–48. I, however, am happy with old-fashioned simplicity. Samian and Cumaean earthenware were inexpensive. **Testae** = the wine jugs that prolong the banquet (**trahant conuiuia**). Tibullus proposes not asceticism but simple pleasures as an antidote to the excesses incited by *praeda*.

49–50. Heu heu marks Tibullus's abrupt about face. If girls, however, rejoice in riches let the booty (**praedae**) pour in! The incongruity is only one of many in the poem. On **gaudere**'s sexual overtones, see 1.5.39–40. Girls thrill to riches.

51–52. Let Nemesis be a sight for all the city with my gifts! Nemesis is named here for the first time. **Incedat** = a stately, leisurely gait.

53–54. Tibullus accepts all the marks of luxury moralists normally condemn. Coan silks were expensive and transparent (**tenues**). See Propertius 1.2.2. This is not the dress of a *matrona*.

Vias here = stripes, but golden roads cannot help but call to mind the previous condemnations of travel as motivated by greed and a sign of the fall from the Golden Age (1.1.25–26, 49–54, 1.4.40–41, 1.5.63–64). These stripes of gold in turn would be the opposite of the humble **rara uia** found in Apollo's cheese-straining basket earlier in the poem (line 16). Coan silk interwoven with gold threads would represent the height of luxury. The use of *uia* to mean stripe is a Tibullan coinage.

Note the assonance between words ending in **-es** and **-as** in this couplet. The style is as ornate as the dress.

55–56. And let her be accompanied by slaves from exotic climes! Slaves were by definition a function of **praeda** since they had their origin in military conquest. The ancient ideology of slavery, unlike that in the American south, was not based on race, but on the notion that people captured in war owe their lives to their captors. The dark color (**fusci**) of Nemesis's Indian slaves thus denotes their exoticism and hence their value as a luxury commodity, rather than their servile status.

India refers to the whole of the East.

Solis et admotis inficit ignis equis: the belief was that the further south one went, the closer the sun drove its chariot to the earth, thus allowing its flame to dye (**inficit**) the skins of the inhabitants. Note again the prominent assonance. Long **-is** and short **-is** endings alternate and are punctuated with intervening **ts**.

57–58. Purple dyes (**colores**) from Carthage (**Africa**) and Tyre (**Tyros**) were expensive and much prized in Rome. There is a play on words between **puniceum** and **purpureumque**. Not only do they echo one another across the caesura of the pentameter, but also **puniceum** literally means "Punic" or

"Carthaginian." *Puniceus*, in turn, is etymologically derived from *Phoeniceus*, indicating the Phoenician origin of Carthage, whose mother city was Tyre. The line thus summarizes the origin and history of these dyes while offering the reader the illusion of covering the whole gamut of oriental luxury from Asia to Africa.

59–60. Tibullus's rival is a freed slave. The poet inveighs not so much against the class system at Rome and the aristocracy it supports as its perceived corruption by freebooting newcomers of low social origin.

Nota loquor = "I say what everybody knows is the case," i.e., girls go for money.

Regnum: the rival reigns supreme.

Saepe: the rival was not sold just once but numerous times, presumably indicating his masters' dissatisfaction. He was not only a slave, but a bad one.

Gypsatos ... pedes: foreign born slaves' feet were marked white with chalk on the auction block. Ironically, Tibullus's dream of *seruitium amoris* has come true. Nemesis's **comes** (line 55) is a foreign slave.

Catasta = the revolving platform on which slaves were exhibited for sale.

61–62. The scene returns to that of the opening lines. Nemesis has gone to the country (lines 1–2). The resulting curses on Bacchus and the Earth are startling to the reader, but follow logically from the proposition that Nemesis has gone to the vast estates (lines 41–42) that her freedman lover (lines 59 60) has acquired through the blood and mayhem that are the necessary corollary of **praeda** (lines 35–40). As the following section makes clear, the Golden Age was not only a time of country pleasures, but also a time before private property and amorous possession.

The curse itself makes use of financial metaphors that are telling of **praeda**'s corruption of the rural ideal found in Book 1. The Earth is prayed to pay back (**persoluat**) with no return (**nulla ... fide**) the seeds that have been loaned to it by the harsh harvest (**dura seges**) that has led Nemesis away from Tibullus and the city. The thought and syntax are tortured.

63–64. As the grain is bid to offer a bitter harvest, so is the grape in the person of Bacchus. Bacchus is **tener** both because he is young and because he is the natural ally of elegiac lovers who often use this adjective as a self-description (see line 10 and 1.2.73–74). It is virtually synonymous with *mollis*. Hence, Bacchus would normally be opposed to the **dura seges**.

Deuotos lacus = "cursed wine vats."

65–66. The poet here offers Bacchus (**pater**) his reasoning as to why the god should turn his back on the new wine (**musta**) of which he is normally the sponsor. **Tristibus agris**: the fields are the producers of Tibullus's unhappiness, but he also prays that they be made sterile and hence *tristis* in themselves.

Abdere = "remove."

Tanti = genitive of value.

67–68. If agriculture brings girls to the country, then let us return to a world of pre-agrarian simplicity. This is a vision of the Golden Age when the earth's spontaneous bounty was sufficient to provide for all our needs.

Ne . . . modo = "not in any way."

Glans: the acorn is the favorite Roman example of a primitive food. See Juvenal's famous description of his forefathers "belching acorns" in the period before Justice left the earth (6.10).

69–70. The picture is comical: old time Romans bolting down acorns and making love here, there, and everywhere (**passim**). Who would miss agriculture (**sulcos . . . satos**) then?

71–72. In the good old days, when Love called, Venus answered with open copulation in the nearest shady vale (**umbrosa . . . ualle**). On **gaudia** as orgasm, see 1.5.39–40.

73–74. The advantages of love alfresco now become clearer. If there were no houses then there could be no guardians (**custos**), no doors (**ianua**), and hence no *exclusi amatores* and no paraclausithyra, but of course that also means there could be no elegy.

Si fas est is an apotropaic prayer formula indicating the possibility of divine disapproval of a return to such a state of affairs.

75–76. The hexameter of this couplet is missing, but the basic sense is clear from the pentameter; men were happier when just animal skins covered them. The contrast with Nemesis's finery described in lines 53–54 is striking.

Horrida recalls **horrere** in line 23, referring to the bristling, unkempt quality of Apollo's hair when he stooped to be the shepherd of Admetus. Emphasis on the shaggy nature of people's bodies serves to reduce the distance between human beings and the animals whose skins they wore in the primitive state of nature. Is the reader to view this as a good thing?

Villosa . . . ueste = hairy animal skins worn as clothing.

77–78. We return to the poet's present predicament. His girl is held under lock and key (**clausa**) and he is allowed to catch sight of her only on rare occasions. In such circumstances, what good does his fine loose-fitting toga (**laxam . . . togam**) do?

For **mea**, assume *puella*.

Copia = opportunity.

79–80. Tibullus therefore proposes to become a true *seruus amoris* and plough his mistress's fields, accepting chains and beatings and thereby renouncing the inviolability of his person that was his right as a Roman equestrian. Note the way **non ego me uinclis** balances **uerberibusque nego.**

SULPICIA

3.13

The first poem of Sulpicia's short collection is programmatic. It announces her theme and makes clear the distance she takes from the male elegists. The daughter of a noted jurist who died early and left his daughter in the charge of her mother's brother, Messalla Corvinus, Sulpicia was not only a woman of aristocratic background and upbringing, she was also privy to the most recent artistic and literary trends. As a young woman in the twenties BCE, she would have heard both Tibullus's poetry recited at her uncle's salons and that of the young Ovid. In such an environment, it is inconceivable that she would not have known the poetry of Catullus and Propertius or that when she sat down to write her own verse she would have done so in a naïve or artless manner. Rather as Santirocco, Lowe, and Tschiedel have shown, by far the most economical assumption is to presume that when Sulpicia deviates from the elegiac norm, she does so consciously and deliberately [14, 45–46]. Thus, where it was once fashionable dismiss her poetry as "feminine" – meaning untutored, unsophisticated, and ungrammatical – it is now possible to view it as a woman's poetry – meaning written from a fundamentally different position from that of Tibullus, Propertius, or Ovid.

This poem offers an important test case for all such readings. Even recent critics often assume that 3.13 has slipped out of its proper order in the collection. Since the poem speaks of a love that has been consummated, many critics find it difficult to square its subject with their preconceived image of Sulpicia as a proper young maiden of good family. They have therefore moved it to the end of the sequence where, they claim, it celebrates Sulpicia's marriage to Cerinthus (Merriam 1990; Tränkle 1990). This interpretation, while transparently ideological, was made easier by a false etymology of Cerinthus's name put forward by Renaissance humanists. Deriving Cerinthus from the Greek *kera* or "horn," they identified him with the Cornutus whose marriage is alluded to in Tibullus 2.2. But *Kerinthos* is both the name of a city in Euboia mentioned in the "Catalog of Ships" (*Iliad* 2.538) and the Greek word for "beebread," a substance fed to young bees that the ancients thought of as a compound of honey and wax. As Roessel (1990) has shown, these qualities identify Cerinthus with both the honey-sweetness that the Greeks from Homer to Callimachus associated with poetry and the wax tablets on which deliberate poetic composition took place. Thus Cerinthus, like Cynthia and Delia, is both the subject of the poetry composed in his name and a synonym for the act of composition and the fame resulting therefrom. It is this fame that is the concern of the opening poem, not the celebration of a marriage. As such, 3.1.13 is well designed to be the opening poem of Sulpicia's sequence.

1–2. Love has finally come and it is of such a sort that it would be more a shame to keep still than to reveal it to everyone. The first clause is simple and straightforward, but Sulpicia immediately plunges us into the syntactical complexity for which her poetry is known. The subject of the indirect question that forms the second clause is **fama**. This is also the subject of the poem as a whole, what shall Sulpicia's reputation be? In conventional elegiac poetry, the love affair must be kept secret since it is either *de facto* or *de iure* adulterous [10–13]. Likewise, a young aristocratic girl, out of *pudor* ("shame"), would conventionally keep an extramarital affair secret and avoid *mala fama*. But Sulpicia argues that this love is of such a quality (**qualem**) that the reputation (**fama**) of having kept it a secret (**texisse**) would be more (**sit magis**) a cause for shame (**pudori**) than would that of having exposed it (**nudasse**). The medium of that exposition, of course, is this very poetry, which in conventional elegiac terms insures her **fama**. As Santirocco (1979) has noted, the predominance of indirect discourse in the poem contributes to its syntactical difficulty while dramatizing the workings of **fama** in all its senses.

Pudori = dative of purpose with **sit mihi**.

3–4. Venus has answered the prayers I have addressed to her through the Muses and placed him in our lap. This emphasis on the fulfillment of love is unusual in male-authored elegy. The sexual image implicit in **sinum** in the same sentence with **exorata meis . . . Camenis** clearly associates Sulpicia's lovemaking with her poetry. The image of Venus coming to Sulpicia's aid recalls Sappho 1.

Cytherea = Venus. Cythera is an island south of the Peloponnesus where Aphrodite had an important shrine. **Camenis** = the name of traditional Italic goddesses who had become identified with the Greek Muses. Note the artful alliteration and learning of ending the hexameter with these two proper names. Their corresponding adjectives, **exorata** and **meis**, begin the line.

5–6. This couplet is addressed to Sulpicia's male counterparts in elegy who constantly bemoan their lack of fulfillment in love. Venus has kept her promises to Sulpicia and let anyone who has had less luck in love recount the story of her joys. Sulpicia here clearly adopts a different model of desire from that of her rivals. On the sexual sense of **gaudia**, see Tibullus 1.5.39–40.

7–8. Sulpicia rejects the elegiac tradition of sealed letters exchanged between lover and beloved in favor of the open publication that is also her declaration of poetic arrival. The postponement of the main verb, **uelim**, to the end of the couplet makes the couplet more difficult but effectively maintains the reader in suspense about the poet's intentions until the last possible moment.
   Mandare = "entrust."
   Assume *amor* with **meus**.
   Line 8 presents numerous textual difficulties. I have chosen to stick with Postgate's reconstruction more out of despair than conviction. Our oldest manuscript reads *me legat id uenio quam meus ante uelim*, which is nonsense. All solutions require surgery of one sort or another.

9–10. Sulpicia proclaims her independence of social convention [14]. **Ferar** = either optative subjunctive or future indicative. The ambiguity is pointed. **Cum ... fuisse:** *cum esse* is a common euphemism for sexual relations.

3.14

This poem is written on the occasion of Sulpicia's birthday. It forms a pair with the following poem and together they look back to Catullus's practice of pairing epigrams (see 70 and 72), with the second always looking at the same phenomenon from a later point in time. This will be one of Ovid's favorite devices as well.
   The birthday poem was a common set piece in Messalla's circle. Tibullus wrote two (1.7 and 2.2). Those pieces are happy occasional verses that celebrate the joys of country life. Sulpicia here playfully inverts the topos making the birthday a source of unhappiness because she will have to spend it in the country away from Cerinthus. Moreover, the cause of her unhappiness is her uncle, the same Messalla whose birthday Tibullus celebrates in 1.7. The joke would have been appreciated by those in the know.

1–2. The statement is unusually straightforward. Its poignancy comes from its inversion of expected values. Cerinthus is named for the first time.

3–4. Like Delia, Sulpicia knows love is not a country pleasure. **Arretino ...
agro** = ablative of location, denoting a wine-growing region of Tuscany.
   Frigidus amnis = the Arno, which comes from the north.

5–6. Messalla's associations with *uiae* and their troublesome nature in love have already been examined in Tibullus (see 1.1.25–26, 1.1.59–54, 1.4.41–42, 1.5.63–64). Tibullus makes the clearest association between Messalla and roads in 1.7.57–62, the birthday poem.

The couplet's repeated use of the vocative (**Messalla . . . studiose** and **propinque**) makes the syntax difficult. **Nimium** modifies **studiose**.

Quiescas = hortatory subjunctive.

Non tempestivae saepe . . . uiae = journeys are often not timely. Assume *sunt*.

7–8. The loss of the senses in love was made famous by Sappho in poem 31 and in Catullus's translation (poem 51). I have restored the reading of the best manuscript in line 8, as opposed to the OCT's unnecessary alterations. *Id* must be assumed and refers to the whole of the previous line.

3.15

This is the companion piece to 3.14. Sulpicia celebrates being allowed to remain in the city for her birthday. The text of the best manuscripts read *tuo* for the last word of the second line, which would make this poem refer to Cerinthus's birthday and defeat the purpose of juxtaposing the two birthday poems. Postgate prints this reading but adds *"vix recte"* in his *apparatus criticus*. Some of the later manuscripts read **suo**, which has been widely adopted. It has the advantages of making good sense, being grammatically correct, and having some textual attestation, however thin.

1–2. Triste looks back to line 2 of the previous poem. **Ex animo** = the journey has ceased to be a source of anxiety. **Romae** is locative.

3–4. "Let that birthday be celebrated by us all, which comes with you perhaps not now expecting it!" The syntax is difficult.

3.16

This sarcastic little poem shows Sulpicia's capacity to turn elegiac convention to her own advantage. The *marita fides* [12] that the elegists claimed to practice in relation to their own, often fickle, mistresses was, of course, more honored in the breach than the observance (see Ovid). Here, however, Sulpicia proclaims her lover's obligation to be faithful to her, not just her to him. She thus deploys elegiac convention while revealing the role reversal implied in it for what it was, a convenient weapon in the arsenal of masculine seduction. In the process, she makes a proud declaration of her own high social standing in relation to Cerinthus's **scortum**, "hussy," and of his consequent obligations to her. Power in Rome was distributed along a variety of intersecting axes; two of the most prominent were gender and social class. Sulpicia's gender may have been traditionally submissive but her social standing was near the top of the aristocratic hierarchy.

1–2. "It is a good thing that you now permit yourself to act without a care for me, otherwise I might have quickly made a most foolish mistake" (i.e., fallen in love with you). This is a very difficult couplet. Sulpicia expresses mock gratitude (**gratum est**) because (**quod**) Cerinthus at this point (**iam**) gives himself such wide latitude (**multum . . . tibi permittis**) that she is able to avoid making a grave mistake (**ne male inepta cadam**).

3–4. The lack of parallelism in the comparison makes this couplet difficult as well. The reader expects **cura** to go with all three terms, but **cura togae** functions as the subject of **sit** in apposition to **pressumque quasillo scortum**, which is then compared to **Sulpicia**, although logically **potior** can only be construed with **cura**. There is also a play on words between **cura** and **securus** (i.e., *sine cura*) in the previous line.

    Sit = a dismissive optative subjunctive.

    Togae: prostitutes were the only women who wore the toga, thereby signifying their transgression of the norms of gender behavior.

    Quasillo: wool spinners were at the bottom of the social hierarchy. Their status should not be confused with the traditional piety associated with women who spin wool and make clothes for their own husbands. Spinners, *quasillariae*, were slaves or freed women given large quantities to spin each day for their *dominae*.

    Serui filia Sulpicia: Sulpicia was the daughter of the patrician Seruius Sulpicius Rufus, himself the son of a famous jurist known to Cicero. He died young after marrying Valeria Messalla, the sister of Tibullus's patron. The latter became the young girl's guardian when her mother refused to remarry. Note the way the formal three-word appellation balances the three-word epithet, **pressumque quasillo scortum**, thereby underlining the differences in status. This is the only pentameter in Sulpicia that does not end in a disyllabic word. This deviation from accepted metrical practice calls attention to her name at the end of the line.

5–6. "There are those who are troubled on our behalf to whom the greatest cause of pain is that I might yield to a humble bed." Cerinthus may be **securus** but there are those who do have **cura** for Sulpicia and they worry lest she be made to yield her position to one of low status, the **scortum** whose bed Cerinthus currently occupies. It cannot be Cerinthus himself since we know from the anonymous poems on Sulpicia and her beloved, which precede her own work in the Tibullan corpus, that Cerinthus was of a sufficiently elevated social status to practice the aristocratic sport of boar hunting (3.9). Nonetheless, there may well be a dig here at Cerinthus having a less exalted pedigree than Sulpicia, or an implication that he has debased himself by consorting with a **scortum**.

Ne cedam = a negative after a clause of fearing. Note the parallel with **ne . . . cadam** in line 2.

3.17

As we have already seen in Tibullus 1.5, the illness of the beloved is a topos that allows both the lover to demonstrate his devotion and the *domina* her ingratitude. Once more, Sulpicia inverts expectations. Here she is ill and her lover far from waiting on her appears distracted, perhaps by the *scortum* of the previous poem.

1–2. The question is straightforward. **Cura** recalls **securus** from the opening line of 3.16. **Calor** = fever.

3–4. The desire for mutuality expressed in 3.13.10 and rearticulated in 3.16's demand for fidelity is here taken to its extreme: I do not wish to recover unless you wish so too. **Optarim** and **putem** = potential subjunctives. **Optarim** = a syncopated form for **optauerim**.

5–6. This couplet restates and expands upon the thought expressed in the previous one. What use is health if you can be happy with me sick? Note the emphatic repetition of **morbos euincere**.

Si tu: it is unusual in later elegiac practice to end the hexameter with two monosyllables.

Prosit = potential subjunctive.

Lento = indifferent.

3.18

The theme of *cura* returns, but in the final poem it is Sulpicia who worries that she has needlessly given Cerinthus cause for anxiety when she fled an encounter in an effort to conceal the height of her passion. The topic of misplaced *pudor* first broached in 3.13 returns here, rounding off the sequence in a form of ring composition. The *feruida cura* of the first line recalls not only the previous poem's *pia cura* but also its *calor*. The burning fever has been transformed into the fire of passion. Each couplet appears to be syntactically complete until the reader reaches the next. The poem thus unfolds as a series of surprises.

1–2. The couplet is difficult. **Sim** = jussive subjunctive. **Aeque . . . ac** = "so . . . as" and modifies **feruida cura**. **Mea lux** = a common term of endearment. "May I not, my love, at any time (**iam**) be so burning a cause

of anxiety [but also "passion"] as I seem to have been a few days before."
Cura is often used as a synonym for the beloved. See Propertius 1.1.35.

3–4. We here realize that the poem is a conditional statement. May I not be a cause of burning passion to you if I have ever done anything so stupid!

Tota . . . iuuenta = ablative of time, emphasizing Sulpicia's youth. She was probably around twenty years old. Her subsequent poetic silence, like that of many of her later renaissance counterparts, was probably the result of marriage.

Fatear = subjunctive in a relative clause of characteristic.

Paenituisse = impersonal with **me** as its object.

Magis = can be taken absolutely, but is revealed to be correlative with **quam** in the following couplet.

5–6. At last, we find the cause of the speaker's embarrassment. **Quod** = causal. The final pentameter almost forms a golden line, with the participle and its complementary infinitive surrounded by its object, **ardorem . . . meum**. The image of flame in **ardorem** recalls **feruida** in line 1.

PROPERTIUS

1.1

This is the programmatic poem for the *Monobiblos* in which the poet's beloved is introduced [49–50]. **Cynthia,** as the first word of the book, would have served as its title. In the same way, the *Aeneid* was known as *arma virumque.* Thus, the identification, and at times down right confusion, between the topic of Propertius's poetry and the poetry itself is immediately introduced. The tone of the poem on the surface is one of unrelieved sorrow and suffering but the text reveals an ironic wit equally characteristic of Propertius. It proceeds by a series of abrupt transitions from one section to the next and makes the reader supply the connections between them. The sharp juxtapositions that characterize Propertian style mark its distinct nature from the more dreamlike nature of Tibullan elegy in which one part of the poem blends almost imperceptibly into the next.

The poem starts with a bare statement of the facts: Propertius has fallen hopelessly in love with Cynthia (lines 1–8). The mythological exemplum of Milanion shows the power of devoted service to win over even the most demanding mistress (lines 9–16), but Propertius's case is hopeless and impervious even to the powers of magic (lines 17–24). He calls on friends to lend aid (lines 25–30), but bids happy lovers keep clear. Let his case be a warning to all (lines 31–38). The reader should note the symmetrical construction. Four out of the five sections are eight lines long, while the fourth is six lines long. Moreover, the first couplet of the last section may just as easily be construed as the last couplet of the penultimate section, thus making the symmetry even more striking while avoiding repetition.

1–2. **Prima** is deliberately ambiguous. Did Cynthia capture Propertius first with her eyes or was she the first to capture him? The pentameter makes clear the answer to both questions is "yes." On love emanating from the beloved's eyes, see Meleager's poem in the *Palatine Anthology* (12.101) on which Propertius based the opening of 1.1.

166

Ocellus = a diminutive, a commonly used form in Catullus to show emotional intimacy.

Contactum = "hit," as by an arrow. It can also mean "infected." Love was often conceived of as a disease in traditional Roman circles (see Catullus 76).

3–4. The contrast between Cynthia's eyes shooting darts of love and Propertius's downcast in dejection is rendered more effective by the image of Amor landing on the poet's head with both feet.

Constantis . . . fastus = genitive of description with **lumina**. The pride of those who think they are immune to love's darts is a common theme in the *Monobiblos*.

Impositis . . . pedibus is a pun. Poetry has imposed metrical feet on the poet's sentiments giving Amor form. This continues the confusion between subject matter and artistic form seen in the first couplet.

5–6. The poet announces his status as one who lives outside the norms of traditional Roman conduct. Love is **improbus**. It makes one hate **castas puellas** and live with **nullo consilio**.

Castas . . . puellas can be interpreted in two ways. On the one hand, the poet has learned to hate the kind of proper young aristocratic women an equestrian would be expected to marry in favor of *meretrices* such as Cynthia [13]. Poem 2.7 provides support for this position. On the other hand, Cynthia is not shown in this poem as yielding to the poet's advances, and so the hatred may be of only those **puellas** who remain **castas** in relation to Propertius. The two interpretations are not mutually exclusive. If Cynthia is a *meretrix* – and no certain identification can be made – she is a high class courtesan and no common prostitute open to all comers.

7–8. The madness of love has gripped him for a year and the gods have shown themselves hostile to the poet's desires. **Furor** in the *Aeneid* represents the opposite of *uirtus* and *pietas* [23].

9–10. The poet introduces the mythological exemplum of Milanion. While the Laudamia myth was a prominent structural device in Catullus 68 and several examples were seen in Tibullus (1.4.63–65, 1.5.45–46, 2.3.11–32), mythological exempla are integral to Propertius's style. The relation between the myth and the content of the poem is often less than straightforward and makes demands upon the reader.

Milanion: a suitor for Atalanta, the daughter of Iasus (**Iasidos**). In the more common version of the story, Atalanta challenged all her suitors to a series of foot races. She eventually lost when Hippomenes distracted her with three golden apples. In the present version, Milanion is supposed to illustrate the value of devoted service in love (*seruitium amoris*). The expected parallel with Propertius, however, is not forthcoming, since, as we learn at the end of this section, the poet's love is unique. The wit of introducing an exemplum only to deny its applicability is characteristic of Propertian irony.

Tullus: one of Propertius's early patrons, the nephew of the consul L. Volcacius Tullus. See poem 1.6.

Saeuitiam refers to both the girl's refusal of Milanion's advances and the tradition that Atalanta had been exposed at birth and suckled by a bear. She is untamed, which in traditional terms also refers to her virginity. See the Greek verb *damazō*, which means both to marry and to break a wild horse. Compare Catullus 68.118.

Durae is a common epithet for the beloved in Propertius. See 2.1.78. It represents an inversion of normative gender roles as the poet inevitably becomes correspondingly *mollis* or *tener* [7, 9, 23, 27].

11–12. Madness (**amens**) and error (**errabat**) are common traits of the elegiac lover who wanders outside the norms of accepted behavior as Milanion ranges through the wilds of Arcadia. **Amens** is also a pun on *amans*, present participle of *amo*.

Partheniis ... antris: Atalanta was exposed and raised on Mount Parthenius.

Videre = infinitive of purpose after a verb of motion, a poetic construction. The notion that Milanion's **labores** consisted in going to see shaggy beasts (**hirsutas ... feras**) is humorous.

13–14. According to the version of the myth followed by Propertius, Atalanta was accosted by the centaurs Hylaeus and Rhoeteus one day while hunting in the Arcadian hills. In Apollodorus, she slays them herself, but in Propertius, Milanion apparently comes to her aid and is wounded (**percussus**) by Hylaeus's club (**rami**).

15–16. Atalanta is moved by Milanion's sacrifice and yields to his advances. The pentameter draws the expected lesson from the story. **Velocem** = "swift," a learned reference to the alternative version of the myth involving the footrace with Hippomenes.

Domuisse = to tame, a verb with clear sexual references; see **saeuitiam** in line 10. The irony of Milanion taming Atalanta through being struck by the aroused Hylaeus's club would not have been lost on Propertius's readers.

17–18. Propertius's case is different. Love refuses to follow marked paths (**notas ... uias**). This is an allusion to Propertius's Callimachean allegiances, which have just been demonstrated in his highly original use of mythological learning [9, 26–30, 53, 55]. See Tibullus 2.3.15–16.

Non ullas cogitat artis = "devises no strategies."

168

19–20. The figure of the witch and her ability to call the moon from the skies (**deductae . . . lunae**), as we have already seen in Tibullus, is proverbial in elegy (see 1.2 and 1.5). **Fallacia** implies not only Propertius's disbelief but foreshadows the inability of practitioners of the black arts to help him.

Piare sacra = to perform sacred rites.

21–22. Pallor is a universal sign of lovesickness in the ancient world. **Ore** = ablative of comparison.

23–24. Another standard list of miracles performed by witches. These would all be easier than making Cynthia fall in love with Propertius.

Crederim uobis = "I would trust in your claims."

Cytaeines = Greek genitive singular, "of Medea," who was born in Cytae, a town in Colchis. She was famous as a witch.

25–26. The poet seeks the aid of his friends. **Sero** = "too late." Assume *me* with **lapsum**.

Non sani pectoris: the metaphor of love as a disease is continued.

27–28. Ferrum saeuos patiemur et ignis: iron and fire allude to cauterization in ancient surgical practices. The implication of the pentameter is that the poet has lost his *libertas*, "aristocratic freedom of speech," through his *seruitium amoris*. Only surgery can cut this cancer out. The poet seeks a restoration to the status his social rank bestows upon him, but of which lovesickness has robbed him. Then, he could express his anger (**ira**), which, at present, fear of his *domina*'s wrath keeps under wraps.

29–30. The poet's friends are called upon to take him to a place where no woman can find him and he will escape love's clutches. Assume *me* as the object of **ferte. Norit** = *nouerit*.

31–32. But those who experience requited love, keep back. The poet finds their presence a reminder of his plight and begs them to keep their distance from his infection.

Sitis et in tuto semper amore pares: he wishes them the mutual love that is both the elegiac ideal and that which by definition can never be if the genre is to exist. Those to whom Amor (**deus**) nods with a receptive ear (**facili . . . aure**) do not write elegy.

33–34. The lover's sleepless nights are an elegiac truism, but note the striking expression. His nights (**noctes**) are bitter (**amaras**) because of Venus's exertions. The active verb vividly portrays the tormented nights of the unsatisfied lover without being unduly specific.

Vacuus = "idle." The adjective is not redundant. Love is by definition in

Rome a kind of *otium* or "idleness" as opposed to the nobler *negotium* of law, warfare, or politics [44]. The sentence, thus, can be translated two ways, either "Idle love rests at no time," or "at no time is Love idle nor does it rest," depending on whether **uacuus** is thought of as predicative or attributive. The first option is grammatically easier but logically contradictory: Love is both idle and never resting. The second is more convoluted in terms of syntax, but logically more consistent. From the perspective of Roman ideology, however, both statements make sense. Finally, this love is literally **uacuus**, "empty," because it is unfulfilled. Such semantic and syntactical complexity is typical of Propertius.

35–36. The poet concludes by striking the pose of the *praeceptor amoris* [7, 58]. **Cura** here, as often in elegy, refers to the object of desire. See Sulpicia (3.16, 3.17, 3.18).

37–38. The poet slyly prophesies his own poetic fame. All those who do not heed his lesson will recall (**referet**) his words with great pain. Thus, he will live on in men's minds both those who first listen and those who do not. This is a clever and appropriate way to end a poem introducing a poet's first collection of poems.

1.3

This poem is well known and widely anthologized because of its complex use of mythology and the sudden reversal of power relations at the poem's end. It begins with a series of comparisons between Cynthia and three mythological figures and ends with a recollection of Penelope, the ever-faithful wife who proved herself not only a match for the suitors but also Odysseus himself.

The scenario is basic. Propertius stumbles home after an evening of carousing to find Cynthia asleep. The besotted poet is overcome with fear and desire. His angry mistress wakes and accuses him of leaving her to find pleasure in the arms of another.

In contrast to 1.1 and later poems, Propertius and Cynthia's relationship seems almost domestic, with Propertius playing the tardy husband coming home late at night. It would be a mistake to expect consistent and realistic treatment from one poem to the next in these collections. Elegies are not autobiography, but highly stylized poetic constructs that investigate the topics of love and desire within the terms permitted by Roman ideology and its contradictions. Elegy offered its audience a field for the aesthetic exploration of possible worlds rather than a simple representation of reality.

1–6. The three mythological exempla, each introduced with **qualis**, share certain themes that prepare the reader for the poem, although no one element is common to all. In the first comparison, we see Ariadne asleep on the beach unaware that Theseus has abandoned her. What is not mentioned, but trad-itional in most retellings of the story, is that when Bacchus subsequently comes upon the distraught heroine, he makes her his bride. Propertius here plays two roles, he is both the cruel Theseus who has abandoned Cynthia and the Bacchus-inspired lover.

The second comparison is more difficult. In our mythological tradition, we know of no scene where Andromeda fell asleep after her rescue by Perseus nor where she was abandoned by a lover. Yet, the imagery implicit in the scene helps make the poet's intent clear. Andromeda was to be sacrificed to the Hydra by her mother and father and was chained naked to a rock. Such a sacrifice is a form of rape or violation. Andromeda was saved at the last moment by Perseus who took her as his bride. Thus, Andromeda's first sleep would have been in the arms of her rescuer. Again, Propertius has two roles. He plays both the monstrous rapist and the legitimate and faithful "husband."

In the final comparison, the Bacchic element implied in the first is made explicit. There are numerous ancient paintings of sleeping nymphs and maenads approached by a satyr, Pan, or Priapus with sexual intent. These idealized rape scenes, including a Pompeian wall painting of a Bacchante asleep by a stream, provide an obvious source for this third couplet, and provide a link between it and the preceding comparison. At the same time, Bacchantes were notoriously vicious when woken. Thus, once again, the image is double. On the one hand, we have Propertius as drunken satyr about to take advantage of the sleeping maenad, on the other her fury if awoken before the act was completed.

1–2. **Thesea cedente carina** = ablative absolute. **Languida** is often used to refer to sexual exhaustion. **Cnosia** = Ariadne.

3–4. The verb **accubuit**, "to recline," in Propertius has an erotic sense. **Cepheia** = daughter of Cepheus, king of Ethiopia.

5–6. **Edonis** = Thracian, an area associated with Bacchic cult. **In herboso ... Apidano**: the Apidanus was a river in Thessaly. The reference is presum-ably to a dry riverbed, a common phenomenon in Greece and Italy during the summer, although **in** + the ablative can on rare occasions mean "beside," but **herboso** is then hard to explain.

7–8. **Visa**: understand *est*. **Mollem spirare quietem** = both "to breathe like one asleep" and more literally "to breath forth soft rest." This is a good example of the condensed nature of Propertius's poetic language.

Caput = a Greek accusative of respect with **nixa**.

Non certis ... manibus = a suggestive phrase alluding to the precarious nature of Cynthia's repose.

9–10. The Bacchic element in the initial comparison here finds a more comical, if prosaic, explanation. **Ebria . . . traherem uestigia** = "I drug my drunken tracks," an image that nicely captures the drunkard's shambling gait.

Quaterent . . . pueri: slaves would shake the torches to keep them alight after burning long into the night (**sera nocte**). The image is suggestive also of the inebriated Propertius's wavering eyesight as well as of a group of cupids (another meaning of **pueri**) fanning the flames of passion. The confused reference is emblematic of the poet's state of mind.

11–12. **Hanc ego**: the hyperbaton draws attention to the two most important elements in the sentence while literally showing the poet drawing close (**adire**) to the sleeping Cynthia.

13–14. **Duplici correptum ardore**: understand *me*. The *ardor* is double because of the twin forces of wine and desire. The fire imagery implicit in *ardor* carries forward the image of the shaken torch.

Liber = an Italian name for Bacchus.

Durus: the sexual pun needs no elaboration.

15–16. The OCT marks the pentameter as corrupt, but only because it cannot make sense of the frank sexuality expressed therein. **Sumere oscula** and **sumere arma** are both recognized expressions. **Sumere oscula** is used here literally while **sumere arma** is metaphorical, making their pairing a "zeugma" or the nonparallel use of one word to modify two others. **Arma**, however, is a common euphemism for penis so the connection between the two expressions is not hard to make. Likewise, the ablative absolute construction, **admota . . . manu** "with my hand having been placed on x," could refer either to **positam**, Cynthia, or to **arma**. This latter possibility, however, is signaled as the more likely by the placement of **admota . . . manu** around **arma**. Lastly, military vocabulary such as **arma** and the figure of *militia amoris* [7, 54–55] are common in love elegy (see Ovid, *Amores* 1.1 and 1.9). **Temptare**, "to make a trial of" or "to assault," is another example.

17–18. Propertius's courage wilts before the final assault. Note the use of **domina** in this context of fear and submission.

19–20. We revert to the mythological comparisons of the poem's opening, but now Propertius has become the passive Argus whose hundred eyes were never supposed to sleep as he watched over Io, a young girl whom Jupiter had turned into a cow to hide his philandering from Juno. That Juno was not fooled and that Argus's hundred eyes were lulled to sleep and he was then slain by Mercury does not augur well for Propertius.

Ignotis cornibus: because she had not had horns before.

Inachidos: Io was the daughter of Inachus, king of Argos.

21–22. The poet is comically transformed from potential rapist to reverent devotee making offerings at the shrine of his goddess. In the process, the close relationship between woman as object of worship and object of violence is revealed.

Corollas: garlands of flowers were often worn at drinking parties and given as love tokens.

23–24. The tenderness of the image of the poet rearranging the sleeping Cynthia's hair is striking in light of the implicit violence at the poem's opening.

Poma: apples were a frequent love offering. **Furtiua** should be taken adverbially.

Cauis ... manibus = ablative, the cupped hands of the drunken Propertius carefully placing the apples in Cynthia's lap.

25–26. Sleep is personified as ungrateful in letting Propertius's offering tumble from Cynthia's lap (**sinu**). The scene presages Cynthia's rejection of the poet's blandishments. **Largibar** = a metrically useful alternative form of the imperfect.

27–28. **Duxti** = a syncopated form of *duxisti*.

Obstupui = "struck dumb."

Vano credulus auspicio = "believing the empty omen."

29–30. This couplet contains two fear clauses dependent on **obstupui: ne qua ... uisa** = "lest any dreams"; **neue quis** = "or anyone." Note that what he fears she is dreaming of is the same kind of rape scenario envisioned in the opening mythological exempla and all but enacted in the first half of the poem. Understand *te* with **inuitam.**

31–32. Cynthia is woken by the light of the moon. This is appropriate since Cynthia is also another name for Diana, goddess of the moon.

Diuersas ... fenestras: there is no general agreement on the meaning of this phrase. The most likely possibilities are: (1) different windows, i.e., one after another; (2) opposite windows, i.e., on the opposite side of the room from Cynthia's bed.

Moraturis ... luminibus: even the moon cannot but linger over the sleeping Cynthia's beauty.

Sedula: from the poet's perspective the moon is overly officious in carrying out its duties.

33–34. **Cubitum** = Greek accusative of respect with **fixa.** Cynthia is propped on her elbow. Note the harshness of **sic ait.**

35–36. It is remarkable how many editors take Cynthia's reproaches as shrewish. One cannot help but wonder if there is any relationship between their sympathy for Propertius's plight and their gender.

Iniuria is a technical term for an injury that would constitute the grounds for the formal dissolution of a *foedus* (see Catullus 72.7–8, Tibullus 1.5.7–8). In that case, it should be taken closely with **nostro . . . lecto**: "has some insult to our bed finally driven you from the closed doors of another, bringing you back?" Propertius has apparently been performing a paraclausithyron before another girl's door.

37–38. The **tempora** were made **longa** by Cynthia's waiting. **Meae . . . noctis** refers both to Cynthia's experience of it and to the fact that Propertius owed it to her rather than another.

Languidus = the opposite of *durus* in the sexual sense. Propertius is spent from his evening in the arms of another. See lines 1–2 and 13–14.

Exactis . . . sideribus = the fading of the stars at dawn. This is a poetic version of the more common *exacta nocte*.

39–40. **Talis** and **qualis** recall the opening series of comparisons in lines 1–8.

41–42. The reference to fooling sleep with weaving recalls Penelope's putting off the suitors by saying that she would choose a husband when she had finished Laertes's shroud. Each night, however, she would unweave what she had done the day before. Cynthia is thus transformed from sleeping Maenad to the icon of wifely fidelity.

Orpheae carmine . . . lyrae: Cynthia is a *docta puella*, the neoteric ideal [35], and probably a poet. Orpheus was from Thrace, the same region as the Edonian girl in lines 5–6.

43–44. Cynthia turns the tables as she becomes the elegiac poet bemoaning her abandonment by a fickle lover.

45–46. The poet ends by giving Cynthia the last word. The first line is a beautiful description of slipping off into sleep. The pentameter is ambiguous. If **illa** is attributive with **cura** then it refers to Cynthia's anxiety at falling asleep before Propertius returned home. If it is the subject and **cura** the predicate then it can refer to the other woman, "She was the final cause of anxiety for my tears."

1.6

In this poem, the inversion of normative gender relations [39] characteristic of elegy is extended to the public realm, as the poet explains how love will not allow him to follow a standard political career like that of his friend Tullus. Instead, like Tibullus, he rejects the life of *uirtus* for that of *militia amoris* [27]. He fears not danger, but his beloved's reproaches. The humor of asserting that Cynthia is more to be feared than foreign service would not have been lost on Propertius's audience. This is a dubious claim for courage.

By the same token, the assertion of either the necessity of the life of love or the superiority of Amor's *uita otiosa* to Roman *negotium* [44] is a common motif in elegy and in part accounts for its image as a subversive or counter-cultural discourse. Yet, as this poem also demonstrates, Propertius operates within a conventional set of references. The elegiac stance is both to accept the existing set of social norms and to refashion or invert them after the fashion of Catullus [38].

1–2. Sailing was generally viewed as a hazardous activity. Propertius here asserts his fearlessness.

Tulle = the nephew of L. Volcacius Tullus (see 1.1.9–10), consul in 33 BCE and proconsul of Asia in 30–29 BCE. Our Tullus was presumably to be part of his uncle's entourage. This kind of expedition would constitute a young man's entrée into political and military life. Tullus's invitation to Propertius to join him – to the extent that it is not a convenient fiction – would have opened the door to a more traditional career for the poet.

Ducere uela = "to set sail."

3–4. This couplet recalls the catalog that opens Catullus 11. **Rhipaeos ... montis** = a mountain range in northern Scythia. **Domos ... Memnonias** = Ethiopia. Propertius would go beyond the northern and southern boundaries of the known universe in Tullus's company.

5–6. "I would love to go, *but.* . . ." **Remorantur** goes with both clauses. **Mutato ... colore** could be either ablative absolute, "often her weighty pleas delayed me when her color had changed," or ablative of attendant circumstances, "often her pleas made weighty by her change of color delayed me." Either way, the image is of Cynthia pleading, turning pale, and flushing.

7–8. **Argutat ... ignis** = speaks at length of her fiery passion. The active form of *arguto* is rare. The deponent is more common.

Queritur nullos esse relicta deos: this is an implied conditional in the form of an indirect statement, "she complains that if she is left behind then no gods exist."

9–10. The onslaught of pronouns and possessive adjectives makes the line difficult but nicely captures the tirade Cynthia is pictured as unleashing:

"She already denies to me that she is mine." The pentameter makes clear that the scene is generic. **Tristis** = both "harsh" and "unhappy."

11–12. The hero who would brave the open seas and cross the very limits of the known world cannot endure an hour of his beloved's complaints. The curse of the pentameter would fall upon anyone who exhibited the traditional Roman values of *grauitas* and self-restraint. **Lentus** = "coolly, dispassionately."

13–14. Propertius could have expected to see these sights if he had accompanied Tullus on his uncle's proconsular mission. **Tanti** = genitive of value.

15–16. **Deducta ... puppi** = ablative absolute, with the ship having been launched. *Puppis* is a common synecdoche (part for the whole) for ship.
    Ora notet: the scratching of one's face is a common gesture of mourning.

17–18. The couplet is difficult. **Esse** must be taken with both **oscula** and **nihil** as subjects of indirect discourse. **Sibi** = ethical dative with **debita**. The simplest way to construe the sentence and the one that requires us to make the least number of assumptions is: "She would say that her kisses are owed to the wind opposed [to my sailing] and that nothing is more unyielding than an unfaithful man."

19–20. The poet's attention returns to Tullus and the traditional accoutrements of power. The exact meaning of the line is disputed. If the meaning of **anteire** is "march before in a ceremonial escort" then why *conor*? Likewise, the entourage normally marched behind the proconsul's lictors. If it means "to surpass," it would seem insolent in relation to Tullus's uncle. Some therefore assume without any evidence that Tullus is being sent on a separate mission from his uncle's, but that is to take the bantering tone of this poem too seriously. The line clearly means something like, "Very well, come on then Tullus, go out and try to surpass your uncle's well-deserved axes."
    Conare = imperative.
    Secures refer to the *fasces* that were the symbols of Tullus's uncle's power.
    Vetera oblitis iura refer sociis: Tullus and his uncle were sent to Asia in the wake of the battle of Actium [23, 49]. See also poems 2.15 and 2.16. Many of Rome's eastern allies had sided with Antony against Octavian. They thus needed to be "reminded" of their obligations.

21–22. Tullus's life has yet to have the leisure (**cessauit**) for love. He has been occupied with the traditional pursuits of the aristocratic young Roman: **armatae cura ... patriae**. To wield arms at this period would have almost certainly meant to fight in the civil wars [9, 23, 48–49, 52].

23–24. You have been spared my suffering! The line would have elicited a wry chuckle from most readers. **Puer** = Amor.

25–26. The poet accepts the label of utter depravity (**extremae . . . nequitiae**) that traditional Romans would attribute to his mode of life and asks only to be able give himself over to it. **Iacere** = "to lie idle."

Hanc animam . . . reddere carries with it the notion of to give over utterly and hence also to yield up, i.e. to die. Propertius's duty is hazardous as well.

27–28. The fantasy of dying for love is recurrent in elegy and one of Propertius's favorites (see 2.1.47–48). Generically, it is linked to the elegiac meter's tie with funereal poems and epitaphs [25]. However, the association of sexuality and death is a constant in the western tradition.

29–30. **Non ego sum laudi**: see Tibullus 1.1.57–58. **Hanc . . . militiam** = *militia amoris* [27, 54–55]. See Tibullus 1.1.73–76. The *locus classicus* is Ovid *Amores* 1.9.

31–32. The Ionian Greeks were famed for their luxurious living and hence were considered *mollis*. The irony of implying that Tullus is the one who will fall prey to *mollitia* in the Greek East while Propertius submits to the rigors of a true *militia* should not be missed.

The **Pactolus** river was famously rich in gold. **Lydia** was the kingdom of Croesus proverbial for eastern wealth.

33–34. **Carpere . . . ibis** = infinitive of purpose after a verb of motion, rather than the more regular supine. The verb **carpere** here, while often used with the meaning of "to move through effortlessly," also means "to seize and enjoy," hence *carpe diem*. This latter sense seems relevant in light of both Tullus's serving on a provincial administration and the previous couplet's emphasis on the luxuries to be had there. That provincial administrators expected to enrich themselves at the expense of the locals was a commonplace. The ambiguity is impossible to translate.

Accepti pars eris imperii: Antony's administration of these provinces was said by Augustan propaganda to have been lax and corrupt. Tullus therefore will be part of a welcome return to the rule of law.

35–36. The litotes of the hyperbolic **si qua . . . non immemor hora** nicely sets up the final pentameter in which Propertius's hard fate (**duro sidere**) is contrasted with the implicit *mollitia* of Tullus's life in luxurious Asia. The inversion of accepted values is now complete.

2.1

The previous inversions of normative gender and social roles are extended to the poetic genres of elegy and epic in this poem. Propertius Book 2 moves from the initial establishment of the poet's style in the *Monobiblos* to its institutionalization and direct engagement with Roman institutional and ideological norms. It is no accident that this book commences with a *recusatio* [53], a form in which the poet refuses a request to write epic or encomiastic verse while nonetheless managing to placate his petitioner. It is also no accident that the figures of Maecenas [51–52] and Augustus loom large over it. Propertius has accepted Maecenas's patronage and has begun to move in the imperial circle. This, however, does not mean that his poetry becomes less oppositional: rather, to the extent that poetry referring to, or refusing to refer to, the emperor, Maecenas, and their coterie is more prominent in this collection, then the pressures of Roman ideology stand in even sharper contrast to the desires for *nequitia* and *inertia* that were at the heart of the *Monobiblos*.

Poem 2.1 is a very complex poem. It is both the opening programmatic poem of Propertius's second book and a text that stages Maecenas's suggesting to the poet that he produce an epic in praise of Augustus. Indeed, some have read 2.1 as a response to a demand for such a poem. It is a poem that at the very least stages the possibility of elegy's direct engagement with political and social power in a way that poem 1.6 refuses. Throughout both this poem and much of Book 2, Propertius founds his project on the simultaneous refusal and embrace of the Augustan regime. As such, the specific difference that constitutes elegiac discourse – its opposition to epic *uirtus*, and *militia* – is directly problematized.

In 2.1, the poet begins by offering his reader a *mollis liber* (2.1.2) that is inspired not by Apollo or the Muses but by the poet's *puella* (2.1.3–4). There then follows a list of possible topics concerning his beloved upon which the poet proposes to write *longae Iliades* (2.1.14). This allusion to epic, so out of place in the programmatically *mollis* genre of elegy, is anticipated by a specific reference to amorous violence in the preceding line (*nuda erepto mecum luctatur amictu* ["Naked she fought with me, her wrap ripped away"], 2.1.13). The overt inversion of genres in this passage is paralleled by an implicit inversion of genders as the epic *hostis* metamorphoses into the *puella* of the poet's *militia amoris*. The conflation of genders and genres becomes complete, and the oxymoronic character of the verse explicit, when later in the same poem the possibility of Propertius producing an encomiastic epic on Augustus is rejected. Such *durus uersus* (2.1.41) would be beyond the compass of the soft poet. At the same time, Cynthia, the subject of the poet's own *mollis liber*, is characterized as *dura* (2.1.78), so that the elegiac beloved is attributed the same traits as epic itself. Where the first part of the poem, lines 1–46, is concerned with Propertius's theory of elegy and its relation to epic, the second part, lines 47–70, puts that theory into practice while recycling many of the themes and motifs from the first section. The poem ends with a coda, lines 71–78, addressed to Maecenas in which the two parts are brought together.

1–2. We have already noted that **mollis** in line 2 is programmatic, referring to the subject matter contained in the **liber** (i.e., elegy). Yet the distinctions become much cloudier when we move on to the question of to whom is the poet referring in the phrase **in ora**, himself or his readers, and what this means. While the majority of readers take the phrase as unproblematically referring to the fame the poet achieves through his verse – he is on the lips of everyone – Goold (1990) interprets it as a question of poetics, "how is it that my book sounds so soft upon the lips?" Yet if we look at the immediately preceding hexameter and the following couplet, it becomes clear that what is most at issue is the question of origins: "whence (**unde**) does my soft book come softly on the lips?" This reading does not invalidate either the majority position or that of Goold, for none of these readings is mutually exclusive, from a logical point of view, and all are grammatically possible owing to the extreme concision of the line. Rather it reveals their interdependence. For the question of the origin of the poetry (whence it came), its nature (soft upon the lips), and its ultimate destination (as a topic of conversation for its audience) are all at issue in this poem.

3–4. The poet seems to tell us that his experience dictates the song he sings, **ingenium nobis ipsa puella facit**. Nevertheless, even this seemingly straightforward line is problematic when read in context, for the poet has just told us that his poetry is not the product of Apollo and the Muse (**Calliope**). The very next words beneath the reader's eyes are **ingenium nobis**. This poetry is not the product of the gods but of the poet's own genius! **Ipsa** does nothing to change our mind, since it could as easily be neuter plural as feminine singular. It is only once we reach **puella** that the process of interpretive revision has to take place. The sequence runs as follows: I need no external source of inspiration; my own innate talents are my girl's creation.

5–16. Her every action is a source of inspiration.

5–6. If Cynthia should wear Coan silks, a fabric known for its see-through qualities (see Tibullus 2.3.53–54), the poet will make an entire book from the fabric. He means not only a volume of erotic titillation, but also a deluxe edition fashioned from the fabric, whose style, like that of Catullus's "*libellum . . . pumice expolitum*" ["slender volume polished with pumice"] (1.1–2), will be as smooth as the material from which it is made. It will be silken inside and out.

†Cogis†: it is very difficult to know why one should have to "force" Cynthia to wear such finery or who the singular "you" would be. Various emendations have been proposed, but none has won wide assent. The prudent course is to follow the OCT and print the reading of the best manuscripts, but mark it with daggers.

7–8. Ad frontem sparsos errare capillos = "scattered locks to curl about her forehead."

Laudatis . . . comis: in his poetry that is.

9–10. Percussit = "plucks." One plucks the song of the lyre by striking its strings. **Ut premat** = an indirect question with **miramur**. I have deleted the comma after **miramur** from the OCT text to make the grammar clearer.

11–12. Seu cum: there is a shift in meaning here. Earlier in the list **seu** and **siue** mean "or if," here **seu** means simply "or." Where the others are hypotheticals, this couplet presents itself as something that regularly happens, "or when. . . ." The difficulty has been noticed and debated by scholars, but similar passages from other authors can be cited and there seems little reason to emend the text. Moreover, it should be noted that no two couplets in the list are completely parallel, but each features subtle variations in grammar and structure. Finally, the shift from the hypothetical to the actual is appropriate to the confident summary tone of the pentameter.

13–14. On the general significance of this couplet and its introduction of the themes of epic and *militia amoris*, see the introductory note to this poem. This couplet, while continuing the list of possible amatory topics begun in line 5, starts the shift toward the *recusatio* proper. The break in the continuity of the list occasioned by **seu cum**, discussed in the note above, helps mark the transition.

15–16. The transition from epic in the previous couplet to **historia** (see 3.4.10) here presages the progression of subjects found in the next section of the poem. The poet moves from a discussion of possible mythological topics to those of distant and finally recent history. Note the irony of creating a **maxima historia de nihilo**.

17–18. Quod = "but."

Heroas ducere in arma manus: this line is generally interpreted as meaning metaphorically "to write epic," but the literal reading, "to lead bands of heroes into arms," should not be forgotten. Propertius was not a soldier, as he makes clear in 1.6, and neither was Maecenas, who served Augustus in a strictly civilian capacity.

19–26. This list of rejected topics constitutes a brief history of the world from its mythological origins to the present.

19–20. Propertius condenses into one couplet two myths that were often conflated: the battle of the Titans with the gods, and the attack of the Giants, Otus and Ephialtes, on heaven. The latter piled Mount Ossa on Olympus, and Pelion on Ossa, before they were defeated. The battle of the Titans was treated by Hesiod in the *Theogony*.

21–22. The story of the Seven against Thebes and of their sons was the subject of an epic cycle. These battles are mentioned in the *Iliad* as occurring in the two generations before the Trojan War. Thus we are moving in chronological order from the Titans to the Giants, to the Theban cycle, to Homer, and to the Persian Wars chronicled by Herodotus. In the process, we move from the earliest forms of mythological epic to **historia** as it was first practiced in Greece.

Xerxis et imperio bina coisse uada: the reference is Xerxes's cutting a canal through the isthmus behind Mount Athos. **Vada** = metonymy for sea.

23–24. The shift from epic to **historia**, or from myth to history, prepares the shift from Greek to Roman subject matter. This couplet contains a brief history of Rome down to the first of the civil wars that, over the course of the first century BCE, would lead to the triumph of the Augustan regime [18–21].

Remi: many commentators see Remus as standing for Romulus, arguing that Romulus is metrically impossible. This is not true. Certainly, *Romuli* could not be merely substituted for **Remi**, but *Romulus* ($-\smile\smile$) could have been used in a dactylic hexameter if Propertius wished. Moreover, since Propertius in the next couplet tells how he would sing *princeps*'s praises if he had the ability, and since Octavian had considered taking the honorific cognomen Romulus rather than Augustus, then Romulus would have seemed a logical choice. It seems best to assume then that Remus was a deliberate choice and this makes sense. Remus, killed by Romulus, was the first victim of fratricidal conflict in Rome, and it is precisely Caesar's deeds in the civil wars that Propertius says he would sing. Likewise, **Remi** in the first half of the hexameter is balanced by **Mari** in the pentameter. Marius's conflict with Sulla marked the beginning of the civil wars.

Animos = "pride" or "ferocity." The defeat of Carthage in the Punic wars established Rome as the undisputed master of the western Mediterranean.

Cimbrorumque minas et bene facta Mari: the Cimbri were an invading German tribe. They were defeated by Marius in 101 BCE on the Raudine plains in the upper Po valley.

25–26. I would not sing of past myths or history but memorialize the deeds (res) and wars (bella) of your friend Caesar (tui . . . Caesaris), and you would be my next object of concern (cura secunda), right after great Caesar (Caesare sub magno).

27–28. While the previous couplet would have appealed to Maecenas and Augustus, the subject matter Propertius proposes to treat is more problematic. All of these victories are over Roman opponents, at a time when Augustus was attempting to put himself forward as *pater patriae*.

Mutinam: a famous battle (43 BCE) in which Octavian at the head of a consular army defeated the forces of Antony when he tried to seize the province of Cisalpine Gaul from its rightful governor. The battle was later remembered for the fact that both consuls, Hirtius and Pansa, were killed fighting on the side of Octavian.

Civilia busta Philippos: Philippi (42 BCE) was the climactic battle between the combined forces of Antony and Octavian and those of Brutus and Cassius, the assassins of Julius Caesar. That Propertius would sing the **busta** or "graves" indicates more a song of mourning than praise.

Siculae classica bella fugae = "the naval war of the Sicilian route," referring to Octavian's defeat of Sextus Pompeius at Naulochus in 36 BCE.

29–30. The first line refers to the Perusine war (41 BCE), Octavian's bloodiest massacre of the civil war and the topic of a pair of short epigrams by Propertius at the end of Book 1 [48–53]. The reference stands out because it is the only topic in the entire list, beginning with the Titans (line 19) and ending with the celebration of Augustus's triumph over Antony and Cleopatra (line 34), that is not in chronological order. The poet thus draws special attention to a topic that Caesar wished to forget.

Ptolemaeei litora capta Phari refers to the capture of Alexandria (30 BCE) after Antony and Cleopatra's defeat at the battle of Actium (31 BCE). Pharos is an island off the coast of Alexandria.

31–32. In 29 BCE, Augustus celebrated a triple triumph for his victories over Pannonia, the naval forces gathered at Actium, and Egypt itself. On the third day, a representation of the captured Nile (**captiuis . . . aquis**) was brought (**attractus**) through the city streets.

Septem: the Nile was said to have seven mouths in its delta.

Note the large number of elisions in the hexameter. The slightly archaic prosody imparts a veneer of solemnity.

33–34. Captured rulers of defeated countries were routinely marched through the streets during the celebration of a triumph. The chains round their necks were gilded to mark them out as royalty. The victory at Actium was celebrated by marching the prows (**rostra**) of captured ships down the Sacred Way as part of the triumphal procession. The image's conjunction of golden chains and of ships in the streets presents the triple triumph as a time of wonders, a time when the natural order of things had been upset.

35–36. The image of Propertius's Muse weaving Maecenas (**te . . . contexeret**) into the fabric of the Augustan military feats just listed (**illis . . . armis**) is striking.

Contexeret = potential subjunctive.

Sumere arma and *ponere arma* are both standard phrases for beginning and ending hostilities. Propertius's substitution of **et sumpta et posita pace** inverts the formula so that war becomes the normal background, which is punctuated by moments of peace, rather than vice versa. He highlights the substitution by placing **armis** at the end of line 35.

Fidele caput is in apposition to **te**.

37–38. This is a very difficult couplet. **Infernis** and **superis** may be either neuter locative ablative or masculine dative. The ambiguity is not resolvable by grammatical means alone, nor does it represent the sole crux. Some take **superis** to mean "in the world of men as opposed to the underworld," others "in the world of the gods." There are problems with each, and both uses are attested, but the force of the present **testatur** indicates ongoing action. Achilles and Theseus not only declared their respective friendships with Patroclus and Pirithous in the past, but continue to do so. The idea of an eternal friendship, in turn, better fits the ostensibly encomiastic context of Propertius immortalizing the friendship of Augustus and Maecenas. In that case, **superis** must refer to the realm of the immortals. In several later versions of the myth, Achilles spends eternity in the Elysian fields or Isles of the Blessed.

Ixioniden = Pirithous, the son of Ixion who went to the underworld with Theseus to carry off Persephone.

Menoetiaden = Patroclus, son of Menoetius, whose death caused Achilles to re-enter the Trojan War and consequently sealed his own fate.

There is no compelling reason to assume a lacuna after this couplet as the OCT does. The shift to mythological parallels recalls the beginning of this section of the poem (lines 19–22) and prepares for the transition from epic subject matter to elegy proper. This movement is completed in the next two couplets with the recollection of the Giants' assault on Mount Olympus (lines 19–20 and 39–40), and the invocation of the authority of Callimachus [9, 25–29].

39–40. Phlegraeos . . . tumultus = the battle on the legendary Phlegraean plain between the gods and the Giants (see 3.11.37–38). **Enceladique** = one of the Giants, struck down by Jupiter's thunderbolt.

Intonet = "thunders", a reference to epic style, which Callimachus says belongs to Jupiter alone.

Angusto pectore: Callimachus was an advocate of the slender style as opposed to what he saw as the bombastic inflation of epic.

Note that both this pentameter and the previous one violate the rule of disyllabic endings. While Propertius in his early work is not strict in his adherence to this rule, a sequence of two couplets in a row calls attention to itself. The Alexandrians did not observe this practice. It is thus perhaps not an accident that the first pentameter ends in a learned, polysyllabic patronymic, **Menoetiaden**, a common feature of Alexandrian poetic diction. The second ends in the name **Callimachus** itself. The only other example of two pentameters in succession ending in words of more than two syllables is where lines 14 and 16 end in **Iliadas** and **historia** respectively. Again, the practice is deliberate, preparing the reader for the close association between the two genres in the section to follow.

41–42. Duro . . . versu = epic, as opposed to Propertius's **mollis liber** (see line 2). Note how terms associated with gender categories are also markers for poetic genres.

Caesaris in Phrygios condere nomen auos: a reference to Augustus's efforts to trace his line to Aeneas. Vergil at this point had already started work on the *Aeneid*. See 2.34.61–66.

43–44. Each man tells of what he knows best.

45–46. The hexameter is very condensed. We must assume *narramus* or its equivalent. **Versantes** can be read as either nominative or accusative meaning both "pursue" and "turn into verse."

Proelia = either the object of the assumed verb or of **uersantes**. It introduces the motif of *militia amoris*. This next section (lines 45–70) will systematically appropriate elements from the previous discussion of possible epic subject matter and turn them into the material of amorous elegy.

Angusto . . . lecto: the bed is narrow because it is Callimachean; see lines 39–40. Note how poetic composition and lovemaking are portrayed as identical.

Pote = colloquial for *potest*.

Conterat = "rub away," hence "spend." The erotic connotation is clear.

47–48. As the soldier receives glory from dying in battle, the lover receives glory from dying in love. See 1.6.29–30 and Tibullus 1.1.57–58. The couplet as a whole contains an implicit syllogism. It is praiseworthy to die in love. It is also praiseworthy to enjoy love while alive. However, to enjoy it while alive means to enjoy it alone without a rival. Therefore, not to be **solus** in love is to be dead.

Uno = dative for *uni*. Analogous forms are found elsewhere in Propertius, 1.20.35. Some people emend the text to read *uni*. Others take **uno** as ablative modifying **amore**. This would then assimilate the elegiac lover to the *matrona*'s ideal of being *uninupta*, married to only a single man. As we have seen, such inversions of gender expectations are frequent in elegy. It may well be that the grammatical ambiguity is intentional.

49–50. In this couplet, Propertius not only recalls lines 13–14, but manages to advance the outrageous claim that elegy (i.e. Cynthia who stands for the poetry) is morally superior to epic. The political irony of this statement coming immediately after the elegist's claim that the Callimachean poet is unable to write an epic on Augustus cannot be avoided.

51–52. This couplet begins an anaphoric sequence in which possible mythological topics are reviewed. The repetition of **seu** in lines 51–54 directly recalls the opening sequence of lines 5–16.

All three of these figures are related. Circe is the paternal aunt of Medea and the maternal aunt of Phaedra.

Nouercae . . . Phaedrae: Phaedra was married to Theseus when she conceived a passion for Hippolytus, his son by Hippolyta.

Pocula = love potions, but also poisons as lines 55–56 make clear. The Greek word *pharmakon* could refer to a beneficial drug, a charm, or a poison. Propertius thus declares his exclusive love for Cynthia and his will to die for her. Though in Euripides's *Hippolytus* Phaedra does not resort to a philter, the scholia on Theocritus mentions other versions of the story where she does. In the version Propertius has in mind the potion is either not drunk or without harmful effect (**non nocitura**).

Priuigno = Hippolytus.

53–54. Circe used *pharmaka* to transform Odysseus's men into pigs, in effect killing them (**pereundem est**).

Colchis = Medea. **Iolciacis** = in *Iolcus* the home of Jason, where Medea killed Pelias by boiling him in a cauldron under the pretext of rejuvenating him.

55–56. "Since one woman alone has stolen my senses, my funeral procession will start from her home": a very odd way of expressing devotion, in which love and death are equated. The image of the loss of the senses in love goes back to Sappho 31. The relationship between love and death is common in Propertius (see 1.6.27–28) and often associated with *militia amoris*. *Praeda* = "booty won in war" (see Tibullus 1.2.65–66, 2.3.35–42). It is a recurring motif in Ovid.

57–58. Solus amor morbi non amat artificiem: this phrase would normally be translated "love alone does not love the maker of the disease," but the sense of the hexameter would seem to require it to mean just the opposite, "love alone does not love the healer of the disease," taking *artifex* as a generic term for a skilled professional. The duality of the maker and healer of disease, while straining normal Latin syntax and usage, is in fact consonant with the double meaning of **pocula** as love potions and poisons. Love is a disease whose cure is poison.

59–64. There follows a list of famously difficult cures drawn from mythology. The irony of both this list and of the preceding mythological exempla from a poet who rejects the themes of epic should not be missed.

59–60. Machaon cures Philoctetes of his snakebite at Troy. Phoenix was cured of blindness by the Centaur Chiron, both of whom were associated with Achilles. Notice how the themes of the *Iliad* recur throughout the poem.

61–62. Deus . . . Epidaurius = Asclepius, son of Apollo and god of healing. Androgeos, son of Minos, met a premature death. Only Propertius has Asclepius restore him to life.

63–64. Mysus = Telephus, king of Mysia, wounded by Achilles. He could only be cured by an application of rust from the same spear.
  Haemonia . . . cuspide = the Thessalian spear, i.e., that of Achilles.

65–66. A series of *adunata* or impossible tasks. Tantalus had tried to feed his son Pelops to the gods. His punishment in Hades was to stand for eternity in a pool of water from which he could not drink and beneath a fruit tree from which he could not eat. He was thus constantly tormented by hunger and thirst. The imagery of the incurable affliction (**uitium**), and of the underworld recalls the earlier images of poison, death, and wounds.

67–68. The Danaids were forever condemned to carry water to fill large storage jars (**dolia**), which leaked as fast as they were filled, because they had killed their husbands on their wedding night at the behest of their father, Danaus.
  Tenera . . . colla: water jars were normally carried on the head.

69–70. Prometheus for the theft of fire from the gods was chained to a mountain in the Caucasus where vultures devoured his eternally regrowing liver. In some versions, he was released by Hercules.

71–72. The final section is addressed to Maecenas. We return to the funeral motif. Propertius has died of love, a fate worthy of epic ambitions but duly commemorated in Callimachean fashion on **exiguo marmore**. Compare line 40, **angusto . . . pectore**, and line 45, **angusto . . . lecto**.

73–74. Nostrae spes inuidiosa iuventae = "envied hope of our youth."

This phrase carries with it three meanings that cannot be disentangled. (1) All the youth of Rome hopes to benefit from the patronage of Maecenas in the same fashion as Propertius. (2) Maecenas is the envy of the young because he shows how high an equestrian may hope to rise. As the nineteenth-century commentators point out, the equestrian order was sometimes referred to as the *iuuenes*. Maecenas while involved in imperial politics made a point of never giving up his equestrian status and becoming a senator. (3) Maecenas is the hope of Propertius's youth specifically. This reading of **nostra** as poetic plural is somewhat strained by the shift to the singular in the pentameter, though by no means excluded.

Gloria is normally a military virtue. See 2.7.17–18 and Tibullus 1.5.1–2. It implicitly continues the mixing of the elegiac and epic genres found throughout the piece.

75–76. Busto recalls line 27. **Esseda ... Britanna** = the British war chariot. This was not a vehicle of machismo. Ovid (*Amores* 2.16.49–50) tells us it is the kind chariot of driven by a woman, a sentiment echoed in Propertius 2.32.5. Cicero treats it as a sign of effeminate luxury (*Att.* 6.1.25; *Phlipp.* 2.24). The transformation from epic battle-car to elegiac chick-chariot, in many ways sums up the entire thrust of this poem.

Caelatis ... iugis = yokes engraved with metalwork. This was a luxury model.

77–78. On the **dura puella**, see the introductory note to this poem.

2.7

This poem is generally read as a celebration of the repeal of one of Augustus's moral reform laws {53} and a declaration of opposition to the Augustan regime's restoring of Rome's ancient virtues. Instead of celebrating the return of the *mos maiorum*, the poet's vision of himself in an exclusive relation with Cynthia, is promoted to the status of a norm (*tu mihi sola places: placeam tibi, Cynthia, solus:* | *hic erit et patrio sanguine pluris amor* ["You alone please me, may I alone please you, Cynthia, and this love will be worth more than a father's blood"] ll.19–20). Yet, this reading of the poem is problematic since, as Badian has shown (1985), none of the laws promoted by Augustus had been passed at this time, let alone repealed. Badian's elegant solution to this historical conundrum is to argue that the poem's actual reference is to the repeal by Augustus of a tax imposed on unmarried men by the second triumvirate in order to raise money for the civil wars. The repeal, then, would represent part of the normalization process undertaken by Augustus, commonly referred to as "the restoration of the republic." Implicit in Badian's reading is the idea that 2.7 rather than being an attack on Augustus's moral reform legislation is actually a celebration of his fiscal restraint.

While Badian's solution to the problem of the legal reference in 2.7 is compelling, it hardly eliminates the interpretive difficulties that beset the poem. What Propertius and Cynthia celebrate is not their ability "to keep what they earn," but their refusal to enter into a recognized marital relationship and to provide citizens for the imperial armies of Rome (*unde mihi Parthis natos praebere triumphis?* | *nullus de nostro sanguine miles erit* ["why should I offer sons for a Parthian triumph? | There will be no soldier from our blood"] 2.7.13–14), neither of which can be seen as supporting Augustus's political program [22, 57]. Hence, Propertius's celebration of Augustus's repeal of the repressive triumviral legislation can still be read as a statement of opposition to Augustan ideology. The poem is deeply ambivalent.

The poem assumes that it would have been impossible for Propertius and Cynthia to marry. This could only be for two reasons: (1) Cynthia is already married to another; (2) Cynthia is a freedwoman living as a *meretrix* and hence of too low a social status to marry an equestrian. There is no positive evidence for number 1 and in poem 1.3 Propertius and Cynthia are portrayed as having a close domestic relationship, which would have been precluded had she been married to another; therefore number 2 is the most economical assumption.

1–2. **Sublatam:** understand *esse*. **Flemus** = a syncopated form of the perfect *fleuimus*, as required by parallelism with **gauisa es** and by the sequence of tenses with **diuideret** in the subordinate clause.

3–4. This couplet is strictly speaking a paradox. If Jupiter himself could not separate them, then why did they have to worry? **Ni** = archaic for *ne*.

5–6. '**At magnus Caesar':** The point of the preceding paradox becomes clear. Caesar is more to be feared than Jupiter, an interlocutor suggests.

Sed magnus Caesar in armis: Propertius's retort is that while Caesar is indeed great, his sphere of influence is limited to arms, which as poem 2.1 observes is the province of epic [6].

7–8. **Citius paterer caput hoc discedere collo:** this line is in the first instance a figure of speech, but in the aftermath of the civil wars the suggestion that Caesar might turn arms against his own people cannot be discounted. Is this an acknowledgement of Caesar's power, an indictment, or both?

Nuptae perdere more faces: this line is much debated. Is Propertius wasting torches in a marriage procession? Is he destroying the torches used for the paraclausithyron on the orders of a hypothetical wife (**Nuptae . . . more**)? Is he dashing the torch of love to humor a new bride? Alternatively, is the text corrupt and should the popular reading of **amore** for **more** be accepted? If we assume that the best manuscripts contain the correct reading, then there is no sure way of distinguishing the various interpretations, and we must conclude that Propertius has artfully created a line in which the torches of the bridal procession, the paraclausithyron, and of passion would be destroyed were he to marry.

9–10. Transirem = "pass by."

11–12. The **tibia** was a flute played in the wedding procession but also the musical instrument most closely associated with the performance of elegy in archaic Greece. The **tuba** was played at funerals, but was also the war trumpet. See Tibullus 1.1.3–4. There is thus a subtle transition in these lines from the wedding procession, which would be the end of Propertius's love for Cynthia and hence of elegy, to the funeral, which is also associated with archaic elegy, to warfare and the theme of *militia amoris* that dominates the last portion of the poem.

13–14. Propertius's refusal to provide a son to fight in such a venture is not only anti-Augustan but un-Roman.

I have replaced the OCT reading *Parthis*, which is a late emendation, with **patriis**, the reading of the best manuscripts and most modern editions.

15–16. Quod = "but."

Magnus Castoris . . . equus: Castor was famed as a horseman and the divine sponsor of the equestrian order. Note that **magnus Castoris** recalls **magnus Caesar** from line 5.

17–18. Martial **gloria** (see 2.1.74) is here replaced by amorous **gloria**.

Borysthenidas = inhabitants of the far northern outpost of Borysthenis on the Dnieper river.

19–20. Places . . . placeam: the distinction between the indicative and the optative subjunctive is instructive.

I have kept the reading of the best manuscripts, **sanguine**, for the OCT's **nomine**. *Sanguis* nicely captures the significance of blood as symbolic of both kinship and warfare that is central to this poem (see line 14).

Pluris = genitive of value.

2.15

Poems 2.15 and 2.16 are important for the two contrasting evaluations of the battle of Actium they present [23, 52–53, 55–56]. Poem 2.15 is a celebration of a night of love with Cynthia. It is one of the few poems of consummated passion in the corpus. It ends with the statement that if only everyone would spend their days in love's embrace then the straits of Actium would now be churning fewer Roman bones. Some have viewed this poem as a statement of Propertius's loyalty to the cause of Marc Antony since his adoption of the pose of Dionysus and his notorious passion for Cleopatra made him the image of anti-Roman decadence in Augustan propaganda. Such a view is oversimplified, since poem 2.16 paints a much less flattering image of Antony. What is key in both of these poems is the way in which the political context, traditional Roman values, gender expectations, and elegy both as a mode of life and a poetic genre are inextricably woven together so that each element in this matrix is only understandable through its complex relation with all the others.

Richardson (1977) notes that the poem can be divided into three parts. Lines 1–24 feature a contrast between elements of light and dark as expressed in the first line's *o nox mihi candida*! The next 24 lines focus on the contrast between the eternal and transient. The last 6 lines form a coda in which these two themes are brought together.

1–2. The hiatus (lack of elision) between **felicem** and **o** is softened because it occurs at the caesura and seems natural after an accusative of exclamation. The contrast with the elision between **candida** and **et** is to be noted. Here the elision emphasizes the linkage indicated by the conjunction.

Lectule: such diminutives are common signs of affection in Catullus.

Deliciis = a euphemism for sexual relations.

3–4. Narramus = historic present.

Rixa = tussle of love, an allusion to the vocabulary of *militia amoris*.

5–6. Est luctata continues the vocabulary of amatory struggle.

Interdum tunica duxit operta moram: "from time to time, having concealed herself with her tunic, she caused me to delay." **Operta** = perfect passive participle from *operio*.

7–8. The reversal of roles as the pursuer becomes the pursued is part of the fun.

Lente = "lazy one."

9–10. The description of changing sexual positions is as explicit as anything found in Propertius. **Mutamus** = historic present.

11–12. The notion that love should be made "with the lights on" was contrary to the norms of modesty expected between a Roman man and his wife, who was only to be approached in darkness.

Si nescis = colloquial, "in case you didn't know."

Note that all the mythological exempla that follow are Greek and deal with extramarital relations.

13–14. Lacaena = Helen, "the woman from Sparta."

Perisse = "to have fallen in love," but also looks forward to Paris's real death because of his adulterous liaison.

15–16. Endymion had fallen asleep in a cave when Luna (**Phoebi ... sororem**) fell in love and lay with him. He later returned to the same cave and fell into a dreamless sleep from which he never awoke, but was preserved just as he was.

17–18. Quod = "but." **Pertendens** = "resisting." **Cubaris** = future perfect of **cubo**.

Manus is ambiguous, meaning both "hands" and "force." The rape fantasy played a prominent role in the Roman masculine erotic imagination.

19–20. Quin etiam indicating the climax of an argument = "but indeed." The implicit violence that is assumed in the Roman erotic imagination is the basis for the metaphor of *militia amoris*.

21–22. Inclinatae ... mammae: the note of vulgar realism would have been comic.

Viderit haec, si quam iam peperisse pudet: "she will have known these things who has experienced the shame of having given birth." *Meretrices*, as Ovid points out, dealt with the threat of pregnancy by self-administered abortions that were not infrequently fatal. As freedwomen whose livelihoods depended on maintaining their attractiveness, *meretrices* could ill afford pregnancy. It was a cause of shame (**pudet**), where for the *matrona* it was a badge of honor promoted by the Augustan regime (see poem 2.7) [15, 22, 53]. **Haec** = neuter plural accusative.

23–24. The previous reminder of the threats of age and pregnancy now modulates into a more standard invocation of the *carpe diem* motif. The pentameter evokes a famous line from Catullus 5.

25–26. Haerentis ... nos = "locked in our embrace." The image is comical and recalls that of Ares and Aphrodite trapped in the golden net of Hephaestus at *Odyssey* 8.295–99.

27–28. For the image of the passionate doves, see Catullus 68.125–28.

29–30. The couplet articulates a paradox. Love is a disease (**uesani ... amoris**) that is defined by its refusal to recognize boundaries (**finem**). Therefore he who seeks a limit (**modum**) in love errs (**errat**), i.e. literally wanders off course or out of bounds. Love is the opposite of the traditional Roman virtue of seriousness and self-control (*grauitas*).

Vesani = a recollection of Catullus 7.

31–32. Love's disorder is the natural order of things. A series of *adunata* follow (see 2.1.65–66). **Falso partu**: the earth will mock the ploughman by producing bizarre or unexpected crops.

The horses of the sun are normally white, while those of the moon are black.

33–34. Rivers reversing course are standard in lists of *adunata*.

35–36. Alio = "elsewhere." **Dolores** = love, which by definition in elegy and traditional Roman morality is a source of pain. Note the elegantly balanced pentameter.

37–38. Quod = "but." A year of such love would be a long life.

39–40. The Greek doctrine of euhemerism held that the gods were once mortals who through the performance of extraordinary acts had been elevated to divine status in the popular imagination. This philosophy in turn provided the rationale for divine kingship in the Hellenistic monarchies and eventually in the empire. Propertius pokes sly humor at this doctrine and its growing currency under the principate by saying that a single night with Cynthia is enough to make anyone (**quiuis**) a god.

41–42. Membra = a Greek accusative of respect with **pressi**. On **mero**, see Tibullus 1.2.1–2.

43–44. The political point here is sharp. It is precisely Roman seriousness and self-control that have led to civil slaughter. If only everyone led a life of drunken debauchery, the Actian sea would not now churn Roman bones. It cannot be ignored that Augustan propaganda depicted Antony as leading such a life. Yet, it is equally hard to believe that Propertius is proposing a serious political policy, and it must be remembered that he is by this time receiving patronage from Maecenas, Augustus's close confidante. The satire is in fact double-edged. No Roman would take such proposals seriously, and this positive picture of Antonian excess is balanced by a negative one in the following poem.

45–46. The note of sorrow here for the civil wars and of Rome's exhaustion is genuine. What Propertius, Horace, and Vergil wanted as much as anything was peace. Augustus's great merit was that he was able to bring it.

The image of Rome beset by its own triumphs (**propriis circum oppugnata triumphis**) can cannot help but recall Augustus's triple triumph celebrated at the conclusion of the Actian campaign. These were portrayed as triumphs over eastern foreigners, but the fact that Antony was a Roman general leading Roman legions as well as eastern allies would have been lost on no one. See 2.1.31–34.

Crinis soluere = a traditional gesture of mourning.

47–48. The young will remember our acts of daring-do. This is a traditional wish for future glory ironically employed for drunken carousing rather than martial valor.

Nullos . . . deos: Antony portrayed himself as the new Dionysus. Augustus took Apollo as his tutelary deity (see poem 4.6). Our cups (**pocula**) would not harm any such gods.

49–50. The *carpe diem* motif returns and Propertius addresses Cynthia directly. The kiss theme recalls the earlier allusions to Catullus 5 and 7.

51–52. This is an extraordinary image of the end of a party, as the dried leaves from the revelers' garlands float on the top of the wine bowl. In the context of the *carpe diem* motif, this is a metaphor for death that also conjures up the image of the bones rolled in the Actian sea from lines 43–44.

53–54. Magnum spiramus = "draw deep breath." **Includet** = "will close."

2.16

The companion piece to 2.15, poem 2.16 presents the end of Propertius's amorous idyll. Cynthia's head has been turned by the elegists' standard antagonist the *diues amator* [44], in this case, a praetor returned with riches from abroad. This poem features a corresponding evocation of the battle Actium to that of 2.15, portraying Antony as a *seruus amoris* whose subjugation to Cleopatra causes the destruction of his fleet. Augustus, in contrast, is praised for his clemency and *uirtus*. One must ask, however, how seriously can such statements be taken in a poem that also condemns mercenary girls and the booty-laden soldiers and public officials who compete with poets for their affections?

1–2. Praetor = most likely a propraetor, a person of praetorian rank assigned to govern a province. Such magistrates were expected to enrich themselves at the expense of the inhabitants, as long as their exactions were not excessive. See 1.6.

On **praeda** as the booty associated with *arma* in elegy, see poem 2.1.55–56 and Tibullus 1.2.65–66, 2.3.35–50. Such statements of poverty on the part of an equestrian should be taken with a large grain of salt [34]. Note the perfectly balanced pentameter.

3–4. If only the praetor had died in a shipwreck! **Saxo ... Cerauno** = Acroceraunia, a rocky promontory on the border of Illyria and northwestern Greece that made navigation treacherous.

5–6. Propertius will become the *exclusus amator*.

7–8. Si sapis = a colloquialism, "if you're smart." **Ne desere** = "do not neglect."
  Stolidum ... carpe pecus: a hilarious variation on the **carpe diem** motif.

9–10. Once Cynthia has fleeced him, she can give him his leave to go ransack other provinces.

11–12. Cynthia cares nothing for the typical Roman man's obsession with the *cursus honorum* or "sequence of offices" a young man was expected to hold as he struggled his way to the top of the political pile. She cares only about the weight of his purse.
  Fascis = accusative plural. See 1.6.19–20.
  Una = she alone, i.e. best of all. Though it would seem more logical to take it adverbially, "she only weighs," the grammar does not support such a reading.
  Sinus = accusative plural, referring to the folds in a toga used as a purse.

13–14. The pentameter is a recollection of the end of Catullus 11 where the poet says Lesbia holds three hundred adulterers at once and bursts their loins (*ilia rumpens*).

15–16. Indigna merce: indigna could be both transfer of epithet from **puella** and a true ablative. **Perit** is ambiguous as well. Does she go bad, die to Propertius's affections, or fall in love? All three are possible. Certainly, a girl who fell in love for an unworthy price would, from Propertius's perspective, have gone bad and (he claims) be dead to his heart.

17–18. Here is the rub. Cynthia is always demanding gifts from Propertius too. **Quaerere** = infinitive of purpose with a verb of motion.
  Ipsa ... Tyro: see Tibullus 2.3.57–58. The sequence of the *diues amator*, followed by the poet himself being sent across the sea in search of riches, and then nostalgia for the Golden Age (lines 19–20) recalls the structure of Tibullus's poem 2.3. While Book 2 of Tibullus (*c.*19 BCE) was published later than Propertius's second book (26–25 BCE), it is impossible to date the composition of individual poems with any precision and to say who is imitating whom.

19–20. Dux = Augustus. Is this a jab at the proclamation of a return to the Golden Age in Vergil and Horace? See Tibullus 2.3.35–36.

21–22. Fieret cana = would grow old.

23–24. Foedo . . . uiro = ablative of place where with **fusa**.

25–26. Peccarim = potential subjunctive, "not because I would be untrue."
Vulgo = "for the common man."
Leuitas = "fickleness, unreliability," the opposite of *grauitas*.
Amica here = "companion," but recalls the more common meaning of
"girlfriend" used in line 21. This last clause is a recollection of Catullus
72.3–4.

27–28. This couplet is an illustration of the **leuitas** described in the previous
line. One moment, the rival is a foreign slave (**barbarus**, compare Tibullus
2.3.59–60) who paces outside the door (**agitat uestigia**), the next (**nunc**), he
rules Propertius's realm (**mea regna tenet**).
Barbarus: it is ambiguous whether this is meant to imply the praetor was
of servile origins, a common charge in Roman political invective, or whether
this is a general statement.
Exclusis . . . lumbis: a humorous note of grotesque realism, "with
his loins locked out." The reference to the trope of the *exclusus amator* is
clear.
Felix = both "happy" and "rich."

29–30. Eriphyla accepted a bribe to force her husband to join the expedition
of the Seven against Thebes. He lost his life and their son took her life in
revenge.
Creusa = the Corinthian princess whom Jason left Medea to marry. She
accepted a cloak and crown of gold as wedding gifts from Medea. They were
steeped in poison and she died in terrible agony.

31–32. Following the pattern of Catullus in poems 72, 75, and 76, the poet
presents himself as embittered by Cynthia's infidelity and incapable of
breaking off the relationship.
Iniuria: see Catullus 72.7–8.

33–34. None of the poet's usual pleasures has been able to distract him.
Campi = Campus Martius where outdoor sports were practiced.

35–42. The case of Antony is offered as exemplary of the destructive power of
love, while Augustus serves as the image of virtue.

35–36. Pudeat: this is the voice of traditional Roman morality, whereas the
normal elegiac stance is Tibullus's **non pudet** 1.1.73–74.
Quod aiunt indicates a proverbial saying.

37–38. Antony becomes emblematic of **turpis amor**, reversing the positive evaluation implicit in poem 2.15. **Ducem** = Antony. **Fremitu . . . inani . . . damnatis . . . militibus**: the cry of Antony's doomed soldiers is empty because it is unheeded by their leader who fled the scene of the battle when Cleopatra withdrew. He thus insured the destruction of his fleet.

39–40. Extremo . . . in orbe: Antony and Cleopatra fled to Egypt where they intended to continue their resistance.

41–42. Augustus is praised for his clemency toward the supporters of Antony after the latter's defeat. Yet, while Propertius grants Augustus *uirtus*, he defines it as the opposite of what it normally means in Roman ideology. As Gurval has recently observed, "The *virtus* and *gloria* come not from his courage in fighting or military success over the enemy but from the pardon that the victor bestowed on the vanquished" (1995: 184–85). For Propertius, Augustus can be said to embody *uirtus*, but only so long as it does not mean *uirtus*.

43–44. The poet turns his attention to the gifts offered by the Illyrian praetor. **Chyrsolithus** = "topaz."

45–46. Haec = object of the infinitive **ferre. In uanum** = "into the void."

47–48. The notion that Jupiter is deaf to the prayers of perjured lovers contradicts the common wisdom represented by Catullus 70 and Tibullus 1.4.21–26.

49–50. The fact that Cynthia has heard thunder and seen lightning hardly proves that Jupiter was punishing perjured lovers.

51–52. Pleiades . . . Orion: these constellations set in October and November, when storms were common.

53–54. Propertius's proof: Jupiter must be punishing lying girls when he thunders because he too has been deceived in love. The irony, of course, is that not only is Propertius's reasoning patently ludicrous, but also Jupiter was notorious for his faithlessness. See Catullus 68.140.

55–56. I have deleted the OCT's comma between **timeas** and **quotiens**.

2.34

In this poem, the poet traces his poetic genealogy and contrasts his project with that of Vergil, thus recapitulating the themes of the inversion of gender and genre norms and Propertius's problematic relation to Augustus. The occasion of the poem is the advances Lynceus has made upon Cynthia. This is best interpreted as a reference to the latter trying his hand at love elegy rather than actual amatory theft. It should be remembered that Cynthia from poem 1.1 on stands both for Propertius's poetry and its source of inspiration. Lynceus was a practitioner of tragic and philosophical poetry and his cross-border raid is the pretext for a lengthy reflection on the nature of elegiac poetry *per se*. This provides a fitting closure to Book 2 that 2.1 opened with a series of equally self-conscious reflections on the nature of elegy.

The first 24 lines have been treated by some editors as a separate poem. They deal exclusively with Lynceus's attempt to poach on Propertius's turf. The last 70 lines concern Propertius's reflections on the nature and history of love elegy. Most modern editions concur in printing 2.34 as a single poem.

1–2. The opening line has puzzled most commentators and some have resorted to emendation. The question is what does it mean to entrust your mistress's beauty to Love. But if we keep in mind the programmatic intent of the poem, Amor's status as the sponsoring deity of elegy (see 1.1.4), and the fact that *Amores* will be the title of Ovid's own collection of elegiac verse, then we can see this as a reference to Propertius's publication of his elegiac verse (see line 25 as well). This publication naturally attracted the attention of admirers and rivals such as Lynceus. Thus, Propertius says that Cynthia and the book that bears her name are the talk of the forum.

3–4. The self-subverting quality of the hexameter is to be savored.
Raro = adverb. **Non** goes with **raro**.

5–6. Ille deus = Amor. Love, as the origin of strife, makes elegy and its themes the condition necessary for the existence of epic. This view is made explicit in the next couplet's invocation of the traditions of the *Iliad* and the *Argonautica*. This is an argument Ovid will expand on in *Tristia* 2. There is a further irony in that Love in most ancient cosmogonies is presented as a force of attraction and hence of harmony rather than strife.

7–8. Hospes adulter = Paris.
Colchis = Medea. **Ignotum . . . uirum** = Jason.

9–10. Lynceus has never been convincingly identified. **Curam** = love, but also any source of anxiety. Hence, it applies equally well to elegy and its subject matter.
Nonne tuae tum cecidere manus: Lynceus has failed in his attempt.

11–12. These lines are more paradoxical than most commentators recognize. What would be the disgrace in which Lynceus would have to live if Cynthia were not so constant and true: the disgrace of betraying Propertius or of living in the same type of irregular relationship as the elegist? In what way is Cynthia faithful? That is not the picture in 2.16. Moreover, were we not just told that it was Lynceus whose strength failed, not Cynthia who rebuffed him?

Of course, the pose of the elegist is that of one who revels in disgrace (see 1.6.25–26). Lynceus is the practitioner of more respectable genres and has been caught poaching on Propertius's turf. Thus, Cynthia as elegy is faithful and true to Propertius. His disgrace is her honor. The poetry of adultery is faithful, even when Lynceus tries his hand.

13–14. Kill me if you must, only leave my mistress alone! **Mihi** = possessive dative with **pectus. Tantum . . . modo** = *tantummodo*.

15–16. We can share everything and you can rule me in all matters.

17–18. Te deprecor = "I beg that you abstain from."

Iovem: if he is unwilling to accept Jupiter as a rival, then he would certainly not accept Lynceus. Jupiter is associated with the serious genres of poetry, such as epic, which Lynceus normally practices.

19–20. Propertius is jealous of his own shadow.

21–22. I will forgive you, if your comments were made because of too much neat wine (**multo . . . mero**). Note that the crime with which Propertius charges Lynceus concerns **uerba**, not *res*.

23–24. Lynceus's air of old Roman severity does not fool Propertius. He charges *grauitas* with being a cover for hypocrisy.

25–26. The change of tone is abrupt, but not inexplicable. Propertius rejoices if Lynceus recognizes Propertius's gods and becomes a sincere convert to the elegiac genre under the master's tutelage. This demonstrates the superiority of elegy to its rivals. The next section, which begins the genealogy of the elegiac genre, serves as Lynceus's initiation into the mysteries of erotic verse.

Amores applies equally well to Propertius's love and his love poetry, but the remainder of the poem clearly favors a literary reading.

27–28. In love, the reading of philosophy will be of no value. **Rerum . . . uias** refers to serious didactic poetry such as Lucretius's *De rerum natura*.

29–30. Erecthei is a speculative reconstruction that has not won universal assent. If it is accepted, it would mean "Athenian" and would therefore presumably refer to tragedy, though some believe that, in combination with **lecta**, it refers to the official recitations of Homer regularly held in the city. It may be deliberately vague.

Vester . . . senex: the old man in love is a stock figure in Roman comedy, a genre related to elegy [6, 24]. Lynceus is portrayed as wrinkled (line 23).

31–32. Philitas was a Hellenistic elegist (340 to *c.*300 BCE). He wrote learned poetry, often on erotic themes. Only fragments of his work survive.

Somnia Callimachi: this is a reference to a famous passage in the prologue to Callimachus's *Aitia* [28–30] in which the narrator receives his poetic initiation from the Muses.

Non inflati refers to Callimachus's famous valuing of brevity and refinement over the bombast typical of epic.

33–34. Here begins a list of topics that Lynceus may no longer treat. All are common in mythological epic. **Licet** = "although."

Aetoli . . . Acheloi: the river Achelous was the largest in Greece. It formed one of the borders of Aetolia. Callimachus in the prologue to the *Aitia* uses the image of the river Euphrates to signify epic bombast as opposed to the pure springs of his inspiration [29].

Magno fractus amore liquor: an allusion to the battle between Hercules and Achelous for the love of Deianira in which the river god lost one of his horns. **Fractus** is also a euphemism for having experienced orgasm, i.e. "spent."

35–36. The Meander is a river in Phrygia that features in the *Iliad*.

37–38. This couplet contains allusions to events connected with the Seven against Thebes, a common topic of epic invention. **Vocalis Arion**: a wondrous horse given to Adrastus (**Adrasti**), king of Argos, who had the gift of speech. **Tristis ad Archemori funera uictor equus**: Archemorus was a child who died during a visit of the Seven to Nemea on the way to Thebes. The Nemean games were established in his honor. Arion was a *uictor* in these first games, though still grieving (**tristis**) over the boy's death.

39–40. Amphiareae as normally scanned ($-\smile\smile--$) is metrically impossible after **non**, hence the OCT prints this line in daggers. All the modern editions agree that the reference to Amphiareus whose chariot was swallowed up by a chasm in the defeat of the Seven against Thebes is correct. The most popular solutions are either assuming a variant scansion for the word or a slight emendation (such as *num* for **non**). No solution has gained wide favor.

Capanei: Capaneus was hit with a thunderbolt from Jupiter as he tried to scale the walls of Thebes.

Grata = predicative.

41–42. The next three couplets make explicit the implicit message of the preceding four: if Lynceus wishes to practice erotic elegy he must give up epic and tragedy. **Coturno:** the buskin or thick-soled boot worn by tragic actors.

Mollis ... choros = soft measures, hence elegiac verse. The elegist is characterized by his *mollitia* [7, 9, 23, 27].

43–44. Angusto ... torno = narrow lathe. See 2.1.39–40 and 45–46.

Ignis = accusative plural. Fire is a common symbol of erotic passion, most easily seen in the various meanings of the word *ardor*.

On **durus** for epic [9], see the introductory note to 2.1.

45–46. Antimachus (active *c.*400 BCE) of Colophon [24–25] wrote an epic on the Seven against Thebes.

Recta puella: the literal meaning is "possessed of a good figure," but the connotation of "proper" or "correct" provides an added irony.

47–48. Oxen were broken to the plough by being tied by the horns to rafters. On images of taming and breaking in elegy, see 1.1.9–10 and 15–16 and Catullus 68.118.

49–50. Per te = by yourself. On the paradox of *durus amor*, see the introductory note to 2.1.

A nobis: Propertius now officially assumes the role of *praeceptor amoris* [7, 58]. The ablative of agent, instead of the more normal dative with the passive periphrastic construction, is due to metrical considerations.

51–52. Harum = *puellarum*. They do not read didactic poetry. See line 28.

Luna laboret: a phrase for the eclipse of the moon found in Cicero, Pliny, and others. **Fraternis ... equis:** causal ablative. Luna's brother is Apollo in his role as god of the sun. Luna is an aspect of Diana.

53–54. Girls do not care about the sort of metaphysical questions debated by the Epicureans and others.

Restabimus undas: the OCT prints the unintelligible manuscript reading, *restabit erumpnas*, with daggers. I have adopted Wassenberg's commonly accepted conjecture.

Consulto = with a purpose.

55–56. *Puellae* do not care about the traditional marks of status in Roman society: wealth and honored ancestors. Here Propertius is clearly contradicting himself, since in 2.16 wealth is one Cynthia's chief preoccupations. Indeed, as has already been noted, for the entire genre the *diues amator* is the elegist's chief antagonist. The purpose of the present passage is to contrast the figure of the elegist with that of the traditional images of Roman prestige. These traditional values, in turn, are associated with the "serious" genres of tragedy, epic, and didactic poetry, all of which Lynceus must abandon if he is to be successful in love.

Relicta est implies that the family fortune was once larger and that it suffered diminution in the proscriptions that took place during the civil wars, perhaps as a result of the role his family played in the events at Perusia [23, 40, 48–51, 53]. As an Umbrian, it is not surprising that none of Propertius's family members had celebrated a triumph (**nullus . . . triumphus**). He, like all the major poets of the period, was a *nouus homo*, a provincial without consular ancestors.

57–58. Propertius reigns over the *puellae* at dinner parties because his verse is recited there. **Ingenio:** see 2.1.3–4.

Quo tibi nunc eleuor = "for which I am now made light of by you."

59–60. Me iuuet hesternis positum languere corollis = "let it be my pleasure to lie exhausted amidst yesterday garlands." The poet rejects *negotium*, the foundation of traditional *uirtus*, in favor of an idleness that produces exhaustion and ultimately impotence. See *languidus* in 1.3.38.

61–80. This section is given over to an examination of Vergil's career. Vergil had started as a poet of love, but was now writing the *Aeneid*. Poem 2.1's picture of Maecenas urging Propertius to take up epic indicates that there were expectations that Propertius's career might follow a similar track. Propertius tactfully indicates that he thinks Vergil has made a mistake.

61–62. The juxtaposition of this couplet's evocation of Actium with the previous couplet's portrait of the remains of the prior evening's party directly recalls the end of poem 2.15 and its statement that if everyone pursued love and drink the waters off Actium would not be grinding the bones of so many Romans. The whole couplet is a reference to Vergil's depiction of the battle of Actium on the shield of Aeneas in *Aeneid* 8.671–728.

63–64. A reference to the plan for the *Aeneid*. See also 2.1.41–42.

65–66. This couplet appears to be a compliment, but in light of the preceding part of the poem it is hard to take at face value. **Maius** can be translated as either "greater" or "larger," and the latter translation would not be a compliment from the perspective of Callimachean aesthetics. See Ezra Pound's famously witty mistranslation:

> Make way, ye Roman authors
>   clear the street, O ye Greeks,
> For a much larger Iliad is in the course of construction.

67–68. Propertius now reviews Vergil's previous career in chronological order, starting with the *Eclogues*, 39–38 BCE, his most erotic work, and hence the closest to elegy. The details of Propertius's allusions are sometimes less than completely accurate. For example, none of the *Eclogues* is set in a pine grove (**pineta**).

Galaesi: a river in the region around Tarentum. Although not mentioned by Vergil in the *Eclogues*, it was celebrated for its sheep and hence was an appropriate pastoral setting.

Thyrsin et . . . Daphnin: Two shepherds featured in *Eclogue* 7.

Attritis . . . harundinibus: Daphnis's panpipes, worn from use, appear in *Eclogue* 5.

69–70. The ten apples (**mala**) and the kid (**haedus**) are love offerings sent to seduce (**corrumpere**) girls. In *Eclogue* 3, ten apples are sent to a boy, but in Vergil's' Greek model, Theocritus, they are sent to a girl.

Vtque: Vergil is cast in the elegiac role of *praeceptor amoris*.

Impressis . . . ab uberibus: the kid is unweaned.

71–72. Cynthia would be impressed by no such humble (**uilis**) gifts. Note the contradiction with line 55. **Huic** = this woman of mine, i.e., Cynthia. **Ingratae** = predicative.

Tityrus = the speaker in *Eclogue* 1, often taken to represent Vergil himself.

73–74. Felix seems an odd epithet for Corydon whose advances are rebuffed by Alexis in *Eclogue* 2, although he resolves by the poem's end to be happy in his pastoral simplicity, even if his desire remains unsatisfied. The pentameter is almost a direct quotation of the opening of *Eclogue* 2.

75–76. This couplet acknowledges that, although Vergil no longer writes pastoral poetry, his *Eclogues* are still read and praised. **Ille's** antecedent is Corydon, but the latter is treated as a mask for Vergil.

77–78. Tu canis recalls line 67 and indicates we are moving from the *Eclogues* to the *Georgics*, 29 BCE. Only two couplets are devoted to this didactic poem on farming, which has less in common with Propertian elegy.

Ascraei = Hesiod of Ascra (seventh century BCE) whose *Works and Days* constituted the *Georgics'* earliest poetic precedent.

79–80. Testudine = a lyre. **Cynthius** = Apollo.

81–82. After discussing the alternative genres of tragedy, epic, and didactic poetry in general, and the example of Vergil, arguably the greatest poet of the day, Propertius argues in the remainder of the poem for the legitimacy of elegy by establishing its genealogy.

Haec: understand *carmina*, hence elegy.

83–84. A difficult couplet: "Nor here with less inspiration does the melodious swan yield to the rude song of the goose, although he may have a smaller mouth," i.e., he may sing songs of lesser length and smaller scope. This is a reassertion of the Callimachean doctrine of preferring the small and the refined to the large and the bombastic.

85–86. Varro of Atax (b. 82 BCE) is offered as a counter-example to Vergil. His career took the opposite path. First he translated Apollonius's *Argonautica*, then turned his attention to erotic verse in the *Leucadia*. None of this latter work survives, and only fragments of his earlier verse have come down to us.

87–88. On Catullus, see the introduction [3, 5, 7, 10–11, 27, 30–39]. **Quis** = ablative plural.

89–90. Calvus (b. 82 BCE) was a fellow neoteric poet and friend of Catullus [35]. He wrote a famous elegy on the death of his beloved, Quintilia. **Docti** refers to literary knowledge and was a term of approbation in neoteric circles.

91–92. Gallus (70–26 BCE) is generally credited with being the first of the elegists proper [5, 13, 50].
Formosa . . . Lycoride = causal ablative.

93–94. Propertius claims poetic immortality if his praises of Cynthia will be ranked among those of his predecessors for their beloveds.
I have adopted the widely accepted **uiuet** for the OCT's *etiam*. Otherwise the verse is missing a verb.

3.4

This is the first of a pair of poems that engages Propertius's ambivalent and conflicted relationship with Augustus. In the first, Caesar is portrayed as a conquering god (*deus*) who will be celebrated in a traditional Roman triumph upon his return. This poem can be read as straightforward encomiastic verse of the kind that will become increasingly common under the empire. Yet, there are many ironic undercurrents lying beneath the surface that make it difficult to accept such a one-dimensional interpretation, not the least of which is the final image of Propertius watching the triumph while resting his head in Cynthia's lap. Still, poem 3.5 presents the biggest obstacle to such simplistic readings. Its opening line clearly parodies the beginning of 3.4. Only this time, *Amor* is the god to be celebrated as the patron of peace. The transmutation of *arma* to *Amor* and the declaration of the poet's loyalty to peace (*pacem*) necessarily make us revisit our understanding of 3.4's portrait of Caesar as the god of war.

The occasion of 3.4 is Propertius's anticipation of Augustus's long-awaited Parthian campaign. Crassus, a member of the first triumvirate with Julius Caesar and Pompey, had undertaken a campaign against the Parthian empire in 55 BCE that ended in disaster at the battle of Carrhae (53 BCE) where the expedition was wiped out and its legionary standards lost. This defeat was a source of humiliation in Rome, and agitation for a new expedition to recapture the lost standards began almost immediately. In the end, however, it never took place, and Augustus negotiated the return of the lost standards in 20 BCE.

1–2. This couplet is interesting and problematic on several levels. **Arma deus Caesar** is a parody of the opening lines of the *Aeneid*, *arma uirumque cano*. That the *uir* in Vergil was the mythological ancestor of Augustus, a fact that Propertius will point to later in this poem, makes the substitution of **deus** both ironic and appropriate.

Deus: it is unclear whether the intent of deifying Caesar is encomiastic. Neither Horace nor Vergil ever goes that far, and Augustus forbade his being worshipped at Rome, although he allowed a cult of his *genius*.

Dites . . . Indos: the emphasis on riches recalls the elegiac truism that the true motivation for war is greed.

3–4. The wages of warfare are great. This is part of elegy's indictment. Yet, the sentiment is traditional in encomiastic poetry as well. **Viri** = vocative.

Tua = Caesar's.

5–6. **Sera sed . . . ueniet** = *sera veniet, sed ueniet*.

Virgis = the rods bound in the *fasces*, traditional symbol of Roman authority.

Partha tropaea = trophies won from the Parthians, as opposed to those taken by the Parthians from Crassus.

7–8. The pentameter is difficult and I have found no two commentators who agree on its interpretation, although the text itself seems sound. I have adopted Fedeli's (1985) reading, which takes **armigeri** as vocative and **equi** as genitive: "Warriors, bring back the accustomed gift of the horse." The Parthians were renowned for their horses and horsemanship.

9–10. **Omina fausta cano**: Propertius adopts the pose of the traditional prophet or *uates* that was common in the poetry of the period.

Piate: includes the idea of both fulfilling one's duty and expiating a wrong.

Consulite = "take care of, have regard for."

11–12. The Vestals were not only the keepers of the sacred hearth fire of Rome, but as the guardians of the phallic deity, *Fascinus*, were directly tied to triumphing Roman generals, who wore an amulet in the shape of the god.

13–14. Axis = accusative plural, refers to the axles of Caesar's triumphal chariot weighted with the spoils of conquest. See 2.1.31–34.

The pentameter is linked by asyndeton (the lack of an expected conjunction) to the hexameter. **Resistere** = "to stop." **Ad ... plausus** = accusative of purpose.

15–16. The evocation of the Augustan triumph is abruptly undercut by the irreverent image of Propertius watching propped in Cynthia's lap.

Titulis oppida capta legam: a reference to the depictions of captured cities carried in the triumphal procession.

17–18. There would also be depictions of the battles themselves. The Parthians were famed for their mounted archers.

Subter ... arma: the captured enemy leaders are seated at the foot of a trophy carried in the procession – a pillar mounted with captured arms and armor.

19–20. *Venus genetrix* was claimed as the ancestor of the *gens Julia*. Augustus, therefore, as the adopted son and nephew of the deified Julius Caesar would be the offspring (**prolem**) of Venus and descendant of Aeneas. This couplet recalls the opening allusion to the *Aeneid*. Compare Ovid *Amores* 1.2.51–52, where the satirical implications are clearer. See also 2.1.41–42.

21–22. This couplet can be read as a statement of traditional Roman values: "Let the prizes goes to those who earn them, for the rest of us there is nothing to do but express our admiration." This is an ideological truism: those who possess wealth and power deserve it. It does not challenge the traditional social order and the system of rewards reserved for *otium* and *negotium* but reaffirms them. Then why say it? The one question the traditional position cannot answer is why someone would choose not to play the game. That someone is the elegist.

On **praeda** in elegy, see Tibullus 1.2.-65–66, 2.3.35–50, Propertius 2.1.55–56, 2.16.1–2, and Ovid *Amores* 1.2. 19–20 and 29–30, 1.3.1.

Sacra ... Via = the road down which triumphal processions progressed.

3.5

This poem is 3.4's companion and the opening lines answer it point for point. The end of the poem clearly recalls the contemplated Parthian expedition that was the occasion for 3.4. Poem 3.5 is also important because it looks forward to the possibility of a poetic career for Propertius after Cynthia. It will be remembered that Cynthia is bid farewell at the end of Book 3 [54] and that Book 4 is substantially different in tone and subject matter than its three predecessors [55–56]. It should also be noted that many of the topics Propertius contemplates taking up in the last half of 3.5 are the ones he rejected at the end of 2.34. Thus, Propertius's real interest in natural philosophy, astronomy, and speculative metaphysics should be taken with a grain of salt.

1–2. The opening clearly recalls that of 3.4.1. The invocation of the *militia amoris* motif in the pentameter's description of the poet's hard battles (**proelia dura**) with his girl translates 3.4's epic vocabulary into the language of elegy. **Proelia dura** contains a sexual *double-entendre*.

3–4. In this couplet, the opposition between love and war in lines 1–2 is treated as analogous to that between greed and contentment.

Gemma diuite recalls **gemmiferi** in 3.4.2 and refers to a bejeweled drinking cup or one cut from semiprecious stone.

5–6. See Tibullus 1.1.1–2. **Iugis** = teams of oxen.

Aera . . . Corinthe, tua: Corinth was famous for its bronze. Corinthian bronze first became common after the sack of the city by the Romans in 146 BCE. Hence, **clade** refers not only to the traditional association of wealth and *praeda* with soldiery but also to the sack of the city.

7–8. Greed is pictured as a form of original sin inherent in our fashioning by Prometheus. Propertius alludes to the myth that human beings were made out of clay by Prometheus.

I have followed the majority of modern editors and kept the manuscript reading **caute** instead of the OCT's *cauti*. **Parum** = "too little" and modifies **caute**.

9–10. The sentiment is Platonic in its exaltation of mind over body and sorts very oddly with the elegiac emphasis on pleasure.

Non uidit = "he did not pay attention to."

In arte = "in his work."

11–12. This is a brilliant passage. The first clause, **nunc maris in tantum uento iactamur**, describes metaphorically the result of Prometheus's shoddy craftsmanship. The way (**uia**) of our soul is not straight (**recta**) and, as a result (**nunc**), we are tossed about by the wind on a sea of passion. In the second clause, **et hostem quaerimus**, that same sea becomes literal as we cross it seeking enemies due to our greed. The third clause, **atque armis nectimus arma noua**, gives the upshot of this behavior: an endless series of wars as one set of captured arms is lashed to the next. Thus, the deformation of our souls produces greed, which forces us to seek new sources of plunder and new enemies. The glance back to poem 3.4 is clear, but the reader should note that Propertius says the fault is inherent in all of us. The elegist's desire is as insatiable as Caesar's.

13–14. Riches are of no value because rich and poor alike face death.

Vehere = future passive.

15–16. The lack of differentiation between victors and vanquished in the underworld tells against the lasting nature of both military glory and infamy.

Mario: Gaius Marius, consul in 107, 104, 103, 102, 101, 100, and 86 BCE, was a noted military commander [20–21, 34].

Iugurtha: king of Numidia, ultimately captured through the intrigue of Marius's lieutenant and later antagonist, Sulla.

17–18. Croesus, king of Lydia, was proverbial for his wealth. **Irus** was a beggar from Ithaca (**Dulichio**) in the *Odyssey*.

Optima mors Parcae quae uenit acta die: "best is the death which comes on the day appointed by fate." This line is vexed. The problem is **Parcae.** The OCT prints the reading of the best manuscripts, *parca*, in daggers. Lachmann (1973) notes that *parca dies* is nonsense in Latin. *Parcae dies*, however, gives excellent sense, is easily explained, and is paralleled in *Aeneid* 12.149. The issue that has impeded its acceptance is one of interpretation: are not all deaths those that come on the day of fate? But if that is the case then what is the point of the distinction Propertius is drawing between the life (and death) of the lover and the soldier? Such a question, however, assumes that Propertius's goal is logical consistency and that the purpose of the passage is to present a distinction between two opposed styles of life, the Augustan and the elegiac. Yet, as numerous commentators have noted, the essence of Propertian style is just the opposite: it does not present the reader with unproblematic rhetorical demonstrations, but sharp juxtapositions, unstated transitions, and ironic reversals.

Moreover, this tidying up of the rhetorical distinctions between the Augustan and the elegiac modes of life is in direct contradiction with thrust of the passage itself, which states that all such categories are invalid in the realm of the dead, **uictor cum uictis pariter miscebitur umbris.** The fact that no matter when or how one dies it is always on the day appointed by fate does not render the passage meaningless, but proves its point. Thus, on the one hand, the poet's message is certainly that the pursuit of wealth is to be shunned since "you can't take it with you." However, on the other, since there are no distinctions in the underworld, then the lover and the soldier, the poor man and the rich man are counted the same.

19–20. Propertius has chosen his mode of life based on what gives him pleasure.

Helicona: a mountain in south-west Boeotia, sacred to the Muses.

21–22. Compare 2.15.41–54 and 2.34.59–60. **Lyaeo** = Bacchus.

23–24. Here for the first time Propertius envisages a poetic future beyond love elegy. We should not take overly seriously the laundry list of possible topics that follows, but it is generally believed that the first five poems of Book 3 were meant to be a programmatic introduction for the book as a whole. As such, they would have been composed after the rest of the book was complete. One way of viewing this list is as a preview of the change of subject matter and tone found in Book 4 [55–56].

25–26. Quis deus hanc mundi temperet arte domum: "who is the god who presides with skill over the household of the world."

27–28. Coactis cornibus = "with it horns having been drawn together," a reference to the moon's waning.

29–30. Vnde = "for what reason." **Superant** = intransitive and indicative instead of the more usual subjunctive with indirect question.

In nubes unde perennis aqua: understand *sit*.

31–32. Sit = deliberative subjunctive. **Subruat** = "batters down."

Bibit: the rainbow was thought to draw up water that came back down as rain.

33–34. Pindi: a mountain chain in Greece. The **Perrhaebi** were a people who dwelled in the area.

Atratis . . . equis: a solar eclipse.

35–36. Serus . . . uersare: understand *est*. The constellation **Bootes** was thought to drive a wagon. Homer calls it "late-setting" because it is visible in the sky throughout the year, going below the horizon only early in the evening near the winter solstice.

Spisso . . . igne: the stars of the Pleiades are so close together that they are almost indistinguishable from one another.

39–40. The next eight lines are concerned with the underworld and the existence of an afterlife, so that the second half of the poem ends with the same topic explored in the first. Compare lines 13–18.

Tormenta gigantum: for the Giants' assault on heaven, see 2.1.19–20. They were punished in the underworld with a variety of torments.

Tisiphone = one of the Furies.

41–42. Understand *sint*. **Alcmaeoniae furiae**: Alcmaeon killed his mother, Eriphyla, to avenge his father, Amphiarus, and was pursued by Furies like Orestes. See 2.34.39–40.

Ieiunia Phinei: Phineus blinded his children and was thereafter kept from eating by Harpies.

Rota = Ixion's punishment for attempting to rape Juno.

Scopulus = poetic license for the boulder endlessly rolled by Sisyphus.

Sitis inter aquas = the punishment of Tantalus. See Tibullus 1.4.63–64 and Propertius 2.1.65–66.

43–44. **Tityo iugera pauca**: understand *sint*. Tityus was one of the Giants. For his attempted rape of Latona he was slain and condemned to be stretched across nine acres in the underworld where a vulture fed on his ever-regenerating liver.

45–46. Do the horrors described above exist in the underworld or are the Epicureans right and the afterlife is but a **fabula**?

47–48. **Exitus** = "issue, remainder." The pentameter looks back to 3.4 and the Parthian campaign.

3.11

Propertius in response to a charge of effeminacy justifies his submission to a woman by citing Antony's to Cleopatra. This poem recalls both 2.15 and 2.16 and their evocations of the battle of Actium. Poem 3.11 is particularly symptomatic of the kind of ideological problems presented by Book 3. The poem closes by celebrating Augustus's power as equal, if not superior, to Jupiter's own (lines 65–66). The statement is problematic. On one level, it is certainly laudatory of Augustus. On another, it borders on sacrilege by exalting the *princeps* above the father of the gods, a position that sorts ill with his preferred image as the restorer of traditional piety. Propertius goes well beyond the more nuanced position staked out by Horace:

> Caelo tonantem credidimus Iovem
> regnare; praesens diuus habebitur
> Augustus adiectis Britannis
> imperio grauibusque Persis

We trust that thundering Jupiter reigns in heaven; Augustus will be considered godlike in the here and now by the conquered Britains and through his power over the dread Persians. (*Odes* 3.5.1–4)

In this closing poem of the Roman Odes, Augustus is a god only to those barbarians at the far edges of the known world who are about to be subjected to Roman *imperium*. In Rome, he is merely the first citizen. His subsequent deification is alluded to by Horace, but his status in this world is clearly that of a man.

The extremity of the Propertian position is deliberately provocative. Is it a compliment or an insult? The question becomes more difficult to answer the closer we look at the poem itself. Jupiter, who is compared to Augustus at the end of 3.11, is earlier in the poem portrayed as one who, like Propertius, disgraces himself and his household through submission to a woman (3.11.27–28). Jupiter like Propertius functions as an analogue to Antony. The poem's mention of Pompey's death on the shores of Egypt not only calls to mind the origins of the civil wars but also reminds the reader of Julius Caesar's submission to Cleopatra (lines 33–38). This last association is especially important because the deification of Augustus's uncle and adoptive father is what established the ground for the *princeps*'s own divine status.

1–2. Why do you wonder at my being a *seruus amoris*?

3–4. Ignauus = inactive and hence effeminate.

5–6. Many editors think the hexameter corrupt, but the sense is clear. As the soldier and sailor knows the dangers of their mode of life, so does the lover.

9–10. The rest of the poem is devoted to mythological and historical examples of heroes and gods subjected to women, culminating in the ultimate figure of female domination in Augustan propaganda, Cleopatra. The poem ends with a celebration of Augustus's virtues as demonstrated in his saving Rome from this danger. The irony, of course, is that all this is part of a poem that is supposed to defend, or at least offer an apology for, Propertius's choice of a lifestyle that is analogous to that of Antony's subjection to Cleopatra. The triumvir's name, however, is never mentioned in the poem.

The assumed subject of this and the following couplet is Jason. **Colchis** = Medea. Jason, with her aid, yoked the fire-breathing bulls (**flagrantis . . . tauros**) and sowed the dragon's teeth from which fully armed soldiers sprang to fight each other (**armigera proelia**).

11–12. Custodis . . . Serpentis = the dragon guarding the golden fleece (**aurea lana**).
Aesonias . . . Domos = the household of Jason's father, Aeson.

13–14. Penthesilea: queen of the Amazons, who were associated with the region around the sea of Azov (**Maeotis**) in central Asia. She fought with the Trojans against the Greeks.

15–16. Achilles was overcome by Penthesilea's beauty when, after slaying her, he stripped (**nudauit**) off her helmet. **Nudauit** also carries more erotic connotations.

17–18. Omphale: queen of Lydia. Hercules served as her literal *seruus amoris*, dressing as a woman and spinning with her maidservants. He thus became a model of the hero as elegist. Propertius treats this theme more fully in poem 4.9. Antony, it should be remembered, claimed descent from Hercules.

Gygaeo tincta puella lacu: Gyges's lake is associated with the gold for which the Lydian kingdom was famous, and Omphale's beauty is emphasized by her being said to have bathed in it.

19–20. Columnas: the straits of Gibraltar were commonly known as the pillars of Hercules. They were erected to celebrate the hero's having rid the world of monsters and brigands. The irony of the subjection of this most manly of heroes to a woman is underlined by the juxtaposition of **dura . . . manu** with **mollia pensa** [7, 9, 23, 27]. See 3.5.1–2.

21–22. Semiramis: legendary founder and queen of Babylon. **Vt . . . Tolleret** = a result clause. **Cocto** = brick. Note that she receives six couplets as opposed to four apiece for the preceding mythological figures. This signals both the end of the catalog and Semiramis's status as an avatar of Cleopatra, another powerful female monarch. Such figures were both fascinating and fearful to traditional Roman ideology. Witness Dido in the *Aeneid*.

23–24. The walls of Babylon were so large that two chariots could be driven on top of them in opposite directions without ever touching. **Possent** must be taken with both **mitti** and **stringere**. It is dependent on the **ut** in the previous couplet.

25–26. Medium, quam condidit, arcis: "through the middle of the city she founded."

Bactra = capital city of Bactria, modern Afghanistan.

27–28. Why should I cite other examples of gods and heroes guilty of subservience to a woman? Jupiter disgraces himself and his family in the same way.

29–30. Quid = "what about?"

Nostris opprobria uexerit armis: the question is why would Cleopatra bring shame to Roman arms? Is this a reference to the fact that Antony's troops were Roman as well, although Augustus in his propaganda always portrayed Actium as a battle against foreign forces of the effeminate East? Was it an insult to Roman arms to have to condescend to engage such a foe?

211

Was the battle itself a source of shame? All are possible readings and all resonate with other portions of the poem and the Propertian corpus as a whole.

Trita: the word has strong sexual connotations. Cleopatra is portrayed as the sexual object of her servants (**famulos**), an inversion of normal power relations that would have proven her perversity in Roman eyes. This, however, is the essence of elegiac *seruitium amoris*.

31–32. Propertius hews close to the Augustan line in portraying the subjection of Rome as the wedding gift Cleopatra demanded from the unnamed Antony.

33–34. This couplet makes reference to the fighting around **Alexandria** during not only Augustus's campaigns, but also Julius Caesar's Alexandrian war (48 BCE) and Pompey's assassination, mentioned in the following couplet. Memphis was not the scene of actual fighting but a traditional residence for the Egyptian monarchy.

35–36. In 48 BCE, after his defeat at the battle of Pharsalus by Julius Caesar, Pompey fled to Egypt where he was murdered as he tried to reach shore in a small boat. His headless corpse was left on the beach (**harena**). The pentameter notes that the shame of Pompey's murder will never be erased and reminds us vividly of the horrors of the civil wars [21–23, 51–53].

Tris ... triumphos: Pompey's three triumphs were celebrated over Numidia (80 BCE), Spain (71 BCE), and Mithridates (61 BCE).

37–38. Phlegraeo ... campo: the Phlegraean plain was the scene of the battle between the gods and the Giants (see 2.1.19–20 and 39–40, and 3.5.39–40). It was traditionally located in one of two places, in Puteoli just outside of Naples and in Thessaly near the site of the battle of Pharsalus. Both were locations where Pompey could have met an honorable death. In 50 BCE, Pompey was seriously ill in Naples, while death at Pharsalus would have been preferable to the end he received. Indeed, as the pentameter makes clear, surrender would have been better. The association of the gods and Giants with Pharsalus is a deft poetic touch.

Socero: Caesar's daughter Julia became Pompey's wife in 59 BCE. Politics were the primary motivation for aristocratic marriages of the first century BCE. Her death in 54 BCE was one of the reasons for the collapse of the first triumvirate.

Datura eras: periphrasis for dedisses.

39–40. The next four couplets evoke the horror of Roman subjection to the effeminate East. The association of gendered traits with ethnicity is typical of Roman ideology and Augustan propaganda.

Meretrix regina: a deliberate oxymoron that on one level describes the perversity of Cleopatra to Roman eyes but on another recalls that Cynthia is portrayed as a *meretrix*. Indeed, it is the subjection of Roman *uirtus* to feminine domination that the passage condemns, but that the poem as a whole seeks to justify.

Canopi: a resort in Egypt famous for its license.

Vna Philippeo sanguine adusta nota: in apposition to the hexameter. Both lines modify the subject of the following couplet. "She alone from the blood of Philip was burned by this brand." The Ptolemies claimed descent from Philip of Macedon, father of Alexander the Great.

41–42. Ausa: understand *est*. *All the subsequent infinitives depend on this verb.*

Latrantem . . . Anubim: the dogheaded Egyptian god.

43–44. Crepitanti . . . sistro = a rattle used in the worship of Isis.

Baridos = Greek genitive. The *baris* was a barge propelled by poles (**contis**).

Rostra Liburna: the swift and maneuverable galleys used by Octavian's admiral, Agrippa, to defeat Antony and Cleopatra's larger fleet at Actium.

45–46. Foedaque Tarpeio conopia tendere saxo: the Tarpeian rock on the Capitoline hill was the heart of Rome. It was from this site that murderers and traitors were hurled. Its being covered with a thin gauze of Egyptian mosquito netting (**conopia**) is the perfect image for Rome's subjection to softer, more effeminate forces.

Arma Mari: the trophies won from Jugurtha by Marius were set up on the Capitoline hill. See 3.5.15–16.

47–48. What would be the value of having thrown off the yoke of the Etruscan kings and founded the republic if Rome had then yielded to a woman? Note how the unusual enjambment into the next couplet with **si mulier patienda fuit** marks submission to a woman as doubly perverse.

Tarquinii . . . nomine quem simili uita superba notat: the last of the Etruscan kings, Tarquinius Superbus. His son's rape of Lucretia led to the expulsion of the Etruscan monarchy by the Roman nobility. Note again the association of sexual and political domination in this poem.

49–50. Si mulier patienda fuit: for a man to be penetrated sexually by another man was referred to as *pati muliebria*. To suffer such an act entailed an essential loss of manhood (*uirtus*) in Roman sexual ideology. To suffer such degradation at the hands of a woman was emasculation to the second power. The juxtaposition of this clause with the hailing of the Augustan triumph is a powerful example of the profound interrelation between the political and the sexual in Rome.

Longum . . . Diem = "long life."

51–52. Cleopatra is now the subject. **Accepere ... manus** is, of course, figurative since Cleopatra committed suicide rather than be captured by Augustus.

53–54. This couplet refers to an image of Cleopatra's death carried in Augustus's triumph.

Occultum ... soporis iter is the subject of **trahere**, a wonderfully evocative line.

55–56. "I was not to be feared by you, Rome, when you had so great a citizen as this." Augustus's preferred title was *princeps*, "first citizen." He studiously avoided the trappings of monarchy.

Lingua sepulta mero: Augustan propaganda consistently portrayed Cleopatra as besotted with wine. But see 2.15.41–44.

57–58. How can I be blamed for my submission to Cynthia when Rome itself feared the threats of a woman? The poet recurs to his opening theme. The next four couplets can be interpreted two ways. (1) Where has Rome's past glory gone, if today Cleopatra strikes fear in its heart? In other words, how did Rome become nothing but a bunch of elegists? (2) What is Rome's past glory in comparison to Augustus's present excellence? The contradiction between the praises of Augustus and justification of elegiac *mollitia* [9, 23, 27] is found throughout the poem.

67–68. The majority of modern commentators have seen the final lines of this poem as problematic. Many have resorted to wholesale emendation and transposition to produce a smoother reading and more logical text. While I remain unconvinced of the absolute necessity of such alterations, the OCT adopts a moderate course accepting only Passerat's transposition of lines 67–68. This yields good sense and provides a smoother transition to the praises of Augustus that occupy the end of the poem. The question is whether smoothness and logical consistency are essential elements of Propertius's poetics.

Nunc ubi: Rome's past victories fade before the thought of having feared a woman.

Scipiadae classes: the fleet by which Scipio Africanus's army was transported to Africa for his final defeat of Hannibal in the Second Punic War (205 BCE).

Signa Camilli: Camillus defeated the Gauls in 387 BCE. The precise reference, however, remains obscure since his standards are not mentioned in surviving accounts.

Bospore, capta: understand *signa* again. The reference is to Pompey's defeat of Mithridates and the capture of his standards (65 BCE).

59–60. The OCT puts daggers around **monumenta**, "statues, trophies," because of its repetition in line 61, but this is hardly the sole such instance in Propertius.

Syphacis = Syphax, king of Numidia and ally of Hannibal.

Pyrrhi: Pyrrhus, king of Epirus, led an unsuccessful expedition to assist Tarentum against Rome (280–75 BCE).

61–62. Curtius: M. Curtius rode a horse into a chasm that opened in the forum in response to a prophecy that this would insure the future of Rome.

Decius: P. Decius, a father (340 BCE) and son (295 BCE) who each saved Rome by riding a horse headlong into enemy lines.

63–64. Coclitis: Horatius Cocles saved Rome from the Etruscans by defending the approach to the bridge over the Tiber while it was torn down behind him. He swam to safety.

M. Valerius Corvinus received his **cognomen** from a crow (*coruus*) that perched on his helmet as he killed a Gaul in single combat.

65–66. On the excessive, almost sacrilegious, nature of the pentameter, see the introductory note to this poem.

69–70. Leucadius ... Apollo: a reference to Apollo's shrine on the island near Actium. Leucas was associated with horrific deaths and human sacrifice in ancient literature. Propertius's choice of this as a memorial to the battle of Actium recalls the gruesome images of 2.15.43–44 and 2.16.37–38.

71–72. The final couplet is deliberately ambiguous as to whether Caesar should be remembered as the sailors' savior or bane.

4.4

An aitiological poem in the manner of Callimachus, this selection introduces the different nature of Book 4 while maintaining the essentially amatory focus {54}. Tarpeia, the daughter of Septimius Tarpeius, the commander of the Roman garrison when the city was attacked by the Sabine Tatius, was a Vestal virgin who, in the story told by Livy (1.11.6), betrayed the city because she coveted the gold bracelets the Sabines wore on their left arms. Her reward was to be buried beneath the Sabines' shields. In Propertius 4.4, although still a Vestal, she becomes a double of the figure of the elegiac lover, betraying the city for love not greed. As such, there has been much debate about how seriously the condemnation of her at the poem's end should be taken.

Nonetheless, what seems clear is that Propertius has managed the difficult feat of combining three separate genres to create a new hybrid unlike anything seen in elegy's past. First, the poem is clearly an amatory elegy, even if the protagonist is not the poet speaking in the first person. Second, the poem is a Callimachean *aition*. It tells how the Tarpeian rock got its name. Third, it is patriotic poetry in the traditional Roman mode, telling the great stories of the past, ostensibly to inspire virtue today. The contradictions in interpretation noted above are in fact a consequence of the poem's complex aesthetic and ideological genealogy. It is difficult to believe that Propertius would have been insensitive to the ironies such hybrid constructions entailed.

Tarpeia herself was a figure of profound ambiguity. A Vestal virgin who betrayed her vow and the city whose hearth fire she was charged with keeping, she nonetheless received yearly sacrifice from the Vestals. Through her crime, she gave her name to the Tarpeian rock, off which traitors were thrown from the top of the Capitoline Hill, while the Capitoline itself was known as the *Mons Tarpeium* and Tarpeia's gravesite was where the temple of Jupiter Capitolinus was built, the religious and political center of the city. Tarpeia was the other whose very existence is constitutive of the same. She was the un-Roman, the un-manly, the un-chaste virgin who made Roman *uirtus* and *pudor* possible. She thus stands for the contradictions that lay at the heart of Roman identity.

1–2. Tarpeium nemus: this grove is mentioned only here.

3–4. Lucus erat felix: the poem begins with an image of the Golden Age transgressed. In it, a vision of a pastoral Rome is evoked. It is a city without walls, haunted by the rustic god, Silvanus, nymphs, and other markers of the *locus amoenus* (line 3–6, 13–14, 25). Nevertheless, that pastoral paradise is already stained by the violence of the Sabine camp (lines 11–12). Thus, at the opening of the poem, the possibility of a Rome without violent confrontation with the other is simultaneously evoked and denied. This paradox is nicely captured in lines 13–14 where the image of Rome as a city without walls is combined with that of a Sabine war-horse drinking from the spring that would later be the site of the **Curia**.

Obstrepit: "rustles in reply."

5–6. Siluani: Silvanus was a primitive god of the forests and countryside.

7–8. As Janan (2000) points out, one of the unanswered questions of this poem is how Tarpeia draws water from this stream that has been walled in by Tatius.

9–10. The contrast between past and present is fundamental to aitiological poetry.

Curetis = nominative masculine singular adjective, derived from **Cures** the chief town of the Sabines, agreeing with **tubicen**.

13–14. Rome's walls at the time were the hills on which it was built.

15–16. The image of the simple clay pot (**fictilis urna**; compare Tibullus 1.1.37–38) weighing down upon Tarpeia's head (**urgebat medium** ... **caput**) combines a vision of primeval purity – only earthenware could be used in the service of Vesta – with the heavy burdens of chastity. Note the juxtaposition of fire and water in this and the following couplet.

17–18. The tone of righteous indignation here is undermined both by Propertius's past poetry and the question of what would it mean to fool Vesta's flames (**flammas fallere**), given that they are said to cause Tarpeia's passion in lines 69–70.

19–20. **Iubas** = the mane of his horse. A striking example of Propertius's visual imagination.

23–24. How a young maid might walk through the palisade round the spring is never explained. This passage is one more example of the way in which this poem problematizes the boundaries and their relation to Roman identity. It is no accident that the vehicle of this problematization is female desire, a concept that traditional Roman sexual ideology both refused to recognize formally (women were *mollis* and hence the passive objects of desire) and feared deeply (witness Dido, Cleopatra, Clodia, and others).

25–26. **Romula** = *Romulea*.

27–28. As subsequent action in the poem makes clear, **primo** ... **fumo** refers to the blowing up of the fires to cook the evening meal.

29–30. **Tarpeia** = ablative singular adjective modifying **arce**, an anticipation of the naming of the *Mons Tarpeius* that resulted from her actions.
   Ab = "away from." Jupiter would not have countenanced (**patienda**) the violation of her Vestal vows betokened by her wounds of desire (**uulnera**). His home was also on the Capitoline.

31–32. It is emblematic that the first word out of Tarpeia's mouth is **ignes**, recalling both the Vestal flames and the "fires" of desire. See 2.34.43–44.

33–34. This couplet has been an interpretive crux. The problem lies with the repetition of the word **captiua**. In line 31 it must agree grammatically with the subject of **sedeam**, but in line 32 it may agree either with the subject of **conspicer**, Tarpeia, or with **ora**, so that we may translate it either "would that I, a captive, might see the face of my Tatius," or "would that I might see the captive face of my Tatius," the latter possibility envisioning a reciprocal love match in which each would be the captive of the other. Neither reading in isolation is completely satisfying. In the first possibility, the anaphora seems peculiarly unproductive, and thus the grammatical tension that attracts **captiua** to **ora** is not obviated. In the second possibility, the repetition of the adjective exhibiting the same morphology, but agreeing with two different nouns, is harsh, since the reader's natural tendency is to interpret the same word in the same manner. There is no way to construe the passage without ambiguity.

35–36. Pudenda = "who ought to be ashamed of my disgrace" or "who is to be shamed by my disgrace." The question of Tarpeia's agency is central to the poem. Both translations are defensible depending on how one translates lines 69–70.

37–38. Reponet: Tarpeia envisions the hoped-for result of her act.
   Dextras . . . iubas: according to Vergil (*Georgics* 3.86) a fine war-horse's mane fell to the right.

39–40. Love produces all sorts of monstrosities. Tarpeia seeks here to justify her irregular contact in much the same way Propertius did in 3.11.
   Scyllam: see Tibullus 1.4.63–64.

41–42. Fraterni . . . Monstri = the Minotaur, whose sister, Ariadne, betrayed him out of love for Theseus, whom she gave a thread (**stamine**) so he could find his way out of the labyrinth (**torta via**). See 1.3.1–2.

45–46. The burning of Vesta's fire guaranteed the safety of Rome. If one of the Vestals broke their vow of chastity the fire would go out, endangering the city. Propertius performs a witty elegiac variation on this piece of religious lore by having the fire extinguished by Tarpeia's tears (**lacrimis**). A Vestal who was convicted of breaking her vow was buried alive.
   Pallados = Greek genitive. The Palladium, or image of Pallas, was said to have been brought by Aeneas from Troy and was kept in the Vestal shrine.

47–48. Tarpeia addresses Tatius directly. **Potabitur** = a reasonable conjecture for the MSS's impossible **pugnabitur**, which makes nonsense out of the later description of the festival of the **Parilia** (lines 74 and following) that was taking place at the time of the attack.

49–50. Tacentes . . . aquas: the cliff-face of the Capitoline is combed with small springs. Note the persistence of water and fire imagery throughout the poem.

51–52. The desire for magic spells parallels the elegiac lover's frequent invocation of witchcraft. See Tibullus 1.2.40–64.

53–54. Toga picta: a crimson toga embroidered with gold worn by triumphing generals. It belonged to Jupiter Capitolinus and was worn by Roman kings.

Quem = Romulus. Propertius alludes to his and Remus's suckling by a she-wolf.

55–56. Sic, hospes, pariamne tua regina sub aula: "In that case, would I not give birth as queen in your palace." The hexameter is much disputed, but as many of the older commentators demonstrate, there is no solid reason not to accept the reading of N, the oldest and best MS. The objection that Tarpeia is a virgin and so would not be giving birth assumes she planned on remaining one. It is precisely the boundaries between various bodies and categories that is at issue in this poem.

57–58. Tatius's assault on Rome was intended to avenge the rape of the Sabine women. Tarpeia proposes that if Tatius is not prepared to have her as queen then he should ravish her in revenge. This is hard to imagine in the mouth of female character created by a woman author. It also demonstrates that Roman purity was compromised from the start, founded on an arbitrary act of sexual violence in which reciprocity can only be conceived of as either betrayal (**prodita Roma**) or another rape in turn.

59–60. Tarpeia envisions her "marriage" with Tatius as the **medium** for Roman and Sabine reconciliation. Her body is to become the site where their forces are mingled and their opposition undone.

Nuptae palla . . . mea: Tarpeia's wedding dress.

61–62. There is a sexual pun here. On **arma** as a euphemism for male genitalia, see 1.3.15–16. On **mollitia**, see Introduction [9, 23, 27].

63–64. The night was divided into four watches. The end of each was marked by a trumpet (**bucina**) blast.

67–68. Tarpeia's speech is done and we return to the narrative. She seeks respite from her passion in sleep but succeeds only in rousing new furies.

69–70. The OCT reads **Vesta** following the MSS. Kraffert proposed *Venus* since Propertius offers no explanation for how Vesta comes "to take on the function of the love goddess" and argued that no interpretation adequately explains this connection. While Kraffert's emendation is supported by none of the manuscripts, the force of its logic has won the assent of a number of scholars. The reading *Venus* is given added authority by the fact that Vergil employs similar imagery to describe Dido in *Aeneid* 4.300–03.

Good cases can be made for both *Venus* and *Vesta*. In terms of Roman ideology, there are two areas of ambiguity, one on the level of image, the other on the level of cult. Fire imagery in Latin literature has been widely studied. Its link to passion has been an important leitmotif in Vergilian scholarship. This evidence would seem to tell in favor of the emendation to *Venus*, who plays a crucial role in the downfall of Dido. Yet, virginity in the *Aeneid* is also associated with violence and passion, so that the fires of Vesta and Venus are not easily distinguished.

This observation brings us to our second area of ambiguity – the Vestal cult. In fact, the virginity of the Vestals in no way segregates them from the realm of Venus. Thus Mary Beard (1980) argues that the debate over whether Vestal cultic practices can be traced to the religious duties of daughters or the wives of the primitive Roman kings conceals a more profound dispute over these women's legal and ideological status as either virgins or *matronae*. Her conclusion is that they represent both, and this liminal status accounts for their sacred nature. Hence, the Vestals and their fire do not represent the opposite of Venus and her fires. Likewise, in Indo-European mythology, abstinence, far from marking the opposite of sexuality, represents a strategy of hoarding vital force that allows the community to stockpile sexual power. Thus, the Vestals not only practiced ritual virginity but kept watch over the phallic god Fascinus. See Miller and Platter (1999).

Iliacae . . . fauillae: the fire of Vesta was said to have been brought from Troy.

71–72. Qualis celerem prope Thermodonta | Strymonis abscisso pectus aperta sinu: an impossible image of female sexual power raging beyond male control. The Thermodon is a river in Cappadocia, home of the Amazons. The Strymon is a river in Thrace. A **Strymonis** is a woman from this area, normally a bacchante. Although bacchantes and Amazons both represent images of female power, they represent two distinct categories of women from two widely separated geographical areas. Propertius combines them to create a hyperbolic metaphor of feminine fury. See Janan (2000).

Note once more, in this and the preceding couplet, the conjunction of fire and water imagery. Note also how the unusual spondaic ending of the hexameter calls attention to the passage.

73–74. On the **Parilia**, see Tibullus 1.1.35–36.

75–76. The rustic trays (**pagana . . . fercula**) overflow with food and drink (**madent . . . diuitiis**).

77–78. Part of the purification rite involved leaping over bonfires placed at regular intervals (**raros**).

79–80. Because of the holiday, Romulus calls off the watch, a very strange action given the presence of the Sabine army on his doorstep.

81–82. Hoc = predicative with **tempus**. **Suum** is attributive with both **tempus** and **hostem**.

Pactis, as Richardson (1976) notes, is both ablative, "by the terms of the agreement," and dative with **comes**, "to those with whom she had reached an agreement."

83–84. The OCT prints the hexameter with daggers, but while the sense is condensed it is not impossible. "The climbing of the mountain was in doubt, but the guard was relaxed on account of the holiday." Enclitic **que** can take an adversative sense after a negation, here implied in **dubius**.

Occupat: the implied subject is *hostis* or Tarpeia.

85–86. The punishment is owed to Jupiter (**poenis . . . suis**), because the hill is sacred to him.

87–88. It would normally be the girl's parents not the bride herself (**ipsa**) who set the day for her marriage. This inversion of normal values would be the natural corollary in Roman ideology to the series of betrayals listed in the hexameter.

89–90. Nube = imperative, "veil yourself" and hence "marry." Tarpeia's bridal veil will be the Sabine shields under which she is crushed.

91–92. Virgo is ironic.

93–94. **Duce Tarpeia** refers to Tarpeia's leading the Sabines up the mountain.

The pentameter is oracular. **Vigil** could refer to Jupiter following lines 85–86, in which case the **praemia** is undeserved because Jupiter was subsequently called *Tarpeius*, though Tarpeia herself deserved no such divine memorial. On the other hand, **uigil** is taken by many to refer to Tarpeia as the guardian of the citadel that later bore her name. Then, she deserved not the honor of the hill being named after her. Finally, Tarpeia's fate is fundamentally unjust (**iniustae . . . sortis**) since she is the innocent pawn of Vesta and the fires of passion. The instability of borders and the ambiguities of origins, agency and justice embodied in final line are central to the problems investigated by the poem.

4.6

This poem on the battle of Actium is read by some as evidence of the poet's reconciliation with Augustus and by others as an exercise in satire. Its ambiguities can be seen as part of the poet's continually evolving response to this battle and its aftermath as explored in poems 2.15, 2.16, and 3.11. What is perhaps most important to appreciate in this controversy, however, is the very impossibility of nailing down the poet's response to the consolidation of the Augustan regime and the beginning of the empire. What does it mean to be a poet, an elegist, and ultimately a citizen in such a polity where the very definition of *ciuis Romanus* has fundamentally changed?

Book 4 is about the displacement of Propertius as the subject of his own experience. In 4.4, the poet as speaker is replaced by Tarpeia, nor is his attitude toward her easy to specify, for she is explicitly condemned within the text of the poem, but her position is also revealed to be the direct analogue of that of the elegist. Similarly, in this poem Augustus is explicitly praised, but the praise is extreme and so at variance with the poet's statements in previous poems that it is impossible to take completely seriously. Yet, hyperbole is not the same as attack. It does not take up a position hostile to the Augustan regime, but one whose place is precisely impossible to locate.

To ask what is the poet's real attitude is the wrong question, rather we should say that Propertius in Book 4, like Ovid after him, speaks from an ironic position that is inherently double. He creates a poetic hall of mirrors in which any given passage can be said to reflect its opposite. In such poetry, there can be no sincerity, only duplicity and wit. This is typical of certain styles of court poetry that would be common in the West through the Enlightenment. Such a position also signals the end of elegy, for elegy always defined itself in contradistinction to certain ideological norms that it both mocked and accepted. If its opposition to those norms can no longer be specified then the genre has lost its reason for being.

4.6 is cast as an aitiological poem on the origin of the cult of Apollo Actiacus Pallatinus. After an introduction in which Propertius assumes the role of *uates*, "poetic priest," much as Horace does in the "Roman Odes" (lines 1–14), there is a description of the battle itself (lines 15–68), including a long central speech of encouragement given by Apollo to Augustus (lines 37–54). It closes with an account of Propertius joining other poets at their wine in celebration of the feats of Augustus (lines 69–86).

1–2. **Sacra facit uates**: Propertius, the poetic priest, offers sacrifice.

Sint ora fauentia: a variation on the traditional formula demanding silence during the performance of the rites to insure that no ill-omened speech escaped.

3–4. This couplet gives the artistic program for the poem. **Serta . . . Romana** would be both the garlands of Roman poets vying with their Greek predecessors and the garlands of the triumphing general that provide the matter for a poem to be executed in the Hellenistic style.

Philiteis . . . corymbis: on Philitas see, 2.34.31–32. Ivy was sacred to Bacchus, patron of elegiac poetry.

Cyrenaeas . . . aquas: Callimachus was from Cyrene. Propertius in this couplet says he will write aitiological poetry on Roman subject matter in the refined Hellenistic style [9, 25–29].

5–6. Propertius gives orders to those assisting in the sacrifice. **Costum** = a costly oriental plant used in perfume.

Laneus orbis = a thin ribbon of wool wound round the altar three times.

7–8. Note the careful interweaving of images of ritual purity with flowing song.

Libet = hortatory subjunctive.

Recentibus aris: altars made for the occasion, probably of piled turf.

Tibia: the traditional accompaniment for elegy.

Mygdoniis: the Mygdones were a tribe from Phrygia, the traditional birthplace of the flute.

9–10. The poet alludes to the image of the untrod path (**nouum . . . iter**) that Callimachus evokes in Apollo's admonition in the preface to the *Aitia* to follow only *keleuthous atriptous* (1.27–28). At the same time, he recognizes the unprecedented nature of this poem in the Propertian corpus. This poem owes much to Callimachus's "Hymn to Apollo."

Alio . . . Aere = "under another sky."

Laurea: a spray of laurel used to sprinkle lustral water for purification. Laurel was also sacred to Apollo, the god of poetry and Augustus's patron at Actium.

11–12. **Palatini . . . Apollinis aedem**: the temple is here associated with the battle of Actium. It was originally vowed as a thanks-offering for Augustus's victory over the naval forces of Sextus Pompeius in 36 BCE. The temple itself opened in 28 BCE, the year after the triumph at Actium was celebrated. It was praised for its artistic treasures by Propertius in 2.31 and housed a library that was an important resource for poets.

Calliope: see 2.1.3.

13–14. Caesar is to be honored in this hymn as superior to the gods. Jupiter himself should pay attention (**Iuppiter ipse uaces**): a hyperbole bordering on sacrilege. It is moments like this that cause readers to see this poem either as a clumsy failure or a deft satire.

15–16. The poem moves from the introduction to its main body with a description of the area around Actium. This kind of description is a common figure in epic, known as *ecphrasis*.

Phoebi fugiens . . . portus: a bold figure of speech. The harbor is **fugiens** because it runs back inland from the open sea. There was a temple of Apollo on the promontory overlooking the Ambracian Gulf.

Athamana ad litora: the harbor's inlet stretched back toward the land of the Athamanes, a tribe living on its shores in Epirus.

Condit = "calms."

17–18. Pelagus monumenta: another daring figure. **Pelagus**, "sea," is in apposition to **portus** and **monumenta** is in apposition to it. The image of the sea as a monument is paradoxical, since monuments are normally stable in opposition to the roiling sea, and grandiose, since the whole vast expanse of water becomes monument to Augustus's fleet.

Iuleae: as the adopted son of Julius Caesar, Octavian became a member of the *gens Iulia*.

Non operosa uia = "a not difficult way."

19–20. Moles pinea: the mass of pinewood ships.

Nec . . . aequa . . . auis: both fleets were not favored by equivalent omens.

21–22. Teucro . . . Quirino: Quirinus was the name of the deified Romulus. Teucer was the son of Scamander, the first king of Troy, hence the Trojans were known as Teucrians. Romulus was a descendant of Aeneas and so of Teucer. All of this emphasizes the legitimacy of the Augustan cause in contradistinction to that of Antony, who is once more effaced behind the figure of Cleopatra (**feminea**). See 3.11.

23–24. Augusta ratis = both "the ship of Augustus" and "the holy ship." Understand *uenit*.

Signaque iam . . . uincere docta: Augustus's standards had learnt to conquer in previous battles.

Patriae suae: the implicit message is clear. Augustus fought for Rome, Antony for a foreign power. Augustus did all he could to portray his victory at Actium as the defeat of the effeminate east, not civil slaughter. But see 2.15.43–46.

25–26. A memorable image of the two fleets lined up for battle. Cassius Dio (50.13) indicates that Augustus's fleet advanced in a concave crescent so as to encircle Antony's fleet. The latter responded by trying to push through the middle of Augustus's fleet, thus forming a convex crescent. Other accounts offer different details. **Nereus** = a god of the sea.

27–28. Se uindice: ablative absolute. It applies equally well to Delos, birthplace of Apollo, and to Augustus's ship (line 29).

Stantem . . . Delon: Delos according to Callimachus's "Hymn to Apollo" was a floating island (**mobilis**) before the god's birth. **Vna**: Delos was the lone such island.

29–30. Noua flamma luxit in obliquam ter sinuata facem = "A strange flame shone that was twisted three times into a slanting torch." The image would appear to be that of a jagged lightning bolt, but the poet is perhaps deliberately vague to underline the omen's preternatural air.

31–32. Apollo did not appear in his aspect as the god of poetry.

33–34. Rather he appeared as the god who showered death on Agamemnon's camp (**castra**) in the first book of the *Iliad*, when his priest Chryses calls down divine wrath because Agamemnon refuses to return the latter's daughter. **Auidis . . . rogis**: the pyres of the dead from the plague Apollo sent.

35–36. Or he seemed the god who slew the Python. **Orbis** = coils.

Imbelles . . . Lyrae = metonymy for the muses who were terrorized by the serpent that guarded Delphi before Apollo came.

37–38. The hyperbole of Apollo's address to Augustus is breathtaking. Such flattery is always by definition ironic, since it necessarily calls attention to itself as flattery rather than as a simple statement of fact.

Longa . . . Alba: an early settlement, traditionally founded by **Iulus**, the son of Aeneas, and namesake of the *gens Iulia*.

Hectoreis . . . auis: i.e., Trojan ancestors.

39–40. Hoc onus = Apollo's quiver.

41–42. Augustus sails with the full support of the Roman public.

43–44. According to the sources, when **Romulus** and **Remus** were deciding either where to found the city of Rome or what to name it, they took auspices or bird signs (**auis**). Remus saw six vultures over the Aventine hill, but Romulus saw twelve over the Palatine, so the initial wall (**murorum**) was built there. Propertius's point is that if Augustus does not defend the city, then Romulus's augury was mistaken (**non bene**). Since this would be inconceivable, Augustus's victory at Actium was therefore predestined. On the other hand, this dispute between Romulus and Remus can be seen as the first example of that fratricidal strife, the culmination of which was Actium. See 2.1.23–24.

45–46. Audent: understand *hostes* as subject.

Te principe: in 27 BCE Augustus was awarded the title *princeps senatus*. This was a traditional republican title for the senior member of the senate. It is a good example of Augustus's preservation of republican forms even as he laid the foundations of the empire. The phrase makes a striking contrast with **regia**, since royalty was associated with tyranny in Roman thought. Augustus studiously avoided the trappings of kingship. See 3.11.55–56.

47–48. More than one critic has remarked on the oddness of Apollo telling Augustus he need not fear. Does this imply that the *princeps* was something less than a fearless leader?

Alis = "oars." **Centenis** probably stands for any large number.

Inuito . . . mari: there were storms at sea that disrupted Antony's fleet.

Labitur is a wonderfully evocative word in this context. It means first "to glide along," but carries with it the secondary meanings of "to sink, decline, perish" and "to be deceived, or in error," all of which are applicable in this context.

49–50. Again the emphasis on Augustus's fear and its baselessness seems out of place. **Minantis** = accusative plural, referring to carved figureheads in the shape of Centaurs throwing rocks on the ships' prows. Augustus's fears are merely painted images (**pictos . . . metus**).

51–52. Excutit arma pudor: many commentators see an allusion here to the high rate of desertion among Antony's troops.

53–54. Laurigera: laurel was both sacred to Apollo and worn by triumphing generals.

57–58. Dat . . . Poenas = "pays the penalty."

59–60. Pater . . . Caesar = the deified Julius, another hyperbolic touch.

Idalio . . . astro: the star is Idalian, because the *gens Iulia* claimed descent from Venus through Aeneas. Idalium is a mountain in Cyprus, an island associated with Venus.

Sum deus: a statement impossible to read without a chuckle.

Fides = "proof."

61–62. Cantu = the note of celebration blown by Triton on his conch-shell trumpet.

Libera signa: the standards of free people as opposed to those of an eastern tyranny. Nonetheless in light of the deification of Julius Caesar, the special favor of Apollo, and the procession of marine deities accompanying the victorious fleet, the difference between the Augustan principate and Cleopatra's divine monarchy is increasingly difficult to specify. The problem becomes all the more vexed when it is recalled that half of the opposing army was made up of Roman soldiers, led by a Roman general whose ties to the deified Julius were as strong as those of Augustus. A Roman reader would have been hard put not to see the irony.

63–64. Hoc unum is in apposition to **Nilum.** Cleopatra sought to escape to Egypt so that she would not be put to death after marching in Augustus's triumph (**iusso . . . die**), as was the custom with captured monarchs.

65–66. A very ambiguous couplet. **Di melius** = "the gods had a better plan," but a better plan than what? Than Cleopatra dying in Egypt or marching in the triumph? If the former, then Cleopatra thwarted the gods themselves. If the latter, then why did the gods not want Cleopatra to march in the triumph? Was she an unworthy opponent or was the battle itself a source of potential shame?

In this light, it is hard not to read **quantus** as sarcastic. If Augustus's victory at Actium is reduced to a triumph over one woman (**mulier . . . una**) as opposed to the mighty **Iugurtha** (see 3.5.16), does that not undercut the encomiastic intent of the poem? Of course, from the elegiac perspective triumph over one woman *is* worth more than Marius's over Jugurtha and all his armies.

67–68. See the introductory note and lines 11–12 above. Apollo's temple at Actium was restored by Augustus.

69–70. Bella satis cecini: an abrupt return to the poet's elegiac persona. Apollo too puts aside arms and resumes his aspect as patron of poetry.

71–72. This is precisely the type of symposiastic atmosphere the poet prescribes as an antidote to Actium's civil slaughter in 2.15.41–54.

Rosae = genitive singular.

73–74. Falernis: Falernian was a superior vintage.

Spica Cilissa: "Cilician saffron" was especially treasured. The **spica** is the pistil of the flower from which it was extracted.

75–76. Positis = "at rest."

77–78. The poets take turns celebrating recent imperial triumphs. **Paludosos . . . seruire Sycambros**: the Sygambri, a tribe from the marshy Rhineland, in fact were anything but enslaved. In 16 BCE, the earliest date for this poem's composition, they had invaded Gaul and defeated M. Lollius. They subsequently withdrew, but were not completely subdued until 9 BCE.

Cepheam ... Meroen: Meroe was an island in the Nile from which the Ethiopians staged raids into southern Egypt. They were defeated by the Roman prefect Petronius in 22 BCE. Cepheus, father of Andromeda, was a legendary king of Ethiopia.

79–80. Sero ... foedere: the adjective *serus* uncomfortably recalls that Crassus's lost standards were only returned once numerous projected military campaigns were scrapped in favor of a diplomatic settlement (20 BCE). See the introductory note to 3.4. As the pentameter points out, the Parthians may have returned the standards they captured, but they retained their own.

Lines 80–84 are best taken as a direct quotation of the poet in question.

81–82. Propertius suggests that perhaps Augustus spares the Parthians so that the glory may go to his heirs, his grandsons Gaius and Lucius Caesar whom he adopted in 17 BCE. One wonders how credible this suggestion was.

Pharetris ... Eois: the Parthians were famed archers.

83–84. The image of Crassus's body lying in the black sands is a powerful reminder of the costs of war, which are glossed over in the description of Actium. That the fruit of Augustus's *foedus* with Parthians was the ability to cross the Euphrates and visit the tombs of those who had died seems a strange note on which to end a poem celebrating victory.

85–86. Patera: a flat dish used for making sacrificial libations. The final image of drink and song until morning light, even if given a ritual cast, recalls the closing of 2.15.

4.7

The poet's final two poems on the affair with Cynthia bid his beloved an ironic farewell. Poems 4.7 and 4.8 are remarkable on several counts. They are the only two poems in Book 4 on Cynthia. They are also the only two poems in the whole of the Propertian corpus in which the beloved speaks. They thus continue the pattern established in 4.4 in which the poet is displaced as speaker and replaced by a woman. In addition, the juxtaposition of 4.6 with 4.7 and 4.8 cannot help but make the reader question the extent to which Propertius's new-found heroic and epic voice is a mask designed to conceal what remains an essentially elegiac and hence nonconformist poetics.

Poem 4.7 features Cynthia returning from the grave to accuse Propertius of neglecting her funeral rites, abusing her slaves, and replacing her with an otherwise unknown Chloris. The poet is never given the occasion to answer these charges. Cynthia's words stand alone. Nonetheless, the traditional stance of the elegist is everywhere apparent in this poem, as Cynthia systematically adopts the complaints of the elegiac lover as her own. Thus, it is

Propertius now who is fickle, greedy, and whose attentions are attracted by a *diues amatrix*.

Moreover, the death and final epitaph of the lover are common motifs throughout elegy in general (see Tibullus 1.159–62) and the Propertian corpus in particular (see 2.1.47–48 and 77–78). But normally it is his own death that the poet narcissistically imagines. Here it is the death of Cynthia. Lastly, where the inability of witches' potions and poisons to help the hapless lover is a frequent topic in elegy, Cynthia here claims to have been poisoned by Propertius's slave. In short, the basic motifs of masculine elegy are put into the mouth of the beloved, to whom they are normally addressed, and systematically inverted. The result is not a new, feminist perspective on the essential elegiac complaint, but rather a mirror image of the masculinist position. Cynthia when she speaks sounds nothing like Sulpicia. Instead, the displacement and inversion of the standard elegiac position evidenced in this poem can be seen as one more piece of testimony for the genre's own progressive effacement from the stage of early imperial culture, as it becomes more and more difficult for the elegist to find a place from which to speak.

1–2. Euictos . . . rogos: the pyre itself is overcome. It does not consume all.

3–4. Fulcrum = the foot of a bed or couch.
Ad = postposition, highly unusual.
Extremae . . . uiae = "at the end of the road." Most commentators prefer "at the edge of the road," but, as Richardson (1977) rightly observes, this notion is already communicated by *ad murmur* and, as we find out later in the poem, Cynthia is buried in Tivoli at the end of the *uia Tiburtina* (line 85).

5–6. The hexameter is a highly poetic line that can be translated "when sleep for me hung from the funeral procession of love," meaning either that he dreamt of Cynthia's funeral or he was unable to sleep from thoughts of the funeral. The ambiguity is productive since it leaves open the question of whether Cynthia was a dream or a waking vision.

The ultimate cold kingdom (**frigida regna**) is the underworld, which is what Propertius's bed has been symbolically transformed into.

7–8. The image of the burnt garment hanging from her flank is both pathetic and erotic.

9–10. The incredible heat of the pyre is made vivid by its capacity to eat away at (**adederat**) the semiprecious beryl (**beryllon**) in her ring. The fact that no damage is done to her body emphasizes the combination of the material and the spiritual that makes this poem so powerful. Cynthia herself is intact, but her physical accoutrements have suffered in the fire.

Summaque Lethaeus triuerat ora liquor: her face has become somehow indistinct as it has been worn away by the waters of "oblivion" (the meaning of Lethe in Greek).

11–12. Spirantisque animos: normally the sign of life, but here the medium of the voice and the sign of a residual inner animation. **Spirantis** is generally taken as a genitive.

At illi pollicibus fragiles increpuere manus: the eerie sound of thumb bones clicking together gives a final chilling note of realism to the scene. Note that **increpuere** can also mean to rebuke. Both meanings are appropriate.

13–14. "Faithless one, nor is any girl to hope for better!"

15–16. The fact that Cynthia herself describes their relationship as **furta** implies that it was essentially adulterous, whether she was cheating on a husband or another lover. The image of secret meetings in the **Subura**, Rome's red light district, clashes with the domesticity described in poem 1.3. On such inconsistencies, see the introductory note to that poem.

19–20. Pectore mixto: a powerful image of passionate embrace that looks forward to line 94.

21–22. On the truism that a lover's promises are not to be trusted, see Catullus 70.3–4 and Tibullus 1.4.13–14.

Foederis heu taciti: Greek exclamatory genitive.

23–24. The hexameter is a difficult line. **Inclamauit** normally takes a person rather than a thing as an object (**oculos**). **Euntis** = accusative plural modifying **oculos**. Propertius refers to the Roman custom of calling out the name of the dying, which was believed to bring them briefly back to life. It is the loss of this extra time (**unum . . . diem**) that Cynthia bemoans in the pentameter.

25–26. Cynthia complains of Propertius's penury even in death. **Fissa . . . harundine custos:** a hired guardian of the corpse supposed to keep away evil spirits by the use of a rattle made from a split reed.

Tegula curta: the image of the beloved's head now propped on a broken tile is a powerful image of abandonment in death.

27–28. The implication seems to be that Propertius either did not attend Cynthia's funeral, which seems unlikely given line 5's **exsequiis**, or that he failed to appear appropriately distraught.

Curuum = "bent over with grief."

29–30. Corpses could not be burned or buried within the walls of Rome. The cortege accompanied the corpse to the gates, but after that only close family and friends continued. Cynthia chastises Propertius for failing to follow her bier beyond the city walls and for not ordering it to move slowly and gently to that point (**illuc**).

At = "still."

31–32. The custom was to call upon the winds to consume the corpse quickly and to anoint it with scented oil (**nardo**).

33–34. Graue = "difficult, an imposition."

Fracto . . . cado: the reference is obscure. The custom of pouring wine on the ashes of the dead to quench the fire is widely attested, but there is no reference to breaking the wine jar. Some see this as transfer of epithet, so that it is the *uina* itself that is *fracta* and hence bad. Others like Richardson see the breaking of the jar as a "natural gesture." Still others see the jar itself as a funereal offering whose cheapness would be attested by its being broken. Finally, citing a passage from Vergil, some see the *cadus* as the actual funeral urn. It is probably best to translate literally and assume that reference is deliberately vague, since appeals to usage and custom are contradictory, and appeals to nature are always suspect.

35–36. Lygdamus = Propertius's personal slave; see 4.8. 37–38 and 79–80.

Lamina = a thin piece of metal heated and used to torture slaves. **Vernae**: see Tibullus 1.5.25–26. **Sensi**: understand *id*. **Insidiis** = poison. **Pallida** = the pallor of death.

37–38. Nomas: an otherwise unknown slave.

Salivas: slimes, and the poisons associated with them.

Dicet: the purpose of slave torture was to extract a confession.

Ignea testa: a pottery shard heated and used for torture.

39–40. Propertius's new love has come into recent riches. Whether she has taken possession of Cynthia's or arrived at them through other means, she represents a female variation on the motif of the *nouveau riche diues amator*. She is thought to be the **Chloris** named in line 72.

Modo = "lately."

Inspecta est publica: implies prostitution, and **uilis . . . noctes** indicates that it was not of a very refined genre.

Aurata cyclade: an elegant gown, with gold embroidery, worn by wealthy women of fashion.

Signat humum: the image of her weighed down by her golden dress like a signet ring in wax is memorable.

41–42. On the **quasillis**, see Sulpicia 3.16.3–4.

43–44. Petale: an otherwise unknown slave of Cynthia.

Codicis: a block of wood to which slaves were bound for punishment.

45–46. Lalage: another unknown slave. Her name means "babbler" and reflects her transgression. **Suspensa capillis**: she is hung by her head to be flogged. **Per nomen**: Lalage dared to seek a favor from Propertius in Cynthia's name.

47–48. Meae . . . imaginis aurum = either a medallion or statuette of gold bearing Cynthia's portrait.

Conflauit = "to kindle" and by metonymy "to melt."

The pentameter is striking for its conflation of Cynthia's funeral pyre with the fire used to smelt the gold and provide Chloris's "dowry" (**dotem**).

49–50. Cynthia exempts Propertius from her reproaches because she long reigned in his books. The use of the perfect (**fuere**) nicely recognizes that she no longer is the prime topic of Propertius's poetry. Rather, this poem and its counterpart, 4.8, embody on the poetic level the scenario imagined on the dramatic level in 4.7, Cynthia's return from the dead.

51–52. Iuro ego Fatorum nulli reuolubile carmen: a poetic construction. Understand *per*. "I swear by the song of the Fates, which can be reversed by no man." Propertius here uses a bold mixed metaphor conflating the song of the Fates, as exemplified in the conclusion of Catullus 64, with the more traditional image of them spinning the thread of each person's life. Note the juxtaposition of the **carmen** of the Fates with Propertius's poetry in the previous couplet.

Tergeminusque canis = Cerberus.

Sic . . . Sonet = a more vivid wish or command construction.

The enjambment of the indirect statement, **me seruasse fidem**, to the next couplet and the resulting hyperbaton call close attention to Cynthia's role in the creation of Propertius's poetic language.

53–54. The double-accusative construction in the indirect statement allows for a nice ambiguity over whether Cynthia preserved her faithfulness (**fidem**) or her faithfulness preserved her. Both would be appropriate things for her to claim, though both are of questionable veracity when one looks at the rest of the corpus. **Si fallo** = "if I am untrue."

55–56. The dead cross the river Styx to two different destinations, based on their virtue in life.

57–58. The text of this couplet is much disputed. The hexameter transmitted by the manuscripts, which I have printed here, has been challenged, since, as lines 55–56 make clear, the dead are divided into two (**gemina**) groups, but where **una** . . . **altera** in the received text seems to create two groups in the underworld, the repetition of **altera** in 59 would add a third. This however is an unnecessary interpretation. **Altera pars** in 59 denotes a completely separate division of the underworld (**Elysium**), where **una** . . . **altera** merely denotes two successive waves carrying two damned heroines to Tartarus. The antecedent of **una** is **aqua** (line 56). The sense of the couplet is: *una aqua portat stuprum Clytaemestrae, altera uehit monstra lignea bouis Cressae mentitae.*

Clytaemestrae stuprum = "the perversity of Clytemnestra," referring to her adultery with Aegisthus and her killing of Agamemnon. **Stuprum** is a strong word, indicating sexual monstrosity.

Cressae . . . mentitae lignea monstra bouis: the reference is to Pasiphae's having Daedalus build a wooden model of a cow so that she could satisfy her lust for Minos's bull. The monster stands by metonymy for the transgression that condemned Pasiphae to Tartarus.

61–62. Numerosa fides = a pun, both the lyre and the praises of fidelity set to meter.

Aera rotunda: cymbal played in the rites of Cybebe, the Great Mother goddess, whose home was in Phrygia, near Lydia.

Cybebes = Greek genitive singular.

Mitratis = wearing the turban associated with Lydia.

63–64. Andromeda: see the introductory note to 1.3.

Hypermestre: the sole one of Danaus's fifty daughters to refuse his command to slay her husband on her wedding night.

65–66. Maternis: Andromeda was chained to the rock to expiate the sin of her mother's boasting that she herself was more beautiful than the Nereids.

67–68. Non ualuisse: an odd way of describing an act of virtue that won Hypermestre a place in paradise.

69–70. While the OCT prints *sancimus* in place of **sanamus**, the reading of the manuscripts, there is no reason to doubt the text. The heroines seek solace for their losses in tales of faithful love, Cynthia alone (**ego**) must lie to conceal Propertius's faithlessness. Of course, as 4.8 reveals, there was perfidy on both sides.

71–72. The focus returns to this world as the poem moves into its final section.

Herba = magic potions.

73–74. **Auara**: the nurse was a frequent go-between for elegiac lovers, who is often portrayed by poets as a greedy *lena*.

75–76. **Cui nomen ab usu: Latris** is Greek for "maidservant."

77–78. **Laudes desine habere meas**: there is an ambiguity here. If Propertius burns his poetry on Cynthia he will literally cease to possess his praises of her, but he will also cease to have the praise that rightly belongs to Cynthia.

79–80. The care and inscription of the male lover's tomb is a frequent motif in elegy. It is significant that ivy is said to be growing over Cynthia's tomb. Ivy was sacred to Bacchus who was traditionally associated with verse.

   Again, there is controversy about the text. The OCT prints *praegnante* for the manuscript reading, **pugnante**. But there is nothing prima facie absurd about portraying the ivy, and by metonymy its clusters of berries, as "struggling" to work its way into the tomb and bind Cynthia's delicate bones (**mollia . . . ossa**).

81–82. The river **Anio** spreads across the plain below Tivoli (*Tibur*) and irrigates orchards (**ramosis . . . aruis**).

   Numquam . . . pallet ebur: it is speculated that the high mineral content of the nearby spring keeps ivory from yellowing.

   Herculeo: Hercules was the founder and patron deity of *Tibur*.

83–84. **Media . . . columna**: the inscription is to be written on a gravestone in the shape of a column. It will be brief enough to be read by a traveler without stopping (**currens**).

87–88. There were gates of ivory and gates of horn from the underworld. True dreams issued from those of horn (**piis . . . portis**) and false from those of ivory.

89–90. **Abiecta . . . sera**: with the bar withdrawn.

91–92. Understand *nos* in the hexameter.
   Nauta = Charon.

93–94. Cynthia concedes to Chloris's reign, since she will possess Propertius in the world beyond.

   Mixtis ossibus ossa teram: a wonderfully macabre image of lovemaking beyond the grave.

95–96. **Querula . . . sub lite peregit**: technical legal terminology, "she had brought her querulous indictment to an end."

The pathos of the shade that slips from the embrace of the living is familiar from both Achilles and Patroclus in the *Iliad* and Aeneas and Anchises in the *Aeneid*.

4.8

As observed in the introductory note to 4.7, 4.8 and its predecessor form a pair that says goodbye to Cynthia. Once again, Cynthia is the primary speaker. While offering a broadly comic treatment of Cynthia's rage and jealousy that provides a clear balance to the pathos of 4.7, 4.8 is an aitiological poem that explains the origins of a disturbance on the Esquiline and of an obscure snake cult in Lanuvium. It thus rejoins one of the major thematic preoccupations of Book 4 [5, 28–30, 55].

Lanuvium was a city off the Appian Way, south-east of Rome. In it was located a shrine of Juno Sospita whose strange rites were regarded as curious even by the Romans. The cult statue depicted a warrior goddess wearing a goatskin. Cynthia in this poem is also depicted as a wild and avenging deity. Connected to the shrine was a cave inhabited by a serpent. Once a year, a group of unmarried girls was selected to bear cakes to it, guided only by a mysterious current of air. If the snake took the offering, then the girls' virginity was proven and the fertility of the community assured. If the snake refused the food, then the wind currents would bring scraps of the cakes to the opening of the cave and the girls would be punished. Propertius himself in this poem is presented as both unfaithful and punished. On the relation between virginity and fertility exemplified in the cult, see the introductory note to 4.4.

The poem is notable for the way in which Cynthia is presented in a clearly masculine role, while Propertius occupies the feminine position. It is Cynthia who journeys out into the world while Propertius stays home. Both lovers are equally faithless to the other, but only Propertius is chastised. It is Cynthia who uses violence and physical force to seek retribution for her betrayal, exercising a masculine prerogative. Lastly, although Propertius seeks to console himself for Cynthia's infidelity by entertaining two high-priced professional women, he is unable to perform because of his preoccupation with Cynthia (lines 47–48). He is thus *mollis* and emasculated [7, 9, 23, 27].

1–2. The poem starts in mock epic manner, promising to teach us what manner of disturbance drove the inhabitants of the Esquiline out of their houses.

Aquosas: three aqueducts crossed the Esquiline.

Nouis . . . agris: the reference is obscure, but most take it as a reference to the new gardens Maecenas [51–54] had built on the site of a former cemetery.

19–20. Most critics agree that this couplet is out of place as transmitted in the manuscripts and printed in the OCT. This transposition makes good sense and is widely adopted, although it is difficult to explain how the couplet fell out of place. Many choose to delete or bracket it.

Arcana . . . taberna: an out-of-the-way cookshop or tavern in which Phyllis and Teia, Cynthia's rivals, sought refuge from her wrath. See line 62.

3–4. The transition is abrupt and immediately foregrounds the poem's more traditional aitiological content.

Tutela is ambiguous, meaning both ward and protector. This nicely captures Lanuvium's relation to the serpent.

Hic ubi tam rarae non perit hora morae = "here where an hour spent on so extraordinary a visit is not wasted."

5–6. **Qua sacer abripitur caeco descensus hiatu** = "where the sacred descent is carried off into a dark chasm." The cavern was completely dark and the young women were guided only by the mysterious breeze coming from its depths.

Virgo, tale iter omne caue: the interjection is otiose unless it is meant to imply that chastity is less common than its proclamation, an idea consonant with the poem as a whole.

The enjambment into the next couplet highlights the wondrous nature of the rite described.

7–8. **Honos** = "rite."

Ex ima sibila torquet humo: the poet associates the hissing of the snake with the breeze emanating from the cavern's depths.

9–10. **Anguino . . . Ore** = locative ablative in place of the more usual dative.

13–14. The clear implication is that if they are found to be *incestae*, they do not return to their parents. Were they immured in the cave in the same fashion as Vestals who broke their vows were entombed in the city walls?

15–16. **Detonsis . . . mannis**: short-clipped Gallic ponies. These are not working animals, but manicured pleasure horses. The juxtaposition with **castae** in the previous couplet is effective.

Iuno = Juno Sospita, a mere pretext for an erotic (**Venus**) outing.

17–18. **Triumphum**: the irony of depicting Cynthia's mad dash (**effusis . . . rotis**) as a triumphal progress is clear.

21–22. Cynthia is presented as transgressing all boundaries of propriety, even physical laws. She is pictured as leaning so far forward as she drives her gig in headlong careen that she hangs over the front of the pole (**primo temone pependit**) to which the horses are attached. At the same time, she is seen driving through areas of low repute (**impuros . . . locos**), whose boundaries a respectable *matrona* would not cross. Lastly, she violates the laws of gender by driving when she has a male escort. The notion that **impuros . . . locos** refers to rough terrain or "mud puddle[s]" (Richardson 1977) is both unparalleled, as Butler and Barber (1969) acknowledge, and out of tune with the opening of the poem, which centers on the purity of the maids who deliver the snake its offering. The juxtaposition with Cynthia's outrageous behavior is part of the point.

23–24. The use of the *praeteritio* ("I won't mention . . . x") recalls the invective of the republican period, when Cicero frequently used the figure. The syntax of this couplet is as ornate as the scene it describes.

Vulsi . . . nepotis: Cynthia's lover is depilated, and hence both an effeminate and wealthy youth.

Colla Molossa: Molossian hounds were highly valued in the period. **Molossa** is transfer of epithet from **canis**. **Colla** is a Greek accusative of respect with **armillatos**.

25–26. The antecedent of **qui** is **nepotis**. The insult is that the now well-plucked golden youth will soon run through his fortune and will give his worthless life (**uenalia fata**) for the meal of a gladiator and the latter's short beard (**barba**). He will, in short, be forced to sell himself into the lowest form of slavery. **Saginae** = literally "stuffing" or feed used to fatten animals. It was commonly used of the food eaten by gladiators.

27–28. Another clever juxtaposition. Propertius's use of **castra** in the *militia amoris* [27, 54–55] motif sets up a contrast between the metaphor and its literalization in his rival's future as a gladiator. See Tibullus 1.1.75–76, Propertius 1.3.15–16, 1.6 introductory note, 2.1 introductory note, and 3.5.1–2.

29–30. The temple of Diana on the Aventine was ancient. Note once again the juxtaposition of presumed virginity (Diana) and promiscuous sexuality (**Phyllis**).

31–32. Tarpeia also combines ritual purity and promiscuous sexuality. See the introductory note to 4.4. **Tarpeios . . . lucos** = the Capitoline.

33–34. **Furta nouare mea** = "to embark on fresh infidelities."

35–36. The tone is deliberately titillating.

37–38. At this elegant little *al fresco* threesome, Lygdamus (see 4.7.35–36) will pour the drinks, using glassware (**uitri**), a luxury reserved for summer (**aestiua**). In winter, silver service would have been the choice.

Methymnaei: Methymna in Lesbos was famed for its wine.

Saliua here = "flavor," but compare 4.7.37–38 where it means poison and is again associated with Lygdamus.

39–40. Not only was there wine and a secluded couch for three, but entertainment. **Phillis** is printed with daggers. It is most unlikely that Phyllis was a paid castanet dancer at a party thrown for her entertainment. No emendation carries conviction. What we want is a name indicating provenance to balance **Nile, tuus**.

Haec facilis spargi munda sine arte rosa = "this one, elegant in her simplicity, is easily sprinkled with rose petals." The scattering of rose petals was common at Roman parties. **Rosa** = ablative.

41–42. The OCT prints the emendation **nanus** for the manuscript reading **Magnus**, but *nanus* is redundant. What is wanted is a proper name to parallel those of the other entertainers. The cruel wit of **Magnus** as the name for the dwarf fits the bill. Dwarfs were a fashionable feature at parties.

Caua buxa = the pipe.

43–44. The party, in spite of Propertius's best preparations, was ill-omened from the start. The lamps would not stay lit and the table kept collapsing. This is a wonderful moment of comic bathos.

45–46. The reference in this couplet is to dicing, a common amusement at Roman dinner parties. The best throw was Venus (**Venerem**), with all four dice showing different numbers. The worst was the dog (**canes**), with all four dice showing ones. There is a clear pun. Propertius has set up this party with Phyllis and Teia to seek Venus or sexual satisfaction, but he craps out.

47–48. The reason for the poet's poor showing in the games of love is made clear. His mind was on Cynthia in Lanuvium.

49–50. The rapid transition from Propertius, **Lanuuii ad portas . . . solus**, to Cynthia bursting through his door is highly effective.

Laris = the Lares who guard the outer entryway to the house where shrines were often found. On the Lares, see Tibullus 1.1.19–20.

51–52. Totas resupinat . . . ualuas: Cynthia breaks down both leaves of the outer door. Her hair is flying (**non operosa comis**), and she is in her element (**decens**) and thus attractive in her fury.

53–54. Palluerantque ipso labra soluta mero: the poet's lips, normally violet with unmixed wine, turn pale with fear as the cup drops from his hand; a wonderful example of Propertius's visual imagination.

55–56. Cynthia's fury is no less than that exhibited in the fall of a city: a neat twist on the traditional elegiac motif of *militia amoris*.

57–58. Vicinas . . . clamat aquas = "cries 'fire!' "

59–60. The whole neighborhood is woken by the ensuing disturbance.

61–62. Cynthia drives Phyllis and Teia into the first open tavern on the dark street. See lines 19–20.

63–64. Cynthia returns home bearing the trophies of her triumph, scraps of hair and clothing, and literally gives Propertius the back of her hand (**peruersa . . . manu**).

65–66. Propertius's ready concession that he deserves (**meruere**) this abuse can be read two ways. First, continuing the inversion of sexual roles, Propertius is in the position of the woman whose infidelities are punished, often violently, while Cynthia occupies the position of the Roman man who philanders with impunity. Second, bites and even slaps are often portrayed in elegy as a form of foreplay. Considering that the estranged lovers wind up in bed, Propertius may be hinting at his own pleasure.

67–69. The enjambment of **eruitur** to line 69 is a stroke of rhetorical brilliance, dramatizing Cynthia's pulling Lygdamus from behind the headboard of the dining couch (**plutei**). **Fulcra** = the inlaid mounting that held the *pluteus*.

69–70. Geniumque meum . . . adorat: in Roman culture every man was protected by a guardian spirit known as his genius (women had a Juno). Augustus, while not allowing prayer or sacrifice to be made directly to him, did permit worship of his genius. It is hard not to see a veiled reference to this rhetorical sleight of hand here. Lygdamus's relation to his master would be the analog of the Roman people's to Augustus.

71–72. Propertius's defeat is complete. He assumes the position of a suppliant in wartime suing for peace (**ad foedera ueni**). Cynthia reluctantly allows him to embrace her feet. The return of the *militia amoris* motif gives the whole scene a suitably comic turn.

73–74. Formula legis = "terms," in technical legal vocabulary.

75–76. Pompeia ... umbra = Pompey's portico, according to Ovid a prime spot for picking up young women. See *Ars* 1.1.67–68.

Harena: the forum was spread with sand on holidays, and games were held there. Such crowded spaces offered opportunities for amorous liaisons. See *Ars* 1.1.163–64.

77–78. Summum ... theatrum: Augustus allowed women to sit only in the upper rows of the theater. Propertius is to keep his eyes on the stage.

Lectica ... Aperta = one whose curtains are not drawn.

79–80. Not only is Propertius's *genius* unable to protect Lygdamus, he consents to the latter's being thrown into chains and sold (**ueneat**). 4.7.35–36 indicates that this action was not followed through on.

83–84. Suffiit = fumigation. Cynthia's ritual purification of Propertius's house recalls the rites at Lanuvium with which the poem began.

87–88. Respondi = "I promised again."

Soluimus arma = "We laid aside arms," but, since *arma* is a common euphemism for penis (see 1.3.15–16), it also means "we released our lust."

OVID

Amores 1.1

This programmatic introduction to the collection focuses, like Propertius 2.1, on the opposition of epic and elegy. The tone here is openly satirical, and the *Aeneid* is the unambiguous object of Ovid's irony. In later poems, other targets come in for similar treatment, including Augustus himself. Ovid's infectious, almost compulsive, irreverence is on display from the poem's first line, which there parodies the *Aeneid*'s *arma uirumque cano*. Yet, Ovid is not subversive in any narrow or simple sense. Where Propertius and Tibullus both imagine and have memories of a world beyond that of the principate, Augustus's world is Ovid's [63]. Because he takes this brave new world for granted in both its vanities and benefits, his irony is self-deconstructing. That even the position of self-subverting ironist was ultimately no longer safe, however, is revealed by the poet's subsequent exile. Ovid's fate is more evidence of the increasing impossibility of the elegist under the imperial regime than it is of his political sympathies.

The opening sequence of poems in the *Amores* is important. Ovid tells us in a separate prefatory epigram that our edition of the *Amores* is a second revised edition. The first was five books long rather than the current three. While little is known of the first edition, it is thought to have been published serially between 20 and 10 BCE. The second edition was published as a single work around 4 BCE, but is dated by some as late as 1 CE. How much rewriting was involved in the second edition is unclear, but, as Ovid acknowledges, it involved substantial editorial pruning and consequent rearrangement of the poems. Thus, we can assume that the order of the opening sequence, as we have it, was deliberately composed. As discussed in the Introduction, this opening proceeds methodically, firmly situating Ovid's work both in relation to the conventions of the elegiac genre and those of its chief competitor epic [62]. This first poem is of decisive importance in setting the tone for the collection as a whole.

The scenario of 1.1 is simple and hilarious. The poet sits down to write epic, but Cupid steals a foot from every other line producing alternating hexameters and pentameters. The result: Ovid becomes an elegist! When he complains that Cupid has overstepped his bounds and trod upon the territory of Apollo and the Muses, the god responds with one of his arrows causing the poet to fall in love. In 1.1, Ovid deliberately reveals the artificiality of the genre by showing the form to precede the content. At the end of the poem, the poet is in love because an elegist must be, but he does not yet have a beloved.

1–2. This couplet introduces an elegant variation on the Callimachean *recusatio* {53} in which the poet explains why he cannot write in a given genre. See the introductory note to Propertius 2.1.

Materia . . . modis: note how the alliteration underlines the notion that form and content should coincide. Ovid places **modis** ("meter") at the end of the pentameter to signal the foot "missing" from the hexameter.

3–4. Note the play on words in **inferior**. The second verse of the couplet was smaller. Elegy was also considered a lesser genre.

5–6. The poet's disrespectful address to the god (**saeue puer**), while typically Ovidian, is rare in ancient poetry, even elegy.

Pieridum: see Tibullus.1.4.61–62.

Vates: see Propertius 3.4.9–10 and the introductory note to 4.6.

7–8. If Cupid can interfere in the realm of Apollo and the Muses, then what is to keep all the gods from trading places?

Praeripiat . . . Venus arma Mineruae: Ovid uses this example to introduce the theme of *militia amoris*, which is one of his favorites. Just as Cupid has taken on Apollo's office, Venus in the *Amores* does take up arms.

9–10. The theme of role reversal continues through the next two couplets. What if **Ceres** and Diana (**pharetratae uirginis**) were to exchange roles? Ceres is the goddess of agricultural fertility (**arua**) and Diana of untamed virginity in the wilds beyond civilization (**siluis . . . iugosis**). Again, the reversal is emblematic of elegiac discourse as whole, whose aim in Ovid is seduction, that is, to tame female virginity and bring it under masculine cultivation. On the metaphor of "taming" virginity, see Catullus 68.118 and Propertius 1.1.9–10 and 15–16.

11–12. The exchange here is between Apollo and Mars, and hence between war and poetry. This too is relevant to the genre, since not only is this poem about the poet's inability to write an epic on war, but also elegy itself appropriates epic's subject matter through the figure of *militia amoris*. Thus, once again the boundaries between these seeming opposites is called into question.

Crinibus insignem: on Apollo's hair, see Tibullus 1.4.37–38, 2.3.23–26.

13–14. Ovid presents the traditional notion that there are discrete realms of experience and discrete poetic genres and that personal, political, and poetic order is best maintained by observing these boundaries. Elegy, however, is the transgressive genre *par excellence*. Cupid refuses to stay put.

15–16. Heliconia tempe: a beautiful valley in Thessaly, here applied to the glens round Mt. Helicon, traditional haunts of the Muses. **Tempe**: Greek neuter plural.

17–18. The hexameter is here pictured as a strong rising meter (**surrexit**), and the pentameter as a weak falling back (**attenuat**). Duncan Kennedy (1993) sees an erotic *double-entendre* in this couplet.

Attenuat: the valuing of the slender or thin is common in Callimachean poetics [29].

19–20. Ovid's complaint that he lacks the subject matter to write elegy (**materia . . . numeris leuioribus apta**) reveals the artificiality of the form and punctures the illusion that it is based on the poet's experience.

Aut puer aut . . . puella: the interchangeability of boys and girls as objects of masculine desire is discussed in the introductory note to Tibullus 1.4.

21–22. Cupid opens his quiver (**pharetra . . . soluta**) and responds to Ovid's complaint with an arrow fashioned for his demise. The motif of Cupid's arrow lends itself well to the recurring theme of *militia amoris*.

In exitium = accusative of purpose.

23–24. Lunauit = to pull back the bow and form it into the shape of a crescent.

25–26. Vror: see Catullus 72.7–8.

Vacuo . . . pectore: Ovid is in love but does not yet have a beloved.

27–28. The rising and falling rhythm of the elegiac couplet is alluded to.

29–30. Ovid bids epic farewell and binds his temples with myrtle, a plant sacred to Venus.

Vndenos . . . Pedes = a hexameter plus a pentameter.

Amores 1.2

In this poem, the triumph is subverted. Cupid marches at its head with the poet in chains behind him. From the time of Augustus's triple triumph in 29 BCE, the sacred rite of Roman victors was a frequent theme of Augustan poetry (see Propertius 2.1.31–34, 2.15.45–46, and the introductory note to 3.4). The poem ends with a recollection of Propertius 3.4.19–20 where Venus is called on to watch over Augustus. Both passages call attention to the presumed kinship of Augustus and Amor. The *gens Julia* claimed descent from Aeneas and therefore had a special devotion to the cult of *Venus genetrix*. The irony of taking such claims literally, however, becomes clear in the elegiac context in which the rejection of war and epic in favor of love and erotic verse are programmatic elements.

Moreover, Augustus the moral reformer sorts ill with Augustus Cupid's cousin. The legislator against adultery makes an odd bedfellow with the god of seduction. Propertius deployed this trope, which was taken directly from Caesarian propaganda, in the context of Augustus's projected campaign to recapture Crassus's lost standards. It was a context that allowed the passage to be read both as serious praise of what would have been a popular campaign and as an ironic undercutting of epic *militia* in favor of elegiac *otium*. Ovid's use of this same trope is very different. The political context of the mid-20s BCE in which the Augustan regime was establishing its uncontested legitimacy is all but gone. The *pax Augusta* is an accepted reality and both civil wars and wars of conquest are to be a thing of the past. Thus, for Ovid, the topical context for the triumph motif, which appears in Propertius 3.4, and the potential political complexity it implies, was vanishing.

In 1.2, Ovid also parodies one of the most unambiguously pro-Augustan passages in the *Aeneid*, Jupiter's prophecy of Rome's coming greatness and of Augustus's closing of the gates of war on the temple of Janus in 27 BCE (*Aeneid* 1.291–96). The Ovidian passage is the exact opposite of Vergil's. In it, *Furor* is set free rather than bound and *Mens Bona* ("Good Sense") and *Pudor* ("Shame") – clear parallels to Vergil's *Fides* and *Vesta* – are made captive (1.2.29–36).

The poem opens with Ovid suffering the pangs of love, but still without a love object and resisting the power of love. By its end he has yielded and is begging for mercy from Caesar's cousin. Love in this poem, as in 1.1, remains primarily a formal device. It offers generic opportunities for irony and boundary crossings of the literary, political, and cultural sort favored by elegy.

1–2. Sleeplessness is a classic symptom of love in ancient literature.

3–4. **Vacuus somno** = "without sleep."
   Versati corporis: a vivid image of tossing and turning.

5–6. The conversational aside is a typical device of Ovidian rhetoric. "Could I be in love without my knowing it?" We are meant to relish the absurdity.
Callidus: understand *Amor*.

7–8. See 1.1.21–26.

9–10. Note the anaphora. The question of domination and submission is central to Ovid's conception of the erotic. As the poet here cedes to Amor, in the next poem he seeks for Corinna to cede to him. Roman sexuality, with its emphasis on the opposition of activity versus passivity, is generally portrayed as a zero-sum game in which for one party to win the other must lose. It is within this ideological framework that the concept of *seruitium amoris* takes on its full significance. See the introductory note to Tibullus 1.4.

11–12. Seneca the Elder tells us that these "personal observations" (*uidi*) were commonplaces taken from Ovid's rhetoric teacher, Porcius Latro.

13–14. For taming as an erotic image, see 1.1.9–10, Catullus 68.118, and Propertius 1.1.9–10 and 15–16.

15–16. Lupatis = a jagged bit, with teeth like those of a wolf (*lupus*), used for taming horses.
Ad arma facit = "acts in accords with his harness." **Arma** = harness, but looks forward to the triumphal motif.

17–18. *Seruitium amoris* is analogized directly to the domestication of animals.

19–20. Praeda: one of Ovid's favorite metaphors for love as conquest. See Tibullus 1.2.65–66, 2.3.35–42, Propertius 2.1.65–66, 2.16.1–2, 3.4.21–22.
Porrigimus uictas ad tua iura manus: Ovid answers in the affirmative his own question from 1.1.5.

21–22. Like Tibullus in 1.1.57–58, Ovid defines elegy as the opposite of **laus**.
Opus est = "is necessary."

23–24. The *triumphator* wore a crown of laurel. On myrtle, see 1.1.29–30.
Maternas . . . columbas: Venus's chariot was drawn by sparrows or doves.
Vitricus = stepfather. Appropriately, the identity of Cupid's father is disputed. Cupid was said by some to be the son of Venus and Jupiter. Jupiter was the god to whom triumphs were dedicated. The traditional procession ended at the shrine of Jupiter Capitolinus. Others said Mars was Cupid's sire and, since triumphs were normally celebrated to commemorate conquest in

war, Mars too can be thought of as supplying Cupid's chariot (**currum**). Venus's legitimate spouse was the misshapen Vulcan who would have built the car. Any one of these three could with reason be referred to as Cupid's **uitricus**. Ovid's allusion to Cupid's doubtful paternity, and his subsequent identification of the god as Caesar's cousin in lines 51–52, cannot have appealed to Augustus's moral or political sensibilities.

25–26. Triumphum: the crowd would call out *io triumphe* as the conquering general's chariot passed.

27–28. Rather than foreign kings and queens, young men and women captured by Love will march behind his triumphal chariot.

29–30. Praeda recens: see lines 19–20.
    The chains of love shackle the mind (**captiua . . . mente**) rather than the body.

31–36. On this passage as a parody of the *Aeneid*, see the introductory note.

31–32. Mens Bona = rational behavior. All the traditional virtues are held captive and the vices set free.

33–34. See lines 25–26.

35–36. In the *Aeneid*, **Furor** is shut within the temple of Janus when the closing of the gates of war by Augustus is foretold. Here, it is Cupid's companion.

37–38. Love is the supreme power over all men and gods, trumping even Caesar's power.
    Nudus eris = a clear *double entendre*.

39–40. Triumphanti: understand *tibi*.

41–42. The **triumphator** was referred to as "golden" (**aureus**) because of the decorations on the *toga picta* he wore. Aphrodite is often termed "golden" in Greek poetry and so this is a fitting epithet for her son as well. See Propertius 4.4.53–54. Cupid's bejeweled hair-do more befits the effeminate elegiac dandy than a traditional Roman general.

43–44. Cupid ceases to be the conquering hero and becomes the ruthless tyrant as he turns on the adoring crowd.

45–46. Where self-control was a Roman military virtue, Cupid displays the elegist's inability to restrain himself (**licet ipse uelis**).

47–48. The intoxications of **Bacchus** and of Love are identified. Bacchus's triumphal chariot was pulled by tigers back to Europe after his conquest of India.
Gravis alitibus: an oxymoron.

49–50. **Perdere** is the complement of **parce**.

51–52. This couplet has been discussed in the introductory note. It also alludes to Propertius 2.16.41–42, *Caesaris haec uirtus et gloria Caesaris haec est:* | *illa, qua uicit, condidit arma manu.* These lines refer to Caesar's clemency and Marc Antony's shameful conduct at the battle of Actium. Walter (1999) has demonstrated that Cupid occupies the position of Antony in Ovid's text. *Amor*, he argues, therefore stands for a dangerous Dionysian excess that is in direct opposition to Augustus's self-chosen model of Apollonian control. Thus in 1.2, *Amor*, the *princeps*'s cognatus, presents a threatening parody of the traditional Roman triumph. He is not the victorious hero who returns to bask in the acclamation of his fellow citizens and reaffirm the integrity of the existing order, but a tyrant whose passion has turned against the adoring crowd, and who treats his own people as a conquered nation. He represents a loss of self-control, the reign of *Furor*. In this Dionysian guise, *Amor* is the perfect model for Antony who in 34 BCE celebrated his triumph over the Armenians in Alexandria with Cleopatra rather than returning to Rome. There he portrayed himself as the New Dionysus. From the perspective of Roman propaganda, this was a major gaffe. It was precisely the kind of "eastern excess" that allowed Augustus to portray himself as the defender of traditional Roman order against the dangers of an orientalizing and effeminate tyranny (see Propertius 3.11).

Amores 1.3

Ovid revels in the artificiality of elegy by deferring the introduction of Corinna to poem 3, although she is still not named. In this poem, Ovid is no longer the *praeda* of Cupid, but of his beloved. Ovid offers her undying love and poetic immortality and claims to be no "sexual circus rider" (*desultor amoris*), but later poems give the lie to his protestations of eternal fidelity (see 2.7 and 2.8).

This poem is notable for its rehearsal of many of elegy's major themes including the *paupertas* of the poet (see Tibullus 1.1) and his *seruitium* to his beloved. All of these emphasize the poet's subservience. Yet, in as much as the poem begins with the image of the *puella praedata* and ends with a series of mythological rapes, Ovid's tongue is firmly in his cheek.

1–2. **Aut amet aut faciat cur ego semper amem**: the interchangeability of true love with its semblance is a consistent Ovidian theme and one consonant with his emphasis on the artificiality of the elegiac genre.

3–4. Tantum = "only."
Audierit = perfect jussive subjunctive.

5–6. Per longos . . . annos: another Ovidian deflation of amatory rhetoric. Only two poems earlier, the poet was struck by Cupid's shot.

Protestations of the poet's *fides* are an elegiac commonplace since Catullus. See poem 76 and note the contrast in tone with Ovid's elegant irony.

7–8. The poet acknowledges his equestrian status, which, while more modest than that of a man from a senatorial family with consular ancestors, was far from mean [34]. See Propertius 2.34.55–56.

9–10. On the hexameter see Tibullus 2.3.41–42 and Propertius 3.5.5–6. The thrifty father is a comic archetype in Rome. Ovid expands it to include both parents.

11–12. Comitesque nouem = the Muses.
Vitisque repertor = Bacchus, whose title, derived from the god's association with wine and hence poetic inspiration, hardly seems designed to inspire *fides*.
Hac faciunt = *hac ex parte faciunt*, "work on this side, support me." **Faciunt** is intransitive.

13–14. Nuda simplicitas = "unadorned simplicity," but the sexual *double entendre* undermines the poet's assertion.
Purpureus pudor = "blushing shame." Note the alliteration.

15–16. Desultor = a trick rider at the circus who jumps from mount to mount. The image itself belies the assertion.
Si qua fides: a pregnant, if conventional, qualification.

17–18. The poet's death and the beloved's mourning are standard elegiac motifs. See Tibullus 1.1.59–60 and Propertius's elegant variation in 4.7.
Sororum = the Fates.

19–20. Materiem felicem: the beloved is to be the subject of Ovid's poetry. Her reward will be immortality, but she is reduced to the passive object of the elegist's poetic imagination.
In carmina: accusative of purpose.

21–24. The mythological exempla of Lo, Leda, and Europa all involve young girls overpowered by an all powerful deity in bestial disguise. They are not the examples designed to reassure a potential lover. Jupiter is the ultimate *desultor amoris*.

21–22. Io: see Propertius 1.3.19–20.

Quam = Leda, whom Jupiter approached in the form of a swan (**fluminea . . . aue**). The result of the encounter was an egg from which Helen and the Dioscuri were born.

23–24. Quaeque = Europa, the Phoenician princess whom Jupiter lured away by taking the form of a bull (**simulato . . . iuuenco**) and then swimming with her on his back to Crete.

25–26. Their fame will be mutual, casting doubt on the purity of the poet's motives. His true desire is poetic achievement.

Amores 1.4

Poem 1.4 of the *Amores* is crucial to our understanding of the collection as a whole. Situated between the opening three avowedly programmatic poems and 1.5 in which Corinna is finally named, 1.4 represents the beginning of the sequence's narrative proper. In this poem, the drama of the *Amores* moves beyond the purely formal game of elegiac love portrayed in 1.1, 1.2, and 1.3.

In it, the poet appears as the *praeceptor amoris* [7, 58] who instructs Corinna in the arts of adultery in order to deceive her *uir*. 1.4 has a companion piece in 2.5 where the poet is hoist on his own petard. There the very same signs, winks, and nods are used against Ovid himself.

The term *uir* is ambiguous and much debated. On the one hand, it suggests that he is Corinna's husband and hence that the relationship portrayed in the *Amores* is adulterous. This reading sees Ovid deliberately flouting Augustus' moral reform and its reconstruction of *uirtus* ("virtue," "courage," but also "manliness") as embodied in the *mos maiorum* [10, 22, 30, 52, 63]. At the same time, the *uir* may refer merely to Corinna's man of the moment and reflect her status as a *meretrix*. What does seem clear, however, is that the ambiguity provides Ovid with plausible deniability, allowing him to appear both subversive and submissive at the same time. Indeed, everyone agrees that the language used in the poem is deliberately deceptive and that through it Ovid is at least suggesting the possibility of violating the *lex Iulia's* ban on adultery [13, 18, 37, 62, 64].

1–2. Roman women unlike their Greek counterparts regularly attended dinner parties with their husbands and lovers.

3–4. Tantum = adverbial. The poet can only look (**aspiciam**). Another will enjoy being touched.

5–6. Apte subiecta = "appropriately snuggled against," but also with the notion of "lain under." The image has sexual connotations while suggesting Corinna's subjection to the power of the *uir*.

Iniciet collo . . . manum: this refers to an embrace, but it also cites a legal formula used later in the poem to assert property rights (see line 40). This implication is reinforced by **cum uolet**.

7–8. The couplet refers to the battle of the Lapiths and the Centaurs. At the wedding of Hippodamia and Pirithous, the Centaurs when they had finished their wine (**posito . . . uino**) were so intoxicated that they attempted to lay hands on the bride. The story became a paradigm of boorish behavior. This image of bestial rape recalls those cited in 1.3.21–24.

Candida . . . Atracis = Hippodamia, the daughter of Atrax, the name of a Thessalian king, as well as a river and a city.

Ambiguous . . . uiros: the Centaurs were half men and half horses. Ovid, in as much as he will later assert the rights due Corinna's *uir*, is in effect himself a *uir ambiguus*. Moreover, the elegist as a man who expressly prefers the *mollis* to the *durus* is always in Roman terms a *uir ambiguus*.

9–10. Vix a te uideor posse tenere manus = "I scarcely seem able to keep my hands off you." Compare line 6. As several commentators note, **tenere manus** more frequently has violent rather than erotic connotations.

11–12. The poet shifts from lamentation to pragmatic instruction.

13–14. Note the anaphoric repetition **ante ueni . . . ueneris ante . . . ante ueni** and the couplet's symmetrical construction. The irony of the poet admitting his own instructions to be useless but insisting on them nonetheless is to be savored. It foreshadows other examples in the collection where the poet turns his irony against himself, revealing the *amator* to be less than he wishes to appear.

15–28. This entire passage is an expansion and systematization of Tibullus 1.2.21–22.

15–16. The guests prepare to take their places at the table. Unlike at modern dinner parties, Romans reclined on couches while eating. There were three diners to a couch and three couches arranged around a square table. The fourth side was left open for serving purposes. Diners propped themselves on one elbow and ate with their free hand. As Corinna makes her way to the couch, she is to touch Ovid's foot. He has arrived first and is already reclining.

17–18. Here commence Ovid's instructions in secret signs.

19–20. Note the anaphora of **uerba**.

Verba digitis . . . notata mero: words drawn with fingers in wine.

21–22. Veneris lasciuia nostrae: the pleasure of our lovemaking.

Purpureas . . . genas = blushing cheeks. Compare **purpureusque pudor** in 1.3.14.

23–24. Pendeat extrema mollis ab aure manus = tug on your ear lobe.

25–26. Digitis = poetic plural.

27–28. Note the progression from the *amator* displeasing his beloved (lines 23–24) to his pleasing her (lines 25–26), to her wishing the *uir* harm.

29–30. With mention of the *uir*, Ovid turns his attention to how his beloved should act toward her escort.

Sapias is ambiguous. If one were to stop reading the line, it would take its original meaning, "taste." It is not until the reader reaches **iubeto** that it becomes clear that it means, "be wise" and hence, in this context, "do not taste."

Iubeto = future imperative.

Leuiter = "quietly."

31–32. Ovid plans to steal a virtual kiss by drinking where Corinna has.

33–34. She shall not eat what the *uir* has tasted lest their mouths meet.

35–36. Ovid over the next three couplets envisions Corinna engaged in love-play with her *uir*, gradually working himself into a jealous frenzy. The irony of the adulterer's jealousy would have been enjoyed by Ovid's audience.

Sinito = future imperative.

37–38. Sinus in this context refers first to the folds in her cloak, but it is also used as a euphemism for "vagina." In the context of heavy petting, this implication cannot be excluded.

Ne uelis + infinitive is a common legal formula. This is the first of a series of technical legal terms. The combination of legal jargon, lessons in adulterous intrigue, and salacious innuendo creates a comic mixture that not only satirizes respectable Roman society, but also elegy itself.

39–40. Manifestus = legal term, meaning "caught in the act," as in the phrase *fur manifestus*. Since love affairs are referred to as *furta* in elegy, this phrase is no doubt being deliberately recalled (see Catullus 68.136, 140, Tibullus 1.2.9–10, 19–20, and 35–36, 1.5.7–8, 69–70, and Propertius

4.7.15–16, 4.8.33–34). **Amator** here is equated with *fur*. It is therefore doubly ironic when in the pentameter the poet invokes the legal process of *manus iniectio*, a form of *uindicatio*, in which stolen property is claimed by its rightful owner.

    Iniciamque manum: the technical legal phrase recalls its earlier more neutral use in line 6.

41–42. Haec tamen aspiciam: Ovid here answers in the affirmative the question he posed in the same terms in lines 3–4. He thus admits that his previous instructions to Corinna will most likely be ignored.

    Pallia: the diners on a couch were provided with a coverlet.

    Caeci: because he cannot see what is happening beneath the covers.

45–46. Ovid's self-subverting irony here comes full circle as the *amator* admits that he fears most what he has already done. There is a charm to Ovid's audacious hypocrisy. Its artifice paradoxically evokes a sense of honesty as it constantly points to its own cynicism, thereby demystifying the position of the elegiac lover while satirizing the petty moralizing of those who are affronted by his manipulations. Of course, the very artificiality of his position precludes that honesty from being more than rhetorical.

47–48. The irony of **iniecta** should not be lost. On a semantic level, it is redundant. Its clear purpose is to remind us of the formula, *inicere manus*, while assimilating it to a quasi-public act of mutual masturbation. When Ovid pursues his **dulce ... opus**, he is both asserting a claim of sexual possession and depicting a transgression of the very law that makes that claim possible. In this light, Ovid's later claim that Corinna's kisses are given to him freely, whereas those given the *uir* are forced by law, rings hollow (lines 63–64).

49–50. Hoc tu non facies: the hypocrisy of the *amator* produces hilarity.

    Conscia de tergo pallia deme tuo: Ovid asks Corinna to remove the coverlet (**pallia**) so he can see what she and the *uir* are up to. The same command could also be used to ask her to remove her cloak (**pallia**).

51–52. The poet rallies his courage and proposes that Corinna get the *uir* drunk so they can pursue their intrigue.

53–54. If he passes out, we will know what to do.

55–56. In medium turbae ... agmen: compare Tibullus 1.5.63.

57–58. Note the extraordinary rhetorical balance of the hexameter. As

McKeown (1989) observes, "Ovid and his mistress are here, as is recommended in line 56, in the middle of the throng."

Mei = partitive genitive.

59–60. Note the immediate reversal from **tange mei** to **me miserum.** Ovid is a master of such ironic transitions. **Me miserum** = accusative of exclamation.

In paucas . . . horas = "for a few hours."

61–62. Nocte uir includet: the **uir** locks the door for the night, rendering Ovid the *exclusus amator* [10] and showing the limits of the instructions he proffers as *praeceptor amoris* [7, 58].

63–64. Quod mihi das furtim, iure coacta dabis: Corinna gives kisses and more to the *uir* because she is under a legal obligation, presumably as his wife, concubine, or contractually obligated *meretrix.* Ovid implies that because those she gives to him are stolen (**furtim**), they are freely given. He thus inverts normal Roman values, portraying transgression as freedom and the law as the site of coercion and implicit violence. Ovid's own bid to assert legal ownership in line 40, however, undercuts his already shaky moral authority.

65–66. "At minimum, submit silently and let the sex be bad" (**sitque maligna Venus**).

Dato = future imperative.

67–68. "That way maybe he won't enjoy it, or at least you won't."

69–70. "But whatever you do tonight, lie to me tomorrow." The poem ends with a typically Ovidian reversal of roles as the deceiver prays to be deceived.

Dedisse = "to have given in."

Amores 1.5

In 1.5, the praeceptor's instructions bear fruit as the affair is consummated in the famous siesta poem in which Corinna is finally named. Compare this delay to the opening line of Propertius's *Monobiblos, Cynthia prima fuit.* Ovid through this and other techniques consistently foregrounds the artificiality of his chosen genre. Nonetheless, this poem appeals because of its seeming realism and its expression of frank joy in an uncomplicated erotic encounter. Such poems are rarities among the elegists, who mostly bemoan their disappointments or rail against rivals. The simplicity of the scenario, however, should not deceive the reader. The encounter is highly staged, filled with knowing winks and rhetorical nods.

1–2. Aestus erat, mediamque dies exegerat horam: Ovid sets the scene. Making love during the day was considered a decadent pursuit by traditional Roman moralists such as Cato the elder, who expelled a senator for embracing his wife in daylight.

Membra leuanda: the sense of "resting" or "lightening one's limbs" conceals a sexual *double entendre*, "raising one's member." Catullus's hendecasyllabic poem 32 on a proposed afternoon encounter with Ipsitilla, which is one of Ovid's models, makes the image more explicit.

3–6. The window is half open allowing a kind of twilight in the afternoon.

Quale fere siluae lumen habere solent: compare 1.4.9–10 and its recollection of the forest home of the centaurs. Poem 1.5 represents the fulfillment of the desires thwarted by the *uir* in 1.4.

7–8. The voice of the *praeceptor amoris* from 1.4 returns.

Verecundis is not an adjective that would normally be associated with girls who would show up for such an encounter.

9–10. Ecce, Corinna uenit: the shift to the present sets Corinna immediately before us.

Recincta = "unbelted." Tunics were normally one-piece garments bound at the waste by a girdle.

Candida: compare Catullus 68.70.

Diuidua colla tegente coma: Roman women normally wore their hair tied up in a knot or bun. Corinna's letting her hair down in this manner invites intimacy in a way hard to square with the term *uerecunda*.

11–12. Sameramis = Semiramis, on whom see Propertius 3.11.21–22.

Lais = a famed Corinthian courtesan. This reference can be seen as connoting the fact that Corinna was a *meretrix*, but it may merely imply that her favors were widely bestowed.

13–14. The rapid shift from the slow and almost reverent description of Corinna's entrance to the violence of **deripui tunicam** is typically Ovidian.

Rara: refers to the loosely woven, transparent quality of the tunic.

Nec multum . . . nocebat: a difficult passage, presumably referring to the fact that Corinna's robe, given its transparent quality, did not much get in Ovid's way, but nonetheless (**sed tamen**) she fought (**pugnabat**) to cover herself with it.

15–16. Indications of amorous violence, as seen in the use of verbs like **deripio** and **pugno**, are common in Ovid (*Amores* 1.7 makes the violence explicit). This couplet's implication that Corinna's refusal of Ovid's advances were (**pugnaret tamquam quae uincere nollet**) not serious, while perhaps

mitigated by the context, reveal the clear imbalances of power that characterized Roman sexuality. It is not clear that Corinna has a right of refusal once
she entered the *amator's* house. Through Ovid's recognition of the reality of
Roman sexual power relations, the pose of *seruitium amoris* is shown in this
and other poems to be a fiction in the service of poetry and masculinist sexual
ideology. Only those who have power can play at not having it.

17–18. Note the distanced tone. Ovid initially approaches the naked
Corinna with the detachment of an art critic.

21–22. Castigato = compressed or restrained, and hence not sagging. The
hexameter indicates that Corinna bore none of the physical marks of
childbirth.

23–24. Singula quid referam: this formula cuts off the description at the
moment when it would have crossed the boundary from the erotic to the
pornographic.

25–26. Cetera quis nescit: a knowing wink that says everything and nothing.
  Lassi: their passion spent.

Amores 2.5

In this companion piece to 1.4, the poet is hoist on his own petard. Corinna
here uses against the *amator* the tricks he taught her to employ against the
uir. Ovid is fond of such pairs of poems. See also 2.7 and 2.8, as well as 2.19
and 3.4. Where Book 1 introduces us to Corinna and foregrounds Ovid's
playful and parodic take on the elegiac genre, Book 2 explores the perils of
erotic relationships, almost always at the lover's expense. He is shown to be
feckless, manipulative, and self-deceiving. Thus, in the immediately preceding poem, Ovid had just explained how every sort of girl is pleasing to him,
tall or short, fat or thin, light or dark.

1–2. The opening couplet is paradox: "no love is worth the promise to die for
it that I have made so many times." **Totiens** immediately signals that the
lover's subsequent protestations should be viewed with suspicion. For if he
has made such vows frequently, then how seriously should they be taken?
Moreover, if he has made them repeatedly we can assume they have not
always been made to the same person.
  Tanti = genitive of value.

3–4. Mihi here does double duty going both with the exclamatory **ei** and
serving as a dative of disadvantage with **malum**. Some editors prefer to
emend the text.

5–6. Deceptae: the meaning of this word is much debated, but if construed in its most literal sense, it would mean something like "intercepted." Lovers often exchanged notes written on wax tablets.

Crimen: here begins the use of legal vocabulary reminiscent of that found in 1.4.

7–8. Ovid's proof of Corinna's **crimen** is too strong for her to be able to deny it easily. It is based not on circumstantial evidence but eyewitness testimony, his own. The humor of course is that normally a lawyer's case cannot be too good, but Ovid, as at the end of 1.4, wishes to be deceived. **Arguerem** = "I would plead my case." **Vincere** = "to win a suit." **Causa** = "a case."

9–10. Quod amat = "what he loves."
Non feci = "I plead not guilty."

11–12. To seek to win cases such as this is to seek one's own pain.
Palma = the regular sign of victory in athletic and forensic contests.
Victa . . . rea = ablative absolute, "with his litigation won."

13–14. Cum me dormire putares: was Ovid pretending to sleep so that he might catch Corinna *in flagrante delicto* or had he dozed off due to wine and the lateness of the hour? The poet claims to have been **sobrius**, but simultaneously notes that the wine had been served (**apposito . . . mero**). See 1.4.7–8.

15–16. Compare 1.4.17 and 1.4.19.

17–18. Compare 1.4.20. The double negative (**nec . . . nulla**) = a strong positive. This is an example of the rhetorical figure of litotes.

19–20. The poet recognized (**agnoui**) the lovers' code.
Sermonem . . . quod non uideatur agentem = "a conversation not doing what it seemed."
Verbaque pro certis iussa ualere notis = "and words ordered to stand for certain agreed-upon things."

21–22. Iamque = "and then."
Frequens . . . conuiua = collective singular, "many a guest."
Compositi = "drowsy." Compare 1.4.53.

23–24. Illa = oscula. These were passionate kisses with the tongue, not friendly pecks.
Liquet in the impersonal is frequent in legal terminology.

25–26. Viro recalls 1.4. The tables have been turned.

27–28. Diana as the goddess of virginal purity is a good example for portraying the kisses a **germana** might offer to her **frater**, whereas the kisses of Venus and Mars were not merely sensual but adulterous.

29–30. Compare 1.4.40. On **gaudia** as orgasm, see Tibullus 1.5.39–40.

31–32. Our **gaudia** are community property in which no third person (**tertius**) has a share.
    In . . . uenit = legal terminology for "to be entitled to."
    Ista . . . bona = a pun. On the one hand, **bona** is a standard legal term for property (as in English "goods"). But the **gaudia** are also **bona**.

33–34. This couplet represents the turning point in the poem. The poet's tirade has produced a blush that inflames his passion. It is instructive to recall Lavinia's blush at *Aeneid* 12.64–70 and its effect on Turnus. Line 37 is an almost direct quote of *Aeneid* 12.67–68. Line 40's mention of stained ivory echoes *Aeneid* 12.66–67. For further Vergilian echoes, see *Amores* 1.1.1 and 1.2.29–36. In each case, Ovid travesties the heroic with the erotic absurd.
    On **purpureus . . . pudor**, see 1.3.14.

35–36. Tithoni coniuge = Aurora, the dawn.
    Sponso uisa puella nouo = the contrast between the young maid with her newly betrothed husband-to-be and Aurora's marriage to Tithonus, who was granted eternal life but not eternal youth and eventually sunk into utter decrepitude, makes a nice rhetorical antithesis. The ironic contrast between the modest blush of the bride-to-be and Corinna's flush of shame makes the simile doubly effective.

37–38. Vbi cantatis, Luna, laborat equis: compare Propertius 2.34.52. The laboring of the moon is used there and elsewhere of its eclipse, during which it often first reddens. An eclipse was thought to be the effect of witchcraft (**cantatis . . . equis**).

39–40. This simile is not only found in the *Aeneid* but also at *Iliad* 4.142–44. **Maeonis** = Lydian and is a transliteration of Homer's Greek. Ovid's parody of epic here becomes complex and multi-layered.
    On the yellowing (**flauescere**) of ivory, see Propertius 4.7.82.

41–42. The hexameter is a wonderfully self-subverting acknowledgment of the excessive nature of Ovid's rhetorical elaboration.

43–44. Note the chiastic arrangement of the hexameter.

45–46. The conjunction of threatened violence and sexual arousal has been discussed above at Propertius 1.3.21–22, in the opening note to 2.1, and at 2.15.19–20, 4.4.57–58, as well as *Amores* 1.5.13–16.

47–48. Corinna's beauty is here portrayed as a form of violence (**armis**) on a par with Ovid's threat in the previous couplet to tear her hair and rip her cheeks.

49–50. Deteriora = worse than those given to his rival.

51–52. The image has slapstick quality. **Tela trisulca:** Jupiter's triply cut thunderbolts.

53–54. The poet returns to the jealousy theme.
   Ne introduces a fear clause after **torqueor.**
   Ex hac . . . nota = "of this vintage." The **nota** was a label on wine casks.

55–56. Corinna must have been taught by another to kiss so well. The *praeceptor amoris* is beaten at his own game.

57–58. At the poem's beginning, Ovid presents the paradox of an advocate whose case is too strong; he ends with that of a lover whose kisses are too good.

59–62. There is only one place Corinna could have learnt such kisses; another's bed. **Magister:** the inversion of roles is complete.

Amores 2.7

Poems 2.7 and 2.8 are a famous pair depicting the *amator*'s dalliance with Corinna's maid, Cypassis. Both are the same length. In the first, the poet strongly denies the accusation and bemoans the fact that Corinna is always casting unjust charges against him. In the second, the poet not only reverses the situation, as in 1.4 and 2.5, he also threatens to blackmail Cypassis by revealing the whole affair to Corinna if she does not continue to submit to his advances.

The exercise of arguing both sides of a question had been a staple of the rhetorical schools since the time of the sophists. One way of understanding Ovid's role in the elegiac tradition is to see the extent to which he applies the principles of the rhetorical schools to the poetry of love. In so doing, while Ovid's content remains outside the norms of Augustan moral discourse, the form is increasingly assimilated to mainstream political and forensic oratory. Catullus, Tibullus, Sulpicia, and Propertius while familiar with the basic principles of a rhetorical education all produce poetic forms whose style and structure are eccentric to the art of speechmaking.

Ovid begins 2.7 by putting himself in the position of a defendant in a law case arguing against a charge. The terminology is legalistic. One of the more hilarious aspects is the tone of self-righteous indignation adopted throughout.

1–2. Reus, crimina, and **uincam** are legal terms familiar from 2.5.5–12. **Sufficiam . . . in** = "provide the material for."

3–4. Marmorei respexi summa theatri: a paraphrase of Propertius 4.8.77. Ovid in the *Ars* lists theaters as good places to find girls.
   Elegis: the two long *es* make it clear that this is the perfect of the verb **eligo** and not a form of the noun **elegi,** "elegiac verses." Nonetheless, the identical spelling and the juxtaposition with **dolere** identifies Corinna's choice of grief (**uelis**) with the standard elegiac pose.

5–6. The reference to tacit codes is incriminating to the reader familiar with 1.4 and 2.5.

7–8. Crimen dissimulare putas: understand *me.* **Crimen** while appropriate to a legal context is often used of infidelity in elegy.

9–10. Pallor is a sign of love in ancient poetry.

11–12. This couplet is perhaps the most outrageous lie in the poem.

13–14. Insimulas = "charge," another word with legal connotations.

15–16. Miserandae sortis = genitive of description. Note that **sortis** and **uerbere** are used in lines 20 and 22 respectively of Cypassis, while **domitus** is cognate with **dominae** in line 18. Cypassis is thus implicitly compared to a beaten donkey.

17–18. Ornare: understand *capillos.*
   Obicitur = a legalism. The passive use with a personal subject is unparalleled in classical Latin.

19–20. Di melius: understand *dent.*
   Si sit . . . libido = "if it were pleasing."

21–22. While sexual relations between free men and slaves were common and recommended by Horace in *Satires* 1.2 as a method of preventing adultery, Ovid is legally correct that someone of servile origin (**famulae**) cannot contract **conubium** or "marriage." **Conubium,** however, can also mean sexual intercourse. This arguing in terms of legal technicalities is typical of the style of forensic argument Ovid parodies here.

Secta uerbere: note the casual brutality.

25–26. The reading of most manuscripts, **quae tam,** is preferable to Kenney's conjecture in the OCT, **quod erat,** which is strained and unduly sarcastic.

Quid, nisi ut indicio iuncta repulsa foret = "why would I do that except in order that rejection be joined with betrayal?"

27–28. The oaths of lovers were proverbially worthless. Swearing by Venus hardly inspires more faith. **Volatilis** = both "able to fly" and "flighty."

The pentameter is a reprisal of verse 1.

Amores 2.8

In this companion piece to 2.7, the *amator*'s cynical threat to expose his sexual relationship with Cypassis to her mistress as a means of insuring her continued compliance paints with brutal realism the image of a true *seruitium amoris*. The poem begins with an ingratiating attempt at flattery. This was a tactic borrowed from the rhetorical schools known as the *captatio beneuolentiae*. The tone, however, soon changes.

1–2. The *captatio beneuolentiae* seems largely aimed at allowing the *amator* to recover from the aspersions he has cast up on Cypassis in the preceding poem. The opening couplet refers back to 2.7.23–24.

3–4. Iucundo non rustica cognita furto = "known to be not unsophisticated in love on the sly." This is another example of litotes. On the sexual implication of *cognoscere*, see Catullus 72.5.

The pentameter refers to 2.7.25–26.

5–6. Index = "informer," a legal term.

Sociati corporis: a bold sexual metaphor.

Concubitus . . . tuos: note that the poet attributes sole responsibility to the party who had the least freedom. She alone faces punishment.

7–8. Num tamen erubui = "I did not blush, did I?" The poet here gives the lie to his claim to possess *purpureus pudor* in 1.3.14.

9–10. Ovid here refers to 2.7.19–22, at which Cypassis would have evidently taken offense.

11–12. Thessalus: Achilles, whose war prize, Briseis, was taken from him by Agamemnon, causing the former to withdraw from the Greek effort against Troy. Women captured in war automatically became slaves.

Mycenaeo . . . duci = Agamemnon, dative of agent.

Phoebas = a Greek nominative singular meaning "priestess of Apollo." The reference is to Cassandra. It is not reassuring that both Cassandra and Agamemnon were slain by his wife Clytemnestra.

Understand *est* in the pentameter.

13–14. **Tantalide:** Agamemnon was the great-grandson of Tantalus.

15–16. **Ut** = "when."

17–18. Understand *eram* in the hexameter. **Praesentior** = "more perspicacious." The poet refers back to 2.7.27–28.

19–20. On lovers' vows, see Catullus 70.3–4. **Animi periuria puri:** the oxymoron reveals the factitious nature of Ovid's claim.

Carpathium . . . mare: a stormy stretch of sea between Crete and Rhodes, surrounding the island of Carpathos.

21–22. The *amator* expects payment for services rendered.

Concubitus . . . tuos is in apposition to **pretium . . . dulce.**

23–24. **Unum** = the object of **emeruisse,** meaning both "to have obliged" and "to have satisfied sexually." Ovid here plays the *dominus* as opposed to the *seruus amoris.*

25–26. Ovid threatens blackmail, using the same terminology with which he opened the poem (**index**).

27–28. He will not only reveal their secrets but also give incriminating details sure to inflame Corinna's anger and heighten Cypassis' punishment.

Modis = sexual positions. Note the ambiguity of **dominae.**

Amores 2.19

2.19 and 3.4 constitute a third pair of poems whose contradictory stances recall 2.7 and 2.8 and whose adulterous subject matter recalls 1.4 and 2.5. The basic scenario in 2.19 is that love needs a challenge. The mistress's husband (*maritus*) should guard her more zealously lest the *amator* lose interest. The sheer perversity is part of the fun. The attempt to make a convincing argument for an unorthodox or illicit thesis was a standard showpiece of rhetorical skills, designed to show the persuasive powers of the speaker. Compare Lysias's first speech in the *Phaedrus.* Poem 3.4 argues that the husband should relax his guard since it is ineffective and only inflames the *amator*'s passion.

Ovid in both poems, as well as in 1.4, appears to be influenced by the *lex Iulia de adulteriis coercendis* of 18 BCE. This law, which was part of the Augustan moral reform, not only criminalized adultery but also specified penalties for complicitous husbands. Ovid in 2.19 makes the argument that those husbands who comply with the law are in fact merely encouraging the activity it was designed to prevent. Whether this satire has a political aim, such as aiding the opposition to Augustus or proposing an alternative policy, is doubtful, but it is hard to see how the *princeps* could have taken it as an endorsement of his policies.

The mistress in these poems is not Corinna, but a *femina noua* who has caught his fancy (lines 19–2) and is compared to Corinna (lines 9–10). These poems prepare the way for the final dissolution of the affair announced at the end of Book 3. Ovid presents a unified work that traces the affair from its beginning to its end.

1–2. Opus est takes the ablative.

At is not adversative but introduces the apodosis of the condition.

3–4. Quod licet, ingratum est; quod non licet, acrius urit = the basic thesis of the poem. What follows is illustrative. Note the political implications of accepting this as a principle of action.

5–6. Note the chiastic arrangement of the hexameter.

7–8. We have to understand a transitive verb in the first clause. Booth (1991) reasonably proposes **uelim**. The pentameter is at once a canny observation on the perils of erotic boredom and a statement of sheer, hilarious perversity.

9–10. Versuta = "crafty."

11–12. Note the spondaic opening of the pentameter as the meter enacts the poet's loitering.

13–14. Note the anaphoric repetition of **a quotiens**.

Poem 2.5 indicates that the unfaithfulness (**culpam**) was not simply feigned (**finxit**). Is this another example of the poet's self-delusion?

Licebat insonti = "although she was innocent."

The use of the nominative **nocens** to modify the subject of **esse** is Greek.

15–16. Vexarat: a syncopated pluperfect. Understand *me*.

17–18. Oscula: compare 2.5.55–62.

19–20. Nostros rapuisti nuper ocellos: this new girl has only lately replaced Corinna as the object of his affections.

Time insidias: if the girl fears traps set by her husband, that will pique the *amator*'s interest.

21–22. The elegiac paraclausithyron is revealed to be a game with agreed-upon rules, as opposed to the victimization of an innocent lover by a callous *domina*.

23–24. Alimenta: the comparison of love to food is continued in the next couplet. Frustration is a kind of condiment.

25–26. Easy love and sweet food both cloy the palate.

27–28. Danae, the daughter of Acrisius was imprisoned in a bronze tower by her father after he received a prophecy that he would be killed by her son. Jupiter turned himself into a shower of gold to gain entrance, whereupon he fathered Perseus.

De Iove: *de* is used here instead of the more common *ex*.

29–30. On Io, see Propertius 1.3.19–20 and *Amores* 1.3.21–24.

31–32. Arbore frondes carpat, i.e. takes that which is available to all and therefore of no special merit or interest.

E magno flumine potet aquam: a paraphrase of Callimachus's admonition in the *Hymn to Apollo* not to drink from the broad Euphrates river, but only from the slender spring of pure inspiration [29]. See also his epigram 28. Ovid with this allusion redirects the reader from the strictly erotic to the poetic challenge he has set himself. Indeed, Ovid here produces a poem such as few would dare. He seeks not access to his mistress, as do the other elegists, but to have that access barred. This is precisely the kind of rhetorical challenge Ovid enjoyed.

33–34. The pentameter is an almost direct quotation of 1.4.45–46. Given the results of the *praeceptor*'s advice there, as shown in its companion poem 2.5, we can assume that the poet will again fail.

35–36. Note the chiastic arrangement of the pentameter.

37–38. Secure = one who is *sine cura* and hence lax.

Note the irony of the poet asking to be made an *exclusus amator*. Once more, Ovid foregrounds the artificiality and gamesmanship that constitutes the traditional elegiac position.

39–40. Furtim: elegiac love is often portrayed as a form of theft [10].

See Catullus 68.136, 140; Tibullus 1.2.9–10, 19–20, and 35–36, 1.5.7–8, 69–70; Propertius 4.7.15–16, 4.8.33–34; and *Amores* 1.4.39–40.

41–42. On **tabellas**, see 2.5.5.

43–44. As poem 1.4 had already demonstrated, the elegiac affair in its very conception is essentially adulterous, without the rival and his superior claims of legitimacy elegiac subterfuge has no reason for existence.

45–46. Ovid makes clear here the legally adulterous nature of his relationship, looking forward to line 57.

47–48. A wonderful *reductio ad absurdum*. *Tua* would normally be expected, not **mea**.

49–50. Ovid turns the image of the long-suffering elegiac lover on its head.
   The balanced construction of the pentameter points to the ideal reciprocity the *amator* demands: you guard the girl so that I can steal her.
   Verba darem: a colloquialism, "to lie or deceive."

51–52. Nulli patienda marito: the *lex Iulia* (see introductory note) expressly forbade husbands from tolerating their wives' adultery on pain of being prosecuted for *lenocinium* or "pimping" [13,18, 52, 62, 64].

53–54. Infelix: normally in elegiac discourse this applies to the locked out lover. Ovid again inverts our expectations.
   Sub nullo uindice: *uindex* is a legal term for one who asserts their property rights through the process of *iniectio manus* (see 1.4.40). The image is of a husband who would assert his rights while Ovid and his mistress are in the act. Hence, Melville (1990) translates "free from threats of vengeance," and Green (1982), "won't you beat me up one night."

57–58. On *lenocinium*, see lines 51–52.
   Gaudia: see Tibullus 1.5.39–40.

59–60. Quin = "why not?" The complicity of all parties in the elaborate charade of elegiac love is here revealed. If the husband wants to continue to play, he must do his part.

Amores 3.4

In this poem, Ovid sees the result of the *maritus* in 2.19 taking his advice. The relationship of this second poem to the first is complex and has been much disputed. It is in essence threefold. First, 3.4 is a brilliant rhetorical display. It takes the same material and same assumptions and argues to the opposite conclusion: the husband should not guard his wife because it only fires the lover's desire. Poem 3.4, therefore, contradicts 2.19 in a fashion reminiscent of 2.8's contradiction of 2.7. Second, 3.4 is a confirmation of 2.19. In 2.19, the poet bade the husband to guard his wife or he would lose interest. The husband has complied and the *amator*'s passion continues unabated. Third, 3.4 is the sequel of 2.19. In the latter, the poet invited the *maritus* to play the elegiac game so that the *amator* might deceive (*uerba dare*) him and he might provide *locum . . . materiamque* for the *amator*'s *dolis*. In 3.4, we see precisely the words and tricks of the lover now deployed against a resistant husband. The game thus has been joined and now can be properly played.

1–2. This first statement in addition to being a rejoinder to and continuation of 2.19 speaks to the futility of efforts such as the *lex Iulia* to legislate morality.

3–4. The question of the mistress's consent was first addressed in 1.4, where the poet argues that Corinna's kisses are given freely to him, the *amator*, but those given to the *uir* are coerced. Ironically, this puts the traditionally virtuous woman who submits to her husband in the same position as the slave (see 2.7 and 2.8). True virtue consists in acting without restraint.

5–6. The distinction between mind and body would appeal to Ovid's medieval Christian apologists who used it to very different ends.

7–8. Omnibus occlusis intus adulter erit: the adulterer within is, in the first place, the desire in the *puella*'s mind, but it also hints that a girl with adultery on her mind will find a suitable partner within the household if one from without is unavailable. This would mean a slave.

9–10. Note the chiastic arrangement.

Potestas refers to formal legal and political power. Thus, as Augustus notes in the *Res Gestae*, his *potestas* was no greater than that of any other magistrate, but he excelled all in his *auctoritas*, "personal political prestige." The *lex Iulia* forbidding adultery was passed in 18 BCE under the aegis of the *princeps*'s *tribunica potestas* and personal *auctoritas*.

Semina nequitiae languidiora: *languidus* is a frequent euphemism for impotence (see Propertius 1.3.1–2, 37–38; 2.16.59–60). The last clause is thus capable of two possible readings: "the very power to sin makes the seeds of wrongdoing weaker"; or "formal political power itself makes one's seed impotent for sexual escapades."

11–12. Inritare = "to excite."

Obsequio uinces: the paradox of conquest through submission is at the heart of the metaphor of *seruitium amoris*.

13–16. The simile of the horse recalls the same image used of the poet himself in 1.2.15–16.
Reluctanti = "struggling against the bit."
Vt primum = "as soon as."

17–18. Interdictis imminet aeger aquis = " the sick man longs for forbidden waters," possibly a reference to the baths.

19–20. Argus guarded Io. Ovid here refers to 2.19.29–30.

21–22. On **Danae**, see 2.19.27–28. She went in a **uirgo**, but came out a **mater**.

23–24. The *amator* presumably does not want to push the **Penelope** analogy too far given the fate of the suitors.

25–26. The end of the pentameter is an almost direct quotation of 2.19.4.

27–28. The hexameter is a statement of deliberately outrageous perversity.
The subject of **ceperit** is *maritus*.

29–30. The subject of **fit** is **adultera**.
By this logic, the *lex Iulia* actually encourages adultery.

33–34. Gentis . . . externae: fear is only appropriate to slaves and freedwomen, who were generally of foreign extraction.

35–36. If the mistress is chaste because a **custos** has been posted to guard her, this inverts the social hierarchy, since the free woman is then acting so that the slave may receive praise. She is subjugated to the will of her social inferior.

37–38. This passage makes Ovid's later claims in the *Ars Amatoria* and *Tristia* not to be promoting adultery ring hollow. Only the bumpkin or *rusticus* objects, the sophisticated *urbanus* takes infidelity in stride.

39–40. Rome was founded on adultery! According to the traditional legend, Ilia, the Vestal virgin who was the mother of Romulus and Remus, was raped by Mars.
Martigenae = masculine, nominative plural, "begotten by Mars."

41–42. Quo tibi formosam, si non nisi casta placebat: the first clause assumes a verb of picking or choosing such as *deligis*. *Tibi* should be taken with *placebat*.

Non possunt ullis ista coire modis = "those things are not able to go together in any fashion," but it should be remembered that *coire* can also mean "to have intercourse" and *modis* can refer to sexual positions.

43–46. Ovid here directly advocates the practice of *lenocinium*.

Gratia: a euphemism for the monetary and political rewards the astute husband would collect from his wife's lovers.

47–48. The husband who acts as his wife's pimp is welcome at every party and sees at his home many gifts that he himself has not given.

Ars Amatoria 1.61–228

This passage from Ovid's manual of seduction [64] not only shows the *praeceptor amoris* at his best, but also prominently features those aspects of the Roman cityscape in which Augustus took particular pride. The *Ars* is in many ways a summation of the *Amores*. It takes the same themes and motifs and presents them in the guise of a systematic treatise on love. The *Ars* gives us elegiac love reduced to a method. The position of the lover is no longer outside norms of Roman life, but can itself be stated according to a set of rules. Those rules, however, are always parodic. The *Ars* is a tremendously funny poem whose sophisticated wit offers no place for the expressiveness of Catullus or Sulpicia, the nostalgia of Tibullus, or the political engagement of a Propertius, but rather marks the spot of the elegiac lover with endlessly self-consuming irony.

Moreover, just as the *Amores* may be read as a parody of the elegiac genre, so too the *Ars* is a parody of didactic poetry. The ancient world was filled with versified manuals of instruction. Aratus's *Phaenomena*, a Greek poem on the ever-popular subject of astrology, received no fewer than three Latin translations, including one by Cicero himself. Some of these works achieved the status of great works of art in themselves, such as Lucretius's *De Rerum Natura* and Vergil's *Georgics*. The didactic form was tailor-made to be parodied by the *praeceptor amoris*. The opening lines of the *Ars* thus read:

> Si quis in hoc artem populo non nouit amandi,
> hoc legat et lecto carmine doctus amet.
> arte citae ueloque rates remoque mouentur,
> arte leues currus: arte regendus Amor.

[If anyone among the people does not know the art of loving, let him read this and, once he has been instructed by this poem, let him love. Swift ships are moved by sail or oar through art, as are swift chariots: Love too is ruled by art.]

Ovid's send-up is all the more effective for his adopting the tone of the serious professor for the trivial subject of love.

. The passage we have chosen instructs the reader on the best places to find a girl. Most of the buildings mentioned in it were erected by Augustus or his entourage and, as the *Res Gestae* (4.19–21) makes clear, the *princeps* regarded his building projects as a point of pride. He could not have looked favorably upon Ovid choosing those same buildings as the site for a program of seduction in direct contradiction to his own program of moral reform. It should be remembered that the *Ars* was one of the reasons cited for Ovid's exile.

61–66. This section opens with Ovid assuring the reader that there are girls to fit every taste in Rome.

61–62. Primis et adhuc crescentibus = "young and still growing," that is, pubescent. **Vera puella** = "a true girl," that is, not a woman.

63–64. Iuuenem = "a young woman."
　Voti = "choice, wish."

65–66. Hoc modifies **agmen.**

67–88. Ovid now lists the local hotspots.

67–68. Pompeia . . . umbra refers to the colonnade attached to Pompey's theater built in 55 BCE. See Propertius 4.8.75–76
　Cum sol Herculei terga leonis adit: the sun enters the sign of Leo in July, the hottest part of the Roman summer when the shaded afforded by the portico would be most sought after. Leo is the Nemean lion killed by Hercules.

69–70. Marcellus, the nephew of Augustus by his sister Octavia, was the heir apparent before his death in 23 BCE. His mother dedicated a library to him and the *princeps* a theater. Sometime after 27 BCE the *Porticus Octavia* was constructed next to where the *Theatrum Marcellum* was later built, this is probably the structure to which Ovid is referring. It is difficult to explain why Ovid says the *porticus* was added on to the theater rather than the other way around.

71–72. The **Porticus Liviae** was built in 7 BCE and named for Augustus's wife.
　Priscis . . . tabellis: such colonnades often housed collections of paintings by old masters.

73–74. Ovid refers to Augustus's crowning achievement, the temple of

Apollo on the Palatine (see Propertius 4.6.11–12) and its *porticus*, which featured fifty statues of the Danaids (see Propertius 2.1.67–68).

Belides: Belus was the father of Danaus and Aegyptus. The daughters of Danaus married their cousins and killed them on their wedding night with one exception.

75–76. The poet switches briefly from monuments to religious occasions where people congregate and the pickings might be good: the Adonia, especially honored by *meretrices*, and the Jewish sabbath, where young women might be expected to gather outside one of the thirteen synagogues in Rome.

77–78. **Linigerae Memphitica templa iuuencae**: Isis, because of her horns, was identified by the Romans with Io, who was in Egypt when turned into a heifer (see Propertius 1.3.19–20; *Amores* 1.3.21–24, 2.19.29–30, and 3.4.19–20). The priests of Isis wore linen.

79–80. The notion that the forums, the political and judicial centers of Rome, and the symbols of *negotium* {44}, should be prime sites to pick up young women is particularly outrageous.

81–82. The poet speaks of the *forum Iulium* where the temple of *Venus Genetrix*, mother of Aeneas and founder of the *gens Iulia* into which the *princeps* had been adopted, was located (see Propertius 3.4.19–20; *Amores* 1.2.51–52). Both the temple and forum were dedicated by Julius Caesar and completed by Augustus.

Appias … aera: a statue of a nymph gracing a fountain standing immediately before (**subdita**) the temple.

83–84. **Consultus**: a technical legal expert as opposed to a forensic orator. This entire passage shows Ovid's fondness for legal vocabulary already seen in the *Amores*.

85–86. **Diserto**: the *disertus* was the counterpart of the *consultus*. As the judicial advocate he should never be at a loss for words.

Resque nouae = "cases without precedent," i.e. the lawyer falls in love for the first time.

Causaque agenda sua est: nonetheless the case must be prosecuted.

87–88. **Patronus**: the patronage system at Rome was a complex system of mutual obligations between social superiors and inferiors. One of the duties of a *patronus* was to represent his *clientes* in court. The *disertus* here seeks Venus to prosecute his case as his *patrona*, thus inverting normal social roles.

Note the telling alliteration of **cupit** and **cliens**.

89–134. The next section focuses on the theaters.

89–90. **Venare** = second person singular imperative of the deponent verb. The hunting metaphor recurs throughout the *Ars*.

Voto . . . tuo = either ablative of comparison or dative of reference.

91–92. **Ames . . . ludere possis . . . tangas . . . tenere uelis** = potential subjunctives. Note the balanced construction with the complementary infinitives. The whole forms a chiasmus, with **ames** and **tenere uelis** referring to longer-term relationships and **ludere possis** and **semel tangas** to brief encounters.

Quod ludere = "to deceive" in the transitive construction. Note the distancing effect of the neuter pronoun throughout the passage.

93–98. As the ant goes back and forth to its hill bearing food and the bee back and forth carrying honey to its hive, so the swarm of women seeking amorous sustenance return again and again to the theater. The image of the bees recalls Vergil's *Georgics*, the premier didactic poem of the period.

Cultissima = "the most refined," but also she who takes the most care of her appearance.

Iudicium = "decision."

99–100. Note the chiastic arrangement.

Spectatum = supine with verb of motion expressing purpose.

101–34. Theaters were founded by Romulus as a ruse to lure in the Sabine women. Rome's very foundation is thus shown to rest on an act of transgressive sexuality. According to the traditional story, Rome was founded by outcasts, farmers, and shepherds. If the city were to sustain itself, women had to be attracted to the settlement. Romulus thus invited the neighboring Sabines to a festival that was actually a trap so that the Romans could kidnap the Sabine women. On the subsequent siege of Rome by the Sabine leader Tatius and the city's betrayal by Tarpeia, see Propertius 4.4.

101–02. **Ludos** = "plays" or any sort of "games."

103–04. Ovid emphasizes the rustic character of the early Roman theater.

Vela = an "awning" to protect spectators from the sun.

Liquido . . . croco: the stage was perfumed with a mixture of wine and saffron.

105–06. **Palatia** = poetic plural.

Positae: understand *fuerunt*.

Scena: an example of asyndeton, the omission of an expected conjunction. In prose, *et* or something similar would introduce the second clause. I have altered the OCT's punctuation for the sake of clarity.

107–08. Ovid's shaggy ancestors sat on piles of turf holding leafy branches to cover their unkempt hair. The poet here pokes fun at the popular nostalgia for a lost golden age. See Tibullus 1.1.

Qualibet . . . fronde . . . tegente = ablative absolute.

109–110. Each shaggy Roman was eyeing a girl for himself and secretly making plans (**tacito pectore multa mouent**).

Respiciunt: Augustus had decreed that women could only occupy the back rows of the theaters.

111–12. Ovid describes a form of early Etruscan dancing.

Rudem praebente modum tibicine Tusco = ablative absolute.

Aequatam . . . humum = the primitive stage.

113–14. The MSS read *petenda* for **petita**, but all modern editors agree this makes no sense. Most adopt Bentley's emendation as I have.

On *praeda*, see Tibullus 1.2.65–66, 2.3.35–50; Propertius 2.1.55–56, 2.16.1–2, 3.4.21–22; *Amores* 1.2.19–20, 29–30, and 1.3.1.

Ovid claims even the applause was primitive.

115–16. Animum . . . fatentes = "declaring their passion."

Iniciuntque manus: see *Amores* 1.4.5–6, 39–40.

119–20. Timuere = *timuerunt*.

121–22. Though all the Sabine women were afraid, they showed their fear in different ways.

Sine mente = "mindlessly," i.e. paralyzed with fear.

125–26. Note how both the rape and the women's fear are described with detached humor.

Genialis = a pun, meaning both "belonging to generation" and "pleasant."

Decere = "to be becoming."

127–28. Si qua repugnarat nimium: the assumption underlying this statement is the same as that seen in *Amores* 1.5. Resistance is merely an amorous ploy on the woman's part. Those who go too far (*nimium*) are carried off by main force.

Repugnarat and **negarat** = *repugnauerat* and *negauerat*.

129–30. The homely explanation of the Sabine women's new found roles as the mothers of Rome is meant to amuse through its naivety.

131–32. When we recall that Octavian considered taking the name *Romulus* instead of *Augustus*, this couplet becomes all the more pointed and funny. It is also pertinent that the *princeps* at this period was having difficulty in recruiting soldiers for the legions.
Commoda = a term commonly used of bonuses given to soldiers.

133–34. The rape of the Sabine women was the precedent that made theaters dangerous to beautiful women (**formosis**).
Sollemni: the OCT's reading *sollemnia* is hard to make sense of and is now rejected even by its editor, Kenney, in favor of Madvig's reading and that of one of the later MSS.

135–62. The poet turns his attention to the *Circus Maximus*. One of the main gathering places in Rome, it could hold up to 150,000 people.

137–38. Here the would-be lover does not need the elaborate system of signs Ovid detailed in *Amores* 1.4 and 2.5 but can speak openly to the girl and sit beside her.

139–40. **Sedeto** = future imperative. The poet, after the excursus on the Rape of the Sabine women, resumes his didactic tone.

141–42. Lines demarcated individual spaces, but the seating was quite cramped.
Et bene: understand *est*.
Si nolis = in this context, "whether you like it or not," a generalizing statement.

143–44. **Hic** = "at this point."
Socii sermonis origo = the beginning of a shared conversation. That is, "start to make small talk."
Publica uerba = as opposed to more intimate topics.

145–46. **Facito** = future imperative, with the following *ut* omitted.
Studiose = "zealous one," vocative modifying the subject of **requiras**.
Mora: understand *sit*.

147–48. **Pompa frequens**: the procession of the gods that opened the games.
Caelestibus ... eburnis: ivory statues of the gods were paraded around the arena. Each deity's devotees applauded as his or her patron went by.

Veneri dominae: Venus is the goddess of lovers. The epithet *domina*, while appropriate to divinity, also looks back to elegiac usage [7, 10, 12].

149–50. An excuse is found for touching the girl. Note the patterned alliteration of **deciderit digitis** and **excutiendus erit**.

151–52. Even if no dust is there, one can always pretend.

153–54. Pallia = a Greek cloak, poetic plural. It was commonly worn by freedwomen and *meretrices*.

155–56. As a reward (**pretium**), you can glance at her legs.
Contingent oculis anticipates what comes after looking.

159–60. Little attentions reap big rewards.
Fuit utile multis: a stock phrase in didactic literature.
Puluinum = "a cushion."

161–62. Tabella: this is the only usage of this word to mean "fan." It is best taken in its normal sense of a "writing tablet" that is here used as a fan. This reading also increases the humor as the would-be lover is portrayed as a would-be poet.
Scamna = "stools."

163–76. Having now covered porticoes, temples, the forums, the theater, and the race track, the poet moves on to the last major site on his list, the gladiatorial games. This will leave just one more venue, for the final section of our excerpt, the triumphal procession. It, however, is less a place than an event.

163–64. A transitional couplet linking **Circusque** and **sparsaque . . . harena** in a "both . . . and" structure.
Sollicito . . . foro: gladiatorial bouts, originally part of the funeral celebrations of noted aristocrats, gradually became institutionalized. They were at first offered in the forums, the open areas of which were covered with sand to absorb the blood. The first amphitheater was built in 29 BCE, but the forums continued to be used for some time. Compare Propertius 4.8.75–76.

165–66. Cupid as gladiator presents an elegant variation on the *militia amoris* motif. It is the spectator who is wounded in his combat with Venus's child, rather than the gladiator himself.
Vulnus habet: the audience would cry *hoc habet*, "he's got it," when one of the gladiators was wounded.

167–68. The subject of **loquitur tangitque . . . poscitque . . . et quaerit** is the same as *habet* in the previous couplet. Suetonius tells us that Augustus did not allow men and women to sit together during the games. Some suggest that these rules were relaxed when the bouts took place in the forum. Otherwise, it is hard to understand the import of these lines.

Libellum = "a program."

Posito pignore = ablative absolute. Betting was common.

169–70. The spectator wounded by Cupid's dart becomes part of the show.

Muneris: *munus* is the regular word for gladiatorial games, reflecting their origins as private gifts given to the people.

171–72. One of the most spectacular of all *munera* was the recreation of the battle of Salamis. It was given by Augustus in 2 BCE to celebrate the dedication of the temple of Mars Ultor ("the Avenger") in fulfillment of a vow made at the battle of Philippi (42 BCE). Fought on an artificial lake, the battle featured over 3,000 gladiators. For Augustus, this was a solemn occasion, ratifying his status as Julius Caesar's rightful heir and reminding the people of both the divine sanction his rule had received and his personal piety. He could not have been pleased by Ovid's turning it into still another occasion to mock the *princeps*'s efforts at moral reform.

Modo cum = "recently when."

Persiadas . . . Cecropiasque rates: the battle of Salamis was the turning point in the second Persian war, when Xerxes's fleet was defeated by the Athenians. *Cecrops* was a mythical king of Athens.

173–74. Young men and women came from both sides of the sea to see the spectacle.

Venere = *uenerunt.*

175–76. Note the ironic mock solemnity of the pentameter. **Aduena** = a masculine noun in apposition to **amor.**

177–228. This passage on how to meet girls at triumphal processions forms a logical extension of the poet's treatment of Augustus's staging of the mock naval battle. In both cases, the *princeps* is the butt of the joke. The section as a whole is an ironic, didactic reworking of Propertius 3.4. Like Propertius's original text, there are elements that are not easily dismissed as negative satire. The propempticon (send-off poem) on the youthful Gaius's expedition to the East (1 BCE) may well be serious (lines 181–212), or at least not intended as mockery. This passage is a good example of why it is a mistake to see Ovid as anti-Augustan in any simplistic sense. He rather is a poet who takes the Augustan settlement for granted and sees it as the natural ground for the exercise of his wit. He neither proposes a return to the republican constitution nor takes Augustan propaganda at its word. His position of sophisticated agnosticism, in which mockery metamorphoses into flattery and vice versa, may be the only authentic position open to a poet under the conditions of an emerging absolutist regime.

177–78. The Parthians, while reaching a diplomatic settlement with Augustus in 20 BCE that resulted in the return of Crassus's standards, remained an independent political and military force on Rome's eastern flank. Gaius's expedition will according to Ovid set matters aright. In fact, it was designed to do nothing more than settle a dispute over the succession to the Parthian and Armenian thrones in 2 BCE.

Caesar: Augustus was supreme commander, as opposed to the young Gaius, his grandson, who would actually take the field.

179–80. Crassus's defeat at Carrhae in 53 BCE left a raw wound in the Roman psyche, despite Augustus's eventual recovery of the standards through diplomatic means. See the introductory note to Propertius 3.4 and 4.6.79–84.

181–82. Primisque ... annis: Gaius was only 19 at the time of the expedition. As Augustus's grandson by Julia and Agrippa, he was the heir apparent and this expedition was supposed to establish his credibility as Augustus's successor. Unfortunately, he died in 4 CE turning Ovid's pleasing flatteries into bitter mockery for the aging *princeps*.

Ducem profitetur = "proclaims himself a military leader."

Puer: dwelling on the heir's precocious accomplishments is a regular part of Hellenistic encomiastic poetry.

183–84. As one does not number the birthdays of the gods, so the accomplishments of a Caesar are not limited by age. There may be an allusion here to Octavian's holding command in the civil wars before the age of 20.

185–86. Ingenium caeleste: *ingenium* is one's in-born character. The fact that Augustus was styled *filius divi*, "son of the deified," because of Julius's elevation to the status of an immortal, means that his heir would necessarily have a "divine" or "heavenly" *ingenium*.

187–88. Tirynthius = Hercules, son of Jupiter by Alcmene. He was famed for strangling snakes sent by Juno to kill him in his crib. He was born in Tiryns. Both he and Bacchus (lines 189–90) were popular in imperial propaganda since each was promoted to the status of divinity based on his achievements.

189–90. Bacchus supposedly conquered the east while still a youth, a fitting parallel for the young Gaius about to set out for Parthia.

Thyrsos: the ivy-wreathed symbols of Bacchic divinity wielded by Maenads.

191–92. Gaius will go out and conquer under the authority of Augustus's age and divine sanction.

Auspiciis = the consultation of bird signs traditionally undertaken by a military officer before a campaign.

193–94. Rudimentum: a technical term for one's initial military service.

Tanto sub nomine: an unusual usage, with *sub* emphasizing Gaius's subordinate position to Augustus.

Iuuenum princeps: Gaius had received this honorary title in 5 BCE.

Future senum: a reference to Augustus's title, *princeps senatus*, which Gaius hoped to inherit.

195–96. Gaius's campaign is presented as an act of filial piety. He is to avenge the wrong done to the four sons of Phraates IV, king of Parthia, by Phraates V, their half-brother. The latter was the son of an Italian slave girl and had killed his father so that he might usurp the throne while his brothers were serving as well-tended hostages in Rome. Gaius's charge was to come to terms with Phraates V and convince him to stop meddling in the Armenian succession. Ovid portrays this as defending the rights of the four brothers and the laws of the father.

Fratres = Lucius and Agrippa Postumus.

197–98. Where Augustus takes up arms for you, your enemy took up arms against his father.

Induit: every published translation reads this as meaning that Augustus clothes Gaius in arms. This would seem to be the sense the context demands, but *induo* does not mean to clothe someone else, but "to assume or put on." If we accept this reading then the antithesis between the hexameter and pentameter becomes sharper. The sense would be that Augustus goes to war (see line 177) to defend the interests of Gaius and his country. Gaius as lines 191–92 make clear is merely his father's proxy.

Genitor patriaeque: in 2 BCE, shortly before the expedition here contemplated, Augustus received the title of *pater patriae* from the senate.

199–200. Gaius's **tela** are **pia** because they serve the cause of filial piety whereas Phraates's arrows serve that of crime. The Parthians were famed for the skill of their mounted archers. The bow, however, was considered a suspect weapon in the ancient world since, unlike the spear, it did not require you to stand and face your opponent. The bow in mythology is the weapon of the crafty, such as Odysseus, and the unmanly, such as Paris. See also Propertius 4.6.79–84.

Iusque piumque = "justice and duty."

203–04. Ovid attributes godhead (**numen**) to Augustus, a move that will be common in the exilic poetry. Augustus had expressly forbidden divine honors so one must always wonder whether such statements are flattery, cheek, or both. See Propertius 3.4.1–2 and the introductory note to 3.11.

Date **numen** = "grant your power."

E uobis alter es, alter eris = "for one of you is and the other will be." Ovid here cautiously retracts Augustus's premature divination.

205–06. Ovid promises an epic poem for the victor's safe return. This is probably tongue in cheek since it would be out of character for the elegist. Nonetheless, the whole passage is out of character, which may be part of the point. Note the pairing of two couplets ending in **eris**, thus implicitly equating Gaius and Augustus.

207–10. Ovid imagines the epic scenes he will recount: Gaius standing fast exhorting his troops, the Parthians fleeing, the Romans pursuing, and the missiles the enemy hurls from a turned horse. The Parthians were famed for their tactic of feigning retreat, then wheeling around and loosing a hail of arrows. See Propertius 3.4.17–18, 4.6.81–82.

O desint animis ne mea uerba tuis = "may my words not fail your courage!"

211–12. The logic of Ovid's argument is far from impeccable. "You who flee so that you might conquer, Parthians, what do you leave behind for the conquered?" Most commentators assume this means that since the Parthians feign flight as a means to victory, real flight is no longer an option. Yet that is a non sequitur. If Ovid hopes to convince us with this statement, he is a far worse rhetorician than he is generally credited to be. On the other hand, since **uicto** does not modify the subject of **relinques**, the sentence could also mean that the Parthians leave behind nothing for those they conquer. This was certainly the case with Crassus and his legions. If we admit the possibility of this reading, then the question of for whom the Parthian style of warfare (**Mars tuus**) is ill-omened remains open.

213–14. Ovid here projects Gaius's coming triumph, which allows him to return to the main theme of this section the *Ars*: where should one go to pick up girls? Such a direct juxtaposition of the politically serious and the sexually frivolous is typically elegiac. It was part of the genre's appeal and also part of what made it unsettling to traditional Roman sensibilities, which saw sexuality as a force to be subordinated to the service of aristocratic male power.

Quattuor in niuies . . . equis: the traditional equipage of the triumphal chariot.

Aureus = the *toga picta*. See Propertius 4.4.53–54 and *Amores* 1.2.41–42.

215–16. On the triumphal procession, see Propertius 2.1.33–34, 3.4.15–22, and *Amores* 1.2.23–53.

Fuga: another allusion to Parthian cavalry tactics.

217–18. Diffundetque animos = "will let spirits run free," an unusual expression.

219–22. The *praeceptor* resumes his instruction. The young Don Juan should read and explain the placards on the floats going by to any young woman willing to listen, and he should be ready to make up details to fill in what he does not know.

223–24. The images of conquered rivers, portrayed as gods, were a common part of triumphal processions. The Tigris and Euphrates were under Parthian control and so would form the objects of Gaius's conquest.

Praecinctus harundine frontem: the banks of the Euphrates were noted for their reeds.

225–26. Facito: the future imperative makes it clear that the *amator* is to improvise as needed.

Danaeia Persis: *Persis* was the province of the Parthian empire from which the Persian kingdom had originally sprung. The Persian kings were said to be the descendants of Perseus, the son of Jupiter and Danae. On Danae, see *Amores* 2.19.27–28 and 3.4.21–22.

Achaemeniis = Achaemenid, the great Persian dynasty that produced Cyrus, Darius, and Xerxes.

227–28. The passage closes with emphasis on the *amator*'s ability to fashion appropriate fictions.

Heroides 7

This example of the elegy as amatory epistle is particularly important for its reworking of the Dido and Aeneas story. Indeed, almost every line in Ovid's epistle can be traced to a parallel passage in *Aeneid* Book 4. Ovid, however, not only inverts the perspective of Vergil's poem, by giving us Dido's side of the story [65], he also removes the tragic grandeur that made Book 4 so powerful. Ovid's Dido frequently takes the very arguments presented for why Aeneas should leave Carthage and turns them to the opposite cause. The result is a rhetorical *tour de force* in which the reader is both invited to sympathize with Dido as victim and yet never allowed to identify fully with her position. The dazzling rhetoric creates a split perspective that at once seeks to convince and yet distances the reader. The artifice of the presentation is such that one finds oneself admiring the wit first and empathizing second.

Ovid does not so much refute the *Aeneid* as refuse to take it seriously. Aeneas is shown to be heartless, and there is no acknowledgment of his larger historical mission. Yet, Dido is no tragic heroine. She is not presented as the victim of Rome's grand destiny. She is simply another abandoned elegiac beloved. Ovid does not counter epic grandeur with epic grandeur, but appropriates epic for elegy. In the process, he creates a poem in which the precise position of the speaking or writing subject becomes ever harder to identify. Is Dido the great Queen, an elegiac *puella*, or a clever rhetorician who slyly appropriates the serious language of her opponent?

The inability to locate a unified perspective from which Dido speaks is symptomatic of a wider shift in elegy. Just as the *amator* of the *Amores* constantly foregrounds the artificiality of his own genre, and the *praeceptor* of the *Ars* represents the role of the lover as reducible to a system, so the *Heroides*, written shortly after the *Amores*, reveals a displacement of the elegiac subject. In the *Heroides*, as in Book 4 of Propertius, the poet no longer speaks in his own voice, but in that of an ironically presented third person. The fact is that the position of the elegist has become increasingly untenable in the late Augustan period. For Dido in *Heroides* 7 to present a unified response to the *Aeneid* would imply that a position outside the imperial system existed. The split nature of Dido's response is revelatory of the very double bind in which the elegist found himself. The result is not tragedy but a depthless, ironic pathos.

1–2. This first couplet is generally bracketed or not printed at all. It appears in a number of MSS, but in only one of the six considered the most reliable. Its summary nature adds little to the poem and has the air of a gloss added by a later copyist or commentator.

3–4. The swan was thought to sing only at the moment before its death. This couplet looks forward to Dido's suicide depicted at the end of *Aeneid* 4.
    Maeandri: on the Meander river, see Propertius 2.34.35–36.

5–6. Dido says she realizes her letter is written in vain, but the shift from the passive **moueri** in the hexameter to the active **mouimus** in the pentameter betrays a lingering hope that Aeneas can be moved.
    Ista = the letter.
    Deo probably = Amor.

7–8. **Merita** = neuter plural accusative. Compare *Aeneid* 4.317.
    Pudicum = *ex commune* with both *corpus* and *animus*.

9–10. Venti uela fidemque ferent: note the alliteration and the zeugma: *ferent* is used in two different senses.

11–12. Nescis: the contrast between Aeneas's certainty and his heading off to an unknown land is highlighted by the juxtaposition of *nescis* with the anaphoric repetition of *certus es*. This is precisely the kind of rhetorical elaboration one would not normally expect from a distraught and suicidal lover.

In the next ten lines, Dido will appeal to Aeneas's self-interest by arguing that he would be better served by taking the bird in the hand.

13–14. This couplet directly recalls and inverts *Aeneid* 4.86–89, *non coeptae adsurgunt turres . . .* | *pendent opera interrupta, minaeque* | *murorum ingentes, aequataque machina caelo* ["towers that begun no longer climb . . . projects are stopped in mid-stream, the huge menaces of the walls and the cranes reaching the sky"]. The recognition of the inversion is part of the wit as Dido turns what in Vergil is a negative characterization into a positive reason for staying.

Note that the couplet is arranged as a tricolon or triple climax, with each succeeding term being more attractive and more specific.

Sceptro = metonymy for sovereignty.

15–16. This couplet begins a series of repeated uses of the gerundive, extending through line 20, meant to contrast the certainties of Aeneas's present situation with the uncertainties of his future. Note the chiastic arrangement of gerundives and past participles in **facta . . . facienda . . . quaerenda . . . quaesita.**

Altera . . . altera = "one . . . another."

17–18. The force of both rhetorical questions is undermined by the fact that Dido did precisely what she implies no one would do.

Vt = concessive.

19–20. The hexameter is much vexed. I have printed the Budé reading in daggers. The manuscripts vary widely. The present reading has the advantage that it yields reasonable sense, every element is attested somewhere in the MS tradition, and it follows the pattern of at least one gerundive in each line that characterizes the passage as a whole. Unfortunately, it scans only if we assume a sense pause after the question mark so great that it vitiates the effect of the double consonant and allows the last syllable of *restat* to be scanned as short. This would be most unusual. The common solution among anglophone editors has been to adopt Diggle's reading, *scilicet alter amor tibi restat et altera Dido,* but *scilicet* appears nowhere in the manuscripts and the excision of the gerundive not only breaks the rhetorical pattern, it also goes against the unanimous testimony of the tradition.

On fides [12, 38], see the introductory note to Catullus 76 and 87.3–4; the introductory note to Sulpicia 3.16; Propertius 4.7.53–54; *Amores* 1.2.29–36, 1.3.5–6. The Romans consistently portrayed the Carthaginians as lacking in *fides*. *Poenica fides* was proverbial for a lack of trustworthiness. Such a concept, however, would be anachronistic at the time of Dido's letter. The recognition of the reversal of the charge and its anachronism is part of the fun for the reader. At the same time, it creates a distancing effect that separates us from a direct identification with the heroine.

21–22. Instar = an indeclinable noun in apposition to **urbem**.

23–24. Even if you found your city, where would you find a wife who would love you as I do?

25–26. Vror recalls **uxor** from the previous line. In the Roman world of arranged marriages, passion was not part of the package. That is the realm of elegy [6]. See Catullus 72.5.

Ceratae ... taedae: as Knox (1995) observes, Ovid has conflated two terms, one for torch (*taeda*) and one for candle (*cereus*). "Dido's choice of image is deliberately ambivalent: the *taeda* . . . had familiar associations with the wedding procession, but the *cereus* was used at funerals."

27–28. He is an ingrate whom, if I were wise, I should be glad to be rid of.

29–30. Note how the last words of each line, **odi** and **amo**, recall the opening of Catullus 85. Dido's position is that of the elegist.

Observe the play on **queror ... questa**.

Peius amo = "love more passionately," but with a clear connotation that this is the worse of two options.

31–32. Ovid's referring to Dido as Venus's daughter-in-law (*nuruus*) is mischievously humorous. On Cupid being Aeneas's brother see *Amores* 1.2.49–52, where there is reference to Augustus as Cupid's cousin. See also Propertius 3.4.19–20.

Castris militet ille tuis: compare *Amores* 1.9.1, *militat omnis amans et habet sua castra Cupido*. Ovid here has Dido invert the elegiac trope of *militia amoris* to make the soldier a lover rather than the lover a soldier. See Propertius 2.7.15–16.

33–34. Quem: the antecedent is **ille** in the pentameter.

Curae: *cura* is a common term for the object of affection in elegiac verse. See Sulpicia 3.18.1–2; and Propertius 1.1.35 and 2.34.9–10.

35–36. Dido retreats from wishful thinking for a more sober assessment.

Ista . . imago = "that vision." **Mihi** can be read as both dative of reference and dative of agent. **Falso** = adverbial.

37–40. One wonders how Augustus would have read this claim that Aeneas could not be the son of Venus, given the *gens Iulia*'s devotion to *Venus genetrix*.

The commonplace of attributing inhuman parents to those exhibiting harsh behavior can be traced to the *Iliad* (16.33–35), but Ovid's more immediate source is Dido's similar charge against Aeneas at *Aeneid* 4.365–67.

Quo . . . ire paras: the mention of the sea leads to this digression (lines 40–44) on the dangers of sea travel. Dido in her struggle to find any argument to convince Aeneas often proceeds by free association.

41–42. Hiemis mihi gratia prosit: this is best read as an aside to Dido herself. As many commentators have noted, the epistolary fiction that serves as a framework for the *Heroides* is little more than a rhetorical convenience enabling the creation of what are in essence dramatic monologues.

Eurus = the east wind.

43–44. Sine = imperative. The pentameter has added poignancy in light of line 39's claim that Aeneas must have been born from the inhuman sea.

45–46. Tanti = genitive of value.

Ut pereas depends on *tanti*.

47–48. The implicit economic metaphor of the previous couplet's genitive of value is continued in such words as **pretiosa, uile,** and the construction of **constantia** with **magno,** an ablative of price.

Dum = "so long as."

49–50. Iam uenti ponent = "at some point the winds will abate." Compare *Aeneid* 7.27, *cum uenti posuere*.

Strataque . . . unda = ablative absolute.

Triton = son of Neptune. In the *Aeneid* 1.144–47, he calms the sea after the storm unleashed by Juno against the Trojans.

51–52. Dido chastises Aeneas for being less **mutabilis** than the wind, and in line 47 she takes him to task for his *constantia*. Conventionally, the faithful lover exhibits *constantia*, while the unfaithful is *mutabilis* like the wind. See Catullus 70.3–4 and Propertius 2.34.11. This line is also meant to recall Mercury's admonition to Aeneas not to tarry since Dido might be plotting against him as *uarium et mutabile semper | femina* (*Aeneid* 4.569–70).

Eris: Dido momentarily believes she will be successful.

53–54. Quid, si nescires insana quid aequora possunt, | expertae totiens tam male credis aquae? "Why do you entrust yourself to the water which has already proven itself ill so many times, as if you did not know that of which the raging sea is capable." Dido recalls the shipwreck that brought Aeneas to her shores. I have altered the punctuation of the Budé edition for the sake of clarity.

Note that *si* plus the imperfect subjunctive is used to introduce an unreal condition.

55–56. Vt pelago suadente etiam retinacula soluas = "even with the open sea persuading you to cast off," i.e., because it is calm. I have omitted the Budé edition's extraneous commas.

57–58. The sea proverbially punished breakers of oaths.

59–60. The irony of course is that the mother of Amor is the mother of Aeneas as well. On Venus being born from the sea, see Tibullus 1.2.39–40.

Cytheriacis ... aquis = the water round Cythera, site of a prominent shrine to Venus. See Sulpicia 3.13.7–8.

61–62. Perdita ne perdam, timeo, noceamue nocenti: a fine example of polyptoton, or the use of the same word in more than one form.

63–64. Do not die at sea, because then you will not be said (**ferere**) to be the cause of my death! Dido refers to her impending suicide. Compare *Aeneid* 4.381–87, where Dido wishes Aeneas death at sea.

65–66. Go ahead picture yourself caught in a storm, what will you think then?

Nullum sit in omine pondus: normally the contemplation of such an event would be considered unlucky.

67–68. Occurrent: understand *tibi*.

Periuria: the faithlessness of the Trojans was proverbial since the rape of Helen. See *Aeneid* 4.541–42.

69–70. Coniugis ... imago: Dido here assumes the role of Aeneas's wife. In the *Aeneid*, Aeneas stands firm on the contention that they were never formally married. This passage is also meant to recall Creusa's appearance to Aeneas after being left behind in Troy (2.772–76).

Effusis ... comis: a standard symbol of mourning.

71–72. "Quicquid id est, totum merui; concedite": Aeneas's address to the phantom. I have added the quotation marks to the Budé edition.

73–74. The comparison of the sea's harshness with Aeneas's is continued. Dido in *Aeneid* 4.429–34 makes a similar plea for a short **spatium**.

75–110. In the next section, Dido calls into question Aeneas's defining virtue, *pietas* or duty to the gods, fatherland, and family. It was his willingness to forego his individual desires in the name of *pietas* [38] that made him the ideal Augustan hero and the antitype to the elegist.

75–76. Tu: understand *es*.

Iulo: Iulus is another name for Ascanius, Aeneas's son. He is the namesake of the *gens Iulia*.

Dido here reverses the argument Mercury makes to Aeneas in *Aeneid* 4.232–43 and 272–75 that he should depart Carthage immediately, if not for his own sake then for Ascanius's.

77–78. Dido refers to Aeneas's rescue of Ascanius and the household gods (**Penates**) during the fall of Troy recounted in Book 2 of the *Aeneid*. Note the clever rhetorical opposition of gods snatched from the fire being drowned at sea.

79–80. Iactas = "throw up to me, boast about."

Pater: the image of Aeneas carrying his father Anchises out of the burning city while leading Ascanius by the hand is one of the most striking images of *pietas* in the *Aeneid* (2.721–25).

For a similar, but more muted questioning of Aeneas's *pietas*, see Dido's statement at *Aeneid* 4.597–99.

81–82. Primaque = *neque prima*.

83–84. A wonderfully pointed jibe. Ascanius's mother, Creusa, is left behind in Troy when Aeneas flees. She later appears in a vision saying the Great Mother goddess had taken her and absolving Aeneas of guilt (*Aeneid* 2.737–95). Nonetheless, as Dido observes, Aeneas has a remarkable ability to shed spouses who no longer serve the purposes of Rome. Augustus had a similar facility, as his first wife, Scribonia, could attest.

85–86. Haec mihi narraras et me mouere. Merentem | ure: minor culpa poena futura mea est: the MS reading is profoundly corrupt. Knox's reading (1995) provides the best sense while doing the least violence to the attested readings. The couplet refers to the whole of Books 2 and 3 of the *Aeneid* in which Aeneas recounts to Dido the fall of Troy and his wanderings.

Narraras = *narraueras*.

Vre = a reference both to Dido's funeral pyre and her passion. See line 25.

87–88. Aeneas's own story of his wanderings show him to be cursed by the gods. Compare *Aeneid* 1.755–56. In a characteristic reversal, Ovid changes Vergil's *aestas* to *hiemps*.

89–90. Compare *Aeneid* 4.373–74.

Vixque bene audito nomine: the ablative absolute construction is suitably ambiguous. Did Dido give Aeneas her kingdom as soon as she heard his name because it was so famous or in spite of the fact that she had not heard it before? The first is the Augustan reading, the second exposes the factitious nature of the entire legend.

91–92. Et mihi concubitus fama sepulta foret = "and the fame of my sleeping with you consigned to oblivion."

93–94. Dido here refers to the famous scene in the cave, *Aeneid* 4.160–72, where her and Aeneas's love was consummated.

Decliue sub antrum = "in a sloping cave."

95–96. Nymphas ululasse putaui: compare *Aeneid* 4.168, *ulularunt . . . Nymphae*. Ovid's more tentative formulation anticipates Aeneas's later denial that it was a real marriage (*Aeneid* 4.338–39). In the process, Ovid draws our attention to the inexcusable nature of Aeneas's behavior in Vergil's own terms.

97–98. Exige, laese pudor, poenas, uiolate Sychaeeu, | ad quem, me miseram, plena pudoris eo: the couplet is highly disputed. Some of the later codices include two interpolated lines, accepted by a minority of editors. I have restored the MS reading *poenas* for the Budé's *poenam et* and altered the punctuation accordingly. Dido refers to her pledge to her deceased husband not to marry again (*Aeneid* 4.15–18).

Eo: anticipating Dido's suicide.

99–102. These lines are a reworking of *Aeneid* 4.457–61 on Dido's shrine to Sychaeus.

99–100. Velleraque alba: garlands of white wool. See Tibullus 1.5.15–16.

101–02. Citari = "to be summoned."
Elissa = another name for Dido.

103–04. Venio, uenio: note the emotionally effective repetition.
Admissi = substantive, "crime."

105–06. Idoneus auctor = a proper authority, and hence someone who would mitigate Dido's fault. There is a pun here as well. The true *auctor* is Vergil.

Inuidiam = "ill will." **Noxae . . . meae** = dative of separation.

107–08. One of Ovid's great ironic couplets. Dido was deceived by Aeneas's *pietas*!

Mansuri . . . uiri = "of a man who would stay."

109–10. Si fuit errandum: understand *mihi*.

Fidem: it is her own lack of *fides* for which Dido is apologizing, by citing Aeneas's reputation for this very virtue. Her *fides* to Sychaeus has, in fact, proven as false as Aeneas's to her. Observe how the sense pause after **fidem**, two syllables before the caesura, creates added emphasis.

Note the artful balance of the two passive periphrastic constructions, the first with the perfect, the second with the future.

111–12. Dido breaks off her address to her dead husband and reflects upon the continuity of her tragic fate.

Fati . . . tenor ("the course of fate") is the subject of **durat** and **prosequitur**.

In extremum: understand *uitae*.

113–14. Dido thinks back to the scene of Sychaeus's slaying at the hands of her brother Pygmalion (*Aeneid* 1.346–51).

Herceas: Heinsius's conjecture for the nonsensical *in terras*. If correct, it refers to a title of Jupiter as protector of the household.

Praemia: the wealth of Sychaeus.

115–16. Compare *Aeneid* 3.10–11 on Aeneas's departure from Troy.

117–18. Adplicor ignotis = "I am brought to unknown shores."

Note the punning parallelism between **fratrique** and **fretoque**.

Perfide, litus emo: the legend of Dido's trickery in buying the land of Carthage is recounted in *Aeneid* 1.367–68. The juxtaposition of this reference with the epithet, *perfidus*, applied to Aeneas is ironic. Ovid has Dido undercut her own argument.

119–22. Dido, as in the *Aeneid*, is surrounded by jealous enemies. Her affair with Aeneas, which should have brought a strengthening alliance with the Trojans, has only made her more isolated and vulnerable.

Rudis is taken variously by editors and translators as nominative singular modifying the subject of **paro**, genitive singular modifying **urbis**, and accusative plural modifying **portas**. Logically, it goes with all three.

123–24. The Budé's emendation of **me** to *in me* is unnecessary. **Me** = subject of the infinitive **praeposuisse**. The whole clause is the object of **querentes**.

Nescio quem = the idiomatic "someone."

125–28. These couplets are based on *Aeneid* 4.325–26.

Gaetulo ... Iarbae: Iarbas is one of Dido's suitors. The Gaetuli were a nomadic tribe in North Africa.

Praebuerim = potential subjunctive.

129–30. Dido speaks as if Aeneas were still carrying the *Penates* he rescued from Troy.

131–32. **Eras ... futurus** = active periphrastic construction indicating the future of the past, "if you were to be."

Elapsis: understand *deis*.

133–38. Observe the rapid transition from one theme to the next, as though Dido were becoming more frantic as the end approached.

In *Aeneid* 4.327–30, Dido wishes that she might be pregnant so that she would have a child to remind her of Aeneas. Ovid turns this into a rhetorical ploy on Dido's part, suggesting that she might be pregnant and that Aeneas would not only be the cause of her death by suicide but also of his own son's.

Nati funeris: note the pointed juxtaposition here and in **una duos**.

139–40. **Sed iubet ire deus**: understand *te*. The line drips with sarcasm.

Vellem uetuisset: note the emphatic alliteration.

141–42. The Budé and many other modern editions punctuate this line with a question mark, but this robs **nempe** of much of its sarcastic force.

Compare Mercury's chiding of Aeneas in *Aeneid* 4.271.

143–44. **Pergama** = the citadel of Troy. The couplet is difficult. Prose word order would be *Pergama si quanta forent {quam} fuere uiuo Hectore, uix tibi tanto labore erant repetenda*, "If Troy were as great as it was when Hector was alive, it would scarcely be worth being sought by you with so much labor [as you expend seeking Rome]." Compare *Aeneid* 4.311–13.

145–46. Why do you seek strange lands where you will be an enemy?

Simoenta = Greek accusative of Simois, a small tributary to the Scamander near Troy.

Thybridas = Greek, adjectival form of *Tiberis*.

Vt = concessive.

147–48. The image of Latium as an ever-receding goal is common in the

Aeneid, but there is an ironic, almost playful, quality to Dido's description that casts Aeneas in the comic role of the aging lover pursuing the *puella* who plays hard to get. See Tibullus 1.2.89–96.

149–50. Dido offers her own people and the riches of her slain husband, which she had brought with her, as dowry.

Ambage remissa: the most basic level of meaning is "with all wanderings put away," but it can also mean "with all ambiguity put aside." In the *Aeneid*, the plot turns on an ambiguity: what Dido considers marriage Aeneas does not. What Dido offers would be a marriage without ambiguity, a notion that Ovid undercuts by using an ambiguous phrase to communicate it.

Pygmalionis opes: Pygmalion had killed Sychaeus in order to steal his riches.

151–52. **Transfer felicius** = "you will more happily move."

153–54. **Suo partus Marte triumphus** = "a triumph procured by his own martial skill."

155–56. We have everything you could want, even lots of enemies to conquer. The deflating of the Roman martial ethos as a personal vanity is directly contrary to the message of the *Aeneid*.

157–58. **Tu modo** = a vocative to be taken with **parce** in 163. The violation of the integrity of couplet here is unusual and harsh in Ovid. It presumably is meant to represent the disorder of Dido's thought as the poem approaches its climax and Dido's suicide nears.

Per matrem . . . deos: Dido piles up deities and attributes on which she bases her plea. The whole list goes with **precor** in line 63. On Venus as Aeneas's mother and Cupid as his brother, see lines 31–32.

159–62. The parenthesis offers the kind of bargain one commonly finds in Roman prayer formulas, if x then y. If you spare my household (**parce . . . domui**, line 163), then may the members of yours be spared as well.

Superent = "may they survive."

Mars ferus . . . ille = the Trojan War.

Modus = predicate nominative, "limit."

Molliter ossa cubent = a standard funereal formula.

163–64. **Tradit habendam**: see line 15.

165–66. I am not your enemy. **Pthia** = the home of Achilles, ablative of origin with **oriunda**. **Magnisque . . . Mycenis** = home of Agamemnon.

Virque paterque: this phrase is out of place, since there was no father and husband that stood against the Trojans (Menelaus was Helen's husband, but her father took no part). Nor is there ever a question of Dido's relations opposing Aeneas. Rather Ovid is engaging here in creative and ironic anachronism by looking forward to Turnus's and Latinus's opposition to Aeneas's marriage to Lavinia, events that Dido could not know about since they take place after her death. The line only makes sense if we assume that Dido has read the *Aeneid* as carefully as Ovid and his readers. Thus, it points to the status of the whole letter as an exercise in self-conscious intertextuality.

167–68. Let's not quarrel over semantics. If you prefer not to call me your wife, I'll be your guest.

169–70. Dido returns to the theme of lines 39–44. Weather conditions are bad and Aeneas should delay his departure.

171–72. Carbasa = Spanish flax and hence sails.
    Eiectam = "driven ashore."
    Leuis . . . alga = seaweed piled on shore by storms at sea. Compare Horace *Odes* 3.17.9–12. The paradox of large warships held by light seaweed is the kind of self-conscious rhetoric that never failed to attract Ovid even when it added nothing discernible to the content of the line.

173–74. Nec te, si cupies, ipsa manere sinam: a line whose sheer unbelievability renders it an example of unrelieved pathos and unmitigated bathos.

175–76. Compare *Aeneid* 4.289, 294–95, 400 and 418, where Aeneas's comrades far from asking him to delay his departure grow more restless with each passing day.

177–78. Pro meritis et siqua tibi debebimus ultra, | pro spe coniugii tempora parua peto: "In return for what I have already deserved from you through past services and anything we shall owe you in the future, in return for the hope of marriage you held out, I seek a little more time." The Latin is very condensed. This and the following couplet are a revision of the message Dido asks her sister, Anna, to carry to Aeneas at *Aeneid* 4.429–34.

179–80. The notion that **usus** tempers love is the premise behind *Amores* 2.19 and 3.4.

181–84. Si minus = "otherwise."
    Animus = "the courage."

Effundere uitam: a graphic image of Dido bleeding to death once she stabs herself with Aeneas's sword (**Troicus ensis**). Compare *Aeneid* 4.646–47.

Crudelis: Dido hurls this epithet against Aeneas with her dying breath at *Aeneid* 4.661–62.

185–86. The image of the sword drenched (**tinctus**) first with tears and then blood is striking.

187–88. Note the bitter sarcasm of the sword as Aeneas's *munus* to Dido and of his building her grave at little expense (**impensa . . . breui**).

189–90. The wound of love is a familiar trope also found in *Aeneid* 4.1–2.

191–92. Anna soror, soror Anna: note the heightened emotion of the chiastic anaphora.

Male conscia: an ambiguous phrase that can be taken either to mean that Anna was wretched in her knowledge of Dido's blame or that she was only poorly conscious of it, i.e., unable to appreciate its true gravity, both of which are true.

Culpae frequently = sexual misconduct.

Vltima dona = burial.

193–94. Inscribar = jussive subjunctive.

195–96. Dido responds to Aeneas's disingenuous question to her in the underworld in Aeneid 6.458, *funeris heu tibi causa fui?*

Tristia 2.207–468

Tristia 2 is Ovid's apology to Augustus. In the first half, he invokes the goodwill and *clementia* of the *princeps* and defends his own personal integrity. In the second half he not only offers a defense of the *Ars Amatoria* but also features a deliberate and provocative recollection of the geography of seduction depicted in our selection from the earlier work [61, 64, 66–67]. If Ovid's real purpose was to win either Augustus's pardon or his permission to move to a more cosmopolitan locale, it is hard to believe that this would be the best strategy. Indeed, in this poem, perhaps more than any other, Ovid chooses to speak the truth to power. While ostensibly offering a humble defense of his life and art, the poet launches into what at times reads more like a satire than a petition for imperial clemency.

Still, Ovid is careful. He never calls into question the legitimacy of Augustan power. The stance in the poem is more ironic than oppositional. Ovid in this poem is most himself when he means the opposite of what he says. He is most authentic when he appropriates the words of others. His creation of this ironic textual subject allows him to be most fully present where he is absent. The Ovid constructed by and through the *Tristia* thus becomes the perfect metaphor for both exile and the subjections of empire, whose simultaneous self-constitution and nonexistence render him an ideal citizen of this brave new republic. Indeed, as the poet himself notes throughout these poems, he is in a real sense dead.

207–08. Carmen et error: the two causes for Ovid's exile [61]. Since he was not allowed to mention the second, he will defend the first.

209–10. My value is not so great (**non sum tanti**) that I would reopen old wounds. The poet acknowledges the position of the emperor by setting himself at a fundamentally different social, if not ontological, level.

211–12. Ovid seeks to narrow the charge by dealing only with the question of whether the *Ars* directly promoted adultery.

213–14. "If you have been convinced of this charge then it is permissible to fool the hearts of the gods, and many things are not worth your notice." The logic of the argument is not the best, but the implication is that you, a god, could only be deceived into believing this because such matters are not worth your attention.
Notitia . . . tua = ablative of comparison.

215–16. Vtque: the analogy between Jupiter's rule in heaven and Augustus's on earth was a staple in the repertoire of the Augustan poets.
Deos caelumque simul sublime = direct object of **tuenti . . . Ioui.**

217–18. De te pendentem = "hanging from you," i.e., in the great chain of being.

219–20. The insinuation is that if Augustus did claim to have read the *Ars*, then he was derelict in his duty.
Imparibus . . . modis = elegiac couplets.

221–24. Non ea . . . moles . . . ut = "not such a burden . . . that." **Non** goes with **tam leue** as well.
Lusibus: *lusus* and *ludus* are synonyms for love and love poetry.
Aduertere numen = "to direct your divinity toward." Real gods have better things to do. The phrase is used in place of the more common and expected *aduertere animum*, "to pay attention to."

225–26. Pannonia was the region stretching from modern Belgrade to Vienna. It became an imperial province in 10 CE. Its revolt in 6 CE was a major crisis that threatened Italy and created political unrest in Rome. The elder Pliny (*Hist. Nat.* 7.149) records that Augustus was rumored to be on the verge of suicide. He certainly didn't have time to be reading elegy at the very moment he was preparing to send Ovid into exile. The Illyrians also revolted in 6 CE. Tiberius restored order.

Raetia = the eastern Alps, site of a smaller rebellion put down by Tiberius and Drusus.

The Thracian rebellion does not seem to have been a serious threat. Ovid paints a picture of a restive empire requiring the *princeps*'s full attention, perhaps explaining the need for a scapegoat.

227–28. The references here are complex. In 20 BCE, Rome had established a pro-Roman monarchy in Armenia. This diplomatic maneuvering had led to the return of Crassus's standards by the Parthians who then feared being outflanked. In 1 BCE, the anti-Roman faction had once more assumed power in Armenia and Augustus's grandson and heir Gaius was dispatched to re-establish stability in the region. He died on the return journey in 4 CE without his mission fully accomplished. See Ovid's allusion to same expedition in *Ars* 1.177–228. This like the previous couplet can be read as hyperbolic praise, a dig at Augustus's recent setbacks, or an argument for why the *princeps* would have been too busy to read the *Ars*.

Arcus: the Parthians were famed archers. See Propertius 3.4.17–19; 4.6.81–84.

229–30. Prole tua = Tiberius, the son of Livia by her first husband, Tiberius Claudius Nero, he was adopted by Augustus in 4 CE, only after the death of Gaius. There is some irony here in Ovid's use of the term *proles* or "offspring."

Obit = "engages in."

231–34. Ovid turns from Augustus's foreign worries to his domestic preoccupations.

Denique = "in addition." **Vt** = "given that."

Corpore = the body of the empire. **Labet** = "is insecure."

Legum . . . tutela tuarum et morum: a direct reference to Augustus's moral reform legislation [53].

Similes quos cupis esse tuis: a suitably ambiguous phrase.

235–36. Praestas = "you guarantee." Elegy is a product of *otium*, not the *negotium* of war and politics [44].

237–38. Ovid here moves to an active defense of the *Ars*. **Mirer** = deliberative subjunctive.

Euoluisse = "to have unrolled," i.e., a papyrus scroll.

239–40. Vacuum = "free time."

243–44. Legum = the *lex Iulia de adulteris coercendis* of 18 BCE. See the introductory note to *Amores* 1.4.

Nurus = "young married women."

245–46. Of course, the warning also functioned as an advertisement.

247–50. The quotation is from *Ars* 1.31–34. Ovid has altered it, substituting **nil nisi legitimum** for *nos Venerem tutam*, making the warning even stronger. Augustus would not presumably notice the difference if he has been too busy with the *negotium* of empire to read the *Ars*.

Vittae = the hair bands worn by freeborn women who either were or would become *matronae*.

Instita = a border sewn to the edge of the *stola* or long robe worn by *matronae*.

Concessa furta: as the excerpt from *Ars* included here shows, Ovid's instructions on seduction make no distinction between various targets of opportunity after this initial, perfunctory gesture toward propriety.

251–52. Ecquid = an interrogative particle.

253–54. Ovid's critics voice the objection that *matronae* might still read the *Ars* and learn the arts of seduction. But Ovid claims all poems can be misread.

Quoque trahat, quamuis non doceatur, habet = "she has that by which she may attract men, even though she was not the one being taught."

257–58. Sinistri = "depravity."

259–60. Annales = the first great Roman epic, written by Ennius in the first half of the second century BCE. It was considered a repository of old-fashioned virtue, though by the Augustan era it was considered stylistically crude (**hirsutius**). It represents the opposite of elegiac *mollitia*.

Ilia = daughter of Aeneas, a Vestal virgin who became the mother of Romulus and Remus when raped by Mars. See *Amores* 3.4.39–40.

261–62. Aeneadum genetrix = Venus. These are the first words of Lucretius's *De rerum natura*, a didactic poem in hexameters on Epicurean philosophy. Note how all of Ovid's examples allude to Augustus and the *gens Iulia*'s claim to descend from Aeneas and to their veneration of *Venus genetrix*. See Propertius 3.4.19–20 and the introductory note to *Amores* 1.2.

263–64. The poet looks ahead to lines 363 and following.

265–66. All things with beneficial effects can also cause harm.

269–70. Interdum, modo = *modo, modo.*

273–74. The example of forensic eloquence is telling since it was normally identified with respectable *negotium* as opposed to elegiac *otium.*

275–76. Recta si mente legatur: the implication is that only those with dirty minds find harmful things in poetry. Would this include Ovid's accusers?

277–78. The imaginary interlocutor, a stand-in for Augustus, returns.

The OCT reading, *uitio*, is nonsense. I have preferred the equally well attested **uitiat**.

279–80. Ovid here begins his review of the temptations offered by the capital. The same terrain, as we have already seen, is covered in *Ars* 1.61–228. In both passages, many of the sites have connections with Augustus and his family.

On theaters, compare *Ars* 1.89–134.

281–82. Owen in his OCT (1915) printed *multis quam*, but in his later commentary (1924) he accepted the MS reading **multi quam**, printed here.

On gladiatorial bouts, compare *Ars* 1.163–76.

283–84. The circus was a favorite theme of Ovid's. Compare *Ars* 1.135–164, which is a reworking of *Amores* 3.2.

285–86. On the colonnades, see *Ars* 1.67–74.

287–88. The poet argues that the *Ars* is no more to blame for vice than other Roman institutions that are susceptible of misuse. This includes temples, and he says with a wink **quis locus est templis augustior?** ["What place is more august than temples"]. The passage is susceptible to three logically – but not rhetorically – mutually exclusive readings. The first reads the statement as tautological, "what place is more holy than temples." The second sees a pun on Augustus's name and notes the wit of associating the *princeps* with places of possible seduction, particularly in a poem that seeks to defend its author against charges of corrupting the morals of young women. According to this interpretation, Ovid is no more to blame for the misuse of the *Ars* than Augustus is for the seductions that occur in holy/august temples. This reading gains in complexity when we realize that the temples the poet names were all constructed or reconstructed by the *princeps* and listed in the *Res Gestae* as among his proudest accomplishments in rebuilding the city and re-establishing traditional religion (19.1–21.1). Thus what could be more like Augustus, *augustior*, than these temples that he himself caused to be built or refurbished? And it is this very play on words that also allows the line to be read as a form of flattery that acknowledges precisely those attributes he claimed for himself. Ovid, according to this third reading, merely defends the *Ars* in its own terms and says even the holiest of places, those most associated with the *princeps*, are subject to misuse and misinterpretation.

On temples, see *Ars* 1.75–88.

289–90. The periphrasis **ille deus** urges us to recall that Ovid frequently equates Jupiter with Augustus in the exilic poems. According to Suetonius and others, Augustus did not always practice what he preached in sexual matters. By the same token, the express purpose of much of Augustus's moral reform legislation was to make "many women mothers."

291–92. Proxima adoranti Iunonis templa subibit = "it will occur to her praying at the nearby temple of Juno."

Paelicibus = the same lovers that Jupiter made mothers in the previous couplet.

293–94. Natum de crimine . . . Erichthonium: Erichthonius was born when Vulcan tried to rape Pallas. He prematurely ejaculated and the child was born from the Earth. Pallas subsequently raised him in secret (**sustulerit**).

295–96. The temple of *Mars Vltor*, dedicated in 2 BCE, was vowed by Augustus in return for his victory over the assassins of Julius Caesar. It featured a statue of Venus, the patron deity of the *gens Iulia*, joined with that of Mars in an allegorical representation of the alliance of the power of war to the imperial clan. **Iuncta** has clear sexual connotations.

Vir = Vulcan, a statue of whom was placed outside. Venus's husband is reduced to the figure of the elegiac *exclusus amator*. Compare *Amores* 1.4.

Note the artistic arrangement of this and the preceding couplet as we move from Vulcan the would-be rapist to Vulcan the outraged husband. We will return to *Venus genetrix* two couplets later.

297–98. Isidis = Isis, often confused by Roman writers with Io, the object of Jupiter's affections and Juno's (**Saturnia**) wrath. See Propertius 1.3.19–20; *Amores* 1.3.21–22, 2.19.29–30, 3.4.19–20; *Ars* 1.1.77–78.

299–300. Anchises = the father of Aeneas, with whom Venus fell in love. The reference is to the shrine of *Venus genetrix* in the *forum Iulium*.

Latmius heros = Endymion. See Propertius 2.15.15–16.

Iasion = son of Jupiter and Electra, lover of Ceres.

305–06. Ovid returns to the temple imagery. **Sinit:** undertand *eam*.
Huic = the priest. He is not guilty of her crime.

307–08. The pentameter can be read in different fashions depending on
whether **licet** is construed as a verb or a concessive adverb, and whether
castae is construed as the nominative subject of **legant** or as a dative of agent
with **facienda**. In all cases, however, a distinction is made between the
permissible in life and in art.

309–10. Nudas = prostitutes who were exhibited nude in the streets of
Rome. If pimps are not punished for exposing *matronae* to such sights how
could Ovid be for the *Ars?* This is one of Ovid's strongest arguments
and suggests that the *error* more than the *carmen* was Augustus's chief
motivation for the poet's exile. Note the clever juxtaposition of **nudas** with
matrona.

311–12. Even the Vestals are regularly exposed to such sights. Roman life
was much more openly and intensely eroticized than modern western life, as
revealed by the wall paintings in Pompeii and the various implements of
daily life on which sexual scenes were routinely depicted.

313–38. Ovid embeds a standard elegiac *recusatio* in his defense. He admits
that his subject matter is not of the highest order, but pleads inability to
write in the epic manner. This passage recalls Propertius 2.1.

317–18. The key term in the couplet is **iterum.** Ovid implies the Trojan
story does not need to be rehashed.

319–20. The Seven against Thebes was a popular epic topic often used as a
foil for elegy. See Propertius 2.1.21–22 and 2.34.39–40. **Fratrum** = Eteocles
and Polynices.

321–22. Pius = an allusion to *pius Aeneas* in Vergil.

323–24. The claim that the poet either planned to write an epic on Caesar's
deeds or would have written one had he been able is common. See Propertius
2.1 and 2.10.

327–28. Arguor inmerito: the phrase can be interpreted in two opposed
fashions. **Inmerito** can be read as ablative of means, "I am convicted by my
lack of merit," or as ablative of manner, "I am convicted without merit, i.e.,
undeservedly."
Tenuis is a common term in Callimachean poetics, indicating the slender
style [29].

329–30. Exiguo has Callimachean connotations. See Tibullus 1.1.29–30 and Propertius 2.1.71–72.

Cumba: on the metaphor of the skiff that stays close to shore as opposed to the ocean-going vessel, see Apollo's warning to Propertius not to try epic themes in 3.3.21–24 as well as 3.9.3–4 and 35–36.

331–34. The *Metamorphoses* shows that Ovid was able to write poetry in hexameters and treat mythological subjects.

335–36. Diuitis ingenii = genitive of description. **Inmania** = either "vast" or "inhuman, savage." **Condere** = "to join together in a composition" or "to hide, cover up." A wickedly ambiguous couplet.

337–38. Ovid claims he tried to write an epic on Caesar but instead of praising his strengths he seemed to detract from them. This can be read in two ways.

339–40. Ovid refers to the *Amores*, explicitly acknowledging that they were fictional.

345–46. Quis = *quibus*.

347–48. Neque . . . **–que** indicates a contrast. On the one hand, no bride learned adultery from me, and on the other, one cannot teach what one does not know. Ovid here returns to the difference between the poet and his poetry. See lines 307–08.

349–50. Delicias et mollia carmina = "soft songs of love," an example of the rhetorical figure of hendiadys (one thing expressed by two).

The pentameter's relation to the hexameter is not clear. If it is a result clause, the poet's present predicament seems to tell against the assertion. If it is a purpose clause, the logic of his rhetorical strategy is more perverse than his poetry. The best solution is to take it as a concessive clause. **Fabula** = "scandal, ill-fame."

351–52. Adeo = "even."

353–54. Note that in making the distinction between his **Musa iocosa** and his **uita uerecunda**, he as much as admits that the *Ars* was immoral. Otherwise, the contrast has no point.

355–56. The subject of **permisit** is **pars**.

357–58. Owen prints **uoluptas** in his later commentary, rather than *uoluntas*, which he accepts in the OCT. **Voluptas** is attested and makes better sense. **Honesta** = "harmless."

Feres = "you will obtain (in the *Ars*)."

359–60. Green (1994) speculates that a couplet containing the protasis of this condition has dropped out.

Accius: tragic poet, 170–86 BCE. **Terentius**: the comic poet Terence, active in the 160s BCE.

361–62. Ovid here begins a mocking literary history with the aim of showing that all poets have written about love, even the epic poets. This, of course, makes elegy the true master genre.

363–64. Lyrici Teia Musa senis: Anacreon, the Greek lyric poet from Teos, sixth century BCE.

365–66. Sappho: the sixth-century BCE poet. Note: **puellas** can be both the subject and the object of **amare**.

367–68. Battiades = Callimachus [26–30]. The reference is to his erotic epigrams.

369–70. Menander: the chief author of Greek New Comedy (343–291 BCE) [24], whose plots always revolved around romance and ended in marriage.

371–72. What is the *Iliad* but a fight between an *amator* and a *uir*?

373–74. The *Iliad* (**illi** = locative) begins with the quarrel between Agamemnon and Achilles over Briseis. Even epic, elegy's generic nemesis, is reread as its precursor.

377–78. Maeonides = Homer, son of Maeon. The story of Hephaestus capturing Aphrodite and Ares *in flagrante delicto* is in *Odyssey* 8.296.

379–80. Calypso and Circe both took Odysseus for a lover. The *Odyssey* is obviously more congenial for Ovid's purposes than the *Iliad*.

381–82. Nothing is more serious than tragedy, and yet it is always about love. Ovid's list of topics (lines 383–406) is exhaustive and exhausting.

383–84. Hippolytus was both the son of Theseus and the title character of Euripides's tragedy on his stepmother (**nouercae**) Phaedra's illicit passion for him.

Canace = daughter of Aeolus, whose love for her brother was treated in a lost tragedy by Euripides. **Nobilis** = "well known."

385–86. Tantalides . . . eburnus = Pelops, who had an ivory shoulder. See Tibullus 1.4.63–64 and Propertius 2.1.65–66. **Pisaeam** = Hippodameia, who was won as bride by Pelops in a chariot race against her father Oenomaus. The latter was killed in the race, thereby fulfilling the prophecy that he would die at the hands of his son in law. The topic was treated in lost tragedies by Sophocles and Euripides. **Currus** = poetic plural.

387–88. Mater = Medea, the subject of a tragedy by Euripides and one by Ovid himself [60]. See Tibullus 1.2.51–52; Propertius 2.16.29–30.

389–90. The Thracian king Tereus married Procne, but later raped her sister Philomela and cut out her tongue to prevent her from revealing the secret. Itys was the son of Procne and Tereus. Philomela used embroidery to communicate her outrage to her sister, who then killed Itys and served him to Tereus for dinner. When Tereus discovered what had happened he pursued both women with an ax, whereupon they were transformed into birds in answer to the young women's prayers. In the Roman version, Tereus became a hoopoe, Philomela a swallow and Procne a nightingale. In some versions, the roles of Philomela and Procne were reversed. Sophocles wrote a tragedy based on the story as did Livius Andronicus and Accius.

391–92. Aeropen = the wife of Atreus who was seduced by Thyestes, his brother (**frater sceleratus**). For revenge, Atreus served Thyestes a banquet of his own children's flesh. The sight was so horrible that even the horses of the sun turned away in horror (**auersos Solis . . . equos**). Numerous tragedies were written on the theme.

393–94. Scylla: see Tibullus 1.4.63–64. The tragedy to which Ovid refers is unknown.

395–96. The story of Orestes and Electra's revenge on their mother, Clytemnestra (**Tyndaridos**), for her murder of Agamemnon and her adultery with Aegisthus was treated in extant tragedies by Aeschylus, Sophocles, and Euripides.

Qui = archiac *quo*.

Egentem mentis Oresten: Orestes was driven mad by the Furies for killing his mother.

397–98. Domitore Chimaerae = Bellerophon. He was accused by his hostess (**fallax hospita**), Anteia, of trying to rape her when she failed to seduce him. He was sent by her husband Proetus to her father, Iobates, to be killed.

The latter set Bellerophon a number of dangerous tasks including slaying the fire-breathing Chimera. The story was treated by Sophocles and Euripides.

399–400. Hermione = the daughter of Menelaus and Helen. She was betrothed to Orestes during the Trojan war, but when Menelaus returned he gave her to Achilles's son, Neoptolemus, instead. Orestes then slew Neoptolemus. The story was treated by Sophocles and Euripides, as well as Ovid himself in *Heroides* 8.

    Schoenica Virgo = Atalanta. See Propertius 1.1.9–16. She was the subject of a tragedy by Aeschylus.

    Mycenaeo Phoebas amata duci = a direct quotation of *Amores* 2.8.12. The story of Cassandra was widely treated in tragedy.

401–02. Danaen: see *Amores* 2.19.27–28, 3.4.21–22. Sophocles and Euripides treat the theme.

    Danaesque nurum = daughter-in-law of Danae, Andromeda, who was saved by Perseus, son of Jupiter and Danae. See the introductory note to Propertius 1.3 as well as 4.6.77–78 and 4.7.63–66. She was the subject of tragedies by Sophocles and Euripides.

    Matremque Lyaei = Semele, the mother of Bacchus (*Lyaeus*) by Jupiter. Aeschylus wrote a tragedy on her destruction. She requested Jupiter to manifest himself without disguise and perished in flames when he did.

    Haemonaque = son of Creon, lover of Antigone.

    Noctes cui coiere duae = Alcmene, wife of Amphitryon and mother of Hercules by Jupiter. Two nights were required for his miraculous begetting. While a common topic for comedy, the Alcmene story also received tragic treatments by the major Athenian tragedians.

403–04. Peliae generum = Admetus, husband of Alcestis, subject of the extant play of the same name by Euripides.

    Pelasgum primus = Protesilaus; see Catullus 68.74. His story was the subject of a tragedy by Euripides.

405–06. Iole = Hercules's beloved. When his wife Deianeira (**Herculis uxor**) discovered the affair she sent him a robe dipped in the blood of the Centaur Nessus. It was supposed to be a charm to return him to her affections, but instead was a poison that produced an agonizing death. Sophocles treats the story in the *Trachiniae*.

    Pyrrhi parens = Deidamia, beloved of Achilles and mother of Pyrrhus, who was also called Neoptolemus. Her story was treated by Euripides.

    Hylas = Hercules's pederastic beloved in the *Argonautica*. We have no record of a tragedy in which he appeared. The story is told in Propertius 1.20.

    Iliacus puer = Ganymede, the son of Tros, carried to heaven by Jupiter on account of his beauty. Sophocles and Euripides both wrote tragedies on this theme.

407–08. Ovid brings his catalog of tragic topics to a close by self-consciously observing that it had become a mere list of names that could continue indefinitely.

409–10. Ovid refers to the satyr-plays performed at the end of each tragic trilogy.

411–12. Sophocles wrote a satyr-play entitled *The Lovers of Achilles*, which depicted this most warlike of heroes as the object pederastic affections and hence *mollis*.

413–14. Aristides (second century BCE) wrote six books of erotic stories set in Miletus.

415–16. Eubius is mentioned only here. **Descripsit corrumpi semina matrum**: his work apparently dealt with abortions, possibly giving advice on how to perform them.

417–18. Sybraritica: an erotic work in verse by Hemitheon of Sybaris, a town known for its licentiousness. As the pentameter indicates, however, erotic and pornographic works were in wide circulation.

419–20. Ovid refers to the great public libraries created in 39 BCE by Asinius Pollio and in 28 BCE by Augustus. The (**ea**) erotic texts, discussed in the previous three couplets, were found there among the works of the learned (**doctorum monumentis mixta uirorum**), and were made available (**patent**) by the generosity of these same generals (**muneribusque ducum**). Augustus is thus indirectly made a purveyor of pornography.

421–22. Ovid turns from Greek literary precedents to Roman.

423–24. Ennius: see lines 259–60.

425–26. Lucretius: see lines 261–62.
    Triplex . . . opus = the universe in its three great divisions, land, sea, and air. **Casurum**: Lucretius predicts the ultimate destruction of the universe.

427–28. Catullus is cited as Ovid's first real predecessor in Roman literature [34–39].

429–30. Adulterium: see the introductory note to Catullus 68.

431–32. Calvus was one of Catullus's contemporaries [35]. **Exigui** = Callimachean refinement. See Tibullus 1.1.29–30 and Propertius 2.1.71–72.

433–34. This passage presents a crux. Many editors, including Owen in his OCT but not in his later commentary, transpose this couplet with 435–36 on the grounds that Ticidas is said by Apuleius to have celebrated Metella under the name of Perilla. Thus they place the present couplet immediately before lines 437–38. There are, however, counter-arguments: (1) the transposition lacks manuscript support; (2) none of the authors mentioned by Apuleius revealed the true name of their beloved in their work, hence Ticidas cannot be referred to in 437–38; (3) if 433–34 and 437–38 belong together, this would be the only example in the catalog stretching from lines 422 to 446 of a single entry running more than one couplet. I leave the manuscript reading unchanged and assume with Owen in his commentary that the poets referred to in 437–38 are not Ticadas and Memmius.

Ticidas was a little-known poet who died in 46 BCE fighting with Caesar against Pompey.

Memmi = Gaius Memmius, governor of Bithynia in 57 BCE. Catullus was a member of his staff. Pliny the younger includes him in a list of men whose lives were "pure" but whose verse was wanton.

Rebus adest nomen nominibusque pudor = "Things are called by their proper names, and those names are shameful."

435–36. Cinna = Gaius Helvius Cinna [35].

Anser = an adherent of Antony. None of his verse survives.

Cornifuci = Q. Cornufucius, a friend of Catullus [35], killed in 42 BCE fighting on the side of the senate against the second triumvirate [40].

Catonis = P. Valerius Cato, a teacher and poet from Cisalpine Gaul. He was an important influence on Catullus and other poets of the period.

437–38. This couplet is troubled. The MS reading of *per illos* is nonsense. I follow the early Italian commentators and Owen in his commentary by printing **Perillae**.

Metelle: a woman took her husband's name upon marriage. The couplet as a whole should read: "and those in whose books she was recently hidden under the name Perilla (she is now called by your name, Metellus)."

439–40. Varro of Atax wrote a translation of Apollonius's *Argonautica* before turning his attention to erotic verse. See Propertius 2.34.85–86. **Phasiacas ... undas** = the river Phasis in Colchis, home of Medea and the Golden Fleece.

441–42. Hortensi = Q. Hortiensius Hortalus, the famous orator and rival of

Cicero, mentioned in Pliny's list of those whose lives were sober but their verse gay.

Serui = possibly Seruius Sulpicius, father of Sulpicia.

443–44. Sissenna: L. Cornelius Sissena, historian, a contemporary of Cicero who translated Aristides. See lines 413–14.

445–46. Ovid now turns to what he sees as the culmination of the literary history he has just produced, erotic elegy. On Gallus and Lycoris, see Introduction [5, 13, 50] and Propertius 2.34.91–92.

447–62. This passage is a reworking of Tibullus 1.6.5–32, with elements from 1.2 and 1.5. Ovid has picked out those parts of Tibullus that most presage his own work.

447–48. Iuranti = the *puella*.
Sic . . . quod = "because thus."

451–52. He would use the excuse of remarking on her jewelry to touch his *domina*'s hand.

453–54. Ovid would later use this scenario to write *Amores* 1.4. Compare Tibullus 1.2.21–22.

455–56. Tibullus taught how to remove hickeys.

457–58. Ovid developed this Tibullan scenario in *Amores* 2.19 and 3.4.

459–60. See Tibullus 1.5.73–74.

461–62. The recurrence of **arte** here and in line 450 reminds us that Ovid's purpose is to defend his own *Ars*.

463–64. Fraudi = "a cause of harm," in a double dative construction. **Te principe:** Octavian received the name *Augustus* from the senate in 27 BCE, around the same time he started officially to use the title *princeps*. Tibullus was well known by this time.

465–66. Propertius taught the same lessons, with the same renown. **Destrictus** = censured.

467–68. Ovid like Juvenal in his first satire will speak only to the dead.

CRITICAL ANTHOLOGY

INTRODUCTION TO *THE LATIN LOVE ELEGY*

Georg Luck

> Schoolmasters have special faces for them. Catullus, whose 'brutal frankness' revealed the suffering of his tormented soul (look of comprehension and pity . . . secret sorrow), irradiated by his delightful humour (wry smile); Tibullus, all rustic grace (pass on); Propertius, difficult – h'm in every sense – precious (*moue* of distaste); Ovid – great facility, bad end; an Augustan Oscar Wilde (Universal Tension).
>
> Cyril Connolly, *The Sunday Times*, 29 November 1959

When we speak of an 'elegy', we usually think of a melancholy and meditative kind of poem. In ancient literature, however, an 'elegy' is defined only by its metre, by the alternating sequence of a dactylic hexameter and pentameter. This metrical pattern has a gentle, yet insistent musical quality. Propertius called it 'soft', *mollis*,[1] and Ovid compared the movement of the elegiac distich to the rise and fall of a jet of water: 'In six numbers let my work rise, and sink again in five.'[2] Elsewhere Ovid describes the personified Elegy as a beautiful woman with perfumed hair, clad in a gauzy robe. The fact that 'one of her feet is longer than the other' only adds to her charm.[3]

The earliest Greek elegies deal with a variety of themes: war, politics, the pleasures and pains of life in general, love, friendship, death. They communicate a variety of moods: joy and sadness, hope and despair, deeply personal beliefs and common thought. Such fragments as we have do not tell a story for the sake of the story; they do not compete with the epic. An early Greek elegy is at the same time more personal and less straightforward than the epic; it reveals more of the poet's personality, his tastes, his experiences, his philosophy of life.

The later history of the ancient elegy is marked by two important developments. (1) In the post-classical period it is adapted more generally to mythological narratives, without losing its personal and, sometimes, highly emotional character. A legend, as told by Callimachus, represents a very colourful and exciting tissue of visual impressions and side-comments. (2)

307

During the Augustan Age at Rome the elegy becomes the preferred medium of love-poetry.

The history of the love-elegy in Rome covers only a few decades. Catullus died shortly after 55 B.C.; Propertius' first book of elegies was published around 29 or 28 B.C.; Tibullus followed with his first book soon after; and the first edition of Ovid's *Amores* appeared shortly after 20 B.C. Within less than fifty years Latin elegiac poetry had compassed an astonishing wealth of themes and situations, styles and techniques. The Greek elegy developed slowly; it had its archaic period, its classical and post-classical age. These categories of literary history seem to lose their meaning when they are applied to the Latin elegy. Everything happened more quickly, at an almost feverish pace.

Ovid, the last of the elegiac love-poets, felt that they had all been 'members of a group', *sodales*. At the end of his funeral lament for Tibullus, he describes how the dead poet meets in the underworld the shades of Catullus and Calvus.[4] In his own autobiography, written in exile, he remembers the 'friendly circle', *convictus*, and the 'comradeship', *sodalicium*, which included himself, Propertius, and two of Propertius' friends.[5] These young men used to read their poems to each other, cultivating a common tradition, proud of being the true disciples of Callimachus and Philetas.

They knew that the life they led and the verse they wrote were not altogether respectable in the eyes of their contemporaries. Obviously they were not concerned with great religious and national issues. Sometimes they make a half-hearted attempt to defend their 'naughtiness', *nequitia*. They always seem to remember that the love-elegy is a 'playful' kind of poetry (*lusus*). This half-affectionate, half-deprecatory term could be applied to lyrics, epigrams, bucolics, satires, but certainly not to tragedies and epics.[6]

Both Horace and Vergil had composed 'playful poems' in their youth, but they had gone on to more serious themes and modes in later years. Tibullus died too soon to follow their example; Propertius, in his 'Roman elegies' (Book IV), and Ovid in his *Fasti* tried to show that the elegiac metre, too, was suitable to more ambitious themes. But this was hardly more than an experiment, in the case of Propertius; and Ovid knew that he would be remembered by posterity as the 'playful author of tender love-poems', *tenerorum lusor amorum*.

The Latin elegists feel more apologetic about their way of life than about the kind of poetry they write. Like Callimachus who 'shaped his verse on a narrow lathe',[7] they claim to be conscious craftsmen. They are trying to raise the elegy to a higher rank, to distinguish it from the epigram and the light improvisation. Hence they avoid certain expressions and phrases which are frequent in the epigram (Catullus, Martial).[8] For 'kiss' they prefer *osculum*; the synonym *savium* belonged to the idiom of comedy (it is found only once, in Propertius 2.29.39).

Some poets were more fastidious than others. Propertius, for example, has many colloquialisms found also in Catullus, but not in Tibullus and Ovid. In Latin, as in many other languages, diminutives have a colloquial ring. They appear frequently, as terms of endearment, or for purely metrical reasons, in Propertius' early poems. Their number decreases in his later books, as his style tends toward the elevated and grandiose. Tibullus uses them rarely, Ovid sparingly.

Occasionally the elegiac style admits of a word that is not exactly 'vulgar', but not dignified enough for the style of the epic and tragedy; for example, *plorare*, 'to cry', instead of *flere*; and *lassus*, 'tired', instead of *fessus*. It seems that the elegiac poets hesitate to divorce their language completely from that of everyday conversation. They dislike using certain words that had disappeared from the spoken language long ago and were (presumably for this very reason) considered effective in epic verse. *Extemplo*, 'immediately', appears ten times in Ovid's *Metamorphoses*, but never in his love-elegies.

Compared to their great contemporaries, Horace and Vergil, the elegiac poets were always at a slight disadvantage. They were read, they had an enthusiastic and devoted audience, but they never rose to the rank of 'classical' authors. Whereas we have various sets of ancient commentaries and notes on Horace and Vergil, the text of Propertius, Ovid and Tibullus is bare of explanations. This could mean that, even in Antiquity, they were read less extensively in schools than Horace and Vergil, partly because they were felt to be less suitable *virginibus puerisque*, and partly because their range of experiences was somewhat limited.

They write about love, their love. For the first time in Roman literature, love is taken seriously. Euripides and Apollonius Rhodius had shown the power of love over a woman. Plautus and Terence had brought enamoured adolescents on to the comic stage, but treated their passion in a conventional manner. The happy ending was inevitable. The other extreme we have in Lucretius. He considers love as a threat to the Epicurean peace of mind.

In Lucretius' own time the attitude toward love in literature changes radically. The society of Catullus begins to pay attention to love and love-affairs, one's own and those of others. Is this a case of literature imitating life or life imitating literature? All the poets of the Augustan Age deal with erotic themes; even Vergil cannot conceive of his serious national epic without a love-intrigue. It is possible that there was a love-intrigue in Naevius' *Bellum Punicum*, but the extant fragments give no indication of its nature, and Vergil was free to omit it if he had found it unsuitable.

This society refused to consider marriage as a happy end, but rather as an intermediary stage, a means to an end. A legal marriage had become a short-termed association for which nothing was necessary but the free assent of both man and woman. No religious ceremonies, no legal formalities were required. It was easy to obtain a divorce. Cicero's daughter Tullia had been divorced three times when she died at the age of thirty-nine. Maecenas' wife Terentia had, as everyone knew, intimate relations with Augustus; her husband divorced her and married her again soon afterwards; 'he had only one wife, but he got married a thousand times', Seneca remarks on their frequent quarrels and reconciliations.[9]

A Roman girl could be engaged at the age of ten and married at twelve to a man chosen by her father. When she grew up to discover the meaning of love, she was no longer free. During the early centuries of the Roman Republic, as long as Rome was a city with a predominantly Roman population, the women must have accepted this situation because it was all they knew. After Rome had risen to political power, foreigners from all parts of the Mediterranean world began to stream into the city, first as traders, visitors or prisoners of war. At the beginning of the second century B.C., many of them had taken permanent residence in the capital and were active in business, or creative in literature and the arts.

With the increase in material prosperity, a taste for new pleasures and luxuries developed. In the first century B.C., we find in Rome a large number of Greek courtesans, many of whom were cultured, well-read, and accomplished dancers and musicians. They were much sought after by the fashionable set of young men. No wonder that the more sensitive and passionate among the native Roman ladies were envious of the glitter and excitements of a different way of life and resented the tedious routine of their households.

During this last century of the Roman Republic, a curious social phenomenon takes place. Ladies of the best families begin to live a rather independent life. It is not always possible to determine whether the women we meet in the love-poetry of this period are Roman matrons or Greek freedwomen. Catullus' Lesbia was a consul's wife, but Cicero speaks with heavy sarcasm of her notorious conduct. In A.D. 19 another Roman lady, the daughter of a distinguished man, registered with the police as a public prostitute. Gallus, the statesman, soldier and poet, fell in love with a Greek freedwoman whom he calls Lycoris in his elegies. Tibullus' Delia and Nemesis may have belonged to the same class. In the case of Propertius, it is not clear whether Cynthia, who lives and behaves in all respects like these other girls, was not actually of an old Roman family. 'Sulpicia, the daughter of Servius', proudly signs her love-poems with her name.

As the traditional ideals of marriage lost their meaning, man and woman alike were seeking love outside marriage. The memory of traditional values such as 'faith', *fides*, 'affection and respect', *pietas*, and 'chastity', *castitas*, were nevertheless still alive; only they were now transferred from the legal union between man and wife to the loose association between the lover and his mistress.

Tibullus paints in idyllic colours the life he wishes to lead in the country at the side of his Delia. Propertius rejoices when he hears that the Emperor has withdrawn one of his marital laws which seemed to threaten his affair with Cynthia, but he speaks of her as 'for ever my mistress and for ever my wife'.[10] In one of his late poems Catullus reminds Lesbia that he loved her 'as a father loves his children'.[11]

To these poets the 'eternal union', *foedus aeternum*, between a man and a woman no longer seems possible nor desirable within a legal marriage; it can only be realized in the ideal love-affair. Ovid swears by all the gods that he will never seek another mistress than Corinna.[12]

The elegiac poets and, later, the satirists and the Christian church fathers, convey only one side of the picture. Many private documents, such as letters and funeral inscriptions, show that among the middle and lower classes the old ideals of loyalty and affection were still alive. Augustus tried to impose them by force on the upper classes, but the conjugal laws which he proclaimed at various times after 28 B.C. met with such violent opposition that he was obliged to postpone their enforcement until A.D. 9. At about the same time, by an act of curious brutality, he showed how determined he was. He banished Ovid, the poet who had symbolized the frivolity of a whole period, on questionable charges, to the Black Sea, where he died obscurely in A.D. 17, without ever seeing Rome again. His exile marks the end of elegiac love-poetry in Rome.

Notes

1 Propertius 1.7.19: *et frustra cupies mollem componere versum*; cf. 2.1.2 and already Hermesianax, quoted by Athen. 13, p. 597 F.
2 Ovid, *Amores* 1.1.27f: *sex mihi surgat opus numeris, in quinque residat.*
3 Ovid, *Amores* 3.1.7ff.
4 Ovid, *Amores* 3.9.16f.
5 Ovid, *Tristia* 4.10.45ff.
6 H. Wagenvoort, '*Ludus poeticus*', now reprinted in: *Studies in Roman Literature, Culture and Religon* (1956), 30ff.
7 Propertius 2.34.43; on the meaning of this image see Richard Bentley's note on Horace, *Ars Poetica* 441.
8 The following remarks are based on B. Axelson, *Unpoetische Wörter* (Lund 1945), 18f, 26, 36.
9 Seneca, *Epistulae*, 114.6.
10 Propertius 2.7, 2.6.42.
11 Catullus 72, 3f.
12 Ovid, *Amores* 3.2.61f.

THE POLITICS OF ELEGY

J. P. Sullivan

We sometimes regret that the Romans were not interested in some of the subjects that interest us or, at least, in the *way* that they interest us. The Romans were interested in money, but not in economics; they were interested in literature, but not interested in literary criticism. Just as, on the other hand, we are interested, to some degree, in oratory, but not in rhetorical theory; we are interested in free speech, but less so in the varied and complex, sometimes devious, forms free speech must take in differing political and social circumstances. Just as the Romans often fail to supply us with proper statistics for our economic analyses, so sometimes, in other areas, we are not as aware as we should be of subtle techniques of dissent and criticism which are necessitated by political situations very different from our own, where we can more or less say *what* we like and *how* we like. We therefore may be guilty of injustice, literary and moral injustice, to certain writers who do not fit our own paradigms of frankness and free expression. With Roman satire, for example, it is unrealistic to expect the savage and specific political criticism of Lucilius in the work of Horace – or, one might add, in Persius and Juvenal. We look in vain in extant Augustan literature for the indecent directness of Catullus' criticism of contemporary politicians and officials such as Julius Caesar, P. Sestius, and C. Memmius.

As a corollary to this, it may well be that we, along with other generations, in our admiration for the directness and frankness of such classics as Aristophanes and Catullus have scanted the credit we allow to other poets who, because of their literary, social, and political circumstances, could not possibly imitate such forthrightness, and who had therefore to cultivate different, perhaps more subtle, virtues and modes of expression in their work.

There is, as we know, something of a tendency among students of the Augustan Age to discuss the literature and the history of the period separately. There are dangers in this, particularly, I would suggest, for the students of literature. The historian, is acutely aware of the gory paths Octavian trod to reach his ascendancy; of the discomfort he felt about the earlier constitutional arrangements; of the plots against him; of his tub-thumping, but ultimately cautious, policy towards Parthia; and of the intermittently softening and hardening of his attitude towards dissent. The literary critic, on the other hand, in his modern, and in many ways proper, regard for the work of art as a thing in itself, the final focus of his attention, may run into certain avoidable difficulties of interpretation if he ignores the approximate dating of different works by the major Augustan writers. An apparent inconsistency of attitude may sometimes be explained by the difference in the times and circumstances. In this respect, Augustan literature is somewhat akin to Soviet literature in the twentieth century. It is therefore particularly important that we should not assume that Roman poets were any more politically naive than modern Soviet writers are, or than their educated Roman contemporaries were: at least we should not assume this without evidence or as a basis for discussion. Surely, if these Augustan poets are so admirable and so durable in other ways, it is fairer to look for development and subtlety in their works than for naivety or crassness.

In discussing the elegists *vis-à-vis* the other Augustan poets such as Virgil and Horace, I see no obvious way of distinguishing entirely between personal predilections, literary principles and conventions, and politics proper; these tend to overlap and reinforce one another, just as they do in certain modern literatures. And the fairly close relationships that existed in this small city of Rome between the various writers of different persuasions will often blur the distinctions I am trying to make here. Horace, we may venture to say, disliked Propertius and was a friend of sorts to Tibullus; Virgil was close to Gallus; and Propertius, overtly at least, admired them both. But, as we know from the case of Hemingway and Scott Fitzgerald, or Robert Frost, personal friendship does not always entail uncritical attitudes among writers.

To illustrate the surface ambiguity of elegiac attitudes, one might consider first the subject of peace. It is generally thought that the elegists, like the U.S. Army Air Force, might well take for their motto: "Peace is our profession." Certainly in elegy 1.10 Tibullus attacks war, praises the benefits of peace, and ends with this appeal:

> at nobis, pax alma, veni spicamque teneto
> profluat et pomis candidus ante sinus.

Yet in the opening elegy of book II, he compliments Messala, his friend and patron, on his victories in Aquitania:

> gentis Aquitanae celeber Messala triumphis.

Indeed, if we can believe the anonymous Life of Tibullus, he actually served with Messala in the Aquitanian war of 31 B.C. and was suitably rewarded. Of course, when he is at death's door in 30 B.C. and Messala is sailing off to

Cilicia, he has to praise the Golden Age when all was peaceful, without armies, war, anger, or armament manufacturers:

> non acies, non ira fuit, non bella, nec ensem
> immiti saevus duxerat arte faber.
>
> (1.3.47–48)

We see then, on the one hand, a rejection of war and conquest, but on the other a very Roman acceptance of these as necessary, indeed glorious, modes of existence. So in proclaiming a preference for *making love, not war*, the elegist must, rather self-consciously, set himself at odds with the premises of his society, but, as is also clear, he cannot become a radical dissenter disrupting the Augustan military machine or criticizing the social status of generals.

With Propertius, this ambiguity is even more complicated and it is, I believe, one of the several reasons for the complexity and the detectable irony in many of his poems. Propertius of course belonged to the circle of Maecenas, Augustus' right-hand man, his minister of state for domestic affairs. Yet quite apart from the conventional elegiac preference for love rather than war, Propertius had personal reasons for his horror of it. His family had been on the wrong side in the Civil War; its property had probably been confiscated; and he had lost at least one relative in the aftermath of the siege of Perusia in 41 B.C.[1] He speaks out very specifically and bitterly against war, and particularly against civil strife. He makes the conventional protestations that he'd be no good as a soldier:

> non ego sum laudi, non natus idoneus armis
>
> (1.6.29)

and that love is the god of peace:

> Pacis Amor deus est, pacem veneramur amantes
>
> (3.5.1)

but this is far short of *Hell No, We Won't Go*, and Propertius has therefore other personal and ironic ways of expressing his dissent. Firstly, he has an insistent way of referring adversely to incidents in the Civil War that Augustus would presumably have far rather forgotten. In the sigillum of Book I, for instance, he asks Tullus if the tombs of his Perusian home are known to him, the pyres of those dark days for Italy when Roman civil strife drove out Rome's own citizens:

> si Perusina tibi patriae sunt nota sepulchra,
> Italiae duris funera temporibus,
> cum Romana suos egit discordia civis.
>
> (1.22.3–5)

In the middle of the opening *recusatio* of the second book, whose basic irony we shall return to, he claims that were he not a love poet, he would be a writer of contemporary epic (like Cornelius Severus) and would celebrate Augustus' wartime exploits; but, *most untactfully*, he alludes to the more painful episodes of the Civil War, to Mutina, to Philippi, and, not least and once again, to the Perusine War, when he refers to the overturned hearths and homes of the ancient Etruscan race:

> eversosque focos antiquae gentis Etruscae
>
> (2.1)

Even Actium, which was to Horace something to celebrate in a great victory ode, is for Propertius an occasion for regretful moralizing. If everyone lived like Propertius, that is, "turning on" with wine and and "dropping out" into Cynthia's arms, then there would be no cold steel, no naval trumpets, the sea off Actium would not be rolling Roman bones, and Rome would not be tired of mourning, besieged on every hand by triumphs over her very own people:

> qualem si cuncti cupere decurrere vitam
> et pressi multo membra iacere mero,
> non ferrum crudele neque esset bellica navis
> nec nostra Actiacum verteret ossa mare,
> nec totiens propriis circum oppugnata triumphis
> lassa foret crinis solvere Roma suos.

Secondly, towards imperial conquest and further wars, which were so much in the air at the time of writing, Propertius' attitude is again subtly but unmistakeably critical. Parthian, Persian, Arabic, or even British expeditions are for Horace opportunities for adulation, boasting, or at very least something that offers a welcome alternative to civil war.[2] Propertius however dismisses such exhortatory or celebratory poetry:

> a valeat, Phoebum quicumque moratur in armis
>
> (3.1.7)

He adds that there will be many to sing Rome's praises in poetic annals and proclaim that Bactria will be the boundary of the Empire, but he himself is offering something one can read *in peace time*:

> multi, Roma, tuas laudes annalibus addent,
> qui finem imperii Bactra futura canent.
> sed, *quod pace legas*, opus hoc de monte sororum
> detulit intacta pagina nostra via.
>
> (3.1.15–20)

As for that very sore point with the Romans, the standards of Crassus taken by the Parthians after that General's defeat and death in 53 B.C., Propertius is almost flippant about them; his poem on Augustus' proposed expedition to India begins with an impressive description of his possible territorial and financial acquisitions. Propertius offers a hasty prayer for its success:

> omina fausta cano. Crassos clademque piate!
> ite et Romanae consulite historiae.
>
> (3.4.9–10)

But the whole effect is undercut when we learn that Propertius will be leaning on his girl-friend's arm and merely *watching* the triumph move along the Sacred Way. A further proof that this celebration of Augustus' military adventures is not seriously meant is that the next poem in the collection announces that Love is the God of Peace:

> Pacis amor deus est. pacem veneramur amantes.
>
> (3.5.1)

Moreover, it is in this poem that we find the most poignant general criticism of what Augustus is doing:

> nunc maris in tantum vento iactamur, et hostem
>   quaerimus, atque armis nectimus arma nova.
> haud ullas portabis opes Acherontis ad undas:
>   nudus in inferna, stulte, vehere rate.
> victor cum victis pariter miscebitur umbris:
>   consule cum Mario, capte Iugurtha, sedes.
>
> (3.5.10–16)

Then the concluding lines of the poem expressly nullify Propertius' earlier prayer for Augustus' success. After a life of love and wine, he says, he'll turn to philosophy; *this* is how his life will end; let those who *prefer* war, let them bring home the standards of Crassus.

> exitus hic vitae superest mihi; vos, quibus arma
>   grata magis, Crassi signa referte domum.
>
> (3.5.47–48)

Anything further from Horace's nationalism: *dulce et decorum est pro patria mori* can hardly be imagined. The general irony and attitude is to some extent reminiscent of Arthur Hugh Clough's lines in *Amours de Voyage*:

Dulce it is, and *decorum*, no doubt, for the country to fall, – to
Offer one's blood an oblation to Freedom, and die for the Cause, yet
Still, individual culture is also something, and no man
Finds quite distinct the assurance that he of all others is called on,
Or would be justified even, in taking away from the world that
Precious creature, himself.

(2.2.1 ff.)

It is this persistent strain of criticism in Propertius, expressed in various modes of irony, indirection, humour, bathos, and elegiac complaint throughout the first three books which makes me unwilling to believe that Propertius' apparent conversion in Book IV to Augustan ideals, particularly in the elegiac hymn celebrating the Battle of Actium (IV.6), is serious; I feel that the features of that puzzling book are open to a different explanation. Again, we must remember that Propertius, like Horace and Virgil, unlike Tibullus and Ovid, was in a rather difficult position: he belonged to Maecenas' circle, but his literary principles and apparently his general social and political views seem radically different. This was to have a definite effect on his poetry and will account partly for its allusive, elliptical, and sometimes difficult and ambiguous character. Like Horace in his *Satires* and like Virgil throughout his work, Propertius must have been subject to various sorts of social and personal pressure, which have left their mark on his poems.

When we come to the last of the great Augustan elegists, we find that Ovid's attitude to the bellicose spirit of the time is typically ingenious. On the one hand, he makes the claim that the life of adulterous leisure (*otium*) is as strenuous as that of the warrior:

militat omnis amans, et habet sua castra Cupido:
Attice, crede mihi, militat omnis amans.

(*Am.* 1.9.1)

On the other hand, the life of love and elegiac poetry secures immortal fame as the dusty rewards of military life do not (*praemia militiae pulverulenta*, as he describes them at *Am.* 1.15.1–8). But it is plain that the practical involvement in military life of Gallus and Tibullus, and the personal bitterness and consequent scepticism about war that we discern in Propertius, are both equally remote from Ovid. Though a knight, he had not served in the army and his family seems not to have taken the wrong side in the Civil Wars. He therefore deploys the now conventional themes and motifs of the elegiac poet, namely, rejecting the glory and rewards of war in favour of battles in the bedroom and boudoir, but he cannot bring the themes to life; they are mere decoration. Coming at the end of the brilliant line of Roman elegiac poets, he develops to their ultimate conclusion, not the elegists' anti-war attitudes or their contempt for military booty and glory, but rather the anti-Augustan moral and social standards implicit in their work.

The picture of the elegist as presented in the surviving corpus of these poets is all too familiar. Briefly, he has turned away from the conventional standards of service and success in a Roman career; he rejects politics, military life, and financial rewards. Whether his preference is for the quiet life of the country like Tibullus, or for starving in a garret in Rome like Propertius, he is dominated by only two driving forces, his mistress (or boy friend) and the writing of a certain type of poetry. In the first instance, he is rejecting also the restrictive but pragmatic norms of sexual behaviour to which most Romans, including Augustus, in his official capacity, at any rate, paid lip service. In the second instance, he is rejecting a dominant tradition of Roman literature at the very period in which it was being assiduously reinvigorated by Virgil, the tradition of Epic.

Let us examine the implicit morality of elegy first. Whether the elegist attributes his misery (or amazing happiness) to madness or witchcraft, he claims to live a very private, if not a disordered and anti-social, life (in Propertius' words, *nullo vivere consilio*, 1.1.6). Horace sums up the attitude of the sensible Roman to such goings-on in the second satire of his first book, where he criticizes those who go mad over freedwomen (presumably the status of Cynthia, Delia, Nemesis, Corinna and the rest), and who waste their money and ruin their good name. The elegist will neither marry (this is the implication of Propertius' hatred of chaste girls of good social standing – *castas odisse puellas*, 1.1.5)[3] nor will he do what Horace advises, enjoy the easily available favours of ordinary prostitutes. One notices, incidentally, that Horace's few references to elegists are slightly contemptuous: he tells both Albius Tibullus and Valgius to stop their unmanly complaints of lost loves, to desist from *flebiles modi* or *miserabiles elegi*:[4] Valgius he even invites to celebrate, as Horace does (despite his occasional love poetry), the new battle honours of Augustus (*nova Augusti trophaea*, *Carm.* 2.9.18–19).

The professed aims and ideals of the elegists, however playfully they are interpreted, clearly and consciously fly in the face of accepted Roman standards of seriousness, sobriety, public service, and personal ambition. This is obvious from the defiant, or half-apologetic, defences that they offer of their way of life. The standard estimate of a poet's social utility and status is best seen in Cicero's defence of Archias, although Archias was admittedly a foreigner by descent.[5] The elegists, by and large, although they have abnegated their Roman duty of "praising famous men" (and cities), direct their aspirations to the sort of fame that few conventional Romans would seriously desire: this, along with their mistresses' affections, is their compensation for any lack of money, military distinction, or political power.

Augustus, however, whatever the deficiencies of his own personal life (and they were many), had set himself seriously to the task of amending Roman public morals. He was troubled by the decay of religion – Polybius, after all, attributed Rome's greatness partly to her dependence on superstition as a means of controlling the populace.[6] Augustus was also disturbed by the decline in sexual morality, by the prevalence of bachelorhood, which he thought responsible for a declining birthrate, and by anti-social behaviour in general; and he was offended by the conspicuous consumption of the upper classes.

The elegists all were, or pretended to be, poor, and so they would scarcely be the target of Augustus' sumptuary laws, but their sexual habits, or at least the sexual attitudes implicit in their work, might well raise the Augustan eyebrows an inch or two. Propertius and Ovid were the main offenders.

Propertius announces his distaste for respectable ladies (1.1.5); he rejects military service because of Cynthia's tears (1.6 etc.); he refuses to produce any public-spirited celebration of the regime's military achievements (2.1 etc.); and, in one of his most straight-forward poems he even complains against Augustan marriage legislation.

In this particular poem (2.7), despite the cautious manner, there is a strong basic criticism of the regime. We are told that Cynthia was overjoyed because the law that might separate the two lovers had been withdrawn. This was, presumably, the proposed *lex de maritandis ordinibus* which would have forced Propertius, a bachelor, to marry. According to Suetonius (*Aug.* 34), this rather strict law could not be passed because of the public protest of those involved, which may indicate that even Augustus had his troubles with dissenters. But Propertius goes on to say that even Jupiter cannot divide two lovers against their will. Caesar may be powerful, but only in war; military conquests count for nothing when it comes to love. Propertius would sooner be condemned to death than betray his beloved and marry. It is not for Propertius to produce arrow-fodder for future military ventures against Parthia. No son of mine, he says, will be a soldier. If Cynthia can love him, then this will be worth more than his duties to family tradition.

The point about this poem is not so much the objection to the proposed legislation, although that is significant enough, but, in the context, the almost gratuitous rejection of the Roman duty to produce sons for the Roman Empire.

This of course is mild by comparison with Ovid's explicit message in the *Ars Amatoria*, which was, after all, the *official* reason for his banishment, even if, as so often with political crimes, there were deeper causes, or other more political poems such as the *Metamorphoses* to take into account.

The anti-Augustan implications of the *Ars Amatoria* may be construed differently. The work may be seen as a parody of Virgil's *Georgics* but aimed at keeping men *in* the city. If the *Georgics* be taken as supporting Augustus' land policies, the *Ars Amatoria* might be taken as doing the opposite for Augustus' moral legislation. But without going so far, we can find in the work, not just the encouragement to anti-social immorality that Augustus professed umbrage at, but more specific and less guarded irreverence about

the larger ideals of the principate. To take an obvious example: in book I of
the *Ars* (177 ff.) Ovid launches into a great apostrophe of Augustus' future
conquests. Caesar plans to add what is missing to the Roman Empire; the
East will finally be ours; the Parthians will pay the penalty for what they did
to Crassus and his son and the lost standards:

> ecce, parat Caesar, domito quod defuit orbi,
>   addere: nunc, Oriens ultime, noster eris.
> Parthe, dabis poenas; Crassi gaudete sepulti
>   signaque barbaricas non bene passa manus.
> (*A.A.* 1.177–180)

The elaboration of the eulogy is long: Ovid is to write thanksgiving poems
about Gaius Caesar's victories and he will of course watch the great triumph.
But suddenly we discover that all of this is prelude to advice on how to pick
up a girl in the crowd watching the procession. The lover is to invent fictitious names and nationalities for sections of the spectacle if necessary; he is
even to use the victory banquets as an occasion for sexual encounters. Ovid, of
course, is using, and elaborating, the Propertian motif of the lover watching
the triumph go by, while he clings to his girl, but there can be no mistaking
the similarly deflating effect of moving from the apparently sublime to the
ridiculously sexual. The Roman reader would be forgiven if he detected therefore an ironic scepticism in Ovid's enthusiasm and praise. Rhetorical inflation
followed by deflation is not a technique peculiar to Juvenal.

In the midst of his advice to the fair sex, for Ovid, within his limits, was
one of the first advocates of Women's Liberation in some matters, Ovid
throws out a perfunctory disclaimer that his didactic treatise is not to be
taken as directed against upper and middle-class marriage. He was, he says,
about to go over the ways to deceive a sharp husband and his watchful
guards, but really wives *should* fear their husbands; brides *should* be watched:
this is proper and this is what the laws, the Emperor, and propriety command. He will therefore direct his advice to the seduction of freed women
(although not a word need be changed to make it applicable to more exalted
ladies):

> nupta virum timeat, rata sit custodia nuptae:
>   hoc decet, hoc leges duxque pudorque iubent.
> (*A.A.* 1.613–614)

The penalty for Ovid was harsh; the punishment did not perhaps fit the
alleged crime; but the anti-Augustanism of the *Ars Amatoria* need not be
glossed over in our pity for Ovid.

So far we have considered the elegists' political and social attitudes in a more

or less straightforward way; when we turn, however, to the politics of literature, other more complex factors enter to blur the picture. Purely personal
considerations of life style, patronage, and past history will no longer suffice
to explain why this poet or that writes in one particular vein. The ground is
treacherous and one must step warily, but it may be possible to discern some
tendencies and connections that will explain certain aspects of the literary
divisions in the Augustan Age.

The word *Augustan*, as is often pointed out, is very slippery, and it might
be preferable, for our purposes here, to use it only as a chronological term.
For in the past it has had a rather lulling effect on classical critics. In another
context, that of English literature, A. R. Humphries has perceptively pointed
to similar dangers in the word: when we dub the century in which *our*
Augustan period came "The Age of Reason," we are creating "the impression
. . . that by some psychological freak three or four generations of Britons
grew up colour-blind to the emotions." He suggested "that if the Augustans
spoke so much of reason it was not because their emotions were weak but
because on the contrary they were strong."[7] Similarly, it is sometimes
forgotten, partly because of the associations of the word *Augustan* in English
literary history, that Virgil, Horace and Propertius emerged not from some
Arcadia, or from the political background of Queen Anne, but from a hard,
dangerous, troubled, and often bloody historical reality: as Tacitus puts it,
*after this there was undoubtedly peace, but it was a bloody peace (pacem sine dubio post
haec, vero cruentam, Annals* 1.10). It has been rightly remarked that classical
literature is often the imposition of form on turbulence, whether it be the
turbulence of Periclean Athens or the post-civil war period in Rome. Again,
because Virgil, Horace and Ovid are our standard Latin classics from this era,
we must not be tempted into assuming that they personally invented and
then unanimously accepted their new unimpeachable standards of art.
It should be borne in mind that Horace's three books of *Odes* met with a
disappointing reception; that many still preferred the satires of Lucilius to
Horace's gentler, if more artistic, brand of *sermones*; that Virgil for his *Aeneid*
was described by Agrippa as the inventor of a new type of bad imitation
(*novae cacozeliae repertorem*), an attack that was followed up by numerous critics
in the next generation, not least by the author of the *Aeneidomastix*. Even
Virgil's *Eclogues* were cruelly parodied by contemporary poets, and Tibullus,
Valgius, and Propertius, it seems, were given short shrift for their elegies by
Horace. In brief, we must bear in mind the excited literary controversies of
the period, the rivalries, the critical backbiting, the disagreements, often
with political implications, out of which were slowly produced the very
different kinds of masterpieces that have come down to us, whose differences,
since they are now all classics, may be easily overlooked. What has to be
done, however tentatively, is to locate on a critical map, as it were, the
positions of the Augustan poets that will do justice to their divergent
principles and the opposing traditions of literature that they embraced. The

political implications of their choices will then perhaps emerge also. The controversies of the period are reminiscent of literary-cum-political fights that were, and are, so prevalent in Soviet literature in the past forty years.

A would-be poet of the Augustan era, about to enter the Battle of the Books, from which he might carry away fame, patronage, and financial rewards, had a number of literary and practical decisions to make. In prose writing, in history, for example, he would have had to decide whether his sympathies lay with the Republican cause or the New Order, a choice which a poet might be able to avoid by taking up a genre which did not involve such considerations. If he looked to his potential public, he would see a choice between the respectable, high-minded older Romans, with their preferences for archaic and Republican literature, and the younger, more permissive, and sophisticated audience at which Ovid's *Ars Amatoria* was so clearly directed. More select audiences included the patrons of literature with their circles – Asinius Pollio, Messala, Maecenas, and, above all, the literate Emperor himself. Augustus had his own critical principles – he hated archaism and Asianism, for example – and he was something of a writer himself, but of course his literary outlook was also affected by concern for his public image, his political status, and his moral legislation. Only the best artists, we know, were allowed to treat of Augustus and his achievements, and both T. Labienus, the supporter of Pompey, and Ovid were the targets of indignant censorship.[8]

Apart from these extrinsic considerations, there were at least two major traditions, not always separable of course, to choose from. In the latter days of the Republic, the most notable poetic movement was the Neoterics, a circle or series of circles that looked to Alexandria, to Callimachus, Philetas, Euphorion, and Theocritus, for their inspiration: these included such writers as Catullus, Varro of Atax, Calvus, Gallus, and others. And it is plausibly argued that the émigré Parthenius of Nicae was an important mediator and teacher of this avant-garde movement.[9] Its preference was for the newer, smaller poetic genres: epigram, elegy, the so-called epyllion, pastoral, didactic and, naturally, gently teasing court poetry. It was, as is well known, characterized by metrical and formal experimentation, oblique and recherché treatment of myth, and, in general, an avoidance of epic, certainly of contemporary and historical epic on a large scale, such as Ennius' *Annales*.

Against this was the older tradition that *looked up* to Ennius, to himself and to later generations the Roman Homer; its supporters admired the writings of Accius and Pacuvius and Lucilius and the antique style in general; they looked for public-spirited poetry on a grand Roman scale. Just as Catullus is contemptuous of the long *Annales* of Volusius, so Cicero, a practitioner himself in this Roman tradition, sneers at the Neoterics, the *Cantores Euphorionis*.

These basic traditions, of course, follow their own development as we enter the Augustan Age. The metrics of each are refined and developed (note, for example, the move in elegy from polysyllabic to dissyllabic pentameter endings); the divisions between them blur; new modes, more difficult to characterize as belonging to one side or another are developed; and poets following their own artistic bent, borrow and blend from each. And it may well be that the more slavish adherents to one tradition or another, the hard core, as it were, of minor poets who, as often, might give us a clearer picture of the basic literary situation than individual and original geniuses, have perished from our ken simply because of this unoriginality. We must not underestimate how much we have lost: how many straight complimentary epics on contemporary wars, such as the *Bellum Aquitanicum* of Cornelius Severus, on the one hand; and how many laborious Alexandrian mythological poems such as the *Zmyrna* of Calvus and *The Grove of Grynium* of Cornelius Gallus.

But despite this, we can detect two opposing tendencies in the undercurrent of critical comments, or even parody, in the poetry that survives from the period. Horace, for example, hews largely to the Roman line for all his own innovations, but he is critical of those who admire only the archaic poets and archaic language, while ignoring those moderns who are producing a newer, more stylish, embodiment of their virtues. His earlier work, the *Sermones*, descended directly from Ennius and Lucilius, but he strenuously objected to those uncritical admirers of Lucilius who did not see Horace's stylistic superiority. Horace's admiration for Greek literature, for Homer and Old Comedy, for example, is of course obvious; he even borrows not a little from the Alexandrian and neo-Alexandrian writers, Callimachus' and Philodemus' epigrams, for instance, for his lighter odes and the satires, but for his more substantial odes and epodes on political and social themes, he preferred to go back to the great age of Greek Lyric, to Pindar, Bacchylides, Sappho and Alcaeus. We have already noticed his dislike or contempt for the most flourishing Alexandrian genre at this time, erotic elegy, whereas he often praises or encourages writers, or potential writers, of epics that would celebrate the war-like achievements of Augustus and his generals.

Virgil, on the contrary, began as an Alexandrian writer, who did his best to reconcile the public themes that the Roman tradition advocated with the stylistic and thematic objectives of his models. Under pressure from his circle and circumstances, if the stories are true in the *Lives of Virgil*, he moved more and more in the direction Horace had taken early. His Theocritean imitations have more politics in them than his model; his *Georgics*, although a didactic poem and acceptable therefore by strict Alexandrian standards, share many of the purposes of Horace's protreptic *Odes* and *Satires*; that is, they conform to the political and social ideas of the regime. This is not, of course, to condemn the work out of hand: not all good literature is the literature of protest. And finally, in the *Aeneid*, although there are many Alexandrian elements in his treatment – one thinks of the Dido episode and the aetiological interest of the story of Hercules and Cacus – Virgil has finally taken his stand with the Roman tradition, producing an epic to the glory of Rome and its great past and present heroes. For all the many heart-searchings and pessimistic doubts about Rome's destiny in Book IV Virgil firmly makes Aeneas choose War, not Love.

On this spectrum of public versus private themes; of Rome versus Alexandria; of Love versus War; of epic versus elegy; of public law versus private disorder, the elegists are clearly to the left of Horace and Virgil. Propertius' poetry shows the tension most clearly. He openly claims as his masters Philetas and Callimachus, whose Roman equivalent he hopes to be; he rejects war, conquest and moneymaking for the private pursuits of love, learning, and poetry. Yet he belongs to Maecenas' circle; he is aware of the power of Augustus and the current Roman ideals of moral reform, the extension of empire, civilization, and the rule of law; he acknowledges the grander scale of epic by comparison with the softer, delicate nature of elegy (epic is *durus* and *grandis*; his verse is *tener*, mollis). For him all this constitutes pressure, internal or external, exaggerated or real. Yet he rejects the pressure, and the manner of his rejection is illuminating both for his poetry and the literary history of the time. His chief reasons, or excuses, are the ineluctable claims of his mistress and the contrary pulls of his own genius and poetic inspiration, generally personified as Apollo (3.3). His main shield is the *recusatio*, the formal poetic rejection of a given theme, which takes various forms, either the elaborate defence of his refusal to write epic or an account of his intention and aim to do so, which is then frustrated by divine warnings. It may even take the form of inviting Maecenas to do so first, or invoking Virgil's earlier Alexandrian work in his defence.[10]

This tension is best seen Books II and III. Book I, except for two short poems at the end, is more like Tibullus' work; the question has not arisen, for Propertius is not yet part of Maecenas' circle. With Book IV, things change. The case generally made is that Propertius, much like Virgil in a different, more extreme way, came to terms with the claims of the regime and the claims of his art. He found that there was one Alexandrian sub-genre of elegy, aetiological elegy on origins, legends, and causes, which was both sanctioned by Callimachean principles, and capable of being adapted to the service of Roman greatness. Hence the series of elegies on Roman deities and religious institutions; on the history of the *spolia opima* (a very important issue at this time); on the story of Tarpeia. They are of course a prototype of Ovid's *Fasti*. This final bowing to imperial pressures, it is thought, is confirmed by the long and strange elegy on Octavian's victory at Actium – described by one scholar as the worst poem in Roman literature.[11] The rest of the elegies in this book, we are told, the poems on Cynthia and related private themes, are not to the point: they are either make-weight, introduced for variety, or else the whole book is a non-unified posthumous compilation by an editor, who gathered together the few finished aetiological poems and added to them poems that belonged to an earlier stage of Propertius' literary career.

But there is much to object to in this account. It involves a complicated explanation of the first long and clearly programmatic elegy – whether this is one poem or a diptych. In this poem Propertius announces his project of an account of Roman religion, festivals, and ancient topographical nomenclature, a project which is hardly justified, anyway, by the few extant aetiological elegies; the poet is then taken to task by the soothsayer Horos and told to write love elegy as before:

> at tu finge elegos, fallax opus: haec tua castra
> scribat ut exemplo cetera turba tuo.
> militiam Veneris blandis patiere sub armis,
> et Veneris pueris utilis hostis eris.
>
> (4.1.135–138)

Moreover, the private poems to Cynthia and on the death of Cornelia are far superior to the aetiological elegies with which they are inmixed, and even these elegies have certain ambiguous features about them, certain elements of humour and anti-Augustanism, which might give us pause before we accept the conventional interpretation.[12] A case may therefore be made that Book IV is in fact Propertius' most elaborate *recusatio*, in which he *proves* that he is not suited to even the most artistically congenial way of supporting the program of the regime. And the strange, *deliberately* or *unavoidably* poor poem on Actium (4.6 at the very centre of the collection) is the final confirmation of his point. Whether we speculate that Propertius genuinely tried to write worthwhile Roman aetiological elegies and then failed; or wrote so few of them because, for all their technical merits, they went against his grain from the beginning; or made them subtly disparaging of their apparent purpose: in any case, the significance of the opening elegy becomes clearer, and the importance for him of the other love poems which stand in the book as proof of his undiminished talent.

Finally, there is Ovid. Ovid, of course, was more than an elegist, but both in his early work and in his later *Metamorphoses* he indicated which tradition he belonged to, for all his facility and poetic versatility. And his eventual fate was to be determined, among other things, by his literary politics. It seems fairly clear, at least until the axe fell in A.D. 8 or so, that Ovid, unlike Propertius and perhaps Tibullus, did not feel the strain of the times; the Civil Wars ended when he was still a mere boy; the clear domination of the *princeps* was a fact of life that he could contrast with no other form of political existence. Deprived of avenues for real ambition, it was natural that the *jeunesse dorée* of Rome, Ovid's contemporaries and audience, would turn to less strenuous amusements and pursuits than the old *cursus honorum*. Were Ovid born in a different time, his virtuosity in poetry might well have been

Notes

1 1.22.7–8.
2 Cf. *Carm.* 1.53–56; 1.35.29–32, 37–40; 2.9.18–20; 3.342–48; 3.5.2–4.
3 For the interpretation, see my "*Castas odisse puellas:* A Reinterpretation of Propertius I, 1," *WS* 74 (1961) 92–118.
4 *Carm.* 2.9.9; 1.33.2 and *passim.*
5 Cf. e.g. *Pro Arch.* 9, 12.
6 Polyb. 6.56.
7 A. R. Humphries, *The Augustan World, Life and Letters* in Eighteenth Century England (London, 1964), p. 189.
8 Cf. in particular Tac. *Ann.* 1.72: *primus Augustus cognitionem de famosis libellis specie legis eius tractavit . . .*
9 See W. V. Clausen, "*Callimachus and Roman Poetry,*" *GRBS* 5 (1964) 193ff.
10 Cf. 3.9, 2.34.68ff.
11 To be quite accurate, G. W. Williams stated in *JRS* 52 (1962) 43: "one of the most ridiculous poems in the Latin language is his celebration of the Battle of Actium." In *Tradition and Originality in Roman Poetry* (Oxford, 1968), p. 51, the statement is somewhat toned down: "Propertius is generally judged to have written a thoroughly bad poem."
12 See Judith P. Hallett, *Book IV: Propertius' Recusatio to Augustus and Augustan Ideals* (unpublished dissertation, Harvard 1971), pp. 92ff. and the literature there cited.
13 See my review of Brooks Otis, *Ovid as Epic Poet* (Cambridge, 1966) in *The Arch* 14.2 (1967) 1–9.

THE ROLE OF WOMEN IN ROMAN ELEGY

Counter-cultural feminism

Judith P. Hallett

Domum servavit. Lanam fecit: "She kept up her household; she made wool."
This was the ideal Roman woman – in the eyes and words of what was
doubtless a male obituary writer, late second century B.C. vintage.[1] Our
information on the role traditionally assigned Roman women – and by *role*,
as distinct from social position and rank, I mean the socially prescribed
pattern of behavior manifested by females when dealing with people who
are not females – suggests that it involved little more than submissiveness,
supportiveness, and stability. By the end of the Roman Republic and the
beginning of the Empire, the men empowered to determine how women
could and could not comport themselves apparently modified certain
inconvenient regulations; nevertheless, they remained remarkably faithful to
the spirit, if not the letter, of earlier laws reducing women to chattel status.
While Roman society undeniably acknowledged the existence of women's
physical charms and mental endowments, for the most part it merely "patron-
ized" females, accepting them only when they adhered to rigidly (and externally) delimited norms of conduct. Women were not as a rule admired for
their individual qualities, much less permitted to function autonomously or
esteemed for so doing.

But very few rules want for exceptions. In Latin love elegy, and the
particular upper and upper-middle class social environment in which it
flourished, we directly encounter a violation of the general behavioral
principles outlined above. The women featured therein managed to attain a
singularly exalted stature, to be appreciated as people in their own right.
Their admirers, moreover, not only glorified them out of genuine adoration,
they were also motivated by a powerful, often mischievously subversive
desire to differentiate themselves and their own system of values from existing forms of conduct. Consequently, the amatory elegists do not restrict
themselves to venerating their beloved. They even cast her in the active,

masterful role customarily played by men. They do not simply conceive of their emotionally-absorbing romantic liaisons as acceptable activities; they consider them, and the poetry emanating from them, no less strenuous and praiseworthy pursuits than conventional Roman careers in business, the military and the law. What is more, they are not satisfied with justifying their behavior; the Augustan elegists even recommend it wholeheartedly to others! By utilizing a new form of art to portray this role-inversion and achieve their sought-after moral conversion, they seem also to characterize themselves as a veritable "counter-culture," a modern term whose applicability to the love elegists deserves further exploration. We should, however, first ascertain the exact role of women in the elegists' Rome so that we can comprehend precisely what they reject and redefine. Then we may redefine. Then we may examine more closely the perversity and proselytism in the elegia poetry of Catullus, Tibullus, Propertius and Ovid.

1. *Mores*

We can marshal abundant and varied evidence to substantiate our initial assertion that Roman society relegated women to a subservient, confined role. Tomb inscriptions, for instance, affirm that wifely obedience (the technical Latin term is *obsequi*),[2] domesticity, chastity and fidelity to one man brought their occupants earthly fulfillment and will qualify them for eternal acclaim.[3] Literary works also portray "nice women" as submissive and docile. Capitalizing upon the permissive, "holiday," mood granted comic performances, the playwright Plautus parodies the conventional Roman marriage formula, which consigns the bride to her husband's tutelage (*Cas.* 815–824). There a male slave, masquerading as a blushing bride, receives instruction from a slave woman on a Roman wife's duties and rights. Like everything else in the scene, however, the advice reverses reality: it depicts the *wife* as the dominant, forceful marriage partner.[4] Of equally great interest is the account which the Augustan historian Livy gives of the first protest demonstration over women's rights (or lack thereof), the insurrection against the *Lex Oppia* in 193 B.C. (34.1–8.3). Even the story's most outspoken liberal, the tribune who successfully agitated for the law's repeal, believes that women are by nature passive and retiring. He seasons his complaints over Roman women's lack of privileges and his demands for their equitable treatment with pious homilies on how women prefer dependence on males to emancipation of any sort (34.7.12–13). In this passage, moreover, we may discern the much-touted Augustan attitude toward women, a crucial component of the emperor's moral rearmament programme. This effort (promoted by wool-spinning among the socially invisible women of the imperial household and repeated claims of the empress' virtue) provides further, historical, corroboration for a view of Roman women as quiet, submissive creatures.[5]

But contradictory evidence confronts us as well. Scholars are quick to point out that, by the first century B.C., Roman women enjoyed considerable power and freedom, particularly when one compares them to their counterparts in fifth century Athens and in the early Roman Republic.[6] Marriage no longer required that a husband possess absolute ownership, *manus*, of his wife. Under the conditions of what was called marriage *sine manu*, wedded women could for all intents and purposes control property they had acquired from their male relatives and thereby retain some sort of individual identity: this arrangement also entitled either party to a divorce if he, *or she*, so wished.[7] And upper class Roman women could lead morally relaxed, independent lives without having to resort to *divortium*. One modern scholar notes that they began emulating the conduct of the exotic émigrées, largely Greek freedwomen, who flooded Rome from the eastern cities of her newly-obtained Mediterranean empire.[8] We can probably attribute such consciously loose behavior to a combination of envy and delayed emotional development: married by their fathers at the onset of puberty, Roman women faced the responsibilities of matronhood before they could cope with the romantic and sexual fantasies of adolescence.[9] Whatever the explanation, some *matronae* from illustrious Roman families so completely adopted the freedwoman's dissolute mode of conduct that students of Latin poetry have never been able to determine the marital status and social class of the Augustan elegists' mistresses with any certainty.[10]

How, then, can we reconcile these two sets of facts? First, by recognizing that Roman society offered its women only a limited and illusory brand of liberation – visible independence, yes; autonomy, no. Limitations first. For one thing, whatever possibilities for emancipation *did* exist only affected a small minority of Roman women, the wealthy and the rootless. For another, even the most emancipated and self-assertive Roman woman lived in a state of bondage if we compare her to the most retiring Roman male. Historians who deal with first century B.C. Republican Rome are prone to talk about the political sway exercised by the ladies of Rome's leading houses.[11] Women with the right connections – such as Fulvia, wife successively of Clodius, Curio, and Antony, or Brutus' mother Servilia – no doubt constituted a political force in their own right.[12] But to wax enthusiastic over the *total impact women as a group* had on the Roman political scene is in many ways tantamount to marvelling over the extent to which house pets influence their owners' living habits. *Quanta erit infelicitas urbis illius, in qua virorum officia mulieres occupabunt*, Cicero is reported to have said – stating unreservedly that woman's place is *not* in the forum.[13] Forbidden to vote or hold political office, women could not have possibly exerted an influence on political affairs that even vaguely approximated their representation in the general population. We should not, moreover, cling to any false notions about Roman women's freedom to come and go as they liked, or imagine that they cast off all sexual restraints. Before the civil wars women invariably stayed at home while their husbands travelled abroad to fight and engage in provincial administration; even after Augustus formally instituted the practice of taking his wife along on journeys, respectable women practically never left Italy without a male escort.[14] And, as Saara Lilja points out, while husbands had the right to philander as they chose – as long as they respected the chastity of a virgin or of another man's wife – wives were legally bound to uphold *fides marita*.[15]

Moving on to the grand illusions, we must not lose sight of the fact that a woman's social class and social acceptability were determined by the men in her life, her "patrons" as it were. The upper class matron owed her eminence – and probably her blueblooded husband – to the wealth, contacts and maneuverings of her father and other male kinsmen; by the end of the Republic, the very survival of a marriage like hers depended upon her attractiveness as a symbol of success.[16] In addition, she was as strongly compelled to gratify men's whims and yield to their demands as was a freedwoman like Volumnia/Cytheris, an actress whose coquetteries gained her the affections of Rome's leading men (among them Antony and the love elegist Cornelius Gallus). A major historical study of the late first century B.C. relates how some women of the upper classes took selfish advantage of existing social opportunities – involving themselves in politics and the arts, managing their own financial affairs – and paid dearly. Such "uppityness" lost them the ability to attract their male peers. "The emancipation of women had its reaction upon the men, who, instead of a partner from their own class, preferred alliance with a freedwoman, or none at all."[17]

This brings us to the second major *trompe-l'oeil* of Roman women's so-called liberation: the fact that women's new freedoms had really evolved in order to render them more serviceable to men and male political ambitions. As marriage without *manus* deprived a wife of claims to her husband's estate, one scholar on Roman law conjectures that it was originally devised by the prospective bridegrooms' families to obtain for their sons the advantage of a marital alliance without the usual obligations.[18] Easy divorce had similar benefits. It permitted fathers and brothers as well as spouses to discard politically useless in-laws in favor of more useful ones. Furthermore, in this world of constantly changing ententes and enmities, where women functioned as temporary cement, the power-hungry males who selected a kinswoman's marital partners often viewed women as things, not sentient, sensitive human beings. They tended to value women *as* mere political assets and not *for* redeeming personal qualities, evincing no concern for any feelings they might have. Witness Julius Caesar's behavior: how he cold-heartedly broke his daughter's engagement so that he might marry her to Pompey, or how he later contemplated shedding his own loyal wife in order to wed Pompey's daughter.[19] Or how his nephew Augustus forced a match between his daughter Julia and stepson Tiberius, at great emotional pain to them both.[20] Or how their legendary ancestor Aeneas abandons Creusa and Dido, two women who deeply love him, the first basically out of loyalty to male relatives, the second so that he may continue upon a political quest. When Aeneas finally decides to commit himself to a lasting relationship with a woman, he selects as his mate a king's daughter who cares nothing for him; he must also destroy much that is beautiful in primitive Italy to achieve this aim.[21] Hot political properties to be sure, but properties nonetheless, women of the late Republic and early Empire essentially reverted to their acquiescent, 'non-person' status under early Roman law. *Plus ça change, plus c'est la même chose.* No wonder women "over-availed" themselves of what freedoms they did have, indulging in clandestine sex or engaging in challenging activities at the risk of losing male approbation!

But we must reconcile the *ideal* of Roman women's seclusion and obsequiousness with the *fact* that many proper Roman women could and did mingle freely in public and have legally sanctioned carnal knowledge of more than one man. We must also come to grips with the patently licentious behavior of freedwomen and with the openly acknowledged demand for unrestrained, free-wheeling women of their type voiced by the men of the propertied classes. The frequent claims of uxorial rectitude on funeral inscriptions, Augustus' efforts to re-affirm the "old" Roman morality – such insistent self-righteousness suggests that its eulogizers are trying to combat a trend in the other direction, to contrast examples of "what should be" to "what actually is." The *princeps'* moral programme – lest we forget – included not only propaganda and financial rewards for child production. Its architect designed it for the express purpose of replenishing the depleted senatorial and equestrian ranks, Rome's ruling élite; it also featured laws requiring intra-class marriage of upper class males and forbidding adultery.[22] Clearly Augustus, notorious exploiter of the new moral freedom though he was, found the conduct of certain upper class men, and the effect that it had upon the females whose lives they controlled, downright subversive.

Suetonius and Cassius Dio tell us that the "new, moneyed" aristocracy, the equestrian rank, opposed Augustus' marriage and moral legislation.[23] We have, in addition, a far more eloquent and extensive protest against the sanctimonious moral assumptions and abusive social conventions of the late Republic and early Empire than ever could have echoed in the halls of the Roman Senate. It is, moreover, readily available and well-known to all students of ancient Roman culture. I refer to Latin love elegy, a form of self-revelation and indirect social criticism created and developed by members of the dissident equestrian class.[24] To be sure, the elegists' personal dissatisfaction with standard *mores* extended far beyond simple disenchantment with women's role – idealized and actual – in contemporary society. Yet Catullus, Tibullus, Propertius and Ovid all reveal discontent with both the traditional Roman view of women as demure, submissive chattels and the current Roman practices which allowed women an ostensible increase in freedom so as to exploit them more fully. They write of a social milieu which pays no heed to common social expectations about female – and, conversely, about male – behavior. The amatory elegists, or at least their literary *personae*,[25] speak on behalf of the people whose iconoclastic actions ultimately struck Augustus as threatening. They constitute what present-day social historians would call a "counter-culture," a movement which seeks to "discover new types of community, new family patterns, new sexual *mores*, new kinds of livelihood, new esthetic forms, new personal identities on the far side of power politics."[26]

I do not employ this current phrase, "counter-culture," simply to sound chic and *au courant*. If the wisdom of the past has anything to teach the present (certainly a belief cherished by all self-aware classicists), then the insights of contemporary man should bear on previous human experience as well. Furthermore, the label I am applying to the Latin love elegists and their coterie could not be more *à propos*. Like the counter-culture which sprang up in the industrialized Western nations during the late 1960's and early 1970's, this particular group was both young and conscious of youth's special privileges,[27] advantaged in terms of social and educational background, and relatively affluent.[28] Their youthful self-assurance, well-placed connections, high degree of intellectual attainment, and financial security enabled them to disdain accepted social practices. While more humble, unschooled and impecunious Romans deemed the "nuclear" family arrangement an economic necessity, the elegists could reject the idea of a subservient, supportive wife who bears multitudinous potentially useful offspring in favor of an exciting, attractive and spiritually inspiring female companion. These same personal advantages also permitted the amatory elegists to display a certain cynicism about politics; Propertius, for example, actually appears to question whether he or *any* individual can influence the governmental processes in what latter-day terminology would call a totalitarian state.[29] Instead, they invested their hopes and energies into maintaining romantic attachments, replacing the loyalty they were expected to pledge their *patria* with undying allegiance to their *puellae*. In addition, the Latin love elegists, like the counter-culturists of today, tried to forge a new, more meaningful set of values, embody them in actions which substituted for conventional social practices, and glorify them through art, the most exalted and effective means of human communication. Their redefinition of female and male roles, our concern here, nicely exemplifies their arch contrariness and wistful inventiveness in all matters; the attractive way in which they generally depict their relationships with women helps recommend their *vitae novae* to others.

2. *Amores*

From the very first, the Latin amatory elegists indicated both their non-compliance with widely-accepted behavioral norms and their bent toward social innovation by consciously and deliberately (if sometimes ironically) inverting conventional sex roles in their poetry. Catullus draws on the language of Roman politics in describing his relationship with Lesbia. He thereby infuses his avowals of love and devotion with a peculiar immediacy for the Roman reader; at the same time he indirectly attempts to question current social assumptions about upper-class male conduct and re-tailor them to accommodate his own emotional needs. Thrice in his elegiac poems, most notably in the closing lines of 109 with *aeternum hoc sanctae foedus amicitiae*, Catullus terms his association with his beloved a *foedus*. The word *foedus* means a bond, a treaty, a political pact made by two equally powerful – in other words, *male* – parties;[30] *amicitia*, moreover, does not only signify friendship in our modern sense, but the political alliance in Catullus' day which substituted for party affiliation and demanded unswerving loyalty.[31] The poet depicts this *foedus* as a hallowed pledge of mutual devotion, requiring efforts of a religious nature to sustain. Thus he attests to his own *pietas* and labels his commitment to his mistress *sancta fides*, *fides* being the late Republican word for "the bond of shared trust making possible political *amicitiae* between equals" (72.2–3).[32] Catullus, then – in direct contrast to many contemporary Roman males who regarded their womenfolk as insensate political pawns – conceives of his Lesbia as a full equal deserving of the deepest trust. What is more, we have no evidence to indicate that Catullus ever revered or deeply involved himself in the late Republican political scene or adopted its underlying values; consequently, we might further conjecture that he is also expressing some doubts as to the ultimate validity of a system in which men's feelings about their personal associates are often respected while women's just as frequently pass unacknowledged. Such an interpretation of Catullus' purpose in utilizing political imagery can also apply to lines 3–4 of poem 72, where Catullus swears that he loves Lesbia *non tantum ut vulgus amicam | sed pater ut gnatos diligit et generos*, "not only as most men love their girlfriends, but as a father loves his sons and sons-in-law."[33] A recent study of Catullan poetic language argues that these lines are also employing the metaphor of political alliance; Roman aristocrats of the late Republic chose sons-in-law (and their own sons' fathers-in-law) with great care.[34] They deemed a suitor's political connections and influence far more important than their daughter's feelings about him, since marriage would join their house with his.[35] In this passage, therefore, Catullus would be comparing his special affection for Lesbia to that which men hold for their closest political allies and "public representatives." His juxtaposition of *gnatos* and *generos* may well, furthermore, imply that while politically ambitious men tend to prize their hand-picked supporters as highly as their natural male offspring, they accord a lesser degree of esteem to their female children, whom they force to function in an adhesive capacity. Whatever Catullus' poetic and social intents, by likening his fondness for Lesbia to paternal pride and support, he distinguishes himself quite trenchantly from most Roman men.

Catullus' poetic vocabulary in his love elegies abounds with other politically-charged words and expressions: *officium, iniuria, bene velle, benefacta.*[36] Inasmuch as the end of the Republic also brought down the curtain on the large-scale political maneuverings by ambitious aristocrats (what Lily Ross Taylor calls "party politics"), we should not be surprised that the Augustan elegists never employ the word *amicitia* for the relationship between poet and mistress and invest the words *foedus* and *fides* with far more imprecise connotations.[37] Yet Catullus delineated his emotions and unusual social behavior through non-political language as well, by inverting an aspect of Roman social reality which endured for far longer than the political machinations of the late Republic. I have already mentioned the obligation imposed upon a Roman wife to remain faithful to her husband alone, though no such pressures impinged upon a male's sexual freedom. In Catullus, and later in Propertius, we find the males adopting the loyal, trustworthy, conventionally female role and even trying to come to terms with their mistresses' real and potential infidelities. The former compares himself – in lines 138–140 of poem 68 – to Juno, who was constantly deceived by her philandering spouse (140 *omnivoli plurima furta Iovis*), just as he is by Lesbia (136 *furta feremus erae*). The latter assumes a traditionally female stance in 2.7, when recounting his beloved Cynthia's joy at the repeal of a law which would have forced him to marry a woman of his own social standing and produce children to increase Rome's triumphs. In lines 7–10 he expresses utter revulsion at the now-remote possibility of marrying another woman. Even more significantly, he does not entertain the idea of adultery, of continuing his liaison with Cynthia despite his change in marital status; he in fact labels his legal involvement with a woman other than Cynthia betrayal (10 *prodita*) of their love. Further on in the same poem Propertius reaffirms his monogamous intentions (19 *tu mihi sola places*) and begs, in the subjunctive, that Cynthia feel the same way about him (*placeam tibi...solus*). One can cite other instances in Propertius' elegies where a male in love assumes the traditional female role of devoted, dependent passivity and imputes masterful, active conduct to his beloved. Most notable is 2.13a.35–36 where the poet asks that his tombstone claim that he was *unius...servus amoris*, the male equivalent of such well-utilized terms for wifely virtue as *univira*.[38] Of greatest importance, however, remains the fact that Propertius, like Catullus, expects faithfulness from men as well as, if not more than from, women and thereby spurns the double standard characterizing Roman male-female relationships.

We now come to the most-commented upon inversion of Roman love elegy, that depicting the mistress as enslaver, *domina*, and the lover as slave. Giving vent to one's darkest, most radically misandrous impulses, one could attempt to trace the source of such an elegiac convention solely to the love elegists' rightful anger at the way Roman men virtually shackled their women; after all, feminist doctrine maintains that patriarchal societies such as that of ancient Rome treat females no better than they do their lowest, most despised slaves. But such does not turn out to be the case. Catullus, Tibullus, Propertius and Ovid do not appear to posit any analogy between the social position of women and that of slaves. Nonetheless, the love elegists' use of the *topos* characterizing a lover as his mistress' slave should not for that reason strike us as any less remarkable or revolutionary. The idea of love-as-servitude, it is true, had circulated for centuries prior to the brief efflorescence of Roman elegy.[39] Yet the specific literary convention portraying one's lover as enslaver has an altogether different history. Formally originating in Alexandrian erotic poetry, it there invariably casts a *male* in the role of enslaver, whether the enslaved be a male, as happens most often, or a woman.[40] By transforming the archetypal erotic slave master into a slave mistress, then, by ascribing so much importance to a woman, the amatory elegists are displaying intellectual courage and originality as well as sheer infatuation. One critic calls this sort of transmutation a "radical break with Alexandrian poetic tradition," suggesting that the elegists were making a conscious rupture with literary as well as social and political orthodoxy.[41] But let us examine the development of this particular idea in the elegists themselves.

One tends to think of the Latin word *domina* as nothing more than a fancy term for "woman" or "lady." Such is the sense conveyed by the word's Romance descendants such as *dame* or *donna*; *domina* already has such a diluted connotation in the later books of Propertius[42] and in the love poetry of Ovid, who employs it in such places as *Amores* 1.4.60 and 3.2.80 as synonymous with *puella*. Its primal meaning, however, is that of "woman in command of household slaves," "the wife of the *dominus* in her capacity as overseer of the operations of the *domus* and its slaves."[43] *Domina* makes its début in Latin love elegy at lines 68 and 158 of Catullus 68. In each of its occurrences it appears in close connection with a *domus* which the lady inhabits, an indication of both its etymological parentage and Catullus' own connection of the word with residence in an impressive abode. But only by extension can we interpret the poet's use of it to describe the enslaving power a *domina* has over her combination lover/house mate. Catullus is, more likely than not, reverting to a socio-political frame of reference, as is his wont: characterizing the *domus* as a woman's particular sphere of influence, an area in which men prove powerless outsiders. Nevertheless, when he *does* talk about his helpless subservience to Lesbia, he calls her an *era* (68.136, in a passage discussed earlier), a word which also means mistress of slaves.[44] *Domina*, then, does not come into its own as a term for "enslaving, tyrannical controller of man's fate as a result of man's adoration for her" until Tibullus and Propertius begin to use it – and then quickly deteriorates into an amatory commonplace.

Tibullus delineates his subjection to a *domina* as, figuratively speaking, a painful, physical state linked with chains and lashings. At 2.3.79–80 he speaks of doing his mistress Nemesis' bidding (*ad imperium dominae*) and thereby accepting *vinclis verberibusque*. He opens the succeeding poem by yielding to *servitium* and his *domina*, here again Nemesis, and bidding farewell to his inherited freedom (*libertas paterna*); he depicts this *servitium* as involving *catenae* and *vincla* (2.4.1–4). *Vincla puellae* also figure in poems referring to Delia; at 1.1.55 and (along with *verbera* and *slavery*) at 1.6.37–38. In the twenty-odd times that *domina* is applied, in the elegies of Propertius, to the poet's mistress, the word lacks Tibullus' characteristic implements of physical torture as escorts. Only five occurrences of *domina*, all in the Monobiblos, even portray Cynthia as imperious.[45] Yet Propertius also views his emotional state as a form of *servitium* (cf. 1.4.4, 1.5.19, 1.12.18; 2.20.20; 3.17.41). At lines 21–30 of 1.10, moreover, he dilates upon what this *servitium* entails: complete role reversal with a dollop of masochism. He himself must constantly endure Cynthia's faithlessness, but can only expect cruel punishment from her if he gives the least sign of infidelity on his own part. Nonetheless, he equates great self-humiliation with deep self-fulfillment in love; in 23–24 of the next poem he proudly attributes his moods to her treatment of him. Although Tibullus' and Propertius' modification of this particular "beloved-as-enslaver" convention serves primarily as a poetic, and not a social, protest, the two poets certainly must have taken cognizance of the extent to which men in Roman society decided the fate and feelings of women. At any event, by having women control them, they are sharply reversing social reality.

A post-script on Ovid and *servitium*. As stated previously, the word *domina* has shed its original connotations of "powerful, absolute rule" in Propertius' later books and in Ovid. What is more, when Ovid does speak of love's slavery in such passages as *Amores* 1.3.5 and 3.11a.12, he never bothers to define his interpretation of the concept; in his elegies it has become a hollow cliché for the idea of a lover's dependency. We can best explain the literal enervation of this once daring, vivid metaphor by saying that as its newness wore off, so did the zeal of its employers to legitimatize it. But there may be more to it than that. A point Ovid stresses in both the *Amores* (1.10.29–36) and the *Ars Amatoria* (2.682 and 727–728) is that both male and female should derive *equal* pleasure from love; in fact, he rejects homosexual practices (*A.A.*2.683–684) for their "undemocratic" nature, in that both parties are not equally gratified by lovemaking. Equal rights to erotic satisfaction – recalling Catullus' use of political imagery to elevate women's status in love to equal that of men – strike him as far preferable to inequality of any sort, regardless of the more powerful individual's sex. Could it be that Ovid is here trying to correct what he sees as emotional and moral imbalance in the attitudes of his Augustan predecessors? Not that he criticizes them outright – far from it. Propertius and Tibullus, especially the former, had to battle fiercely in order to establish the validity of love poetry and its practitioners' devotion to it (a point to which I want to return later); overstatement and exaggeration of the beloved's power apparently helped gain love elegy popular acceptance. But, after the battle had been waged and won, Ovid could tone down amatory elegy's polemic excesses and rethink its assumptions. To me, at least, it seems likely that he both recognizes and resents the ability of either sex to control or exploit the other *and* wants to resolve all sexual rivalries and tensions through equality in sex.

Finally, the most important inversion of all, one greatly facilitated by the love elegists' comfortable backgrounds and, in the case of the Augustans, by their feeling that they were not vitally needed in the Roman governing and expanding process. I am referring to the elegists' substitution of their mistresses and the pleasures derived from celebrating them for traditional Roman careers and their rewards. Their poetry describes *otium*, love and elegy (free time, women and song?) as activities which in importance rival accepted pursuits: the law and politics, financial acquisition, and the military, all pursuits which, in addition, supplied the elegists' male peers with livelihood, challenge, glory and security. To most Roman men of the elegists' station, women served as a means to one or several of the above ends. To the elegists, their mistresses and the satisfactions – sensual, artistic and emotional – they provided were end enough.[46] Catullus concludes 68 with the remark that Lesbia makes his life sweet, even though his adored brother is dead (159–160).[47] Tibullus proclaims at 1.1.57–58 that he does not care about praise; as long as he is with Delia, he can be labelled sluggish and lazy by ambitious men. What is more, at 2.5.111 he maintains that he could not write at all, were it not for Nemesis. Propertius, who at 2.1.4 calls his mistress his very *ingenium*, at 1.7.9–12 insists, like today's proud-to-be-unliberated suburban housewife, that he only desires identity through his beloved. Ovid ascribes his poetic talent to his mistress' inspiration (*Am.* 1.3.19; 2.17.34; 3.12.16); at *Amores* 1.15.1–6 he maintains that his poetry will grant him as much renown as military, legal and political careers do others.

What is more, all of the elegists use the language of "establishment practices," i.e. politics, law, finance and warfare, to portray their love affairs. Catullus, of course, speaks about his liaison as if it were a political alliance. Tibullus, Propertius and Ovid also employ political and juridical imagery.[48] Tibullus with *leges* at 1.6.69 and *lege* at 2.4.52; Propertius in such elegies as 3.20 (15–16 *foedera . . . iura | lex*, 21 *foedere*, 25 *foedera*) and 4.8 (71 *foedera*, 74 *formula legis*, 81 *legibus*); Ovid with *Amores* 2.4.48 (*noster in has omnis ambitiosus amor*), 2.7, and 2.17.23–24 (*in quaslibet accipe leges; | te deceat medio iura dedisse foro*). We find the Augustan elegists all defending their love life as a respectable replacement for rank and wealth: Tibullus at 1.1.51ff., Propertius in 1.8a and at 2.34.55–58, Ovid petulantly in *Amores* 3.8. Most common of all, however, is the time-honored depiction of love as an equivalent of military service.[49] One calls to mind Tibullus 1.1.75; Propertius 1.6.30, 2.7.15–18, 2.14.24, 4.1b.135–138, 4.8.63–70; Ovid *Amores* 2.12.1, 2.18.2 and especially 1.9 (*Militat omnis amans*).

By using the "mainstream" language of conventional Roman careers to represent the devotion they bestow upon and the rewards which accrue to them from their mistresses, the amatory elegists are trying to make their feelings understandable to "straight" readers, those who have not undergone the same experiences that they have. They aim for comprehensibility, chiefly so that they can justify their life styles to individuals (and possibly even to portions of their own psyches) who subscribe to conventional assumptions, believing love and love elegy something worthless, "*nequitia.*" Yet the Augustan elegists also appear to be struggling toward a greater goal: the conversion of others to their beliefs and behavior. Ovid's attempts to turn potential lovers into practicing ones need no lengthy documentation; his self-styled tenure as *praeceptor amoris* managed to terminate both his stay in Rome and the Latin love elegy. Tibullus soft-pedals his approach in such elegies as 1.1. 1.5, and 1.6: he simply paints his rural idylls with Delia so attractively as to entice his audience away from their tawdry existences. One immediately thinks of Charles Reich's lyrical, though often infantile and over-simplified, evocations of Consciousness III in *The Greening of America*.

But it is Propertius that should concern us here, since he, more than any of the elegists, fought to convince and succeeded in convincing the Roman literary public of love poetry's worth (without Propertius' victory, we should never have had an Ovid).[50] Furthermore, Propertius' efforts to justify his life style and recommend it to others deal to a large extent with specifying what personal qualities and traits he admires in the woman he loves. In further clarification of these ideals, he wrote his most spirited defense of and exhortation to his *raison de vivre*, the fourth and final book of his elegies. There, the poet devotes considerable attention to women who are *not* his love objects – something heretofore rather unusual in Latin love elegy. There, through contrasting the behavioral roles and personal values of these various women, both legendary and contemporary figures, with those of his mistress Cynthia, Propertius voices his general discontent with Augustan beliefs and reaffirms the validity of his own.

A word on the special character of Book 4, which in many ways represents a new phase in Propertius' poetic development. Cynthia, omnipresent in Book 1, highly visible in Books 2 and 3, is offstage more than on in Book 4. If any one figure can be said to hold center stage it is Rome – featured in aetiological elegies about her holy shrines, festivals, topography and in love elegies about her inhabitants, past and present. Yet, as stated above, Book 4 introduces several "other women," all in some way Roman, all quite different from Cynthia. Elegy 3 stars the contemporary *nupta relicta*, Arethusa, who bemoans the fact that her husband has left her to fight Augustus' campaigns. 4 is about the fabled traitress Tarpeia, depicted by Propertius as betraying the Roman citadel to the Sabines out of love for their commander, and not, as most accounts do, out of avarice for Sabine golden ornaments. In 5 and 11 Propertius delineates, through speeches delivered in the first person, two newly-dead women: the greedy procuress Acanthis and the idealized noble matron Cornelia. Cynthia's rivals (her successor Chloris in 7, the courtesans Phyllis and Teia in 8) and the Bona Dea worshippers barring Hercules from their shrine in 9 also play substantial parts within the book, not to mention such cameo roles as Arria and Cinara in 1b, Cleopatra in 6.

Cynthia, however, is still very much a presence in Book 4. Elegy 7, in the fashion of elegies 5 and 11, features a *post-mortem* on her; it largely consists of her own words to Propertius when her ghost appears to him in a dream. She is also dealt with explicitly in 8, implicitly in 1 and probably in 5. Furthermore, Propertius' characterization of Cynthia in Book 4 is perfectly consistent with that presented in Books 1, 2 and 3: a *dura puella*, masterful, assertive and ultimately successful in her attempts to maintain complete control of Propertius. On the contrary, none of Book 4's other leading ladies – Arethusa, Tarpeia, Acanthis, Cornelia – are shown to be truly vigorous, strong-minded individuals who in the last analysis succeed in their endeavors. All pale in comparison beside the incandescent Cynthia: Acanthis and Tarpeia are described as utter failures (5.66–74; 4.89–92), Arethusa and Cornelia as self-obsessed and dependent (cf. 3.11–16, 29–62; 11.29ff., esp. 61–72). And, most important of all, while Cynthia represents the very kind of woman Augustus – judging from the purport of his moral legislation – would have liked to eliminate, the other, "inadequate," females in Book 4 in one way or another embrace or even embody conventional Roman, that is to say Augustan, beliefs about woman's role. Her triumph implies their defeat, or at least casts considerable doubt on the worth of their conduct and their values.

3. *Clamores*

The plight of the young bride Arethusa in 4.3 poignantly illustrates the dire consequences of war, particularly Augustus' expansionistic campaigns and the enforced estrangements between men and their loved ones that they wrought. An off-and-on nine-year separation from her husband Lycotas[51] has rendered Arethusa querulous, hyper-emotional and neurotic; although she gives evidence throughout the poem that she is basically a stable, self-reliant and resourceful individual (17, 18, 33–40, 57–62), she melodramatically describes herself in a letter to her husband as a weak, minimally functioning creature who is perishing from loneliness (2, 3, 41–42, 55–56). Propertius paints Arethusa with love and sympathy. He intends, I think, that his readers laugh indulgently at Arethusa's efforts to bring her husband home through arousing his pity. Yet Propertius also wants to bring home to his audience the basic incompatibility between the demands placed upon women – to live in seclusion, faithful all the while to one man – and those placed upon men – to abandon the women they love and prove their virility through dangerous warfare abroad. Women in Arethusa's situation have every good reason to become unrealistic about themselves, purposely childlike, ultimately ridiculous. Elegy 9, moreover, serves as a structural and contentual counterpart of 3; it shows how men's adoption of brutal, warlike postures can alienate them from women of sensitivity and principles: Hercules' testimony to his past conquests avails him not in obtaining access to the spring of the Bona Dea worshippers.

Tarpeia in 4.4 also possesses qualities commonly found in respectable Roman women. By profession a Vestal virgin, she is basically a passive, sheltered girl who values herself solely in terms of the material advantages she can give her prospective bridegroom: Propertius' Tarpeia's exact word is *dos*, dowry (56); this dowry is Rome betrayed. Propertius does not, moreover, blame her tragic end on her moral impropriety, her defiling her vows of chastity. In fact, he portrays her compassionately, even to the point of assigning her guardian goddess Vesta and ruler Romulus complicity in her crime (69–70, 79–80). What he does see as responsible for her undoing are her materialistic, altogether inadequate, definition of her worth as a person *and* her total miscalculation of her idolized Tatius' nature resulting from her abysmal self-ignorance. In lines 55–60, when listing her qualifications for marriage to Tatius, she never bothers to document her all-consuming love for him. She blindly assumes that her *dos* alone can win him; in lines 57–60 she even claims that ravishing her alone would revenge the rape of the Sabine women – clearly deeming herself an invaluable political asset. Tatius, so noble that he would not honor crime (89), kills her as a traitress. The word employed for his punishment of her is again *dos* (92); Propertius thus stresses the potentially disastrous consequences of women's naive reliance upon connections rather than internal strengths for social acceptance.

In elegy 5, the poet represents the bawd Acanthis as a woman who prizes the conventional, outward signs of manly – and, in his day, Roman – valor ... material acquisition and military glory. What is more, not only does Acanthis consider material rewards the sole worthwhile incentives in life (21–26) and encourage a client, probably Cynthia, to accept the advances of well-paying soldiers and sailors and slaves (49–53); not only does Acanthis conceive of women's beauty and charms as highly marketable qualities (59–62), valuable only if lucratively capitalized upon, she also views the events customarily comprising a love affair, those which frequently serve as subjects for amatory elegists' poems – quarrels (31–32), observance of Isis' rites (34), involvements with other men (29, 39–40) and one's birthday (36) – as opportunities for a girl to squeeze money out of her admirer. She also tells her client to be dishonest at any, and for every, price, beginning with advice to *sperne fidem* in 27 (cf. also 28, 29, 34, 41–42, 45). Predictably, she also disdains poetry and its practitioners because they lack material rewards (54–58). Acanthis, then, epitomizes the attitudes Propertius and his fellow elegists opposed: esteem for money and the external indications of "manliness" (in the word's narrowest sense); "reification" of women as potentially profitable items; acceptance of unfaithfulness and mutual exploitation as part and parcel of male–female relationships; scorn for poetry and its spiritual benefits. At the close of 5, Propertius and his ideals are vindicated: Acanthis dies penniless and unmourned. Like other women in Book 4 who care inordinately for money – Arria in 1, even Cynthia's rival Chloris in 7 – or war – Cleopatra in 6 – she has been doomed to failure, punished for her faulty appraisal of what really matters in life.

Propertius no doubt admires Cornelia, the noble matron featured in the closing elegy of Book 4, for strictly adhering to the behavioral code prescribed for women of her class. But her portrait, a defense of her life which she herself delivers from the grave, is not, upon close inspection and after comparison with the similar posthumous address given by Cynthia in 7, altogether flattering. Although Cornelia makes much of her lifelong fidelity to one man (11, 35–36), although she has virtuously followed the rigid patterns of conduct set forth for "nice" Roman women (cf. especially 33–34, 45–46, 60–64), although she takes great pride in the fact that her male relatives have done all the right things in war and politics (29–32, 37–42, 65–66), although she can congratulate herself on the moral rectitude of her female ancestors (51–54), nevertheless Cornelia is totally devoid of real personality and utterly lacking in substance. In 7.53 and 70 Cynthia speaks openly of her faithfulness to and love for Propertius, a surprising avowal for a a *demi-mondaine*; yet we never hear Cornelia say what one might expect from a devoted wife and mother, that she *loved* her husband or her children. One gets the impression, in fact, that Cornelia has no true emotions, just acquisitive impulses. She imagines the events and people in her life as material possessions, describing them either by the physical objects connected with them (11 *currus*, 29 *tropaea*, 32 *titulis*, 33 *praetexta*, 34 *vitta*, 61 *generosos vestis* etc.) or, in the case of her children (12, 73), as financial entities, *pignora*. She herself does not want to be judged as a person; instead, she derives her entire sense of self-worth from her ancestry (11, 23–32, 37–40), the accomplishments of her living relatives – including her mother's brief and unhappy marriage to Augustus (55–60, 65–66), and her own possession of a socially prominent husband and the three requisite children (61–64, 64–70). Furthermore, she carries this materialistic evaluation of herself and her colorless behavior to unrealistic extremes: she demands privileged treatment in the underworld (19–26), predicts that her family will be beset with unendurable grief over her loss (77–84), and expects special status in the afterlife (101–102). Propertius has portrayed Cornelia as the ideal wife of both longstanding Roman tradition and contemporary political reality: chaste, fecund, retiring, loyal; rich in political connections and associations with Republican Rome. Yet, when one compares her to Cynthia as she is depicted in Book 4, one understands quite clearly that, and why, Cornelia is not Propertius' kind of woman.

And what is Propertius' kind of woman? Self-sufficient, forthright, unmaterialistic in her desires and self-image. Within the confines of Book 4, we encounter Cynthia rejecting wealthy admirers in favor of Propertius, criticizing the greed of her successor Chloris, expressing her own wants as plain ones, and forcing Propertius himself to abandon luxurious habits (8.51–52, 7.39–40, 7.73–76 and 79–86, 8.75–78). She wants to be cherished for her own personal qualities, notably her honesty and deep affection – not purchased as one would a material commodity. Appearing in Propertius' dreams after her demise, she recalls how she remained faithful to him *in her fashion* (7.52 *me servasse fidem*), thereby winning an ultimate resting place beside Andromede and Hypermestre, both wronged, *sine fraude maritae* (7.62 ff.). Yet she does not hesitate to chide Propertius for his ungrateful and unfaithful conduct (7.13–32, 8.73–80). Furthermore, her unabashed frankness extends beyond her displays of passion and temper to her realization that mere complaining does no good in effecting reconciliations with a wayward lover. In 8, while alive, she singlehandedly stages an actual military siege to expel rivals (51–66); in 7, posthumously, she coolly declares that death will soon reunite the temporarily errant Propertius with her (93–94). Cynthia may be willful, unpredictable, domineering; to Propertius she seems sensuous, unaffected, exciting. What better advertisement for his unconventional life style could he have selected than his portraits of her in 4.7 and 4.8, surrounded as they are by pictures of more conventional, far less interesting, female types? What better cause for living counter to standard *mores* than a female companion who defies the expectations of what is ultimately an inequitable, hypocritical society and affords inspiration for a simple, honest and rewarding life?[52]

Notes

1 *ILS* 8403; cf. also M. I. Finley, "The Silent Women of Rome," collected in his *Aspects of Antiquity* (London 1968) 130–131.

2 See G. Williams, *JRS* 48 (1958) 25, for instances of *obsequi* on the gravestones of Roman women from varied social backgrounds and historical periods.

3 Cf. *CIL* 6, 1527=31670, the so-called *Laudatio Turiae*; cf. also *CE* 81 and 968 and the inscriptions quoted by Williams (above, n. 2) 21 n. 20.

4 So Williams (above, n. 2) 17–18.

5 See R. Syme, *The Roman Revolution* (Oxford 1939) 335, 443–445; cf. also Horace, *Odes* 3.14.5.

6 For example, Syme (above, n. 5) 445; G. Luck, *The Latin Love Elegy*, 2nd edition (London 1969) 22–24; S. Lilja, *The Roman Love Elegists' Attitude to Women* (Helsinki 1965) 31–42.

7 On the difference between *manus*-marriage and marriage *sine manu*, see Cicero, *Topica* 3.14 and, *inter alios*, P. E. Corbett, *The Roman Law of Marriage* (Oxford 1930) 68–106, 113.

8 So Luck (above, n. 6) 23–24. In dissuading his (male) readers from sexual intrigues with respectable married women, Horace (*Satires* 1.2) implies that adultery, often of a promiscuous variety, on the part of matrons from the best families was a well-acknowledged fact of Roman life in the late first century B.C.

Horace condemns such intrigues as dangerous and inconvenient for the men involved – not as immoral in themselves!

9 On the standard age of marriage for Roman women, see J. A. Crook, *Law and Life of Rome* (Ithaca 1967) 100 n. 9, who cites M. K. Hopkins, *Population Studies* 1965, 309ff.

10 See the discussion of Lilja (above, n.6) 37–41, from which one may choose to conclude that the Augustan love elegists deliberately left the social status of their mistresses vague.

11 Cf. Syme (above, n. 5) 12, 384ff., 414.

12 For their political wheeling and dealing, see, *inter alios*, Cicero, *ad Att.* 2.11.2; Velleius Paterculus 74.2.3.

13 The remark is quoted by Lactantius, *Epit.* 33(38)5. See K. Ziegler's fifth Teubner edition of the *De Republica* (1960).

14 See J. P. V. D. Balsdon, *Life and Leisure in Ancient Rome* (New York 1969) 237.

15 See Lilja (above, n. 6) 176–177, who in turn cites T. Mommsen, *Römische Staatsrecht* (Leipzig 1899) 22f., 688f. and 691. See also Balsdon, *Roman Women* (London 1962) 214, who calls attention to the elder Cato's dogged championship of a double standard already codified in law, and Cato's own remarks on the topic given by Aulus Gellius (*Noct. Att.* 10.23.5).

16 See C. L. Babcock, *AJP* 81 (1965) 1–32, on Fulvia, the aforementioned female "politico"; he ascribes her ability to attract three prominent and powerful spouses to her consular stepfather and considerable wealth.

17 Syme (above, n. 5) 445.

18 Crook (above, n. 9) 104. Marriage without *manus* also enabled the male members of a woman's own family to retain control of her property after her marriage. Admittedly, such an arrangement benefitted women in certain respects. Their husbands no longer held complete sway over them; they could appeal to their fathers against their husbands and vice-versa. But it also permitted and in fact encouraged male relatives to interfere in "personal," conjugal relationships whenever they felt it in their interest.

19 Plutarch, *Caesar* 14.4–5; Suetonius, *Julius* 27.1.

20 Suetonius, *Augustus* 63.2 and 65; *Tiberius* 7.2–3.

21 See K. Rogers, *The Troublesome Helpmate. A History of Misogyny in Literature* (Seattle 1965) 44, who notes Aeneas' imperviousness to female charms, "male chauvinism," and Lavinia's utter vacuity. In all fairness to Vergil's Aeneas, however, it should be said that Creusa's ghost justifies – *ex post facto* – Aeneas' abandonment of her as divinely ordained (*Aen.* 2.776ff.).

22 Cf. Suetonius, *Augustus* 34.1; Cassius Dio 54.16; Horace, *Carm. Saec.* 17–20; also the review of Balsdon (above, n. 14) by T. J. Cadoux, *JRS* 52 (1963) 207.

23 Suetonius, *Augustus* 34.2; Cassius Dio 56.1.2.

24 For a summary of the evidence for the elegists' social standing, see Lilja (above, n. 6) 10–16.

25 On the issue of sincerity in the Roman elegists, see A. W. Allen, *CPh* 25 (1950) 145–160. While the elegists' allegedly autobiographical poetry may not be telling the exact truth about their personal lives, it at least presents an internally consistent picture of the "characters" which the elegists assume *gratia artis*. Latin love poetry also must have purposely contained enough general social realism to strike a chord of recognition in readers' hearts; i.e. the Roman literary public must have known other men who acted as Tibullus, Propertius and Ovid claimed to behave. See also Lilja (above, n. 6) 23–30.

26 T. Roszak, *The Making of a Counter Culture* (Garden City 1969) 66; cf. also C. Reich's similar descriptions of Consciousness III in *The Greening of America* (New

York 1971) 233–285. Counter cultures have blossomed in other historical eras too – recall the medieval Goliards and their revolt against ecclesiastical moral strictures.

27 So Propertius at 2.10.7ff., Ovid at *Amores* 3.1.26 and 68 label love poetry an art form for young artists.

28 See again the evidence assembled by Lilja (above, n. 6) 10–16 about the backgrounds of the Latin love elegists; see Roszak (above, n. 26) 26–41 on those of the 1970-style counter-culturists. From what the elegists tell us about their origins and imply about their education and social contacts, we should, I think, infer that the "poverty" of which they speak (e.g. Tibullus 1.1.19–22; Propertius 4.1b. 128–130, 4.5.54–58) is either fictitious or a voluntary form of social protest against the materialistic occupations and preoccupations of the equestrian class.

29 See, for example, his unwillingness to participate in the emperor's military campaigns and the national military spirit in 3.4.15–22. Cf. also two recent studies: J. P. Hallett, *Book IV: Propertius' Recusatio to Augustus and Augustan Ideals* (unpublished dissertation, Harvard 1971) 98–102, on 4.2, which details Vertumnus' futile pleas for continued forum residence in the face of the emperor's projected expansion of the Basilica Julia; J. P. Sullivan, *Arethusa* 5 (1972) 17–25.

30 See D. Ross, *Style and Tradition in Catullus* (Cambridge, Mass. 1969) 85.

31 So L. R. Taylor, *Party Politics in the Age of Caesar* (Berkeley 1949) 7–8.

32 Ross (above, n. 30) 85, who cites M. Gelzer, *Die Nobilität der Römischen Republik* (*Kl. Schr.* 1.71–73).

33 *gnatos* can, of course, mean both male and female children, but its juxtaposition with *generos*, which can only signify husband of a daughter or female relative, strongly suggests that it here refers to sons.

34 Ross (above, n. 30) 89.

35 See discussion in Taylor (above, n. 31) 33–44; see also the evidence regarding Caesar cited in n. 19 above.

36 See discussion in Ross (above, n. 30) 86–88.

37 At 1.11.23, in fact, Propertius calls Cynthia his *domus* and *parentes*; at 2.18b.34 he expresses a desire to be her *filius* or *frater*. In so doing he recalls the words of Andromache at *Iliad* 6.429–430 and of Tecmessa at 518ff. of Sophocles' *Ajax*, both of whom liken their relationship with their husbands to that a child enjoys with his parents. Yet Propertius is here assuming the dependent, helpless role of these defenseless women and not the protective one of their heroic spouses. Instead of seeking in Cynthia an equal with whom he can carry on an adult relationship of mutual respect, he looks to her for nurturance and protection, roots and direction. See the discussion below on the mistress as *domina* and as a replacement for worldly satisfactions as the logical extention of Propertius' submissive yearnings.

38 Cf., for example, 2.27.13–16, where the mythical plight of Eurydice is assigned to a male lover, the behavior of Orpheus to his *puella* – an observation made by Luck (above, n. 6) 128–129; cf. also 1.11.23 and 2.18b.34, discussed in the preceding note.

39 Cf., for example, Euripides, fr. 132; Plato, *Symposium* 183a.

40 See F. O. Copley, *TAPA* 78 (1947) 285ff.; A. La Penna, *Maia* 4 (1951) 187ff.; Lilja (above, n. 6) 76ff.

41 Luck (above, n. 6) 129.

42 2.3.42; 2.9.45; 2.17.17 are good examples.

43 Cf. A. Ernout and E. Meillet, *Dictionnaire étymologique de la langue latine*, 3rd edition (Paris 1951) I 326ff. s.v. "*dominus.*" Lilja (above, n. 6) 81 notes that we have no Republican examples of the word *domina* to describe a *dominus'* relation-

ship with his wife – the word only refers to relationships between slaves and their mistresses.
44 Cf., for example, Ennius, 287 Vahl. (Medea described by her household staff); Plautus, *Cas.* 311.
45 1.21, 3.17, 4.2, 7.6, 17.15.
46 Cf. also J. E. Fontenrose, *CPCP* 13 (1949) 371–388.
47 The interpretation of these lines given by K. Quinn in his commentary on Catullus (London and Basingstoke 1970) 396.
48 For a fuller discussion of "establishment imagery" in the Augustan elegists, see Lilja (above, n. 6) 63–73.
49 The earliest occurrence of the theme is *Anacreonta* 26 A. For the tradition of *militia amoris*, cf. A. Spies, *Militat omnis amans* (Diss. Tubingen, 1930).
50 On Propertius as "ur-Ovid" (so L. A. Richardson and K. Quinn) or on Ovid as "Propertius vulgarized" (so J. P. Sullivan), see the *entretiens* of the American Philological Association-Propertius colloquium, December 29, 1971, recorded by D. N. Levin, 422 and 426 respectively.
51 29–20 B.C. Line 9 refers to the war against the Getae waged by M. Crassus in 29 B.C. and to Augustus' planned invasion of Britain in 25 B.C.; lines 7 and 63 describe a proposed campaign against the Parthians, just prior to Augustus' recovery of long lost Roman standards from them in 20 B.C.
52 I would like to thank the following for assistance and encouragement: Sheila Dickison, Katherine Geffcken, Carol Kline, Donald N. Levin, Mary Lefkowitz, Jane Loeffler, John Sullivan and Dorothea Wender.

THE LIFE OF LOVE

R. O. A. M. Lyne

1. Introductory

When Propertius' *monobiblos* appeared in the early 20s the civil wars had brought an end to the republic and the door was open for regular imperial government. It had been a time of revolutionary political activity, fervour, and change.

Changes in moral and sexual attitudes were of a different kind; in a way they did not really change. Attitudes simply became more entrenched, the separating lines more clear-cut. And the manner of making one's views felt changed. Conservative traditionalism acquired a formidable advocate. Already in the 30s, it seems, Octavian (the future Augustus) was turning his thoughts to moral regeneration. And he was prepared to lend traditional veneration for family, *patria*, and honour the muscle of an autocrat: where the *maiores* had for the most part observed, exhorted, praised, or deplored, Octavian was prepared to punish and compel. He *organized* morality as everything else and brought it into the scope of public law.[1]

Opponents shifted their emphasis. Rather than simply defy accusations of immorality, they argued their case as an alternative morality; what was implicit became explicit. The generation of Catullus became the generation of the Elegists. The 'life of love' was codified.[2]

2. The life of love (1): eternity

It had been Catullus' aspiration that love should be for life. Note too the implications of poem 5, *uiuamus, mea Lesbia, atque amemus*. The attitude assumed here (simple though it may seem) is important. If we recall the conventional view that love was properly a *ludus*, a *ludus* belonging to youth (responsible men had more important things to do), we shall realize that Catullus' position has a provocativeness (moral, philosophical, and social) that is easy to miss.

The early Elegists adopt the Catullan view and broadcast it. Neither fickle time nor even the onset of age (but see below) will change their love. It is hoped with greater or lesser confidence that the beloved will be similarly devoted, cf. e.g. Prop. 1. 12. 19 f.:

> mi neque amare aliam neque ab hac desistere
> fas est
> Cynthia prima fuit, Cynthia finis erit.

> For me it is not right to love another or stop
> loving her.
> Cynthia was the first, Cynthia will be the end.

Cf. too 1. 15. 29 ff., 2. 6. 41 f., 7. 19, 21. 19–20. Lines 2. 1. 65 f. phrase the idea differently; as often (cf. below) Propertius adopts the condemnatory terms that society might use:

> hoc si quis uitium poterit mihi demere, solus
> Tantaleae poterit tradere poma manu.

> If anyone could remove this vice from me,
> he could put fruit in Tantalus' hand.

That is, it is impossible. 2. 15. 36 is characteristic in another way:

> huius ero uiuus, mortuus huius ero.

> I shall be hers in life and hers in death.

Love until *death* is a favoured Propertian emphasis. He can consider love after death too.

One fact to notice (it is psychologically very plausible and therefore revealing) is that although Propertius is committed to love's surviving for life, he does not as a rule face the full implications of that commitment. His own and Cynthia's *ageing* is usually ignored. Exceptions to this are few and interesting.[3] One sees Propertius' point. Horace confronted the fact of ageing and came to a very different view of life and love (pp. 204–15). Romantic aspiration needs the indulgence of a blind eye.

Unless (apparently) you are Tibullus: Tibullan commitment to lifelong love can, it seems, more easily accommodate the problem of age. Cf. 1. 6. 85–6:

> nos, Delia, amoris
> exemplum cana simus uterque coma.

> Delia, you & I
> must be Love's paradigm when we are both
> white-haired.

> (Lee)

And 1. 1. 59–62

> te spectem suprema mihi cum uenerit hora;
>> te teneam moriens deficiente manu.
> flebis et arsuro positum me, Delia, lecto,
>> tristibus et lacrimis oscula mixta dabis.

> O let me gaze at you, when my last hour comes –
> hold you, as I die, in my failing grasp!
> Delia, you will weep for me laid on the bed of
>> burning
> and you will give me kisses mixed with bitter tears.
>
> (Lee)

is followed in 69 ff. by these 'Horatian' lines:

> interea, dum fata sinunt, iungamus amores:
>> iam ueniet tenebris Mors adoperta caput;
> iam subrepet iners aetas, neque amare decebit,
>> dicere nec cano blanditias capite.

> Meanwhile, with Fate's permission, let us unite and love.
> Tomorrow Death will come, head hooded – in the dark,
> or useless Age creep up, and it will not be seemly
> to make white-headed love or pretty speeches.
>
> (Lee)

But perhaps 1. 1. 59 ff. and 69 ff. are inconsistent. There is a point worth attention here.[4]

3. The life of love (2): the lover and society
(*militia amoris*)

Attitudes to life implicit in Catullus' poetry (including 'love is forever') amounted, we could say, to a virtual alternative social creed; his romanticism had public as well as private implications.

Catullus served a spell in the entourage of the governor in Bithynia.[5] This (*militia*, 'military service') was as we shall see exactly the sort of thing a young man of Catullus' class should do if he had a proper, conventional career in mind. For Catullus it was clearly no more than a distasteful brush with convention.[6] His priorities and values were different. He was profoundly and provocatively devoted to occupations of leisure (*otium*), to poetry, and (in particular) to love. Years of effort lavished on a poem is a matter for praise;[7] solemn protestations of deeply Roman obligation are uttered to a girl-friend; the girl-friend is called his 'life', and the implications of that term are accepted. Catullus ignores the normal rewards and honour that a man of his class could expect in *negotium*, to court the rewards of *otium*. Love is not only to last for life, it is the most serious occupation of life; love and poetry are his *negotium*, for which he sacrifices virtually all else. Here was a set of values – romantic values – to enrage conventional opinion; we should remember (for example) Cicero's careful qualification of the role of love in life. And we have evidence that the Catullan phenomenon did actually enrage Cicero: in his oration *Pro Sestio* (56 BC) Cicero vilifies an idle society of pleasure in terms that sound very like a jaundiced and malevolent misrepresentation of the world we see reflected in Catullus' poems.[8]

By the time we get to the first books of the early Elegists we find a renunciation of conventional life explicitly and formally declared. An alternative social creed finds and emblazons itself.

Interestingly the two Elegists put it (at this stage) in rather different ways, or at least moods. Tibullus, whose first book is published a little after Propertius' *monobiblos*, makes the more unequivocal statement. His first poem is virtually programmatic. In the opening lines he expresses hopes for a *uita iners*, a life without *negotium*, in the country (a typically Tibullan emphasis) and derides the wealth that *labor* in military service brings. In 45–52 wealth, which demands effort, is judged inferior to love and serenity in comparative idleness. In 53–8 Tibullus directly expresses his preference for a life of love with Delia to a life of honourable military action. He starts politely (because he is contrasting himself with his patron, the great Messalla) but nevertheless firmly:

> te bellare decet terra, Messalla, marique
> 	ut domus hostiles praeferat exuuias.
> me retinent uinctum formosae uincla puellae . . .

> It befits you, Messalla, to make war by land and sea
> so that your house may display spoils taken from the enemy.
> But the bonds of a lovely girl hold me, a prisoner . . .

He concludes with an enthusiastic statement of his own commitment to love and unmanly *otium*:

> non ego laudari curo, mea Delia: tecum
> 	dum modo sim, quaeso segnis inersque uocer.

> I don't care about esteem, Delia.
> Provided that I am with you, I court the name idle, inactive.

And the life of love with Delia is also (it is hoped) to be in truth lifelong, as we saw above (lines 59–60).

Many more such passages could be cited from this and other poems. But the message is clear and for the moment adequately illustrated. Tibullus is explicitly advocating inactivity, *otium*, and love in contrast to conventionally proper and honourable pursuits: military service, the pursuit of esteem and wealth. And he provocatively accepts for himself society's pejorative terms, positively emblazoning what Cicero, for example, had derided (this had *not* been a Catullan habit).[9] The Elegist's declaration is designed as a deliberate affront. Catullan attitudes have been codified into a flagrantly provocative creed.

Propertius argues for the life of love in his first book as explicitly as Tibullus. But he acknowledges more complexity; and (a fact not unconnected with this: see below) he doesn't talk in generalities but considers a specific case, that of himself and his friend Tullus.

In poem 6 he rejects an invitation from Tullus, nephew of the proconsul of Asia in 30–29 BC, to accompany him as a member of his uncle's staff, and in the course of the poem contrasts his own life of love with Tullus' approaching life of military action. He commits himself, like Tibullus, to his life of love, which he avows to be disreputable, and rejects Tullus' honourable course. But his espousal of the dishonourable is less enthusiastic than Tibullus' (25 f.):

> me sine quem semper uoluit fortuna iacere
> hanc animam extremae reddere nequitiae

> Allow me, whom fortune always wished me be low,
> to surrender this life to utter depravity.

Cf. to 29 f.:

> non ego sum laudi, non natus idoneus armis
> hanc me militiam fata subire uolunt.

> I was not born for esteem and arms.
> The fates want me to undergo *this* soldiering [i.e love].

Meanwhile there is no derision at, nor even overt criticism of, Tullus' life of military action – rather indeed the contrary (21–4). Like Tibullus, Propertius is committed to the life of love for life: cf. 26 above; also 27 f.:

> multi longinquo periere in amore libenter
> in quorum numero me quoque terra tegat.

> Many have willingly died in a long love.
> Among this number may earth also cover me.

But unlike Tibullus, as these lines show (and cf. 2. 1. 65 f.) , he does not seem too overjoyed about it.

We find the same general pattern in poem 14 where Propertius contrasts love and wealth, an obvious achievement of a conventionally successful life. Again it is discussed in the specific situation – Propertius' love and Tullus' wealth; and again there is no obvious criticism of Tullus' portion and far from unequivocal praise of love. So in these two poems Propertius emerges, like Tibullus, explicitly committed to the life of love; and he takes upon himself society's condemnatory terms – he does so more strikingly in 1. 1 (also addressed to Tullus) where he represents himself as subject to degradation, disease, folly, and madness.[10] But he suggests that his way is more of a painful necessity than a happy and clear-cut choice; his acceptance of condemnatory terms seems to be much less cheerful.

Propertius will in later books argue the superiority of the life of love with more confidence and vigour; and Tibullus will admit to more pain, problems, and compulsion in his choice.[11] In their first books in fact we catch an interesting moment. Propertius is perhaps the earliest poet so explicitly to argue so unorthodox a life. For him the issue is very topical and still *specific*; he is not yet interested in – he perhaps has not yet thought of – generalizing. That is one reason why his decision is difficult and his attitude more complex. A friend's career and achievements are not to be simply dismissed or decried; his own love which he admits to that same friend is painful and humiliating cannot be glibly preferred without some acknowledgement of the objections to such a preference. Tibullus writes in the wake of these Propertian beginnings; he formulates the life of love more generally; and while generalizing he can desire it more unequivocally. And perhaps his love-life was easier.

Militia amoris (the soldiering of love)

The Elegists found one distinct and telling method of projecting their creed which we should notice: *militia amoris*. (And approaching the figure from this, the proper direction, we shall be able to give a truer account of it than exists in the standard books.)[12]

Military imagery of love had been sparingly used in Greek (Hellenistic) poetry. Its growth and development was particularly Roman. We find it mainly in Roman Comedy – and then in the Elegists (it is not for example Catullan). Literary historians might have scrutinized this peculiar distribution with profit.

The general attraction of such imagery for Romans is comprehensible. Military life and customs were very close to ordinary Roman citizens – closer than to Hellenistic readers of Hellenistic literature.[13] Soldiering therefore offered lively and immediate illustrations that might be wittily discordant or unexpectedly and amusingly appropriate – love is both violent and supremely non-violent. These considerations account for the popularity of the image in the very Roman comedian Plautus.

They account partially for the popularity of the image with Propertius and Tibullus. But a comedian making fictional characters speak of the soldiering of love (when soldiers were often on stage) is something rather different from, rather more obvious than, personal love poets speaking of themselves in those terms. We remember that Catullus, the great progenitor of the elegy, did not; and among the Alexandrian erotic epigrammatists it was a fairly insignificant conceit. Yet with the Augustan Elegists it suddenly becomes (it seems) fashionable. There must be particular reasons for this new interest. There are. They lie in the reality of *militia*, in what real 'soldiering' stood for at the time when the Elegists wrote and what its implications for them were.

In the first place *militia*, service under a provincial governor or general on campaign was, as has often been said above, a standard stage in the career of an ambitious young man. Whether or not he intended his ultimate *negotium* to be military in emphasis, *militia* was a wise course for him – for a time – to follow: it offered valuable experience, financial benefits, and a chance to secure the friendship and support of important people. This could be demonstrated countless times over. An interesting and amusing illustration is offered by letters of Cicero to a protégé, the jurist Trebatius Testa (known to us also from Horace, *Satires*, II. 1). Cicero had secured a position for Trebatius on the staff of Julius Caesar in Gaul. But Trebatius was none too thrilled with his golden opportunity, either before or during it, having a strong taste for the town; and Cicero had to write to him repeatedly, strengthening his resolve and pointing out the advantages. (When Trebatius was finally reconciled to his *militia*, Cicero wrote to him again, with some humour, praising him for his fortitude: 'your letter showed that you are now bearing *militia* with firmness of purpose and that you are a brave and stout fellow (*esse fortem uirum et constantem*).')[14]

Here, in the fact that *militia* was a standard stage in a conventional career, lies one important reason for the popularity of the *militia amoris* figure with the Elegists. They were organizing and proclaiming the life of love as an alternative to conventional life; *militia* was symptomatic of conventional life; by professing their own *militia* the Elegists might neatly declare their dissociation. With bland insolence or subtler irony the figure could demonstrate that the life of love was *by definition* incompatible with, an aggressive alternative to, the life decreed by society.

Let us recall Tibullus' programmatic poem (1. 1), where Tibullus dissociates himself (at first very tactfully) from Messalla's military life of action:

te bellare decet terra, Messalla, marique . . .

It befits you, Messalla, to make war by land and sea . . .

Some lines later (75–7) he writes:

354

> hic ego dux milesque bonus: uos signa tubaeque
>   ite procul, cupidis uulnera ferte uiris,
> ferte et opes.

> Here [i.e. amidst the boisterous brawls of love]
>   I am general and stout soldier. You
>   standards and trumpets [of real; militia]
> hence far away! Take your wounds to greedy men,
> take wealth too!

Tibullus' attitude to a life of military action ultimately becomes clear and less tactful. He strikes a neatly provocative stance by transferring its esteemed terms to his own dishonourable but cherished life.

Tibullus we should note had an especial stimulus to use this particular method of provocatively stating his creed. At some time around this period he *did* himself do the standard thing and perform real *militia*: he was present on Messalla's Aquitanian campaign, and started with Messalla for other campaigns in the East but was prevented by sickness.[15] For Tibullus therefore, the one-time or occasional and no doubt pretty unwilling *miles*, the *militia amoris* must have been a particularly enjoyable, certainly a very relevant, way to present an unorthodox philosophy of comparative idleness.[16]

Propertius has only one manifest example of the image in the *monobiblos* but it is very prominent (since Propertius was never a *miles* himself, the image might not have suggested itself so immediately to him as to Tibullus). It occurs in the sixth poem, the poem to Tullus opting for the life of love rather than conventional life in the form of, precisely, *militia*. To Tullus he says (19):

> tu patrui meritas conare anteire securis

> Do you make ready to march before your uncle's well-earned *fasces*.

As for himself (29–30):

> non ego sum laudi, non natus idoneus armis
>   hanc me militiam fata subire uolunt.

> I was not born suited for esteem and arms.
> The fates want me to undergo this *militia* [i.e. love].

His use of *militia amoris* allows him *in a word* to show that the life of love is a rival to, completely incompatible with, a conventional and honourable life. It is itself *militia*.

At this interim point we may notice an incidental but interesting difference in Propertius' and Tibullus' understanding of the *militia amoris*. For Tibullus the stuff of erotic soldiering is, typically, the often physical quarrels lovers may have with their beloveds; he seems in fact to have found these unusually spicy. Propertius has in mind the act of love or the strategy leading to love as well as quarrels.

That was another aspect of real *militia* and another plank in the platform of the life of love which made the *militia* figure magnetic. *Militia* broadly considered might mean violence, savagery, and death; but the life of love proclaimed a virtual pacifism – something quite different incidentally from orthodox Augustan eulogies of Augustus' peace. The Elegists used *militia amoris* to declare their dissociation from war. The conventional world made wars and wars were frightful; 'war' existed in the life of love but was something other, and more or less delightful. Offering their own kind and definition of war the elegists neatly demonstrated the incompatibility of real war with the life of love.

In 1. 3 Tibullus praises the Golden Age and castigates present times thus (47–50):

> non acies, non ira fuit, non bella, nec ensem
>   immiti saeuus duxerat arte faber.
> nunc Ioue sub domino caedes et uulnera semper,
>   nunc mare, nunc leti mille repente uiae.

> Anger and armies and war were not yet known:
> no blacksmith's cruel craft had forged the sword.
> But now, in Jove's dominion, it is always wounds & slaughter;
> now there is the sea and sudden Death's one thousand roads.

>   (Lee)

Soon after he is describing Elysium, where lovers live their afterlife in bliss. He includes these two lines (63 f.):

> ac iuuenum series teneris immixta puellis
>   ludit, et assidue proelia miscet Amor.

> Young men and tender girls make sport, lined up together,
> continually engaging in the battles of Love.

>   (Lee)

Love, the implication is, offers its own battles, harmless indeed pleasurable battles, alternative and obviously preferable battles to those of the real *militia* earlier evoked.

Tibullus opposes *bella Veneris* more directly to real war, carefully defining them and distinguishing them from military violence, in 1. 10. First note lines 1–4:

quis fuit horrendos primus qui protulit enses?
  quam ferus, et uere ferreus, ille fuit!
tum caedes hominum generi, tum proelia nata;
  tum breuior dirae mortis aperta uia est.

Tell me, who invented the terrifying sword?
Hard he must have been and truly iron-hearted.
War that day & slaughter were born to humanity;
that day there was opened a short cut to grim death.

(Lee)

Then 51 ff. (the aftermath of a country festival):

rusticus e lucoque uehit, male sobrius ipse,
  uxorem plaustro progeniemque domum.
sed Veneris tunc bella calent, scissosque capillos
  femina perfractas conqueriturque fores.
flet teneras subtusa genas, sed uictor et ipse
  flet sibi dementes tam ualuisse manus.
at lasciuus Amor rixae mala uerba ministrat,
  inter et iratum lentus utrumque sedet.
a lapis est ferrumque, suam quicumque puellam
  uerberat: e caelo deripit ille deos.
sit satis e membris tenuem rescindere uestem,
  sit satis ornatus dissoluisse comae,
sit lacrimas mouisse satis. quater ille beatus
  cui tenera irato flere puella potest.
sed manibus qui saeuus erit, scutumque sudemque
  is gerat et miti sit procul a Venere.

Home from the sacred grove the farmer far from sober
drives wife and children in the wagon.
Then Venus' war flares up. The woman then bewailing
torn hair and broken door
weeps for soft cheeks bruised, & the winner also weeps
for the mad strength in his hands.
But Love, the mischief-maker, feeds the brawling
    with abuse
& sits there obstinate between the angry pair.
Ah stone is he & steel who strikes his girl:
he drags down Gods from heaven.
It is enough to rip off the thin dress,
enough to disarrange the well-set hair,
enough to draw her tears. O four times happy he
whose anger makes a tender woman weep!

> But the cruel-handed should carry shield & stake
> & soldier far away from gentle Venus.
>
> (Lee)

Love's 'war' is placed by Tibullus both implicitly and explicitly in complete opposition to real war; the life of love is totally (therefore) incompatible with it.

Propertius uses *militia amoris* to pacifist effect (for Propertius' pacifism see the splendid lines 2. 15. 41 ff.)[17] More boldly than Tibullus (though not in the *monobiblos*); his use also tends to be more general and inclusive, combining an effectively pacifist dissociation from war with a dissident dissociation from current patriotic posturing. E.g. 3. 5. 1–2:

> pacis Amor deus est, pacem ueneramur amantes:
> stant mihi cum domina proelia dura mea.

> Love is a god of peace, we lovers revere peace:
> my hard battles are with my mistress.

That is not only effectively pacifist, it is bravely pacifist: it alludes to and passes mute comment on Propertius' previous poem, ostensibly a jubilant reaction to Augustus' military preparations (3. 4. 1):

> arma deus Caesar dites meditatur ad Indos.

> Divine Caesar plans arms against the rich East

pacis Amor deus est picks up and thus undermines the sincerity of *arma deus Caesar*. Note too 2. 14. 21–4:

> pulsabant alii frustra dominamque uocabant:
> mecum habuit positum lenta puella caput.
> haec mihi deuictis potior uictoria Parthis,
> haec spolia, haec reges, haec mihi currus erunt.

> Others knocked on the door in vain and called her 'mistress';
> relaxed, my girl rested her head by mine.
> This victory for me will be more potent than the conquering
>   of Parthians,
> this will be my spoils, this my [captive] kings, this my
>   triumphal chariot.

That implies a triumphant rejection of war (as a career as well as generally) and decries contemporary military aspirations. Finally let us look at 2. 7. 13–18:

unde mihi patriis natos praebere triumphis?
  nullus de nostro sanguine miles erit.
quod si uera meae comitarem castra puellae,
  non mihi sat magnus Castoris iret equus.
hinc etenim tantum meruit mea gloria nomen,
  gloria ad hibernos lata Borysthenidas.

How should I furnish sons for our country's triumphs?
No one of my blood will be a soldier.
But if the soldiering for me was the true kind, soldiering
  under my mistress,[18]
Castor's horse would not be big enough for me.
From love-soldiering my glory has earned its great renown,
glory that has been carried to the wintry inhabitants of
  Borysthenis [on the Dnieper].

These brave lines also combine dissociation from current patriotic causes
with a general rejection of war. They do it with splendid and brave insolence
(*true* war is love-making . . .). And, as in the passages above, the *militia
amoris* figure implies that the views uttered are part and parcel of the life
of love. The life of love being war rules out cruder conceptions of war by
definition.

4. The life of love (3): the lover and his beloved
(*seruitium amoris*)

We have seen that Catullus' poetry embodied a romantic attitude toward
society, and that the early Elegists then organized and emblazoned it. Catullus' attitude towards his beloved was also in a defined sense romantic. This
the Elegists took up, but they also intensified it, and emblazoned their
intensified form. We remember that Catullus introduced three main areas of
non-erotic life to illuminate his feelings for, and attitudes towards, his
beloved: marriage, family relations, and *amicitia*. Two of these provided
Propertius with notable assistance.

First, the family. 1. 11. 21:

an mihi nunc maior carae custodia matris?

Would I guard more anxiously my own dear mother?

This implies a disinterested, protective concern analogous to that expressed
in Catullus 72 (*sed pater ut gnatos diligit et generos*). Two lines later in the same
poem we find a more general expression of devotion that uses family
imagery:

> tu mihi sola domus, tu, Cynthia, sola parentes.

> You only, Cynthia, are my home, you only my parents.

We might notice that *tu sola parentes* implies devoted *dependence* rather than protectiveness, almost in fact the opposite emphasis to line 21 and Catullus 72.

Propertius is fond of marriage terminology, particularly in his second book. I quote two examples, one obvious, one not so. At the end of 2. 6 (which throughout views Cynthia rather as a wife)[19] he protests devotion in these unambiguous terms:

> nos uxor numquam, numquam seducet amica.
> semper amica mihi, semper et uxor eris.

> Never will a wife, never will a girl-friend separate me from
>   you.
> You will always be my girl-friend and always my wife.

The lines not only of course illuminate Propertius' feelings for Cynthia; they are also socially and politically provocative, against a background of legislation to enforce marriage: cf. 2. 7 and above, p. 348 (with note). In poem 13 he prophesies Cynthia's devotion to himself after his death (lines 51–2; some wishful or rhetorical thinking here):

> tu tamen amisso non numquam flebis amico.
> fas est praeteritos semper amare uiros.

> Sometimes you will weep for your lost lover.
> It is right to love departed men/husbands for always.

Discreetly Propertius claims to be no more than a friend. But in his heart he feels that he is, or he wants to be, Cynthia's *husband*. Though *uir* is an ambiguous term ('man' or 'husband', like German *Mann*), it was 'right' (*fas*, that is, right and proper according to divine or natural law) for a woman to continue love for a deceased husband, not lover: that way she remained honourably *uniuira*. In fact Propertius seems here to slip into marriage *thinking* rather than adopt marriage terminology. It is often his way: this Catullan mode of devotion was most congenial and natural to him, and is frequently discernible.[20] We can discern it (but not family imagery) in Tibullus too: it shapes (possibly) the way Tibullus imagines Delia waiting for him in 1. 3 (lines 83 ff.); it shapes his vision of Delia officiating at the beloved country estate (1. 5. 21 ff.).

Catullus' third area of non-erotic language, *amicitia*, was in some ways his most revealing. It expressed his romanticism most definably: Catullus offered the full and resonant equality of *amicitia* to a lover. The language of *amicitia* does not play a very significant role in Propertius and Tibullus; to be more precise, they are *not* customarily disposed to represent their relationships fully, systematically as *amicitiae*.[21] On the contrary. Their romanticism now took a different direction – a direction incompatible in fact with their marriage dreams, but we should not look for consistency in romantics.

Conventional folk had derided or vilified abject lovers as sick, insane, and debased. The early Elegists, provocative spokesmen of an alternative morality, admitted as their inescapable (and, as we soon infer, elected) portion sickness or madness,[22] and, too, debasement. And here, in debasement, was the material of a new romanticism, a possible trump. Catullus had offered the sacrifice of traditional superiority; Propertius and Tibullus would surrender equality. The altered emphasis that we observed in Propertius' use of family imagery was significant; but the Elegists found a more striking, a shocking way to play their trump.

The surrender of equality was emblazoned. Just as a telling method of projecting the lover's attitude towards society had been developed (*militia amoris*), so a way was evolved of concretely proclaiming the flagrantly provocative relation of the lover to his mistress – the personal condition of the life of love. Catullus had aspired to be the 'friend' of Lesbia; Propertius and Tibullus, debased and subject beyond such dreams, were their lovers' professed *slaves*. The *seruitium amoris*, 'slavery of love', takes shape.[23]

The emphases of the two poets in their use of the 'figure' (so to call it)[24] are again different, and characteristic. In his first book Propertius professes his slavery as something that he bears unwillingly; and he concentrates on servile loss of free speech. He would even, he says (in a neat paradox, conveyed by ambiguity),[25] submit to servile punishments, provided that he gained the opportunity to speak what his anger prompted – to speak as a free man (1. 1. 27–28). In fact he only finds such liberty when he is alone in a forest and far from Cynthia (1. 18). Note too his comments on love and its servile effects on poems to Ponticus (1. 9) and Gallus (1. 10). Tibullus concentrates on servile physical humiliations – which he embraces almost masochistically. The two poets' difference in emphasis is neatly demonstrated by Tibull. 1. 5, where Tibullus *repents* of an outburst of brave, free words and *invites* servile punishments to prevent another such occurrence (lines 5–6).

> ure ferum et torque, libeat ne dicere quicquam
>   magnificum posthac: horrida uerba doma.

> Brand me for my wildness, rack me lest it please me to speak
>   anything
> grandiloquent again. Tame my rough words.

We see therefore (among other things) a by now familiar variation in the degree to which the poets acquiesce in their state. But slavery as the state of both of them is sure and admitted. It is their most characteristic personal posture, proclaimed with increasing explicitness and generality.[26] It was, I think, Propertius and Tibullus who popularized, who gave effective shape to the *seruitium amoris* 'figure' as we know it. In it they found a concrete and provocative way of declaring the lover's avowed abjectness, the personal condition of the life of love, the new romanticism. The lover a self-confessed slave! Here was a focus for the appalled attentions of conventional sensibilities and a delightfully awful programme for the unconventional to rally to.

Notes

1 For Augustus' moral legislation (his law to curb adultery, the *Lex Iulia de adulteriis*, and his law to encourage marriage, the *Lex Iulia de maritandis ordinibus* are those that particularly concern us) see *Cambridge Ancient History*, vol. x, 441 ff.; P. A. Brunt, *Italian Manpower* (Oxford, 1971), 558 ff.; also Stroh, *Ovids Liebeskunst*.

2 Very helpful on this topic are Boucher's first chapter, Burck, Stroh, *Liebeselegie*, 222 ff.

3 18B is an interesting poem. Aurora who loved the (explicitly) aged Tithonus is held up as an *exemplum* for Cynthia. But the *exemplum* encourages her to love (it questions why she does not love) the *youthful* Propertius. Propertius' own old age is merely an hypothesis: *quid mea si canis aetas candesceret aetas?* Here Propertius admits the full implications of love surviving into age but at one remove, in myth (in the *romantic* world). The admission is uncharacteristic – but not total. The poem is also uncharacteristic at the end. Bitterness makes Propertius advert brutally to Cynthia's coming old age (19) in Horatian fashion; he does this again in his bitter concluding poem: 3. 25. 11 ff. (cf. especially Horace, *Odes* 1. 25).

   Cf. too Prop. 2. 25. 9–10:

   > at me ab amore tuo deducet nulla senectus
   > siue ego Tithonus, siue ego Nestor ero.

   > But no old age will lead me from my love of you,
   > whether I shall be Tithonus or whether Nestor.

   Propertius refers to his possible old age but romanticizes it (puts it in mythical terms); and of course the main point of *senectus* is not to evoke love accommodating senility but love enduring through life – a fabulously long life. He is in fact making his usual sort of romantic declaration, but choosing an unfortunate or half-honest word to do so.

   3. 10. 17 shows a suppressed appreciation of Time's winged chariot: see *GR 20* (1973), 43. The tenderness and sensitivity of this partial admission is in eloquent contrast to 3. 25. 11 ff.

4 If it is not *decens* to love in old age and make 'pretty speeches with white hair', it is difficult to justify 1. 1. 59 ff. and (even more) 1. 6. 85–6. It is evident in fact that Tibullus had – at least he expresses – quite strong Horatian sympathies on the topic of Age and Love, Time and Love. Horatian beliefs are implicit at 1. 2. 89 ff., 1. 5. 70, 1. 8. 47 f., 2. 1. 73 f. (cf. also Bright, 234–5, Geiger, 11) and explicitly uttered by Priapus at 1. 4. 27 ff. Tibullus' romantic aspiration does seem odd

alongside these passages. It is of course not at all impossible that he should be inconsistent; or perhaps he means to distinguish more carefully than his language actually does between *acts* of love and affection-love. Or perhaps we have another and different spot of evidence that Tibullus' romanticism is not quite as earnest as may first appear: it may have its histrionic aspect.

5 Cf. poems 10, 28, 31, and 46.

6 It wasn't even profitable, as Catullus is not too romantic to point out: 10. 5 ff., 28, 7–10. Poems 46 and 31 capture Catullus' sense of relief and happiness at the ending of his provincial duty.

7 Cf. poem 95.

8 Note especially *Pro Sestio*, 136 ff.

9 When Catullus talks positively about a 'life of love' he uses neutral words (poem 5) or his own special positive vocabulary (109). When love torments him he can use conventional pejorative terms from a conventional point of view; he does not more or less willingly accept and emblazon 'disease' or 'madness' like Propertius or Tibullus (on this aspect of Propertius and Tibullus see further below): see poem 76. In this connection poem 51 is interesting. According to my reading of the poem, Catullus feels uncomfortable about the jealous feelings he describes in the first three stanzas – he feels uncomfortable about the effects of his romantic love – and in consequence reads a moralizing lesson to himself: 'you've got too much *otium* on your hands, Catullus', i.e. too much time to indulge in love (cf. Ov. *Rem. Am.* 139 ff., *otia si tollas, periere Cupidinis arcus . . .*). The choice of the word *otium* here, the assumption it implies that love is properly a marginal, leisure occupation, shows Catullus thinking again in conventionally moral terms. Catullus' attitude to a 'life of love' is natural, fluid, never tendentious.

10 Cf. Allen esp. sect. II, F. Cairns, *CQ* n.s. 24 (1974), 102–7. For condemnations of romantic love from a more or less conventional viewpoint cf. Lucr. 4, 1073 ff. and Cic. *Tusc.* 4. 68–76. Cf. also Plato, *Phaedrus 231 C–D, Symposium* 183A, etc.

11 e.g. Prop. 2. 15.41 ff., the delightful 2. 30B; Tibull. 2. 4.

12 Useful references on *militia amoris* in E. Spies, *Militat omnis amans* (Diss. Tübingen, 1930), Burck, *passim* esp. 177, Lilja (but she interprets them very oddly), 64–7. For Plautus' and Terence's use of the figure see G. E. Duckworth, *The Nature of Roman Comedy* (Princeton, 1952), 337 with refs. And bibliography, E. Fantham, *Comparative Studies in Republican Latin Imagery* (Toronto, 1972), 26–33 and 84.

13 It is interesting to observe that Apuleius uses *military* images for sex where the Greek author of *Lucius or the Ass* uses *wrestling* images (Met. 2. 17; L. o. A, 9, printed in Loeb edn of Lucian, vol. viii): we can gain insight here into the difference between Greek and Roman tastes.

14 Cicero's letters to Trebatius: *Fam.* 7. 6, 17, 18.

15 Cf. Tibull. 1. 3, 7. 9–12, 10. 11–13.

16 It seems likely to me that Cornelius Gallus encouraged the efflorescence of the *militia amoris* figure. He appears to have felt and expressed the rival claims of love and soldiering strongly – this is indicated by Verg. *Ecl.* 10 (note particularly the problematic lines 44 f.) And the famous Servian note on line 46. The *militia* figure could have provided him with some neat ironies and paradoxes.

17 It may be in fact that these lines exploit *militia amoris*: Camps thinks we should read Fontein's *proelia* instead of *pocula* in line 48.

18 Shackleton Bailey, 75 well explains this line. He concludes: 'Translate then "But were I following my mistress' camp – real warfare that – then . . . " . . . The condition, it may be urged, is unwarranted since Propertius *is* already a soldier in this sense. True. He "contaminates" two ideas, one positive, "I follow my mistress'

camp, the true camp for me", the other conditional, "If Caesar's camp were the camp of my mistress, then I should be a mighty soldier." The couplet is influenced by both but properly expresses neither.'

19 Cf. Camps, *Propertius Book II*, 92.

20 Cf. too 2. 5. 17, 8. 29, 9. 3 ff. and 17, 15. 27 f., 16. 22; also 1. 3.

21 Prop. 3. 20 which employs much *amicitia* vocabulary is from more than one point of view a special case (I do not think it concerns Cynthia). It is interesting that Cynthia uses *iniuria* sarcastically at 1. 3. 35. *fides* is quite common in both poets but is too vague to suggest *amicitia* without supporting words; the same applies to an unqualified use of *amicus* or *amica*: Catullus 72.3 (for example) shows how casual *amica* can be. In 2. 9 Propertius talks more in *amicitia* terms than in most poems.

22 Cf. too Tibull. 2. 5. 110, *et faueo morbo, quin iuuat ipse dolor*.

23 I have discussed *seruitium amoris* at length in *CQ* n.s. 29 (1979), 117 ff. and I allow myself to be brief in the text – on admittedly contentious topics. I still do not believe that *seruitium amoris* had very significant currency before Propertius, but a couple of qualifications need making (the article in *CQ* omits a few Greek references (see Stroh, *Liebeselegie*, 218 ff.) but my argument easily accommodates them). I omitted to mention that Lucilius (730 M) seems to have called one of his mistresses *domina*; and the new fragment of Cornelius Gallus (see *JRS* 69, 1979) shows that Gallus referred to Lycoris thus. This makes it more likely that part of the efflorescence of the 'figure' is due to Gallus. But Gallus may have had no more developed a system of *seruitium* than Catullus, who refers to Lesbia as *era*; and for the reasons mentioned in my paper I still think that the efflorescence is largely to be put down to Propertius.

24 I explain my reasons for being chary of calling *seruitium amoris* a figure, loc. cit. I also further discuss the difference between Propertius and Tibullus in their use of *seruitium*.

25 On the interpretation of Prop. 1. 1. 27–8 see *CQ* n.s. 29 (1979), 129.

26 Cf. Prop. 2. 13. 36. Tibull. 2. 3. 5 f. and the concluding couplet; also 2. 4. Note how when Propertius 'renounces' romantic love in 2. 23 *seruitium* occurs to him as, clearly, its most significant manifestation.

Works cited

Works which may be referred to simply by the author's name or name and abbreviated title. Other items will be cited at relevant points in the text or notes. Abbreviations of periodical titles generally follow the normal conventions of *L'Année philologique*.

Allen, A. W., '*Sunt qui Propertium malint*', in: *Critical Essays on Roman Literature*, ed. J. P. Sullivan (London, 1962), 107–48.

Boucher, J.-P., *Études sur Properce* (Paris, 1965).

Bright, D. F., *HAEC MIHI FINGEBAM: Tibullus in his World* (Leiden, 1978).

Burck, E., 'Römische Wesenszüge in der augusteischen Liebeselegie', *Hermes* 80 (1952), 163–200.

Camps, W. A., *Propertius Elegies Book I, II, III, IV* (Cambridge, 1961, 1967, 1966, 1965).

Geiger, H., *Interpretationen zur Gestalt Amors bei Tibull* (Zürich, 1978).

Lee, A. G., *Ovid's Amores* (London, 1968).

Lilja, S., *The Roman Elegists' Attitude to Women* (Helsinki, 1965).

Shackleton Bailey, D. R., *Propertiana* (Cambridge, 1956).

Stroh, W., *Die römische Liebeselegie als werbende Dichtung* (Amsterdam, 1971).

The Latin texts which I cite are based on Mynors's Oxford Classical Text of Catullus (1958), Camps's editions of Propertius, Lee's Tibullus and Ovid, and the Wickham–Garrod Oxford Classical Text of Horace (1901). I permit myself to select different readings where I think it is appropriate.

The most convenient commentaries in English are Fordyce and Quinn, *Catullus, The Poems* (Catullus), Camps (Propertius), Smith (Tibullus), Nisbet and Hubbard, Wickham, and Williams *The Third Book* (Horace), Barsby, *Ovid Amores Book I* (on Ovid *Am.* 1: there is nothing convenient in English on *Am.* 2 and 3; Brandt's German commentary is still very useful).

THE PASTORAL IN CITY
CLOTHES

Paul Veyne

The aesthetic pleasure of a playful triumph over weightiness, over the taste for sentimentality and human interest, Roman erotic elegy retains from our reality just a few banal and vague givens (a noble libertine, an irregular) and then transforms them into fictional beings who lead a dream life. The internal logic of this world, which is not our world, is that one lives in it only to sing of and suffer from love. Not being in the country, these shepherds without a cloak sigh over not being there. Elegy sings not of passion but of the fiction of a life that is exclusively poetic and amorous. As Fränkel says, "the main assumption of the poet is this: Love is no mere incidental event, flavoring an otherwise normal life; it is a preoccupation which molds the whole being of the victim into a new and peculiar sphere apart from the rest of mankind, with a different horizon, climate, and atmosphere."[1] Passion's victim, in other words, wishes to know no other duty than love, no other delight than being in love.

Is this the choice of some lifestyle, refusal to embrace a career in public affairs? No, it is a change in nature – or rather the passage from reality to fiction. What becomes of a person, once in this other world? Such a person becomes an amorous poet, which is something more than a hybrid of being a poet and being in love as it is for the rest of us. The amorous poet is a living species that can be found only in this other world, as we shall see. Elegy seems to take as its theater the streets of Rome, Tivoli, the small port cities of Latium or the Neopolitan coast, but in reality it takes place outside the world, just like bucolic poetry. However, whereas such pastoral fiction never fooled anyone, elegiac fiction can no longer count its victims.

There is something unjust about this. Ancient bucolic ought to have deceived more people, for it is different from the affected pastoral poetry of modern authors, Ronsard's *Bocage royal*, *Astrée*, or *Pastor fido*. Indeed, it is their opposite. If a comparison must be drawn, it should be with *Porgy and Bess*, set in the world of American blacks with their accent and language. No one took the bucolic seriously because it was set in no less puerile and subaltern a world, that of the slaves – a world so subordinate that it becomes innocent and idyllic. Whether slave-holding or racist, a similar distinction between "us" and "them" served as material for an aesthetic construction. The modern pastoral takes noblemen and turns them into shepherds. Gershwin's opera and the ancient bucolic take blacks or slaves, leaves them their coarseness, their jokes, their sexual promiscuity, but transforms them into lovers by profession (who in the bucolic are also poets).

In bucolic, therefore, slave shepherds consubstantially become amorous poets; in elegy, Roman knights do the same, and no less consubstantially. In fact, it suffices, or almost suffices, that a knight from an elegy become a shepherd for him to become a character in a bucolic. And this is precisely the literary experiment that, by taking things literally, Virgil attempted and pulled off in the tenth and last of his *Bucolics*.

This second-degree text, this palimpsest, as Genette will call it, would be by far the most beautiful of the Roman elegies if it were written in elegiac meter instead of in hexameters, the bucolic meter, and if, precisely, it were nothing more than an elegy in the second degree. Virgil is amusing himself by writing an elegy in hexameters.[2] To this metric transposition is added a double transference in meaning. In this poem, Gallus, a well-known elegiac poet of the time, becomes a bucolic poet by the very fact that Virgil is imagining what would happen to Gallus's Ego if he left the city and its vexations to take refuge in pastoral solitude. He would become a hunter and a shepherd, taking up the shepherd's mantle. But on one point the metamorphosis would not be complete: faithful to his elegiac role, in his solitude, Gallus would continue to suffer from love and to sing of his griefs. He would remain the poet he was.

A text written about another text or, more accurately, about another literary genre,[3] the tenth *Bucolic* is a dazzling poem (bursts of applause break out in the reader's head at every line), but, as Jacques Perret writes, it is less pathetic than it first seems to be. This tour de force of one virtuoso over another lays bare those very rules of the game that elegy so carefully avoids. At the time, Gallus was a hallowed author and the father of Roman elegy. The young Virgil, who sensed that his *Bucolics* would echo down to posterity like a cannon shot, dared to pastiche his predecessor and, under the colors of doing him homage, asserted himself to be Gallus's equal in a different genre. Let us recall that Gallus had as his mistress the beauty Volumnia Cytheris, with whom Cicero was so proud and shocked to dine. In his elegies, Gallus sang of the sufferings a certain Lycoris inflicted upon his Ego, and, as will be obvious, Roman readers were highly unlikely to take light poetry so seriously as to attribute to a poet the idiocy of publishing his intimate set backs. Lycoris makes Ego suffer because elegy liked to clothe itself in mourning and normally had tears in its eyes.

More precisely, Gallus's despair had something to do with elegy as a genre. His Lycoris, who lives in high circles, has agreed to accompany one of her lovers to the provinces where he will be a governor. Owing to the force of circumstances, she will be everything to this rival. Such a misfortune did not befall either Propertius or Tibullus. Ego, who is delicacy itself, laments her whose tender feet will crush the snows of the Barbarian countries on the frontiers of the empire. And, in leaving the city, along with its pomp and circumstance, Ego takes refuge among the hills and the scrub, there to share the life of those who haunt these solitudes: shepherds, hunters, and the rustic gods. They all come to console him, each group in turn. Ego is watching over a flock of goats, but does he not blush at so servile an occupation? Virgil implores him not to feel such shame, and then, a few lines later, gives him an activity more suitable for a knight – the hunt (which presupposes a long immersion in raw nature, like hunting with hounds in later years). And Gallus dreams vainly that Lycoris, who has turned faithful (only the city makes irregulars), comes to rejoin him, and they grow old together. One day Tibullus will construct the same dream for his Delia.

The bucolic world knows only simple and innocent misfortunes; pain will break the crystal of this dream. Gallus is well aware that few cruel men and women are to be found in this countryside. Philis is ready to weave flowers into his hair, and the dark Amyntas will play music for him – for servile promiscuity is a dream about paradisical availability. But a lover does not so easily give up his morose delights, and a poet has his formulas. Among these pastoral folk, Gallus will retell his elegiac sufferings from an earlier time. He remains the slave of love, and the country cannot console him. Virgil has only to conclude his poem and lead his flock back to the farm, now that the day of poetic labor is ended: "Home! The goblet is full, night is descending – let's go, my goats!" I do not for an instant believe that, with this epilogue, Virgil meant to deliver a "message" to us, to draw melancholy conclusions about "the final failure of poetry, unable to purge the passions." What reader would think of taking a poetic fiction for some moralist's guidebook, drawing such a clear lesson from it? This epilogue merely signifies that, the pastiche being ended, the two poets again become what eternity will change them into. Gallus once more becomes the elegist he always was. The confusion of genres was only a momentary game, the flock can reenter its fold.

Is Virgil therefore the guardian of this flock? Yes, since a poet passed for what he sang. If he sang of shepherds, he was one himself.[4] Was it not the principal concern of shepherds to sing? They gather up their flock at night, at the moment of quitting their poetry. The case of Tibullus or of Propertius is almost the same. Their Ego is a knight who does not think much about his career or taking care of his lands. He hardly thinks of anything but love and poetry.

Since, for them, the man reflects the poet (just the opposite is true in our eyes), an amorous poet will not be involved in politics, nor will he be a man of affairs. This does not mean in practice that an individual cannot also do these things at the same time, but simply that the guiding themes are different. Erotic poetry is not patriotic poetry, and bucolic pays no attention to wealth of public honors. But, whereas bucolic always abstracts itself from reality, erotic elegy, which does the same thing only in order to reattach itself to reality, must therefore expressly reflect what the pastoral can pass over in silence. Except that the elegy does so so insistently; it goes on at such length about the delights of love[5] that, by all evidence, it finds some pleasure in this rejection: the pleasure of jeering at social conventions, of defying the rules, of inverting values; inverting them so as to laugh. The elegiac instrument has no string for sounding more serious notes. Indeed, in the comedies of Hellenistic theater, the life of lazy libertines had already slaked the imaginations of honest spectators.

What were the rules that could be defied? The elegiac Ego is obviously a member of high society, a knight, and it was from the nobility that the government team – practically speaking, the senate – was recruited.[6] Every young knight, therefore, found himself confronted with a choice: live off his revenues and do nothing, or enter a public career with its functions and honors. If he took the second option, he would become an army commander, a judge, or a provincial governor, and, above all, he would take a place in the senate, which was the highest executive body, the deliberative body, and a sort of academy and conservatory of the political arts all at the same time. In so doing, he would enrich himself immensely, if not honestly. Every knight did not enter such a career, far from it. There were not enough posts for everyone, but it was one thing to stay outside, as did the majority, and another to refuse to take up such a career and to shout it from the housetops.

The elegists cry that no military service is so harsh as the service of love, where one has constantly to be on guard, to be active, to obey one's mistress blindly, handing her her umbrella and her mirror, serving her like a slave,[7] entering into nocturnal combat – this is how one wins glory.[8] Like a soldier, a lover lives from day to day and is never sure about tomorrow. The elegists cry even louder that they know no other service than that of love. For "Love is the god of peace, and we lovers venerate peace" (Propertius, III.5).[9] Good citizenship is for others:

> Work, friend, to advance yourself in your career further than your uncle, the consul; reestablish our vassals' privileges, which they no longer dare to dream of.[10] For, in your life, you have no time to love, you have never thought of anything but your country and war. Let me follow the small fortune that is my lot forever; let me die like a good-for-nothing. Many have died satisfied with having loved for a long time – let me rejoin them in the tomb! I am not made for war and glory, my vocation is to enroll in the army of love (I.6).[11]

I am not of the race that gives birth to soldiers (II.7).[12] Despite this haughty sterility, the poet may know a night of glory:

> Others have knocked at Cynthia's door and said they were her slaves, she did not hurry to open it for them, but left her head next to mine. Here is a victory that I prefer. I would not have been so happy to rout the Barbarians (II.14).[13]

I should add that any political career was necessarily mixed. One took turns at being a general, then an administrator. In order to reject such a career in its entirety, the elegists designate it by its most obvious part, military service.

Not having such a career, the ethics of the nobility allowed for another praiseworthy option: to enrich oneself (for the Roman aristocracy had economic attitudes that one would be mistaken in attributing solely to the bourgeoisie). "If a young noble is good for anything, apart from serving the city, he will increase his family's patrimony."[14] That is why Tibullus brags as much about his poverty as his service to love. Poverty? We need to be clear on this point. In our language, this word refers to all of society, in which there is a minority of rich people and a majority of poor people. In Latin, the word referred only to the privileged minority, designating its ordinary members as opposed to some fabulously wealthy ones. The majority of the population, whom we would call the poor, formed an alien species. Tibullus, or rather his Ego, is poor in the sense that one might be a wine grower and simple landowner in the time of Paul-Louis Courier; that is, he lived on his private income. He was also poor for another reason: he had no career, he did not practice "the senatorial manner of making a fortune,"[15] which was to rob those under his administration: "Heaps of yellow gold, country acres, I leave to others, whom fear keeps awake when the enemy is not far off and who awake to the sound of his trumpets. Let my poverty allow me to traverse existence in a leisurely fashion! It suffices for me if my fire does not die out in my hearth" (Tibullus, I.I).[16] Poverty is the same as the delights of love.

Nothing could be more glorious than this reversal of values. The elegists are vice's braggarts, they are proud to live differently than the rest of humanity. The beloved, moreover, is as sacrosanct as the poet. "No one dares to touch those who love. They are inviolable and thus may safely cross lands where there are robbers. . . . The moon is their light, the stars will show them any pitfalls, Love in person will carry his torch before them, fanning its flame, and angry dogs will turn away their snarling jaws" (Propertius, III.16).[17] Another poet, Horace, asserts that a man of integrity, a man who has nothing to reproach himself for, can cross deserts and mountains safe and sound; but, despite these words, Horace may be thinking more of an amorous poet than of an upright man.[18] For, citing himself as an example (along with the required smile), he tells us that one day as he was out walking he met a wolf, a wolf as big as a lion, at a moment when he was dreaming about love poetry, and the beast did not do a thing to him. The anecdote must be genuine, and Horace must have believed that he owed this miraculous protection to his talent, for the poem ends differently than it began: "Whether I am in the desert, at the equator, or at the pole," he writes in effect, "I will be no less a lover." There are ages when talent has a superstitious kind of pride and, like Bonaparte, believes in its lucky star.

A poet feels himself to be different from other people, as Horace once again can testify:

> There are those whose pleasure is to kick up the dust in the olympic stadium, and not to go off course with their fiery wheels (for such as these, the victory palm is their apotheosis); for others, what counts is that the inconstant mass of electors raise them triumphally to the highest honors; another will want to fill his granary with the wheat of a whole province. . . . As for me, I feel as though I'm in the seventh heaven if I have the poet's crown.[19]

We should bow before these lines. With their "as for me," which sets itself up against everyone else, these lines ally themselves with one of the most universal textual structures, from ancient India, to China, right down to Victor Hugo.[20] Philologists calls it the *priamel*.[21] This structure allows an individual to find a new place for himself, in terms of his difference, on the list of other individual differences, yet also to take a step back from himself.[22] Depending on the case, he extols his difference, or gives himself, on the contrary, a lesson in modesty,[23] or even, as here, authorizes himself to proclaim his particularity, since all the others have their own particularities, and he can put his on the same scale as theirs so as not to impinge on the pride of these others and thus to be tolerated by them.

More precisely, Propertius makes use of the *priamel* on several occasions in order to speak of his particularity among lovers, which is to be the poet of his love: "The sailor tells of winds, the farm laborer of his cattle; the soldier lists his wounds, and the shepherd his sheep; I myself, the vicissitudes of combat in a narrow bed" (II.1).[24] After all, everyone talks about what he is. But Propertius has a sensitive heart: "You ask me, O Demophön, why I cannot resist any woman? A poor question. In love there is never any why. Are there not people who slash their arms with the sacred knife and mutilate themselves to the rhythms of Phrygia? Nature assigns each person his way, and my fate is to always have love on my mind" (II.22).[25] Such a fate also means that the poet speaks only of love. A poet like Propertius is not made for epic; his vocation is the amorous or national elegy (III.9).

We are on the scent of something now. The Roman elegists are more concerned about their verses than about their mistresses. Propertius polemicizes against other poets, defends elegy against the imperialism of other well-known genres. His various poems are addressed to his comrades in pleasure and to other poets when they are not directed to Cynthia or some other unknown woman. The picture of a milieu? No. The amorous poet is not a social type. He is a literary genre personified. "Epic exists for you, oh Ponticus," Propertius writes to a friend,

> and sings of Thebes and its fratricidal war. And here, let me die if the only remaining rival you still have to best is not Homer! As for me, during that time, following my old habit, I shall occupy myself only with my loves [or: my *Loves*], I shall look for the the words that will move my inflexible mistress. I have no other choice. I am no less at the service of my talent than my unfortunate passion, and I deplore being at the cruelest age of life. This is the path I follow, it is my claim to fame, and I know that my poetry gets its fame from it. May it be acknowledged that I knew how to please a lettered woman, knew how to submit again and again to her unjust[26] reproaches, and that will be enough![27] Later, let scorned lovers not put my book down and let them learn to read my unhappiness! (I.7)[28]

Propertius lives for love and Ponticus writes a *Thebaid*. To be in love is the opposite of writing an epic. We can sense some disdain for that artificial and pompous genre. To sing of love is to be in love, but to sing of Achilles is not to become an Achilles oneself. The class dunce is a poet, while poor Ponticus is just someone good at writing on assigned themes.[29]

To love is to be an elegiac poet, not an epic poet. Now this does not necessarily mean to choose to be a pure literary type and to reject public service; there is nothing to prevent one from doing both. Gallus and Tibullus did so.[30] And although we are not told whether Propertius took up a public career, if he did not, he was only following the example of the majority of his equals. Only a small fraction of knights entered public life. Furthermore, among these knights, careerists or otherwise, was a group of golden youth who unduly prolonged the period of misbehavior permitted to adolescents by the indulgent Roman morality. These young men, who lost their virginity at the age of fourteen or fifteen,[31] went wenching in the hot streets, thrashed any bourgeois they happened to meet at night for a few laughs,[32] or, always in groups, broke down the door of a woman with a bad reputation and gang-raped her.[33] Around the age of twenty, they either settled down or took up a career – except for a handful of libertines who had many lower-class mistresses or one flashy one.[34]

Were the elegists part of these happy few? It is possible, but that is not what they talk about. They depict themselves in terms of features that combine love and the poet's ideal, and when they use the word "love," we can always hear "amorous poetry" at the same time. This quite deliberate double meaning is present in every line in Propertius's elegy to Ponticus and in many others as well. It is one of the most constant and noteworthy features of his work. After all, what is a poet? He is not someone who, among other things, sets out to write verses one day; he is someone who is born a poet as a king is born a king, who wears this mantle in the city and who submits to this honor as a fate imposed from without. Propertius and Tibullus do not affirm forthrightly and in the imperative, "Let us disdain power and money in favor of poetry and love." Instead, they indicate negatively and in the indicative that poets do not take up a career: that is the way they are; it is the discovery of an exceptional destiny rather than the choice of a lifestyle.

The distance that separates Roman erotic elegy from reality thus appears as large as that which separates it from bucolic. There were about as many poets who were like Ego in the literary circles of Rome as there were shepherd-poets such as are depicted as in the bucolics in the Italian countryside. For the combination of a love poet and an amorous man is the product of a fictional alchemy. Ego the poet is supposed to be amorous by the same logic that holds that the author of *Pantagruel* must have been a drunkard because he talks so much about drinking, if we are to believe this epitaph attributed to Ronsard:

> Good old Rabelais, who was always Drinking,
> So long as he lived;
> Never did the sun see him,
> Even at morning, when he was not drinking
> And never in the evening when night was dark,
> However late it was, was he seen when he wasn't drinking.[35]

The arbitrariness with which the elegy and the bucolic weave pieces of reality into their fiction is that complete.

When Ronsard thinks of Rabelais as one of his contemporaries, he well knows that the Touraine doctor is not a drunkard; yet as soon as he has to talk about Rabelais as a writer, he loses sight of this and falls into the *topos* that holds that the man must reflect the writer. Even though some sense of reality or coherence might have drawn him away from this dream, Ronsard, somewhat ill at ease, would not have known how else to express himself regarding the author of *Pantagruel* in order to hail his immortality. The same thing applied in Rome. When they thought about a writer, especially an author of love poetry, they drew upon two contrary ideas which, despite their appearances, were equally unrealistic. We are familiar with the first: a poet, considered from the point of view of eternity, must necessarily have been a lover if he sang of love. Yet the same poet, considered as a man and a citizen, will not be held responsible for the sins and libertinage he brags about in his verses. He will be presumed to have spoken this way for laughs and not for having loved.

The poet is assumed to have lied, thanks to a decision by the public conscience, which has decided it does not want to know. The factual question, whether or not a poet was inspired by his experience, is not asked. Yet the presumption of innocence does not immediately impose itself. In Catullus's day, an accused man absolved himself by reading to the jury some verses in which his accuser, "out of poetic playfulness, brags of having seduced a freeborn boy and a girl from a good family."[36] The jurors certainly did not believe in the reality of these monstrosities, but must have thought that the author of such verses ought not to be taken seriously. Catullus himself tries to warn against this mistrust of light verse by proclaiming that it "suffices that a poet should live chastely – his verses can be as unchaste as they please." He asks the same presumption of innocence for them as for their author.[37]

Is there a hint of immoral behavior here, or merely the offense of literary obscenity? Ovid pretends to confuse these two wrongs by defending himself against both in order to make us forget the offense in expression by justifying the more serious one of misconduct.[38] The offense in expression, moreover, is more than just one thing. Under the empire, a meter called hendecasyllable, different from that of elegy, was traditionally reserved for light verse.[39] The highest of personages, senators, the most serious of whom was Pliny the younger, wrote brilliant light verse in this form in order to get away from concerns about the public good and more learned labors, and no one saw anything wrong in it. Pliny was proud of his hendecasyllables and willingly conceded that they were daring, filled with jokes, love affairs, pains, and laments. His collection had such success that his verses were set to music.[40] Knowing that no one would take his poetic confessions seriously, Pliny was merely following the example of Cicero, who sang of the kisses he gathered from the lips of his slave and secretary Tiro.[41] To protest modestly that so classical an author could not have committed such an atrocity would require considerable ignorance of ancient realities.[42] But to swear that Cicero wrote such verses only once would require equal ignorance of the literary conventions of the day. The reader has no right to know, for to be a poet is to disguise oneself, not to express oneself. This was the operative principle. As Genette says, imitation, mimesis, is not a reproduction but a fiction; to imitate is to make something that looks like something.[43]

This principle is open to two interpretations. Either the poet's mantle is but a lovely mask and not the actual man, and Pliny is innocent of his light verses, or the cloak makes the poet and he no longer is an individual. The man is nothing more than the poet, like a priest or a king. Here the modern idea of sincerity makes no sense, or rather just the opposite is true. The individual cuts himself out according to the pattern of the poetic role; he does not go beyond the pattern but fills it out. The individual and the work are not two distinct instances linked by a causal relation, as when we assume that one makes poetry out of one's experiences or, conversely, that one becomes, from *mal du siècle*, what one sings about. There is no clear distinction; in the city, the Muses' performer continues to produce things while in costume. In other words, since erotic elegy is a kind of joke, our poets pretend to take seriously their role as the Muses' priest, knowing full well they will not be taken literally. Whence their pompous air. They come on stage in their poetry wearing their poet's mantle. "The sacred poets are turned into her image by their art. We lack ambition and cupidity, we prefer the darkness of a bed to the brilliance of public life. But we feel no repugnance at attaching ourselves to someone, and we love long and sincerely."[44] Indeed, there is nothing more intimate and inseparable than the attachment of a group of elegies to the beauty who is sung about in them.

To be a poet is not a profession but rather to belong to a somewhat odd species. Ego is a poet as a swan is a swan, now and for always. It would be vain to ask when he became a poet or what his first verses were. Ego is not a poet because he has written some verses; on the contrary, he writes verses because he is a poet. Just as a triangle has three angles by definition, to be a poet is an essence, but therefore it is also an abstraction: "Do not set him on the same footing as the nobles, the rich," says Propertius (II.24).[45] Can a poet then not be wealthy, wellborn, a Roman knight? Yes, concretely, but not in his poetic role. The noble's role was different. The knight Propertius probably gave money to more than one Cynthia in the lower world; the poet Propertius pays his Cynthia by immortalizing her.

That is why poetry was not distinguished from that which it sang. The poet, that performer of mimesis, that *mime* who "pretends," identifies himself by his role, lives his character. He is amorous just as he is a poet – in essence or outside of time.[46] Ego is not a man who became a poet because he happened to fall in love, any more than he is a poet who fell in love and then took his flame as the subject of his new pieces. He is eternally amorous, as a kind of orthodoxy. One is not a love poet because one has written erotic verses. On the contrary, one writes them because one is an amorous poet and only writes such things, just as an apple tree only gives apples.

Love and poetry are indistinguishable not just because the one goes along with the other but, insofar as the poet's head seems to be filled with such ideas, because he says things about love that can only be true in poetry and vice versa. A soothsayer tells Propertius his fate, and tells it in the imperative, as a fatality he cannot escape and a vocation he must follow:

> Forge elegies, those deceptive works – doing this will be your military service – so that the throng of other poets will follow your example. You will know[47] the warlike blandishments of Venus, you will serve under her, and you will be an ideal target for the Loves, her children. (IV.1)[48]

In that age, when the streets served as cemeteries, and when travelers leaving cities had to walk between two rows of tombs, the haughty poet does not want to follow the common route:

> My God, do not allow my Cynthia [or: my *Cynthia*] to put my ashes in some busy place where crowds are constantly passing by! When a lover is under the ground, that would be to dishonor him. Better to be buried at the foot of a tree, far from the highway, or even under the anonymous protection of a pile of dirt. I do not want to have a name for great routes. (III.16)[49]

The refined poet wants no part of vulgar glory. Coming from the lover he claims to be, this wish makes little sense. It is the wish of a haughty poet who does not believe immortality lies along the way of mere versifiers.

Cynthia is a book. To love is to write and to be loved, to be read. In the end, Cynthia is both the book, what the book talks about, and its reader. The poet immortalizes himself by immortalizing her, and *Cynthia* will outlive him.[50] Thus two themes that are harped on by the elegists are superimposable: the service of love, through which the poet refuses any other career than loving, and the refusal to write an epic, or the *recusatio*, through which he indicates that he will only write verses about love. Every lover militates in his own way and pines for his love, says Ovid (1.9), but so does every poet. He is too occupied with his verses to take up the service of the state (1.15). Which means that Roman erotic elegy has no other referent than itself. The poet is in love because the love he speaks about exists only in his verses.[51]

"Not marble, nor the gilded monuments of princes shall outlive this powerful rhyme." This is how Shakespeare promised immortality to his young beloved, wanting to see her fragile grace as immortal. Ronsard promised immortality to real women because the flesh is responsive to celebrity and because immortality makes one think about death, which is not far off, and the thought of death incites one to taste the joys of life. Propertius, in two lovely lines, promises immortality to his Cynthia and brags about the imperishable monument he has erected to her beauty — and also to his own talent:

> Happy the woman that my book has been able to celebrate! These verses are as monuments to your beauty. For neither the Pyramids, which lift their cost to the skies, nor the temple of Jupiter of Olympus, which is as high as the sky, nor the opulent luxury of Mausolus's tomb can escape the final obligation of dying. Fire or rain will wipe away their glory, the shock of the years will pull down their overly weighty mass. But a great name acquired through talent will not fall

out of the flow of time[52] – the glory reserved for talent does not perish. (III.2)[53]

By putting Cynthia among the ranks of literary heroines, along with Catullus's Lesbia and Gallus's Lycoris, Propertius "gloriously takes his place alongside these poets" (II.34).[54]

Love affairs of the writing desk, which end when the poet elevates himself to a higher species. For Propertius, who dreams of Empedocles or Lucretius more than of Homer, this higher genre is not epic but philosophy, "physics."[55] "When the weight of years cuts short my pleasures and the gray of old age is scattered among my dark hair, then it shall be my purpose to study the ways of Nature and how[56] the god can govern the whole household of the cosmos" (III.5).[57] Toward the end of book III, it looks as though the decision to abandon Cynthia and light poetry for higher intellectual pursuits has been taken: "I must take the great voyage to learned Athens, so that the long route will free me from the weight of love."[58] There he will listen to the lessons given by Plato's successors, study Demosthenes and Menander, and admire statues and paintings (III.21). Cynthia, who only existed because of love and Propertius's verses, will fall back into nonexistence: "You are wrong, woman, to count so much on your beauty and to have become so arrogant for having been seen by my eyes.[59] It was from my passion, Cynthia, that your merits came to you; you do not like to think that your celebrity comes from my verses."[60] For the luster of Cynthia's face is a borrowed one (III.24).

Love has poetry as its referent. Let us be clear about what we mean. The Roman elegists were not fools, they were amused by their deliberate confusions. In fact, one of their predecessors, a Hellenistic poet, had pushed the joke even further. He pretended that Homer was in love with Penelope; he must have been, having sung so well of that heroine and her fidelity.[61] But all that these witty games did was pleasantly to exaggerate everyone's idea about an author and the relations between a man and his work.

A work does not resemble its author. Just the opposite, they held. When one thought of a writer – a Homer, a Propertius, or later a Rabelais – one did not imagine a flesh-and-blood person with all those human weaknesses so dear to Sainte-Beuve or a person who, like all craftsmen, maintained a rather distant and complicated relationship with his productions. One imagined a poet in full costume, on stage, bearing all the attributes of his role, the cup of the Pantagruelic drunkard or the tears and scars of love. One did not infer from the work, in the name of some theory of expression, that the author must have been a lover; one was *looking* at a lover who sang.

By a deceptive coincidence, both ancient and modern readers seem similarly convinced that the elegists must have sung of their feelings. It is a false unanimity, however, for their reasons are just the opposite of each other. Moderns would pooh-pooh the idea that Homer loved Penelope since he sang of her, but hold that Propertius sang of Cynthia because he loved her (or so they believe). The ancient conception and that of modern readers ought to meet on one point, however, since they come at each other from opposite directions. The ancients start from mimesis. Like a king, the individual cannot be distinguished from his public role, and they take his disguise for the man himself. Moderns, on the other hand, start from the romantic idea of sincerity: far from disguising himself, the individual expresses his truth through his work.

Ancients and moderns, therefore, read two contrary truths in a famous piece of commentary on the elegists propounded by the philology of antiquity. According to this ancient key, "Catullus employed the pseudonym of Lesbia for the real name Clodia, Propertius gave Cynthia as a pseudonym for a Hostia, and Tibullus was thinking of a certain Plania when he wrote the name Delia in his verses."[62] For the ancients, Cynthia was this Hostia; for moderns, a certain Hostia was the reason for the poetic creation of Cynthia. The ancients thought of an immediate equivalence and looked no further; for moderns, the passage from Hostia to Cynthia implies a whole elaboration, full of all the mysteries of creation and expression; it is not enough, when faced with the pseudonym Cynthia, simply to fill the blank on a questionnaire, telling what her "real name" was. What is important for modern readers is to have some confirmation (or so they believe) that Propertius opened his heart to us, thanks to our knowledge about the existence of a model for Cynthia. The ancients did not go so far. When they tell us that Lesbia was a certain Clodia, they are handing us a key comparable to the many keys bequeathed to us by the seventeenth century for La Bruyère: Who was the real Distrait? The real bird collector? This makes us smile. We will exclaim that an artist like La Bruyère synthesized, stylized, or imagined things more than he copied nature. In the studios of painters and sculptors, the "model" serves more as a reminder. In short, the "key" in our eyes is a starting point; for the ancients, it was the last word as regards knowledge, the key to the riddle. What was important to their taste for erudition was to know what Cynthia's real name was, for readers had understood a work when they knew *what it was talking about*. As Riffaterre says, "the whole effort of philology was to reconstitute lost realities," or to perpetuate their memory, "for fear that the poem would die along with its referent."[63]

Whereas for us a poet is someone who expresses himself, the ancients collapsed these two cases, which is why Catullus, Propertius, and Tibullus give their Ego their own name. "Are you going to die of love, then, oh Propertius," Cynthia's lover asks himself, bringing his everyday name into the scene, whereas a modern poet is a person who uses the convenience of the scene in order to tell everyone about his or her human truth. Propertius and Ronsard play at being amorous poets,[64] Hugo and Shelley are lovers who express themselves sincerely. Every society looks at literature in terms of its conception of the author. The ancients believed that Propertius or even

Homer loved Cynthia or even Penelope. We ourselves have believed that Aragon adored Elsa for forty years, without ever tiring of her, but for a contrary reason. Far from confusing the mask with the face, we hold that poetry that is merely a mask is an insincere form poetry, not a serious form. The hypothesis of an insincere form of poetry is intolerable to our sensibility. We did sense something false in the case of Aragon, and Ronsard ought to have been somewhat bothered by the idea of Rabelais as a drunkard, but, lacking a framework to think about it, the idea remained buried in our unconscious. When the death of Elsa was not followed by the deluge of alexandrines that everyone expected and awaited, a few frustrated natures held it personally against Aragon that they had been fooled by him for such a long time – or rather had fooled themselves.

One quick, final word about an issue that must intrigue the typical reader, that of the origins of Roman erotic elegy. Either we ask a superficial question: who invented the use of "I" in an elegiac meter for talk about love? Or we ask ourselves where the essence of this type of elegy comes from, that is, the whole semiotic described in this and the preceding chapter: the pastoral in city clothes, the identification of the man with his profession as poet, the mirror play and contradictions presented to the reader, the jestingly grand passion for an irregular, etc. In the second case, the answer is a formal one: this quite peculiar and ingenious semiotics was a Hellenistic creation. For a good reason: it is already to be found, fully armed from head to toe, before Propertius and Tibullus, in the work of someone twenty years older than they, the poet Horace, who made use of it in lyric or iambic meters, in his *Epodes* and *Odes*. In other words, for a Roman poet this semiotics was already a consecrated and traditional instrument. For a Roman, Greek culture went without saying. It was culture per se. It is this same semiotic instrument that Virgil pastiched in his tenth bucolic, when Propertius was ten years old. Or, to be more precise, this semiotics was already sketched out in the oldest erotic poets of the *Greek Anthology*, a century or two before our Roman authors. The brevity of their little poems, which were often elegiac, prevented these poets from fully unfolding its whole structure, but the essential is there: the displaying of libertinism and the humor.

Notes

1 H. Fränkel, *Ovid, ein Dichter zwischen zwei Welten* (Darmstadt: 1970), p. 25.
2 *Bucolics*, X.50–51. The Sicilian poet must be the bucolic writer Theocrites, the one from Chalcis, the elegist Euphorion.
3 As Genette writes, people never pastiche, parody, or imitate a text but only the genre or style the text represents. (G. Genette, *Palimpsestes: La littérature au second degré*, (Paris: 1982), p. 82.)
4 "What Virgil does in *Buc.* 10 is to maintain the ambiguity between *writing bucolic poetry* and *being a shepherd*" (G. Williams, *Tradition and Originality in Roman Poetry* (Oxford: 1968), p. 237, his emphasis).

5 On the literary theme of the delights of love, see the selections in Spies, *Militat omnis amans*; cf. N. Zagagi, *Tradition and Originality in Plautus: Studies in Amatory Motifs in Plautine Comedy* (Göttingen: 1980), pp. 109ff. On the actual lifestyle that may have corresponded to this *topos*, see J.-P. Boucher, *Etudes sur Properce: Problèmes d'inspiration et d'art* (Paris: 1965), pp. 17–23.

6 "Senators and knights, they are two orders but one class" (R. Syme, *History in Ovid* (Oxford: 1978) p. 114).

7 Ovid, *Ars Amatoria*, II.233, cf. 216; *Amores*, 1.9 in toto.

8 Horace, *Odes*, III:26: "My vocation was the service of young women and my service record was not without its glory. As a votive offering, here are my veteran's arms, that is, my lyre." Here once again, making love and singing about it are mixed together.

9 *Pacis Amor deus est, pacem veneramur amantes.* (Prop., p. 188)

10 We may understand this as follows: "Make our vassals return to the duty they have forgotten." However, this image of a harsh leader would be less flattering than that of a just one, merciful toward the empire's subjects. The indications in Dio Cassius, LIII.14.6, point in the same direction.

11 *Tu patrui meritas conare anteire secures,*
   et vetera oblitis iura refer sociis.
nam tua non aetas umquam cessavit amori,
   semper et armatae cura fuit patriae;
et tibi non umquam nostros puer iste labores
   afferat et lacrimis omnia nota meis!
me sine, quem semper voluit fortuna iacere,
   hanc animam extremae reddere nequitiae.
multi longinquo periere in amore libenter,
   in quorum numero me quoque terra tegat.
non ego sum laudi, non natus idoneus armis:
   hanc me militiam fata subire volunt.
                    (Prop., pp. 16–18)

12 *Nullus de nostro sanguine miles erit.* (Prop., p. 82)

13 *Pulsabant alii frustra dominamque vocabant:*
   mecum habuit positum lenta puella caput.
haec mihi devictis potior victoria Parthis,
   haec spolia, haec reges, haec mihi currus erunt.
                    (Prop., p. 102)

14 Cicero, *De Oratore*, II.55.224.

15 Cicero, *In Verrem*, III.96.224: *genus cogendae pecuniae senatorium*. In Propertius, III.12, Postumus abandons his young wife out of vanity as well as greed, to go make a career in some province.

16 *Divitias alius fulvo sibi congerat auro*
   et teneat culti iugera multa soli,
quem labor adsiduus vicino terreat hoste,
   Martia cui somnos classica pulsa fugent:
me mea paupertas vita traducat inerti,
   dum meus adsiduo luceat igne focus.
                    (Tib., p. 192)

17 *Nec tamen est quisquam, sacros qui laedat amantes:*
   Scironis media sic licet ire via. . . .

luna ministrat iter, demonstrant astra salebras,
  ipse Amor accensas praecutit ante faces,
saeva canum rabies morsus avertit hiantis.

(Prop., p. 234)

18 Horace, *Odes*, I.22; cf. Fränkel, *Horace*, p. 186.

19 Horace, *Odes*, I.1.

20 "Varied truly are our thoughts. Varied are the ways of men. The joiner wants to find a breakage, the medicine-man an accident, the brāhmin-priest a worshipper" (*Rig Veda*, IX.112 [trans. Thomas, in *A Source Book in Indian Philosophy*, ed. Sarvepalli Radhakrishnan and Charles Moore, p. 35]). "The man who knows how to seduce his contemporaries will have the favor of the court, the man who gives satisfaction to the people will be an administrator, the soldier will love war, the jurists will expand their power of government. . . . In sum, all people have their own occupations and cannot fail to act" (Chuang-Tzu, trans. Kia Hway [Paris: Gallimard, 1969], p. 197). "Those who are in love will sing of their love. . . . Those who love the arts, the sciences, will say so. . . . I, who am unhappy, I will complain about my unhappiness" (Du Bellay, *Regrets*, VI). "Seamen, seamen! unfurl your sails! . . . Envious ones, grovel at the bases of statues. . . . I will contemplate God, the father of the world" (Hugo, *Les Rayons et les Ombres*, XVI). "Everyone works in his own way" (Solon, fragment 1.44 of his *Elegies*).

21 U. Schmid, *Der Priamel der Werte im Griechischen von Homer bis Paulus* (Wiesbaden: 1964); H. Fränkel, *Early Greek Poetry and Philosophy: A History of Greek Epic, Lyric and Prose to the Middle of the Fifth Century*, trans. Moses Hadas and James Willis (New York: 1975), pp. 459, 471, 487; idem, *Wege und Formen frühgriechischen Denkens*, 2nd edn. (Munich: 1960), p. 90, cf. p. 68; E. Bréguet, "Le Thème 'alius-ego' chez les poètes latins," *Revue des études latines* 40 (1962): p. 128. W. Kröhling, *Die Priamel (Beispielreihurg) als Stilmittel in der griechischen-römischen Dichtung* (Greifswald: 1935). A list of questions dear to ancient Greek poetry has to be distinguished from the *priamel*: "What is the most beautiful thing, the most just, the largest, etc., in the world?"

22 The *priamel* "is itself an elaborately casual way of making a point about oneself by considering first the contrasting ideas of the rest of the world" (Williams, *Tradition and Originality*, p. 763).

23 In Pindar's ninth Olympian Ode, at the end, the *priamel* is a lesson in modesty: human beings are not all called to the same vocation, but in any vocation perfection is difficult to attain. In the first Pythian Ode, recalling the good points of all men (the victories over the Medes by Athens and Sparta, that over the Etruscans by the Cumaeans) is a way of not making them jealous over the praise being given.

24 *Navita de ventis, de tauris narrat arator,*
  enumerat miles vulnera, pastor oves;
nos contra angusto versantes proelia lecto.

(Prop., pp. 64–66)

25 *Quaeris, Demophoon, cur sim tam mollis in omnis?*
  quod quaeris, "quare" non habet ullus amor.
cur aliquis sacris laniat sua bracchia cultris
  et Phrygis insanos caeditur ad numeros?
uni cuique dedit vitium natura creato:
  mi fortuna aliquid semper amare dedit.

(Prop., p. 124)

26 These are quite calculated equivocations: "to please a female reader," "to please a female lover." The lover, moreover, is both the reader and the book itself (Cynthia

reads *Cynthia*, which talks about Cynthia). This literary activity (reading and writing at the same time) is put on the same level as love: to write or read about love are not to be distinguished from making it. Unhappy love: loving gets confused with suffering and being a slave. To make love is to be a slave and a poet – this is the complete system of Propertius's relations.

27 Here *solum* has to be an adverb, in the sense of *tantum*, as in 11.34.26.

28 *Dum tibi Cadmeae dicuntur, Pontice, Thebae*
  armaque fraternae tristia militiae,
 atque, ita sim felix, primo contendis Homero,
  (sint modo fata tuis mollia carminibus:)
 nos, ut consuemus, nostros agitamus amores,
  atque aliquid duram quaerimus in dominam;
 nec tantum ingenio quantum servire dolori
  cogor et actatis tempora dura queri.
 hic mihi conteritur vitae modus, haec mea fama est,
  hinc cupio nomen carminis ire mei.
 me laudent doctae solum placuisse puellae,
  Pontice, et iniustas saepe tulisse minas;
 me legat assidue post haec neglectus amator,
  et prosint illi cognita nostra mala.
  (Prop., p. 18)

29 Here is the end of this elegy, which is of capital importance for seeing the perpetual game Propertius makes of talking about love and being in love: If you yourself, oh Ponticus, should fall in love (which I do not wish for you, since love is a plague), you will quickly forget Thebes [that is, your *Thebaid*, an epic poem about Thebes – a poem is not to be distinguished from what it talks about]. Then you will want to write verses about love, but too late – the age of learning [or loving?] will have passed for you. Then you will be jealous of me. As a lover? Propertius does not say so. He says, as a love poet. For I shall be admired and young people will say at my tomb: you were the poet who wrote about our passions. Therefore do not scorn my verses, otherwise Love will avenge me by making you suffer love in spades: whoever loves late loves all the more.

Te quoque si certo puer hic concusserit arcu,
  (quod nolim nostros evoluisse deos)
 longe castra tibi, longe miser agmina septem
  flebis in aeterno surda iacere situ;
 et frustra cupies mollem componere versum,
  nec tibi subiciet carmina serus Amor.
 tum me non humilem mirabere saepe poetam,
  tunc ego Romanis praeferar ingeniis;
 nec poterunt iuvenes nostro reticere sepulcro
  "Ardoris nostri magne poeta, iaces."
 tu cave nostra tuo contemnas carmina fastu:
  saepe venit magno faenore tardus Amor.
  (Prop., pp. 18–20)

30 Gallus was one of the great politicians during the reign of Augustus. On the career of Tibullus (*Aquitanico bello militaribus donis donatus*, says his *Vita*, which means that he was a general, and a general when it came to talent), see for example, Williams, *Tradition and Originality*, p. 559; F. Cairns, *Tibullus: A Hellenistic Poet at Rome* (Cambridge: 1979), p. 145. In his verses, even while professing his service to love, Tibullus does not hesitate to let it be understood that, by

disobeying the laws of Love, he made the error of having a career. There is no relation between this theme of service to love and his biography.

31 The custom was that boys fourteen or fifteen years old, as soon as they had put on their men's clothing (the "virile toga"), went straight to the low life quarter (Subura). For example, Propertius himself, III.15.3–4; Martial, XI.78.11; Persius, V.30. Physicians quite naturally identified the age of puberty with that of initial sexual relations (Rufus of Ephesus in Oribasius, VI.38), and for Celsus, *De medicina*, III.23, the first sexual relation for boys is paralleled to the menses of girls. But not for long. From the age of Seneca onward, a sort of children's crusade gets under way to delay the age when boys lose their virginity (cf. Seneca, *Ad Marciam*, XXIV.3); Marcus Aurelius, I.17, praises himself for not having performed the virile act until as late as possible. On such praises to the *sera Venus*, delayed love, see A. D. Nock, *Essays on Religion in the Ancient World*, ed. Z. Stewart (Oxford: 1973), 1:479. Tacitus's Germans, those splendid types, only made Venus's acquaintance in this way at a late date (Tacitus, *Germania*, XX.4). Physicians advised gymnastics for impatient young people (Soranos, *Gynaikeia*, chap. XCII, p. 209 [Dietz]), for premature sexual relations hamper the development of soul and body (Athenais, in Oribasio, vol. III, p. 165 [Bussemaker-Daremberg]). Whence the custom of the *infibulatio*, well known to Martial and Celsus. A small matter perhaps, but it illustrates in its domain the passage from the *homo politicus* to the *homo interior* (as Pierre Hadot puts it) that characterized the years 50–300 of our era, for which Christianity is just one factor (and in no way the cause).

32 On these folkloric kinds of violence, see P. Veyne "Le Folklore à Rome et les droits de la conscience publique sur la conduite individuelle," *Latomus* 42 (1983): 3–30. Undoubtedly they ended up as gang rape.

33 The Hellenistic bucolic, the Roman ode, and the Roman elegy often allude to the nocturnal custom of young men attacking the door of a courtesan and forcing their way in, probably to pay their compliments to her. Some may reproach these folkloric kinds of violence, which were traditional and tolerated among the young, particularly the custom of gang rape: what is soiled may be soiled with impunity. This is a custom that still exists today in Lebanon (for example), and it was well known in ancient France (J. Rossiaud, "La Prostitution dans les villes françaises au XVe siècle," *Communications* 35 (1982): p. 75). Such an attack on houses of ill repute was known in Rome: Aulus-Gellius, IV.14; *Digest*, XLVII.2.39 (40).

34 On the showy mistress, see all of Cicero's *Pro Caelio*. For the idea that youth must pass, see ibid., XII.28, and Tacitus, *Annales*, XIII.12–13, where we find Seneca approving of Nero's adultery with Acte, for it is better that the adolescent emperor deceive his wife Octavia with a freedwoman than with the wife of some senator. On the *delicata juventus* in the time of Cicero, see J. Griffin, "Augustan Poetry and the Life of Luxury," *Journal of Roman Studies* 46 (1976): pp. 89–90, who writes that in Cicero's eyes this group of young libertines, ready for political violence, "almost . . . constituted a political party," rightly or wrongly.

35 This epitaph for Rabelais was one of the poems that were later suppressed in the *Bocage royal* of 1544.

36 Valerius-Maximus, VIII.1, abs. 8.

37 Catullus, XVI.4; cf. Martial, XI.15; Apuleius, *Apology*, XI; Pliny, *Epistulae*, IV. 14.3; Ovid, *Tristes*, II.354.

38 Ovid, *Tristes*, II.421f.; II.339ff. His main claim is that his exile was based on a misunderstanding – his life was censured for the doubtful faith expressed in his verses (*Tristes*, II.7).

39 Quintilian, 1.8.6.

40 Pliny, *Epistulae*, IV.14.5; VII.4.6; VII.26.2; on the light verses of Arruntius, see Pliny, IV.3.3–4; IV.18; V.15; Statius, *Silvae*, I.2.100 and 197.

41 Cicero, quoted by Pliny, *Epistulae*, VII.4.6.

42 He was pushed into doing it.

43 G. Genette, *Introduction à l'architexte*, (Paris: 1979), p. 42.

44 Ovid, *Ars Amatoria*, III.539.

45   *Quamvis nec sanguine avito*
nobilis et quamvis non ita dives eras.
(Prop., p. 132)

46 Propertius (II.22), who thereby wrongly seems unfaithful to Cynthia, says that he always has some love or other on his mind. We are to understand that he is eternally in love, just as a triangle is, by definition, eternally a triangle.

47 "You will know the service of love," *militiam Veneris patiere*. Literally, "your fate will be to serve under Venus." *Patior* means "this or that happened to me," like the Greek *paschein* (in Aristotle, the accident that a substance undergoes "happens" to it); *kakos pascho* means "some misfortune happened to me," and *miranda patior*: "something extraordinary happened to me."

48 *At tu finge elegos, fallax opus: — haec tua castra!—*
scribat ut exemplo cetera turba tuo.
militiam Veneris blandis patiere sub armis,
et Veneris pueris utilis hostis eris.
(Prop., p. 274)

49 *Di faciant, mea ne terra locet ossa frequenti,*
qua facit assiduo tramite vulgus iter!
post mortem tumuli sic infamantur amantum.
me tegat arborea devia terra coma,
aut humer ignotae cumulis vallatus harenae:
non iuvat in media nomen habere via.
(Prop., p. 234)

50 We have already pointed out this confusion above, in note 26, regarding Propertius 1.7; see also II.11; II.13; II.26b. It is the theme of Cynthia as a literate young woman.

51 The confusion was facilitated by the ancient way of titling books. Often the title was merely a designation of its contents, as when a bottle of wine has the word "wine" on its lable. In that age, a "treatise on physics" would be titled *Nature, De Natura Rerum*; a treatise on acoustics would be *On Sounds*, for to "study acoustics" was to "study sounds." When someone told of his loves, the collection was titled *Loves*.

52 The meaning is unclear. It may also mean "not fall away from the effect of the flow of time."

53 *Fortunata, meo si qua est celebrata libello!*
carmina erunt formae tot monumenta tuae.
nam neque Pyramidum sumptus ad sidera ducti,
nec Iovis Elei caelum imitata domus,
nec Mausolei dives fortuna sepulcri
mortis ab extrema condicione vacant.
aut illis flamma aut imber subducit honores,
annorum aut ictus pondere victa ruent.
at non ingenio quaesitum nomen ab aevo
excidet: ingenio stat sine morte decus.
(Prop., p. 180)

54 *Hos inter si me ponere Fama volet.* (Prop., p. 172)
55 Similarly, the author of *Ciris*, in his prologue, admits future philosophical ambitions.
56 "How the god," and not "what god." For this sense of *quis*, see F. Bader, "De Lat. 'arduus' à Lat. 'orior,'" *Revue de philologie* 54 (1980): p. 274, nn. 32, 34.
57 *Atque ubi iam Venerem gravis interceperit aetas,*
   sparserit et nigras alba senecta comas,
   tum mihi naturae libeat perdiscere mores,
   quis deus hanc mundi temperet arte domum.
                    (Prop., p. 190)
58 *Magnum iter ad doctas proficisci cogor Athenas,*
   ut me longa gravi solvat amore via.
                    (Prop., p. 246)
59 This seems to me to be the meaning of this line.
60 *Falsa est ista tuae, mulier, fiducia formae,*
   olim oculis nimium facta superba meis.
   noster amor tales tribuit tibi, Cynthia, laudes.
   versibus insignem te pudet esse meis?
                    (Prop., p. 256)
61 Hermesianax, *Elegies*, in Athenaeus, XIII.597EF.
62 Apuleius, *Apology*, X.2.
63 M. Riffaterre, *La Production du texte*, (Paris: 1979), p. 176.
64 Consider also the few autobiographies that have come down to us of ancient poets. They do not tell about their private life, or even their poetic career, but rather the way in which they upheld the role of poets. See G. Misch, *Geschichte der Autobiographie*. 3rd edn. (Bern: 1949), I:1, pp. 299ff.

MISTRESS AND METAPHOR IN AUGUSTAN ELEGY

Maria Wyke

1. Written and living women

A pressing problem confronts work on the women of ancient Rome: a need to determine the relation between the realities of women's lives and their representation in literature. Several of the volumes on women in antiquity that have appeared in the 1980s expose the methodological problems associated with any study of women in literary texts,[1] but few of their papers have yet investigated the written women of Rome.[2] In any study of the relations between written and living women, however, the heroines of Augustan elegy deserve particular scrutiny because the discourse in which they appear purports to be an author's personal confession of love for his mistress. The texts of Latin love poetry are frequently constructed as first-person, authorial narratives of desire for women who are individuated by name, physique, and temperament. This poetic technique tempts us to suppose that, in some measure, elegy's female subjects reflect the lives of specific Augustan women.

Moreover, in presenting a first-person narrator who is indifferent to marriage and subject to a mistress, the elegiac texts pose a question of important social dimensions: if Augustan love poetry focuses on a female subject who apparently operates outside the traditional constraints of marriage and motherhood, could it constitute the literary articulation of an unorthodox place for women in the world? This question has generated considerable controversy, as the debate between Judith Hallett and Aya Betensky in *Arethusa* (1973, 1974) reveals.[3]

In particular, the corpus of Propertian poems seems to hold out the hope that we may read *through* the written woman, Cynthia, to a living mistress. Poem 1.3, for example, conjures up before its readers a vision of an autobiographical event. The first-person narrator recalls the night he arrived late and drunk by his mistress's bed. The remembered occasion unfolds through time, from the moment of the lover's arrival to his beloved's awakening. The details of the beloved's sleeping posture, her past cruelty, and her present words of reproach all seem further to authenticate the tale. The portrait of a Cynthia possessed of a beautiful body, a bad temper, and direct speech inclines us to believe that she once lived beyond the poetic world as a flesh and blood mistress of an Augustan poet.[4]

Even the existence of Cynthia within a literary work appears to be explained away. Poem 1.8 creates the illusion that it constitutes a fragment of a real conversation. The persistent employment of the second-person pronoun, the punctuation of the text by questions and wishes that center on "you," turns the poem itself into an event. As we read, Cynthia is being implored to remain at Rome with her poet. Subsequently, we are told that this poetic act of persuasion has been successful:

> hanc ego non auro, non Indis flectere conchis,
> sed potui blandi carminis obsequio.
> sunt igitur Musae, neque amanti tardus Apollo,
> quis ego fretus amo: Cynthia rara mea est!

> Her I, not with gold, not with Indian pearls, could
> turn, but with a caressing song's compliance.
> There are Muses then, and, for a lover, Apollo is not slow:
> on these I relying love: rare Cynthia is mine! (1.8.39–42)[5]

Writing poetry, on this account, is only the instrument of an act of courtship. The text itself encourages us to overlook its status as an Augustan poetry-book and to search beyond it for the living mistress it seems to woo.

There are, however, some recognized dangers in responding to Propertian poetry in this way, for the apparently personal confession of a poet's love is permeated with literary concerns and expressed in highly stylized and conventional terms. Even the female figures of the elegiac corpus – Propertius's Cynthia, Tibullus's Delia and Nemesis, Ovid's Corinna – display highly artful features.[6] Thus, once we acknowledge that elegy's debt to poetic conventions and Hellenistic writing practices is so extensive as to include in its compass the depiction of elegy's heroines, we are forced to call into question any simple relation between elegiac representations and the realities of women's lives in Augustan Rome. But if the relation between representation and reality is not a simple one, what then is its nature?

In the last few decades one answer to this question has gained particular currency. The extreme biographical methodology of the nineteenth and early twentieth centuries – the search for close correspondences between the individual characters and events of the text and those of its author and his milieu – has long since been abandoned. Nor has the opposite view, that elegy's ladies are entirely artificial constructs, proved satisfactory; for, like the Platonic assessment of literary processes, the theory that Latin erotic discourse is modelled on Hellenistic literature, which is itself modelled on Hellenistic life, leaves Augustan poetry and its female subjects at several removes from reality. Recently, critics have preferred to seek accounts of the relation between representation and reality that accommodate the literariness of elegiac writing and yet keep elegy's written women placed firmly on the map of the Augustan world.

Poets, we are told, deal in "verbal artefacts," yet their poetry "adumbrates," "embodies," or "emblazons" life.[7] Love elegy, it is argued, is neither an open window affording glimpses of individual Roman lives, nor a mirror offering their clear reflection, but a *picture* of Roman realities over which has been painted a dignifying, idealizing veneer of poetic devices.[8] Idioms such as these form the ingredients of a critical discourse that does not treat elegiac poems as accurate, chronological documents of an author's affairs, but still describes their stylized heroines as somehow concealing specific Augustan girlfriends.[9] In the vocabulary of this revised critical language, Cynthia, and possibly Delia, are not the mirror images of living women, but their transposed reflections.

Thus the realism of the elegiac texts continues to tempt us. While reading of women who possess some realistic features, we may think that – once we make some allowances for the distortions that a male lover's perspective and a poet's self-conscious literary concerns may impose – we still have an opportunity to reconstruct the lives of some real Augustan mistresses. Controversy arises, however, when we ask exactly what allowances should be made. Is the process of relating women in poetic texts to women in society simply a matter of removing a veneer of poetic devices to disclose the true picture of living women concealed beneath?

It is precisely because readers of Cynthia have encountered such difficulties as these that I propose to explore aspects of the problematic relations between women in texts and women in society by focusing on the Propertian corpus of elegiac poems. My purpose is, first, to survey approaches to the issue of elegiac realism and by placing renewed emphasis on Cynthia as a *written* woman to argue that she should be related not to the love life of her poet but to the "grammar" of his poetry; second, to demonstrate that the poetic discourse of which she forms a part is firmly engaged with and shaped by the political, moral, and literary discourses of the Augustan period, and therefore that to deny Cynthia an existence outside poetry is not to deny her a relation to society; and, third, to suggest that a study of elegiac metaphors and their application to elegiac mistresses may provide a fruitful means of reassessing one particular set of relations between written and living women.

2. Augustan girl friends/elegiac women

The first-person narratives of the elegiac texts and their partial realism entice us. They lead us to suppose that these texts form poetic paintings of reality and their female subjects poetic portraits of real women. Yet realism itself is a quality of a text, not a direct manifestation of a "real" world. Analysis of textual realism discloses that it is not natural but conventional. To create the aesthetic effect of an open window onto a "reality" lying just beyond, literary works employ a number of formal strategies that change through time and between discourses.[10]

As early as the 1950s, Archibald Allen drew attention to this disjunction between realism and reality in the production of Augustan elegy. He noted that the realism of the Propertian corpus is partial since, for example, it does not extend to the provision of a convincing chronology for a supposedly extratextual affair. And, focusing on the issue of "sincerity," Allen argued that the ancient world was capable of drawing a distinction that we should continue to observe, between a poet's art and his life. From Catullus to Apuleius, ancient writers could claim that poetry was distinct from its poet and ancient readers could construe "sincere" expressions of personal passion as a function of poetic style.[11]

More recently, Paul Veyne has pursued the idea that the *I* of ancient poets belongs to a different order than do later '*Is*' and has suggested that *ego* confers a naturalness on elegy that ancient readers would have recognized as spurious. Exploring the quality of *ego* in elegy's narrative, Veyne further argues that the ancient stylistic rules for "sincerity" observed in the Catullan corpus were scarcely obeyed in Augustan love elegy. Full of traditional poetic conceits, literary games, mannerisms, and inconsistencies, the texts themselves raise doubts about their potential as autobiography.[12]

Both these readings of elegiac first-person narratives warn us to be cautious in equating a stylistic realism with Augustan reality. But what of the particular realist devices used to depict women? Some modern critics think, for example, that the elegiac texts do offer sufficient materials from which to sketch the characteristics and habits of their authors' girlfriends or, at the very least, contain scattered details that together make up plausible portraits. From couplets of the Propertian corpus, John Sullivan assembles a physique for Cynthia:

> She had a milk-and-roses complexion. Her long blonde hair was either over-elaborately groomed or else, in less guarded moments, it strayed over her forehead in disarray . . . Those attractive eyes were black. She was tall, with long slim fingers.[13]

Oliver Lyne adds credible psychological characteristics:

> We find a woman of fine artistic accomplishments who is also fond of the lower sympotic pleasures; superstitious, imperious, wilful, fearsome in temper – but plaintive if she chooses, or feels threatened; pleasurably passionate – again if she chooses. I could go on: Propertius provides a lot of detail, direct and circumstantial. But the point I

simply want to make is that the figure who emerges is rounded and credible: a compelling 'coúrtesan' amateur or professional.[14]

An ancient tradition seems to provide some justification for this process of extracting plausible portraits of Augustan girlfriends out of the features of elegiac poetry-books. Some two centuries after the production of elegy's written women, in *Apologia* 10, Apuleius listed the "real" names that he claimed lay behind the elegiac labels *Cynthia* and *Delia*. Propertius, we are informed, hid his mistress Hostia behind *Cynthia* and Tibullus had Plania in mind when he put *Delia* in verse. If we accept these identifications then, however stylized, idealized, or mythicized the elegiac women Cynthia and Delia may be, their titles are to be read as pseudonyms and their textual characteristics as reflections of the features of two extratextual mistresses.[15]

There are, however, a number of problems that attach themselves to this procedure, for the process of extricating real women from realist techniques involves methodological inconsistencies. Beginning with an ancient tradition that does not offer "real" names to substitute for *Nemesis* or *Corinna*, the procedure is not uniformly applied. The inappropriateness of attempting to assimilate Ovid's Corinna to a living woman is generally recognized. Because the text in which she appears easily reads as a playful travesty of earlier love elegy, most commentators would agree with the view that Corinna is not a poetic depiction of a particular person, but a generalized figure of the Mistress.[16]

As a poeticized girlfriend, a transposed reflection of reality, the second Tibullan heroine has likewise aroused suspicion. David Bright offers detailed support for an earlier reading of Nemesis "as a shadowy background for conventional motifs."[17] Nor does he find that this fictive Mistress is preceded by at least one poeticized girlfriend in the Tibullan corpus. The first Tibullan heroine, Delia, also seems to be entangled in elegy's literary concerns, as the characteristics of Nemesis in Tibullus's second poetry-book are counterbalanced by the characteristics of Delia in the first to produce a poetic polarity. Delia is goddess of Day, Nemesis daughter of Night.[18] Bright states: "The flexibility of fundamental characteristics and the meaning of the two names, indicates that Delia and Nemesis should be regarded as essentially literary creations."[19] Faced with such readings, we may want to ask whether Propertian realism is anchored any more securely to reality than that of Ovid and Tibullus. Does Cynthia offer a close link with a real woman only to be followed by a series of fictive females?

Realist portraits of a mistress do not seem to have so bold an outline, or so persistent a presence, in Propertian poetry as to guarantee for Cynthia a life beyond the elegiac world, because realism is not consistently employed in the corpus and sometimes is challenged or undermined by other narrative devices. Even in Propertius's first poetry-book the apparent confession of an author's love is not everywhere sustained. Poem 1.16, for example, interrupts the realistic use of a first-person narrative. At this point the narrative *I* ceases to be plausible because it is not identifible with an author and is voiced by a door. Poem 1.20 substitutes for expressions of personal passion the mythic tale of Hercules' tragic love for the boy Hylas. The poetry-book closes with the narrator establishing his identity (*qualis*) in terms not of a mistress but of the site of civil war.

The formal strategies that produce for us the sense of an Augustan reality and an extratextual affair are even less prominent or coherent in Propertius's second poetry-book. The *ego* often speaks without such apparently authenticating details as a location, an occasion, or a named addressee. The object of desire is not always specified and sometimes clearly excludes identification with Cynthia.[20] The margins of the poetry-book and its core are peopled by patrons and poets or take for their landscape the Greek mountains and brooks of poetic inspiration. At these points, the text's evident concern is not to delineate a mistress but to define its author's poetic practice.[21]

By the third and fourth poetry-books a realistically depicted, individuated mistress has ceased to be a narrative focus of Propertian elegy. The third poetry-book claims as its inspiration not a girlfriend but another poet. Callimachus has replaced Cynthia as the motivating force for poetic production. The title *Cynthia* appears only as the text looks back at the initial poems of the corpus and draws Cynthia-centered erotic discourse to an apparent close. Far more frequently the first-person authorial narrator speaks of love without specifying a beloved, and poetic eroticism takes on a less personal mode.

In the fourth book there is not even a consistent lover's perspective. Several poems are concerned with new themes, such as the aetiology of *Roma*, rather than the motivations for *amor*. And the narrative *I* fluctuates between a reassuring authorial viewpoint and the implausible voices of a statue, a soldier's wife, and a dead *matrona*. When the more familiar mistress appears, the sequence of poems does not follow a realistic chronology but moves from the stratagems of a dead Cynthia who haunts the underworld (4.7) to those of a living Cynthia who raids a dinner party (4.8).[22]

These inconsistencies and developments in the Propertian mode of incorporating a mistress into elegiac discourse cannot be imputed merely to an author's unhappy experiences in love – to Propertius's progressive disillusionment with a Hostia – for each of the poetry-books and their Cynthias seem to be responding to changes in the public world of writing. The general shift from personal confessions of love toward more impersonal histories of Rome may be determined partially by changes in the material processes of patronage in the Augustan era, from the gradual establishment of Maecenas's circle through to the unmediated patronage of the *princeps*,[23] and the particular character of individual poetry-books by the progressive publication of other poetic discourses such as Tibullan elegy, Horatian lyric, and Virgilian epic.[24] But are the individual, realistically depicted Cynthias of the Propertian corpus then immune from such influences?

Literary concerns permeate even the activities and habits of the Cynthias who appear in the first two books. Poem 1.8, for example, implores its Cynthia not to depart for foreign climes and asks: *tu pedibus teneris positas fulcire pruinas, | tu potes insolitas, Cynthia, ferre nives?* ("Can you on delicate feet support settled frost? Can you Cynthia, strange, snows endure?" 1.8.7–8) The Gallan character of this, Cynthia, and the trip from which she is dissuaded, is well known. In Virgil's tenth *Eclogue*, attention already had been focused on the laments of the earlier elegiac poet over the absence of another snow-bound elegiac mistress. Propertius caps the Virgilian Gallus, in the field of erotic writing, by contrasting his ultimately loyal Cynthia with the faithless Lycoris.[25] Cynthia's delicate feet both recall and surpass the *teneras plantas* of the wandering Lycoris (*Ecl.* 10.49). Simultaneously, they give her a realizable shape and mark a new place in the Roman tradition for written mistresses.

Similarly, it has been observed that the disturbing narrative techniques of the second book – its discursiveness, parentheses, and abrupt transitions – constitute a response to the publication of Tibullus's first elegiac book.[26] And the process of transforming Propertian elegy in response to another erotic discourse again extends to realist depictions of the elegiac beloved. Poem 2.19 presents a Tibullanized Cynthia, closer in kind to the images of Delia in the countryside than to the first formulation of Cynthia in the *Monobiblos*:

> etsi me inuito discedis, Cynthia, Roma,
> laetor quod sine me devia rura coles . . .
> sola eris et solos spectabis, Cynthia, montis
> et pecus et finis pauperis agricolae.

> Even though against my will you leave, Cynthia, Rome,
> I'm glad that without me you'll cultivate wayward fields . . .
> Alone you'll be and the lonely mountains, Cynthia, you'll watch
> and the sheep and the borders of the poor farmer. (2.19.1–2, 7–8)

Tibullus began his fanciful sketch of a countrified mistress – the guardian (*custos*) of a country estate – with the words *rura colam* (1.5.21). So here *rura coles* begins Cynthia's departure from the generally urban terrain of Propertian discourse. The apparently realistic reference to Cynthia's country visit contains within its terms a challenge to the textual characteristics of a rustic Delia.

The Cynthias of the third and fourth books also disclose the influence of recently published literary works. The third Propertian poetry-book initiates an occasionally playful accommodation of Horatian lyric within erotic elegy. This literary challenge is articulated not only through the enlargement of poetic themes to include social commentary and the elevation of the poet to the rank of priest,[27] but also through the alteration of the elegiac mistress's physique.

The book opens with an erotic twist to the Horatian claim that poetry is an everlasting monument to the poet. For, at 3.2.17–24, Propertian poetry is said to immortalize female beauty (*forma*).[28] The book closes appropriately with the dissolution of that monument to beauty and the threatened construction of one to ugliness:

> exclusa inque uicem fastus patiare superbos,
>   et quae fecisti facta queraris anus!
> has tibi fatalis cecinit mea pagina diras:
>   euentum formae disce timere tuae!

> Shut out in turn – may you suffer arrogant contempt,
>   and of deeds which you've done may you complain –
> an old hag!
> These curses deadly for you my page has sung:
>   the outcome of your beauty learn to fear! (3.25.15–18)

The threatened transformation of Cynthia on the page from beauty to hag – the dissolution of the familiar elegiac edifice – mirrors similar predictions made about the Horatian Lydia in *Odes* 1.25.9–10.[29]

The two Cynthias of the fourth book take on Homeric rather than Horatian shapes. Although multiple literary influences on the features of these Cynthias may be noted – such as comedy, aetiology, tragedy, epigram, and mime – their pairing takes up the literary challenge recently issued by Virgil. Just as the Virgilian epic narrative conflates an Odyssean and an Iliadic hero in the character of Aeneas, so the Propertian elegiac narrative constructs a Cynthia who becomes first an Iliadic Patroclus returning from the grave (4.7) and then a vengeful Odysseus returning from the war (4.8).

In the last book of the Propertian corpus, the precarious status of realism is put on display. Whole incidents in the lives of a poet and his mistress now reproduce the plots of the Homeric poems, while their details echo passages of the *Aeneid*. In poem 4.7, the first-person authorial narrator recalls the occasion on which he had a vision of his dead mistress. Her reproaches are replete with apparently authenticating incidentals such as a busy red light district of Rome, worn-down windows, warming cloaks, branded slaves, ex-prostitutes, and wool work. But the ghost's arrival and departure, her appearance, and her reproofs sustain persistent links with the heroic world of *Iliad* 23 and the general conventions of epic discourse on visions of the dead. Similarly, in poem 4.8, the first-person narrator recalls the night when Cynthia caught him in the company of other women. The narrative of that night is also littered with apparently authenticating details such as the setting on the Esquiline, local girls, a dwarf, dice, a slave cowering behind a couch, and orders not to stroll in Pompey's portico. But Cynthia's sudden return finds her playing the role of an Odysseus to her poet's aberrant Penelope. Echoes of *Odyssey* 22 dissolve the poetic edifice of a real Roman event.[30]

When critics attempt to provide a plausible portrait of Cynthia, they must undertake an active process of building a rounded and consistent character out of physical and psychological characteristics that are scattered throughout the corpus and are often fragmentary, sometimes contradictory, and usually entangled in mythological and highly literary lore. But the discovery of Gallan, Tibullan, Horatian, and Virgilian Cynthias in the Propertian corpus argues against the helpfulness of this process. The strategies employed in the construction of a realistic mistress appear to change according to the requirements of a poetic project that commences in rivalry with the elegists Gallus and Tibullus and ends in appropriation of the terms of Horatian lyric and Virgilian epic.

It is misleading, therefore, to disengage the textual features of an elegiac mistress from their context in a poetry-book, so as to reshape them into the plausible portrait of an Augustan girlfriend, for even the physical features, psychological characteristics, direct speeches, and erotic activities with which Cynthia is provided often seem subject to literary concerns. Thus the realist devices of the Propertian corpus map out only a precarious pathway to the realities of women's lives in Augustan society and often direct us instead toward the features and habits of characters in other Augustan texts.

The repetition of the title *Cynthia* through the course of the Propertian poetry-books may still create the impression of a series of poems about one consistent female figure.[31] Does support remain, then, for a direct link between Cynthia and a Roman woman in the ancient tradition that *Cynthia* operates in elegy as a pseudonym for a living mistress Hostia?

On entry into the Propertian corpus, the epithet *Cynthia* brings with it a history as the marker of a poetic programme. Mount Cynthus on Delos had been linked with Apollo as the mouthpiece of a poetic creed by the Hellenistic poet Callimachus. That association was reproduced in Virgil's sixth *Eclogue* where the god directing Virgilian discourse away from epic material was given the cult title *Cynthius*.[32] The Propertian text itself, draws attention to that history at, for example, the close of the second poetry-book where in the course of poem 2.34, Callimachus, Virgil, Cynthius, and Cynthia are all associated with writing-styles. First, Callimachean elegy is suggested as a suitable model for poetic production (2.34.31–32); then, in a direct address to Virgil, *Cynthius* is employed as the epithet of a god with whose artistry the works of Virgil are explicitly compared: *tale facis carmen docta testudine quale* | *Cynthius impositis temperat articulis* ("Such song you make, on the learned lyre, as | Cynthius with applied fingers controls," 2.34.79–80). Finally, a reference to *Cynthia* closes the poem and its catalogue of the male authors and female subjects of earlier Latin love poetry: *Cynthia quin etiam uersu laudata Properti* –

| *hos inter si me ponere Fama uolet* ("Cynthia also praised in verse of Propertius –
| if among these men Fame shall wish to place me," 2.34.93–94).

The alignment within a single poem of Callimachus, Virgil, Cynthius, and Cynthia constructs for Propertian elegy and its elegiac mistress a literary ancestry. The title *Cynthia* may be read as a term in the statement of a poetics, as a proper name for the erotic embodiment of a particular poetic creed. In a corpus of poems that frequently voices a preference for elegiac over epic styles of writing that use a critical discourse inherited from Callimachus and developed in Virgil's *Eclogues*,[33] the title *Cynthia* contributes significantly to the expression of literary concerns.[34]

The name of the elegiac mistress does not offer us a route out of a literary world to the realities of women's lives at Rome. But, as with her other apparently plausible features, her name is inextricably entangled in issues of poetic practice. Any attempt to read through the name *Cynthia* to a living mistress, therefore, overlooks its place in the "grammar" of elegiac poetry where *Propertius* and *Cynthia* do not perform the same semantic operations. In the language of elegy, a poet generates a different range and level of connotation than his mistress.

The issue of the elegiac mistress's social status further elucidates the peculiar role women play in the poetic language of Augustan love poetry; for, when attempts have been made to reconstruct a real girlfriend out of Cynthia's features, no clear clues have been found in the poems to the social status of a living mistress and conclusions have ranged from Roman wife[35] to foreign prostitute,[36] or the evident textual ambiguities have been read as reflections of the fluidity of social status to be expected within an Augustan *demi-monde*.[37]

In Propertius 2.7, for example, the narrator describes his mistress as having rejoiced at the removal of a law which would have separated the lovers. He declares that he prefers death to marriage:

> nam citius paterer caput hoc discedere collo
> quam possem nuptae perdere more faces,
> aut ego transirem tua limina clausa maritus,
> respiciens udis prodita luminibus.[38]

> For faster would I suffer this head and neck to part
> than be able at a bride's humor to squander torches,
> or myself a husband pass your shut doors,
> looking back at their betrayal with moist eyes. (2.7.7–10)

And he rejects his civic duty to produce children who would then participate in Augustus Caesar's wars: *unde mihi Parthis natos praebere triumphis? | nullus de nostro sanguine miles erit* ("From what cause for Parthian triumphs to offer my sons? | None from my blood will be a soldier," 2.7.13–14). Here, if nowhere else in Augustan elegy, we might expect to find a clearly defined social status allocated to the elegiac mistress, because, at this point in the elegiac corpus, the text seems to be directly challenging legal constraints on sexual behaviour.

Nevertheless, even when the elegiac narrative takes as its central focus a legislative issue, no clear social position is allocated to Cynthia. We learn instead that men and women play different semantic roles in this poetic discourse. The female is employed in the text only as a means to defining the male. Her social status is not clearly defined because the dominating perspective is that of the male narrator. What matters is his social and political position as a man who in having a mistress refuses to be a *maritus* or the father of *milites*.[39]

What this analysis of elegiac realism seems to reveal is that the notion of *concealment* – the idea that the stylized heroines of elegy somehow conceal the identities of specific Augustan girlfriends – is not a helpful term in critical discourse on elegiac women. Perhaps Apuleius's identification of Cynthia with a Hostia is suspect, since it forms part of a theatrical self-defence and should be read in the light of a long-standing interest in biographical speculation. (We do not now accept, for example, Apuleius's identification of Corydon with Virgil or of Alexis with a slave boy of Pollio.[40]) But the point is that, whether or not a Hostia existed who was associated with Propertius, the Cynthia of our text is part of no simple act of concealment.

While the combination of realist techniques and parodic strategies in the Ovidian corpus is thought to deny Corinna any reality, the realist strategies of the Propertian corpus have been isolated from other narrative techniques and left largely unexplored in order to secure for Cynthia an existence outside the text in which we meet her. But I have argued that, however, even the realist devices of Propertian elegy can disclose the unreality of elegiac mistresses. Cynthia too is a poetic fiction: a woman in a text, whose physique, temperament, name, and status are all subject to the idiom of that text. So, as part of a poetic language of love, Cynthia should not be related to the love life of her poet but to the "grammar" of his poetry.

The Propertian elegiac narrative does not, then, celebrate a Hostia, but creates a fictive female whose minimally defined status as mistress, physical characteristics, and name are all determined by the grammar of the erotic discourse in which she appears. The employment of terms like "pseudonym" in modern critical discourse overlooks the positive act of creation involved in the depiction of elegy's mistresses.[41] Therefore, when reading Augustan elegy, it seems most appropriate to talk not of pseudonyms and poeticized girlfriends but of poetic or elegiac women.

3. Metaphors

So the bond between elegiac women and particular Augustan girlfriends has proved to be very fragile. The realistic features of elegy's heroines seem to owe a greater debt to poetic programmes than to the realities of female forms. But if we deny to Cynthia an existence outside poetry, are we also denying her any relation to society? If elegiac narratives are concerned with fictive females, how do women enter their discourse? What relation might still hold between women in Augustan society and women in its poetic texts? And what function could a realistically depicted yet fictive mistress serve in elegy's aesthetics?

A possible approach to some of these questions has already been suggested, as I have argued that the characteristics of elegiac women are determined by the general idioms of the elegiac discourse of which they form a part and that Cynthia should be read as firmly shaped by the Propertian poetic project. But elegiac discourses and poetic projects are, in turn, firmly engaged with and shaped by the political, moral, and aesthetic discourses of the Augustan period. And so it is through the relation of elegiac narratives to all the other cultural discourses of the specific period in which they were produced that we can at last see a more secure fit between women in elegiac texts and women in Augustan society.

A. Cultural discourses

The general idioms peculiar to elegiac writing have been as intriguing to the reader as the specific attributes provided for women at various points in the elegiac corpus, for they seem to be offering a challenging new role for the female, a poetic break away from the traditional duties of marriage and motherhood.

First of all, features of the elegiac vocabulary seem to overturn the traditional Roman discourses of sexuality. In the poetic texts the elegiac hero is frequently portrayed as sexually loyal while his mistress is not.[42] The Propertian lover protests: *tu mihi sola places: placeam tibi, Cynthia, solus* ("You alone please me: may I alone please you, Cynthia," 2.7.19). He desires as the wording on his epitaph: *unius hic quondam seruus amoris erat* ("Of a single love this man once was the slave," 2.13.36). Now this elegiac expectation of eternal male faithfulness, according to one analysis, "spurns the double standard characterizing Roman male–female relationships" because traditionally, extramarital sex was acceptable for husbands while their wives were legally required to uphold the principle of *fides marita*.[43] It was the ideal of a woman's faithfulness to one man that was most frequently expressed on Roman epitaphs and, furthermore, it was expressed in the same terms as the elegiac ideal: *solo contenta marito, uno contenta marito* ("content with her husband alone," "content with but one husband").[44]

Another feature commonly cited as evidence for an elegiac transformation of traditional sexual roles is the application of the *seruitium amoris* metaphor to a heterosexual liaison.[45] A parallel for the *topos* of the lover-as-enslaver can be found in Hellenistic erotic writing, but Augustan elegy's casting of the female in the dominant sexual role seems to work against the operations of other Roman sexual discourses. The Propertian narrator asks: *quid mirare, meam si uersat femina uitam | et trahit addictum sub sua iura uirum?* ("Why are you surprised, if my life a woman directs | and drags bound under her own laws a man?", 3.11.1–2).

The male narrator is portrayed as enslaved, the female narrative subject as his enslaver. The Tibullan lover, for example, says farewell to his freedom: *hic mihi seruitium uideo dominamque paratam: | iam mihi, libertas illa paterna, uale* ("Here for me I see slavery and a mistress at the ready: | now from me, that fathers' freedom, adieu," 2.4.1–2). Thus the control of household slaves, a woman's version of the economic status of a *dominus*, has been transformed figuratively into the erotic condition of control over sexual slaves. The sexual domain of the elegiac *domina* contrasts with that traditionally prescribed for Roman wives, namely, keeping house and working wool.[46]

A third significant feature of this poetic discourse is the declaration that the pursuit of love and poetry is a worthy alternative to more traditional equestrian careers. This elegiac declaration is best known in its formulation as the *militia amoris* metaphor.[47] The elegiac hero is portrayed as already enlisted in a kind of military service, battling with love or his beloved. The Propertian narrator receives the following instructions:

> at tu finge elegos, fallax opus: haec tua castra!–
> scribat ut exemplo cetera turba tuo.
> militiam Veneris blandis patiere sub armis,
> et Veneris pueris utilis hostis eris.
> nam tibi uictrices quascumque labore parasti,
> eludit palmas una puella tuas.

> But you, devise elegies, a tricky task: this is your camp!–
> That they, the remaining crowd, write at your example.
> The warfare of Venus you'll endure under alluring weapons
> and to Venus's boys a profitable enemy you'll be.
> Because for you whatever Victorias your effort's procured,
> escapes your awards one girl. (4.1.135–40)

Similarly an Ovidian poem entirely dedicated to the exploration of the metaphor of *militia* begins: *militat omnis amans, et habet sua castra Cupido* ("Every lover soldiers, and Cupid has his own barracks," *Am.* 1.9.1).

Augustan elegy represents its hero as faithful to his usually disloyal mistress, and as engaged metaphorically in either sexual servitude or erotic battles. But the unconventional sexual role bestowed, through poetic metaphor, on the elegiac male seems to implicate the elegiac female in equally unconventional behaviour: he slights the responsibilities of being citizen and soldier, while she operates outside the conventional roles of wife and mother.

So, if specific features of the elegiac mistresses do not seem to reflect the realities of particular women's lives, might not the general idioms employed about them nevertheless reflect general conditions for the female in Augustan society? Is the elegiac woman unconventional because there are now some unconventional women in the world?

Once again, the elegiac texts tempt us: if, as Georg Luck has argued, "the woman's role in the Roman society of the first century BC explains to a large extent the unique character of the love poetry of that period,"[48] then elegy would be invested with a social dimension of substantial interest to the student of women in antiquity. The mistresses stylized in elegy might then constitute poetic representatives of a whole movement of sexually liberated ladies and may be read as "symbolic of the new freedom for women in Rome's social life in the first century BC."[49]

To establish such a connection between elegiac mistresses and Augustan women it is first necessary to find parallel portraits of the female outside the poetic sphere. If external evidence can be found for the gradual emergence of a breed of "emancipated" women, then it might be possible to argue that such women *provoked* elegiac production.

Sallust's description of an unconventional Sempronia provides the most frequently cited historical parallel for the elegiac heroines:

> litteris Graecis et Latinis docta, psallere, saltare elegantius quam necesse est probae, multa alia, quae instrumenta luxuriae sunt. Sed ei cariora semper omnia quam decus atque pudicitia fuit; . . . lubido sic accensa ut saepius peteret uiros quam peteretur.

> Well educated in Greek and Latin literature, she had greater skill in lyre-playing and dancing than there is any need for a respectable woman to acquire, besides many other accomplishments such as minister to dissipation. There was nothing that she set a smaller value on than seemliness and chastity . . . Her passions were so ardent that she more often made advances to men than they did to her.[50]

Similarly, the Clodia Metelli who appears in Cicero's forensic speech *pro Caelio* is often adduced as an example of the kind of emancipated woman with whom Roman poets fell in love in the first century BC and about whom (thus inspired) they composed erotic verse. The early identification of Clodia Metelli with Catullus's *Lesbia* seems to strengthen such a link between living and written women and to bind the habits of a late

Republican noblewoman – as evidenced by Cicero's *pro Caelio* – to poetic depictions of a mistress in the Catullan corpus.[51]

But the process of matching love poetry's heroines with a new breed of "emancipated" women raises methodological problems. Sallust's Sempronia and Cicero's Clodia have often been employed as evidence for the phenomenon of the New Woman – as elegy's historical twin is sometimes called.[52] It is important to observe that, even outside the poetic sphere, our principal evidence for the lives of ancient women is still on the level of representations, not realities. We encounter not real women, but representations shaped by the conventions of wall-paintings, tombstones, and, most frequently, texts. Any comparison between elegiac women and emancipated ladies tends, therefore, to be a comparison between two forms of discourse about the female.

Sempronia and Clodia are both to be found in texts. And as written women, they are – like their elegiac sisters – no accurate reflection of particular female lives. Sallust's Sempronia is written into a particular form of literary discourse, for, in the context of his historical monograph, she is structured as a female counterpart to Catiline.[53] Her features also belong to a larger historiographic tradition in which the decline of Roman *uirtus* and the rise of *luxuria* are commonly associated with aberrant female sexuality. Sempronia's qualities contradict the norms for a *matrona*. She is whorish because a whore embodies degeneracy and thus discredits the Catilinarian conspiracy.[54]

Clodia is also written into a text. The villainous features of this prosecution witness are put together from the stock characteristics of the comic *meretrix* and the tragic Medea. Cicero's Clodia is a *proterua meretrix procaxque* (*pro Cael.* 49) because sexual promiscuity was a long-standing *topos* in the invective tradition against women. As part of a forensic discourse, the sexually active woman is designed to sway a jury. The rapaciousness of this supposedly injured party turns the young, male defendant into a victim and her sexual guilt thus underscores his innocence.[55]

When attempting to reconstruct the lives of ancient women from textual materials, some critics have drawn upon a kind of hierarchy of discourses graded according to their usefulness as evidence. Marilyn Skinner, for example, argues that Cicero's letters offer a less tendentious version of Clodia Metelli than does his oratory. And the Clodia she recuperates from that source is one concerned not with sexual debauchery, but with the political activities of her brother and husband and with property management.[56] Perhaps this picture of a wealthy, public woman is a better guide to the new opportunities of the first century BC, but it is not the picture of female behavior that Augustan elegy paints. The term *domina* could identify a woman of property, an owner of household slaves. But within the discourse of Augustan elegy, it takes on an erotic, not an economic, significance. The female subject that the poetic narrative constructs is not an independent woman of property but one dependent on men for gifts: *Cynthia non sequitur fascis nec curat honores,* | *semper amatorum ponderat una sinus* ("Cynthia doesn't pursue power or care for glory, | always her lovers' pockets she only weighs," 2.16.11–12). Augustan elegy, then, does not seem to be a response to the lives of particular emancipated women, but another manifestation of a particular patterning of female sexuality to be found in the cultural discourses of Rome.

Now Rome was essentially a patriarchal society sustained by a familial ideology. The basic Roman social unit was the *familia* whose head was the father (*pater*): "a woman, even if legally independent, socially and politically had no function in Roman society in the way that a man, as actual or potential head of a *familia*, did."[57] Consequently, in the conceptual framework of Roman society, female sexuality takes on positive value only when ordered in terms that will be socially effective for patriarchy. Sexually unrestrained women are marginalized. Displaced from a central position in cultural categories, they are associated with social disruption.

Using the Ciceronian Clodia as her starting-point, Mary Lefkowitz has documented the prevalence of this way of structuring femininity in antiquity. Praise or blame of women, Lefkowitz argues, is customarily articulated with reference to their biological role, assigned according to their conformity with male norms for female behaviour. The good woman is lauded for her chastity, her fertility, her loyalty to her husband, and her selfless concern for others. The bad woman is constantly vilified for her faithlessness, her inattentiveness to household duties, and her selfish disregard for others.[58]

A notable example of this polarization of women into the chaste and the depraved occurs at the beginning of the Principate: "In the propaganda which represented Octavian's war with Antony as a crusade, it was convenient to depict [Octavia] as a deeply wronged woman, the chaste Roman foil of the voluptuous foreigner Cleopatra."[59]

This patterning of discourses about the female can be grounded in history. A figure like Sempronia was not articulated in Roman texts before the middle of the second century BC, after Rome's rise to empire – and its consequent wealth and Hellenization – had brought with it significant social and cultural change.[60] From this period there began a proliferation of moral discourses associating female sexual misconduct with social and political disorder. And by the first century BC childlessness, procreation, marriage, and adultery were appearing regularly as subjects for social concern in the texts of writers such as Cicero, Sallust, Horace, and Livy.[61]

So persuasive have these discourses on the female been that they have often been taken for truth. Many of the histories on which elegy's commentators once relied for reconstructions of Rome's New Woman invested their accounts of changes in women's social position with elements of moral turpitude transferred wholesale from the writings of the Roman moralists. For example, the *Cambridge Ancient History* claimed that "by the last century of the Republic, females had in practice obtained their independence, and nothing but social convention and a sense of responsibility barred the way to a dangerous exploitation of their privilege."[62] Similarly, Balsdon's *Roman Women* stated emphatically: "Women emancipated themselves. They acquired liberty, then with the late Republic and the Empire they enjoyed unrestrained licence."[63] Thus in the ready association of liberty with licence, the strictures of Roman moralists were turned into the realities of Republican lives.[64]

One particular form of discourse about female sexuality had considerable and significant currency during the period in which elegiac eroticism was produced. From 18 BC on, legislation began to appear that criminalized adultery and offered inducements to reproduce. But the production of elegy's female figures cannot be read as a direct poetic protest against this social legislation, although it appears to be the subject of one Propertian poem:

> gauisa est certe sublatam Cynthia legem,
> > qua quondam edicta flemus uterque diu,
> ni nos diuideret.

> She was delighted for sure at the law's removal – Cynthia –
> > over whose publication once we both cried long,
> in case it should part us. (2.7.1–3)

Since the tradition of erotic writing to which the Propertian Cynthia belongs stretched back at least as far as the Gallan corpus, the earliest examples of the elegiac mistress considerably predate the legislation.[65] But the appearance of the Augustan domestic legislation from 18 BC demonstrates that the discourses about female sexuality with which elegy was already engaged were now being institutionalized. Female sexual practice was now enshrined in law as a problematic issue with which the whole state should be concerned.[66]

Augustan elegy and its mistresses constitute, therefore, a response to, and a part of, a multiplication of discourses about, the female, which occurred in the late Republic and earlier Empire. Similarly, in his first volume on the history of sexuality, Michel Foucault demonstrates that, when "population" emerged as an economic and political problem in the eighteenth century, "between the state and the individual, sex became an issue, and a public issue no less: a whole web of discourses, special knowledges, analyses, and injunctions settled upon it."[67] In the first century BC, at a time when female sexuality was seen as a highly problematic and public concern, the poetic depiction of the elegiac hero's subjection to a mistress would have carried a wide range of social and political connotations. And the elegiac mistress, in particular, would have brought to her poetic discourse a considerable potential as metaphor for danger and social disruption.

B. *Metaphoric mistresses*

A brief outline of the operations of realism and of metaphor in Augustan elegy discloses that elegy's mistresses do not enter literary language reflecting the realities of women's lives at Rome. An examination of their characteristics reveals that they are fictive females engaged with at least two broad – but not necessarily distinct – categories of discourse. Shaped by developments in the production of literary texts and in the social construction of female sexuality, they possess potential as metaphors for both poetic projects and political order.

The second of these two categories will be further explored in the remainder of this article; for it is the range of connotations that the elegiac mistress gains as a result of her association with the erotic metaphors of *seruitium* and *militia*, rather than those arising from her identification with the Muse and the practice of writing elegy, that may most intrigue the student of women in antiquity.[68] Amy Richlin argues that on entry into a variety of Rome's poetic and prose genres such as invective and satire, the ordering of female sexuality is determined by the central narrative viewpoint which is that of a sexually active, adult male.[69] So, in depicting their hero as subject to and in the service of a sexually unrestrained mistress, do the elegiac texts offer any challenging new role for the female, or for the male alone?

Some critics have made much of the boldness of appropriating the term *laus* for the erotic sphere and *fides* for male sexual behaviour, but their descriptions of such strategies are seriously misleading. The Propertian narrator declares: *laus in amore mori: laus altera, si datur uno | posse frui: fruar o solus amore meo!* ("Glorious in love to die: glorious again, if granted one love | to enjoy: o may I enjoy alone my love!", 2.1.47–48). Both Judith Hallett and Margaret Hubbard, for example, frequently refer to such material as involving a bold reversal or inversion of sex roles – the elegiac hero sheds male public virtues and takes on the female domestic virtue of sexual loyalty.[70] Such terminology suggests, erroneously, that in elegiac poetry the female subject gains a position of social responsibility at the same time as it is removed from the male.

But it is not the concern of elegiac poetry to upgrade the political position of women, only to portray the male narrator as alienated from positions of power and to differentiate him from other, socially responsible male types. For example, in the same poem of Propertius's second book, the narrator's erotic battles are contrasted with the activities of the *nauita*, the *arator*, the *miles*, and the *pastor*, without any reference to a female partner:

> nauita de uentis, de tauris narrat arator,
>   enumerat miles uulnera, pastor ouis;
> nos contra angusto uersantes proelia lecto:
>   qua pote quisque, in ea conterat arte diem.

403

The sailor tells of winds, of bulls the farmer,
  numbers the soldier his wounds, the shepherd his flock;
we instead turning battles on a narrow bed:
  in what each can, in that art let him wear down the day. (2.1.43–46)

Similarly, in the first poetry-book the Propertian lover expresses, in the abstract terms of an erotic militancy, his difference from the soldier Tullus (1.6.19–36).

Furthermore, the elegiac texts take little interest in elaborating their metaphors in terms of female power but explore, rather, the concept of male dependency. The elegiac mistress may possess a camp in which her lover parades (Prop. 2.7.15–16) or choose her lovers like a general chooses his soldiers (*Am.* 1.9.5–6), but generally the elegiac metaphors are more generally concerned with male servitude not female mastery, and with male military service not female generalship. In *Amores* 1.2 it is Cupid who leads a triumphal procession of captive lovers, not the Ovidian mistress, and in *Amores* 1.9 it is the equation *miles/amans* not *domina/dux* that receives the fullest treatment.

The metaphors of *servitium* and *militia amoris* thus disclose the ideological repercussions for a man of association with a realistically depicted mistress. In a society that depended on a slave mode of production and in which citizenship carried the obligation of military service, these two metaphors define the elegiac male as socially irresponsible. As a slave to love he is precluded from participating in the customary occupations of male citizens. As a soldier of love he is not available to fight military campaigns.

The heterodoxy of the elegiac portrayal of love, therefore, lies in the absence of a political or social role for the male narrator, not in any attempt to provide or demand a political role for the female subject. The temporary alignment with a sexually unrestrained mistress that Augustan elegy depicts does not bestow on the female a new, challenging role but alienates the male from his traditional responsibilities. The elegiac poets exploit the traditional methods of ordering female sexuality which locate the sexually unrestrained and therefore socially ineffective female on the margins of society, in order to portray their first-person heroes as displaced from a central position in the social categories of Augustan Rome. And, moreover, they evaluate that displacement in conventional terms. At the beginning of the second book of the *Amores*, the poet is introduced as *ille ego nequitiae Naso poeta meae* ("I, Naso, that poet of my own depravity," 2.1.2) and in the Propertian corpus the lover and poet of Cynthia is also associated with the scandal of *nequitia* ("vice" or "depravity," 1.6.26 and 2.24.6). Thus, the poetic depiction of subjection to a mistress is aligned, in a conventional moral framework, with depravity.

Finally, despite claims of eternal devotion, none of the elegiac poets maintain this pose consistently or indefinitely. At the end of the third poetry-book, the Propertian lover repudiates his heroine and describes himself as restored to Good Sense (*Mens Bona*). At the end of his first poetry-book, the Tibullan hero finds himself dragged off to war. And, toward the end of the *Amores*, the appearance of a *coniunx* on the elegiac scene disrupts the dramatic pretence that the narrator is a romantic lover involved in an obsessive and exclusive relationship.[71]

4. Conclusion

The purpose of this article has been to suggest that, when looking at the relations between women in Augustan elegy and women in Augustan society, we should not describe the literary image of a mistress as a kind of poetic painting whose surface we can remove to reveal a real Roman woman hidden underneath. Instead, an exploration of the idioms of realism and metaphor has demonstrated that elegiac mistresses are inextricably entangled in and shaped by a whole range of discourses, which bestow on them a potential as metaphors for the poetic projects and political interests of their authors.

I hope that such an analysis proves not the conclusion of, but only the starting-point for, a critical study of elegy's heroines and their constructive power as metaphors for poetic and political concerns. But one aspect of this analysis may still seem unsatisfactory or unsatisfying, for it seems to offer no adequate place for living Augustan women in the production of elegiac poetry. Further questions confront us. How did women read or even write such male-oriented verse? Would a female reader be drawn into the male narrative perspective? And how did a female writer, such as Sulpicia, construct her *ego* and its male beloved? In such a context, would the erotic metaphors of *seruitium* and *militia* be appropriate or have the same range of connotative power?

Notes

An earlier version of this paper was read in 1987 to Oxford's seminar group on Women in Antiquity. I am very grateful to the participants for the comments they made at the time and to all those who have commented on or criticized the paper since, including C. Edwards, J. Henderson, E. Rawson, A. Scafuro, J. P. Sullivan, and the *Helios* referees.
1 See, for example, the comments of Foley in her preface to *Reflections of Women in Antiquity* (1981), and the articles of Skinner and Culham in *Helios* (1986.2).
2 The bias in favour of Greek material is observed by Fantham (1986), 5–6.
3 Hallett (1973), 103–24, and (1974), 211–17; Betensky (1973), 267–69, and (1974), 217–19.
4 See Wyke (1987a), 47.
5 Quotations from the elegiac corpus follow the most recent editions of the Oxford Classical Texts.
6 For the problematic artifice of Augustan poetry see Griffin (1985), ix. On the genre of personal love elegy see Du Quesnay (1973), 1–2.

7 Lyne (1980), viii and *passim*.
8 The idiom belongs to Griffin (1985), for example, 105.
9 See, for example, Williams (1968), 542.
10 A classic exposition of the disjunction between textual realism and reality and a detailed exploration of the strategies of nineteenth-century French realist writing can be found in Barthes' *S/Z* (1975). For the importance of this work see Hawkes (1977), 106–22.
11 Allen (1950), 145–60.
12 Veyne (1983).
13 Sullivan (1976), 80.
14 Lyne (1980), 62.
15 For Cynthia and Delia as pseudonyms, see, for example, Williams (1968), 526–42.
16 Bright (1978), 104. Cf. Wyke (forthcoming), but contrast McKeown (1987), 19–24.
17 Williams (1968), 537.
18 Bright (1978), 99–123.
19 *Ibid.*, 123.
20 See Veyne (1983), 67 and 71, and Papanghelis (1987), 93–97.
21 Wyke (1987a).
22 For the narrative techniques of Books 3 and 4 see Wyke (1987b), 153–78.
23 See, for example, Stahl (1985).
24 See, for example, Hubbard (1974).
25 For a convenient summary of views on this literary relationship, see Fedeli (1980), 203–5 and 211.
26 For example, Hubbard (1974), 57–58, and Lyne (1980), 132.
27 See, for example, Nethercut (1970), 385–407.
28 For the comparison with *Odes* 3.30.1–7, see Nethercut (1970), 387, and Fedeli (1985), 90.
29 Fedeli (1985), 674 and 692–93.
30 For references to the extensive literature on these two poems, see Wyke (1987b), 168–70, and Papanghelis (1987), 145–98.
31 Cf. Veyne (1983), 60 on *Delia*.
32 See Clausen (1976), 245–47, and Boyance (1956), 172–75.
33 See, for example, Wimmel (1960).
34 For the intimate association of Cynthia and Callimachus in the Propertian corpus, see Wyke (1987a).
35 Williams (1968), 529–35.
36 Cairns (1972), 156–57.
37 Griffin (1985), 27–28.
38 The interpretation of verse 8 is open to much dispute.
39 See especially Veyne (1983), who argues that it is sufficient for elegy's purposes to locate its *ego* "chez les marginales."
40 See, for example, Fairweather (1974), 232–36.
41 Bright (1978), 103–04.
42 For references to male faithfulness in the elegiac corpus, see Lilja (1965), 172–86, and Lyne (1980), 65–67.
43 Hallett (1973), III; cf. *ibid.*, 106.
44 *Carm. Epigr.* 455 and 643.5, for which see Williams (1958), 23–25.
45 For references to erotic *servitium* in the elegiac corpus, see Lilja (1965), 76–89; Copley (1947), 285–300; Lyne (1979), 117–30.
46 Hallett (1973), 103, contrasts the epitaph of Claudia (*ILS* 8403): *domum seruauit, lanam fecit.*

47 For references to erotic *militia* in the elegiac corpus, see Lilja (1965), 64–66, and Lyne (1980), 67–78.
48 Luck (1974), 15.
49 King (1976), 70.
50 Sallust, *Cat.* 25.2–4 (Budé edition, ed. A. Ernout 1964). The translation is that of Lefkowitz and Fant (1982), 205. For Sempronia's use as part of the social backdrop for elegiac production, see Lyne (1980), 14, and King (1976), 70 and n. 7.
51 See, for example, Lyne (1980), 8–18, and Griffin (1985), 15–28.
52 Balsdon (1962), 45.
53 Paul (1966), 92.
54 Boyd (1987).
55 Lefkowitz (1981), 32–40, and Skinner (1983), 275–76.
56 Skinner (1983).
57 Gardner (1986), 77.
58 Lefkowitz (1981), 32–40.
59 Balsdon (1952), 69. Griffin (1985), 32–47, also draws attention to correspondences between representations of Antony and the Propertian narrator.
60 I am indebted to Elizabeth Rawson for this observation.
61 See, for example, Richlin (1981), 379–404.
62 Last (1934), 440.
63 Balsdon (1952), 14–15.
64 Cf. Gardner (1986), 261.
65 For the details of the Augustan legislation see Last (1934), 441–56, and Brunt (1971), 558–66. Badian (1985), 82–98, doubts that even by the time Propertius's second book was published any attempt had yet been made to introduce the legislation concerning marriage. For the relation between Augustan elegy and the moral legislation, see also Wallace-Hadrill (1985), 180–84.
66 I am very grateful to Catherine Edwards for giving me access to an unpublished paper on the subject of adultery and the Augustan legislation.
67 Foucault (1981), 26.
68 For the elegiac mistress as a metaphor for her author's poetics, see, for example, Veyne (1983), and Wyke (1987a).
69 Richlin (1983).
70 Hallett (1973) and Hubbard (1974).
71 Cf. Butrica (1982), 87.

Works cited

Quotations from Propertius, Tibullus, and Ovid follow the Oxford Classical Texts of E. A. Barber (1960), J. P. Postgate (1915), and E. J. Kenney (1961), respectively.

Allen, A. "'Sincerity' and the Roman Elegists." *CP* 45 (1950): 145–60.
Badian, E. "A Phantom Marriage Law." *Philologus* 129 (1985): 82–98.
Baldson, J. P. V. D. *Roman Women.* London: The Bodley Head, 1962.
Barthes, R. *S/Z.* Trans. R. Miller, London: Jonathan Cape, 1975.
Betensky, A. "Forum." *Arethusa* 6 (1973): 267–69.
—— "A Further Reply." *Arethusa* 7 (1974): 211–17.
Boyancé, P. *L'influence grecque sur la poésie latine de Catulle à Ovide.* Entretiens Hardt 2. Geneva: Fondation Hardt, 1956.
Boyd, B. "Virtus Effeminata and Sallust's Sempronia." *TAPA* 117 (1987): 183–201.

Bright, D. F. *Haec mihi Fingebam: Tibullus in his World.* Leiden: Cincinnati Classical Studies, New Series 3, 1978.

Brunt, P. A. *Italian Manpower*, Oxford: Clarendon Press, 1971.

Butrica, J. "Review Article: the Latin Love Poets." *EMC* n.s. 1 (1982): 82–95.

Cairns, F. *Generic Composition in Greek and Roman Poetry.* Edinburgh: Edinburgh University Press, 1972.

Clausen, W. "Cynthius." *AJP* 97 (1976): 245–47.

Copley, F. O. "Servitium Amoris in the Roman Elegists," *TAPA* 78 (1947): 285–300.

. Culham, P. "Ten Years after Pomeroy: Studies of the Image and Reality of Women in Antiquity." *Helios* 13.2 (1986): 9–30.

Du Quesnay, I. M. Le M. "The Amores." In *Greek and Latin Studies, Classical Literature and its Influence: Ovid,* ed. J. W. Binns: 1–48. London: Routledge and Kegan Paul, 1973.

Fairweather, J. "Fiction in the Biographies of Ancient Writers." *Ancient Society* 5 (1974): 231–75.

Fantham, E. "Women in Antiquity: A Selective (and Subjective) Survey 1979–84." *EMC* 5.1 (1986): 1–24.

Fedeli, P. *Sesto Properzio: Il Primo Libro delle Elegie.* Florence: Accademia Toscana Studi 53, 1980.

—— *Properzio: Il Libro Terzo delle Elegie.* Bari: Adriatica Editrice, 1985.

Foley, H. P. *Reflections of Women in Antiquity*, ed. H. P. Foley. New York, London and Paris: Gordon and Breach, 1981.

Foucault, M. *The History of Sexuality.* Volume 1: *An Introduction.* Middlesex: Pelican Books, 1981. Reprint and translation of 1976 edition.

Gardner, J. F. *Women in Roman Law and Society.* London: Croom Helm, 1986.

Griffin, J. *Latin Poetry and Roman Life.* London: Duckworth, 1985.

Hallett, J. P. "The Role of Women in Roman Elegy: Counter-Cultural Feminism." *Arethusa* 6 (1973): 103–24.

—— "Women in Roman Elegy: A Reply." *Arethusa* 7 (1974); 211–17.

Hawkes, T. *Structuralism and Semiotics.* London: Methuen, 1977.

Hubbard, M. *Propertius.* London: Duckworth, 1974.

King, J. K. "Sophistication vs. Chastity in Propertius' Latin Love Elegy." *Helios* 4 (1976): 67–76.

Last, H. "The Social Policy of Augustus." In *Cambridge Ancient History*, vol. 10: 425–64. Cambridge: Cambridge University Press, 1934.

Lefkowitz, M. R. *Heroines and Hysterics.* London: Duckworth, 1981.

Lefkowitz, M. R. and M. B. Fant. *Women's Life in Greece and Rome.* London: Duckworth, 1982.

Lilja, S. *The Roman Elegists' Attitude to Women.* Helsinki: Suomalainen Tideakatemia, 1965.

Luck, G. "The Woman's Role in Latin Love Poetry." In *Perspectives of Roman Poetry*, ed. G. K. Galinsky: 15–31. Austin. TX: University of Texas Press, 1974.

Lyne, R. O. A. M. "Servitium Amoris." *CQ* 29 (1979): 117–30.

—— *The Latin Love Poets: from Catullus to Horace.* Oxford: Clarendon Press, 1980.

McKeown, J. C. *Ovid: Amores.* Volume 1, *Text and Prolegomena.* Liverpool: Arca Classical and Medieval Texts, Papers and Monographs 20, 1987.

Nethercut, W. R. "The Ironic Priest. Propertius' 'Roman Elegies' iii, 1–5: Imitations of Horace and Vergil." *AJP* 91 (1970): 385–407.

Papanghelis, T. *Propertius: A Hellenistic Poet on Love and Death*. Cambridge: Cambridge University Press, 1987.

Paul, G. M. "Sallust." In *Latin Historians*, ed. T. A. Dorey: London: Routledge and Kegan Paul, 1966.

Richlin, A. "Approaches to the Sources on Adultery at Rome." In *Reflections of Women in Antiquity*, ed. H. P. Foley: 379–404.

—— *The Garden of Priapus: Sexuality and Aggression in Roman Humour*. New Haven and London: Yale University Press, 1983.

Skinner, M. "Clodia Metelli." *TAPA* 113 (1983): 273–87.

—— "Rescuing Creusa: New Approaches to Women in Antiquity." *Helios* 13.2 (1986): 1–8.

Stahl, H.-P. *Propertius: "Love" and "War." Individual and State under Augustus*. Berkeley and Los Angeles: University of California Press, 1985.

Sullivan, J. *Propertius. A Critical Introduction*. Cambridge: Cambridge University Press, 1976.

Veyne, P. *L'Élégie érotique romaine*. Paris: Éditions du Seuil, 1983.

Wallace-Hadrill, A. "Propaganda and Dissent?" *Klio* 67 (1985): 180–84.

Williams, G. "Some Aspects of Marriage Ceremonies and Ideals." *JRS* 48 (1958): 16–29.

—— *Tradition and Originality in Roman Poetry*. Oxford: Clarendon Press, 1968.

Wimmel, W. *Kallimachos in Rom*. Wiesbaden: Hermes Einzelschriften 16, 1960.

Wyke, M. "Written Women: Propertius' Scripta Puella." *JRS* 77 (1987a): 47–61.

—— "The Elegiac Woman at Rome." *PCPS* 213, n. s. 33 (1987b): 153–78.

—— "Reading Female Flesh: *Amores* 3.1." In *History as Text*, ed. Averil Cameron. London: Duckworth, forthcoming.

REPRESENTATION AND THE
RHETORIC OF REALITY

Duncan Kennedy

The notion of representation plays a prominent role in aesthetic criticism. The relational sense of the term, that of 'representing', 'standing for', opens up a characteristic disjunction, expressed as between 'art' and 'the world', or 'literature' and 'life'. Another characteristic distinction generated by the term is that between the 'means' and the 'object' of representation. The capacity of representational art to elide these disjunctions, indeed the projection of this on occasions as an ideal of such art, is remarked upon in the story of Pygmalion in Ovid's *Metamorphoses*: Pygmalion creates an ivory statue with such skill that he comes to think of it as a flesh-and-blood woman, 'to such an extent does artistry lie hidden by means of its own artistry' (*ars adeo latet arte sua*, 10.252). From the perspective of semiotics (the discourse of the sign, which also invokes representation as a foundational concept in its assertion that a sign 'stands for' something else). Roland Barthes has treated in detail of the means by which a text can draw attention away from itself as text so as to create the 'reality effect', the sense of direct contact with the real.[1] Contrariwise, the distinction between means and object can lead to emphasis on the former (formalism), as the represented object recedes whilst the medium turns itself back on its own codes and conventions and engages in self-reflexive play. As is the case with all terms projected as autonomous opposites, these distinctions are open to deconstruction, but generate meaning to the extent to which, in what ways, and to what ends, they are kept distinct. Texts work within such distinctions, even when they endeavour to collapse them. Criticism and its object, often projected as separate, can also be seen as operating within similar assumptions and implicated in the same discursive strategies, by viewing them as two examples of 'the same thing', as, say, 'kinds of writing'; their very projection as separate instances of discrete phenomena can be one of the means whereby this complicity is disguised.

The terms of this discourse of representation are much in evidence in current discussion of Roman love elegy. In the Introduction to his *Latin Poets*

410

and Roman Life. Jasper Griffin locates himself within this discourse and adopts a particular perspective:

> This book aims to illustrate and clarify the relationship between Augustan poetry and the world in which it was produced and enjoyed. Many readers of Augustan poetry have difficulty with an obvious and central feature: the highly polished verbal style and the brilliant metrical expertise are accompanied by highly stylised conventions of situation and attitude. Yet behind the conventional devices – the pastoral scenes, the songs sung outside closed doors, the Greek myths – the reader feels the presence of emotional truth. How is this effect produced, and what is the relation of the finished poem to the raw stuff of life?[2]

The particularly sharp distinction drawn here between 'poetry' and 'the world' generates its own problematic, the 'relationship' between the 'means' (the highly polished verbal style, the highly stylized conventions of situation and attitude, the conventional devices, the finished poem) and the 'object', which is also the ostensible *object*, the end, of the enquiry, the raw stuff of life, the achievement of which is signalled by the term 'presence'. The verbal texture of the poetry is thus presented as a barrier; Griffin's text holds out the hope of passing through that barrier to achieve a direct experience of reality. Drawing attention to the problems posed by the formal texture of Augustan poetry serves to suppress the involvement of Griffin's own text in the rhetorical strategies of representation he seeks to describe: under what circumstances will we be deemed to be in the 'presence' of 'reality'? At what point will the verbal texture of Griffin's own text claim to have elided itself?

In the course of discussing 'Augustan poetry and the life of luxury', Griffin asks of Horace, *Odes* 1.17: 'Is this musical *fête champêtre* a transparent fiction?'[3] He thinks it is not, and that 'we can trace it through a less exalted stylisation to reality'. Adducing *Odes* 2.11.13ff., he remarks: 'Here we are less grand: here alone in the *Odes* the low word *scortum* appears . . . Yet the ingredients are all the same: a girl, music, drink, in the country.' As further evidence, it is stated that:

> we come down to realism in Ovid's account of the holiday in honour of Anna Perenna, *Fasti* 3.523 ff.: on the banks of the Tiber,
>
> plebs venit ac virides passim disiecta per herbas
> potat, et accumbit cum pare quisque sua
>
> 'The common people come and lie about on the grass and drink, each man stretched out with his girl' . . . This unromantic and plebeian

scene is, presumably, 'realistic' enough, and shows that one could have a picnic in Augustan Italy without becoming a poetical fiction.

The progressive condescension ('Here we are less grand'; 'the low word *scortum*'; 'we come down to realism'; 'this unromantic and plebeian scene is presumably "realistic" enough') tends to associate reality with, and seeks to find it in, the *plebs*, the common people. But Griffin resists using the word 'reality' here, preferring for the moment 'realism' and 'realistic', the latter betraying some anxiety by its enclosure within inverted commas. When the 'reality effect' is working, the text seems to be elided and the reader seems to belong to the world depicted; conversely, the invocation of the term 'realism' indicates, albeit expressed as a residual awareness of the act of representation, both a sense of fascination for what is depicted and of being an observer rather than a participant, of 'seeing', perhaps, rather than 'being present'. The works of Petronius and Juvenal, which are often held to depict a world peopled by lower social groups and viewed from their perspective, are constantly praised for their 'realism'. Critics who use the term project themselves as interlopers, however much they enjoy the temporary frisson of seeing how the other half lives from the safe confines, and through the window, of a racy textual vehicle. The milieu of Augustan poetry is, by contrast, characterized as predominantly aristocratic, and the world it depicts as viewed from that perspective. 'The poem then', Griffin concludes as he safely returns to *Odes* 1.17, 'is not a fantasy in no relation to life, a "dream", but a stylised and refined version of reality.' In the word 'refined', which seamlessly combines the discourses of artistic and social differentiation, Griffin finds the reassuring sense of 'presence' which licenses the use of the master term 'reality'. And curiously, those very conventional devices which were projected as a barrier to reality are now coming to take on the role of reality, a critical position Griffin is elsewhere very keen to distance himself from when he discusses 'Genre and real life in Latin poetry'.[4] Curiously too, the act of emphasizing the fundamental difference between the musical *fête champêtre* and the plebeian picnic, the difference which is held to constitute reality, has involved the projection of the two as instances of the same thing . . .

The strategy of grounding 'reality' in a discourse of social and aesthetic differentiation whilst the author coalesces with a point of view emerges again when Griffin turns to contemplate the pleasures of nakedness. Discussing devices to justify the representation of naked women (the bath and the presence of molesting satyrs are the examples adduced),[5] Griffin observes that 'the application to the nude of some trappings of mythology could make a great difference to its respectability', and points to Alma Tadema's Roman ladies in the bath and Lord Leighton's Greek nudes to suggest the similarity of Victorian practice.[6] He suggests a similar dignifying function for Propertius' use of the Judgement of Paris to suggest the beauty of Cynthia in 2.2.13–14:

cedite iam, divae, quas pastor viderat olim
Idaeis tunieas ponere verticibus

Yield now, you goddesses, whom once the shepherd saw undress on
Mount Ida

He adduces the parallel of *Ars* 1.247–8[7] as Ovid drawing 'the frank moral
from the story that, as Paris looked the goddesses over thoroughly before
making his choice, so his male readers, too, should look carefully before
choosing a girl', which leads immediately to the following reverie: 'the picture of a Roman man about town, running an eye over the girls on offer in
some louche establishment, is almost tangibly present'.[8] The rhetorical strategy underpinning the discourse of 'reality', culminating in the phrase 'almost
tangibly present', is by now familiar. The perspective adopted (explicitly
figured in terms of 'running an eye over') is that of a 'man about town'
visiting 'some louche establishment' – overtly male, overtly privileged. But
what Griffin holds out to us here is not reality but, explicitly, a *picture*,
another representation, just as, in retrospect, the musical *fête champêtre* of
Horace, *Odes* 1.17 was a stylized and refined *version* of reality. The rhetoric of
'reality' is invoked and manipulated to justify another representation, the
object of which is in this case the body of a lower-class female. A discourse of
constraints, of 'respectability', *enables* a representation, encoding a particular
ideological perspective, in the text of Griffin no less, according to his
assertion, than in the works of Alma Tadema or Lord Leighton.

Maria Wyke, in analysing reading practices that seek to look 'through' the
texts of elegy to a 'reality' of what she terms 'flesh-and-blood' women, also
locates herself within the discourse of representation. Again, the relational
structure of the term 'representation' defines the problematic, 'a need to
determine the relation between the realities of women's lives and their representation in literature'.[9] Granting that the poetic technique of elegy tempts
its readers to suppose that to some degree its female subjects reflect the lives
of specific Augustan women (and thus suggesting that poetic technique and
reading practice have colluded to produce a congruence of past and contemporary perspectives), she argues that 'realism itself is a quality of the text,
not a direct manifestation of a "real" world', and that 'to create the aesthetic
effect of an open window onto a "reality" lying just beyond, literary works
employ a number of formal strategies that change through time and between
discourses'.[10] Thus Cynthia's reproaches in Prop. 4.7 are 'replete with apparently authenticating incidentals such as a busy red light district of Rome,
worn-down windows, warming cloaks, branded slaves, ex-prostitutes, and
wool work'.[11] Sensitive to the way that the strategies of realism and the
invocation of that term render the rhetoric of 'reality' problematic, she
nonetheless acknowledges the legitimizing power of the term as she warns
that 'the realist devices of the Propertian corpus map out only a precarious

pathway to the realities of women's lives in Augustan society'.[12] Other path-
ways are explored only to be rejected, for example finding 'parallel portraits
of the female outside the poetic sphere',[13] such as Sallust's Sempronia or
Clodia Metelli; but 'these are on the level of representations, not realities –
any comparison tends to be a comparison between two forms of discourse
about the female'.[14] 'So persuasive have these discourses on the female been',
she continues, 'that they have often been taken for truth.'[15] In the course of
her meticulous search, 'representation' has taken over the rhetorical space
which 'reality' was presumed to occupy. The 'flesh-and-blood *woman*' produced by one reading practice is significantly replaced by the 'female *form*' of
another: the written women of elegy are 'to be read as signifiers of moral and
political ideologies'.[16]

The increasing concentration on means rather than object raises a crucial
question that can be framed in terms of the 'reality effect': where does it
stop? Any assertion that a particular statement in a text represents reality is
open to the counter-assertion that it is an instance of the reality effect, that
what is *represented* as reality is precisely that, another representation. Within a
discourse of representation, increasing formalist emphasis on 'means' at the
expense of 'object' produces disturbances within the rhetoric of reality and
contamination of categories assumed to be discrete: what were assumed to be
different turn out to be instances of the same thing, and *vice versa*. The
'conventional devices' which were initially presented as a barrier between
'life' and 'literature' start to take on the role of 'reality'; if the notion of
representation is recuperated under these circumstances, it leads to a reversal
of categories: 'life' imitates 'literature'. A favourite Ovidian motif, of
course,[17] incorporated into the *persona* of the Ovidian lover who, in the
received critical tradition, 'takes on the role(s)' of his elegiac predecessors.[18]
Griffin presents us ostensibly with a Propertius who models his lover's
behaviour on the lifestyle of Antony; but Antony's life*style* turns out to be
modelled on the 'role' of the dissolute man of action represented in literature.[19] As the formalist turn is pressed, the opposition between 'life' and
'literature', from which the traditional discourse of representation takes its
bearings, starts to fall apart and categories become unstable to the extent of
being inverted: 'life' and the practices assumed to constitute it (the musical
fête champêtre, songs sung outside doors etc) become 'texts', discourses we
inhabit; rhetoric is 'reality', *il n'y a pas de hors-texte*, the man is the style, and
reality is experienced as a network of representations – seemingly endless, for
any representation of reality is open in turn to representation as an instance
of the reality effect. However, although the categories have been destabilized,
we do not therefore stand outside the discourse of representation. The relation of 'standing for' has not been excluded or foreclosed: the discourse of
reality becomes the locus for the construction and contestation of ideologies
of class, gender and so on; the network of representations now 'stands for'
ideological differences. But ideology in turn is not a thing-in-itself: the term

'ideology' is itself precisely determined by the notion of 'perspectival representation' ... The reader will by now be getting the picture, that 'things' are never *just, simply, merely* what they seem 'to be', that the 'thing-in-itself', presumed to be an object of representation, becomes in the process itself a representation.

Griffin and Wyke each have their story to tell of Roman love elegy, each producing a textual construct at once itself a representation and itself open to representation. My representation of their texts as 'stories' may seem initially paradoxical, but it does enable further leverage to be exerted on the rhetoric of reality. For in their search for the 'raw stuff of life' and the 'realities of women's lives' at Rome, they invoke the notion of, and inscribe themselves within, a discourse of history, which seeks to ground itself in the actuality of the past; but it is here that the challenge textuality offers to the rhetoric of reality is at its most acute. History constitutes itself as a heuristic discourse by generating, amongst other distinctions, one between the past and the present, the object of history being to recapture the absent past: the past is thus represented as different from the present. But its means of doing so is textual: history fashions *representations* of the past, which create the illusion of reality and make the past 'present'. There is nothing outside the discourses of history by which representations of the past can be checked, no independent access to historical actuality. There is no escape in an appeal to so-called '*Realien*', for they too are open to being represented not as things-in-themselves, as the historicist might wish, but as textually constituted, signifiers never identical with themselves. Hard historicism, which in its purest form would wish to show the past 'as it really was', posits the independent existence of extratextual 'facts', a process of reification rhetorically underpinned by the employment of metaphors that, in speaking of '*hard* facts', '*material* practices', '*flesh-and-blood* women', 'the *raw* stuff of life' and so on, offer immediate and sometimes somewhat sinister sensual gratification. Hard historicism attempts to maintain its position in the face of the textualist emphasis that all 'facts' are discursively constituted as such, all 'events' are always already 'under description' (which is not, incidentally, to deny the actuality of the past but to suggest the process of its discursive organization). In striving to represent the past 'as it really was', to make the past 'present', historicism gestures towards a non-perspectival objectivity despite textualist assertions that history's characterizing structure is teleological,[20] that events are discursively selected, shaped and organized 'under the shadow of the end',[21] that, far from being disinterested, history does precisely make the past 'present' in the sense of accommodating the past to present interests. At its most occlusive, historicism creates 'objective' representations of the past that in their 'immediacy', 'relevance' or 'presence' serve to throw back consoling or affirming self-images; but as textualism encroaches, the distinction between past and present becomes less clearly demarcated, and depictions of the past become more overtly representative of the present. If historicism achieved its aim of understanding a culture of the past 'in its own terms', the result would be totally unintelligible except to but that culture and moment. And arguably not even to that, for a culture is articulated at any point by the contested historicity of its constitutive terms. Far from past being made 'present', it would be rendered totally foreign and impenetrably alien.[22] History cannot present the past in its own terms; it must act to some extent as a translator, an interpreter. The past, even if ostensibly represented as 'different', must also at some level be represented as the 'same'.

History is inextricably locked into the projection, under one guise or another, of 'extratextual realities', and as hard historicism is obliged to soften under the pressure of textualist awareness and critiques, the practice of history reforms itself. As its 'facts' are acknowledged to be textually constituted and its representational devices and modes become visible as such, so rhetorically it creates fresh reifications whose textuality is not immediately apparent, as in 'ideologies'. Realist modes of representation are jettisoned in favour of experimental styles, whilst realism migrates so as to inform other discourses such as sociology or anthropology (or to blur the barriers between them, creating a mixing of genres) – until the next textualist challenge comes along.

The issue of limit and control now becomes pressing, for the anxiety that formalist or textualist approaches raise most starkly is: at what point are such analyses to be *stopped*? At what point *will* they be stopped, since they *can* (apparently) be pressed to the point where categories collapse into an undifferentiated textuality? There lies, we are told, silence or madness. Every discursive intervention (including the Nietzschean) attempts or effects a closure of a sort with greater or lesser success, figured in the (illusion of) fulfilment of the desire which informs the intervention. Pygmalion creates a statue; the story 'ends' with it becoming a 'real' woman. However, a sign 'stands' not for reality, but for another sign in a continuing chain of signification. A statue stands for the female body, but the female body is a signifier in its turn; and so on. It is the function and effect of rhetoric to efface itself, to dissolve the distinction between 'illusion' and 'reality' (*ars adeo latet arte sua*). The object of such rhetorical persuasion may be its exponent no less than its audience. Pygmalion's statue 'becomes' a 'real' woman; her 'reality' is beyond question because she 'represents' nothing beyond the fulfilment of his desire. If the female body is the 'object' of representation in Griffin's text, the female form proves too large for the end he wishes to impose. The capacity of signifiers to signify sooner or later evades our control, except in our fantasies; but our sense of control is created *in* our stories, *in* our pictures, *in* our representations. But it is always open to others to tell their stories in their way. Beyond the ostensible *object* of representation, reality as represented by Maria Wyke becomes the locus for the construction and contestation of ideologies of class, gender etc. She seeks in 'ideology' a closural term, but it provides not the destination that the rhetoric promises, but only another resting-place. Closure is provisionally imposed, and the term 'reality' comes into play, when we assert that something stands only for itself, seemingly circumscribed and reflecting our will to control, when the application of a term is deemed a sufficient description, when the verb 'to be' is invoked, an identity asserted, and we say that something *is* something, the 'be-all and end-all'. But just as it looks as though history is set to collapse into an undifferentiated textuality, it comes back with a vengeance and issues its own challenge, that the term 'textuality' itself has a history, that it organizes its discourse teleologically to celebrate its own triumph, that it 'proves' its case by writing . . . history. Just as history 'ends up' (that is, finds the closure it requires to remain usefully operative) talking textuality, so textuality 'ends up' talking history, though always striving to retain the guise of one or the other. Sooner or later (the issue may be represented as one of *deferral*), the contradictions within a term become disablingly obtrusive and can only be resolved by recourse to an appeal to another term to which the first is ostensibly opposed. Thus 'difference' at some level invokes 'sameness' (recall the musical *fête champêtre* and the plebeian picnic), and *vice versa*. The purest of 'textualizing' definitions of history, 'a kind of storytelling towards the present, a textual construct at once itself, an interpretation and itself open to interpretation',[23] turns out on further inspection to be the most historicizing as well. For to define, to set within limits, to impose closure, to inscribe in a teleological framework, is to historicize.

Textualism allowed to run loose, we are assured, turns all distinctions into undifferentiated textuality, even the reification by which textuality is congealed into texts. Historicism allowed to run loose renders unintelligible even the historical moment it seeks to represent. If the impossible were to happen, if either were to be brought to its 'logical' conclusion (and this can be represented as a possibility only insofar as the terms are projected as extratextual realities), meaning would indeed cease: a text could never reach either horizon without there being total noise or total silence. But the horizon constantly recedes as one approaches, and we are left circumnavigating another hermeneutical circle. Invoking the word 'indeterminacy' is a fine way of making the flesh creep, or creating a warm glow; but its utterance as a meaningful term should offer immediate reassurance, or disappointment, that we haven't got to that stage, and won't, so long as it can create those effects. So, we are not faced with a choice – textuality *or* history – but must live with them both, for it is only in the making and manipulation of such distinctions that meanings can be generated – to the extent to which, in what ways, and to what ends, such terms are kept distinct. Distinctions are often represented as *determining*, but they can also be represented as *enabling*.

There can, then, be no representation without accommodation, no interpretation without appropriation; but equally, there can be no appropriation without interpretation, no accommodation without representation. Any reading, any act of interpretation of a text (of whatever description), is analysable in terms of on the one hand a hermeneutics, which seeks out an originary meaning for a text, and on the other the appropriation of the text by, and its accommodation to, the matrix of practices and beliefs out of which the reading is produced, including the role of the text in the authorization of those beliefs and practices which inform the reading. In establishing its desired goal, the closure to which it is ideally directed, an interpretation sets up a series of distinctions which characteristically incorporate a hierarchy of value, according privilege to one term at the expense of the other in furtherance of the ostensible end. A historicizing hermeneutical approach works to open up a distinction between text and context, projecting the second as ancillary to the first. The tendency of this is to locate the meaning of a text in the original moment of inscription and to represent all previous contextualizations as detachable, closed 'episodes' in the text's *Nachleben*, thus projecting the present contextualization as the 'truth', the 'real meaning'. A discourse of appropriation works to blur any distinction between text and context in its emphasis on the contextual construction of textual meaning – that every context is precisely another text, a construction open to interpretation – and stresses the multiplicity of contexts. But although this approach emphasizes that all readings are equally rhetorical, it baulks at the suggestion that all readings are therefore equally true; an agenda is no less at work here, leading to its own *telos*. The 'most plausible' or 'best' reading from this perspective is that which sees in the text the closest figuration of present preoccupations, and previous contextualizations are retrospectively seen as accommodated to the preoccupations of their periods – now treated by the imposition of closure as 'episodes', their awkward openness now (apparently) safely under control. The more strongly the figuration is felt, the more emphatic the assertion that it is objectively 'there' in the text, and has been 'present' in it all along, albeit locally suppressed and awaiting recovery. By contrast, a 'historicizing' rhetoric will tend to occlude notions of appropriation. But however much an approach succeeds in marginalizing one term at the expense of the other, the other always remains operative within it, however occluded, and renders the reading available for recuperation for and in the very terms occluded. Allowing the occluded terms to bounce back relativizes the findings (not necessarily refuting them – for all findings depend on distinctions being operative and are validated or negated only within the terms of the discourse which produces them – but rendering them open to recontextualization); reveals the pretensions of the previous reading, its claims to authority as presenting the 'truth'; and exposes the provisionality of closures represented as final, opening up the discourse to further acts of interpretation.

The issue of how far one term is going to be pressed at the expense of the other constitutes the politics of interpretation, that is, the discourse representing positionality 'inside' and 'outside' the formation of scholarship. Thus to represent recent criticism of Roman love elegy as historicizing emerges as a truism (for how could it fail to be so in some fashion?) and as a claim to a position within the scholarly formation. What is represented as 'historicism' (or 'textualism') is never *simply* an example of historicism or textualism (since one incorporates the other at some level), but also includes the perspectival positionality of the term's use, in the continuing (but not *end*less) contestation over what are to be projected as the 'norms' of interpretation – a struggle in which one's own approach will be represented as 'truths to be defended' and 'firmly-grounded methodologies' and one's opponent's as 'ideologies to be uncovered' and strategies of evasion, domestication, recuperation, accommodation and so on.

A 'reading' is not a closed system, identical with itself, however much it seeks to impose, or succeeds in imposing, closure on the chain of representations. It is always more or less accommodated to the context in which it appears, and for which it has been invoked, ordered and shaped, as is clearly the case with my readings of Griffin and Wyke no less than of the Pygmalion story in Ovid or the Tibullan readings to follow, which make 'Griffin', 'Wyke', 'Ovid' and 'Tibullus' *representative* of particular perspectives. A reading is thus, beyond its ostensible function as *explication du texte*, an allegory of itself and a justification of its own procedures, constitutive of the discourse of representation which seeks to represent it. If the Pygmalion story 'responds' to a discourse of representation, it can hardly do otherwise when it is re-constituted as a projection of it. Attempts to formalize, to systematize, run up against this problem sooner or later. It can only be deferred, so long as *a* reading can be made to appear *the* meaning of a text.

Any text, be it a Roman elegy or this one, must present itself at some level as having a 'universal' or transhistorical aspect even as it addresses a specific moment, if it is to be interpreted at all. What Thucydides presents as polar opposites (1.22), works written *es to parachrēma* rather than designed to stand as a *ktēma es aiei* (but then, as a self-styled historicist he has an interest in opening up this distinction, just as a self-styled textualist has an interest in closing it), are of necessity ingredients of any intelligible text. The universality occurs when a text projects, or is interpreted as projecting, a term as of universal validity or applicability, identical with itself, an essentialism. In order to depict and argue for the multiplicity of representations, it is necessary to project 'representation' as a foundational term of transhistorical validity, a preoccupation 'present' in the texts of the past; in order to argue for 'differences' it is necessary to posit sameness or identity, and *vice versa*. A discourse of 'representation' provides a set of terms which enable and determine the articulation of issues of reality, identity, control etc. With all this in mind, let us examine some texts of elegy from the (inevitably restricted) viewpoint (sic) of representation.

A prominent place has been given in recent critical writing to elegies which concentrate realist devices within the framework of a narrative description delivered in the first person and identified with the author, to the extent that this mode is projected as representative of elegy as a whole; Propertius 1.3, 2.15, 4.8 and Ovid, *Amores* 1.5 are repeatedly adduced as the classic examples. This does scant justice, it should be said, to the variety of representational strategies explored in the genre. One might adduce, for example, the contrasting narrators and expository styles of Book 4 of Propertius,[24] the use of a mythical female narrator within an epistolary framework in Ovid's *Heroides*, or the contrasting perspectives offered by the male friend of Sulpicia and by Sulpicia of Sulpicia's relationship with Cerinthus in [Tib.] 4.2–6 and 7–12 respectively. One of the most sustained, searching and sophisticated experiments in representational strategy is formed by the Delia poems of Tibullus (1.1–3, 5 and 6). This cycle can be read in such a way as to render problematic precisely what is 'taken for granted' in readings of elegy, the first-person male authorial *persona*. These poems have often been dismissed as disorganized concatenations of motifs, and, although this is a view which has become increasingly difficult to defend,[25] they are tantalizingly elusive. The first poem seems to be a monologue of some sort, representing the words or thoughts of what for the moment I shall refer to as its 'speaker'. The opening lines express a willingness that others may face the hardships and dangers of war abroad in pursuit of great wealth in contrast to the speaker's wish for a life of inglorious inactivity at home (1–6). But who is this speaker? His identity is available to us only through his words, and thus far we have heard only the expression of desire via a series of subjunctive verbs. The circumstances, the 'facts', the 'realities' which have prompted the expression of these desires, or are preventing their fulfilment, have not yet been divulged and will only emerge in the speaker's words. But for the moment, the subjunctives continue. As a *rusticus*, a peasant (7–8), he would set vines with expertise, nor would his hopes play him false, but deliver a bumper vintage. His words have not made clear whether he does, or does not, regard himself as a *rusticus*, and, if so, what is standing in the way of him accomplishing what he wishes, but his wishes for a bumper vintage are characterized by an undoubted confidence in their fulfilment, for he says, employing an indicative at last in his first explicit self-characterization, that he *is* a man of piety (*veneror*, 'I pay homage', 11), and his further description of the piety he represents as characteristic of himself reveals through another indicative (*ponitur*, 14) that he *is* a country property-owner of some sort ('and a portion of whatever fruit the new harvest brings forth for me *is* placed before the farmer god', 13–14). The speaker's 'real' circumstances are emerging in his words. What, then, is preventing the fulfilment of his wishes of 5–8, and of the promises he subsequently makes to honour Ceres, the goddess who would guarantee such fruitfulness, and Priapus, the god who would guard it (15–18)? The address in the indicative to the Lares that follows (19–22) reveals in passing another important circumstantial detail, that the speaker's property, which was once huge, is now greatly reduced. The optative subjunctives that resume in 25–6,

> iam modo, iam possim contentus vivere parvo
> nec semper longae deditus esse viae . . .

if only now, now at last, I may be able to live content with little, and not always be given up to the long march . . .

reveal obliquely the reason why the speaker is unable to tend his reduced estate: 'if only I may not always be given up to the long march' implies that that is precisely what he is, a soldier duty-bound to serve far from home. His reasons for becoming a soldier are not made explicit, but his opening expression of willingness that others should go away to war in pursuit of wealth so long as he might be able to stay at home in his reduced circumstances can be read retrospectively in this light. Similarly, the serving soldier's reverie about making love to a mistress on the familiar couch at home while the storm rages outside (43–50) turns out in retrospect to have been prompted in relation to a specific individual, *mea Delia* (57), and the elaborate series of plays throughout the text on words applicable to both warfare and love-making[26] can be seen as 'generated' out of the solider/lover's 'experience' and articulating the ironies and conflict of values involved in his situation.

The text is thus, obliquely, providing its own context, a 'reality' notion-ally 'outside' it against which the speaker's identity can be constructed, his character delineated and his perspectives assessed, and it is possible to con-struct a very detailed 'context' (as for example Cairns does for 1.5, setting out in tabular form the ' "historical" order' of events and their 'actual order of presentation'[27]), and to explore the ramifying discrepancies and reson-ances between the text and its 'context'. The addresses to Messalla (53ff.) and Delia (57ff.) suggest a dramatic aspect to the monologue, but if the 'setting' is, as lines 25–6 seem to imply, abroad on military service, the possibility that both of them are envisaged as present to hear it seems to be excluded, leaving it probable that neither is to be thought of as listening. Rather the implication is that the text represents the sequence of the 'speaker's' thought, and that we read it as eavesdroppers on a stream of consciousness, thus involving us in the piquant circularity of extrapolating 'reality' from the text and then using it to assess the viewpoint from which that 'reality' has been presented. The address to Messalla serves, apparently, to anchor the text's ostensible context in turn in specific historical 'reality', whether we wish to represent that as the undoubted physical existence of Messalla, or the ideological values he is represented as embodying so successfully (53–4).

However, the Delia cycle does not fold itself unproblematically into that specific historical 'reality'. 1.3 projects its 'setting' as the soldier/lover falling ill on the way to the campaign with Messalla and in danger of dying. Again the addresses to both Messalla (1f.) and Delia (82ff.), who is repeatedly represented as having been left behind, suggest that we are eavesdropping on a monologue in the mind. The soldier/lover has fallen ill on the island of 'Phaeacia' (3). There were a number of contemporary discourses which sought to identify the Homeric Phaeacia with the island of Corcyra,[28] but contextualizations which seek to ground themselves in the 'realities' of the poet's biography or the immediate circumstances of composition and substitute 'Corcyra' for 'Phaeacia', often without comment, thereby sidestep the very issue of the distinction between 'truth' and 'fiction', the 'real' and the 'fictive' which the name 'Phaeacia' problematizes. It will not do to seek a final meaning in the signifier 'Tibullus', for what is signified by 'Tibullus' is one of the points at issue. We eavesdrop on the thoughts of 'Tibullus' as he believes he is about to die. He reviews what happened between him and Delia immediately before his departure from that perspective – under the shadow of the end, we might say – (9–22), revealing the way his representation of the past is structured around his present concerns, and his interpretations of the 'same' event fluctuate through changing circumstances. Immediately before his departure, Delia, he recalls, is said (*dicitur*, 10) to have consulted all the gods about his prospects of return: *dicitur* implies he was not present and knew this only by report. All the omens (*par excellence* a discourse of signs whose interpretation is contingent upon circumstance) promised his safe return (13), although Delia's behaviour gave every indication that she was not convinced by them. At that juncture his casual attitude to the omens (sought by Delia and not by him) was determined by the desire to use them, and Delia's reaction to them, in order to cast himself in the role of *solator* (15), a comforter, and, after the last farewell, separated from Delia, to seek in them a (now anxious) excuse for not going just yet (15–16). Following his departure, which involved a stumble in the gateway (20), changing circumstances lead him increasingly (cf. *quotiens*, 19) to brood upon these signs and to deem them unlucky (*tristia*, 20), a chain of interpretation seemingly validated by his present plight. His self-identification as a lover within this monologue provides the explanation and the moral to be drawn: let no-one dare to depart from a lover who doesn't wish it, or he will know that he has gone against the prohibition of the god (21–2). The implied circumstances and self-image of the lover determine the details of the escapist fantasy of a Golden Age in the past, when there were no long roads for marches (*longas . . . vias*, 36), no ships to take men overseas in search of wealth, no warfare, no doors to houses (37–48). This is similarly the case when he seeks refuge from his helplessness in weaving elaborate fantasies about a heaven for those who have died young in love (57–66) and a hell for anyone who would wish to desecrate not, as it transpires, love in general, but his own affair (67–82), this last fading into an Odyssean fantasy of the welcome he might receive from Delia should he return safely (83–92).

What emerges from this ostensibly private stream of consciousness upon which we eavesdrop is a complex mixture of fantasy and oblique narrative emplotted from the perspective of one whose circumstance is impending death and whose self-image is overwhelmingly that of a lover. Nonetheless, at one point this monologue contemplates projecting out into the 'world' a 'text' which offers a quite different perspective. Fearful of the imminence of death, the lover composes his epitaph, which will be open to 'public' scrutiny in a way that his 'thoughts' will not be:

> hic iacet immiti consumptus morte Tibullus
> Messallam terra dum sequiturque mari (55–6)

> Here lies Tibullus taken off by a cruel death while serving with Messalla on land and sea

For 'public' consumption, the lover who imagines himself cavorting around the Elysian Fields or returning to the arms of his rapturous beloved, wishes to be seen (fantasizes being seen?) as the model of a loyal soldier, following his commander even to his death. Giving to the lover/soldier the name 'Tibullus' further complicates the issue. Which constitutes the 'real' identity, the lover or the soldier (or the person his friends 'know' as 'the poet'; compare the contrasting representations in Horace, *Odes* 1.33 and *Epistles* 1.4)? Or does the 'real' identity lie in the incongruity and conflict between the roles? From where does the definition of our identity arise? From the interpretations by others of our actions and words? In the face of the entanglement in (oftentimes bewildering, dangerous or distasteful) circumstance which the social pressures on the construction of our identities exert, fantasy seems to offer a reassuring sense of control by allowing desire untrammelled freedom. However, fantasy is not separate from reality but helps to constitute it, and only becomes perceived as separate and open to representation as 'fantasy' when the closure it seeks to impose is superseded and becomes untenable. In 1.5, the setting for which is the street outside Delia's door up and down which he walks, the locked-out lover recalls how he used to fashion a future for himself and Delia (21–34), an idyllic existence in the country in which Delia would grow accustomed to rural life, to the extent that she could take over the running of everything (29–30), and be the perfect hostess to Messalla on his visits (31 4), *consuescet* (25) tempts one to extrapolate about the 'reality' of Delia's character which the lover's fantasy was at that stage striving to override. Changed perception (which now appropriates for itself the role of 'reality') has rendered this picture untenable, a 'fantasy'; the verbatim recollection is framed between two uses of the verb *fingebam*, 'I used to imagine' (20, 35), and to the first of these the lover appends from his present perspective the adjective *demens*, representing himself from the perspective of now as 'out of his mind' then – precisely when, it could be argued, he was most *in* it. The dominant theme of the Delia cycle on this reading is *real*ization, the rendering of 'reality' to oneself.

It is high time, however, that some pressure were exerted on the rhetoric of this form of analysis, the way the argument has been structured to suggest that 'in reality' these poems are monologues, that the text generates within itself a context against which it might be read and so forth. This can be done by looking at another of the Delia poems which can be interpreted in such a way as to render visible some of the rhetorical strategies involved in this reading. The poems thus far examined have been read as projecting as their 'setting' a particular moment and place from which the lover emplots the events of the past and projects his vision of the future. 1.2 has placed considerable difficulties in the path of a similar analysis. Guy Lee has summarized the problem well:

> This long elegy appears to have a dramatic setting, but readers differ over what that setting is. Some think the whole thing takes place at Delia's closed door (the wine referred to in line 1 could be served there, cf. Plautus *Curculio* 82–85). Others think that it takes place at a drinking-party, at which the poet from line 7 on falls into a reverie, possibly (as Leo suggested) coming out of it at line 89 when someone present laughs. Still others think that the poet is at home, soliloquizing after initially addressing a servant; a variant of this would be that he falls asleep after line 6 and what follows represents his thoughts in a vivid dream.[29]

Let us take a hint from Lee's use of the phrase 'dramatic setting' and explore the poem as the projection of, and response to, not one particular moment and place but a developing series of situations which the lover both responds to and prompts – a fully-fledged dramatic monologue, that is. His opening words represent him as trying to get drunk in response to *novos . . . dolores*, new miseries (1), the adjective implying perhaps that this is not the first time things have gone wrong. He finds himself outside his girl's firmly bolted door (5–6), to which he addresses a typical lover's lament (7–14): where elsewhere the lover's words were addressed only to himself, in his mind, his lament we may imagine him as uttering aloud. His initial curse directed at the door on finding it locked (7–8) turns immediately into an obsequious apology to it (9–12), and then, in the hope that it may yet open to let him in, into a reminder of the many times he has decorated it with garlands – frequently the action of a lover who has had to depart unsuccessfully,[30] and so an oblique confirmation of

424

the situation adumbrated in the phrase *novos . . . dolores* (1). Delia is then addressed through the door (15–24). She may have another man or she may be under guard to prevent her meeting the lover; he assumes the alternative that offers him greater hope, and addresses encouragement to her which articulates his image of her desired behaviour: the goddess of love favours lovers who show courage in overcoming the obstacles to furtive love-making, but not to everyone, only those whom 'fear does not stop getting up in the dark of the night' (*quos . . . nec vetat obscura surgere nocte timor*, 23–4). *en* (25) usually draws attention to action happening at the precise moment of its utterance, and *ego cum tenebris tota vagor anxius urbe* ('when I wander distraught throughout the city in the dark'), uttered from the lover's perspective as demonstrative proof that Venus protects brave lovers, seems to indicate as well that he has now left the doorstep; his point of departure may be signalled in *surgere* (24), for the action signified there could instigate his departure from the door just as much as describe the behaviour desired of Delia. Venus renders courageous lovers inviolable, the lover tells himself (29–30), as he catalogues the possible dangers faced by a lover wandering the streets alone at night, the first which occurs to him being assault and theft (27–8). But whether it be the dangers of mugging or the frost and rain, any hardship, he tells himself, is worthwhile if only Delia will invite him in (33–4). The startled exclamation *parcite luminibus* (35; eyes or torches?), presumably prompted by his first encounter with another person, seems to give the lie to the lover's much-vaunted courage. His following words combine an attempt to recuperate that self-image with a warning to anyone who might recognize him to keep his mouth shut, implying that recognition *as* a lover is chief amongst his anxieties (37–42). Not that Delia's *coniunx* will believe an informer anyway, he tells himself (43; the reason for the lover's earlier exclusion is becoming clearer with the lover's explicit allusion to this character *as* Delia's *coniunx*, her partner), since the lover has obtained a spell from a witch so that he won't believe his eyes, even if he catches the lover and Delia in bed together (55–8); but the lover's anxieties about Delia's attachment to him emerge as he adds that the spell will only work for him, not for other potential or actual lovers (59–60). His faith in the witch seems total as he recalls to himself the demonstration of her powers that he witnessed (45–54), but on further reflection (61–6) his faith rapidly evaporates, as he recalls that the witch promised to free him from his love and carried out ceremonies to do so. But her failure is hardly surprising, since it immediately transpires that while all this was going on, the lover himself was praying (cf. *orabam*, 66) not that his love should go away, but that it should be mutual, and that he shouldn't be able to live without Delia.

The lover's capacity for self-delusion seems boundless, as every successive utterance works to undermine the realities he has previously unfolded for himself. Another figure now enters his thoughts, an iron-hearted man who, when he had Delia for the asking, preferred, the fool (*stultus*, 68), to go abroad to war in the successful pursuit of plunder and glory (67–72). The lover contrasts his aspirations starkly with those of the soldier, if only *he* had the opportunity to be with Delia (*mea si tecum modo Delia*, 73), and they are his characterizing dream of life and love in the country (73–6). What, he asks himself, is the point of luxurious bedding, feather pillows and the soothing sound of running water, if you spend the night awake crying (77–80)? The iron-hearted man is not explicitly identified, but the account of his activities in 67–70 has a ring of familiarity, and the details of the remorse attributed to him in 77–80 are remarkably specific. Can it be that this is the lover's *alter ego*, whose behaviour is now so unaccountable to him that he can only refer to it as though it were that of another person entirely? The account of the luxurious bedding in 77 arises out of, and in contrast to, the lover's dream of making love to Delia in the country, and his assertion that *his* sleep (cf. *mihi*) would be *mollis*, soft, on the uncultivated ground (76). The adjective carries the connotation that this would be the sleep that follows on love-making.[31]

We only ever 'see' Delia through the words of the lover, and must construct our image of what she is 'really' like from the perspectives these offer; but from his previous references to *molli . . . lecto* (19) and *molli . . . toro* (58), in both of which the figure of Delia is implicated, it is at least open to us to wonder what her reaction to the prospect of making love on the uncultivated ground might be, let alone her attitude to a lover who went away to war to enrich himself when he could have had her for the asking. The lover turns to wondering whether his present predicament could be the result of displeasing the goddess of love (81–4); if so, he wouldn't hesitate to crawl on his hands and knees and beat his head against the door of her temple (85–8). At this point he addresses a warning: 'but you who complacently laugh at my woes, beware; your turn will come' (89–90). Presumably his attention has been caught by the sound of laughter and he realizes that he is the object of it. What dramatically will have prompted the laughter? What, indeed, prompted the thought in 81ff. that he might have displeased Venus? Is it that on his nocturnal ramblings he has arrived at the temple of Venus, and is carrying out the actions he refers to as his penance? It is to address her that he turns once more (99–100) when he has delivered his warning to the person who derided him (91–8).

Doubtless this reading could be altered, supplemented or challenged; it presents itself as one more or less plausible 'contextualization' of the text. But to what extent is it 'outside' the text, as the term 'contextualization' seems to suggest? We have already seen the way the other Delia poems 'invade' their possible contextualizations in such a way as to blur the distinction between text and context. Lee's use of the term 'dramatic setting'[32] can be developed to produce a reading of the poem as the representation of action, the subject-matter and rapid changes of scene being reminiscent of mime, a genre with which elegy has a number of affinities.[33] Possibly Tibullus 1.2 was amenable to some form of dramatic performance, as Virgil's *Eclogues* reportedly were. That is an intriguing possibility, but neither its establishment nor its refutation would 'fix' or guarantee the meaning of the text. The notion of 'performance' entailed by and encoded in a phrase like 'dramatic setting' can serve a variety of rhetorical functions, and its attendant terminology is available for appropriation in various ways to underpin differing types of interpretation with differing interests. From one perspective, performance is 'outside' the text, an interpretation of it: the term 'performance' enacts a distinction between a 'transcendent' text and the specific, imperfect *interpretations, embodiments, representations, realizations* of it. But from another perspective, performance of a text is the means of self-exploration or self-expression on the part of the performers.[34] This perspective informs, for example, criticism of drama which seeks the 'meaning' of a play not in the 'transcendent text', but in its specific performances, seen, say, as ritual or the enactment of civic ideology. This sort of criticism seeks a closure in the representation of drama as an *embodiment*, the material 'presence' of the body being seen as the guarantor of meaning. But the closure is a provisional one, for the body is not a self-evident 'reality' signifying nothing beyond itself, and performance in this scheme is itself an enactment of something further (religious belief or civic ideology), and thus itself a 'text' to be interpreted. As a text 'dramatizes' action, it becomes part of this chain of signification, and we discover ourselves in a delightful world of ironic resonances in which the 'reality' of one text dramatizing action finds rhetorical corroboration in the 'realism' of another, as when Margaret Hubbard says of Propertius 4.8: 'we could not be . . . more firmly located in the *verismo* of the mime'.[35] Within this chain of representations, all the world's a stage, and the discourses we inhabit are 'scripts' so 'real' to those involved that they 'act' upon them. One cannot impose a closure on Tibullus 1.2 by referring to the person Tibullus, for 'Tibullus' is an exploration of the roles, poetic and erotic, the elegy dramatizes. Elegy's place in this chain of signification is encoded in Ovid's warning to the censorious at the beginning of the second book of the *Amores* (2.1.3–4):

> procul hinc, procul este, severi:
> non estis teneris apta *theatra* modis

> Away with you from here, those of you with puritan views: you are
> not a fit *audience* for erotic strains

A text (of whatever description) cannot seal itself off from, it can only occlude its own involvement in, the terms of analysis it seeks to impose.

In ostensibly talking *about* representation and the terminology it involves, I have not been able to escape using it myself; the opening sentence of this chapter read 'the notion of representation *plays a prominent role* in aesthetic criticism', and the language of 'seeing' (perspective, viewpoint, ostensibly, etc.) pervades it. It is possible to articulate only within the terms of a discourse, but if this is determining from one perspective, it can also be represented as enabling. One can devise strategies of provisional evasion, such as I have done in talking about the '*discourse* of representation' which projects a position 'outside' from which the illusion of control can be created and suggests that certain terms 'within' it (notably 'representation') are foundational and not problematic, and in manipulating terminology (e.g. 'closure') in such a way as to suggest it lies beyond sceptical scrutiny. The distinctions imposed in any discourse are always arbitrary in the sense that they cannot be grounded in any appeal to something 'outside' the discourse, but never arbitrary in the sense that the distinctions are discursively produced. In criticizing the 'rhetoric' of reality (that is, the way *others* use the term), one cannot avoid creating a 'reality' within which one's own discourse is ostensibly grounded. The reader may care to look again at the indicative statements in this chapter. It is salutary to see in every 'answer' another question, in every 'disavowal of authority' the construction of another 'authority', to regard the time one thinks one is right as the time to think again. Indicative statements; but indicative of what?

Notes

1 Barthes (1974).
2 Griffin (1985), ix.
3 Griffin (1985), 20.
4 Griffin (1985), 49.
5 Griffin (1985), 103.
6 Griffin (1985), 104.
7 *luce deas caeloque Paris spectavit aperto,|cum dixit Veneri 'vincis utramque, Venus'.* ('Paris viewed the goddesses in broad daylight when he said to Venus "You beat them both, Venus".')
8 Griffin (1985), 105.
9 Wyke (1989a), 25 [reprinted in this volume, pp. 386–409].
10 Wyke (1989a), 27.
11 Wyke (1989a), 32.
12 Wyke (1989a), 33.
13 Wyke (1989a), 37.
14 Wyke (1989a), 38.
15 Wyke (1989a), 40.
16 Wyke (1989b), 128.
17 Cf. e.g. *Ars* 2.313, 3.155, 164, 210, *Met.* 11.235–6.
18 See Davis (1989).
19 Griffin (1985), 32, 47.

20 See Attridge, Bennington and Young (1987), 9.
21 Kermode (1966), 5.
22 See Felperin (1990), 14.
23 Felperin (1990), 159.
24 See Wyke (1987).
25 See Cairns (1979), 192.
26 See Lee (1974).
27 Cairns (1979), 176, 8.
28 See Cairns (1979), 44–6.
29 Lee (1990), 116. I have used Lee's text and enumeration in the following discussion.
30 See Smith (1913), 210, ad loc.
31 See Cairns (1979), 102.
32 Comparable terms are found elsewhere of this poem, e.g. Smith speaks of its 'mise-en-scène' (1913, 45).
33 See McKeown (1979).
34 See Sayre (1990).
35 Hubbard (1974), 151.

Works cited

Attridge, D., Bennington, G. and Young, R. (eds) (1987) *Post-structuralism and the Question of History*. Cambridge.

Barthes, R. (1974) *S/Z*, trans. R. Miller. London.

Cairns, F. (1979) *Tibullus: a Hellenistic Poet at Rome*. Cambridge.

Davis, J.T. (1989) *Fictus Adulter: Poet as Actor in the Amores*. Amsterdam.

Felperin, H. (1990) *The Uses of the Canon*. Oxford.

Griffin, J. (1985) *Latin Poets and Roman Life*. London.

Hubbard, M. (1974) *Propertius*. London.

Kermode, F. (1966) *The Sense of an Ending*. Oxford.

Lee, G. (1974) '*Otium cum indignitate*: Tibullus 1.1', in A.J. Woodman and D.A. West (eds.), *Quality and Pleasure in Latin Poetry*. Cambridge.

—— (1990) *Tibullus: Elegies*. Leeds.

McKeown, J.C. (1979) 'Augustan elegy and mime', *PCPhS* 25. 71–84.

Sayre, H. (1990) 'Performance', in Lentricchia and McLaughlin (eds.) (1990) *Critical Terms for Literary Study, Chicago*.

Smith, K.F. (1913) *The Elegies of Albius Tibullus*. New York.

Wyke, M. (1987) 'The elegiac woman at Rome', *PCPhS* 33. 153–178.

—— (1989a) 'Mistress and metaphor in Augustan elegy', *Helios* 16. 25–47.

—— (1989b) 'Reading female flesh: *Amores* 3.1', in A. Cameron (ed.), *History as Text*, London.

"BUT ARIADNE WAS NEVER THERE IN THE FIRST PLACE"

Finding the female in Roman poetry

Barbara K. Gold

Or, if you prefer, for a culture busy unraveling itself from within an imaginary labyrinth, Ariadne remains just around the corner. But Ariadne, like Truth, was never really there in the first place (Jardine 1985: 47).

"It's a shame that more people don't take an interest in what you people write." "It's a shame that we don't write for you to read" (Richlin 1990: 176).

Feminist literary criticism is currently undergoing an identity crisis. In her 1977 book *A Literature of Their Own* and her 1979 study "Towards a Feminist Poetics," Elaine Showalter distinguished between *feminist critique* (woman as the consumer of male-produced literature) and *gynocritics* (feminist criticism concerned with "woman as writer – woman as the producer of textual meaning, and the history, themes, genres and structures of literature by women"; Showalter 1979: 25). Showalter advocated that feminist criticism should develop "new models based on the study of female experience," and should include among its subjects linguistics and the problem of a female language, and individual or collective literary careers and histories, rather than analyzing male experience in order to try to understand the presentation of women in his texts (Showalter 1977).

Similarly Annette Kolodny attempted to define what feminist literary criticism might mean. She distinguished three types of women readers: women who write about "men's books," women who write about "women's books," and "any criticism written by a woman no matter what the subject" (Kolodny 1975: 75). In her classification of modes of understanding "woman" or "women," there are two broad distinctions to be made: women as readers versus women as writers and women reading male texts versus women reading female texts. We should now add to these distinctions the current focus on plurality in feminism and the need to take account of both white feminists and feminists of color (Lugones 1991).

Recently, Showalter has turned her attention to "gender studies," arguing that feminists should, with considerable caution, consider questions of masculinity and be willing to focus on male texts, "not as documents of sexism and misogyny, but as inscriptions of gender and 'renditions of sexual difference'" (Showalter 1989: 5). Given the fact that nearly all classical texts still extant are male authored, the gender-studies approach would seem to be a fruitful hermeneutic for most classical feminist scholars, but it is important here to note Modleski's observations on the dangers of allowing gender studies to supersede feminist studies (Modleski 1991). If male critics coopt and bury feminist studies or exploit them for their own advantage, feminist studies will be marginalized and increasingly lost to view and, as Modleski points out, feminism will become "a conduit to the more comprehensive field of gender studies" (Modleski 1991: 5).

Except for Sappho (and even most of her poems have come down to us in a fragmentary state), all of the female writers in antiquity such as Corinna, Erinna, Anyte, Nossis, and the two Sulpicias are known to us from short and incomplete snippets or from late or unreliable testimonies about them (Lefkowitz 1981). Classicists have thus tended to focus on male-authored texts (see Hallett's (1993) article in this volume for suggestions on how we might broaden our curriculum to include a wider range of noncanonical authors and different combinations of canonical and noncanonical texts). As increasing numbers of feminist scholars attempt to map the female consciousness of antiquity, more and more attention has been paid to using the admittedly scanty remains of female writers such as those mentioned above to learn about how and what women thought from their own words and to try to re-create the social contexts in which they operated (Hallett 1979, 1993; Winkler 1981; Skinner 1989a, 1991a, 1991b, 1993; Snyder 1989, 1991; Stehle 1990; Pomeroy 1991a, 1991b).

A serious debate has recently arisen among feminist classical scholars about the validity of using male-authored, canonical texts, which are labeled as "tribal totems for classicists" in Phyllis Culham's "Decentering the Text: The Case of Ovid" (Culham 1990: 161). This article forms the introduction to and basis of a debate on the choice of a male author, Ovid, by the Women's Classical Caucus for its 1985 panel at the annual meeting of the American Philological Association (for the debate, see *Helios* 17[1990]). Here Culham argues that we would do far better to work at recovering women's lived reality by reading female authors themselves when possible and by paying close attention to the historical, material context which will reveal, as male-authored literary texts do not, the disparity of male and female experience (see also Culham 1987: 9–30; Pomeroy 1991a: 265).[1] The focus on material culture, according to Culham, would reintroduce working women into the picture, highlight the importance of lived reality over ahistorical, constructed texts that are often regarded as transcendent entities, and help us to provide explanations of social phenomena and to investigate the origins and propagation of Western culture (Culham 1990: 165). Other feminists argue that lived reality is always mediated and its representation always textual (Hallett 1973, 1993; Gamel 1989, 1990; Richlin 1990, 1992b). They further maintain that, even in discussing male writers of antiquity, we are not excluding ancient women since all the events depicted and attitudes voiced in canonical texts "bear on the lives of the women who heard [Ovid's] poems and live(d) in the sign system that produced the canon" (Richlin 1992b: 159). They contend as well that reading several male-authored ancient texts about women against other ancient evidence about women can help to illuminate the social, political, artistic, and erotic aspirations of the women pictured there, especially when we have no other evidence (Hallett 1973, 1993).

Since so few female-authored texts are available, classicists who are interested in "retrieving the bones of our foremothers" (Richlin 1990: 177) need to make creative connections and to use the skills developed by feminist researchers operating in other disciplines in order to find sensitive and successful approaches to elucidating women's actions, thoughts, and desires in antiquity from the male-authored texts that have come down to us. Toward this end, I would like to look at what French and Anglo-American criticism of the last twenty years have to offer us and then to move on to a model that I find a useful hermeneutic for reading certain male-authored Roman texts, namely Alice Jardine's concept of "gynesis" (Jardine 1985). Jardine's approach works particularly well for Roman elegy, a genre of poetry written in Rome in the first century BCE as a reaction to the clearly developed but already collapsing moralistic patriarchal value system of that society. The conditions under which the Roman elegists worked parallel the conditions of contemporary Western life that Jardine discusses precisely because of the unsettled political climate, the concomitant shakeup of societal values, and the search for an individual response to the failure of the patriarchal state in Rome at that time.

Before testing Jardine's gynesis on one of the Roman elegists, Propertius (who lived from some time in the early 40s BCE to some time before 2 CE), I will give a brief historical survey of two major "schools" of feminist thought which have been important to the development of Jardine's argument: the French feminists/poststructuralists and the Anglo-Americans, many of whom have tended to follow a more empirical approach that is somewhat akin to the historical empiricism characteristic of Anglo-American classical scholarship. It should be made clear at the outset that the French feminist positions that I will outline here were articulated in the 1970s (see works cited at the end of this chapter). A great deal of fundamental work was done in that period by critics such as Kristeva, Cixous, and Irigaray, but French feminist thought today has changed and is now quite different. Nonetheless, the ideas of these critics have had an enormous effect on Anglo-American feminists and on Jardine in particular, and they continue to produce reactions in many feminist quarters.

Using the ideas of the French and the Anglo-American feminists, I will try to show what benefit we can gain from each "school," how classics fits into these approaches, and how Jardine's discussion might help us continue the dialogue on women in Roman elegy started by Hallett, Wyke, et al., by further developing our thinking on the depiction of women in this genre. I am proposing to proceed in this way with the full knowledge that post-structuralism did not exist (or at least was not recognized as a mode of analysis) in antiquity and that Jardine herself is not talking about antiquity but about modernity. Yet what she says about male writers in our own period can help us to understand the place of "woman" in ancient elegy, and to confirm, as I have proposed above, that modern modes of representing the feminine can be seen in antiquity in such writers as Propertius. It is import-ant that we learn to "reread the past from the unavoidable perspective of present cultural influences . . . without denying the specificity and difference of the past," on the one hand, or our preconceptions of the present, on the other (Belsey and Moore 1989: 223; Beer 1989: 67).

Contempory critical approaches can certainly help us to elucidate classical texts in new ways that will help the feminist/classicist project. But openness to contemporary criticism should work both ways. An understanding of the feminist possibilities in classical texts adds a historical depth to the current feminist debates. Such classical texts are capable of illuminating the contemporary texts they have influenced by showing that contemporary representations of women have close parallels in literatures from the past. To put the alterations of and repetitions of these representations in a historical context is vital if we are to be able to determine which means of challenging texts produced by a heavily patriarchal tradition will be of most use for the feminist approach. Only by examining the long development of attitudes toward language and representation that have limited women's self-knowledge and expression can we shake off the effects of centuries of patriarchal control.

To the uninitiated, feminist theory may seem a monolithic set of ideas designed to interpret the world and its texts in ways which provide an alter-native to or undermine the existent male-generated approaches. But nothing could be further from the truth. Feminist critics would appear to agree on only one thing: the importance of dismantling traditionally male ways of seeing. But questions of how to achieve this goal and what the major focal points of debate should be have proliferated with the development of femi-nist theory over the past twenty years. As feminism has become more developed and more complex, it has naturally spawned different "schools" of thought on such fundamental issues as the definition of gender identity, the role of language in determining or defining gender, the nature and import-ance of the unconscious, the importance of the speaking subject, and the desirability of an empirical versus a theoretical mode of analysis. Two of the more polarized stands on such issues have been taken by certain

Anglo-American and French feminists (see Moi 1985; Jones 1985). As Jardine points out, "any generic description of either French or American feminism would immediately homogenize, colonialize, and neutralize the specificities of struggles that are often of quite epic proportions" (Jardine 1985: 15), so that what I will say here should be regarded as necessarily schematic and not as an attempt to describe with any specificity each individual French or Anglo-American feminist critic or to generalize unfairly about them.

The central dividing line for French and American feminists has been the French emphasis on the importance of *language* to the exclusion of all else. For the French feminists, there was no world outside of the texts; the text was everything, everything was language, and that language was identified with and dominated by the masculine (Marks 1978: 842; Jones 1985). They were therefore interested in seeing women somehow gain control over language or invent a new kind of writing, writing that was not logocentric, that did not contain preestablished, easily accessible meanings, and that liberated women from the repression of phallocentric language. *Phallocentrism* or *phallogocentrism* (or *phallologocentrism*) is the term French feminists have used to describe and critique a cultural framework in which concepts have an independent existence, the truth of an idea is found outside of language in the subjectivity of the individual, and language itself privileges the phallus as the symbol or source of power. In their view, primacy of place has been given to the male and male forms of discourse; women have been forced either to participate in masculine, phallocentric language or to invent their own form of discourse, which is characterized by lack and marginalizes them even further. The French feminists "have reformulated Freud's question 'What does a woman want?' to, 'What does a woman write?' "(Marks 1978: 842).

The three best-known contemporary French feminists are Luce Irigaray, Hélène Cixous, and Julia Kristeva, all deeply influenced by psychoanalytic and poststructuralist thought and heavily indebted to Lacan and Derrida. To this group I would also add Monique Wittig (for a good summary of contemporary French feminism, see Jones 1985; Moi 1985). These French theorists cannot be lumped together into one category since they vary widely in their approaches and orientations, but they do have certain things in common. All have rejected language as a "natural" communicative function and the belief in any specific correspondence of the signifier to the signified. The idea that there can be a self-contained individual characterized by specific attributes, a special historical, cultural, or biological identity, or a separate consciousness is exposed and revealed to be a fiction of earlier humanist discourse.[2] It also follows that we cannot expect to find in the "subject" (or speaker or author) any individual authorial intentions on which we might rely to discover the meaning of the text or discourse because the "subject" is a construct grounded in social discourse beyond any individual control. Instead of hunting for an authentic individual beneath the cultural and ideological overlay, the French feminists would posit a subject constructed by discourse and inscribed in culture through language.

Thus many of the French feminists (Kristeva and Wittig in particular), like other poststructuralists, have insisted that language does not and cannot guarantee identity or meaning and that therefore subjectivity and identity are not fixed but are always in process; further, the long-accepted idea of the unified subject that controls and fixes meaning must be questioned. According to Kristeva, women cannot be defined and should not be defined since the term "woman" is a social, not a natural construct. Wittig quotes de Beauvoir's famous statement: "One is not born, but becomes a woman. No biological, psychological, or economic fate predetermines the figure that the human female presents in society; it is civilization as a whole that produces this creature, intermediate between male and eunuch, which is described as feminine" (Wittig 1981: 47). The poststructuralist feminists thus problematize the whole notion of a historicized or "real" figure in literature who is characterizable by a specific personality and particularities of experience. For them, "woman" and the "feminine" are metaphors, linguistic categories, terms "in process."

Kristeva, Cixous, and Irigaray each take a very different approach to these fundamental issues. One of the main arguments among them concerns the development of a woman's language and the link between anatomy and verbal destiny (Gilbert and Gubar 1988: 227–71). Kristeva has taken a much criticized position, opposing both women's participation in phallocentric discourse and the development of a special woman's language (Kristeva 1974; Marks 1978; see Gautier 1974 for an insistence that women must develop their own language). She is suspicious of trying to develop a language that only women can use, and she contends that the only power women can have is to disrupt the system from within. She says, "What we must do is to help women to understand that these modern breaks with tradition and the development of new forms of discourse are harmonious with the women's cause. By participation in this activity of subversion (which exists on a linguistic, family, and social level) and in the growth of new epistemes they will be able to see this as well" (Féral 1976: 17). In her eyes, the only possible feminism is a negative feminism; according to her, "A woman cannot be; it is something which does not even belong in the order of being. It follows that a feminist practice can only be negative, at odds with what already exists so that we may say 'that's not it' and 'that's still not it' " (Kristeva 1974: 137).

Cixous and Irigaray are like each other in insisting on a difference in male and female language based on the difference between male and female "libidinal economies," one of which has been allowed to develop culturally (the male) and the other of which has been repressed (the female) (Marks 1978). Both Cixous and Irigaray believe that an essential feminine exists historically and cross culturally and further that language is closely tied to sexuality. But, unlike Kristeva, they move from male theorists (mainly Lacan for Irigaray and Derrida for Cixous) to develop a language peculiarly feminine which women can use to challenge the effects of a patriarchal order. Cixous's *écriture féminine* is a feminist discourse that is accessible to both male and female to use for dismantling phallocentric discourse; women, however, have a more immediate relationship to this language (Cixous and Clément 1975: 85–89, 91–99; Cixous 1976). Indeed, Cixous's own writing at times exemplifies what she must mean by *écriture féminine*: "Writing is the passageway, the entrance, the exit, the dwelling place of the other in me – the other that I am and am not, that I don't know how to be, but that I feel passing, that makes me live – that tears me apart, changes me, who? – a feminine one, a masculine one, some? – several, some unknown, which is indeed what gives me the desire to know and from which all life soars" (Cixous and Clément 1975: 85–86); or "You only have to look at the Medusa straight on to see her. And she's not deadly. She's beautiful and she's laughing" (Cixous 1976: 855).

Irigaray's *parler femme* ("womanspeak") is a female language produced from female sexuality as unfixed and not locatable in one organ; thus female language is nonlinear, irrational, and incomprehensible (to men) (Irigaray 1977: 28–29). Therefore, her *parler femme* belongs largely to women (although certain male writers such as Genêt have been included in this group) (Irigaray 1974, 1977, 1980). Neither Irigaray nor Cixous emphasizes the effects of culture and history; their theory of language as a force which is rooted in sexuality leaves little room for social or political change (Jardine modulates this position by the introduction of the more action-based Anglo-American feminism).

Many Anglo-American feminists, on the other hand, continue to talk about women's reality, women's experience, and women's history as if they were discussing a set of knowable facts rather than verbal constructs that carry with them an overlay of ideologies and values and specific cultural perspectives (Draine 1989: 147). They are often more interested in seeing women freed from political and social oppression than from the repression of phallocentric language. Some have accepted a more biological or essentialist approach, identifying "woman" as a transparent signifier of a biological female in history, not a metaphor of her sex. For them, "woman" does not signify a process that disrupts symbolic structures in male discourse (as the French would have it); rather, women can be defined by their activities and attributes in their cultural milieu. "Woman" would thus signify, for example, a biological person, a bearer of children, someone who worries about child care, who is an object of male sexuality, who speaks in a different voice. Many of the Anglo-American feminists eschew Freud and Lacan, highlighting and valorizing "natural reality" over the unconscious, and privileging the self and empirical evidence of women's "speech-acts" (Jardine

1985: 42, 44, 47; Lakoff 1975). Language is emphasized by them, but only as a communicative, natural function. Anglo-American feminists have not in the past engaged as much in the same kind of radical rethinking of the male and female subjects' relationship to the real, the imaginary, and the symbolic as have the French feminists, who have focused more on psychoanalysis and the role of the unconscious; an increasing number of Anglo-American feminists (for instance Gallop, Miller, Kamuf, Schor, and Jardine) have begun to think in psychoanalytical terms.

In sum, many Anglo-American feminists, in answer to Simone de Beauvoir's question "are there women?" would respond "yes" and try to define women by their cultural attributes and activities, taking a more empirical and activist stance. Most new French feminists and poststructuralists would answer "no" and attack the very category of "woman" by examining language and its effect on the subject (see Wittig, Delphy, and other materialists). As Marks puts it, "where American women cry out 'male chauvinist pig,' the French women inscribe 'phallologocentric'" (Marks 1978).

Problems abound, of course, with each of these two broadly defined approaches, particularly for classicists. The more empirical approach taken by many American feminists emphasizes the truth value of everyday experience and "natural" reality, but does not give enough attention to the importance of cultural determinations and language. The French poststructuralist theorists' insistence on woman as process, social construct, and fiction downplays the biological aspect of the female, discounts individual and experiential intersections with the imprint of history, and deconstructs the feminine subject to such an extent that feminism has little or no meaning and allows no possibility for action (Kristeva 1974: 137; 1979: 33–34). As Martin (1982), Hartsock (1990), Richlin (1991), and others have pointed out, poststructuralism and Foucauldian thought undercut activist feminism by getting rid of subjectivity, making totalizing discourse impossible, and treating sexual identity as a fiction. The question of the oppression of women becomes muted because the emphasis on linguistic and thus symbolic process, on abstractions, and on categories neutralizes sexual difference and constantly denies or defers the importance of everyday experience. We thus face the difficult task of exploding and undermining traditional categories without either losing the particularity of "women" or forfeiting our right to struggle against the oppression of women. As Bordo says, however, poststructuralism is useful for feminism, but more as an interpretive tool and historical critique than as a theoretical framework to be adopted and applied wholesale (Bordo 1990: 153–54).

Some feminists have tried to offer a *tertium quid* that might allow us to take the best from both theoretical stances and to combine the equally valid but conflicting ideas of "*woman as* (linguistic) *process*" and "*woman as* (biological) *sexual identity*" (Jardine 1985: 41). This compromise position gives us a valuable tool with which to analyze the Roman poetry of the first century BCE. For example, Teresa de Lauretis tries to bridge the gap between woman as poststructuralist genderless subject (woman) and woman as a historicized subject (women); such an approach would allow us to look at the figures in Roman poetry both as they are constructed in language and as they intersect with their social/historical contexts. She uses the term "experience," not in "the individualistic, idiosyncratic sense of something belonging to one and exclusively her own," but "in the general sense of a *process* by which, for all social beings, subjectivity is constructed" (de Lauretis 1984: 159). She thus allows for an intersection of women and their positions in relation to shifting interpersonal and political contexts.[3] For her, language is not the sole locus of meaning; she also places importance on the subjective, individual interpretation of social and historical relations through which meaning can be constructed, and she gives the subject an identity (de Lauretis 1987, 1990: 267).

Like de Lauretis, Alice Jardine, in her 1985 study *Gynesis*, tries to maintain the alliance between feminism and postmodernism and to describe the compromise position that has evolved out of the deconstructive and the essentialist positions by introducing a process which she calls "gynesis." Jardine searches for a theory that can combine the American feminist focus on ethics, practice, and sexual identity with the French idea of woman as a process that disrupts symbolic structures. I will maintain that Propertius and other elegiac poets of the first century BCE use women and gender in just this way: to disrupt the structures of their society and to produce in the process a new formulation of gender. Jardine's gynesis involves "the putting into discourse of 'woman' or 'the feminine'"; gynesis is the process of requestioning and destructuring the traditional Western master narratives, the accounts of the world that have attempted to explain to us "Man, the Subject, Truth, History, Meaning" (Jardine 1985: 25).

In her questioning of the foundations of Western critical thought, Jardine examines the texts of some contemporary French male theorists of modernity, who employ the textual image of woman in their quest to denaturalize concepts like "experience," "the Natural," "the Ethical," "the Good," "the True," and to revalorize what the master Western texts have posited as unknown, uncertain, unnatural, unmanageable. Jardine would focus on what has been left out of, deemphasized, or denied articulation in the master texts (Jardine 1985: 36). This lost object, represented so often but almost impossible to represent (Heath 1978), is manifested in texts in the discourse of uncertainty and unfixity that has traditionally connoted femininity and been coded as "woman" in these master texts. But Jardine points out that this "femininity" is a stereotype of traditional male ways of seeing women, "an excess of patriarchal history" (Belsey and Moore 1989: 19), a product of patriarchal control over language, culture, and texts, and it has nothing to do with biological women (Jardine 1985: 25–26, 36–38).

While the male theorists of modernity in many ways simply reinforce stereotypes of women as passive, uncertain, powerless, and devious, their discourse is still useful for feminism because it points to a space in the text, an area of uncertainty that has feminine connotations and is a place of the unknown, a space over which the narratives have lost control (Jardine 1985: 25). This "space" allows us to problematize and to question anew the representations of women in these texts. Jardine demonstrates the need for women to "enter and renovate the discourse of modernity on a nonsexist basis," "to make something utterly new of/in the discourse, theory, and praxis of modernity, as an alternative to the repetition forced on to traditional feminist discourse by the dominant ideology in the West" (Draine 1989: 156; Jardine 1985: 258).

Jardine asks whether both the concept and the practice of feminism might not be productively redefined in light of the new conceptual paths opened up by the texts of modernity. Such male-engendered texts might offer new directions through which women can conceptually rework "male" and "female" and force us to imagine a new kind of hermeneutics "able to give up its quest for truth and capable of self-reflection on its own complicity with inherited systems of representation" (Draine 1989: 158).

Theories like Jardine's that are clearly grounded in contemporary culture can help us to interpret or to understand texts from other periods as well. Feminists are now studying the structuring of gender and the implied female reader in literatures from many different eras (for example, Krueger for the medieval period; Poovey for the Victorian age). So too, the analysis of gender structuring and definition that gynesis supplies can be done in certain classical texts. The "master narratives" that we might examine from antiquity, analogous to Jardine's Western "master narratives," would be any male-authored text that has received, transmitted, and influenced the traditional male-centered system of representation (for example, Homer, Sophocles, Cicero, Vergil). In these master narratives from antiquity, the authors have naturalized and normalized all of our most fundamental concepts (the good, the true, the natural) according to a particular masculine and aristocratic ideology, and they have created and subsequently reinforced all of the stereotypes of women that Jardine finds in the twentieth-century texts she discusses (passivity, treachery, powerlessness, fluidity). In certain authors, however, we can see a "space" in the fabric, where there is an uneasiness in the representation of gender for both the author and reader, where the language seems to have more potentiality to be interpreted from many different perspectives, where the marginalized characters seem to be trying to "speak," and where there are border challengings (voices speaking against the text).[4] Not only Sappho's explicit rereadings of Homer, or Sulpicia's of elegy, but such figures as the women of Aristophanes's *Lysistrata*, *Thesmophoriazousai*, and *Ekklesiazousai*; the female characters of Euripides; the freed slaves of Petronius's *Satyricon*; Vergil's Dido and Statius's Hypsipyle; the native leader Calgacus who speaks against Rome in Tacitus's *Agricola* – all these have been seen, or could be seen, as places where the mute are pushing through the fabric of the text.[5]

One place where we find such spaces is in Roman elegy, a genre of personalized lyric poetry that owes much to its Greek predecessors but survived in a peculiarly Roman form for less than a century, from about 55 BCE, when our first extant Roman elegiac poet Catullus was writing, until about 17 CE, when Ovid, the last classical practitioner of this genre probably died (Luck 1959). The origins and development of elegy are buried in mystery since there are many missing links in the tradition. Technically defined as poetry written in elegiac couplets, elegy was written by the Greeks at least as far back as the seventh century BCE. It may have been used for funeral dirges, but it seems to have accommodated from the beginning a wide variety of topics, themes, and purposes (for example, war, drinking, politics, and mythological stories). It was connected rather closely with love stories from mythology by some of its Hellenistic practitioners in the fourth through first centuries BCE, but these love stories, although often addressed to female lovers (for example, Antimachus of Colophon to his wife Lyde in about 400 BCE), were probably about the love affairs of others or at least cast as mythological narratives rather than as personal experiences. The first poets to have used elegy for the purpose of writing a personal account of their own love affairs to their own mistresses were Catullus and perhaps Cornelius Gallus, a figure from the mid-first century BCE who survives in ten lines (nine of which are disputed and the remaining one of which has nothing to do with love at all; Ross 1975; Anderson 1979). Gallus is one of those tantalizing transitional figures whom we suspect is a key link in the tradition but can only recreate with a considerable amount of speculation and guesswork.

The surviving elegists in the first century BCE are Catullus, Propertius, Tibullus, and Ovid. Catullus, more often called a lyric poet because he wrote many of his 116 poems in lyric meters, wrote 52 poems in elegiac meter. Many of these poems focus on love, either Catullus's love for his mistress, whom he calls Lesbia, or someone else's love (whether mythical or contemporary). Catullus is the first extant Roman poet to write ostensibly sincere, intense, passionate outpourings of desire and emotion to his mistress, the first to call his mistress by a poetic pseudonym (Lesbia for Clodia), the first to intermix mythologems of love with his own personal amatory relationship and to let the mythological stories illuminate his own story, the first to question gender roles and to portray himself, the male, as the weak, passive, and helpless member of the duo (Skinner 1989b, Janan 1994; see also Fitzgerald 1988, Oliensis 1991 on gender and sexuality in the poet Horace). Catullus combines what would later become many of the standard qualities of Roman elegy, albeit still in vestigial form (his poem 68 is the only poem in which all of the later elegiac traits are combined but they are there in an uneasy mix), and his influence on the three later elegists is enormous. Propertius, Tibullus, and Ovid all follow Catullus in their use of meter (employing

440

elegiac meter exclusively for their love poetry), their overtly personal displays of affection toward their mistresses, who are also the addressees of many of their poems, and their use of poetic pseudonyms for their lovers (Cynthia, Delia, and Corinna, respectively).

I have chosen Roman elegy for my exploration of gynesis in ancient literature because it is here that we find both the ways of questioning gender constructions and the problematic areas in the text that Jardine identifies in contemporary male writers who attempt to denaturalize traditional concepts and to recast the representations of gender. Elegy offers a fertile ground for such an exploration because it combines traditional ways of seeing love and female lovers with a new sense of male/female relationships and gender redefinitions. And, in contrast to authors such as Vergil, the elegists are more self-conscious in their treatment of gender reversals. The redefinitions of gender found in elegy were developed in response to both the heavily moralistic patriarchal value system that had existed in Rome for centuries and the breakdown of societal values at the end of the first century BCE. The spaces present in the texts connote uncertainty, the unknown, the unreal – qualities that are traditionally ascribed to women by male authors and that thus might be viewed with distrust by feminist readers looking for new ways to reconceptualize "male" and "female" in our texts. Yet, if we do not fall into the trap of focusing on and being influenced by only the traditional representations of women in our texts, but see these "spaces" as a way of problematizing and reconceptualizing "woman" both as a concept and as an identity, we might be able to reevaluate our idea of what "truth" we are looking for and, without complicity with the representations transmitted by the authors of antiquity, read differently the stories we have been "forced to live" (Jardine 1985: 258).

One problem that we will face is that in such an approach to the texts, "women" cease to be historically identifiable subjects and become surrounded by and buried in quotation marks. Women become "woman," a process that designates the encased word as a rhetorical or ideological construct. Thus women as thinking, writing subjects are left in the position of wondering whether they are seeking to reconceptualize and identify "women" or "woman," their written *bodies* (real, biological entities) or their *written* bodies (cultural constructions).[6] In either case, we are giving up some part of women's/woman's identity. Jardine says that, although "the attempt to analyze, to separate ideological and cultural determinations of the 'feminine' from the 'real woman'" may be the most logical path for a feminist to follow, it may also be the most interminable process, "one in which women become not only figuratively but also literally impossible" (Jardine 1985: 37). Her way out of this trap is to use "gynesis" as it is described above, not the now-traditional male way of reading women but a more controlled, more careful feminist version of this in which the concept of woman will be identified with difference, with incompleteness, with the unknown.[7]

Gynesis allows us to focus on the male-generated texts that comprise a very large percentage of our available evidence, but to look in them for something different. Jardine proposes for modernity – and I propose for antiquity – that we look in our texts for what is hidden, deemphasized, left out, or denied articulation, and try to make evident the spaces produced in these texts over which the writer has no control and in which "woman" can be found. Jardine's description of the process of requestioning and destabilizing of the Western master narratives, of the concern for the incomplete rather than the whole, for different modes of production rather than representation, and for difference rather than identity,[8] and of "the putting into discourse of women" (Jardine 1985: 25, 36), can, I believe, be helpful to feminists who are searching for a new way to "find" the female in ancient texts. Many classicists of course have already read the text against itself and uncovered spaces and new levels of meaning for women by making use of new critical methodologies (see, for example, Skinner 1983 [for Catullus]; Richlin 1983: 32–56; 1984 [for elegy and satire]; 1992b [for Ovid]; Wyke 1987, 1989 [for Propertius]; Hallett 1989a [for Roman literature]; Ancona 1989 [for Horace]; Nugent 1990 [for Ovid]; Janan forthcoming [for Catullus]). My use of French feminist critics to elucidate the elegies of Propertius owes a great debt in many different ways to these ground-breaking studies. Some of them, however, come to quite different conclusions than I do and find no positive evidence for women in these texts; the various readings against the text that are beginning to be done show a multiplicity of voices and attitudes.

While "woman" has long been seen, since the beginnings of Western literature as we know it, as a problematic object and the locus of contradictions (Miller 1980: 74), contemporary feminist critics now see the contradiction operating not only in the referent but also in the signifier "woman" itself. I am concerned with the *language* in these texts and with the ways in which the spaces left in our texts, after we have questioned and destabilized them, can help us to understand these texts differently. We can thus challenge the idea that sexuality and subjectivity are fixed, and we can open up the fixed identities assigned to fictionalized female characters by authors who are burdened with the cultural, historical, and conceptual limitations inherited from their patriarchal history. This is not to say, of course, that a feminist reader does not have her own limitations, but at the very least we can problematize "woman" as both a concept and an identity, shake up representations that have been accepted as givens for such a long time within the dominant tradition, and question our own complicity with these inherited ideas.

How then can we, who are trying to determine something about "women" and "woman" from ancient, male-authored texts, put these insights to work? How can we read "woman" in a text like Propertius's elegiac poetry, which centers on a woman but springs from a male imagination and a patriarchal culture? How can we apply Alice Jardine's theory of gynesis, or the putting into discourse of "woman" or the "feminine" as problematic, to such a text? One potential pitfall in applying such questions to a male-authored text is that articulated by Spivak in "Displacement and the Discourse of Woman" (Spivak 1983): can we ask a male writer who is embedded in such a hege-monic discourse and who is in total control of his subjects (objects) to provide us with concepts and strategies that do not "appropriate or displace the figure of woman" (Spivak 1983: 170)? If the writer can problematize but never fully discard his own subjectivity, can he ever allow to his object her own subjectivity?

Keeping this potential hazard in mind, I would like to suggest some questions that we might ask about Propertius's text and the "Cynthia" which (who) is presented there (taking Cynthia as a "woman" and not as a particu-lar, historicized woman). I hope that these questions will allow us to con-tinue to problematize the female figure, to eschew the belief that language can reproduce reality and that women can have a material and knowable essence, and to avoid the impulse to try to turn characters like Cynthia into historical figures.

I take as a given that "Cynthia" is constructed as a fictional figure and that, if a real Roman woman did exist under the pseudonym, this information would not alter our understanding of the text.[9] In fact, even if Cynthia were called by her real name in Propertius's text, she would still be a fictionalized character.[10] The Roman writer Apuleius started the hunt for the "real women" underneath the pseudonyms given in Roman elegy by giving a list of the real names corresponding to these pseudonyms (Apuleius *Apology* 10). Taking their cue from Apuleius, readers of these classical texts have tried to historicize the characters in them and to formulate biographies from "histor-ical details" in the poetry. It is interesting to note in this regard that Proper-tius's first book of elegies has been called the *Cynthia* by both ancient and modern writers.[11] She is identified both by the author himself and by later male critics (ancient and modern) not only *with* his poetry but *as* his poetry. This is quite a deliberate ploy by the poet: her name appears in the first line of the first poem (and thus was used as a title for the book), and, in another book of his elegies, Propertius claims that he was taunted with the fact that his Cynthia "was being read all over the city" (*tua sit toto Cynthia lecta foro,* Prop. 2.24.2), thus producing an image of Cynthia as a sexually passive object (the written woman).

"Cynthia" then is absolutely vital to Propertius's poetry because, accord-ing to him, she constitutes his text. She becomes his book that is the "talk of the town" (Prop. 2.24.1) passed around as an object of exchange, and finally lost or destroyed (*ergo tam doctae nobis periere tabellae,* Prop 3.23.1).[12] But she is also constituted by the text and exists as an object within it. Propertius can manipulate her time, her space, and her attributes. He can project her impos-sibly into the past (Prop. 3.24) or into the future (Prop. 2.18.19–20; 3.25), even going so far as to resurrect her from the grave (Prop. 4.7). He can place her in Rome (Prop. 1.6), abroad (1.8), back again (1.8.27ff.), at a seaside resort (1.11), or on a journey (1.12; 2.19). She can be portrayed as a faithful Penelope (Prop. 1.3) or a faithless hussy (1.16), made into a categorized "woman" by being cast in a preset role in a mythologem. She is endlessly adaptable by the poet because she is a projection of his desires and anxieties, as unstable and slippery as his thoughts (Prop. 2.1.4; *ingenium nobis ipsa puella facit*). She is – or becomes – what Propertius wants or fears for himself, and her identity in the poetry changes depending upon whether she is the fulfillment of his erotic desires or the embodiment of all the traits that men fear in women (instability, fickleness, violence, inscrutability, wiliness, deception).

She is thus seen as both an internal object (an element in the poetry) and an external object (an objectification of the poetry book and separable from it), forming an important part of Propertius's "plot" (though never getting to write her own), and eventually become identified with the book itself. She is called a story (*fabula*, Prop. 2.24.1; *historia*, 2.1.16), a fictionalized object put to the service of the poet so that she may perform a thousand different roles.

How does Jardine's gynesis help us to analyze what a character like Cynthia means to Propertius's poetry? If we examine her roles and destabilize the identity that Propertius has created for her, we might identify a new space in the text by our questioning of Propertius's traditional categories and from this space gain a clearer understanding of what it meant for a "woman" to be the apparent center and anchor of such a male text. We might say that Propertius himself is unwittingly destabilizing the whole question of gender by appearing to lose control of what "Cynthia" represents and by putting his own representation into play as the feminine in a way that gives him a role parallel to Cynthia's (although Spivak's warning about displacement must be considered here). From the outset he makes Cynthia an element of his poetry that is at the same time essential to its meaning but also absent and elusive. At every opportunity Propertius reminds us of her importance, but he also often characterizes her as absolutely powerless. In addition, he cracks open the traditional identifications of "male" and "female" codes of behavior by casting himself frequently in nontraditional male roles, in fact, in roles that we would usually assign to women. A comparison of Cynthia to Vergil's Carthaginian queen Dido or Aeneas's Trojan wife Creusa, for example, or to Livy's self-effacing heroines Lucretia and Verginia, reveals by contrast the unstable, nontraditional character of the place assigned to Cynthia. Such conventional Roman female figures as Dido, Creusa, Lucretia, and Verginia remain imprisoned in their roles: passive, beloved, models of seemly behavior, and willing in the end to kill themselves or let themselves die for their men, their honor (as defined by their men), and the patriarchy (see Perkell 1981 on Dido and Creusa; Hemker 1985, Joplin 1990, and Joshel 1992a on Livy). In the case of Cynthia, however, I believe that we are justified in saying that Propertius, unlike his contemporaries Vergil and Livy, does at least temporarily destabilize the feminine in such a way that his readers can see in his text new possibilities for gender reversals and gender confusions.[13]

Propertius adopts as his major identity the part of hero/lover, and in this role, which is clearly relational, he needs an "other" to complement him.[14] Cynthia's chief purpose is to play the "other" to Propertius's hero. This is not to say that Propertius pretends to give her any independence in her role, but he does make her an essential element in his story. The text depends upon her presence for its meaning, but her presence and identity are not definable in the same way that the poet's character is. He appears to have (or portrays himself as having) a consistency, a completeness, and a fixed identity. Although he plays a number of different parts, they are all variations on the character of hero.

Therefore, as the story unfolds, Propertius's identity is consistent whereas Cynthia is never really given a (one) persona. Her position is relational and is defined entirely by the parts he plays; she is a foil to him. She plays the Penelope to his Odysseus (Prop. 1.3), the Ariadne to his Theseus (1.3), the virago to his abandoned lover (1.15), the wronged woman to his faithless rake (4.8). Often her qualities are summarized and categorized by the use of mythological figures, which are in themselves attempted representations of the unrepresentable (woman), but the frequent changes of representation (sometimes several within one poem) call into question the possibility of so easily confining her to a set mythological character.

Further, many of the bewildering number of roles assigned to Cynthia operate in conflict. Propertius calls Cynthia his parents (a term more focused on the paternal than the maternal aspect) and his household, thus perpetuating the traditional connection of the woman to household (Prop. 1.11.23). In this poem, she is said to contain him and to be his source, an extension of the timeworn idea of the woman as mother, first being, nurturer, creator, womb. Although he never explicitly allows her the maternal role (too dangerous?) and in fact sometimes explicitly denies her this role (Prop. 2.7, 2.15), he draws an analogy between his feelings for her and for his mother (1.11.21–22),[15] and elsewhere he pledges himself to her as her brother and son (2.18.33–34). Thus she is, by strong implication, the force who has created him, the woman who is at once dangerous because of her maternal powers, confined to her chaste, matronal role (Prop. 2.18.33–34), and the object of his affection over whom he watches like a guardian.

In other contexts, Propertius moves beyond his Oedipal role and regards Cynthia in nonfamilial roles as both mistress and wife (*semper amica mihi, semper et uxor eris*, Prop. 2.6.42). Further, she is responsible not only for his birth, existence, and sexuality, but also for his identity as a poet. She plays the literary critic (Prop. 2.13.14), the secure voice of reason (*domina iudice tutus ero*) to counterbalance the "babble of the crowd" (*populi confusa fabula*,

2.13.13–14); she is responsible for his poetic genius (*ingenium nobis ipsa puella facit*, 2.1.4; cf. 1.10.19–20), and she even takes on the role of his patron.[16]

Thus the character of Cynthia is almost infinitely open to adaptation; it (she) can expand to play all the parts that Propertius requires and he can exchange them at his will. Cynthia becomes for the reader an interesting and problematic combination of elements of an "essential woman"; she is a familiar figure, defined by the traditional roles and duties of a Roman woman of the first century BCE. She is a literary, sexual, and historical construct, shaped by the poet and by the male members and readers of his Roman society to be the kind of "woman" they want to valorize and privilege. By giving Cynthia so many attributes and by questioning the traditional tropes of the feminine used in writers of his time and before him, Propertius seems to create in his text the kind of "space" that Jardine finds in male texts of modernity. While Propertius himself is certainly not valorizing a "new" kind of woman, I suggest that he is destabilizing the traditional roles and qualities assigned to women by casting both her and himself in so many different and conflicting roles and by problematizing his representation of her.

My reading of Propertius relies on earlier work that opened up new approaches to Roman elegy and helped to dismantle traditional interpretations of it. In a 1973 article [reprinted in this volume, pp. 329–47], Judith Hallett suggested that male Roman love elegists such as Catullus and Propertius adopted a "counter-culture" persona which repudiated the socially prescribed patterns of behavior for males and females of the Roman elite. In this inversion of gender roles, the poet is often presented as subservient, passive, devoted to one lover alone, defiant of orthodox values, uninterested in politics and war, and obsessed instead with love and life's finer pleasures. His lady takes the dominant role; she is self-sufficient, forthright, and frank about her intentions (amorous and otherwise) to the point of becoming a warrior herself at times (see also Hallett 1993b).

Since Hallett first set in motion this type of approach to elegy, superseding the older biographical and aesthetic readings, much interesting work has been done (see, for example, Wyke 1987, 1989). Recently Gutzwiller and Michelini, in an article that investigates and supplements from a feminist perspective the traditional interpretations of the gender systems operating in classical Greece, Hellenistic Greece, and first-century BCE Rome, have argued that elegiac poets like Catullus do indeed reverse traditional gender roles, borrowing on an already available Hellenistic tradition in which women were valued more positively than in an earlier time (Gutzwiller and Michelini 1991). However, they contend that the Roman poets used the subversive Hellenistic view to "effect a covert reversion to the masculine ethos" and thus reasserted traditional male dominance over the women in question (Gutzwiller and Michelini 1991: 76). Two strains can therefore be seen in this poetry: the Hellenistic view that presented a female-oriented value system and the Roman manipulation of this system that uses it to persuade and control the female subject, recipient, and reader.

In my reading of the elegists (and specifically of Propertius), I would agree with Hallett's suggestion that Propertius is voicing "an eloquent if subtle critique of . . . 'establishment' Roman cultural and literary values" (Hallett 1993b) and might even agree that Propertius's work could in some ways be characterized as "feminist" or at least have been seen that way by certain sympathetic female readers (see Hallett 1993).[17] Gutzwiller and Michelini are right to point out that the Roman elegists were not, however, really interested in asserting a new gender structure, but rather in reverting to a traditional form of masculine behavior and roles encoded in earlier Greek literature.

I have chosen to focus specifically on Propertius (and not on Roman elegists in general) because I see Propertius as a particularly interesting and unique case of a Roman writer who is not a "feminist" in the modern sense and who is not quite creating a reversal of gender codes or a new kind of gender structure, but who – whether consciously or unconsciously – has left us a text that destabilizes traditionally assigned male and female roles and that is in some ways strikingly feminist in its nature and in its treatment of women.

It is because of Propertius's unparalleled treatment of the feminine in his poetry that we can apply Jardine's gynesis to his work. Propertius seems to me to "use gynesis" in a very special way, putting himself into play as the feminine and himself filling the space that has been created in the text for "woman." Propertius removes from Cynthia traits that would have been traditionally ascribed to females such as devotion, submissiveness, loyalty, subservience, passivity, and procreativity, and he appropriates them for himself. He becomes the loyal and devoted slave (Prop. 1.1; 1.6.25–30; 3.11.1–8; 3.25.1–4), the passive husband waiting at home (1.15; 2.8; 2.9), the faithful lover even after death (3.15.46), the one who gives birth to poetry (1.7; 2.1.1–4; 3.17; 3.24). Cynthia, on the other hand, has attributes that are a mimesis of the values recognized in the classical tradition by and for the male: she is demanding, faithless, hard-hearted, domineering, self-absorbed, and interested in competition and rivalry (Prop. 1.1; 1.7; 1.10.21–30; 3.8). Propertius's fixed identity and consistency thus are problematized in the same way that Cynthia's identity is.

This lack of presence or fixed identity of the feminine and the male writer's putting himself into play as the feminine can of course be read in a number of ways; the double-voiced nature of the text is a major problem for the feminist critique, but not an insurmountable one. As Claudine Herrmann has well pointed out, in literature "women have learned to see women through the eyes of men",[18] we have learned by necessity – and are constantly learning – strategies to cope with the sources we do have (and coping is exactly what many of us do), to move beyond the inherited, traditional systems of representation, and to "recognize the ways in which we surround ourselves with our fictions" (Jardine 1985: 47; Richlin 1992b: 161). Feminist scholars and female readers are looking for new ways to think about sexual difference without resorting to the sets of ideas and assumptions transmitted to us by previous thinkers and writers. We can do this partly by looking more closely at how meanings are produced and organized in language. Women in fact may have the advantage here, because some of us are not burdened so heavily by the inherited traditions of past generations and have, because of our position in two worlds at once (the dominant male tradition and our own "muted" female tradition), an opportunity to subvert the texts and to reread them in a different light (Ardener 1972; Fetterley 1978). As feminists have long been urging, women writers need to be "thieves of language" in order to define a truly female self and to rewrite the history of the world (Cixous and Clément 1975; Herrmann 1976; Ostriker 1985; Showalter 1985: 261).[19] As Marks says, "women have the élan and the energy borrowed from male techniques for demystifying and deconstructing, but they also have somewhere to go, to an unknown place, the place of the woman from which she can now begin to write" (Marks 1978: 835; see also Weedon 1987, Moi 1985, on the political imperative for feminist critics and the need to avoid traditional patriarchal categories).

Alice Jardine's amalgamation of French, poststructuralist and Anglo-American feminist ideas is useful because it allows us to avoid the pitfalls of earlier approaches that lead us into blind alleys and to find in texts like the Roman elegies spaces which are filled by "woman" as put into discourse by a male writer. Although Propertius never really relinquishes control over his material, he opens up spaces in his text in which we can feel and see the presence of "woman" and in which he interacts with her (see Williams 1991: 19, on finding the shape of the woman described by her absence). This is not to say that Propertius is performing a radical act by simply putting into play the female, any more than certain contemporary male authors are (Spivak 1983; Jardine 1985: 257).[20] But he does show us new ways of organizing and reading sexual difference by portraying two characters, male and female, who exchange gender roles and are defined by flexibility, lack of identity (difference), incompleteness, and lack of representation (or over representation since each has characteristics of both genders). The space is created in the text by this indeterminacy of role assignment and by the author casting himself as the other gender.

We are thus forced to rethink our known categories of what "woman" or "the female" might mean in Roman elegy. Traditionally "woman" has been represented or understood as the unknown, the mysterious, the unreal, the unrecognizable, the ever-elusive element. Although the figure of Cynthia seems to start out as the representation of traditional female qualities, she and Propertius soon begin to exchange roles, an act that problematizes these traditional traits and puts into question what definition exactly we might wish to give to "male" and "female" here. Propertius does not seem to valorize one set of traits over another; I question whether we can even say that there are two definable "sets" of traits that can be assigned to the genders. Propertius's figure of the female defies any identification and, at least by that act of defying identification, manages to elude the traditional categories that have been used to describe the female in Western literature. Using Jardine's gynesis as our entry into Roman elegy in general and into Propertius's elegy in particular, we can continue the work of feminist scholars like Hallett and Wyke[21] in order to discover how "woman" or "the feminine" is put into discourse in these texts.

To shift now back to my opening quotation from Richlin: it is indeed a shame that more people, especially more women, do not read what feminist classical scholars have to say about "their" texts; more to the point, it is a shame that up until recently, classicists, even feminists, have not been interested in writing articles and books about ancient texts that have been accessible to nonclassicists. My hope is that this article will be a step in rectifying this situation, will put us in closer touch with our sister scholars in other disciplines, will open up ideas for our epigones to pursue (if it is right to think in such hierarchical or linear terms), and will add a historical depth to current feminist projects, thereby benefiting them as much as we have benefited from them.

Notes

This paper would not have been conceived or written without the help of many friends and colleagues in the Women's Classical Caucus, who have redefined the word "patron." I would like to give special thanks to the editors and to Judith Hallett, Shelley Haley, and Carl Rubino.

1 See Wyke's remark that "realism is not equivalent to reality nor a realistically constructed beloved equivalent to a real woman" (Wyke 1987:61).
2 For a discussion of the positions taken by the poststructuralists (who have many things in common with the French feminists), see Alcoff 1988: 415–22.
3 de Lauretis 1984, 1987; see also "Feminist Studies/Critical Studies: Issues, Terms, Contexts," in de Lauretis 1986: 8–9; Flax 1986, 1987.
4 Hélène Cixous unsettles the question of gender and speaks about male figures such as Achilles with whom she has identified from the past (1975: 73–74).
5 For work on border challengings, see Zweig 1993, and Rabinowitz 1993, on Euripides; Foley 1982, and Zeitlin 1981, on Aristophanes; Joshel 1992b, on Roman freed slaves' expressions of subjectivity; Perkell 1981, on Dido; Skinner 1987; 1–8.
6 Jardine 1985: 37. Jardine makes a distinction between the metonymic "discourse *about* women" and the metaphoric "discourse *by, through, as* woman" (Jardine 1985: 36–37).
7 See Stephen Heath, who says that "the woman can only be 'the woman,' *different from*" (Heath 1978: 57).

8 Judith Hallett has problematized the concepts of difference and identity for Roman women in an article on "Women as 'Same' and 'Other' in the Classical Roman Elite" (Hallett 1989b).

9 For a discussion of Cynthia as a historical person, see, for example, Butler and Barber 1933: xxi–xxiii; Williams 1968: 526–42.

10 See Maria Wyke, who says that Cynthia "should not be related to the love life of her poet but to the 'grammar' of his poetry" (Wyke 1989: 35).

11 Ancient writers: Ovid *Rem. Am.* 764; Martial 14.189; modern writers: Butler and Barber 1933: xxxiv; Richmond 1928: appendix A. 1, 388; Enk 1946: part 1, 77; Richardson 1977: 8 (who refers to Propertius 2.24.2).

12 His books are called *doctae* here; Cynthia is called *docta* in Prop. 2.11.6 and 2.13.11; cf. also 1.7.11; 1.10–19: *Cynthia me docuit*.

13 See Hallett (1993), who, in a discussion of the satirist Sulpicia's possible appropriations of Propertian language and eroticism, proposes not only that this is a feminist gesture on Sulpicia's part but also an implicit characterization by her of Propertius expressing feminist views. Hallett would also compare Propertius's representations of Cynthia to his representation in 4.11 of Cornelia, a stable, elite woman, and she views this contrast as further evidence of his characterization of Cynthia as a feminist gesture (Hallett 1973).

14 In some poems, for example, Prop. 1.1, Propertius is the anti-hero, unable to perform the feats of his mythic model, but even in these poems, he is defined by his relationship to a standard set of heroic traits (whether positively or negatively).

15 Oddly, Propertius takes on a sort of maternal role himself in Prop. 1.11.21–22 when he says that the protection of his dear mother would be of no greater concern to him than the protection of Cynthia. For Cynthia as his source, see Prop. 1.11.26: *Cynthia causa fuit*.

16 I discuss this in an essay (Gold 1993) entitled "The Master Mistress of My Passion: The Lady as Patron in Ancient and Renaissance Literature."

17 Whether or not there were women who read or heard the poems of the elegists and to what extent these poems were intended for the ears of a female audience is a vexing issue with no easy answers. Various of the Roman poets certainly do address women as if they would hear or read and respond to these poems. See, for example, Propertius 1.11, 1.15, 1.19, 2.13 (where he talks about reading his poetry while lying in the arms of his learned lady [*doctae puellae*, 11] and calls Cynthia the "judge" of his writings in line 14), 3.8, 3.10, and throughout; Ovid *Tristia* 3.7, addressed to Perilla, whose poetry Ovid claims to have fostered; *Amores* 2.1.5, where Ovid says that he wants a young maiden who is inflamed at the sight of her lover (*in sponsi facie non frigida virgo*) to read his love poetry; *Ars Amatoria* 1.31–34, where Ovid warns respectable Roman matrons away from his tales of love; and Book 3, which is dedicated to the "Amazons" of Rome, "Penthesilea and her crowd" (*Ars Amatoria* 3.1–2). Certainly, we can say that a female audience is strongly implied in these works and must have been expected to read, digest, and engage with the poetry.

18 See Herrmann 1976, cited by Jardine 1985: 38.

19 See Cixous: "What would become of logocentrism, of the great philosophical systems, of world order in general if the rock upon which they founded their church were to crumble? If it were to come out in a new day that the logocentric project had been, undeniably, to found (fund) phallocentrism, to insure for masculine order a rationale equal to history itself? Then all the stories would have to be told differently, the future would be incalculable, the historical forces would, will, change hands, bodies, another thinking, as yet not thinkable, will transform the functioning of all society" (Cixous, "Sorties," *La Jeune Née*, as cited by Ostriker 1985: 314).

450

20 The male writer most often mentioned as writing woman into his text is Jean Genêt; see Cixous and Clément 1975 as discussed by Belsey and Moore 1989: 103.
21 Wyke refers to Propertius and Cynthia as "the Elegiac Man" and "the Elegiac Woman" (Wyke 1987: 48), and she dismantles the idea that Cynthia is meant to be a pseudonym for a real woman, but she still employs the traditional categories by which males and females have traditionally been judged in her assessment of what Propertius meant Cynthia to represent.

Works cited

Alcoff, Linda. 1988. "Cultural Feminism versus Post-Structuralism: The Identity Crisis in Feminist Theory." *Signs* 13: 405–36.

Ancona, Ronnie. 1989. "The Subterfuge of Reason: Horace, *Odes* 1.23 and the Construction of Male Desire." *Helios* 16: 49–57.

Anderson, R. D., P. J. Parson, and R. G. M. Nisbet. 1979. "Elegiacs by Gallus from Qasr Ibrîm." *Journal of Roman Studies* 69: 125–55.

Ardener, Edwin. 1972. "Belief and the Problem of Women." In Shirley Ardener, ed., *Perceiving Women*, 1–17. New York: Halsted Press (division of John Wiley and Sons Inc.), 1978.

Beer, Gillian. 1989. "Representing Women: Re-presenting the Past." In Belsey and Moore 1989, 63–80.

Belsey, Catherine, and Jane Moore, eds. 1989. *The Feminist Reader: Essays in Gender and the Politics of Literary Criticism.* New York: Basil Blackwell.

Bordo, Susan. 1990. "Feminism, Postmodernism, and Gender-Scepticism." In Nicholson 1990, 133–56.

Butler, Harold Edgeworth, and Eric Arthur Barber, eds. 1933. *The Elegies of Propertius.* Oxford: Clarendon Press. Reprinted 1969. Hildesheim: George Olms.

Butler, Judith. 1990. *Gender Trouble: Feminism and the Subversion of Identity.* New York: Routledge.

Cixous, Hélène. 1976. "The Laugh of the Medusa." Translated by Keith Cohen and Paula Cohen. *Signs* 1: 875–93.

Cixous, Hélène, and Catherine Clément. 1975. *La jeune née.* Paris: Union Générale d'Éditions. Translated by Betsy Wing (1986). *The Newly Born Woman.* Minneapolis. University of Minnesota Press. References are to the translation.

Culham, Phyllis. 1987. "Ten Years after Pomeroy: Studies of the Image and Reality of Women in Antiquity." In Skinner 1987b, 9–30.

—— 1990. "Decentering the Text: The Case of Ovid." *Helios* 17: 161–70.

de Lauretis, Teresa. 1984. *Alice Doesn't: Feminism, Semiotics, Cinema.* Bloomington: Indiana University Press.

—— ed. 1986. *Feminist Studies/Critical Studies.* Bloomington: Indiana University Press.

—— 1987. *Technologies of Gender: Essays on Theory, Film, and Fiction.* Bloomington: Indiana University Press.

—— 1990. "Upping the Anti (sic) in Feminist Theory." In Marianne Hirsch and Evelyn Fox Keller, eds., *Conflicts in Feminism*, 255–70. New York: Routledge.

Derrida, Jacques. 1978. *Éperons: Les styles de Nietzsche.* Paris: Flammarion. Translated by Barbara Harlow (1979). *Spurs: Nietzsche's Styles.* Chicago: University of Chicago Press.

Delphy, Christine. 1984. *Close to Home: A Materialist Analysis of Women's Oppression.* Translated by Diana Leonard. Amherst: University of Massachusetts Press.

Draine, Betsy. 1989. "Refusing the Wisdom of Solomon: Some Recent Feminist Literary Theory." *Signs* 15: 144–70.

Enk, P.J., ed. 1946. *Sexti Propertii Elegiarum. Liber I (Monobiblos).* Leiden: E.J. Brill.

Féral, Josett. 1976. "China, Women and the Symbolic: An Interview with Julia Kristeva." Translated by Penny Kritzman. *Sub-Stance* 13: 9–18.

Fetterley, Judith. 1978. *The Resisting Reader: A Feminist Approach to American Fiction.* Bloomington: Indiana University Press.

Fitzgerald, William. 1988. "Power and Impotence in Horace's *Epodes.*" *Ramus* 17: 176–91.

Flax, Jane. 1986. "Gender as a Problem: In and For Feminist Theory." *American Studies/ Amerika Studien* 31: 193–213.

—— 1987. "Postmodernism and Gender Relations in Feminist Theory." *Signs* 12: 621–43.

Foley, Helene P. ed. 1981. *Reflections of Women in Antiquity.* New York: Gordon and Breach Science Publishers.

—— 1982. "The 'Female Intruder' Reconsidered: Women in Aristophanes' *Lysistrata* and *Ecclesiazusae.*" *Classical Philology* 77: 1–21.

Foucault, Michel. 1977. "Nietzsche, Genealogy, History." In Donald F. Bouchard, ed., *Language, Counter-Memory, Practice: Selected Essays and Interviews.* Translated by Donald F. Bouchard and Sherry Simon. Ithaca: Cornell University Press. Also found in Paul Rabinow, ed., *The Foucault Reader*, 76–100. New York: Pantheon Books, 1984. (I have cited the Rabinow version in the text.)

Gamel, Mary-Kay. 1989. "*Non sine caede:* Abortion Politics and Poetics in Ovid's *Amores.*" *Helios* 16: 183–206.

—— 1990. "Reading 'Reality'." *Helios* 17: 171–74.

Gallop, Jane. 1982. *The Daughter's Seduction: Feminism and Psychoanalysis.* Ithaca: Cornell University Press.

Gauthier, Xavière. 1974. "Is There Such a Thing as Women's Writing?" In Marks and de Courtivron 1980, 161–64.

Gilbert, Sandra M. and Susan Gubar. 1988. *No Man's Land: The Place of the Woman Writer in the Twentieth Century*, Vol. 1. New Haven: Yale University Press.

Gold, Barbara K. 1993. "The Master Mistress of My Passion: The Lady as Patron in Ancient and Renaissance Literature." In Mary DeForest, ed., *Essays in Honor of Joy King.* Chicago: Bolchazy-Carducci.

Gutzwiller, Kathryn J., and Ann N. Michelini. 1991. "Women and Other Strangers: Feminist Perspectives in Classical Literature." In Joan E. Hartman and Ellen Messer-Davidow, eds., *(En)Gendering Knowledge: Feminists in Academe*, 66–84. Knoxville: University of Tennessee Press.

Hallett, Judith P. 1973. "The Role of Women in Roman Elegy: Counter-Cultural Feminism." *Arethusa* 6.1. Reprinted in John Peradotto and J.P. Sullivan, eds., *Women in the Ancient World: The Arethusa Papers*, 241–62. Albany: State University of New York Press. (Also in this volume, pp. 329–47.)

—— 1979. "Sappho and Her Social Context: Sense and Sensuality." *Signs* 4: 447–64.

—— 1989a. "Female Homoeroticism and the Denial of Roman Reality in Latin Literature." *Yale Journal of Criticism* 3: 209–27.

—— 1989b. "Women as *Same* and *Other* in the Classical Roman Elite. *Helios* 16: 59–78.

—— 1993. "Martial's Sulpicia and Propertius' Cynthia." In Mary DeForest, ed., *Essays in Honor of Joy King*. Chicago: Bolchazy-Carducci.

—— 1993b. "Feminist Theory, Historical Periods, Literary Canons, and the Study of Greco-Roman Antiquity." In Nancy Sorkin Rabinowitz and Amy Richlin, eds., *Feminist Theory and the Classics*. New York: Routledge, 44–72.

Hartsock, Nancy. 1990. "Foucault on Power: A Theory for Women?" In Nicholson 1990, 157–75.

Heath, Stephen. 1978. "Difference." *Screen* 19: 51–113.

Hemker, Julie. 1985. "Rape and the Founding of Rome." *Helios* 12: 41–48.

Herrmann, Claudine. 1976. *Les voleuses de langue*. Paris: des Femmes.

Irigaray Luce. 1974. *Speculum de l'autre femme*. Paris: Éditions de Minuit. Translated by Gillian C. Gill (1985). *Speculum of the Other Woman*. Ithaca: Cornell University Press. References are to the translation.

—— 1977. *Ce sexe qui n'en est pas un*. Paris. Éditions de Minuit. Translated by Catherine Porter with Carolyn Burke (1985). *This Sex Which Is Not One*. Ithaca: Cornell University Press. References are to the translation.

—— 1980. "When Our Lips Speak Together." Translated by Carolyn Burke. *Signs* 6: 69–79.

Jacobus, Mary, ed. 1979. *Women Writing and Writing about Women*. London: Croom Helm.

Janan, Micaela. 1994. *"When the Lamp is Shattered": Desire in the Poetry of Catullus*. Carbondale: Southern Illinois University Press.

—— In process. *Biography and Textual Controversy in Catullus Studies: Re-evaluation and a New Approach*.

Jardine, Alice. 1985. *Gynesis: Configurations of Woman and Modernity*. Ithaca: Cornell University Press.

Jones, Ann Rosalind. 1985. "Writing the Body: Toward an Understanding of *l'Écriture féminine*." In Showalter 1985, 361–77.

Joplin, Patricia K. 1990. "Ritual Work on Human Flesh: Livy's Lucretia and the Rape of the Body Politic." *Helios* 17: 51–70.

Joshel, Sandra R. 1992a. "The Body Female and the Body Politic: Livy's Lucretia and Verginia." In Richlin 1992a, 112–30.

—— 1992b. *Work, Identity, and Legal Status at Rome: A Study of the Occupational Inscriptions*. Norman and London: University of Oklahoma Press.

Kamuf, Peggy. 1980. "Writing Like a Woman." In Sally McConnell-Ginet, Ruth Borker, Nelly Furman, eds., *Women and Language in Literature and Society*, 284–99. New York: Praeger.

Kolodny, Annette. 1975. "Some Notes on Defining a 'Feminist Literary Criticism.'" *Critical Inquiry* 2: 75–92.

Kristeva, Julia. 1974. "La femme, ce n'est jamais ça." *Tel quel*. Translated by Marilyn A. August (1980). "Woman Can Never be Defined." In Marks and de Courtivron 1980, 137–41.

—— 1979. "Les temps des femmes." 34/44: *Cahiers de recherche de sciences des textes et documents* 5. Translated by Alice Jardine and Harry Blake (1981). "Women's Time." *Signs* 7: 13–35.

Krueger, Roberta. 1993. *The Lady in the Frame: Women Readers and the Ideology of*

Gender in Twelfth- and Thirteenth-Century Old French Romance. Cambridge: Cambridge University Press.

Lakoff, Robin. 1975. *LANGUAGE and Woman's Place.* New York: Harper and Row.

Lefkowitz, Mary. 1981. *The Lives of the Greek Poets.* Baltimore: Johns Hopkins University Press.

Luck, Georg. 1959. *The Latin Love Elegy.* London: Methuen and Co. Ltd.

Lugones, María C. 1991. "On the Logic of Pluralist Feminism." In Claudia Card, ed., *Feminist Ethics*, 35–44. Lawrence: University Press of Kansas.

Marks, Elaine, and Isabelle de Courtivron, eds. 1980. *New French Feminisms.* Amherst: University of Massachusetts Press.

Martin, Biddy. 1982. "Feminism, Criticism, and Foucault." *New German Critique* 27: 3–30.

Miller, Nancy, 1980. *The Heroine's Text: Readings in the French and English Novel, 1722–1782.* New York: Columbia University Press.

Modleski, Tania. 1991. *Feminism without Women: Culture and Criticism in a "Postfeminist" Age.* New York: Routledge.

Moi, Toril. 1985. *Sexual/Textual Politics: Feminist Literary Theory.* London: Methuen and Co. Ltd.

Nicholson, Linda, ed. 1990. *Feminism/Postmodernism.* New York: Routledge.

Nugent, Georgia. 1990. "This Sex Which is Not One: De-Constructing Ovid's Hermaphrodite." *differences* 2.1: 160–85.

Oliensis, Ellen. 1991. "Canidia, Canicula, and the Decorum of Horace's *Epodes.*" *Arethusa* 24: 107–38.

Ostriker, Alicia. 1985. "The Thieves of Language: Women Poets and Revisionist Mythmaking." In Showalter 1985, 314–38.

Perkell, Christine. 1981. "On Cruesa, Dido, and the Quality of Victory in Virgil's *Aeneid.*" In Foley 1981, 355–77.

Pomeroy, Sarah. 1991a. "Brief Mention: The Study of Women in Antiquity: Past, Present, and Future." *American Journal of Philology* 112: 263–68.

—— ed. 1991b. *Women's History and Ancient History.* Chapel Hill: University of North Carolina Press.

Poovey, Mary, 1984. *The Proper Lady and the Woman Writer: Ideology as Style in the Works of Mary Wollstonecraft, Mary Shelley and Jane Austen.* Chicago: University of Chicago Press.

Rabinowitz, Nancy Sorkin. 1993. *Anxiety Veiled: Euripedes and the Traffic in Women.* Ithaca: Cornell University Press.

Richardson, Lawrence, Jr., ed. 1977. *Propertius Elegies I–IV.* Norman: University of Oklahoma Press.

Richlin, Amy. 1983. *The Garden of Priapus: Sexuality and Aggression in Roman Humor.* New Haven: Yale University Press.

—— 1984. "Invective against Women in Roman Satire." *Arethusa* 17: 67–80.

—— 1990. "Hijacking the Palladion." *Helios* 17: 175–85.

—— 1991. "Zeus and Metis: Foucault, Feminism, Classics." *Helios* 18: 160–80.

—— ed. 1992a. *Pornography and Representation in Greece and Rome.* New York: Oxford University Press.

—— 1992b. "Reading Ovid's Rapes." In Richlin 1992a, 158–79.

Richmond, O.L. ed. 1928. *Sexti Properti quae supersunt opera.* Cambridge: Cambridge University Press.

Riley, Denise. 1988. *Am I That Name? Feminism and the Category of "Women" in History*, Minneapolis: University of Minnesota Press.

Ross, David O. 1975. *Backgrounds to Augustan Poetry: Gallus, Elegy and Rome*. Cambridge: Cambridge University Press.

Santirocco, Matthew. 1979. "Sulpicia Reconsidered." *Classical Journal* 74: 229–39.

Schor, Naomi. 1989. "This Essentialism Which is Not One: Coming to Grips with Irigaray." *differences* 1.2: 38–58.

Showalter, Elaine. 1977. *A Literature of Their Own: British Women Novelists from Brontë to Lessing*. Princeton: Princeton University Press.

—— 1979. "Towards a Feminist Poetics." In Jacobus 1979, 22–41.

—— ed. 1985. *The New Feminist Criticism: Essays on Women, Literature and Theory*. New York: Pantheon Books.

—— 1989. "Introduction: The Rise of Gender." In Elaine Showalter, ed., *Speaking of Gender*, 1–13. New York: Routledge.

Skinner, Marilyn B. 1983. "Clodia Metelli." *Transactions of the American Philological Association* 113:273–87.

—— ed. 1986. *Rescuing Creusa: New Methodological Approaches to Women in Antiquity. Helios* 13.

—— 1989a. "Sapphic Nossis." *Arethusa* 22: 5–18.

—— 1989b. *"Ut Decuit Cinaediorem:* Power, Gender, and Urbanity in Catullus 10." *Helios* 16: 7–23.

—— 1991a. "Aphrodite Garlanded: *Erôs* and Poetic Creativity in Sappho and Nossis." In Francesco de Martino, ed., *Rose di Pieria*, 79–96. Bari: Levante Editori.

—— 1991b. *"Nossis Thêlyglôssos:* The Private Text and the Public Book." In Pomeroy 1991b, 20–47.

—— 1993. "Woman and Language in Archaic Greece, or, Why is Sappho a Woman?" In Nancy Sorkin Rabinowitz and Amy Richlin, eds., *Feminist Theory and the Classics*. New York: Routledge.

Snyder, Jane McIntosh. 1989. *The Woman and the Lyre: Women Writers in Classical Greece and Rome*. Carbondale: Southern Illinois University Press.

—— 1991. "Public Occasion and Private Passion in the Lyrics of Sappho of Lesbos." In Pomeroy 1991b, 1–19.

Spivak, Gayatri Chakravorty. 1983. "Displacement and the Discourse of Woman." In Mark Krupnick, ed., *Displacement: Derrida and After*, 169–95. Bloomington: Indiana University Press.

Stehle, Eva. 1990. "Sappho's Gaze: Fantasies of a Goddess and Young Man." *differences* 2: 88–125.

Weedon, Chris. 1987. *Feminist Practice and Poststructuralist Theory*. Oxford: Basil Blackwell Ltd.

Williams, Gordon. 1968. *Tradition and Originality in Roman Poetry*. Oxford: Clarendon Press.

Williams, Patricia. 1991. *The Alchemy of Race and Rights*. Cambridge: Harvard University Press.

Winkler, Jack. 1981. "Gardens of Nymphs: Public and Private in Sappho's Lyrics." *Women's Studies* 8. Reprinted in Foley 1981, 63–89.

Wittig, Monique. 1981. "One is Not Born a Woman." *Feminist Issues* 1.2: 47–54.

Wyke, Maria. 1987. "Written Women: Propertius' *Scripta Puella*." *Journal of Roman Studies* 77: 47–61.

—— 1989. "Mistress and Metaphor in Augustan Elegy." *Helios* 16: 25–47.

Zeitlin, Froma I. 1981. "Travesties of Gender and Genre in Aristophanes' *Thesmophoriazousae*." In Foley 1981, 169–217.

Zweig, Bella. 1993. "The Primal Mind: Using Native American Models for the Study of Women in Ancient Greece." In Nancy Sorkin Rabinowitz and Amy Richlin, eds., *Feminist Theory and the Classics*. New York: Routledge.

READING BROKEN SKIN

Violence in Roman elegy

David Fredrick

Let the captive girl go sadly before, hair undone,
  body all white – if her beaten cheeks would allow it.
A bruise pressed in by my lips would have been more fitting,
  her neck marked by the caress of my teeth.

(Ovid, *Amores*)

Ovid is not simply being flippant when, in *Amores* 1.7, he suggests an amorous bite as the alternative to beating his mistress. Torn dresses, pulled hair, scratches, and bruises are scattered throughout Roman elegy, often in association with lovemaking. If this genre employs the female body as a metaphor for its Alexandrian poetic qualities, how should this broken skin be read? Does violence betray its attempts at "taking the woman's part," confirming that it is an "obstinately male" genre?[1] This essay situates elegiac violence in the context of two distinct ways of representing the mistress: erotic description, which fashions an incomplete but aesthetically perfect body as poetic metaphor (*candida puella*); and jealous suspicion, which produces a degraded body liable to verbal or physical aggression (*dura puella*). These modes converge in the genre's often professed (but rarely obtained) goal of intercourse with the *puella*, where Callimachean metaphor apparently becomes penetrable flesh. Such an approach points toward the reclaiming of epic as a genre closely associated with elite masculinity. But masculinity, as defined through political and social competition, was at the end of the first century BCE an increasingly hollow form of theater, "a loathsome and bitter burlesque," as Carlin Barton has put it.[2] Its recuperation in elegy is therefore parodic, but not simply funny; for its male authors, elegy's wounds are ambiguous metaphors for the transformation of elite masculinity into text.

Fascination and anger: scopophilia and voyeurism

haec sed forma mei pars est extrema furoris;
sunt maiora, quibus, Basse, perire iuvat:
ingenuus color et multis decus artibus, et quae
gaudia sub tacita ducere veste libet.
(Propertius 1.4.11–14)

me iuvenum pictae facies, me nomina laedunt,
me tener in cunis et sine voce puer;
me laedet, si multa tibi dabit oscula mater,
me soror et cum quae dormit amica simul:
omnia me laedent: timidus sum (ignosce timori)
et miser in tunica suspicor esse virum.[3]
(Propertius 2.6.9–14)

Elegy frequently oscillates between fascination and suspicion. Since either posture can be read as "feminine" or "masculine," the genre's gender identification is unstable. It is plausible to argue that laudatory erotic description seeks to endow the *amator* with Callimachean *mollitia* (softness), which the *servitium amoris* confirms; it is equally plausible to argue that such descriptions objectify the mistress, and so express male discursive mastery, which the *amator*'s anger confirms.[4] But if gender cannot be unambiguously assigned to the fascinated or jealous *amator*, the two poses present clear contradictions in the type of female body each constructs.

The "fascination versus jealousy" pattern is familiar from Western representations of women alternatively as virgins or whores, and a useful critical model is provided by Laura Mulvey's "Visual Pleasure and Narrative Cinema."[5] Mulvey assigns each half of the dichotomy, as it appears in mainstream cinema, a distinct representational strategy: "fetishistic scopophilia" (=virgin) and "sadistic voyeurism" (=whore). The two are not interchangeable. Scopophilia presents the woman as a collection of desirable fragments that suggest but still conceal the anatomical difference between the sexes; it "builds up the beauty of the object, transforming it into something satisfying in itself." Voyeurism, on the other hand, presents sexual difference as the woman's castration, constructing a plot to expose her crime and justify the penalty: "Pleasure lies in ascertaining guilt . . . asserting control and subjugating the guilty person through punishment or forgiveness."[6]

Mulvey emphasizes that scopophilia and voyeurism are contradictory in their approach to narrative time and space:

[The fetishized woman] tends to work against the development of a storyline, to freeze the flow of action in moments of erotic contemplation . . . One part of a fragmented body destroys the Renaissance space, the illusion of depth demanded by the narrative, it gives flatness, the quality of a cut-out or icon, rather than verisimilitude, to the screen.[7]

Mulvey's analysis is apposite to elegy's fascination and its suspicion. Each pose constructs its own map (or metaphor) for the female body according to different assumptions about her anatomy, and correspondingly different rules of narrative time and space. For the *candida puella* as slender poetic icon, from whose description genitals are significantly lacking, time stops and space is collapsed into a gratifying visual presence.[8] The *dura puella*, on the other hand, is separated from the *amator* by an almost endless series of barriers (doors, rivers, dinner parties, old nurses, voyages abroad, eunuchs). Behind these lies her sexual experience with other men, which makes her "iron," "bloody," and "wild," reintroducing spatial depth and a temporal plot focused on exposure followed by forgiveness or punishment.[9] The *candida puella* is aesthetically pleasing but physically inviolable: "The parts of her body that evoke desire in the poet form a sort of circle around the genitalia . . . it is as if there were a blank space in the middle of the woman."[10] This blank space effectively precludes sexual or violent penetration, and, in generic terms, epic. Voyeurism, meanwhile, reinscribes penetrability in the blank space, allowing the representation of physical contact with the *puella*, where, as the epigraph from Ovid indicates, violence overlaps with sex, and military images are frequently used.[11]

Callimachean (Greek) *phthonos* and Lesbia

One of elegy's most important literary models is Callimachus, not only in the avoidance of epic, but in the use of the erotic body – in Callimachus's case, usually an adolescent male – to represent desired poetic qualities.[12] But Callimachus is not always Callimachean. The *pais*, like the elegiac *puella*, both represents programmatic attributes and transgresses them through infidelity; consequently, the poet's persona slides back and forth between opposite sides of envy (*phthonos*), its dew-sipping object in the prologue to the *Aetia*, its angry subject in several erotic epigrams. However, the disfiguring effect of *phthonos* is internalized by the poet, leaving no marks on the body of the *pais*, a strategy that contrasts with the verbal staining or beating of the female body in Catullus and Roman elegy.

In *Aetia* fr. 1, the poet complains that the Telchines, "malignant gnomes," are muttering at him again; he condemns them as "a race that understands only how to melt (*tēkein*) its own liver," and tells the "destructive breed of Jealousy (*Baskaniēs*)" to be gone.[13] *Baskania* is virtually a synonym for *phthonos*, and *tēkein* is the Greek verb typically used to describe the effect of *phthonos*. That the Telchines, while muttering against the poet, also melt their own livers is consistent with the double-edged condition of the *phthoneros*: "The malice that is inherent in *phthonos* rebound[s] upon the *phthoneros*."[14] At the end of the *Hymn to Apollo*, *phthonos* itself addresses Apollo, whispering secretly into his ear that he disdains the singer who does not sing as much as the sea; Apollo kicks Envy while replying that the Assyrian River is immense but polluted, and that bees do not bring moisture to Demeter from just any source, but from the pure, high, unmixed, trickling stream. The poet concludes by bidding Blame (*Mōmos*) go where *Phthonos* has gone.[15]

The *phthoneros* is characterized internally by "wasting and emaciation, pallor and sunken eyes; the frowning brow and gnashing teeth of rage; and perhaps physical distortions such as a hunched back," and externally by "the *phthoneros* strangling himself, choking, or bursting, or some clearly visible rendering of the self-inflicted wound or internal torture."[16] A desirable object always stands in opposition to this tortured body. In the *Aetia* prologue and the *Hymn to Apollo*, this object is the Callimachean text itself, characterized by lightness, brightness, delicate wings, and childlike purity. In the erotic epigrams, however, the desired body is represented by a *pais* whom the poet typically loses (*Epigr.* 28 [Pfeiffer]):

Ἐχθαίρω τὸ ποίημα τὸ κυκλικόν. οὐδὲ κελεύθῳ
χαίρω. τίς πολλοὺς ὧδε καὶ ὧδε φέρει
μισέω καὶ περίφοιτον ἐρώμενον. οὐδ' ἀπὸ κρήνης
πίνω. σικχαίνω πάντα τὰ δημόσια.
Λυσανίη. σὺ δὲ ναίχι καλὸς καλός – ἀλλὰ πρὶν εἰπεῖν
τοῦτο σαφῶς, Ἠχώ φησί τις. "ἄλλος ἔχει."[17]

I detest the Cyclic poems, I'm not happy on the highway that carries a crowd here and there. I hate the boy-love who cheats, and I don't drink from the common well. I'm disgusted at everything public. Lysanias, yes, you are handsome – so handsome – but it's barely spoken when an echo comes back: "Another man has him."

This poem partly conforms to the contrast between the polluted body/text and Callimachus: the clumsy epic poem, the heavily traveled highway, and the public well are all rejected. However, the "boy-love who cheats" has muddied the position of the poet. He detests, hates, and is disgusted at everything public, an accumulation of visceral emotion that contradicts the image of the delicate, dew-sipping cicada. The distorted echo of *kalos kalos* by *allos ekhei* matches the transformation of Callimachus's own persona from *erastēs* to *phthoneros*.

In the fourteen erotic epigrams, *phthonos* persistently attends desire.[18] The object of *Baskania* or *phthonos* in the *Aetia* prologue, the *Hymn to Apollo*, and epigram 21, the poet becomes its subject as the *pais* paradoxically represents Callimachean poetics and betrays them by being beyond the reach of the poet – by implication possessed by someone else. The *pais* shifts abruptly from a metaphor for Callimachean poetics to its opposite, *kalos* but corrupt, attractive but polluted: "I know my empty hands hold no riches, but Menippus, by the Graces don't tell my own dream to me. It's agony to hear this bitter word, dear boy, the most disenchanting (*anerastotaton*) thing you've said" (*Epigr: 32*).

Setting the stage for elegy, Catullus adapts for Latin poetry many of Callimachus's programmatic themes, including the use of the erotic object as a metaphor for desirable literary qualities. Like the Callimachean *pais*, Lesbia is depicted ambiguously: a model of erotic/aesthetic perfection, but sexually corrupt. However, the disfiguring effect of jealousy is projected, through Catullus's invective, onto her body. Unlike Callimachus's epigrams, and in contrast to the poems on the infidelity of the *puer* Juventius (24 and 81), Catullus's attacks on Lesbia focus on specific sexual acts and the anatomy involved (11.15–20):

> pauca nuntiate meae puellae
>   non bona dicta.
> cum suis vivat valeatque moechis,
> quos simul complexa tenet trecentos,
> nullum amans vere, sed identidem omnium
>   ilia rumpens.

Announce to my girl a few words, not so good to hear: May she live and prosper with her adulterers, holding in her embrace three hundred at a time, loving none truly, but bursting their groins again and again.

Catullus 11 is a violent representation, not because it depicts an exchange of blows but because the action it attributes to Lesbia – hundreds of partners with the obvious implication of genital, anal, and oral penetration – is viewed as extremely demeaning in Roman society. Moreover, the poem claims that this is a role she willingly assumes; she is "guilty" because of her uncontrolled desire.[19] Poem 11 shares this insistence on physical detail and specificity with several others, such as poem 58: "Caelius, our Lesbia, that Lesbia, that Lesbia whom Catullus loved alone more than himself and all his friends, now in the crossroads and back alleys slips back the foreskins of the descendants of great-hearted Remus."

In their graphic content, poems 11 and 58 are comparable to the invectives directed at Gellius, Mamurra, and others, which equate the cravings for food, money, and sexual pleasure. The upper and lower strata of the body are confused, producing a "grotesque body," voracious in penetrating and being penetrated.[20] Poem 11 reduces Lesbia to a collection of interchangeable holes, while the use of the stem *vor(ax), vor(o)* ("voracious," "devour") in poems 29,

461

33, and 80 similarly assimilates the mouth, anus, and genitals, culminating in Gellius's mouth devouring Victor's penis (80.5–8):

> nescio quid certe est: an vere fama susurrat
> grandia te medii tenta vorare viri?
> sic certe est: clamant Victoris rupta miselli
> ilia, et emulso labra notata sero.[21]

There's something going on: does rumor whisper truly that you devour the impressive hard-ons of a man's crotch? It's true: the burst groin of poor little Victor shouts it, and your lips smeared white with milked-out sperm.

As the echo between 11 (*ilia rumpens*) and 80 (*ilia rupta*) suggests, Lesbia is implicated in the larger treatment of the body in Catullan invective; specifically, Gellius's "stain" here will spread to her when she becomes his lover in poem 91. Similarly, Egnatius's habit of drinking his own urine in poem 37 is particularly offensive to Catullus because Egnatius is identified as one of her lovers, in language that echoes the charges made in 11 and 58: "All you great good fellows make love to her, and, what's really ignoble, all you small-time back-alley fuckers, too."

At the same time, Catullus's poetry constructs a Callimachean body (*lepidus, elegans, suavis, mollis, pura*) closely associated with Lesbia and Juventius. This body represents an "aesthetic of slimness."[22] The physical contact allowed to it is oblique; in comparison with the invective poems, the thousands of kisses in poems 5, 7, and 48, like the sparrow in 2 and 3, defer a more substantial meeting of the flesh. This deferral becomes, through metaphor, infinite: more kisses than the sands of the Libyan desert, more kisses than the stars, kisses denser than fields of ripe grain.

Marilyn Skinner has emphasized the dichotomy in Catullus between the "social virility of the iambicist" and the "emotional vulnerability of the *amator*."[23] But the *amator*'s vulnerability, like the iambicist's virility, depends on the penetration of the object. For the *amator* to suffer and forgive, or suffer and attack, Catullus as poet must first represent Lesbia's violation. In addition, anger remains an important constituent of the amatory *ego* in later elegy, where violence steps into the gap left by Catullan invective. Catullus's shift to a female object consequently reflects more than the fact that Greek and Roman males could be indifferent to the gender of those whom they penetrated. It foregrounds sexual difference, rather than promiscuous behavior alone, a difference marked on the body, rather than a difference evident in behavior but unmarked physically (e.g., the penetrability of the *pais*). Callimachus's echo, "Some other man has him," is inscribed on Lesbia's anatomy: some other man has her *qua* "her." The contradiction between peripheral characteristics (face, eyes, breasts, feet) as metaphors for aesthetic perfection and genitals as the site of corruption and loss will be construed in elegy along generic lines, so that the closer one moves from the former toward the latter, the closer one approaches (mock) epic.

As Foucault put it, in the Hellenistic world, "The agonistic game by which one sought to manifest and ensure one's superiority over others . . . had to be integrated into a far more extensive and complex field of power relations."[24] There is no question that competition within and between city-states was subordinated to struggles between Hellenistic kingdoms; moreover, the citizen's physical role in this political game had changed. The hoplite-*kinaidos* opposition fundamental to the classical construction of the male body appealed to widely shared military experience. By the third century BCE, however, warfare had diversified beyond the limits of the classical phalanx, and mercenaries were widely used for both heavily armed and lighter armed troops. To put it bluntly, the Hellenistic citizen did not customarily expect to put on the armor and kill or be killed.[25] This suggests a changed relation to the ensemble of institutions inherited from the polis, a slippage of the male body from its prior definition through collective warfare.

One of the institutions affected by this transformation was poetry. Considerable attention has been given to the shift of emphasis in Alexandrian poetry from oral to textual performance, a shift whereby the poets measured, self-consciously, their separation from the cultural past. Cameron has recently taken this view to task as "modern dogma," and he demonstrates convincingly that festivals and symposia continued to be relevant for poetry. However, the issue of "oral versus written" involves more than weighing the Library against traditional venues for composition and reception. It bears on poetry's relation, as one of the avenues through which gender was constructed and performed, to civic life, which had changed dramatically in the area of military service. This change was fundamental politically because of the importance of hoplite warfare in defining the male citizen, and fundamental poetically because of Homer. Cameron is consequently less successful in maintaining that there was no conflict between Callimachus's technique and the oral forms and contexts of the classical period.[26] Most importantly, Callimachus rejected the Homeric combination of narrative realism and military/historical content. Whether its target is epic in general, or Antimachus's use of epic realism in elegy, this poetic rejection is what made Callimachus "revolutionary" for his own day and for later Roman poets (who did read it as a rejection of epic). If, as Cameron claims, "the problem was how to de-epicize elegy," this is essentially connected to the "de-epicization" of the citizen through his increased distance from warfare, a citizen for whom the epic battlefield has faded into text that no longer intersects lived experience.[27]

The self-definition of the Roman male elite was similarly dependent on political competition and military accomplishment, and similarly disturbed when Republican institutions crumbled. In framing their reaction, Roman poets found a convenient precedent in Hellenistic poetry. As Martha Malamud has put it, "The adoption of . . . Callimachean poetics in particular provided [Augustan poets] with a sophisticated mechanism for exploring political and social dissonance."[28] Again, epic functioned as the literary analogue for the construction of masculinity through political and military action. Propertius (3.9), noting that he desires only to be found pleasing compared with Callimachus, declares that he will write epic when Maecenas pulls himself out of the shade and leads armies into battle; Ovid (*Am.* 1.1, 1 15, 2.1) rejects epic together with military, legal, and political pursuits.

The elegiac poets embrace the fragmented aesthetic of Callimachus and repudiate the realistic, linear narrative of epic. However, they employ a female rather than a male erotic object in the great majority of their poems. The *recusatio* of epic is thus mapped onto an idealized circle of body parts and attributes that exclude the mistress's genitals – a process of representation that also suspends temporal movement and spatial depth. Jealousy is also mapped onto the female body in the form of bruises and bites that represent, through displacement, the sexual difference avoided in scopophilic description. The genre's trajectory leads from the intangible wound of the *amator* as he falls under the mistress's charms and so departs from epic narrative, to a second wound, the suspicion of infidelity that breaks the fetishistic spell, to the physical wounding of the mistress, which marks the poet's (always temporary) realignment with both masculinity and epic.[29] The wound on female flesh is thus a blot on the self-representation of the poet, a transgression of his aesthetic principles.

Violent Venus

The process is particularly well illustrated in the first fifteen poems of Propertius's second book. Poem 2.1, in its movement from erotic-poetic fetishism and the *recusatio* of epic to the incurable wound inflicted by the *dura puella*, and then to the representation of sex as war, lays out the themes that will dominate the next fourteen poems.

Lines 1–16 programmatically equate Cynthia and the text. The *amores* are written (*scribantur*) and the book is *mollis*; Cynthia substitutes for Calliope and Apollo, the familiar inspirations of Callimachus and of Vergil's *Eclogues*; if she walks in Coan silk (a probable reference to Philitas), the papyrus scroll (*volumen*) becomes all silk; she plays the lyre with ivory fingers (*digitis . . . eburnis*) that suggest her status as constructed art object. She also plays it with skill (*arte*), implying the familiar programmatic term *docta*, "learned." However, lines 13–14 disturb the equivalence between Cynthia and the Callimachean text: *seu nuda erepto mecum luctantur amictu,* | *tum vero longas condimus Iliadas.* With her clothing torn away, she struggles nude with the poet, and they "compose very long *Iliads.*" The word *nuda* jeopardizes scopophilic poetics by calling attention to the *puella*'s genitals, which lack any Callimachean programmatic vocabulary. Moreover, beneath the parodic humor, the violence of epic remains, and by the middle of the poem, infidelity will be its motivation.

The poem continues (17–50) with a *recusatio* of epic addressed to Maecenas and specifically mentioning Callimachus, a progression that would seem to make clear the opposition of Callimachean erotic description to epic narrative. However, the problem of sex as epic violence is raised again in lines 45–50. As the alternative to other subjects, the *amator* claims that he "versifies battles on the narrow bed," but his wish that he alone enjoy his love reveals the potential for aggression behind the military metaphor. He remembers that Cynthia condemns the entire *Iliad* on account of Helen, a reminiscence of the sexual *Iliads* of lines 14–15 with uncomfortable implications for Cynthia's role. By lines 57–78, the *amator* suffers a wound worse than that endured by any epic hero, and finally requests that Maccenas weep over his epitaph: *huic misero fatum dura puella fuit* ("A hard mistress was this poor man's doom"). *Dura* negates the *puella*'s Callimachean qualities, and suggests that, as *nuda*, she is something the poet rarely obtains: to do so, he must break through the barriers that both conceal and represent her sexuality with other men.

Oscillation between Callimachean scopophilia and mock-epic voyeurism dominates Propertius 2.2–2.13. In 2.2, the poet declares that he thought himself free, only to be recaptured by the *puella*'s beauty, elaborated by a set of mythological comparisons; in 2.3 he scolds himself for his lack of will, and then lists the charms he found impossible to resist. Her face is like white lilies, like snow mixed with vermillion, like rose petals floating in milk; her eyes are like torches and stars; her body glistens in Arabian silk; she dances like Ariadne; she is *docta* in playing the Aganippean lyre; her writings (*scripta*) match those of the poet Corinna. Poem 2.4 underscores the importance of sexual difference for the use of the erotic body as metaphor: *ego* laments the *delicta dominae* ("crimes of the mistress") that compel him to *ira*; he prays that his friends love boys, rather than girls, since the former are persuaded by a single word, while the latter "will scarcely become soft even by blood itself" (*altera vix ipso sanguine mollis erit*).

In 2.5, violence is considered, but found to be poetically incorrect (21–26):

> nec tibi periuro scindam de corpore vestis,
> nec mea praeclusas fregerit ira fores,
> nec tibi conexos iratus carpere crinis,
> nec duris ausim laedere pollicibus:
> rusticus haec aliquis tam turpia proelia quaerat,
> cuius non hederae circuiere caput.

I will not rip the dress from your perjured body, nor will my anger smash down your closed doors, nor will I tear apart, in my rage, your woven coiffure, nor dare to hurt you with my harsh thumbs: let some rustic seek such shameful battles, whose head the ivy does not encircle.

The *amator* chooses the Callimachean alternative: "I will write, therefore, what no age will ever efface, 'Cynthia, a powerful beauty, Cynthia, light in words' – believe me, although you disdain the murmurs of rumor, this verse, Cynthia, will turn you pale." This *scripta puella*, injured by verse rather than blows, recalls in strategy if not in explicit language Catullus's invectives against Lesbia.

Poem 2.6 repeats the theme of jealousy, but ends with a statement of eternal devotion: "You will always be my girlfriend, you will always be my wife." In 2.7, movement away from anger toward reconciliation is confirmed from the outside, as Augustus's marital legislation is withdrawn and the lovers rejoice. However in 2.8 the pendulum swings back: Cynthia is again "iron" (*ferrea*), and the *amator* claims that he will kill himself, and her, too (25–28):

> sed non effugies: mecum moriaris oportet;
> hoc eodem ferro stillet uterque cruor.
> quamvis ista mihi mors est inhonesta futura:
> mors inhonesta quidem, tu moriere tamen.

But you will not escape: you should die with me; the blood of both will drip from the same sword, although that murder will disgrace me – it may be a disgrace, but you will die just the same.

In lines 29–38, he compares his grief to Achilles' after the loss of Briseis, a *dolor* that "rages" (*saevit*). In poem 2.10, he tries on more epic masks, declaring his willingness to kill and to die fighting his rival, like Polyneices and Eteocles.

Maria Wyke has demonstrated the inseparability of Callimachean metaphor from the description of the *puella* in Propertius 2.10–2.13, poems that contemplate a switch to epic poetry only to be driven back to elegy by the *puella*'s beauty.[30] As such they fit the general pattern of poems 2.1–2.9, which alternate between increasingly violent dismay at Cynthia's unfaithfulness (voyeurism) and reassertions of erotic/poetic devotion (scopophilia).

The pattern comes to a generically loaded climax in poems 2.14 and 2.15. Poem 2.14 begins by comparing lovemaking to Agamemnon's victory over Troy – as in 2.1, sex equals the *Iliad*, and Cynthia by implication equals Helen. In line 24, this erotic triumph is worth more than victory over the Parthians: "This my spoils, this my conquered kings, this my chariots will be" (*haec spolia, haec reges, haec mihi currus erit*). In 2.15.1–20, the *amator* presents his moment of triumph in detail, using violent language (*rixa*, "quarrels"; *luctata*, "struggling") to describe lovemaking. His account moves significantly from secondary erotic details (her exposed nipples, her self-concealment, her kisses on his eyelids, their entwined arms, their kisses) to a declaration of the importance of visual pleasure ("the eyes are love's leaders") and complete exposure, appealing to the effect that the nudity of Helen and Endymion had on Paris and the goddess Selene (*nuda Lacaena, nudus Endymion, nudae deae*). The *amator* anticipates resistance and violence (17–20):

> quod si pertendens animo vestita cubaris,
>   scissa veste meas experiere manus:
> quin etiam, si me ulterius provexerit ira,
>   ostendes matri bracchia laesa tuae.

But if you are stubborn, and lie down clothed, with your tunic torn away you will know my hands. Still more, if anger provokes me further: you will show your mother the bruises on your arms.

Movement beyond the limits of Callimachean description toward the "blank space" is matched by movement toward *ira*. The torn-off tunic, as obstacle, stands in for all the other obstacles that define the *dura puella*, whose emotional inaccessibility is matched by so many physical barriers. Full disclosure of sexual difference in the bedroom overlaps with elegy's obsession with discovering the *puella*'s guilt, the equivalent of breaking down the doors to find her with another man. Scopophilia is transformed into voyeurism, and looking becomes a blow; the display of sexual difference is transposed into the bruised arms Cynthia shows to her mother.

This shift is not atypical of the genre. The "fascination-jealousy" pattern occupies numerous elegies, and scenes of violent contact, while infrequent, are not for that reason incidental.[31] Ovid gives a particularly clear (to the point of generic self-parody) demonstration of this in *Amores* 1.5 through 1.7. In 1.5, Corinna appears to the poet during a nap on a hot afternoon; the shades are shut, and the (dim) light is just right for the display of "modest girls." As this paradox suggests, everything is halfway in lines 1–10: midday, partly drawn shades, half-light, partly open dress, hair that covers and reveals her neck. The fetishizing technique continues in lines 17–22:

> ut stetit ante oculos posito velamine nostros,
>   in toto nusquam corpore menda fuit.
> quos umeros, quales vidi tetigique lacertos!
>   forma papillarum quam fuit apta premi!
> quam castigato planus sub pectore venter!
>   quantum et quale latus! quam iuvenale femur!

As she stood before our eyes, her dress cast aside, in her whole body there was nowhere a flaw. What shoulders, what arms I saw and I touched! The nipples' shape just right to be pressed! How flat the stomach beneath the perfectly pure breast! Her flank – its size and quality! What a youthful thigh!

At this point he declares, "Why mention the details?" (*singula quid referam*); nude body is pressed to nude body, and "Who doesn't know the rest?" (*cetera quis nescit*). This poem is especially clear in its presentation of the "circling of the look," and representative of the descriptive strategy that transforms the *puella*'s body into an icon, Wyke's Callimachean metaphor.

Menda can be used of a physical blemish, a literary fault, or a slip of the pen – but if there is no flaw, no *menda*, why does the description halt? If the *amator* saw nothing unworthy of praise (*nil non laudabile vidi*), why does one part lack its *laus*? The hint that there is something to be hidden or corrected in this body is confirmed by the use of *castigato* to describe her breasts (*pectore*), which suggests not simply "flawless," but "punished"; the literal meaning of the word is "compelled to be chaste" (*castum* + *ago*). It is important, then, to note the battle over Corinna's tunic in lines 13–16: the poet tears it away (*deripui tunicam*), and although it does not cover much, she battles (*pugnabat*) to keep it on, struggling like someone who wishes to lose. This battle is preceded by a comparison of Corinna to Lais, "loved by many men" (*multis Lais amata viris*).

Amores 1.6 follows with a lengthy appeal to Corinna's doorkeeper, who keeps the door firmly shut in the *amator*'s face, although the latter points out that he does not come as a soldier with an army, but as a lover. Magnifying the less tangible frames of dress and description around her genitals in 1.5, the closed door of the *puella*'s house in 1.6 suggests, as usual, that the mistress is with another man. The *amator* refuses the "epic" action of breaking down the door, but in *Amores* 1.7 he replaces this with a physical assault that disfigures the *puella*'s body and blots the poet's Callimacheanism. The mock triumph in 1.7.35–42 must be cross-referenced specifically with the fetishism of 1.5:

> i nunc, magnificos victor molire triumphos,
> cinge comam lauro votaque redde Iovi,
> quaeque tuos currus comitantum turba sequetur,
> clamet, "io, forti victa puella viro est!"
> ante eat effuso tristis captiva capillo,
> si sinerent laesae, candida tota, genae.
> aptius inpressis fuerat livere labellis
> et collum blandi dentis habere notam.

Go, victor, celebrate your magnificent triumph, wreathe your head

with laurel, give thanks to Jupiter, and let the crowd that follows
your chariot cry, "Io, a girl has been conquered by a brave man!" Let
the captive girl go sadly before, hair undone, body *all white* – if her
beaten cheeks would allow it. A bruise pressed in by my lips would
have been more fitting, her neck marked by the caress of my teeth.

The description in 1.5 emphasizes its omission of her genitals; here in 1.7,
she would be *tota candida* if not for her battered cheeks. Moreover, the poet
suggests that even in lovemaking he would have bitten her neck; the resulting bruise (*livor*) would be the proof of sex, the erstwhile goal of the genre,
and yet it is discoloring, aesthetically at odds with the pristine appearance of
the *puella* as metaphor.[32]

The same basic pattern is found in *Amores* 2.12–15, which move from
triumphant sex, to Corinna's abortion, to the *amator's* description of her from
the privileged perspective of her signet ring. In 2.12 the *amator* claims that
his lovemaking with Corinna is a triumph that "lacks blood" and is "without
slaughter." However, the relation between the Callimachean metaphor and
epicized sex (or beating) suggests that the latter displays what the former has
left out – female genitals as a wound. Lines 17–24 compare lovemaking
to the wars (hardly bloodless) between Trojans and Greeks, Lapiths and
Centaurs, Latins and Trojans, Romans and Sabines, using the repeated
line-opening *femina* to emphasize that women were the cause. The next two
poems describe Corinna's abortion as warfare and gladiatorial combat.[33] Thus
2.15 (1–8):

> Quid iuvat Inmunes belli cessare puellas,
>   nec fera peltatas agmina velle sequi,
> si sine Marte suis patiuntur vulnera telis,
>   et caecas armant in sua fata manus?
> quae prima instituit teneros convellere fetus,
>   militia fuerat digna perire sua.
> scilicet, ut careat rugarum crimine venter,
>   sternetur pugnae tristis harena tuae?

What is the gain for defenseless girls to escape war, and choose not to
follow the savage ranks with shields, if without Mars they suffer
wounds by their own weapons, and they arm blind hands for their
own destruction? Whichever girl first began to tear out tender
offspring, she deserved to die in her own warfare. So that your belly
may lack reproachful wrinkles, perhaps, is the grim sand scattered
for your battle?

These lines fill in the blank space as wound, underscore its opposition to
Callimachean description, and associate it generically with epic. While the

amator describes sex as a triumph without blood, the *nuda puella* remains the site of violent penetration just the same; *Amores* 2.13 and 2.14 are at least as voyeuristic as the poems representing sex or beating. In 2.14.39–40, the *amator* observes that the girl who attempts abortion often perishes, and as she is carried to the pyre, with hair unbound (*resoluta capillos*, 2.14.39 = *effuso capillo*, 1.7.39), all who see her cry out (*clamant*, 2.14.40 = *clamet*, 1.7.38), "She deserved it" (*merito*). There is an equation that runs between the poet's triumph after beating the *puella*, his triumph after making love to her, and this funeral procession after an abortion attempt. Like the husband, guard, and locked door Ovid boasted of overcoming in 2.12.3, abortion is another barrier representing the mistress's independent sexuality, her transgression of Callimachean *mollitia* and the limits of aesthetic fetishism – an "independence" and a transgression constructed for her by the genre.

From the female body as the locus for abortion, *Amores* 2.15 returns immediately to scopophilic description: the *amator* prays to become Corinna's signet ring – a tender burden she could never refuse to bear – so that he can ride on her finger, slip in between her breasts, be moistened by her lips, and accompany her to her bath. Here the description ends, as the sight of *te nuda* would cause the ring to get an erection and play the part of a man.[34] A similar movement from violence back to fetishism is found in 1.7. After wondering why he did not simply scream at the girl and tear away her tunic down to the waist, the *amator* describes how he, "iron-hearted," scratched her face with his fingernail (49–58):

> at nunc sustinui raptis a fronte capillis
>   ferreus ingenuas ungue notare genas.
> astitit illa amens albo et sine sanguine vultu,
>   caeduntur Pariis qualia saxa iugis;
> exanimis artus et membra trementia vidi,
>   ut cum populeas ventilat aura comas,
> ut leni Zephyro gracilis vibratur harundo
>   summave cum tepido stringitur unda Noto;
> suspensaeque diu lacrimae fluxere per ora,
>   qualiter abiecta de nive manat aqua.

She stood stunned, her face white without blood, like marble blocks cut from the slopes of Paros. I saw her lifeless joints and her limbs trembling, as when the wind ruffles the leaves on a poplar, as when a graceful reed whispers gently with the Zephyr, or when wavetops ripple with the warm south wind; her tears hung suspended, then flowed down her face, as water trickles down from melting snow.

The action freezes, and the mistress's body is taken apart into a graceful, trembling, whispering landscape; *aura, leni, tepido, gracilis,* and *manat* all

convey, with appropriately Callimachean artifice, a gentle, soothing "nature."
As the comparison to Parian marble suggests, the mistress is once again an
icon, and the representational mode has shifted back to erotic contemplation.
The *amator* is overwhelmed, and falls before her feet.

Ovid's use of landscape to make a Callimachean metaphor of the *puella*'s
body in 1.7 offers an interesting comparison with a third elegist, Tibullus.
Tibullus's sixteen elegies show the same oscillation between fascination and
suspicion, but they have very little description of the charms of Delia or
Nemesis, which should make it difficult for them to function as the poetic
metaphor suggested by Wyke.[35] However, Tibullus substitutes ekphrases of
an idealized countryside for the mistress's body. In the bucolic setting of 1.1,
the *parva hostia, exiguum pecus*, and *pura fictilia* are contrasted to excessive
wealth, the cause of war; the Golden Age of 1.3.35–48 and the fantasy of
Delia in the country in 1.5.21–36 or 1.10.15–24 are also contrasted to the
horrors of war and epic.

But if landscape rather than the female body is the *materia* for Tibullus's
descriptive passages, the same process makes his landscapes "pastoral" and the
elegiac *puella* "Callimachean." The *puella* without *pudenda*, with the blank
space in the middle, is a lot like the Golden Age landscape, without labor,
disease, greed, or war. The discovery of infidelity parallels the irruption of all
of these woes; it amounts to a return to the city and an opportunity for
mock-epic violence. At the end of 1.10, the drunken farmer and his wife go
back from the rural festival to their bedroom, where their lovemaking repro-
duces the epicized sex found in Propertius and Ovid. In these "wars of Venus,"
the woman's hair is torn out and the door is broken down; her cheeks are
beaten and the man, as "victor," laments that his demented hands were too
strong.[36] Tibullus then condemns the beating, suggesting (61–66).

> sit satis e membris tenuem rescindere vestem,
>   sit satis ornatus dissoluisse comae,
> sit lacrimas movisse satis: quater ille beatus
>   quo tenera irato flere puella potest.
> sed manibus qui saevus erit, scutumque sudemque
>   is gerat et miti sit procul a Venere.

It's enough to tear the thin dress from her body, enough to wreck her
elegant curls, enough to reduce her to tears: that man is four times
blessed at whose anger a delicate girl can weep. But whoever rages
with his fists, let him carry a shield and spear, exiled far from gentle
Venus.

What began as rustic rape – the blessings of Golden Age peace end at the
shattered bedroom door – shifts to familiar elegiac ground. *Lascivus Amor*,
thin dresses, and elegant curls all suggest the urban settings used by Tibullus

when the mistress is being unfaithful. Reinforcing the movement from countryside to city, the woman is first called *uxor*, then *femina*, then *puella*.[37] The passage does not state explicitly why the lover beats her, but in elegy unfaithfulness is *the* cause of anger. Tibullus, like Propertius and Ovid, condemns outright beating, but recommends tearing off the girl's dress, wrecking her hair, and making her cry; not only is this permissible, it brings the greatest pleasure. However, even this ideal of limited violence is transgressed here, as it is elsewhere in elegy.

With one significant exception: Sulpicia, whose poems are the only surviving evidence of what elegy often suggests, that women were interested readers and not infrequently writers of this genre.[38] Sulpicia's corpus resembles male elegy in some respects. Her lover's name, Cerinthus, has associations with bees, wax, and writing, which suggests that he is, like the *puella*, a metaphor for Callimachean poetic composition – a *scriptus vir* (or *puer*?).[39] Poems 4.7 and 4.12 also portray their lovemaking as delayed, though in the latter poem the cause is Sulpicia's own fear of revealing the strength of her desire, not the interposition of a rival. In poem 4.10, however, Sulpicia as female lover accuses Cerinthus of being preoccupied with a prostitute, while she herself is *Servi filia Sulpicia*. The reassertion of her superior name and status is perhaps comparable to the male elegists' reconsideration of epic in the face of their mistresses's infidelity.

Sulpicia's poems do not contain scopophilic lists of Cerinthus's attributes; they do not contain the military language consistently present in the male elegists, nor is there any reference to bites or blows. However, by associating their object with Callimachean text (Cerinthus = writing tablet), the poems imply elegy's scopophilic mode of erotic description. Cerinthus is not only written upon, he is the means through which Sulpicia exposes her poetic self to the readers' gaze, as a public rather than a private text (4.7.7–9):

> non ego signatis quicquam mandare tabellis,
>   *me legat* ut nemo quam meus ante, velim,
> sed peccasse iuvat.

> I would not wish to entrust anything to sealed letters, so that no one might *read me* before my lover, but it is pleasing to have erred.

In these closed tablets, Sulpicia's lover would "read" her before anyone else – but she has become an unsealed text. Placed in her lap (4.7.4, *in nostrum deposuitque sinum*), Cerinthus affords a perspective from which to read "Sulpicia" that anticipates Ovid's ring.[40] This produces a similarly contradictory movement between exposure and concealment: while Sulpicia's *ego* would be more ashamed to cover up (*texisse*) than to lay bare (*nudasse*) her love in 4.7, in 4.13 she has left Cerinthus for a night because she "desires to conceal her ardor" (*ardorem cupiens dissimulare meum*).

472

Sulpicia thus exploits not only an instability of gender intrinsic to elegy, but a confusion of the inscriptive metaphor itself: Callimachean writing, in the male elegists, is an extended disavowal of sexual penetration – which should, according to the metaphor, be analogous to inscription. A *scripta puella* is already wounded, though the male elegists seek to present her as an unblemished surface. But if Ovid as ring portrays a mistress with a blank space in the middle, denying the violence of his own writing, Sulpicia, by casting Cerinthus as tablet and herself as a text to be read, has underscored the ambiguity of the writing metaphor itself: in the center, for herself and for the male elegists, there is both text (wound) and pen.

The problem confronted by the male elegists (the status of the body when elite competition had ceased to provide a reliable definition for it) is not irrelevant for elite women. The stereotypical expectations for elite women – early, arranged marriage and childbirth; chastity; careful management of the household; discipline in the raising of children – were, like those of men, tied to political competition. Women were not emancipated from these expectations during the late Republic, but their meaning was placed in doubt, no less than the meaning of being a senator or a consul.[41] For Sulpicia to offer "herself" to be read (in the act of inscribing her lover/text Cerinthus) seems no less a metaphor for this vulnerability, both political and corporeal, than for Propertius or Ovid to write elegy.

Wyke's emphasis on metaphor establishes a clear break from reading elegy's mistresses as real. However, this point can be granted without allowing the word "metaphor" to neutralize differences between the *candida* and the *dura puella*. Alongside the cheeks like snow and the eyes like stars there are torn dresses, bites, bruises, and abortions. Elegy consistently portrays sex not only as violent penetration, but also as the violation of its own poetic values; the mistress's wound is made a metaphor for epic. But what kind of "metaphor" is this, particularly in the context of Augustan Rome? Is the *ira* that produces elegiac violence itself completely semiotic, as Veyne's reading suggests?[42]

The very notion of bodies used as texts seems a central problem here. The oscillation between Callimachean metaphor and (mock) epic wound strongly suggests an oscillation between the ideal and the "real." If the former turns flesh into idealized text, then the latter, by restoring narrative realism, should make text back into flesh; if the circle of positive attributes is constructed by denial of the "real" of sexual difference, the blank space must be where that "reality" is revealed. But elegy consistently textualizes its violence by presenting it as mock epic, a transgression of Callimacheanism that is nevertheless not "real" violence (i.e., violence offered for straightforward identification). At the end of *Amores* 1.7 the *amator* declares, "Put your recomposed hair back in place" (*puella, pone recompositas in statione comas*), suggesting that the poem has been a transparent play on the extremes of the genre; its violence, like its fascination, was only a surface effect. This does not remove the aggression, but it does complicate its meaning.

Augustan Rome did not enjoy an easy relation with the real, particularly with respect to the elite male body. As Walters argues in this volume, the upper-class *vir* was defined by his freedom from penetration, sexual or violent, in all contexts except military service. This was the guarantee of his social reality, distinguishing independent political action from an empty show under compulsion. As Cicero glumly observed in 55 BCE (*Fam.* 1.8.1–4):

> Commutata tota ratio est senatus, iudiciorum, rei totius publicae; otium nobis exoptandum est, quod ii qui potiuntur rerum praestaturi videntur, si quidam homines patientius eorum potentiam ferre potuerint; dignitatem quidem illam consularem fortis et constantis senatoris nihil est quod cogitemus.

> The entire nature of the senate, the courts, and the Republic itself has changed. Leisure is what we should hope for, and those in power seem ready to grant it, if certain men were able to bear their power more patiently. We should imagine that the consular dignity of a brave and steadfast senator is nothing.

The *vir*, Cicero not the least, was penetrable indeed; in the Principate, Republican institutions became a palpable fiction. Tacitus (*Ann.* 4.19) remarks of the trial of Gaius Silius under Tiberius: "Therefore with much seriousness, as if Silius were being treated in accordance with the law, as if Varro were a real consul, or *that thing* (*illud*) were a Republic, the senate was collected."

In the transformation of Republic into Principate, confusions of status went hand-in-hand with the blurring of divisions between the stage and reality, which sheds additional light on elegy's disturbing mixture of Callimachean metaphor with sexual violence. Two social categories were confused whose separation had been crucial: senator and actor. The latter's penetrability, as a slave, guaranteed that his public words and deeds, onstage, were not "real," while the former's inviolability gave his words and deeds "proper weight and authority."[43] This confusion was explored theatrically through the appearance of upper-class Romans on the stage or in gladiatorial spectacles, and through "fatal charades" where an actor physically suffered in a supposedly fictional situation (e.g., a condemned Prometheus is really eaten by vultures; a boy-actor Icarus really falls to his death).[44] Such confusions of status and reality are instructive for elegy. Elegy opposes Callimachean metaphor to epic, the generic stand-in for elite masculinity and its privileged relation to the "real" defined as political power. Extravagantly artificial, it assumes the glamorous but shameful status of the act.[45] It simultaneously pursues a sadistic narrative reminiscent of the genre it had seemed to reject and inscribes a wound on female flesh to represent this narrative. When it then says of the wound, "This too is text," elegy exposes the semiotic dilemma of the male body defined by a vanishing capacity for political action.

Notes

I would like to thank the editors for their patient and helpful criticism. Thanks also to Stanley Lombardo, Martha Malamud, and Amy Richlin for their responses to earlier versions of this argument. Unless otherwise noted, the translations here are my own.

1 For the *puella* as Callimachean metaphor, see Wyke 1987, 1989b, 1989c, Keith 1994. For "gynesis" and "taking the woman's part," see Gold 1993 [reprinted in this volume, pp. 430–456] for the genre of elegy as "obstinately male," see Lowe 1988, and Wyke 1994. Instances of violence in elegy challenge the general impression of the lover as summarized by Wyke (1994: 120): "He submits, not imposes, is weaponless rather than armed, soft not hard, and feminine not masculine."

2 Barton 1993: 46.

3 "But her form is the least part of my madness – there are greater things, Bassus, for which it's a pleasure to die: her natural color, her skill in many arts, and those joys better discussed under silent sheets." "The faces of young men in pictures wound me, their names too, the tender baby in the crib with no voice wounds me; it wounds me if your mother smothers you in kisses, or if your sister or a girl-friend sleeps beside you. Everything wounds me: I'm scared (forgive me) and in torment I suspect that under that dress there's a man."

4 Kennedy 1993, and Wyke 1994, who notes that the Sulpician narrator's "adoption of both masculine and feminine subject positions . . . is not unparalleled elsewhere in the corpus of elegiac poems" (115).

5 Mulvey [1975] 1989. For the debate in film theory provoked by Mulvey's essay, see Fredrick 1995: 270 n. 13. Mulvey's theory was applied systematically to representations of women in visual art by Pollock 1988; for additional uses in art, literary criticism, and classics, see Fredrick 1995: 269 n. 12.

6 Mulvey [1975] 1989: 21–22.

7 Ibid.: 19–20; cf. 26, "The structure of looking in narrative fictional film contains a contradiction of its own premises: the female image as a castration threat constantly endangers the unity of the diegesis and bursts through the world of illusion as an intrusive, static, one-dimensional fetish."

8 An excellent illustration is provided by Prop. 1.3.1–20, lines that consist entirely of the poet's immobile contemplation of Cynthia's sleeping form, summed up in the closing distich: *sic intentis haerebam fixus ocellis | Argus ut ignotis cornibus Inachi-dos* ("Thus I was frozen, transfixed with intent eyes, like Argus fixed on Io with her unfamiliar horns").

9 E.g., Prop. 2.8.12, *illa . . . ferrea*; 2.17.1–2, *mentiri noctem, promissis ducere amantem, | hoc erit infectas sanguine habere manus*; 2.18c.23. *nunc etiam infectos demens imitare Britannos.*

10 Richlin 1992: 47.

11 See Cahoon 1988 for an analysis of military metaphors and language in the *Amores*.

12 Keith (1994: 39–40) notes the use of the erotic object to represent the poetic text, but does not observe that this object is, in Callimachus, usually male. Cameron (1995: 303–38) argues that Callimachus does not reject epic per se but rather Antimachus's improper use of epic style in his elegiac *Lyde*.

13 *Aetia* fr. 1.1–17 [Pfeiffer]; translation of *Telchines* by Lombardo and Rayor (1988). For the association between the Telchines and the evil eye, see Hopkinson 1988: 91.
14 Dunbabin and Dickie 1983: 9, cf. 15.
15 See F. Williams 1978 and Hopkinson 1988: 85–91. Cf. *Epigr.* 21 [Pfeiffer], where Callimachus is said to have sang "poems stronger than Spite (*Baskaniēs*)."
16 Dunbabin and Dickie 1983: 19.
17 Downplaying connections between this poem, the highway in the *Aetia* prologue, and the muddy river in the *Hymn to Apollo*, Cameron concludes, "The primary purpose of the poem is surely erotic rather than literary" (1995: 399). It seems unnecessary to insist on one meaning to the exclusion of the other, especially since Cameron's own discussion of the *Lyde* (303–38) demonstrates the use of erotic objects as literary metaphors.
18 *Epigr.* 25, 28–32, 41–46, 52, 63 [Pfeiffer].
19 This accusation is repeated in poem 37, and is implicit in other poems that remark upon her infidelity (70, 72, 75, 76, 85). For the concept of "staining" associated particularly with oral–genital contact, see Richlin 1992: 26–31.
20 The phrase "grotesque body" comes from Bakhtin; for discussion in connection with Roman literature, see Gowers 1993: 30, 55. Examples: poems 21, 29, 32, 37, 39, 47, 57, 59, 74, 78, 79, 88–91, 110, 114, 115.
21 Catullus presents the image of Gellius fellating himself in poem 88.
22 Gowers 1993: 44. She concludes that the movement in poem 13 from the tangible *cena* to the intangible odor of the *unguentum* "is a guide to the balance of real and insubstantial in Catullus' work as a whole" (240–42).
23 Skinner 1991: 6.
24 Foucault 1986: 95. He adds that the transformations of the Hellenistic period "brought about, in a much more general and essential way, a problematization of political activity" (86) that extended into the early centuries of Roman rule.
25 On the hoplite-*kinaidos* opposition, see Vidal-Naquet 1986: 85–156 and Winkler 1990: 45–70. On the movement away from classical hoplite warfare, in both tactics and the use of mercenaries, see Griffith 1935: 1–7, 317–24; Ober 1991: 190–92; and V. D. Hanson 1991: 253–56. For the reorientation of the *gymnasion* away from the training of future soldiers and toward intellectual and physical pleasure, see Giovannini 1993: 268–74.
26 Cameron 1995: 3–103. For writing and Hellenistic poetry, see Bing 1988: 10–48; Lombardo 1989, and Lombardo and Rayor 1988.
27 Cameron 1995: 407. Lazenby (1991: 106) points out that Homer remained the "Bible" of the Greeks because of the shared experience of hoplite warfare, nothing that "hoplites were 'the nation in arms' . . . in states where those who could not afford such service were excluded from full civic rights."
28 Malamud 1993: 156; cf. Gutzwiller and Michelini 1991. For the effect of the "Roman revolution" on concepts of the self among the elite, see Barton 1993; Skinner 1991, 1993; Hopkins 1983. For the importance of competition and status in domestic life (housing, furnishing, dining), see Clarke 1991: 1–24, 369–71; D'Arms 1990; Fredrick 1995; and Wallace-Hadrill 1994: 1–61.
29 See especially Ov. *Am.* 1.1 and 2.1; for the wounding of the *amator* by infidelity, see, e.g., Prop. 2.1.57–70, where the speaker compares his injury to those of Philoctetes, Phoenix, Androgeos, Telephus, and Prometheus, and pronounces it much worse because it is incurable.
30 Wyke 1987, who concludes that this group of poems "re-establishes an allegiance to a politically unorthodox, Callimachean poetic practice" (60).
31 For erotic fascination vs. jealous anger, see Prop. 1.1–1.9, 1.11–1.16, 2.16–2.19,

2.24–2.26, 2.29–2.29a, 2.30, 2.32–2.34, 3.1–3.6, 3.10–3.14, 3.16–3.17, 3.19–3.20, 3.23–3.25; and Ov. *Am.* 1.1–1.10, 1.14, 2.1, 2.5, 2.9–2.11, 2.16–2.19, 3.1–3.4, 3.7–3.8, 3.11–3.12, 3.14.

32 For biting in elegiac lovemaking, see also Tib. 1.6.13–14 and Prop. 3.8.21–22.

33 On these two poems, see Gamel 1989.

34 *Am.* 2.15.25: *sed, puto, te nuda mea membra libidine surgent | et peragam partes anulus ille viri.*

35 E.g., Tib. 1.2, 1.4–1.6, 1.9, 2.3–2.4, 2.6.

36 Tib. 1.10.51–60: *rusticus e lucoque vehit, male sobrius ipse | uxorem plaustro progeniemque domum. | sed veneris tunc bella calent, scissosque capillos | femina, perfractas conqueriturque fores; | flet teneras subtusa genas: sed victor et ipse | flet sibi dementes tam valuisse manus. | at lascivus Amor rixae mala verba ministrat, | inter et iratum lentus utrumque sedet. | a lapis est ferrumque, suam quicumque puellam | verberat: e caelo deripit ille deos.*

37 See Tib. 1.5.47–76, 1.6.1–41, 2.3, 2.4.

38 See Hallett 1992: 350–51. On Sulpicia in the context of elegy, see Hinds 1987; Lowe 1988; Roessel 1990; Santirocco 1979; and Wyke 1994.

39 Cf. Roessel 1990: 247, "Sulpicia writes on her lover, both figuratively and literally." For Cerinthus there is no masculine counterpart to the epithet *puella*, although Sulpicia does address him as *mea lux* (4.12.1) and designates herself *tua puella* (4.11.1).

40 Ovid may have had Sulpicia's poem specifically in mind in *Am.* 2.15.15, *idem ego ut arcanas possim signare tabellas*, which partly echoes Sulpicia's line, *non ego signatis quicquam mandare tabellis* (4.7.7).

41 See Bradley 1991: 125–204; Dixon 1988: 41–140, 168–209, and 1992: 36–97; Treggiari 1991: 205–61. For a skeptical view of women's alleged "emancipation" during the late Republic, see Gardner 1986: 257–66.

42 Veyne 1988: 85–115; but Wyke (1989a) questions Veyne's separation of elegy's semiotic code from Rome's social history.

43 Edwards 1993: 85. She there summarizes the actor's position as a paradigm of low status and the implications of Nero's reign as actor-emperor, which "causes everyone to dissemble"; see also Bartsch 1994: 36–62.

44 Coleman 1990.

45 Edwards 1993; she remarks that "acting . . . was seen as incompatible with virtually anything that was admirable in a Roman citizen" (86). This is also the self-proclaimed position of the elegist.

Works cited

Bakhtin, M. 1984. *Rabelais and His World*. H. Iswolsky. Bloomington, Ind.

Barton, C. A. 1993. *The Sorrows of the Ancient Romans: The Gladiator and the Monster*. Princeton.

Bartsch, S. 1994. *Actors in the Audience: Theatricality and Doublespeak from Nero to Hadrian*. Cambridge, Mass.

Bing, P. 1988. *The Well-Read Muse: Present and Past in Callimachus and the Hellenistic Poets*. Göttingen.

Bradley, K. R. 1991. *Discovering the Roman Family: Studies in Roman Social History*. New York and Oxford.

Cahoon, L. 1988. "The Bed as Battlefield: Erotic Conquest and Military Metaphor in Ovid's Amores." *Transactions of the American Philological Association* 118: 293–307.

Cameron, A. 1995. *Callimachus and His Critics*. Princeton.

Clarke, J. R. 1991. *The Houses of Roman Italy, 100 B.C.–A.D. 250: Ritual, Space, and Decoration.* Berkeley.

Coleman, K. M. 1990. "Fatal Charades: Roman Executions Staged as Mythological Enactments." *Journal of Roman Studies* 80: 44–73.

D'Arms, J. 1990. "The Roman Convivium and the Idea of Equality." In O. Murray, ed., *Sympotica: A Symposium on the Symposium,* 308–20. Oxford.

Dixon, S. 1988. *The Roman Mother.* Norman, Okla.

—— 1992. *The Roman Family.* Baltimore.

Dunbabin, K. M. D. and M. W. Dickie. 1983. "*Invida Rumprantur Pectora*: The Iconography of Phthonus/Invidia in Graeco-Roman Art." *Jarhbuch für Antike und Christentum* 26: 7–37.

Edwards. 1993. *The Politics of Immortality in Ancient Rome.* Ithaca, N.Y.

Foucault, M. 1986. *The Care of the Self.* Vol. 3, *The History of Sexuality.* Trans. R. Hurley. New York.

Fredrick, D. 1995. "Beyond the Atrium to Ariadne: Erotic Painting and Visual Pleasure in the Roman House." *Classical Antiquity* 14.2: 266–87.

Gamel, M. -K. 1989. "*Non sine caede*: Abortion, Politics And Poetics in Ovid's *Amores.*" *Helios* 16.2: 183–206.

Gardner, J. F. 1986. *Women in Roman Law and Society.* Bloomington and Indianapolis, Ind.

Giovannini, A. 1993. "Greek Cities and Greek Commonwealth." In A. Bulloch, E. S. Gruen, A. A. Long, and A. Stewart, eds., *Images and Ideologies: Self-Definition in the Hellenistic World,* 265–86. Berkeley and Los Angeles.

Gold, B. K. 1993. "'But Ariadne Was Never There in the First Place': Finding the Female in Roman Poetry." In N. S. Rabinowitz and A. Richlin, eds., *Feminist Theory and the Classics,* 75–101. New York. (Also this volume, pp. 430–56.)

Gowers, E. 1993. *The Loaded Table: Representations of Food in Roman Literature.* Oxford.

Griffith, G. T. 1935. *Mercenaries in the Hellenistic World.* Cambridge.

Gutzwiller, K. J. and A. N. Michelini. 1991. "Women and Other Strangers: Feminist Perspectives in Classical Literature." In J. E. Hartman and E. Messer-Davidow, eds., *(En)Gendering Knowledge,* 66–84. Knoxville, Tenn.

Hallet, J. P. 1992. "Heeding Our Native Informants: The Uses of Latin Literary Texts in Recovering Elite Roman Attitudes Toward Age, Gender, and Social Status." *Échos du monde clasique* 11.3: 333–55.

Hanson, V. D. 1991. "The Future of Greek Military History." In V. D. Hanson, ed., *Hoplites: The Classical Greek Battle Experience,* 253–56. London.

Hinds, S. 1987. "The Poetess and the Reader: Further Steps toward Sulpicia." *Hermathena* 143: 29–46.

Hopkins, M. K. 1983. *Death and Renewal.* Cambridge.

Hopkinson, N. 1988. *A Hellenistic Anthology.* Cambridge.

Keith, A. M. 1994. "*Corpus eroticum*: Elegiac Poetics and Elegiac *puellae* in Ovid's Amores," *Classical World* 88.1: 27–40.

Kennedy, D. F. 1993. *The Arts of Love: Five Studies in the Discourse of Roman Love Elegy.* Cambridge.

Lazenby, J. 1991. "The Killing Zone." In V. D. Hanson, ed., *Hoplites: The Classical Greek Battle Experience,* 87–109. London.

Lombardo, S. 1989. "Technopaegnia: Hellenistic Pattern Poetry." *Tremblor* 10: 200–204.

Lombardo, S., and D. Raynor, trans. 1988. *Callimachus: Hymns, Epigrams, Select Fragments*. Baltimore.

Lowe, N. J. 1988. "Sulpicia's Syntax." *Classical Quarterly* 38: 193–205.

Malamud, M. 1993. "Vandalising Epic." *Ramus* 22.2: 155–73.

Mulvey, L. [1975] 1989. "Visual Pleasure and Narrative Cinema." In L. Mulvey, ed., *Visual and Other Pleasures*, 14–26. Bloomington, Ind. (Originally published in *Screen* 16.3: 6–18).

Ober, J. 1991. "Hoplites and Obstacles." In V. D. Hanson, ed., *Hoplites: The Classical Greek Battle Experience*, 173–96. London.

Pollock, G. 1988. *Vision and Difference: Femininity, Feminism, and the Histories of Art* London.

Richlin, A. 1992. *The Garden of Priapus*. Rev. ed. New York.

Roessel, David. 1990. "The Significance of the Name Cerinthus in the poems of Sulpicia." *Transactions of the American Philological Association* 120: 243–50.

Sanitrocco, M. S. 1979. "Sulpicia Reconsidered." *Classical Journal* 74: 229–39.

Skinner, M. B. 1991. "The Dynamics of Catullan Obscenity: cc. 37, 58 and 11." *Syllecta classica* 3: 1–11.

—— 1993. "Woman and Language in Archaic Greece, or, Why Is Sappho a Woman?" In N. S. Rabinowitz and A. Richlin, eds., *Feminist Theory and the Classics*, 125–44. New York.

Treggiari, S. 1991. *Roman Marriage: Iusti Coniuges from the Time of Cicero to the Time of Ulpian*. Oxford.

Veyne, P. 1988. *Roman Erotic Elegy: Love Poetry and the West*. Trans. D. Pellauer. Chicago.

Vidal-Naquet, P. 1986. "The Black Hunter and the Origin of the Athenian Ephebia." In *The Black Hunter: Forms of Thought and Forms of Society in the Greek World*, trans. A. Szegedy-Mazak, 85–156. Baltimore.

Wallace-Hadrill, A. 1994. *Houses and Society in Pompeii and Herculaneum*. Princeton.

Williams, F. 1978. *Callimachus: Hymn to Apollo: A Commentary*. Oxford.

Winkler, J. J. 1990. *The Constraints of Desire*. New York.

Wyke, M. 1987. "Written Woman: Propertius' *scripta puella*." *Journal of Roman Studies* 77: 47–61.

—— 1989a. "In Pursuit of Love, the Poetic Self and a Process of Reading: Augustan Elegy in the 1980s." *Journal of Roman Studies* 77: 47–61.

—— 1989b. "Mistress and Metaphor in Augustan Elegy." *Helios* 16: 25–47.

—— 1989c. "Reading Female Flesh: *Amores* 3.1." In A. Cameron, ed., *History as Text: The Writing of Ancient History*, 113–43. London.

—— 1994. "Taking the Woman's Part: Engendering Roman Love Elegy." *Ramus* 23.1–2: 110–28.

INDEX